SUNRISE . . . SUNSET

HARVARD BUSINESS REVIEW EXECUTIVE BOOK SERIES

SUNRISE . . . SUNSET

CHALLENGING THE MYTH OF INDUSTRIAL OBSOLESCENCE

ALAN M. KANTROW

Editor

JOHN WILEY & SONS

New York · Chichester · Brisbane · Toronto · Singapore

Library of Congress Cataloging in Publication Data:

Main entry under title:

Sunrise . . . sunset.

   (Harvard business review executive book series, ISSN
0275-2492)
   Bibliography: p.
   Includes indexes
   1. Industrial management—Addresses, essays, lectures.
2. Competition, International—Addresses, essays,
lectures.   I. Kantrow, Alan M., 1947—   .   II. Series.

HD31.S764 1985   658.4   84-19580
ISBN 0-471-80573-4

Printed in the United States of America

10 9 8 7 6 5 4 3 2 1

Foreword

For sixty years, the *Harvard Business Review* has been the farthest reaching executive program of the Harvard Business School. It is devoted to the continuing education of executives and aspiring managers primarily in business organizations, but also in not-for-profit institutions, in government, and in the professions. Through its publishing partners, reprints, and translation programs, it finds an audience in many languages in most of the countries in the world, occasionally penetrating even the barrier between East and West.

The *Harvard Business Review* draws on the talents of the most creative people in modern business and in management education. About half of its content comes from practicing managers, the rest from professional people and university researchers. Everything *HBR* publishes has something to do with the skills, attitudes, and knowledge essential to the competent and ethical practice of management.

This book consists of 32 articles dealing with the very different kinds of challenges managers face when they are operating in start-up, high growth, and mature industry settings. All too often, the advice given to managers reads as if it were equally applicable to all three settings. It is the purpose of these articles to correct that too easy assumption of universality and to identify the relevant contexts of managerial decision-making. Neither abstruse nor superficial, the articles chosen for this volume are intended to be usefully analytical, challenging, and carefully prescriptive. Every well-informed businessperson can follow the exposition in its path away from the obvious and into the territory of independent thought. I hope that readers will find these ideas stimulating and helpful in making their professional careers more productive.

KENNETH R. ANDREWS, Editor
Harvard Business Review

Contents

Part Three   Managing the Mature Company

Part Four   Getting Out, Buying In

Part Five   Managing the Growth Company

SUNRISE . . . SUNSET

Introduction

ALAN M. KANTROW

Of all the misconceptions surrounding the work of management, few have proven more stubbornly resistant to correction than the notion that the key tasks of management are—or should be—everywhere the same. This view of things is troublesome because it ignores the profound changes now taking place in the competitive structure of many industries. It is also troublesome because it rests on the assumption that company-to-company differences in business environment have less effect on what managers have to be good at than does the simple fact of their membership in the same general profession. In recent years this lack of sensitivity to the relations between competitive environment and managerial responsibility has been most clearly visible in the predicament of so-called mature industries.

It was the best of concepts; it was the worst of concepts. It was the gospel of enlightenment; it was the fount of error. It allowed managers to plan intelligently for the allocation of corporate assets; it led managers to view their businesses as generalized types of enterprise important only as users or suppliers of those assets. It offered the work of strategic planning an unprecedented level of analytic rigor; it substituted facility with quantitative measures for "hands-on" knowledge as the benchmark of managerial competence. It kept scarce resources away from the bottomless hole of dead-end investment; it starved vital businesses first into apathy and then into decline.

Indeed, for a generation and more, the concept of maturity has dominated the way American managers think about the products and markets for which they are responsible. Evidence mounts, however, that the various proxies for maturity commonly in use—sales growth, industry concentration, and market segmentation among them—are, at best, inexact and, at worst, seriously misleading. More than that, many of the assumptions on which those proxies rest—assumptions, in particular, about the ways in which industries evolve—are themselves woefully incomplete and downright confusing.

1

Is heightened concentration, for example, more properly interpreted as a sign of maturity already established, as but one of many factors conspiring to bring maturity about, or as part and parcel of an industry's movement toward a revitalization of competition? In the history of the automobile industry, periods of concentration occurred not when technology was most stable and the terms of competition most tightly fixed but, rather, when technology was least stable and the terms of competition most in flux. In fact, the more disruptive of production competence a given technical change was, the more that change went to the heart of the production system then in place, and the greater the likelihood that industry concentration would increase. What, then, of easy generalizations linking concentration to maturity?

In its most virulent form, the concept of maturity had—and continues to have—the force of a self-fulfilling prophecy. If the process of decay is inevitable, why try to shore up the mere outward shell of a once vigorous enterprise? Why not direct resources toward more promising undertakings, preferably those still in the heady flush of youth? So persuasive is this line of reasoning in practice that its not surprising result has been to encourage the premature exodus of management energies and attention from businesses viewed, correctly or not, as mature. This exodus has not been without immense economic and human costs, many of them hidden—not least, the tendency to hasten the decline that all concerned would most like to postpone. In industry as in scripture, it is possible to sell one's birthright for a mess of pottage.

Research confirms what common sense has long suspected: not every product or industry must march through the same inflexible, one-way sequence of evolutionary stages, or even march in the same direction. Not every business that is healthy today must grow aged and infirm tomorrow. Some will, of course, but the salient fact, the fact often overlooked, is that no infallible rule exists for telling in advance which will or, for that matter, the precise sequence in which they will. No single generalization, no pat formula or matrix holds for all circumstances. Hence, the managerial challenge is to understand in all their particularity the dynamics of a given industry or product so as to be able to judge accurately how it is evolving or might evolve.

Today, a number of developments, some economic and some political, has given the task of interpreting maturity correctly a special urgency. A period of lagging performance in international competition has encouraged managers, workers, and policymakers alike to explore the remedial options provided by some version of an industrial policy. Indeed, the historical moment is such that we might well be on the brink of major government initiatives toward industry that will have the same long-lasting effects as did the last significant wave of federal intervention during the New Deal. Recent upheavals in the transportation, telecommunications, and financial services industries brought about by deregulation are only the first sign of how unsettling those initiatives can be.

At the same time, of course, the overall structure of the nation's economy is itself undergoing wrenching change. Not only are familiar industry boundaries crumbling; the percentage of both GNP and employment accounted for by the manufacturing sector trails farther and farther behind the percentage associated with the service sector. Geographic areas long dependent on once-thriving industries like steel face a continual erosion of their economic base; other areas, many of them either near cheap labor markets or in close proximity to university-linked expertise in science and technology, confront the opposite problems of too-rapid growth. Fundamental pieces of the nation's industrial infrastructure—bridges, roads, and power generation systems—show the unmistakable signs of prolonged neglect, and experts puzzle over workable means to finance their repair or replacement. Ever more efficient capital markets place heightened pressure on capital-intensive industries to show quick returns on investment, yet an important development in those markets—the massive availability of venture capital—channels investment dollars toward newer, technology-intensive industries.

Markets that had for years been the safe preserve of domestic producers find themselves increasingly thrown open to foreign competition, and domestic companies that had rarely looked to do business abroad are now forced to devise strategies for competing on a global, not just a multinational, basis. Flurries of mergers and acquisitions pass rapidly into flurries of divestitures, spin-offs, leveraged buyouts, and corporate "streamlining." Exposure to foreign debt risks eats away at the root of the industrial pyramid, and politically inviolable commitments to defense and entitlement programs render that pyramid vulnerable to any shock or dislocation.

The litany is familiar but no less troubling for that. It opens the way for the moderate reception of extreme proposals. In this, as in other periods of discontinuous structural change, recommendations lie thick upon the ground to reconfigure the nation's industrial posture. In practice, of course, the call to reconfigure is often a call to phase out or abandon what are perceived as mature industries, and to nurture in their place the high-growth (today, read "high-tech") industries of the future. Events, then, conspire to make the popular understanding of maturity a matter of great public as well as corporate urgency.

Let there be one, two, three, many Silicon Valleys—or so runs the modern catechism of the high-tech enthusiasts. No one would argue with the vital importance of cutting-edge technology to an advanced industrial economy. The way enthusiasts often pose the issue, however, such technology and the programs that support it are the only things that matter. Against narrow-minded extremism of this sort, it is good to remember that many high-tech industries are themselves, in much of what they do, little more than old-fashioned metal benders and assemblers and that the supposedly dated industries that they are to replace are not only quite technically sophisticated but also the largest customers for what they produce. It is also

Exhibit 1.   High Tech's Output Will Grow Fast Compared with Other Industries . . .

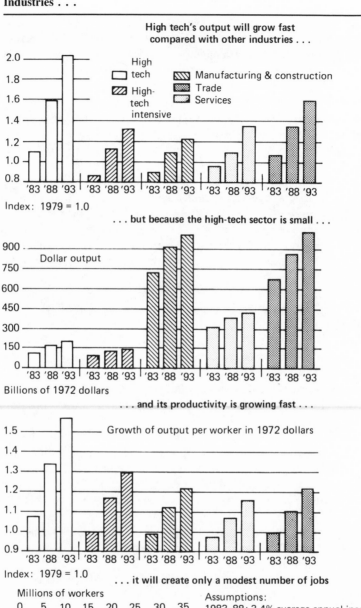

High tech's output will grow fast
compared with other industries . . .

Index: 1979 = 1.0

. . . but because the high-tech sector is small . . .

Dollar output

Billions of 1972 dollars

. . . and its productivity is growing fast . . .

Growth of output per worker in 1972 dollars

Index: 1979 = 1.0

. . . it will create only a modest number of jobs

Millions of workers

Employment
☐ 1983
■ 1993

Assumptions:
1983–88: 3.4% average annual increase in gross national product; 5.7% average annual increase in consumer prices; 2.1% average annual increase in nonfarm employment

1988–93: 2.7% average annual increase in gross national product; 6.4% average annual increase in consumer prices; 1.2% average annual increase in nonfarm employment

Data: Data Resources Inc.

Reprinted from the March 28, 1983 issue of *Business Week* by special permission, © 1983 by McGraw-Hill, Inc.

Exhibit 2. Most New Jobs in High Tech Will Not Be Technical

| | Growth 1980–83 | |
Occupation	Number of jobs	Percent
Operatives	226,183	22%
Managers & clerical workers	149,650	22
Engineers	110,930	40
Craft & related workers	98,121	21
Engineering & science technicians	70,693	37
Professionals, except managers & clericals	33,305	22

Data: Data Resources Inc.

good to remember that, in terms of employment, high technology leaves much to be desired, as Exhibits 1 and 2 make clear.

Neither at the level of policy nor at the level of managerial action does it make sense to write off in knee-jerk fashion products or industries thought to be mature. In the first place, they are not so easily excised from a company's or a nation's economy as all that, nor is the massive rearrangement of assets without its costs in organizational effectiveness as well as in dollars. Even where the diagnosis of maturity is correct, the shifting of effort and resources is a slow process requiring careful management, not something speedily finished with a phone call to the investment bankers or the relocation experts. In the second place, ample experience should have taught us that the diagnosis is much harder to make than it seems to be. Judging maturity accurately is not a simple, obvious matter like telling a blue flower from a yellow tree. It is a much more difficult analytic task, like telling one species of flower from another of the same color that, at first sight, it closely resembles.

If the most vocal proponents of writing off mature operations were superstitious, they would long since have expired from the shock of seeing so many of their dear departed spring back to life. In the 1960s, for example, most consumer electronics companies in the United States began acting as if their businesses had entered the mature phase of development characterized by slow growth, technical stability, vertical integration, and high scale economies. No one, however, managed to convince SONY or Matsushita that their efforts to transistorize pocket radios or miniaturize television sets were too little, too late. During the same period, North American Rockwell (now known as Rockwell International) acquired what it regarded as a flush but stodgy cash cow in Draper, then the world leader in weaving loom capacity for textiles. Efforts to milk Draper for cash necessarily starved its explorations of the new process technologies—water jets, air jets, and the like—that revolutionized the industry within a decade. Only after being divested by Rockwell in 1982 did the company begin to stage a technology-based comeback.

These examples are by no means unusual. In the late 1960s, the major domestic producers of metal cans, then in the midst of a large-scale effort to diversify, were actively harvesting their apparently mature can operations for cash. Two aluminum companies, Alcoa and Reynolds, stood things on their head by developing a process for making two-piece non-soldered aluminum cans, which offered great benefits in both manufacturing and marketing. Twenty years ago, American railroads were the typical superannuated industrial dinosaur; today, with the exception of the system owned by the federal government, most railroads are thriving high-tech businesses. The domestic shoe industry, long considered a terminal case, has recently seen a technology-driven revival in the running shoe and outdoor/casual shoe segments of the market. More familiar, perhaps, is the new vitality brought to the automobile tire industry when radial tires began to replace the standard bias-ply construction.

Not in every case, of course, but in enough instances to document the possibility, changes in market linkages, technology, or both gave operations that had seemed mature—a new lease on life, a new vitality, a chance to revitalize themselves. Some companies were able to grasp the opportunity; others not. Some industries were able to grasp the opportunity; others saw their traditional preserves invaded by competitors based elsewhere. The point is inescapable: a reversal of the drift toward maturity can happen—and often has. The opportunity exists.

Perhaps the most dramatic instance of such a reversal in action is provided by the domestic automobile industry during the 1970s and early 1980s. By the middle of the 1960s, the major American producers had long since fallen into a competitive posture that was quite lucrative in terms of profit but was fully characteristic of the mature stage of industry development. What innovation there was had very little to do with substantial changes in the product itself; for the most part, technical change was directed toward minor incremental improvements in the production process. Consumers did not yet value most technical dimensions of high product performance, nor were they overly concerned with fuel economy or air pollution or safety. What sold cars was not quality of construction but styling, the way sheet metal was stamped and painted, the luxuriousness of interior trim. Lee Iacocca's 1973 view of the importance of innovation at Ford was broadly representative of the whole industry's thinking: "Give them [American consumers] leather. They can smell it."

Since that time, two wrenching oil shocks, stringent government regulation, changing consumer preferences, and vigorous foreign competition have shaken the industry out of its post-World War II lethargy. By 1980, a Japanese producer could put a subcompact car on an American dealer's lot for roughly $1,800 less—conservatively estimated—than could an American producer. As imports, especially from Japan, quickly rose from a mere blip on the horizon to more than a quarter of the domestic market, it became clear that American consumers had grown vitally interested in far more than the smell of leather upholstery.

Statistical evidence confirms this shift in consumer preferences. For one thing, buyers have increasingly become willing to pay a market premium for new product technology. In the 1977–78 period, for example, cars with front-wheel drive sold at a discount of some $315 relative to cars with rear-wheel drive; after the oil shock in 1979, that discount turned into a premium of $416. In the earlier period, diesel engines carried a market discount of $853; in the latter, a premium of $301. In addition to the heightened value of new technology, the domestic industry has witnessed a sizable increase in the diversity of technology available for sale. Exhibit 3 cites data on the growing variety between 1970 and 1980 of engine and drive-train technology on regular production vehicles. Exhibit 4 translates that data into a "diversity index" of sorts, a measure that grows larger as the market shares of each

Exhibit 3. Production Shares of Selected Engine and Drive-Train Characteristics in U.S.-Produced Automobiles (1970–1980)

Characteristic	70	71	72	73	74	75	76	77	78	79	80
Engine Parameters											
I. Cylinder Configuration											
4 Cyl	.02	.08	.06	.07	.12	.09	.07	.06	.13	.22	.29
6 Cyl	.16	.11	.10	.10	.20	.22	.23	.17	.22	.24	.39
8 Cyl	.82	.81	.84	.83	.68	.69	.70	.77	.65	.54	.32
Valve/Camshaft Arrangement											
OHV IL	.18	.19	.16	.17	.31	.30	.27	.18	.25	.16	.23
OHC IL	.00	.00	.00	.00	.00	.00	.00	.00	.00	.17	.18
OHV V	.82	.81	.84	.83	.69	.70	.73	.82	.75	.67	.59
Fuel											
Diesel	.00	.00	.00	.00	.00	.00	.00	.00	.00	.00	.03
Gasoline	1.00	1.00	1.00	1.00	1.00	1.00	1.00	1.00	1.00	1.00	.97
Fuel Delivery											
1 Bbl	.17	.19	.16	.15	.27	.28	.22	.14	.15	.12	.10
2 Bbl	.61	.59	.60	.65	.53	.52	.62	.65	.72	.59	.77
EFI	.00	.00	.00	.00	.00	.01	.00	.01	.01	.09	.05
4 Bbl	.22	.22	.18	.20	.20	.19	.16	.20	.12	.18	.07
Turbo 2	.00	.00	.00	.00	.00	.00	.00	.00	.00	.00	.00
Turbo 4	.00	.00	.00	.00	.00	.00	.00	.00	.00	.00	.01
II. Drive-Train Parameters											
Wheels-Driven											
FWD	.00	.01	.01	.01	.01	.01	.01	.01	.07	.10	.23
RWD	1.00	.99	.99	.99	.99	.99	.99	.99	.93	.89	.76
4WD	.00	.00	.00	.00	.00	.00	.00	.00	.00	.01	.01
Engine Orientation											
Transverse	.00	.00	.00	.00	.00	.00	.00	.00	.04	.09	.21
Longitudinal	1.00	1.00	1.00	1.00	1.00	1.00	1.00	1.00	.96	.91	.79

SOURCE: *From Industrial Renaissance* by William J. Abernathy, Kim B. Clark, and Alan M. Kantrow, © 1983 by Basic Books, Inc. Reprinted by permission of the publisher.
NOTE: The following definitions are used in the table.
OHV IL: overhead valve—in line; OHC IL: overhead cam—in line; OHV V: overhead valve—V-configuration; Bbl: barrel; EFI: electronic fuel injection; Turbo: turbocharger; FWD: front-wheel drive; RWD: rear-wheel drive; 4WD: four-wheel drive.

Exhibit 4. Diversity of Selected Engine/Drive-Train Packages (1970–1980)

Category	70	71	72	73	74	Year 75	76	77	78	79	80
I. Total Market											
Diversity Index	1.67	1.70	1.51	1.64	2.07	2.21	1.89	1.81	1.86	3.76	4.91
No. of Configurations	6	5	5	8	7	10	9	9	13	15	21
II. Market Segments											
Small Cars											
Diversity Index	1.82	2.59	2.02	2.38	2.34	2.17	2.95	2.94	3.55	3.54	3.64
No. of Configurations	5	4	3	6	6	6	6	6	8	9	11
Medium Cars											
Diversity Index	1.31	1.46	1.28	1.25	1.52	1.93	1.96	1.89	2.05	3.41	2.12
No. of Configurations	3	3	4	4	3	3	5	6	7	9	10
Large Cars											
Diversity Index	1.46	1.42	1.36	1.44	1.49	1.71	1.41	1.55	1.20	1.72	2.58
No. of Configurations	4	4	4	5	4	7	6	7	6	7	10

SOURCE: *From Industrial Renaissance* by William J. Abernathy, Kim B. Clark, and Alan M. Kantrow © 1983 by Basic Books, Inc. Reprinted by permission of the publisher
NOTE: A configuration is a combination of engine type (fuel, number of cylinders, carburetion) and drive train (front or rear drive, engine orientation). The diversity index measures both the number of different configurations and their relative importance in the market. Small, medium, and large are defined in terms of weight, with breakpoints being 3,198 pounds and 3,660 pounds respectively.

available configuration (four, six, or eight cylinders, for example) for a given technology-based design parameter (the number of cylinders in an engine) approach equality. Exhibit 4 also indicates that, during the 1970s, not only did the diversity index rise, but the actual number of "packages" (configurations of technology) rose as well.[1]

These statistics give partial but striking evidence of how an industry once thought to be irrevocably mature can find itself in the throes of a process of de-maturity, a movement back toward the vigorous competitive dynamics of an earlier stage of industry development. Indeed, market linkages and production systems that had been locked so tightly into place as to strangle disruptive change in technology or the organization of work can themselves be vulnerable to far-reaching change by upheavals in work organization or technology. Again, the relevant point here is not that developments comparable to those in the automobile industry are likely or even possible for all other industries regarded as mature. The point is that such processes of de-maturity can happen, and that the challenge for managers in this industry or that is to see *if* these processes are happening and *how* they are happening.

This call to action is not intended as a simple plea that managers be awake and aware when the tidal wave hits. There are things to be done betimes. What the experience of de-maturity clearly shows about the shifting terms of competition in many industries is that the character of effort required of managers is not a constant. It changes as the competitive environment changes. Moreover, as noted earlier, if that character of effort—what managers have to be good at—is not in harmony with external circumstances, it can lead to grossly inappropriate or inadequate actions. Recently, of course, this problem has taken the form of managers acting as if they were in an inescapably mature industry setting when, if fact, they were not. But it has taken other forms as well.

One of the by-products of a national economy undergoing pronounced structural change is that, in addition to pockets of both genuinely mature and de-maturing industries, there are pockets of very rapid industrial growth. These high growth areas—some of them linked to cutting-edge advances in technology, but many tied to technologically familiar service activities— pose managerial challenges every bit as difficult as those in operations that are essentially stagnant or in the process of revitalization. In a de-maturing context, for example, managers must accommodate the entrenched price and quality expectations of customers while, at the same time, adjust to disruptive changes in product and process technology. In a high-growth industry, by contrast, the likelihood is that customer expectations are still in enough flux that managers have a great deal more flexibility in their experimentation with product design, fabrication, and marketing. Nonetheless, the huge number of companies that never make the transition from booming start-up to profitable mid-sized operation offers eloquent testimony to just how difficult that transition is.

The preceding pages stress the ill effects of a too-facile diagnosis of maturity because such diagnoses are still far too common, but not because most managers find themselves in a de-maturing context. Calling into question certain long-familiar assumptions about industry evolution is but one way to introduce the central issue to which this collection of articles addresses itself: helping managers be more sensitive to what the competitive environment in which they operate demands of them by way of strategy as well as tactics. If we can be sure of anything in the years ahead, it is that the upheavals now taking place in the nation's industrial base will boost, not diminish, the differences in the managerial challenges posed by different operating environments. Thus, the overriding importance of interpreting the nature of those environments correctly.

The 33 articles reprinted here from *HBR* speak directly to the problems of today's managers who face a growing need to adapt their efforts to quite various sets of industry circumstance. To be sure, it is nothing new for a modern economy to contain at the same time both ascending and declining industries. Freshly minted high-tech companies in Massachusetts occupy the buildings that, until recently, housed textile mills and shoe factories. Indeed, not since the pre-modern days of peasant agriculture have the conditions of economic life continued virtually unchanged from year to year or from generation to generation. What is new, however, is the degree to which a mixture of sunrise and sunset industries permeates the whole of the industrial landscape. No longer are there genuinely isolated pockets of boom or bust. No area is immune, and none is entirely without hope.

In practical terms, this loss of isolation means that economic conditions once only glimpsed from afar are now a part of immediate surroundings. Just as the communications media have broken down many of the old barriers of geographic distance, so the newly fluid checkerboard of industry growth and decline has worked to break down the old barriers of limited managerial experience. It has been said of the American South that its crushing defeat in the Civil War and its bitter endurance of a military occupation have given the region a heritage that is "far more closely in line with the common lot of mankind than the national legends of opulence and success and innocence."[2] In much the same fashion, the intimate coexistence of industrial growth and decay is not a violation of some historical norm. It is, by contrast, a return of American experience to the common pattern of industrial society from the aberrant general prosperity of the post-war years.

Accordingly, "The Changing Environment"—the first grouping or cluster of articles in this volume—has as its primary goal the careful depiction of the unfamiliar landscape, now just coming into view, through which American managers must find their way. "The New Industrial Competition," which begins this section, outlines the altered terms of competition confronting manufacturing industries, especially those exposed to attacks based on price and/or quality by companies located abroad. These attacks, which in turn rest upon mastery of a technology-driven strategy, efficient production, and innovative work force management, have in many cases—the automobile industry being only the most obvious example—unsettled the entrenched competitive dynamics of supposedly mature industries. Here, then, is detailed evidence that the possibility of de-maturity exists, but the question remains open whether that possibility will prove more threat than opportunity for American managers.

Raymond Vernon's thoughtful arguments in "Gone are the Cash Cows of Yesteryear" work to define more clearly the opportunity thus presented. With past advantages in cost structure, factors of production, and secure domestic markets rapidly disappearing, American companies have since 1970 faced the need to participate more fully in an increasingly integrated world economy. As Vernon sees it, the basic lesson for American managers is that they can no longer "either suppose that the innovations of other countries are irrelevant to American needs or expect that American innovations will hold a lead for any length of time over foreign competition." Consequently, their biggest challenge is "to create a scanning capability to survey the advances taking place in other countries and . . . to incorporate those advances whenever they are relevant to [domestic] needs."

But as Ted Levitt suggests in "The Globalization of Markets," required changes in the thinking of American managers go deeper still, to the very way they conceptualize the nature of international markets. Notwithstanding their immense cultural differences, most national markets are showing themselves to be highly responsive to reliable, low cost, standardized products. "Gone," Levitt tells us, "are accustomed differences in national or regional

preference. Gone are the days when a company could sell last year's models—
or lesser versions of advanced products—in the less-developed world."

Nonetheless, if isolationism in industry as in politics is no longer an
acceptable posture, the task of developing a workable internationalist viewpoint has been greatly complicated by unsettling changes at home. Not least
among these is the great reversal during the past few years of the long-term
secular trend since the 1930s toward an ever more stringent regulation of
business. As previously unheard of upheavals in the banking, transportation,
and communications industries make clear, it is no mean feat for managers
to lead their companies successfully through so precarious a transtition. In
"Deregulation: Surviving the Transition," Robertson, Ward, and Caldwell
chart the main obstacles to the development of the kind of market-oriented
thinking essential to survival in a world of deregulated competition.

Two articles by Bruce Scott, "Can Industry Survive the Welfare State?"
and "A National Strategy for Stronger U.S. Competitiveness," conclude
this section of the book. Taken together, they forge a significant interpretive
link between macroeconomic conditions at home and the competitiveness
of U.S. industry abroad. Relying on his extensive research in comparative
economics, Scott proposes a new way to think about economic strategy at
the national level. For Scott, to look at domestic industry in terms of a
theory of dynamic competitive advantage is to see how long-standing political
commitments and institutional arrangements, if not effectively challenged,
will lead inevitably to a decline in competitiveness and, by extension, in the
standard of living.

These, then, are the main features of the new environment in which
today's managers must operate. The second group of articles—"Re-exam-
ining the Conventional Wisdom"—asks, in effect, whether these features
work to challenge or confirm long-held assumptions about various aspects
of managerial practice. The first article—Bruce Scott's "The New Industrial
State: Old Myths and New Realities"—raises pointed questions about the
levels of performance that can legitimately be expected from different kinds
of business units. The second, Lawrence Revsine's "Let's Stop Eating our
Seed Corn," argues that unless accounting systems and the fiscal policies
to which they give rise accurately reflect the costs of maintaining physical
capital over time, even the best-intentioned moves to inflation-adjusted systems can rob a company of its ability to stay competitive.

Given the environmental changes noted above, many of the old managerial rules of thumb no longer apply as well as they once did. Moreover,
the costs—opportunity or otherwise—of mistakenly following them as a
quick-fix solution to pressing difficulties have escalated dramatically. At a
time when so many things are in flux, to act blindly on familiar assumptions
is to take the one sure road to disaster. For instance, "Can More Capital
Buy Higher Productivity?" asks Bradley Gale, who knows full well that
many, perhaps most, managers instinctively view a rapid infusion of capital
investment as a prime guarantee of improved returns. The evidence shows,

however, that a boost in capital investment per employee tends to raise levels of overall return only for companies with certain identifiable characteristics—low unionization, say, and low volume of sales from new products. It is simply not the case that a strategy of ever-increasing mechanization will work for everyone. More is not always better.

Nor, as Robert Buzzell demonstrates in "Is Vertical Integration Profitable?" does a strategy based on integration lead inexorably to better performance. In Buzzell's own summary, it is often the case that "rising investment requirements offset the higher profit margins associated with intensified vertical integration. If integration can somehow be achieved without the penalty of a proportionately higher investment base, then increasing vertical integration should be extremely beneficial." In other words, it depends. Much the same verdict emerges from Robert Leone and John Meyer's analysis of "Capacity Strategies for the 1980s." Managers accustomed to an investment environment marked by stable or declining costs will favor pre-emptive additions of large capacity increments in advance of growth in demand. By contrast, an environment marked by rising costs calls for small-scale capacity increments that lag behind demand growth. Given the levels of investment involved, the financial consequences of not adjusting capacity strategy to a changed environment can be catastrophic.

Having acknowledged these changes and their implications for management thought and practice, we then turn in the third section of the book to a detailed consideration of "Managing the Mature Company." The key point to remember here, of course, is not to allow perfectly reasonable advice about managing a mature business to become a self-fulfilling prophecy, that is, to "lock in" conditions of maturity that would not otherwise exist. Merely because a business is no longer characterized by rapid growth does not mean that all significant growth is over or that a period of revitalization is impossible. It is a bad mistake to assume that over many a corporate door hangs the invisible sign, Abandon hope, all ye who enter here.

In his early but still timely comments on "Diseases that Make Whole Industries Sick," Louis Newman challenges the readiness of managers in well-established industries to assume their businesses are volume- rather than price-sensitive and to compensate their sales force on that basis. When coupled with the inadequacies of most cost accounting systems, which often do not allow competitors to understand the logic behind each other's pricing policies, this volume orientation leads rather directly to an across-the-board depression of prices. As William Hall documents in "Survival Strategies in a Hostile Environment," stagnant industry conditions need not produce such self-defeating behavior at the company level. Even in troubled industries like steel or tires or home appliances, it is possible to earn eminently respectable returns, provided a company is able to achieve a leadership position in terms either of cost or of differentiation in product or service. Drawing on an extensive study of eight basic industries, Hall argues that with adequate planning managers can do more with mature businesses than simply milk them for cash.

Additional research, some of which appears in Carolyn Woo and Arnold Cooper's "The Surprising Case for Low Market Share," takes this line of argument further. Indeed, Woo and Cooper present clear evidence that in certain industry settings—low-growth markets with standardized products that are frequently purchased but infrequently changed—low-share businesses can be quite profitable. In "Strategies for Low Market Share Businesses," Hamermesh, Anderson, and Harris give attention to those strategic emphases—careful segmentation, efficient use of R&D, cautious growth— that give the lie to simplistic planning formulas that equate low share with low profit. The authors' judgment: "Simply put, not all low share businesses are 'dogs.'" In a second article, "How to Compete in Stagnant Industries," Hamermesh (with coauthor Steven Silk) outlines the strategic routes to high performance in such industries. The companies that do well "identify, create, and exploit growth segments . . . emphasize product quality and innovative product improvement . . . and improve the efficiency of their production and distribution systems." No surprises here, just good management.

To conclude this section, Kathryn Harrigan and Michael Porter draw from Porter's important work on competitive analysis a provocative set of "End-game Strategies for Declining Industries." Managers confronted by inexorably declining markets need to know how an industry declines, what the industry's exit barriers are, which pockets of demand remain, and how well their own strengths match those pockets of demand. Because accurate knowledge can lead to handsome opportunities for profit, managers ought to treat an industry's end-game as but another phase of development to be understood and mastered, not as something to drop out of as quickly as possible.

The fourth group of articles—"Getting Out, Buying In"—pushes these considerations one step further by addressing the difficult choices managers face when strategic necessity mandates change in the structure of assets. By way of introduction, Richard Hillman's advice on "How to Redeploy Assets" explicitly rejects the notion that integration is, in itself, a good thing that should not under any circumstances be upset. Effective modes of analysis are available to tell whether industry developments would give assets greater leverage if they were deployed differently. To the extent that redeployment implies the sale of assets, Arthur Bettauer's "Strategy for Divestments" offers early but still timely pointers. A more sophisticated rationale for divestiture as an integral part of strategy follows in "New Emphasis on Divestment Opportunities" by Robert Hayes.

The other side of the coin, of course, is the effort to redeploy assets through acquisition. Several times in the past quarter century, American business has witnessed an immense flurry of mergers and acquisitions. For their part, the press and the public have voiced great suspicion about the long-term value of such massive financial upheavals, and the business community has by and large responded by citing the penny-pinching economy of acquiring assets in this manner. History offers the stern reminder that, although some of these arrangements do turn out well, many do not and that the sheer waste involved, the inefficiencies and the human costs, can be extraordinarily large. On what basis, then, should managers approach acquisition decisions? How can they tell if the deal that looks so very appealing is, in fact, a disaster waiting to happen?

Drawing on their extensive research, Malcolm Salter and Wolf Weinhold advance a hard-headed argument in "Diversification via Acquisition: Creating Value." Their thesis: top management should undertake only those acquisitions that create value for shareholders. It is simply not the case that active diversification policies, especially into areas unrelated to a company's main line of business, tend to raise a company's overall economic performance. The proof, therefore, rests with those who want to show that a given acquisition would, indeed, create value for shareholders. In a second article, "Choosing Compatible Acquisitions," the same authors provide a detailed set of guidelines for screening proposed candidates. No matter how well this screening process is accomplished, companies can still go wrong in their determination both of how much to pay for an acquisition and of how to finance it. Alfred Rappaport considers these issues head-on in "Strategic Analysis for More Profitable Acquisitions," which leads the reader step-by-step through the necessary financial analyses.

There are, to be sure, still other modes of asset redeployment. In "Venturing Corporations—Think Small to Stay Strong," Mark Hanan makes the classic case for diversification through internal ventures. When even well-planned efforts failed in the past, more often than not managers were unable to see that, as Hanan puts it, "new business ventures are best treated as small start-up businesses, not as large businesses in miniature." And when managers did understand this distinction, they often had unrealistic expectations about the speed with which a new venture would begin to show returns competitive with those of mature businesses. Based on a study of some 200 companies in the *Fortune* "500" and of the PIMS data base, Ralph Biggadike finds that it takes a successful new venture 10 to 12 years before its ROI reaches such levels. These findings, summarized in "The Risky Business of Diversification," are ripe with implications for the appropriate scale of new venture activities. "New Ventures for Corporate Growth" by Edward Roberts comes at these questions from a different angle, as it charts the range of venture strategies available and the particular demands each makes on management.

The final group of articles—"Managing the Growth Company"—completes the circuit of thought defined at the outset, namely, the pressing need for managers to adapt both concept and behavior to the environmental context in which deep-seated structural changes in industry have placed them. Donald Clifford's examination of the "Growth Pains of the Threshold Company" provides a careful overview of the challenges confronting managers as they try to guide their companies into the ranks of the *Fortune* "500." Informal modes of organization are no longer sufficient, but the mere introduction of formal systems, without a substantial change in the way managers think, is not enough to get a company successfully over the threshold.

Especially when operating in this no man's land, managers who do not have a firm sense of strategic purpose all too easily succumb to the notion of "growth at any price." As when riding a bicycle downhill, they think they have to keep going faster in order just to keep from falling off. William Fruhan's sober assessment in "How Fast Should Your Company Grow?" confirms what common sense has long suspected: fast growth without profitability is a good way to destroy a company's market valuation. If projections of future ROE do not exceed the cost of equity capital, a policy of rapid growth is counterproductive. In Fruhan's blunt summary, "In short, the key to value is profitability. If you've got it, flaunt it. If you haven't got it, try to get it. If you can't get it, get out."

Even where growth is desirable, there are strict internal limits on the rate of growth a company can reasonably afford. Knowing what those limits are, however, especially during a period of inflation, is no easy matter. Alfred Rappaport's "Measuring Company Growth Capacity During Inflation" addresses this tricky problem by developing a "distributable funds measure" (the maximum amount a company can pay out to its shareholders without compromising its business capability). According to Rappaport, using replacement cost accounting is not enough to give managers of growth companies all the information they need. Bradley Gale and Ben Branch's "Cash Flow Analysis: More Important than Ever" supplements Rappaport's argument by providing a coherent method for understanding the cash flow implications—and requirements—of different growth strategies.

Equally important is rapid growth, in the form of a quest for high market share, always of strategic value (provided, of course, it does not wreak havoc with corporate finances or market valuation)? In other words, if a company can afford it, is the god of market share a god always worth following? Paul Bloom and Philip Kotler answer no in their "Strategies for High Market-share Companies." There are risks that dog the steps of high-share companies, and managers must take them fully into account before embarking on a share-driven strategy. Overambition can spell lasting trouble, as William Fruhan illustrates in "Pyrrhic Victories in Fights for Market Share." There is no substitute for managers developing an intimate understanding of their own companies and of the industries in which they compete. No abstract rule that "share is good" ought triumph over sound professional knowledge of what is possible and appropriate. Here, again, the question is one of fit—of assuring the proper match of a company's abilities with its strategic choices in a given environment.

Such, then, is the logic behind this collection of articles from *HBR*. We offer them to you on their individual merits but also in the hope that their arrangement together gives useful emphasis to the sensitivity with which today's managers must evaluate the unsettled and unsettling operating environments in which circumstance has placed them. As Raymond Vernon quite rightly insists in an article reprinted here, "In the end, U.S. business will have to accept the fact that its competitive position in world markets has changed profoundly. . . . Changes in attitude come slowly, but I am betting that many U.S. enterprises will be able to make the shift.'' This volume is part of *HBR*'s commitment to helping that change in attitude take place—and take hold.

Notes

1.   Exhibits 3 and 4 are taken from William J. Abernathy, Kim B. Clark, and Alan M. Kantrow, *Industrial Renaissance* (New York, Basic Books, 1983), chapter 8 and appendix C.

2.   C. Vann Woodward, *The Burden of Southern History* (New York: New American Library, revised edition, 1969), p. 31.

PART ONE

THE CHANGING ENVIRONMENT

AN OVERVIEW

In the political universe of the eighteenth century, there was an immense difference in characterizing a series of events as belonging to a rebellion or as belonging to a revolution. The former term implied chaotic action, a violent upheaval in the proper nature of things; the latter, drawn from the sciences of mechanics and astronomy, implied a more orderly reversal of fortunes in a world otherwise undisturbed. Of late, as one follows accounts in the business press and management literature of the profound structural changes occurring in the industrial sphere, what one hears by and large is that we are in the midst of a revolution (in the older sense of the term), not a rebellion. For all the variations in rules and participants, the basic nature of the contest remains unaltered.

For many American managers, these reports have seemed a bit of good news. If it is business as usual except that the name of the person at the top of the heap is Japanese and not English, then all responsible executives need to do is try to improve what they are doing already. As the articles in this section make clear, however, such reports are false. It is not business as usual. The changes are not in surface appearance only. What we are facing is a genuine rebellion (again, in the older sense of the term) against the established dynamics of industrial competition. In structural terms, the economic world is no longer as it was even as recently as a quarter century ago. Somewhere in the experience of the past decade or two, future historians will draw a line and say, That is where one industrial era ended and another began.

The six articles that follow attempt, each in its own way, to make practical sense of the transition now in train. Their arguments and emphases vary, but they speak with a single voice in their recognition that the kinds of adjustments required of managers and policymakers alike are not once-and-for-all adaptations to a new, fixed set of circumstances. Instead, they call for a hitherto unfamiliar capacity of ongoing adaptation to constant change. The modern world is not about to replace one industrial *ancien régime* with another; it offers, rather, the more troubling prospect of a continual state of rebellion.

"Henry Ford, as Alfred P. Sloan recalled him" (runs the conclusion of "The New Industrial Competition"), "was a man who had had '. . . many brilliant insights in his earlier years, [but] seemed never to understand how completely the market had changed from the one in which he had made his name and to which he was accustomed. . . . The old master failed to master change.' That is still the crucial challenge—and opportunity."

1

The New Industrial Competition

WILLIAM J. ABERNATHY, KIM B. CLARK,
and ALAN M. KANTROW

The results of Japanese competition in U.S. markets are evident to all Americans. Repercussions from competitive pressures exerted by European and Japanese manufacturers have been or are being felt by U.S. producers of cars, machine tools, minicomputers, commercial aircraft, textile machinery, and color TV sets, to name a few traditional businesses. Taking auto manufacture as their case example, the authors of this article attribute the Japanese carmakers' success to superiority in the manufacturing plant, especially in their process systems and work force management.

The authors describe the current dilemma of U.S. car manufacturers, who find themselves at a crossroads because this struggle has changed the rules of the game. Now these producers face a situation in which advancing technology and the momentous changes it wreaks—instead of the incremental changes through styling, marketing, and service to which U.S. manufacturers are accustomed—will determine the winners and losers. As often happens in a mature industry when a new phase of competition appears, the auto industry may well undergo a renewal that transforms it. The challenge for U.S. companies in endangered industries is to recognize the altered situation, adjust to it, and learn to manage change.

It is barely possible that in some remote corner of the United States a latter-day Rip Van Winkle awoke this morning fresh with shining images of American industry in the 1950s still fixed in his head. But it is not very likely. Who, after all, during the past few years could have slept undisturbed through the general chorus of lament about the economy? Who could have remained unaware that much of U.S. industry—especially the mature manufacturing sector—has fallen on hard times?

Published 1981.

And who did not have a surefire remedy? Born-again supply-siders argued for the massive formation of capital; "new class" advocates of a more systematic industrial policy, for better allocation of existing capital; industrial economists, for enhanced productivity; organized labor, for a coherent effort at reindustrialization; subdued (if unrepentant) Keynesians, for more artful demand management; boisterous Lafferites, for a massive tax cut; congressional experts, for carefully targeted tax breaks on depreciation and investment; Friedmanites, for tight money; and Naderites, for an anti-corporate economic democracy.

This loudly divided counsel on the best strategy for managing economic change reflects inadequacy in both perception and understanding: our current industrial malaise defies the usual interpretations and resists the usual prescriptions. Managing change successfully has proved difficult because policymakers in business and government, trained in an old economic calculus, have found it hard to see the new competitive realities for what they are— or to identify the best terms in which to analyze them.

Policymakers fail to understand that the old rules of thumb and worn assumptions no longer hold. Similarly, the traditional structural arrangements in many industries—the familiar relationship between, say, labor and management or producer and supplier—no longer square with the facts of competitive life. As a result, decision makers who continue to act as if nothing has happened are, at best, ineffective and, at worst, inadvertent agents of economic disaster.

Levers of Change

What has happened? The two principal changes have been greater exposure to international competition and technical advances that alter competition. For a start, let's look at two basic major manufacturing industries that have experienced these forces.

☐ This industry was confronted with new competitors who emphasized high productivity, reliability, quality, and competent design (but not innovative design, except for Sony).

☐ Many competitors—Warwick, Motorola, and Admiral among them— did not survive the foreign thrust and were either taken over or went out of business.

☐ Foreign competitors' emphasis on manufacturing, a critical element, was transferred to their U.S. operations—witness Sanyo's management of the previously unsuccessful old Warwick plant, with many of the same employees and U.S. middle managers.

☐ Now technological changes have created a situation of potential renewal of the product life cycle—developments in videocassette recorders, videodiscs, flat high-resolution screens, telecommunications, and computers may combine to revolutionize the television business.

And another is textile machinery:

☐ Before the 1960s a few U.S. manufacturers (e.g., Draper) dominated this business; conglomerates acquired them (e.g., Rockwell International took over Draper).

☐ The U.S. manufacturers began to lose business primarily because of deterioration in product performance relative to European and Japanese models and failure to remain at the cutting edge of new technology.

☐ Because of insufficient investment (conglomerates treated them as cash cows), the once-dominant U.S. manufacturers have lost technical and market leadership to the Swiss, Germans, and Japanese.

Now consider two other industries that are facing the new forces of international competition.

One of them is computers:

☐ Fujitsu has introduced a mainframe computer that attacks IBM where its strength is—service. Fujitsu is doing this by building a high-quality reliable machine that can *guarantee* 99% uptime. In a test run of strategy, Fujitsu has taken on IBM in Australia with this approach and bested the U.S. giant in obtaining some mainframe contracts. The experience there to date: 99.8% uptime.

☐ In minicomputers and home computers the Japanese are entering the U.S. market. Producers like Mitsubishi, Nippon Electric, and Hitachi will soon offer high-quality products that are cost competitive.

And another is machine tools:

☐ Japanese producers have entered this market with a strategy built around a very reliable, high-quality product. Recently, for instance, a U.S. auto producer ordered transfer lines from an established U.S. machine tool manufacturer and from Toyota. The lines arrived at the U.S. plant at the same time. Toyota sent two engineers who had the equipment running and fully debugged in two weeks, while the competitor's team of eight engineers spent several months getting its line operational.

☐ Developments in new technology—electronics, optical and tactile sensors, lasers, and robotics—are creating opportunities for improved metalworking operations and are opening up new applications in areas like assembly and inspection, where mechanization and automation have hardly played a role. Integration of these advances with computerized design and manufacturing could change the very concepts on which traditional machine tools are founded.

A number of other long-stable U.S. manufacturing industries no doubt will be shaken in the not-distant future by these pressures. One is the air compressor field, which a few companies have dominated. A Japanese producer, Hokuetsu, entered its domestic market five years ago and now rules it. Among the companies left in its wake is Ingersoll-Rand, whose market share in Japan plunged from well over 50% to zero. Hokuetsu offers a dependable good-quality product at half the cost of the comparable U.S. compressor.

Still another field is major household appliances, which the Japanese have slated for heavy export activity in this decade. Sanyo, Toshiba, and other companies are setting up U.S. plants and distribution systems. General Electric, for one, is worried; GE has begun a program designed to improve greatly the quality and productivity of its Louisville appliance complex.

The list of endangered industries goes on: jet engines, commercial aircraft, small forklift trucks, steel, electric motors, lawnmowers, and chainsaws, to name just a few.

Character of the New Competition

Let us focus on a single industry to show in detail the character of the conditions that the imperiled U.S. industries face. An inkling of these conditions has entered the consciousness of all Americans as they witnessed Japan's extraordinary success in capturing a large share of the automobile market from the entrenched Big Three domestic producers. In this article we go beyond the previously known facts and show exactly how the Japanese implemented their strategy on the plant floor, on the engineers' design boards, and in the executive offices.

Until recently, developments in the U.S. auto industry were determined mostly by government policies and economic forces peculiar to North America. The sheer extent of the U.S. market and its productive base had long guaranteed the industry a largely self-contained posture. Over the past 15 years, however, the competitive boundaries have expanded drastically until now they are virtually worldwide in scope.

Accompanying this expansion has been a rapid increase in the number of healthy competitors. These new international players, moreover, have quite a different approach from that of the U.S. Big Three; their plan consists of radically new strategies, modes of operation, and production experience.

More to the point, the novel competitive challenge they present cannot be overcome by the familiar responses U.S. companies have long used against each other. Strategically, the Big Three are well prepared to fight not this new war, but the last one.

Many observers believe that the perceived low quality of Detroit's vehicles is a simple function of lethargy and past practice. This view ignores the close connection between poor quality and a disadvantage in costs. The productive capacity of some new entrants, notably the Japanese, enjoys a significant cost advantage over that of the Americans. The Japanese have been especially skillful in exploiting this advantage by adding performance and quality to their cars. This combination of competitive price and high quality has proved tremendously successful in reaching consumers in the American market.

What makes this advantage particularly troublesome is that it does not represent primarily an investment problem; if it did, it would be far easier to remedy. Instead, it arises to some extent from differences in wage rates and, more significant, from differences in productivity and management of operations.

In 1973, when Lee A. Iacocca was asked about the competitive advantage of innovation as perceived by Ford, he responded simply, "Give them [American consumers] leather. They can smell it." In Ford's reading of the U.S. market, innovation did not pay; styling did. Things are quite different today: technology matters.

In the 1950s and 1960s, product technology was competitively neutral. No auto company sought a competitive advantage through significant innovation. In the 1980s, however, the necessity for advantage through innovation is steadily growing. In fact, consumer preference for small fuel-efficient automobiles has developed faster in the United States than it did earlier in Europe or Japan. Beset by unfortunate decisions in the past, the continued absence of a workable long-term energy policy, conflicting regulatory requirements, and the massive financial demands posed by a retooling of production capacity, U.S. producers find themselves at a serious technological disadvantage.

But this is not all. The edge that U.S. companies have long enjoyed in mass production technology and in the resulting economies of scale—an edge long believed essential to competitive success—no longer obtains. Most of the standard U.S. technology is either already widely diffused or easily transferable. Moreover, the process technology for the new smaller autos is subtly but significantly different from that now in place. In other words, changing market preferences and changing rates of technology diffusion have diluted, perhaps destroyed, the established scale economies of U.S. producers.

Premium on Management

Two main distinctions have largely provided the structure for discussions of manufacturing competitiveness. The first is the division between analysis and prescription of a "macro" sort (that is, having to do with such overarching questions of economic management as fiscal and monetary policy and tax incentives) and those of a "micro" sort (that is, having to do with issues relating to the management of particular companies). The second is the division between analysis and prescription based on "hardware" (equipment, buildings, and machinery) and those based on "software" (people management, organizational systems, and corporate strategies).

Considered together, these distinctions form the simple matrix shown in Exhibit 1. Although the distinctions among these quadrants are rough, they are nonetheless useful. In practice, however, they are often neglected, which has left the unfortunate impression in some minds that the current industrial difficulties are composed equally—and indistinguishably—of problems in all the quadrants.

This impression has been mischievous, for these difficulties and their remedies are distributed unevenly about the matrix. In the auto industry the key measures for meeting the new competition fall primarily into Quadrant 4.

Exhibit 1.   Key Elements in Manufacturing Competitiveness

	Macro	Micro
Hardware	1. Government fiscal and monetary policies Taxation Capital markets Savings	2. Production capability Plant Equipment
Software	3. Socioeconomic environment Work ethic Regulation Education	4. Corporate management Organization Administration Production systems

Japanese Micromanagement

The Japanese advantage in production costs and product quality in the auto industry, as well as many other established U.S. industries, is not only a fact defining the new competitive reality but also the result of a carefully honed approach to management—the stuff of Quadrant 4. Americans' talk of overregulation, and underdepreciation, pervasive national culture, and markedly absent government support is misplaced.

Costs of Production

Several estimates have placed the landed cost advantage in U.S. markets of Japanese-produced subcompact cars in the $400 to $600 range per vehicle. For example, Abraham Katz, then assistant secretary of commerce for international economic policy, testified last year that "the apparent cost advantage to Japanese producers may have been $560 per car in 1979."[1]

These estimates, in our view, seriously understate the advantage. In the first place, they fail to reflect both current rates of labor compensation and, perhaps more important, the great differences in productivity between Japanese and American manufacturers. Furthermore, they are often based on a narrow definition of the productive units to be compared, for they assume that the relevant comparison is between two original equipment manufacturers—say, Ford and Toyota—even though the really meaningful comparison lies between two productive systems, or "confederations"— that is, an OEM and its constellation of suppliers.

To get a truer picture of the Japanese cost advantage, we must therefore produce estimates that account for productivity differentials, labor costs, and industry structure.

The first step in developing these improved estimates is to update assessments of differential labor productivity. We know that in 1974 output per labor hour in the Japanese auto industry—OEMs and suppliers—was 88% of the level in the United States (that is, the ratio of Japanese to U.S. productivity was 0.88). Published data suggest that growth in labor productivity in the Japanese auto industry (motor vehicles and parts) averaged 8% to 9% in the 1970s; the comparable figure for the United States was 3% to 4%. Using a midrange estimate of the difference (5%), we arrive at a 1980 productivity ratio of 1.18. This means that in 1980 Japanese producers operated at a productivity level almost 20% above that of their American competitors.

This rapid growth was offset in part by higher rates of wage increase: in 1974 Japanese hourly compensation rates were about 37% of those in the United States, while in 1980 they were roughly 50%. Dividing the compensation ratio (0.5) by the productivity ratio (1.18) yields a unit labor cost ratio of 0.424—a figure that has remained more or less constant during the entire 1974–1980 period.

Table A in the Appendix translates this steady labor cost ratio into a Japanese advantage of $1,673. Subtracting $400 for freight and tariff costs yields a landed cost advantage of $1,273 on a 1980 subcompact that sells in the American market for about $5,500—a cost advantage of 23%.

Although the calculations in Table A are based on a number of un-documented assumptions about cost structure and labor content, reasonable adjustment of these assumptions would not affect the order of magnitude of the Japanese cost advantage. Indeed, we were biased conservatively throughout in estimating that cost advantage. Moreover, inclusion of general adminis-trative and selling expenses, as well as the costs of capital and salaried personnel, would leave the Japanese cost advantage intact. So we figure that Japanese producers enjoy a $1,200 landed cost advantage on every small vehicle sold in the United States.

We can to some extent check these numbers against information in the annual reports of major U.S. and Japanese producers. These reports yield data on the costs of nonlabor inputs and salaried personnel but none on the labor embodied in components or materials.

Getting at these data, however, presents several analytic problems. Perhaps the most serious is the great difference between U.S. and Japanese OEMs in their degree of vertical integration and in the nature of their re-lationships with suppliers. At Toyota, for example, purchases account for almost 80% of the value of sales; but because Toyota holds an equity interest in many of its suppliers, this figure is somewhat misleading. Comparable data for U.S. companies show much less reliance on suppliers; GM, for instance, has a purchase-to-sale ratio of less than 50%.

A second problem is the quite different product mix of U.S. and Jap-anese OEMs. The data we use come from 1979, when medium-size cars dominated the U.S. Big Three's product lines. The Japanese were producing a much narrower range of vehicles and, of course, were emphasizing the subcompact segment.

Table B in the Appendix shows estimates of total employee costs per vehicle in 1979 at Ford and Toyo Kogyo (Mazda). Our calculations suggest that assembly of the average Ford vehicle required 112.5 employee hours; a Toyo Kogyo vehicle, only 47. Employee costs in building the Ford vehicle were $2,464; for Toyo Kogyo, $491.

As already noted, this sizable cost gap reflects differences in product mix and vertical integration as well as in labor costs and productivity. In-formation on value added in the annual reports and discussions with industry sources suggest that the Toyo Kogyo results should be increased by 15% to 20% to adjust for vertical integration. Using these higher estimates yields a per-vehicle total of 56 hours instead of 47. (To correct for product mix, we have estimated the cost to Ford of producing the Toyo Kogyo product mix. These calculations are presented in Table C in the Appendix.)

Our analysis of annual report data suggests that in 1979 the difference between Ford and Toyo Kogyo employee costs per small vehicle was about $1,300. Updating this figure to 1980 might increase the absolute dollar amount somewhat, but the evidence we cited on relative growth rates in productivity and compensation implies that the percentage gap would not change much.

Adjustment for changes in exchange rates would also have a negligible effect. Using a rate of 200 yen to the dollar (the approximate rate at the end of 1980) instead of 218 would reduce the gap by only $50. And when we adjust this $1,300 to reflect the U.S. advantage in administrative and selling expenses, the 2.9% tariff with the relevant freight costs for Japanese imports, and the Japanese productivity edge at the supplier level, we emerge with a landed cost advantage for Japanese OEMs of about $1,400.

Exhibit 2.   Evidence on Assembly Quality of U.S. Autos Versus Certain Imports

	Vehicle Category	Condition at Delivery[a]	Condition After One Month of Service[b]
	Aggregates	**Domestic**	**Imports**
	Subcompact	6.4	7.9
	Compact	6.2	7.7
	Midsize	6.6	8.1
	Standard	6.8	—
Models	**Domestic**		
	Omni	7.4	4.10
	Chevette	7.2	3.00
	Pinto	6.5	3.70
	Rabbit (U.S.)[a]	7.8	2.13
	Horizon	7.5	NA
	Imports		
	Civic	8.0	1.23[b]
	Fiesta	7.9	NA
	Colt	7.8	NA
	Corolla	7.8	0.71[c]

Source: Aggregates—Rogers National Research, *Buyer Profiles*, 1979; models—industry sources.
[a]Scale of 1–10; 10 is excellent.
[b]Number of defects per vehicle shipped.
[c]European Rabbit averages 1.42 defects per vehicle shipped.
[d]Honda average.
[e]Toyota average.

Contrasts in Product Quality

It is, of course, true that the competitively important dimensions of auto quality are established not by experts but by the market. And many American consumers, who place a high value on quality of assembly workmanship (what the industry calls "fits and finishes"), on reliability, and on durability, seem to believe that Japanese cars are superior in each of these dimensions.

Exhibit 2, which presents industry data on assembly quality, suggests that consumer perceptions are consistent with experience. Buyers rated the imports as a group superior in quality to the domestically produced cars, while the top Japanese models were ranked first and third among the nine rated. Japanese makes also had fewer defects after one month of service.

Similarly, subscribers to *Consumer Reports* gave high ratings to Japanese autos for reliability as measured by the incidence of repairs (see Exhibit 3). Nevertheless, what little evidence exists indicates that U.S.-built vehicles

Exhibit 3.   Ratings of Body and Mechanical Repair Frequency[a]

Make All Models	Body 1980	Mechanical 1980
Domestic		
Buick	9.3	9.4
Chevrolet	8.4	8.9
Dodge	10.0	10.0
Ford	7.2	9.2
Lincoln	8.1	8.4
Oldsmobile	8.4	9.3
Volkswagen	11.3	8.6
Imports		
Datsun	15.3	10.8
Honda	16.0	11.1
Mazda	17.5	12.7
Toyota	16.9	12.4
Volkswagen	11.3	10.0
Volvo	11.9	10.5

Source: *Consumer Reports* annual auto issue, April 1981.

[a]Average = 10; maximum = 20; minimum = 0.

The data cover repair frequency of mechanical systems, components, and body (structure and finish). Ratings are given in five categories: average, below average, far below average, above average, and far above average. Beginning with a score of zero for far below average, we have assigned values of 5, 10, 15, and 20 to the other categories. The sum of the scores on body and mechanical systems gives the total score.

Exhibit 4. Customer Loyalty[a]

	Domestic	Imports	Total
Subcompact	77.2	91.6	81.2
Compact	74.2	91.4	72.4
Midsize	75.3	94.5	76.9
Standard	81.8	—	—
Luxury	86.6	94.6	87.2
Weighted average	78.7	91.8	—

Source: Rogers National Research, *Buyer Profiles*, 1979.
[a]Percent who would buy same make/model again.

have superior corrosion protection and longer-lived components and systems.

At any rate, American automobiles enjoy much less customer loyalty than do Japanese imports. Exhibit 4, which summarizes the data on loyalty, gives perhaps the clearest evidence of the differential customer perception of product value for each dollar spent.

Lessons of Quadrant 4

Most explanations of this Japanese advantage in production costs and product quality emphasize the impact of automation, the strong support of the central government, and the pervasive influence of national culture. No doubt these factors have played an important role, but the primary sources of this advantage are found instead in the Japanese producers' mastery of Quadrant 4—that is, in their execution of a well-designed strategy based on the shrewd use of manufacturing excellence.

It may seem odd to think of manufacturing as anything other than a competitive weapon, yet the history of the U.S. auto market shows that by the late 1950s manufacturing had become a competitively neutral factor. It was not, of course, unimportant, but none of the major American producers sought great advantage through superior manufacturing performance. Except perhaps for their reliance on economies of scale, they tended to compete by means of styling, marketing, and dealership networks.

The Japanese cost and quality advantage, however, originates in painstaking strategic management of people, materials, and equipment—that is, in superior manufacturing performance. This approach, in our view, arose from the Japanese pattern of domestic competition and the need for an effective strategy to enter the U.S. market.

At that time the Japanese realized it would be foolish to compete head-

on with the established domestic producers' competence in making elabo-
rately (and annually) styled large cars with a "boulevard ride." They lacked
the experience, the manufacturing base, and the resources. Instead, taking
a lesson from Volkswagen's success, the Japanese concentrated on producing a reliable, high-quality, solid-performance small automobile and on back-
ing it up with a responsible network of dealers.

Exhibit 5 outlines the seven factors most responsible for successful
productivity performance and compares the Japanese practice in each with
the American. On the basis of extensive discussions with U.S. industry
executives, engineers, and consultants, we have ranked these factors in the
order of their importance in determining the current state of the industry
and have given them approximate relative weights.

Surprisingly, the hardware associated with technology—new automation and product design—proves relatively insignificant in assessing the
competitive difficulties of the U.S. manufacturers, although its importance
for the future of the industry grows ever larger. Despite the publicity given
Japan's experimentation with industrial robots and advanced assembly plants
like Nissan's Zama facility, the evidence suggests that U.S. producers have
so far maintained roughly comparable levels of process equipment. However
appealing they may be, Quadrant 2 explanations cannot themselves account
for U.S.–Japanese differentials in manufacturing productivity.

Focus on "Process Yield"

To the contrary, a valid explanation must start with the factor of "process
yield," an amalgam of management practices and systems connected with
production planning and control. This yield category reflects Japanese superiority in operating processes at high levels of efficiency and output over
long periods of time. Although certain engineering considerations (machine
cycles, plant layouts, and the like) are significant here, the Japanese advantage has far more to do with the interaction of materials control systems,
maintenance practices, and employee involvement. Exhibit 6 attempts to
make this interaction clear.

At the heart of the Japanese manufacturing system is the concept of
"just in time" production. Often called *Kanban* (after the cards or tickets
used to trigger production), the system is designed so that materials, parts,
and components are produced or delivered just before they are needed. Tight
coupling of the manufacturing stages reduces the need for work-in-process
inventory. This reduction helps expose any waste of time or materials, use
of defective parts, or improper operation of equipment.[2]

Furthermore, because the system will not work if frequent or lengthy
breakdowns occur, it creates inescapable pressure for maximizing uptime
and minimizing defects. This pressure, in turn, supports a vigorous maintenance program. Most Japanese plants operate with only two shifts, which
allows for thorough servicing of equipment during nonproductive time and

Exhibit 5.   Seven Factors Affecting Productivity: Comparison of Technology, Management, and Organization

Factor, with Ranking and Relative Weights	Definition	Comparative Practice, Japan Relative to United States
Process systems Process yield 1 (40%)	Output rate variations in conventional manufacturing lines; good parts per hour from a line, press, work group, or process line. Key determinants are machine cycle times, system uptime, and reliability, affected by materials control methods, maintenance practices, and operating patterns.	Production-materials control minimizes inventory, reduces scrap, exposes problems. Line stops highlight problems and help eliminate defects. Operators perform routine maintenance; scheduling of two shifts instead of three leaves time for better maintenance.
Quality systems 5 (9%)	Series of controls and inspection plans to ensure that products are built to specifications.	Japanese use fewer inspectors. Some authority and responsibility are vested in production worker and supervisor; good relationship with supplier and very high standards lead to less incoming inspection.
Technology Process automation 4 (10%)	Introduction and adaptation of advanced, state-of-the-art manufacturing equipment.	Overall, state of technology is comparable. Japanese use more robots; their stamping facilities appear somewhat more automated than average U.S. facilities.
Product design 6 (7%)	Differences in the way the car is designed for a given market segment; aspects affecting productivity: tolerances, number of parts, fastening methods, etc.	Japanese have more experience in small car production and have emphasized design for manufacturability (i.e., productivity and quality). Newer U.S. models

Exhibit 5. *(Continued)*

Factor, with Ranking and Relative Weights	Definition	Comparative Practice, Japan Relative to United States
		(Escort, GM J-car) are first models with design/ manufacturing specifications comparable to Japanese.
Work force management		
Absenteeism 3 (12%)	All employee time away from the workplace, including excused, unexcused, medical, personal, contractual and other reasons.	Levels of contractual time off are comparable; unexcused absences are much higher in United States.
Job structure 2 (18%)	Tasks and responsibilities included in job definitions.	Japanese practice is to create jobs with more breadth (more tasks or skill per job) and depth (more involvement in planning and control of operations); labor classifications are broader; regular production workers perform more skilled tasks; management layers are fewer.
Work pace 7 (4%)	Speed at which operators perform tasks.	Evidence is inconclusive; some lines run faster, some appear to run more slowly.

Exhibit 6. Determinants of Process Yield

Rated machine speed		Uptime		1-Defect Rate		Annual Output of Good Parts
	×	Hours per year	×	Good parts/	=	
Total parts per hour				Total parts		

results in a much lower rate of machine breakdown and failure than in the United States.

Pressure for elimination of defects makes itself felt not in maintenance schedules but in the relationships of producers with suppliers and in work practices on the line. Just-in-time production does not permit extensive inspection of incoming parts. Suppliers must, therefore, maintain consistently high levels of quality, and workers must have the authority to stop operations if they spot defects or other production problems.

Worker-initiated line stoppages are central to the concept of *Jidoka* (making a just-surfaced problem visible to everyone by bringing operations to a halt), which—along with Kanban—helps direct energy and attention to elimination of waste, discovery of problems, and conservation of resources.

It is difficult, of course, to separate the effects of Kanban-Jidoka on process yield from the effects of, say, job structure and quality systems—factors given a somewhat lower ranking by the experts we consulted (see Exhibit 5). It is also difficult to separate them from the benefits of having a loyal work force (Japanese factories have little unexcused absenteeism). Taken together, these aspects of work force management clearly account for much of the Japanese advantage in production.

It is sometimes argued, by the way, that the union–management relationship in the United States helps explain the superior Japanese performance in productivity and product quality. There is no doubt that the industrial relations system in the U.S. auto industry is a critical element in its performance. Nor is there any doubt that many aspects of that system do not square with the new facts of competitive life. Yet to lay these problems at the door of the union—and only there—is misleading.

Employment contracts and collective bargaining relationships do not just happen. Indeed, a contract provision that a company today finds dysfunctional often was initiated by management some time in the past. Moreover, the production philosophy embodied in a contract may have had its origins in the very early days of the industry, long before unionization. Finally, many of the systems and practices that inhibit performance have little to do with a collective bargaining agrement.

Superior manufacturing performance, the key to the Japanese producers' competitive success, is therefore not the fruit of government policy, technical hardware, or national culture (Quadrants 1, 2, and 3). Instead it derives simply from the way people and operations are organized and managed (Quadrant 4).

Technological Renewal

Having looked at causes, we now turn our attention to cures. In a time of expensive energy, by their success in the marketplace Japanese producers have rekindled interest in the automobile—especially the small, fuel-efficient automobile—as a product and thus have opened the way for technology to become the relevant basis of competition in the American market. As one General Motors executive remarked, "We took a look at the Honda Accord and we knew that the game had changed."

But does the American auto industry—or, for that matter, do government bureaucrats, lenders, and suppliers—really understand that the game has changed? Our investigation indicates that it has not—yet. We often hear two interpretations of the current crisis, both of them deeply flawed. By extension, both of these interpretations can apply to other sectors of the U.S. industrial economy.

Misperceptions of Causes

The first of these interpretations, which we call "the natural consequences of maturity," holds that what has happened is the natural consequence of life cycle processes operating internationally on mature industrial sectors. Once an industry reaches the point where its production process has been embodied in equipment available for purchase—that is, once its mode of production is stable and well known—the location of factories becomes a simple matter of exploiting geographic advantages in the relative costs of production. In this view, it makes perfect sense to move these facilities out of the United States as lower cost opportunities become available elsewhere.

Many economists argue that rather than coming to the aid of threatened industries, government and management should follow the path of least resistance, so to speak, and let the life cycle work its will. They recommend a policy not of intervention but, in the phrase of Edward M. Graham, of "positive adjustment." "Government should not," he writes, "protect or subsidize industries that are threatened by imports or [are otherwise] noncompetitive internationally, but should take concrete steps to encourage the transfer of resources from less into more competitive industries."[3]

The question of who is sufficiently infallible to be entrusted with the nasty job of picking winners and losers is, of course, conveniently left unanswered. The evidence to date suggests that no one is.

The second line of interpretation, which we call "transient economic misfortune," is a considerably more optimistic point of view. It holds that the present difficulties with automobiles are temporary, the result of rapid changes in oil prices and consumer preferences. Cost or quality is not the problem, but inappropriate capacity: too many facilities for building big cars.

The forces needed to right the competitive balance are even now locked into place, their happy result merely a matter of time and of bringing the needed capacity on line. Understandably, this view of things appealed strongly to many in the Carter administration, who could use it to rationalize a firm policy of doing nothing.

Both of these interpretive schemes are inadequate—not only because they ignore differences in Quadrant 4 management but also because they count on future stability in technology. Adherents of the maturity thesis assume an irreversible tendency of products to become standardized—that is, technologically stable over time. Adherents of the misfortune thesis, assuming that all outstanding technological problems have been solved, see the industry as needing only to bring the requisite capacity on line to recapture its competitive standing.

Both groups of adherents argue from a set of familiar but outdated assumptions about the relation of technology to industrial development. Looking back on the years since World War II as a period of competition in autos based mainly on economies of scale, styling, and service networks, they persist in viewing the car manufacturers as constituting a typical mature industry, in which any innovation is incremental, never radical, and is thus—in marketing terms—virtually invisible.

Fluidity Versus Stability

Times have changed. Environmental concerns and the escalating price of oil have combined since the oil shock of 1979 to change the structure of market demand fundamentally. Technological innovation—in its radical as well as its incremental forms—again has vital competitive significance.

Changes in product technology have become at once more rapid and more extreme. Unlike most of the postwar period, recent technical advances have spawned a marked diversity in available systems and components. In engines alone, the once dominant V-8 has been joined by engines with four, five, and six cylinders, diesel engines, rotary engines, and engines with turbocharging and computer feedback control.

Moreover, these kinds of product innovation are increasingly radical in their effects on production processes. We have moved from a period in which product innovation focused on the refinement and extension of existing concepts to a period in which completely new concepts are developed and introduced. And this transition from a time of little change in production systems to a time of great turbulence in equipment, processes, skills, and organization is only beginning.

If our assessment is right, this shift in the nature of innovation will have far-reaching implications for the structure of the industry, the strategic decisions of companies, and the character of international trade. The supposedly mature auto industry now has the opportunity to embark on a technology-based process of rejuvenation in which the industry could recover the open-ended dynamics of its youth when competitive advantage was based largely on the ability to innovate.

Research has shown that manufacturing processes, no less than the products turned out, go through a life cycle evolution. As products evolve from low-volume, unstandardized one-of-a-kind items toward high-volume, standardized, commoditylike items, the associated processes likewise evolve from individual job-shop production toward continuous-flow production. In other words, a product–process configuration, or productive unit that is initially fluid (relatively inefficient, flexible, and open to radical change), gradually becomes stable (relatively efficient, inflexible, and open only to incremental change).

This seemingly inexorable movement toward technological stability has long been the fate of the auto industry. Economies of scale on massive production lines have for more than a generation dictated the search for ever-greater product standardization and more streamlined production. Radical change in the underlying technology of either became competitively dysfunctional; the production unit was too finely tuned to wring out the last increment of marginal cost reduction—and its management too focused on organizational coordination and control—to allow the entrepreneurially fertile disruptions caused by radically new technology.[4]

The new industrial competition, however, has dated this older logic by rewarding the ability to compete on technological grounds. It has precipitated a technological ferment, which has in turn been supported by the market's post-1979 willingness to pay a premium for vehicles boasting new technology.

Consider, for example, the rapid market adoption of General Motors' X-bodies with their transaxle and transverse mounted engines, the popularity of enhanced four-cylinder engines like Ford's compound-valve hemispherical head, or the appeal of such fuel-saving materials as graphite fibers, dual-phased steel, and advanced plastics. As a result, the industry has begun to revitalize itself in a movement back to a more fluid process–product configuration in the companies and a more lively technology-based competition among them.

Technology-Driven Strategies

The following factors are the prime elements in the renewal of the auto industry: (1) an increasing premium in the marketplace on innovation, (2) a growing diversity in the technology of components and production processes, and (3) an increasingly radical effect of factors 1 and 2 on long-established configurations in the productive unit as a whole. These developments, in turn, have begun to define the structure and competitive dynamics of the industry in the years ahead—and the corporate strategies best suited to both.

The conventional wisdom about industry structure and strategy accepts an implicit equation between concentration and maturity. When technology-based competition heats up, this logic runs, industry concentration loosens. In such a case, car manufacturers will know how to adjust their strategies accordingly.

To be sure, in a capital-intensive industry with great economies of scale, a period of ferment in product technology often allows manufacturers to offer an increasing variety of products at or below the cost of the old product mix. Especially when the production technology is well understood and easily procurable (in the form of equipment or human skills), companies on the fringe of the industry and fresh entrants can identify and exploit new market niches. Technological activity, market growth, and industry deconcentration usually go hand in hand.

When, however, the ferment in product technology is so extreme that it causes fundamental alterations in process technology, the same degree of activity may have very different results. In this case the immediate effect of a process-linked industry renewal may well be to *increase* the degree and the stability of concentration—that is, as many believe, to push industry structure apparently in the direction of *greater* maturity.

Where these observers go wrong is in failing to distinguish concentration from maturity or, said another way, in assuming that all evidence of frozen or rising concentration is evidence of movement toward maturity. This may, but need not, be the case.

In the auto field, for example, some corporate responses to the prospect of radical process innovation probably will take the industry farther along the road to maturity. Because truly radical product changes are still some years off and because commitments to existing process technology are large (especially in the standard model segment), it is reasonable to expect producers with experience in the older technologies to defend their positions through technical alterations that reduce costs or improve performance but do not make their processes obsolete.

Such a strategy requires the high volumes necessary for scale economies. As a result, the strategy may help concentrate production—either through greater use of joint ventures or, if the scale effects are great enough, through mergers and like forms of mature industry consolidation.

Other corporate responses to process-linked renewal may have the opposite effect. Major innovations in products that are linked to innovations in process technology often permit drastic reductions in production costs or improvements in performance, thus making possible the higher volumes necessary to expand market share. These innovations, however, usually involve large capital outlays as well as development of hard-to-acquire skills on the part of workers and management. So they require large increases in volume to offset the greater investment. As a result, only the leading producers may be able to profit from the process innovations and thus, temporarily at least, enhance their market share and reinforce industry concentration.

Though this pattern of concentration may appear identical to the one we have described, nothing could be further from the truth. Here a consolidation of the market serves to throw the industry into technological ferment that stimulates further technological competition—not to lock it into older process technology.

In time, this upheaval in process technology may even provide the competitive basis for new entrants to the field. Depending on the nature of process advances in auto production, companies in related industries (electronics, for example, or engines or energy) may find invasion of the market an attractive strategic option. But even if a decade from now these new entrants have not materialized, the forces that made their participation possible will have changed the competitive structure of the industry in two fundamental ways:

☐ Whatever its immediate tendency, industry concentration will in the long run have become far less stable than at present.

☐ The basis of competition will have changed to reflect the now crucial importance of technology-driven strategies.

The Challenge to Management

Once U.S. auto manufacturers understand that energy prices and internationalization of competition have altered the industry's old competitive dynamics, they have to decide how they want to compete under the new rules of the game. It may be best for them to avoid duplicating the Japanese pattern of competition. At any rate, after decades of the maturing process, the basis for competing is in flux for U.S. producers and radical rethinking about strategy—not blind imitation—is in order.

The industrial landscape in America is littered with the remains of once-successful companies that could not adapt their strategic vision to altered conditions of competition. If the automobile producers prove unequal to the new reality that confronts them, their massive, teeming plants will become the ghost towns of late twentieth century America. The same, of course, holds true for all companies, large and small, in those old-line manufacturing industries exposed to assault from abroad. Only those able to see the new industrial competition for what it is and to devise appropriate strategies for participating in it will survive.

Managers must recognize that they have entered a period of competition that requires of them a technology-driven strategy, a mastery of efficient production, and an unprecedented capacity for work force management. They cannot simply copy what others do but must find their own way. No solutions are certain, no strategies assured of success. But the nature of the challenge is clear.

Henry Ford, as Alfred P. Sloan recalled him, was a man who had had

. . . many brilliant insights in [his] earlier years, [but] seemed never to understand how completely the market had changed from the one in which he had made his name and to which he was accustomed. . . . The old master failed to master change.[5]

That is still the crucial challenge—and opportunity.

Notes

1. Statement before the Subcommittee on Trade of the House Ways and Means Committee. March 18, 1980.

2. See Robert H. Hayes, "Why Japanese Factories Work," *HBR*, July–August 1981, p. 56.

3. Edward M. Graham, "Technological Innovation and the Dynamics of the U.S. Competitive Advantage in International Trade," in *Technological Innovation for a Dynamic Economy*, edited by Christopher T. Hill and James M. Utterback (Elmsford, NY, Pergamon Press, 1979), p. 152.

4. For a discussion of the evolution toward industrial maturity, see James M. Utterback and William J. Abernathy, "A Dynamic Model of Process and Product Innovation," *Omega*, 1975, Vol. 3, p. 639.

5. Alfred P. Sloan, Jr., *My Years with General Motors* (Garden City, NY, Doubleday, 1964), pp. 186–187.

Appendix: The Japanese Cost Advantage

Table A Calculation of U.S. and Japanese Labor Costs for a Subcompact Vehicle

	1 Share in OEM Manufac- turing Costs	2 Average OEM Hours per Vehicle	3 Estimated OEM Employee Cost per Hour ($)	4 Estimated Cost per Vehicle ($)	5 Labor Content (%)	6 [4 × 5] Labor Cost per Vehicle ($)	7 [6 × .575] U.S.– Japan Differ- ence ($)
OEM labor .24 Hourly	.24	65	18	1,170	100	1,170	673
Salaried .08	.08	15	21	315	100	315	181
Purchased .39 components	.39	NA	NA	1,901	66	1,255	721
Purchased .14 materials	.14	NA	NA	683	25	171	98
Total —	—	—	—	4,875	NA	2,911	1,673

Notes: OEM hourly labor is defined as total nonexempt and includes direct and indirect production workers. The calculations assume an exchange rate of 218 yen per dollar. The method of calculation and sources of data are as follows:

Column 1 contains estimates of the share of total manufacturing cost accounted for by direct and indirect production labor (at the OEM level), purchased components, and materials. These estimates do not reflect the experience of any one company but approximate an industry average. They are based on data prepared for the National Research Council's Committee on Motor Vehicle Emissions as well as on discussions with industry sources. The latter have also provided us with the data in columns 2, 3, and 5.

We made the calculation of U.S.–Japan cost differences in three steps. We first used the data in columns 2 and 3 to get an OEM labor cost per vehicle of $1,170, then extrapolated using the cost shares (column 1) to arrive at a total manufactured cost and the cost of purchased components and materials (column 4). We next multiplied the cost per vehicle in column 4 by an estimate of the labor content of the three categories presented in column 5. The data imply, for example, that $1,255 of the $1,901 cost of components is labor cost. Finally, we calculated the Japan–U.S. labor cost gap by multiplying the U.S. data in column 6 by 0.575, the adjustment factor derived from our estimate of the Japan-to-U.S. unit labor cost ratio.* Thus column 7 provides an estimate of the difference in the cost of producing a subcompact vehicle in the United States and Japan due to differences in unit labor costs, not only at the OEM level but also at the supplier level.

*Let $C(US)$ and $C(J)$ indicate unit labor costs in the United States and Japan. We estimate $C(J)/C(US) = .425$. We want to know $C(US) - C(J)$. Column 6 gives us $C(US)$. Thus, $C(US)$

$$- C(J) = \left(\left(1 \frac{C(J)}{C(US)} \right) \right) \times \text{column 6; this result is in column 7.}$$

Table B   Ford and Toyo Kogyo's Estimated Per-Vehicle Employee Costs in 1979

	Ford	Toyo Kogyo
Domestic car and truck production in millions	3,163	0.983
Total domestic employment†		
Automotive	219,599	24,318
Nonautomotive	19,876	2,490
Total domestic employee hours‡		
Automotive in millions	355.75	46.20
Total employee costs§		
Automotive in millions	$7,794.50	$482.20
Employee hours per vehicle	112.5	47.0
Employee cost per vehicle	$2,464	$491

*Ford figure excludes 65,000 imported vehicles; Toyo Kogyo figure is adjusted for production of knock-down assembly kits.

†Data on automotive employment and costs were obtained by assuming that the ratio of automotive employment to total employment was the same as the ratio of sales. The same assumption was made to obtain Ford employment costs.

‡Ford hours were determined by assuming that each employee worked 1,620 hours per year; Toyo Kogyo hours assum 1,900 hours. These adjustments reflect vacations, holidays, leaves, and absences.

§Data include salaries, wages, and fringe benefits. Toyo Kogyo compensation data were derived by updating a 1976 figure using compensation growth rates at Toyota. An exchange rate of 218 yen/$ (1979 average) was used to convert yen.

Table C Product Mix Adjustment

	Ford	Toyo Kogyo
1. Ratio of car to total vehicle production	0.645	0.652
2. Production shares by size		
Small	0.11	0.83
Medium	0.68	0.17
Large	0.21	—
3. Relative manufacturing cost by size		
Small	1.00	NA
Medium	1.35	NA
Large	1.71	NA
4. Weighted average of relative manufacturing cost small = 1.00	1.38	1.06
5. Production of Toyo Kogyo mix at Ford level of integration		
Employee cost per vehicle	$1,893	$589
Employee hours per vehicle	87	56

Notes: Line 2 for Ford assumes that only Pinto and Bobcat models are small; Mustang and Capri sales were placed in the medium category.

Line 5 for Ford is obtained by multiplying lines 6 and 7 in Exhibit B by (1.06/1.38).

Table B uses the data on manufacturing costs by vehicle size developed for the Committee on Motor Vehicle Emissions of the National Research Council in 1974. We derived estimates of the cost to Ford of producing the Toyo Kogyo mix by first computing a weighted average of the relative manufacturing cost indices with Ford's 1979 production shares by size as weights. The ratio of the comparable Toyo Kogyo weighted average (1.06) to the Ford weighted average (1.38) was used to adjust both costs and productivity as a means of estimating the effect of product mix on Ford's average cost and labor hours per vehicle. After these adjustments we estimate that Ford would require 87 employee hours to produce the average-size vehicle in the Toyo Kogyo product line, compared with 56 hours in the Japanese company. Labor cost per vehicle is just over $1,300 higher at Ford. These comparisons are based on the average-size vehicle at Toyo Kogyo. For a small vehicle (i.e., Pinto vs. Mazda GLC), the Ford estimate is 82 hours per vehicle, while the comparable Toyo Kogyo figure is 53; the corresponding costs per vehicle are $1,785 (Ford) and $566 (Toyo Kogyo). Even this adjustment may overstate costs and hours required to produce the Toyo Kogyo mix at Ford if the trucks and commercial vehicles produced by the two companies differ substantially.

2

Gone Are the Cash Cows of Yesteryear

RAYMOND VERNON

Here is one note of optimism in the overwhelmingly negative chorus of criticism currently aimed at American industry. This author argues not only that critics rail against the wrong thing but also that their hue and cry helps obscure some of the real possibilities and opportunities U.S. companies still enjoy. By using their foreign subsidiaries as conduits, American businesses can obtain information on the latest competitive developments in product, process, and market. Then they can realistically begin to assess the needs and wants of the world market

Suddenly, we are told, the great American juggernaut has run out of steam. No longer can the United States generate the supply of Edisons, Fords, and Salks who for a century or more had given the country its formidable worldwide technological lead. The United States is the newest victim of the English disease—too much government, too little incentive, too little commitment. American industry, which only yesterday could think of the world as its succulent oyster, must now respond to the mounting tide of competitors from newer, more energetic lands.

Those who worry that the United States is drifting downhill in its innovative or productive capacities base their case on more than surmise. They point to figures on the decline in the nation's output per worker, the number of patents issued to American inventors, and the amount spent on R&D. But those figures, studied in detail, convey a complicated and uncertain message. We cannot say that American workers have grown lazier

Published 1980.

over the past 10 years or that American engineers and scientists have lost their creative capabilities (see the Appendix following this article). But U.S. companies *are* losing competitive ground. To reverse the trend, we must first understand why.

To that end, it helps to explore the origins of our vaunted role—dating back to the second half of the nineteenth century—as the world's leader in industrial technology. That role did not result from an unusual abundance of skills. Although the Americans of that period were relatively literate and skilled, so were the British, the French, and the Germans. Indeed, outstanding scientists and engineers were more commonly found in Europe than in the United States. Americans, however, had other advantages: cheap and abundant raw materials, a large internal market, and almost no governmental restraints on the pursuit of profits.

How Did It All Begin?

Only one fly contaminated the economic ointment of the American entrepreneurs. Because opportunities in the United States were so rich, labor was scarce; farming, lumbering, and mining drew off some of the available skilled labor, including immigrant carpenters and metal workers who had made their way to America from Europe. America's businesspeople therefore faced a tantalizing opportunity. With a market there for the taking, they had to find new production methods that could overcome both the scarcity and high cost of skilled workers in the United States.

Driven by the extraordinary challenge, proprietors of textile plants, iron foundries, glass factories, and machine shops produced such devices as sewing machines, glass-blowing machines, automatic woodworking and metalworking machines, and automatic railway signaling devices. Having broken the skilled labor bottleneck, they went on to develop and market a new generation of products, including the electric light, the telephone, the low-priced automobile, and the vacuum cleaner—all appropriate to the tastes of the richest mass market in the world.

Americans have not monopolized industrial innovations over the past century. But their innovations have differed from those of the Europeans in some important respects. In industrial goods, Europeans tended to stress innovation that would conserve capital and raw materials, such as the use of oxygen in blast furnaces and fuel injection in automobile motors. Americans tended to concentrate on labor-saving innovations and were profligate with energy and raw materials. In consumer goods, the United States ground out a stream of new products that could satisfy an apparently unlimited appetite for novelty and comfort. On the other hand, Europe (and later Japan) concentrated on smaller, cheaper, and more durable versions of the same dishwashers and television sets that had first been produced in the United States.

American innovations continued to exhibit their labor-saving, income-serving characteristics during the three decades following World War II (see Exhibit 1). Through the end of the 1960s, many American enterprises felt secure and well entrenched. Here and there, some industries such as automobiles and steel evidenced a certain amount of uneasiness. But by and large, American companies were contentedly herding and milking their cash cows, convinced that they were the most innovative and efficient producers on the face of the earth.

Thinning the Herd

The 1970s began to obliterate features that had distinguished the United States from other industrialized countries. For one thing, European and Japanese income levels were rising rapidly and no longer trailed far behind those of the Americans. Accordingly, foreign consumers' demands in food, household goods, transportation, recreation, safety, and health drew abreast of those in the United States. These foreign markets were no longer small or fragmented, and with the strengthening of the European Community, they began to rival the United States in size and buying power.

Gone, too, were the differences in cost structures that had distinguished the United States from the other countries. Labor was almost as

Exhibit 1. Perceived Advantages of Innovations Introduced in the United States, Europe, and Japan, 1945–1974[a]

Perceived advantage	United States		Europe including Britain		Japan	
	No.	Percent	No.	Percent	No.	Percent
Labor saving	331	40.1	120	12.7	6	6.4
Material saving	175	21.2	444	46.9	32	34.1
Capital saving	58	7.0	104	11.0	7	7.4
Novel function	106	12.8	83	8.8	12	12.8
Safety	50	6.1	60	6.3	7	7.4
Other	106	12.8	135	14.3	30	31.9
	826	100.0	946	100.0	94	100.0

Source: Adapted from W.H. Davidson, "Patterns of Factor-Saving Innovation in the Industrialized World," *European Economic Review*, Vol. 8, 1976, p. 214.

[a]Based on a sample of 1,916 innovations.

expensive in Europe as in the United States. Capital, thanks partly to the burgeoning Euromoney market, was plentiful on both sides of the Atlantic. And as Americans began to rely increasingly on imported raw materials, their historic advantage in the prices of such materials was also evaporating. Therefore, American business no longer had the unique advantage of operating in the environment of the future in its home markets. For once, it was obliged to start off even with its European and Japanese competitors.

Indeed, in one critical respect, the conditions of the 1970s gave the rivals of the United States an edge. Long-time trends in production costs were reversed: for once, raw materials and capital became more expensive all over the world, outdistancing increases in labor costs. Now European and Japanese innovations were in demand, with their emphasis on conserving capital, raw materials, and fuel. Italian oil burners designed for fuel economy found markets in American homes and factories; the cast-aluminum engines of the Japanese and Europeans, designed to reduce overall automobile weight, found American markets as well.

Alas for America's cash cows. The size and productivity of the herd had largely depended on America's technological lead. With good luck and the advantages of the experience curve, American innovators had been able to ride the crest of growing world demand, profiting from a product well into its senescence. Now, however, the experience curve offers Americans little advantage; indeed, in some cases, the advantage lies with their rivals. So the cash cows, we can be reasonably sure, will be fewer and not quite so plump.

What of Our Calving Rates?

America is losing its competitive edge partly because it can no longer count on the advantages of an experience curve. But the deeper worry is that the country may also be suffering from a falling off in the ability of its scientists and engineers to innovate as well as in the willingness of its business community to underwrite those innovative efforts. For instance, a larger proportion of the total patents issued each year by the U.S. Patent Office goes to foreigners, and a smaller proportion of the patents issued by foreign patent offices goes to U.S. inventors. Moreover, R&D expenditures in the United States, calculated as a percentage of the country's GNP, have drifted downward over the past five years or more, whereas the same ratios for other key countries such as Germany and Japan have remained more or less constant for the same period.

Nevertheless, it is not at all clear that America's scientists and engineers have lost their creative abilities (see the Appendix). True, we have been diverting some of our innovative efforts in various ways: our capacity to make better battle tanks is increasing more rapidly than our ability to make better automobiles. Moreover, some U.S. companies have transferred their efforts to other countries, with some U.S. drug companies moving their laboratories to England to escape FDA regulations and IBM shifting some of its development work to Europe to keep French ministers happy. But the most important difference in the position of U.S. companies is the increase in the relevance of the technological work being done in Europe and Japan.

Look to Foreign Markets

Americans need to practice what the Japanese and Europeans have been doing all along—that is, making both cheaper and more durable goods to appeal to the tastes of foreign markets. In fact, the emphasis on the amount and quality of U.S. R&D threatens to be a red herring, diverting attention from more important factors that could boost U.S. industrial performance. History shows repeatedly that countries with an outstanding record in science and technology are not necessarily those that shine in productivity and competitiveness.

The United Kingdom is the outstanding case in point. Surrounded by industrial decay, British scientists continue to perform remarkably. And although Japan's scientific and technological efforts have been increasing, these efforts are still not very impressive when measured by normal quantitative yardsticks.

Clearly, the United Kingdom does not use effectively all the information it generates, whereas Japan manages to apply a lot of the world's information which it had no hand in generating. A good example of Japan's integrative capability is the Nikon camera. Nikon has absorbed technology from all over the world: it uses—imaginatively and well—shutter electronics developed by a Minneapolis company and a single lens reflex mechanism copied from the Germans.

In addition, we must consider that about half the world's present industrial output is generated by MNCs with widespread productive facilities. Accordingly, the flashes of genius produced by an engineer in Morristown, New Jersey could show up on an assembly line in Jakarta as readily as in nearby Newark. By the same token, the ideas first expressed in a laboratory in Fontainebleau can swiftly be brought across the Atlantic provided, of course, that American business has both the antennas to learn about those ideas and the wit to recognize their value.

Therein lie the basic lessons: no longer can we either suppose that the innovations of other countries are irrelevant to American needs or expect that American innovations will hold a lead for any length of time over foreign competition. The biggest challenge for U.S. business is to create a scanning capability to survey the advances taking place in other countries and a managerial capability to incorporate those advances wherever they are relevant to our needs.

Scanning Our Neighbors' Pastures

A visitor from a distant planet observing the great network of U.S. subsidiaries in foreign lands might readily assume that Americans already had a highly developed capability for scanning their foreign markets. These subsidiaries number in the thousands, carry millions of employees on their payrolls, and account for a substantial proportion of the profits of their American parents. No other country's overseas contingent amounts to more than a fraction of America's establishment.

There are signs, however, that these networks are wired mostly for one-way transmission—the center issues commands, but the periphery has trouble transmitting unsolicited data back to the center. Most U.S.-owned subsidiaries operating abroad manufacture a range of products conceived in Toledo or Kankakee. The main task of the subsidiaries is to convince the local populace that these products are exactly what it needs.

Here and there, to be sure, U.S.-owned subsidiaries have adapted successfully to the foreign markets in which they operate. The special skills and knowledge of such subsidiaries, however, are rarely allowed to penetrate the main network of the company. Each of America's big three automobile companies, for example, contains in its network at least one European subsidiary that has long mastered the technology of small-car construction. But Detroit has been remarkably slow to absorb those hard-won skills.

Why Not Listen?

Several factors explain the American propensity for one-way transmission over its multinational networks. Most important, these subsidiaries were created during a period in which U.S.-based companies characteristically enjoyed a technological lead over their competitors, generating and selling products that would represent the market of the future. As long as U.S. companies were secure in their innovative leads, there was not great need to use foreign subsidiaries as listening posts.

A second factor has been the premature obliteration of international divisions in many U.S. companies. As the foreign interests of American companies grew and flourished in the postwar period, the international divisions were often the star performers. But their success was eventually their undoing. By the middle 1960s, one American company after another reorganized itself to acknowledge the increased importance of its foreign business. According to one study undertaken in the early 1970s, the typical pattern consisted of abolishing the international division and setting up a series of so-called global product divisions to do the worrying about foreign markets.

In a recent study covering a group of 57 large U.S.-based multinationals, a colleague and I ran into some disturbing indications suggesting that some of these reorganizations may have been wildly counterproductive. A subset of our sample organized along global product lines, exhibited rather striking characteristics. This group of companies seemed to show decidedly less interest in its foreign operations than those with an international division. Ten years after they had introduced their new products into the United States, the global product companies were only producing about 50% of those products in overseas locations. By contrast, the other companies in the sample were manufacturing more than 80% of their new products in foreign plants. At least in the case of this sample, the demise of the international division and the creation of a global product division suggested a sharp decline in interest in foreign operations.[1]

That result may not be as surprising as it first seems. When managers of domestic product divisions in the United States assume responsibility for global product divisions, the change in perspective may go no deeper than the title on their business cards. In training and outlook, they may still be as American as the Dallas Cowboys and apple pie. And unlike the international specialists that they have replaced, these managers may shrink from confronting unfamiliar problems, which can range anywhere from transacting business in pesos to wrestling with Belgian labor laws.

Some companies have recognized the danger in the newer organizational form and are returning to the old way of doing things. A prime example is Westinghouse, which went form an international to a global product division and back to an international division again.

Getting Out of Dairying

It may seem paradoxical at first that the country with the world's most extensive network of foreign manufacturing subsidiaries should be so parochial in its approach to foreign environments. But the explanation for the apparent contradiction is obvious: very few U.S. companies actively study or understand the particular needs of their foreign markets.

Most U.S. companies were swept into those markets either on the strength of their domestic industrial innovations or by the desire to best their American competitors. Many European and practically all Japanese managers, on the other hand, have always believed that they must export to survive. That difference in viewpoint has produced a change in attitude toward studying the surprises and uncertainties of foreign markets.

But American manufacturers no longer have a choice of entering foreign markets or leaving them alone. Whether they go to foreigners or not, foreigners will come to them—if not through imports then through the output of manufacturing subsidiaries located in the United States.

When citizen band radios suddenly grew popular in the United States, the Japanese built better cheaper models and now have almost captured the leadership in that market. Volkswagen's little Pennsylvania plant cannot keep up with the demand. Honda will soon be a prime competitor on these shores. And Hitachi also plans to conquer the color television market from a new manufacturing base in the West. There is no longer a place where American business can hide.

Responding to the Challenge

That ineluctable fact is just beginning to dawn on many U.S. managers. Once it becomes crystal clear, American companies may also realize that they still operate from a position of considerable strength. Their foreign subsidiaries are grossly underused sources of such strength. U.S. business can turn those subsidiaries into two-way conduits, relaying back to the parent information about the latest developments in product, process, and market that bear on America's competitive position. And the challenge for headquarters is to learn how to listen, to incorporate the foreign advances that are succeeding, and to try to improve on those advances.

A few companies already are rising to the challenge. Du Pont is one enterprise adept at scanning its foreign subsidiaries and using the results in other parts of its organization. A miniplant in Argentina, for instance, generates process innovations that can be used for other small plants in Africa.

For most companies, developing the new capability will take some time, but it will be worth it. The efforts of Ford and General Motors to develop a "world car," for instance, reflect their realization that what other markets want may really matter. There are, to be sure, certain inherent dangers—for example, the so-called world model could turn out to be a sham effort to dress up the preferred U.S. product in another guise. Nevertheless, some part of the world product response will be worthwhile, especially if it represents a genuine effort to respond to the tastes and needs of other markets.

Another strength on which U.S. business can draw is its formidable scientific and technological establishment, still by all odds the world's largest and best. Some of its current efforts seem misdirected, and those developments that are on target are unlikely to provide the same degree of technological lead as in the past. But it remains a formidable resource, unmatched in total strength by any other country.

In the end, U.S. business will have to accept the fact that its competitive position in world markets has changed profoundly. After American businesses have carefully studied the world's markets, after they have absorbed and incorporated the best that can be gleaned from the rest of the world, that effort will do not more than keep them abreast of their nearest competitors.

At that point, the race will be won by those enterprises with the best price, the best quality, and the best after-sales service. This emphasis will be new to many Americans—accustomed to offering the newest, most unusual products and hoping to turn a few of them into the proverbial cash cow. Changes in attitude come slowly, but I am betting that many U.S. enterprises will be able to make the shift.

Notes

1. Raymond Vernon and W. H. Davidson, "Foreign Production of Technology-Intensive Product by U.S.-Based Multinational Enterprises," Working Paper 79-5, Harvard Business School, 1979

Appendix

The Meaning of Productivity

What is so difficult about interpreting the meaning of *productivity*: especially in terms of output per worker?

Until about 10 years ago, industrial plants increased their measured output while destroying the recreational value of lakes, rivers, and open spaces; reducing the potability of water; and increasing the health hazards from befouled air. Should we have reduced measured output in the past to reflect those unmeasured uses of our natural resources? Should we regard U.S. workers as less productive if some of their efforts are now used to reduce these hitherto unmeasured costs?

Next there is the problem of defining a worker. Over the past decade, untrained youths and women of all ages have augmented the work force in unprecedented numbers. Does the entry of this untrained contingent mean that U.S. workers, as a whole, should be regarded as less productive?

Finally, there is the problem of combining different kinds of output in an overall measure that makes sense. The output of the United States increasingly takes the form of services, including contributions of health, safety, recreation, and education. Most of these services do not come in measurable units; many have no market price. We measure this part of U.S. output in ways that say little or nothing about the diligence or energy of U.S. workers.

Importance of Patents

If U.S. inventors are getting fewer patents relative to foreigners both at home and abroad, why is this not conclusive evidence of declining innovative capabilities? There are two main factors to consider:

1. Inventors take out patents in a foreign country only if they plan to exploit the invention there. Formerly, many of the European and Japanese

innovations had little application to the U.S. market; meanwhile, U.S. innovations had strong promise in the markets of Europe and Japan. More recently, however, the characteristic lines of innovation stressed by the Europeans and Japanese have become more relevant to the U.S. market, while U.S. lines of innovation have lost some of their uniqueness in foreign markets. These trends could well be producing the observed shifts in patenting.

2. The number of patents issued is probably losing its value as an indicator of innovation. With a speeding up in technological change, some companies prefer to keep their innovations to themselves rather than publish their results. Moreover, the shift in innovation from creating novel products to developing cost-reducing products and processes also tends to reduce the innovators' willingness to patent. Another major change is the tendency to create innovations by putting together familiar systems in new configurations—for instance, attaching microchips and electric circuits to electric ovens or washing machines. Innovations of this sort, useful though they may be, are commonly not patentable.

The Basic Formula for Business Success*

We have found over many years that the key to business success in any country is to consult with the people who are there, both the officials in charge of economic policy and the private sector people who have a sense of the people's wants and needs. Find out what they are trying to do—their priorities, their plans for the nation, their most urgent needs, their rules for participation in the local economy. Then figure out the best way to make your capabilities and products and services fit their needs and regulations. If a company takes the trouble to do this groundwork, then the odds are in favor of business success because both parties—the company and the host country—*want* the venture to succeed.

Relationships between companies and countries do not develop suddenly, on the whim of some corporate tycoon who suddenly decides he has to have a big operation in Lower Slobovia. Usually it's an evolutionary process.

*From Reginald H. Jones, chairman and chief executive officer, General Electric Company, "The Transnational Enterprise and World Economic Development," a speech delivered to the summer seminar entitled "The Corporation: A Theological Inquiry," cosponsored by American Enterprise Institute and Syracuse University Department of Religion at Airlie House, Airlie, VA, on July 10, 1980. Reprinted with permission.

3

The Globalization of Markets

THEODORE LEVITT

Many companies have become disillusioned with sales in the international market-place as old markets become saturated and new ones must be found. How can they customize products for the demands of new markets? Which items will consumers want? With wily international competitors breathing down their necks, many organizations think that the game just isn't worth the effort.

In this powerful essay, the author asserts that well-managed companies have moved from emphasis on customizing items to offering globally standardized products that are advanced, functional, reliable—and low priced. Multinational companies that concentrated on idiosyncratic consumer preferences have become befuddled and unable to take in the forest because of the trees. Only global companies will achieve long-term success by concentrating on what everyone wants rather than worrying about the details of what everyone *thinks* they might like.

A powerful force drives the world toward a converging commonality, and that force is technology. It has proletarianized communication, transport, and travel. It has made isolated places and impoverished peoples eager for modernity's allurements. Almost everyone everywhere wants all the things they have heard about, seen, or experienced via the new technologies.

The result is a new commercial reality—the emergence of global markets for standardized consumer products on a previously unimagined scale of magnitude. Corporations geared to this new reality benefit from enormous economies of scale in production, distribution, marketing, and management. By translating these benefits into reduced world prices, they can decimate

Published 1983.

competitors that still live in the disabling grip of old assumptions about how the world works.

Gone are accustomed differences in national or regional preference. Gone are the days when a company could sell last year's models—or lesser versions of advanced products—in the less-developed world. And gone are the days when prices, margins, and profits abroad were generally higher than at home.

The globalization of markets is at hand. With that, the multinational commercial world nears its end, and so does the multinational corporation.

The multinational and the global corporation are not the same thing. The multinational corporation operates in a number of countries, and adjusts its products and practices in each—at high relative costs. The global corporation operates with resolute constancy—at low relative cost—as if the entire world (or major regions of it) were a single entity; it sells the same things in the same way everywhere.

Which strategy is better is not a matter of opinion but of necessity. Worldwide communications carry everywhere the constant drumbeat of modern possibilities to lighten and enhance work, raise living standards, divert, and entertain. The same countries that ask the world to recognize and respect the individuality of their cultures insist on the wholesale transfer to them of modern goods, services, and technologies. Modernity is not just a wish but also a widespread practice among those who cling, with unyielding passion or religious fervor, to ancient attitudes and heritages.

Who can forget the televised scenes during the 1979 Iranian uprisings of young men in fashionable French-cut trousers and silky body shirts thirsting with raised modern weapons for blood in the name of Islamic fundamentalism?

In Brazil, thousands swarm daily from pre-industrial Bahian darkness into exploding coastal cities, there quickly to install television sets in crowded corrugated huts and, next to battered Volkswagens, make sacrificial offerings of fruit and fresh-killed chickens to Macumban spirits by candlelight.

During Biafra's fratricidal war against the Ibos, daily televised reports showed soldiers carrying bloodstained swords and listening to transistor radios while drinking Coca-Cola.

In the isolated Siberian city of Krasnoyarsk, with no paved streets and censored news, occasional Western travelers are stealthily propositioned for cigarettes, digital watches, and even the clothes off their backs.

The organized smuggling of electronic equipment, used automobiles, western clothing, cosmetics, and pirated movies into primitive places exceeds even the thriving underground trade in modern weapons and their military mercenaries.

A thousand suggestive ways attest to the ubiquity of the desire for the most advanced things that the world makes and sells—goods of the best quality and reliability at the lowest price. The world's needs and desires have been irrevocably homogenized. This makes the multinational corporation obsolete and the global corporation absolute.

Living in the Republic of Technology

Daniel J. Boorstin, author of the monumental trilogy *The Americans*, characterized our age as driven by "the Republic of Technology [whose] supreme law . . . is convergence, the tendency for everything to become more like everything else."

In business, this trend has pushed markets toward global commonality. Corporations sell standardized products in the same way everywhere—autos, steel, chemicals, petroleum, cement, agricultural commodities and equipment, industrial and commercial construction, banking and insurance services, computers, semiconductors, transport, electronic instruments, pharmaceuticals, and telecommunications, to mention some of the obvious.

Nor is the sweeping gale of globalization confined to these raw material or high-tech products, where the universal language of customers and users facilitates standardization. The transforming winds whipped up by the proletarianization of communication and travel enter every crevice of life.

Commercially, nothing confirms this as much as the success of McDonald's from the Champs Elysées to the Ginza, of Coca-Cola in Bahrain and Pepsi-Cola in Moscow, and of rock music, Greek salad, Hollywood movies, Revlon cosmetics, Sony televisions, and Levi jeans everywhere. "High-touch" products are as ubiquitous as high-tech.

Starting from opposing sides, the high-tech and the high-touch ends of the commercial spectrum gradually consume the undistributed middle in their cosmopolitan orbit. No one is exempt and nothing can stop the process. Everywhere everything gets more and more like everything else as the world's preference structure is relentlessly homogenized.

Consider the cases of Coca-Cola and Pepsi-Cola, which are globally standardized products sold everywhere and welcomed by everyone. Both successfully cross multitudes of national, regional, and ethnic taste buds trained to a variety of deeply ingrained local preferences of taste, flavor, consistency, effervescence, and aftertaste. Everywhere both sell well. Cigarettes, too, especially American-made, make year-to-year global inroads on territories previously held in the firm grip of other, mostly local, blends.

These are not exceptional examples. (Indeed their global reach would be even greater were it not for artificial trade barriers.) They exemplify a general drift toward the homogenization of the world and how companies distribute, finance, and price products.[1] Nothing is exempt. The products and methods of the industrialized world play a single tune for all the world, and all the world eagerly dances to it.

Ancient differences in national tastes or modes of doing business disappear. The commonality of preference leads inescapably to the standardization of products, manufacturing, and the institutions of trade and commerce. Small nation-based markets transmogrify and expand. Success in world competition turns on efficiency in production, distribution, marketing, and management, and inevitably becomes focused on price.

The most effective world competitors incorporate superior quality and reliability into their cost structures. They sell in all national markets the same kind of products sold at home or in their largest export market. They compete on the basis of appropriate value—the best combinations of price, quality, reliability, and delivery for products that are globally identical with respect to design, function, and even fashion.

That, and little else, explains the surging success of Japanese companies dealing worldwide in a vast variety of products—both tangible products like steel, cars, motorcycles, hi-fi equipment, farm machinery, robots, microprocessors, carbon fibers, and now even textiles, and intangibles like banking, shipping, general contracting, and soon computer software. Nor are high-quality and low-cost operations incompatible, as a host of consulting organizations and data engineers argue with vigorous vacuity. The reported data are incomplete, wrongly analyzed, and contradictory. The truth is that low-cost operations are the hallmark of corporate cultures that require and produce quality in all that they do. High quality and low costs are not opposing postures. They are compatible, twin identities of superior practice.[2]

To say that Japan's companies are not global because they export cars with left-side drives to the United States and the European continent, while those in Japan have right-side drives, or because they sell office machines through distributors in the United States but directly at home, or speak Portuguese in Brazil, is to mistake a difference for a distinction. The same is true of Safeway and Southland retail chains operating effectively in the Middle East, and to not only native but also imported populations from Korea, the Philippines, Pakistan, India, Thailand, Britain, and the United States. National rules of the road differ, and so do distribution channels and languages. Japan's distinction is its unrelenting push for economy and value enhancement. That translates into a drive for standardization at high quality levels.

Vindication of the Model T

If a company forces costs and prices down and pushes quality and reliability up—while maintaining reasonable concern for suitability—customers will prefer its world-standardized products. The theory holds, at this stage in the evolution of globalization, no matter what conventional market research and even common sense may suggest about different national and regional tastes, preferences, needs, and institutions. The Japanese have repeatedly vindicated this theory, as did Henry Ford with the Model T. Most important, so have their imitators, including companies from South Korea (television sets and heavy construction), Malaysia (personal calculators and microcomputers), Brazil (auto parts and tools), Colombia (apparel), Singapore (optical equipment), and yes, even from the United States (office copiers, computers, bicycles, castings), Western Europe (automatic washing machines), Rumania (housewares), Hungary (apparel), Yugoslavia (furniture), and Israel (pagination equipment).

Of course, large companies operating in a single nation or even a single city don't standardize everything they make, sell, or do. They have product lines instead of a single product version, and multiple distribution channels. There are neighborhood, local, regional, ethnic, and institutional differences, even within metropolitan areas. But although companies customize products for particular market segments, they know that success in a world with homogenized demand requires a search for sales opportunities in similar segments across the globe in order to achieve the economies of scale necessary to compete.

Such a search works because a market segment in one country is seldom unique; it has close cousins everywhere precisely because technology has homogenized the globe. Even small local segments have their global equivalents everywhere and become subject to global competition, especially on price.

Global competitors will seek constantly to standardize their offerings everywhere. They will digress from this standardization only after exhausting all possibilities to retain it, and they will push for reinstatement of standardization whenever digression and divergence have occurred. They will never assume that the customer is a king who knows his own wishes.

Trouble increasingly stalks companies that lack clarified global focus and remain inattentive to the economics of simplicity and standardization. The most endangered companies in the rapidly evolving world tend to be those that dominate rather small domestic markets with high value-added products for which there are smaller markets elsewhere. With transportation costs proportionately low, distant competitors will enter the now-sheltered markets of those companies with goods produced more cheaply under scale-efficient conditions. Global competition spells the end of domestic territoriality, no matter how diminutive the territory may be.

When the global producer offers his lower costs internationally, his patronage expands exponentially. He not only reaches into distant markets but also attracts customers who previously held to local preferences and now capitulate to the attractions of lesser prices. The strategy of standardization not only responds to worldwide homogenized markets but also expands those markets with aggressive low pricing. The new technological juggernaut taps an ancient motivation—to make one's money go as far as possible. This is universal—not simply a motivation but actually a need.

The Hedgehog Knows

The difference between the hedgehog and the fox, wrote Sir Isaiah Berlin in distinguishing between Dostoevski and Tolstoy, is that the fox knows a lot about a great many things, but the hedgehog knows everything about one great thing. The multinational corporation knows a lot about a great many countries and congenially adapts to supposed differences. It willingly accepts vestigial national differences, not questioning the possibility of their transformation, not recognizing how the world is ready and eager for the benefit of modernity, especially when the price is right. The multinational corporation's accommodating mode to visible national differences is medieval.

By contrast, the global corporation knows everything about one great thing. It knows about the absolute need to be competitive on a worldwide basis as well as nationally and seeks constantly to drive down prices by standardizing what it sells and how it operates. It treats the world as composed of few standardized markets rather than many customized markets. It actively seeks and vigorously works toward global convergence. Its mission is modernity and its mode, price competition, even when it sells top-of-the-line, high-end products. It knows about the one great thing all nations and people have in common: scarcity.

Nobody takes scarcity lying down; everyone wants more. This in part explains division of labor and specialization of production. They enable people and nations to optimize their conditions through trade. The median is usually money.

Experience teaches that money has three special qualities: scarcity, difficulty of acquisition, and transience. People understandably treat it with respect. Everyone in the increasingly homogenized world market wants products and features that everybody else wants. If the price is low enough, they will take highly standardized world products, even if these aren't exactly what mother said was suitable, what immemorial custom decreed was right, or what market-research fabulists asserted was preferred.

The implacable truth of all modern production—whether of tangible or intangible goods—is that large-scale production of standardized items is generally cheaper within a wide range of volume than small-scale production. Some argue that CAD/CAM will allow companies to manufacture customized products on a small scale—but cheaply. But the argument misses the point. (For a more detailed discussion, see the insert, "Economies of Scope.") If a company treats the world as one or two distinctive product markets, it can serve the world more economically than if it treats it as three, four, or five product markets.

Why Remaining Differences?

Different cultural preferences, national tastes and standards, and business institutions are vestiges of the past. Some inheritances die gradually; others prosper and expand into mainstream global preferences. So-called ethnic markets are a good example. Chinese food, pita bread, country and western music, pizza, and jazz are everywhere. They are market segments that exist in worldwide proportions. They don't deny or contradict global homogenization but confirm it.

Many of today's differences among nations as to products and their features actually reflect the respectful accommodation of multinational corporations to what they believe are fixed local preferences. They *believe* preferences are fixed, not because they are but because of rigid habits of thinking about what actually is. Most executives in multinational corporations are thoughtlessly accommodating. They falsely presume that marketing means giving the customer what he says he wants rather than trying to understand exactly what he'd like. So they persist with high-cost, customized multinational products and practices instead of pressing hard and pressing properly for global standardization.

I do not advocate the systematic disregard of local or national differences. But a company's sensitivity to such differences does not require that it ignore the possibilities of doing things differently or better.

There are, for example, enormous differences among Middle Eastern countries. Some are socialist, some monarchies, some republics. Some take their legal heritage from the Napoleonic Code, some from the Ottoman Empire, and some from the British common law; except for Israel, all are influenced by Islam. Doing business means personalizing the business relationship in an obsessively intimate fashion. During the month of Ramadan, business discussions can start only after 10 o'clock at night, when people are tired and full of food after a day of fasting. A company must almost certainly have a local partner; a local lawyer is required (as, say, in New York), and irrevocable letters of credit are essential. Yet, as Coca-Cola's Senior Vice President Sam Ayoub noted, "Arabs are much more capable of making distinctions between cultural and religious purposes on the one hand and economic realities on the other than is generally assumed. Islam is compatible with science and modern times."

Barriers to globalization are not confined to the Middle East. The free transfer of technology and data across the boundaries of the European Common Market countries are hampered by legal and financial impediments. And there is resistance to radio and television interference ("pollution") among neighboring European countries.

But the past is a good guide to the future. With persistence and appropriate means, barriers against superior technologies and economics have always fallen. There is no recorded exception where reasonable effort has been made to overcome them. It is very much a matter of time and effort.

A Failure in Global Imagination

Many companies have tried to standardize world practice by exporting domestic products and processes without accommodation or change—and have failed miserably. Their deficiencies have been seized on as evidence of bovine stupidity in the face of abject impossibility. Advocates of global standardization see them as examples of failures in execution.

In fact, poor execution is often an important cause. More important, however, is failure of nerve—failure of imagination.

Consider the case for the introduction of fully automatic home laundry equipment in Western Europe at a time when few homes had even semiautomatic machines. Hoover, Ltd., whose parent company was headquartered in North Canton, Ohio, had a prominent presence in Britain as a producer of vacuum cleaners and washing machines. Due to insufficient demand in the home market and low exports to the European continent, the large washing machine plant in England operated far below capacity. The company needed to sell more of its semiautomatic or automatic machines.

Because it had a "proper" marketing orientation, Hoover conducted consumer preference studies in Britain and each major continental country. The results showed feature preferences clearly enough among several countries (see the Exhibit 1).

The incremental unit variable costs (in pounds sterling) of customizing to meet just a few of the national preferences were:

	£	s.	d.
Stainless steel vs. enamel drum	1	0	0
Porthole window		10	0
Spin speed of 800 rpm vs. 700 rpm		15	0
Water heater	2	15	0
6 vs. 5 kilos capacity	1	10	0
	£6	10s	0d

$18.20 at the exchange rate of that time.

Considerable plant investment was needed to meet other preferences.

The lowest retail prices (in pounds sterling) of leading locally produced brands in the various countries were approximately:

U.K.	£110
France	114
West Germany	113
Sweden	134
Italy	57

Product customization in each country would have put Hoover in a poor competitive position on the basis of price, mostly due to the higher manufacturing costs incurred by short production runs for separate features. Because Common Market tariff reduction programs were then incomplete, Hoover also paid tariff duties in each continental country.

How to Make a Creative Analysis

In the Hoover case, an imaginative analysis of automatic washing machine sales in each country would have revealed that:

1   Italian automatics, small in capacity and size, low-powered, without built-in heaters, with porcelain enamel tubs, were priced aggres-

Exhibit 1.   Consumer Preferences as to Automatic Washing Machine Features in the 1960s

Features	Great Britain	Italy	West Germany	France	Sweden
Shell dimensions*	34" and narrow	Low and narrow	34" and wide	34" and narrow	34" and wide
Drum material	Enamel	Enamel	Stainless steel	Enamel	Stainless steel
Loading	Top	Front	Front	Front	Front
Front porthole	Yes/no	Yes	Yes	Yes	Yes
Capacity	5 kilos	4 kilos	6 kilos	5 kilos	6 kilos
Spin speed	700 rpm	400 rpm	850 rpm	600 rpm	800 rpm
Water-heating system	No†	Yes	Yes††	Yes	No†
Washing action	Agitator	Tumble	Tumble	Agitator	Tumble
Styling features	Inconspicuous appearance	Brightly colored	Indestructible appearance	Elegant appearance	Strong appearance

*34" height was (in the process of being adopted as) a standard work-surface height in Europe.

†Most British and Swedish homes had centrally heated hot water.

††West Germans preferred to launder at temperatures higher than generally provided centrally.

sively low and were gaining large market shares in all countries, including West Germany.

2   The best-selling automatics in West Germany were heavily advertised (three times more than the next most promoted brand), were ideally suited to national tastes, and were also by far the highest priced machines available in that country.

3   Italy, with the lowest penetration of washing machines of any kind (manual, semiautomatic, or automatic), was rapidly going directly to automatics, skipping the pattern of first buying hand-wringer, manually assisted machines and then semiautomatics.

4   Detergent manufacturers were just beginning to promote the technique of cold-water and tepid-water laundering then used in the United States.

The growing success of small, low-powered, low-speed, low-capacity, low-priced Italian machines, even against the preferred but highly priced and highly promoted brand in West Germany, was significant. It contained a powerful message that was lost on managers confidently wedded to a distorted version of the marketing concept according to which you give the customer what he says he wants. In fact the customers *said* they wanted certain features, but their behavior demonstrated they'd take other features provided the price and the promotion were right.

In this case it was obvious that, under prevailing conditions, people preferred a low-priced automatic over any kind of manual or semiautomatic machine and certainly over higher priced automatics, even though the low-priced automatics failed to fulfill all their expressed preferences. The supposedly meticulous and demanding German consumers violated all expectations by buying the simple, low-priced Italian machines.

It was equally clear that people were profoundly influenced by promotions of automatic washers; in West Germany, the most heavily promoted ideal machine also had the largest market share despite its high price. Two things clearly influenced customers to buy: low price regardless of feature preferences and heavy promotion regardless of price. Both factors helped homemakers get what they most wanted—the superior benefits bestowed by fully automatic machines.

Hoover should have aggressively sold a simple, standardized high-quality machine at a low price (afforded by the 17% variable cost reduction that the elimination of £6-10-0 worth of extra features made possible). The suggested retail prices could have been somewhat less than £100. The extra funds "saved" by avoiding unnecessary plant modifications would have supported an extended service network and aggressive media promotions.

Hoover's media message should have been: *this* is the machine that you, the homemaker, *deserve* to have to reduce the repetitive heavy daily household burdens, so that *you* may have more constructive time to spend with your children and your husband. The promotion should also have targeted the husband to give him, preferably in the presence of his wife, a sense of obligation to provide an automatic washer for her even before he bought an automobile for himself. An aggressively low price, combined with heavy promotion of this kind, would have overcome previously expressed preferences for particular features.

The Hoover case illustrates how the perverse practice of the marketing concept and the absence of any kind of marketing imagination let multinational attitudes survive when customers actually want the benefits of global standardization. The whole project got off on the wrong foot. It asked people what features they wanted in a washing machine rather than what they wanted out of life. Selling a line of products individually tailored to each nation is thoughtless. Managers who took pride in practicing the marketing concept to the fullest did not, in fact, practice it at all. Hoover asked the wrong questions, then applied neither thought nor imagination to the answers. Such companies are like the ethnocentricists in the Middle Ages who saw with everyday clarity the sun revolving around the earth and offered it as Truth. With no additional data but a more searching mind, Copernicus, like the hedgehog, interpreted a more compelling and accurate reality. Data do not yield information except with the intervention of the mind. Information does not yield meaning except with the intervention of imagination.

Accepting the Inevitable

The global corporation accepts for better or for worse that technology drives consumers relentlessly toward the same common goals—alleviation of life's burdens and the expansion of discretionary time and spending power. Its role is profoundly different from what it has been for the ordinary corporation during its brief, turbulent, and remarkably protean history. It orchestrates the twin vectors of technology and globalization for the world's benefit. Neither fate, nor nature, nor God but rather the necessity of commerce created this role.

In the United States two industries became global long before they were consciously aware of it. After over a generation of persistent and acrimonious labor shutdowns, the United Steelworkers of America have not called an industrywide strike since 1959; the United Auto Workers have not shut down General Motors since 1970. Both unions realize that they have become global—shutting down all or most of U.S. manufacturing would not shut out U.S. customers. Overseas suppliers are there to supply the market.

Cracking the Code of Western Markets

Since the theory of the marketing concept emerged a quarter of a century ago, the more managerially advanced corporations have been eager to offer what customers clearly wanted rather than what was merely convenient. They have created marketing departments supported by professional market researchers of awesome and often costly proportions. And they have proliferated extraordinary numbers of operations and product lines—highly tailored products and delivery systems for many different markets, market segments, and nations.

Significantly, Japanese companies operate almost entirely without marketing departments or market research of the kind so prevalent in the West. Yet, in the colorful words of General Electric's chairman John F. Welch, Jr., the Japanese, coming from a small cluster of resource-poor islands, with an entirely alien culture and an almost impenetrably complex language, have cracked the code of Western markets. They have done it not by looking with mechanistic thoroughness at the way markets are different but rather by searching for meaning with a deeper wisdom. They have discovered the one great thing all markets have in common—an overwhelming desire for dependable, world-standard modernity in all things, at aggressively low prices. In response, they deliver irresistible value everywhere, attracting people with products that market-research technocrats described with superficial certainty as being unsuitable and uncompetitive.

The wider a company's global reach, the greater the number of regional and national preferences it will encounter for certain product features, distribution systems, or promotional media. There will always need to be some accommodation to differences. But the widely prevailing and often unthinking belief in the immutability of these differences is generally mistaken. Evidence of business failure because of lack of accommodation is often evidence of other shortcomings.

Take the case of Revlon in Japan. The company unnecessarily alienated retailers and confused customers by selling world-standardized cosmetics only in elite outlets; then it tried to recover with low-priced world-standardized products in broader distribution, followed by a change in the company president and cutbacks in distribution as costs rose faster than sales. The problem was not that Revlon didn't understand the Japanese market; it didn't do the job right, wavered in its programs, and was impatient to boot.

By contrast, the Outboard Marine Corporation, with imagination, push, and persistence, collapsed long-established three-tiered distribution channels in Europe into a more focused and controllable two-step system—and did so despite the vociferous warnings of local trade groups. It also reduced the number and types of retail outlets. The result was greater improvement in credit and product-installation service to customers, major cost reductions, and sales advances.

In its highly successful introduction of Contac 600 (the timed-released decongestant) into Japan, SmithKline Corporation used 35 wholesalers instead of the 1,000-plus that established practice required. Daily contacts with the wholesalers and key retailers, also in violation of established practice, supplemented the plan, and it worked.

Denied access to established distribution institutions in the United States, Komatsu, the Japanese manufacturer of lightweight farm machinery, entered the market through over-the-road construction equipment dealers in rural areas of the Sunbelt, where farms are smaller, the soil sandier and easier to work. Here inexperienced distributors were able to attract customers on the basis of Komatsu's product and price appropriateness.

In cases of successful challenge to prevailing institutions and practices, a combination of product reliability and quality, strong and sustained support systems, aggressively low prices, and sales-compensation packages, as well as audacity and implacability, circumvented, shattered, and transformed very different distribution systems. Instead of resentment, there was admiration.

Still, some differences between nations are unyielding, even in a world of microprocessors. In the United States almost all manufacturers of microprocessors check them for reliability through a so-called parallel system of testing. Japan prefers the totally different sequential testing system. So Teradyne Corporation, the world's largest producer of microprocessor test equipment, makes one line for the United States and one for Japan. That's easy.

What's not so easy for Teradyne is to know how best to organize and manage, in this instance, its marketing effort. Companies can organize by product, region, function, or by using some combination of these. A company can have separate marketing organizations for Japan and for the United States, or it can have separate product groups, one working largely in Japan and the other in the United States. A single manufacturing facility or marketing operation might service both markets, or a company might use separate marketing operations for each.

Questions arise if the company organizes by product. In the case of Teradyne, should the group handling the parallel system, whose major market is the United States, sell in Japan and compete with the group focused on the Japanese market? If the company organizes regionally, how do regional groups divide their efforts between promoting the parallel vs. the sequential system? If the company organizes in terms of function, how does it get commitment in marketing, for example, for one line instead of the other?

There is no one reliably right answer—no one formula by which to get it. There isn't even a satisfactory contingent answer.[3] What works well for one company or one place may fail for another in precisely the same place, depending on the capabilities, histories, reputations, resources, and even the cultures of both.

The Earth Is Flat

The differences that persist throughout the world despite its globalization affirm an ancient dictum of economics—that things are driven by what happens at the margin, not at the core. Thus, in ordinary competitive analysis, what's important is not the average price but the marginal price; what happens not in the usual case but at the interface of newly erupting conditions. What counts in commercial affairs is what happens at the cutting edge. What is most striking today is the underlying similarities of what is happening now to national preferences at the margin. These similarities at the cutting edge cumulatively form an overwhelming, predominant commonality everywhere.

To refer to the persistence of economic nationalism (protective and subsidized trade practices, special tax aids, or restrictions for home market producers) as a barrier to the globalization of markets is to make a valid point. Economic nationalism does have a powerful persistence. But, as with the present almost totally smooth internationalization of investment capital, the past alone does not shape or predict the future. (For reflections on the internationalization of capital, see the insert, "The shortening of Japanese horizons.")

Reality is not a fixed paradigm, dominated by immemorial customs and derived attitudes, heedless of powerful and abundant new forces. The world is becoming increasingly informed about the liberating and enhancing possibilities of modernity. The persistence of the inherited varieties of national preferences rests uneasily on increasing evidence of, and restlessness regarding, their inefficiency, costliness, and confinement. The historic past, and the national differences respecting commerce and industry it spawned and fostered everywhere, is now subject to relatively easy transformation.

Cosmopolitanism is no longer the monopoly of the intellectual and leisure classes; it is becoming the established property and defining characteristic of all sectors everywhere in the world. Gradually and irresistibly it breaks down the walls of economic insularity, nationalism, and chauvinism. What we see today as escalating commercial nationalism is simply the last violent death rattle of an obsolete institution.

Companies that adapt to and capitalize on economic convergence can still make distinctions and adjustments in different markets. Persistent differences in the world are consistent with fundamental underlying commonalities; they often complement rather than oppose each other—in business as they do in physics. There is, in physics, simultaneously matter and anti-matter working in symbiotic harmony.

The earth is round, but for most purposes it's sensible to treat it as flat. Space is curved, but not much for everyday life here on earth.

Divergence from established practice happens all the time. But the multinational mind, warped into circumspection and timidity by years of stumbles and transnational troubles, now rarely challenges existing overseas practices. More often it considers any departure from inherited domestic routines as mindless, disrespectful, or impossible. It is the mind of a bygone day.

The successful global corporation does not abjure customization or differentiation for the requirements of markets that differ in product preferences, spending patterns, shopping preferences, and institutional or legal arrangements. But the global corporation accepts and adjusts to these differences only reluctantly, only after relentlessly testing their immutability, after trying in various ways to circumvent and reshape them as we saw in the cases of Outboard Marine in Europe, SmithKline in Japan, and Komatsu in the United States.

There is only one significant respect in which a company's activities around the world are important, and this is in what it produces and how it sells. Everything else derives from, and is subsidiary to, these activities.

The purpose of business is to get and keep a customer. Or, to use Peter Drucker's more refined construction, to *create* and keep a customer. A company must be wedded to the ideal of innovation—offering better or more preferred products in such combinations of ways, means, places, and at such prices that prospects *prefer* doing business with the company rather than with others.

Preferences are constantly shaped and reshaped. Within our global commonality enormous variety constantly asserts itself and thrives, as can be seen within the world's single largest domestic market, the United States. But in the process of world homogenization, modern markets expand to reach cost-reducing global proportions. With better and cheaper communication and transport, even small local market segments hitherto protected from distant competitors now feel the pressure of their presence. Nobody is safe from global reach and the irresistible economies of scale.

Two vectors shape the world—technology and globalization. The first helps determine human preferences; the second, economic realities. Regardless of how much preferences evolve and diverge, they also gradually converge and form markets where economies of scale lead to reduction of costs and prices.

The modern global corporation contrasts powerfully with the aging multinational corporation. Instead of adapting to superficial and even entrenched differences within and between nations, it will seek sensibly to force suitably standardized products and practices on the entire globe. They are exactly what the world will take, if they come also with low prices, high quality, and blessed reliability. The global company will operate, in this regard, precisely as Henry Kissinger wrote in *Years of Upheaval* about the continuing Japanese economic success—"voracious in its collection of information, impervious to pressure, and implacable in execution."

Given what is everywhere the purpose of commerce, the global company will shape the vectors of technology and globalization into its great strategic fecundity. It will systematically push these vectors toward their own convergence, offering everyone simultaneously high-quality, more or less standardized products at optimally low prices, thereby achieving for itself vastly expanded markets and profits. Companies that do not adapt to the new global realities will become victims of those that do.

Notes

1. In a landmark article, Robert D. Buzzell pointed out the rapidity with which barriers to standardization were falling. In all cases they succumbed to more and cheaper advanced ways of doing things. See "Can You Standardize Multinational Marketing?" *HBR*, November-December 1968, p. 102.

2. There is powerful new evidence for this, even though the opposite has been urged by analysts of PIMS data for nearly a decade. See "Product Quality: Cost Production and Business Performance—A Test of Some Key Hypotheses," by Lynn W. Phillips, Dae Chang, and Robert D. Buzzell, Harvard Business School Working Paper No. 83-13.

3. For a discussion of multinational reorganization, see Christopher A. Bartlett, "MNCs: Get Off the Reorganization Merry-Go-Round," *HBR*, March-April 1983, p. 138.

Appendix A: Economies of Scope

One argument that opposes globalization says that flexible factory automation will enable plants of massive size to change products and product features quickly, without stopping the manufacturing process. These factories of the future could thus produce broad lines of customized products without sacrificing the scale economies that come from long production runs of standardized items. Computer-aided design and manufacturing (CAD/CAM), combined with robotics, will create a new equipment and process technology (EPT) that will make small plants located close to their markets as efficient as large ones located distantly. Economies of scale will not dominate, but rather economies of scope—the ability of either large or small plants to produce great varieties of relatively customized products at remarkably low costs. If that happens, customers will have no need to abandon special preferences.

I will not deny the power of these possibilities. But possibilities do not make probabilities. There is no conceivable way in which flexible factory automation can achieve the scale economies of a modernized plant dedicated to mass production of standardized lines. The new digitized equipment and process technologies are available to all. Manufacturers with minimal customization and narrow product-line breadth will have costs far below those with more customization and wider lines.

Appendix B: The Shortening of Japanese Horizons

One of the most powerful yet least celebrated forces driving commerce toward global standardization is the monetary system, along with the international investment process.

Today money is simply electronic impulses. With the speed of light it moves effortlessly between distant centers (and even lesser places). A change of ten basis points in the price of a bond causes an instant and massive shift of money from London to Tokyo. The system has profound impact on the way companies operate throughout the world.

Take Japan, where high debt-to-equity balance sheets are "guaranteed" by various societal presumptions about the virtue of "a long view," or by government policy in other ways. Even here, upward shifts in interest rates in other parts of the world attract capital out of the country in powerful proportions. In recent years more and more Japanese global corporations have gone to the world's equity markets for funds. Debt is too remunerative in high-yielding countries to keep capital at home to feed the Japanese need. As interest rates rise, equity becomes a more attractive option for the issuer.

The long-term impact on Japanese enterprise will be transforming. As the equity proportion of Japanese corporate capitalization rises, companies will respond to the shorter-term investment horizons of the equity markets. Thus the much-vaunted Japanese corporate practice to taking the long view will gradually disappear.

4
Deregulation
Surviving the Transition

**THOMAS S. ROBERTSON, SCOTT WARD, and
WILLIAM M. CALDWELL IV**

As the regulatory apparatus of the past quarter century falls increasingly by the wayside, managers in affected industries are discovering that adapting to the new world of deregulation is no simple task. What the authors call the "regulatory mentality" of such managers—a lack of market focus, a lack of concern for costs or accountability, a cooperative attitude toward competitors, and an undue concentration on the decision-making process itself—plays hob with their efforts to adjust to the new business climate in which they find themselves. Only by seeing this mentality for what it is and by abandoning it for an orientation more in keeping with the demands of market competition can these managers hope to make their transition to deregulation a success.

> Before, we were operation-oriented. We worried if the shipper fit into our regulated structure. Now we have to be market-oriented and adjust our structure to fit the shipper's needs.*

As the de-emphasis of the federal regulatory process begun in the Carter administration proceeds during the Reagan regime, many companies in regulated industries recognize their potential weaknesses in a competitive en-

---

Published 1982.
*John Smith, executive vice president of CRST Inc., a Cedar Rapids, Iowa trucker, quoted in the *New York Times*, January 24, 1982.

vironment. They view deregulation with something less than enthusiasm or are even lobbying against it.

Nevertheless, the direction toward loosening of the rules, if not outright abandonment of them, seems clear. Duplicating the experience of the transportation industries, the telecommunications, insurance, stock brokerage, banking, and energy industries all face the challenge of switching from a regulation mentality to a market-oriented, competitive mentality.

While companies will feel the impact in different ways—depending on the degree of regulation experienced and on the speed and scope of deregulation—all will encounter common problems in making the transition to the new environment. The transition for established companies will indeed be painful since they must change deeply held values and long-entrenched business practices.

Deregulation is likely to provoke a period of considerable market disequilibrium caused by new competitors, new products, new pricing structures, and new strategic options. The most dramatic aspect of disequilibrium is the collapse of barriers to entry and the consequent appearance of new competitors. The airline industry is in turmoil as old rivals face challenges from People Express, Air Florida, New York Air, Muse Air, and Midway Airlines—just when the industry is already in the financial doldrums.

These entrants often have the advantage of lower costs per seat-mile due to absence of unionization, higher labor productivity, fewer fixed costs in terminals, and newer, smaller (sometimes more efficient) aircraft. In almost all cases, the newcomers choose price as their major entry weapon and cream-skim in the high-volume market segments while leaving the low-volume segments to the entrenched carriers.

As of this writing, Braniff has failed and such established competitors as Pan American, Western, and Continental have been suffering heavy losses, and many of the new entrants have yet to turn a profit. Obviously, a shakeout is in the offing. Survival in the airlines or in other industries facing deregulation will depend on the ability to handle a dynamic situation and to anticipate competitors' actions.

The Regulation Mentality

The origins of the regulation mentality can be traced to the creation of federal and, in many cases, state watchdog agencies, beginning with the Interstate Commerce Commission in 1887. The chief characteristic of this mentality is a company's focus on the regulator rather than on the ultimate consumer. Since regulatory agencies provide a buffer between companies and the feared effects of competition and environmental change, it is little wonder that some company executives are ambivalent toward—or outright against—

deregulation. Suddenly their domain is not so clearly defined; their skills in negotiating with governmental bodies are no longer as important as skills in strategic planning or consumer and competitive analysis.

The regulation mentality is identified by:

- ☐ Focus on regulators rather than the market.
- ☐ Lack of concern with growth and satisfaction with adequacy.
- ☐ Lack of concern for costs.
- ☐ Lack of accountability.
- ☐ Paternalistic attitude toward consumers and employees.
- ☐ Cooperative attitude toward competitors.
- ☐ Myopic concern for process.

Let us look at these characteristics in turn. (Exhibit 1 compares the regulation mentality with the market-oriented mentality in terms of elements of corporate operations.)

Exhibit 1. Regulation versus Market-Oriented Mentalities

Focus	Regulation Mentality	Market-Oriented Mentality
The customer	The regulatory agency may be viewed as the most important customer.	The ultimate customer is the focal point of the company's direction.
Objectives	Generally slow, manageable growth.	Moderate or high growth.
Costs	Cross-subsidization of products and services, and often a lack of cost sensitivity since costs are part of the rate base.	Costs kept by product and (often) markets served.
Accountability	Managers often feel a lack of accountability since the regulators may have the final decision power.	Managers are responsible for their own actions.
Employees	A paternalistic orientation.	A results orientation.
Competition	Regulation is used to limit competition among members of the industry.	Product superiority and cost efficiency are used to rebuff competition.
Decision style	Concern with the process of decision making (i.e., forms and procedures)	Concern with the decision outcome.

Focus on Regulators

In a regulated industry it is all too easy for the agency, rather than the users of the product or service, to become the customer. Managements become more concerned with adequate preparation for hearings before commissions than with sounding out consumer needs and anticipating competitive actions.

Until the mid-1970s, many transportation companies concentrated their marketing efforts on rates, tariffs, and regulatory affairs. At the time of the restructuring of a number of railroads into Conrail, hundreds of people were employed in filing and interpreting rates but only a few were in such functions as strategy formulation, marketing research, or advertising and promotion.

As a result of this focus, regulated companies have often lost market opportunities to enterprising new companies that monitored and responded to market needs. In making overnight delivery of small packages with its Courier Pak and Priority One services, Federal Express filled a customer need, and it bypassed regulations by using airplanes too small to come under the rules. Rolm Corporation and Mitel Corporation succeeded because AT&T was not providing a leading-edge technology and a focused marketing strategy for the small telephone switchboard segment of the market. Commercial banks' emphasis on a limited portfolio of checking and savings options has hindered their growth and allowed money market funds to capture large market shares. New financial combinations, such as Shearson-American Express and Prudential-Bache, are further threatening the status quo in commercial banking.

Lack of Concern with Growth

Many regulated industries need not be concerned with growth; they are assured of a "fair" rate of return when providing adequate service. (This is not true in transportation, where guidelines on rates of return have been established subject to competitive performance.)

Growth occurs as service needs increase, and the regulators determine the pace. Growth is not seen as a vehicle for profit generation. Indeed, some industries downplay growth because of fears of criticism by regulators and the public.

In view of the structural restrictions on many regulated businesses, the lack of concern for growth is hardly surprising. The Civil Aeronautics Board used to take years to rule on a route case and at least several months to rule on a rate case. Adequacy has been demanded of most regulated industries in the past, and adequacy is what they have tried to deliver. As one executive of an East Coast power utility put it, "We call our people 'service representatives' rather than 'sales representatives,' and that's symptomatic of our problem."

Lack of Concern for Costs

Inasmuch as the allowable rate of return is largely based on costs, many industries have little incentive to be cost efficient. Costs can always be passed along. In many regulated companies the officers do not even know the costs of particular products or services. When the competition enters a product category, the regulated company may infer that the product must therefore be profitable.

Most companies under regulation don't adequately analyze joint costs and cross-elasticities of demand. Rates for a certain product or market segment often have nothing to do with the actual costs of serving that segment.

The established, previously regulated company is very vulnerable in this respect. The competition will generally plunge in where the existing company is "overcharging," the rate being based on average costs and not segment costs. MCI did this in its initial entry against AT&T in the high-density Chicago-St. Louis market, as did Southwest Airlines against Braniff in the high-density Dallas-Houston-San Antonio triangle. In both cases, because the entrenched company was pricing based on system costs, not segment costs, the new competitor enjoyed considerable price leverage.

Lack of Accountability

The very nature of regulation involves other forces in the decision process, thus reducing executives' latitude and responsibility—and therefore accountability. Managers may, however, perceive less discretion in decision making than exists. As Richard H. Steiner, Conrail's vice president of marketing, put it, "Regulation was a very convenient crutch for the railroad managers because they could always blame 'those crazies down at 12th and Constitution.' "

Paternalistic Attitude

Employment in a regulated industry often has been one step short of civil service: workers have secure positions, with little demand for creative decision making. When the value system is risk averse and job security is a main concern, the transition to a deregulated environment is difficult.

Regulated companies also tend to view their customers paternalistically: "We know what is good for you." Consolidated Edison aroused the ire of many New York City drivers confronted with street excavations marked with "Dig We Must" signs. The rail industry advertised: "America's railroads—Who needs them? America, that's who."

This attitude springs from the habit of viewing the regulatory agency as the customer. Supposedly, the ultimate consumers fail to appreciate the burden of providing service (often under antiquated regulatory structures and with aging equipment). And consumers are expected to keep quiet, although these days they are often quite vocal.

Cooperation with Competitors

Because of the exclusivity of franchises or divisions of markets served—whether air routes, truck lanes, or banking areas—"competitors" under regulation frequently are not actual rivals. Therefore, the parties may have a mutually cooperative attitude. Regulation provides a sense of order for the division of markets, price setting, and product offerings. When a competitor violates this informal order, the community is outraged. For example, Citicorp felt the wrath of other banks when it mailed Visa applications to consumers in those banks' territories.

Deregulation provides no substitute order except the ultimate market equilibrium established through competition. But this process takes time, and the former "colleagues" may suffer much pain before the dust settles. Following trucking deregulation, Roadway Express, the leading carrier, has entered the Pacific Northwest market and is now head-to-head with number two, Consolidated Freightways, which has invaded Roadway's strongholds in the East. The dust in this nationwide struggle has not yet settled.

Concern with Process

Common to many companies in a regulated environment (and perhaps because of regulation) is an endless concern with process rather than content. The strategic planning process supplants the actual formulation and implementation of strategic plans. The need to be consistent and precisely right—perhaps due to regulatory scrutiny—forces a focus on details and myopic attention to matters that might not be important after all.

Business Not as Usual

For companies fresh off the regulatory treadmill, success will come from abandonment of the regulation mentality and adoption of a competitive frame of mind. Adjustment to the new corporate climate, with its stress on performance, expediency, risk taking, functional specialties, and cross-fertilization from other industries, will be difficult for many managers.

The reward structure may have to be revised to encourage risk taking rather than smooth system maintenance. Skills in strategic planning will be at a premium. To meet changing market needs and competitive situations, deregulated companies will require more flexible organizational structures.

Indeed, senior management must recognize that the very essence of the business may change. In industries such as financial services, transportation, and telecommunications, companies face options undreamt of until now. Business as usual for many companies may be a road to obsolescence and irrelevance.

5

Can Industry Survive the Welfare State?

BRUCE R. SCOTT

The recession dogging the U. S. economy is only symptomatic of the long-term decline suffered by many of our industries since the beginning of the 1970s. The evidence is everywhere, from sagging profitability—and even bankruptcy—of once-dynamic companies to chronic unemployment that reaches far beyond the 10% level for certain areas of the country and population segments. Furthermore, the same symptoms afflict all of the other major economies of the North Atlantic area.

In this article, Bruce Scott argues that despite the degree of decline, no government has proposed a substantive or workable plan to reverse it. Using comparative economic analysis, he shows how the newly industrialized nations of East Asia have prospered just as the industrialized West has declined. Then he explains how the United States can begin the often-painful process of revitalization—not simply by implementing an industrial policy but by adopting a new way of thinking about a country's economic strategy in much the same way a company thinks about its strategy. The idea is revolutionary because, to make it work, government and labor will have to concede certain ground gained in the welfare reforms promulgated since the Great Depression. And for their part, corporations will have to take back some of the responsibility for the rights and security of their employees.

Stagflation has affected the North Atlantic area for almost ten years. We may be able to explain continuous inflation at historically high levels in the face of slack demand in terms of successive oil price shocks, wage settlements that far outpace productivity gains, and excessive money creation (particularly U.S. dollars).

Published 1982.

Author's note: Much of my thinking in the area of corporate governance has been greatly influenced by the writings of Professor George C. Lodge, a colleague.

But what about economic stagnation? The "oil tax" levied by OPEC is part of the explanation. A slowdown in technological innovation may also be a contributing cause. But in addition to these exogenous or noncontrollable developments, it may be that the economic policies of the industrial countries themselves bear a major responsibility. We cannot ignore the growing tax take of the welfare state, particularly when the state uses those revenues for social welfare programs and transfer payments that are "entitlements" unconnected to any productive contribution to society. Deficit financing of these programs makes government an increasingly important competitor for public savings, crowding out more directly productive investments.

Despite the possibility that government policy may have been a major cause of the stagflation problem, a growing sense exists that governments can and should "solve" it. And it is no coincidence that, since 1976, voters have rejected all major Western governments except that of Chancellor Schmidt. New governments are experimenting with radically different programs from supply-side economics in the United States and the United Kingdom to more socialism in France. Each can look to its share of economic experts for support. Consensus on the diagnosis seems almost as elusive as on the most appropriate remedies.

Understandably, much of the attention thus far has focused on the obvious symptoms of unemployment and inflation. But it is time the policymakers of the major countries in the North Atlantic area turned their attention to the more fundamental problems of: (1) weakened industrial performance (declines in the growth of investments, productivity, jobs, and trade balances), (2) the shifting distribution of income that preceded it (toward wages and away from profits), and (3) the increasing vulnerability of the traditional industrial countries to the unprecedented challenge from Japan and the four "new Japans" of East Asia—Hong Kong, Korea, Singapore, and Taiwan.

One important aspect of the new competition is the speed with which it has developed. Japan started to industrialize little more than 100 years ago, while the others began only 30 years ago. But more significant, none of the newcomers has a base of natural resources on which to build an industrial society, and Japan is the only one with a large home market. They have succeeded by mobilizing human and financial resources through different policies and institutions.

While the North Atlantic countries have viewed economic growth in terms of exploitation of natural resources enhanced by trade, the East Asians have created a model that does not require any significant endowment of natural resources. Unwilling to accept the conventional Western idea that their role is to specialize in goods based on cheap labor (their major resource), the East Asians have forged a dynamic theory of comparative advantage that allows them to allocate human and financial resources toward jobs with high value added in growing industries and, for example, to succeed in steel despite a lack of both coal and iron.

This new industrial competition is the most important challenge facing the entire North Atlantic area. Whether economic growth recovers somewhat in the 1980s, the traditional industrial nations will continue to lose industrial competitiveness and industrial jobs unless they respond to it. A successful response will include policy changes to promote increased investment, more rapid adaptation by industry, and increased mobility of labor. These changes will require recognition of the disincentives to work, save, and invest that have become the hallmarks of the welfare state. And in the United States, we must address a special set of problems ascribed to an "adversarial relationship" between business and government.

None of these changes will come easily. Nor should the challenge be a pretext for turning the economic clock back to nineteenth-century private enterprise capitalism. Just as we need to rethink the goals and policies of the welfare state we need also to rethink the governance process of the corporation. If we expect government to revive its commitment to the value of work, saving, and investment, business must recognize investments made by employees as well as shareholders and accept a governance process that effectively reflects the essential rights of both.

Strategies of Economic Growth

Before accepting this "gloomy" or "challenging" diagnosis, we should review comparative performance data to check the severity of the alleged symptoms. In terms of rising incomes and an improvement in distribution of wealth on a worldwide basis, the rapid rise of the East Asians is a positive development. Stagnation in the North Atlantic area, on the other hand, is not, particularly as we witness unemployment rates at levels unheard of since the 1930s. Continued weakness in the industrial sector threatens the loss not only of vital exports but also of highly productive jobs in mass production industries.

Some observers seem to regard industrial decline as a step forward toward a service-based "postindustrial" society. While it is important to recognize the growing importance of the service sector, the vision of a postindustrial society may well turn out to have been an elegant rationalization for failure to maintain a competitive industrial base. Before accepting industrial decline as an inevitable sign of sophistication and progress, we should reexamine how it has happened and the extent to which it may have been caused by differences in economic strategies among countries rather than by inevitable historical forces.

Classical economics has long taught that economic growth was built on the rational uses of resources, with each country building on comparative advantage through trade. Worked out by Ricardo in the early 1800s, when competitive advantages were based on natural resources, the theory was essentially static. The advantages were "given"; there was little room or need for a strategy.

This static notion of comparative advantage has had a profound influence on economic thought throughout the North Atlantic area. Americans, in particular, are not used to thinking of government as needing an explicit economic strategy. The American economy became the most productive in the world without one. Blessed with the world's first "common market" and some of its richest resources, the United States grew by conquering the frontier via private enterprise, without an active government strategy. At least that is what we think. We should not forget that one of the critical elements of success was the Interstate Commerce Clause of the Constitution that prohibited trade barriers among the states; another was the use of land grants to speed the opening of the West via the transcontinental railroads. Even the United States had a strategy of sorts.

Today, however, the static notion of comparative advantage is no longer relevant. The United States still has rich and abundant farmland and is the world's number one exporter of agricultural goods. But the United States no longer has an advantage in the size of its market. Europe has a market of roughly the same size, and Japan's is almost half as large. Raw materials have been found around the globe, and for many applications it is cheaper to import foreign ores than to exploit domestic ones. As a result, most of the natural advantages that were the sources of American economic strength are no longer of critical importance. Increasingly the vital resources are those we create through the organized exploitation of various technologies.

American experts misperceived postwar Japan's potential in large part because of the notion of static comparative advantage. In the 1950s it led Edwin Reischauer to conclude that "Japan's situation is basically similar to England's, but infinitely worse. She is far less richly endowed with the vital resources of coal and iron. . . . She is far less highly industrialized. She has no overseas empire to aid her . . . and she has almost twice the population of Great Britain to support on her more meager resources."[1]

In the 30 years since Reischauer made this assessment, Japan has grown at a rate roughly triple that of the United Kingdom. Economists now recognize that Japan's greatest resource is its population; yet that largely misses the point. India and China have larger populations but have not generated economic performance that is remotely comparable. The Japanese have created a strategy and a set of institutional relationships to implement it. Mobility of capital has been one key, labor mobility another. By promoting savings and investing in the most modern technologies, Japan and the other countries of East Asia have shown that countries can create comparative advantages in almost any industry they choose. Their capacity to abandon older industries as they create new ones shows that a trained, disciplined, and relatively mobile labor force can be a nation's most important real resource.

In contrast, labor mobility and discipline of the older industrial states are declining. Unemployment benefits and various forms of adjustment assistance, however meritorious on other grounds, give added support to individuals who refuse to relocate, while increasingly generous health insurance plans—particularly in Europe—allow employees to be absent from work at almost no cost to themselves. Meanwhile, a variety of subsidies, such as "safe harbor leasing," help prop up losing ventures. Taxes to finance these programs become an added burden on all companies located in these countries and another competitive disadvantage. As growth industries, such as electronics, become more knowledge intensive and as companies transfer technology anywhere on the globe, a nation's economic success hinges on the way it manages its human and financial resources. Under these circumstances, where the key to successful performance is mobility of capital and labor, Ricardo's theory no longer provides much of a framework for formulating public policy.

Recent experience in Korea, Taiwan, Hong Kong, and Singapore demonstrates that Japan is not unique. Without significant natural resources, these countries have achieved rapid growth by developing efficient, specialized manufacturing organizations backed by a system of social and economic incentives designed to promote work, saving, risk taking, investment, and labor mobility. Like Japan, they have built success by organizing human and financial resources and by not banking on the good fortune of natural resources. Their rapid industrialization has grown out of an economic strategy designed to promote productivity while sharply limiting the development of the welfare state.

Welfare vs. Productivity Strategies

Like companies, countries have strategies, or goals and policies, to orient the actions of their respective "managers." Some strategies are more explicit, some more coherent, some more effective. Because the United States is an extreme example of an implicit rather than explicit strategy and at times has a political rhetoric that proclaims the virtues of a government with no economic strategy at all, it may help to use the Japanese example as a starting point.

The goal of the Japanese has long been to catch and then surpass all others in economic performance. To achieve that goal, they have created a strategy to generate rising incomes by using the latest technology and equipment and employing mass production and marketing techniques to reach world markets. The Japanese strategy requires a high level of investment, hence access to a high level of savings. Rejecting Western advice about borrowing heavily or inviting foreign capital, they have chosen to finance their investment from domestic savings. For some years the Japanese have saved roughly 20% of personal disposable income (the current American rate is 5%). They save not because of high interest rates on bank deposits; indeed, when adjusted for inflation the rates have been negative through most of the 1970s. The Japanese save because they must if they are to make major purchases and provide for old age. The government restricts consumer credit. And pensions are only a fraction of American levels. The Japanese receive greater deductions for interest income than Americans, but they receive no tax deductions for interest payments. Japanese banks receive the savings, and because they cannot easily lend to consumers, they must lend to industry if they are to grow.

The Japanese have shaped their policies in housing, banking, and social welfare to support a strategy of raising the standard of living by raising savings, investment, and productivity. Labor policy is part of the strategy. Lifetime employment in large companies means employees are sharing the productivity gains rather than being displaced by them.

No Strategy Is Good Strategy

The problem in the United States is that our strategy is largely implicit and forged in reaction to economic misfortunes. Until the Great Depression, the goal was a rising standarding of living based on the Yankee virtues of work, saving, and investment. The government allowed companies a reasonable chance to compete and refereed the competition as it unfolded. Americans raised their standard of living both as producers and as consumers of goods and services delivered at reasonable prices in a competitive system.

The Depression led not only to a new economics of demand management based on Keynes's ideas but also to a gradual, steady shift in the economic strategies of all the North Atlantic countries.

The priorities shifted toward short-term consumer welfare. Productivity was downgraded, however implicitly. The Employment Act of 1946 commited the U.S. government to use its powers to stimulate demand to ensure a high level of employment. Subsequent legislation established penalty taxes on interest and dividends to help redistribute income from the rich to the poor. Taxes on consumption (sales or excise taxes) were rejected as regressive, and the federal government was financed largely by personal and corporate income taxes and social security contributions.

Although a nominal amount of interest and dividend income went tax free, interest payments on homes, consumer durables, and even credit card purchases became tax deductible. In this way, the United States promoted a higher standard of living through subsidies to consumption. Progressive income taxes designed in part to redistribute the income eroded traditional incentives to work, save, and invest. Ever-increasing levels of entitlements support short-term consumer welfare at the expense of those who work and pay taxes. The result is a system that takes productivity for granted and tries to promote rising levels of consumption.

We can compare the welfare strategies of the North Atlantic area with the productivity strategies found in East Asia using a simple matrix (see Exhibit 1). The East Asians place high priority on productivity and deliberately limit the growth of the welfare state. The North Atlantic countries have done the reverse. Many of the less-developed countries have done little of either, so they are positioned at the lower right.

Exhibit 1. Strategy Matrix by Country

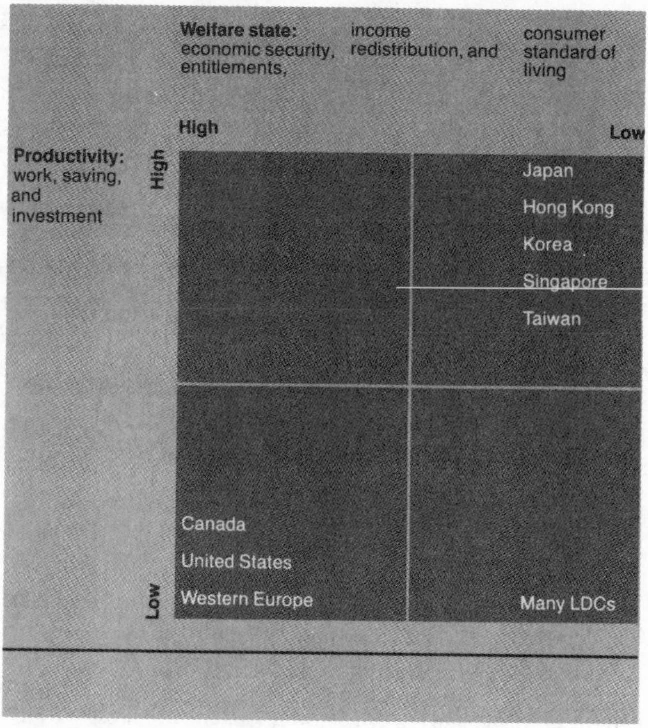

	Welfare state: economic security, entitlements,	income redistribution, and	consumer standard of living
	High		**Low**
Productivity: work, saving, and investment **High**			Japan Hong Kong Korea Singapore Taiwan
Low	Canada United States Western Europe		Many LDCs

The box at the upper left, though blank, suggests a strategy promoting both productivity and welfare. Until recently, Germany would be one country in the upper left box. After World War II, Germany exempted overtime earnings from taxation and gave tax exemptions both for savings and for interest income. On the other hand, it began creating a welfare state under Bismarck. With the victory of the Social Democrats in 1969, the Germans shifted in favor of the welfare state and now belong in the lower left-hand box, even if they are less firmly entrenched there than in Belgium, Holland, the Scandinavian countries, or the United Kingdom.

Worldwide Prospects

If you use this conceptual scheme both to compare economic strategies and to think about the prospects for industries throughout the world, the implications are not reassuring. Unless strategies change, the welfare states of the North Atlantic are likely to be increasingly less competitive with the productivity-oriented countries of East Asia. They will suffer from lower levels of saving and investment and from a variety of disincentives to work. Entitlements, progressive income taxes, and subsidies for consumption will make them increasingly less competitive as locations for any industries where product values allow international trade. The problem is not so much with themselves as with the newly industrialized countries (NICs).

More important, today's NICs will not be alone for long. Since the continuing success of the East Asians does *not* require any natural resources, or even a large home market, other less-developed countries can copy it. Indeed, Malaysia and Thailand appear to be moving toward similar strategies, and a related process has brought rapid progress to Brazil.

A Dynamic Theory of Comparative Advantage

The implications of the world economic picture are clear. In industrial terms, the star performers of the last 30 years are a group of countries whose critical resources are not land or minerals but rather people and savings—and the policies and institutions to mobilize and periodically redirect both.

To be able to direct our own economic strategy in the United States, we need to construct a way of thinking that will foster this mobility. It will help to postulate that countries, like companies, have "portfolios" of businesses or industries. They can influence not only the mix in the portfolio at any time but also the rate of new business development, the redeployment of human and capital resources to growth sectors, and the withdrawal of those same resources from declining sectors. In fact, dynamic industrial policy should promote all three.

Several schemes have been developed for corporations looking at their portfolios of businesses. The Boston Consulting Group pioneered in this field, and I think governments would find a variant of its growth-share matrix useful (see Exhibit 2). Based on industry growth rate and corporate market share, the original matrix related high market share to increased output, cumulative experience, and lower costs. For comparable products, lower costs mean higher margins.

The lower left-hand corner of the matrix symbolizes high share in a slow-growth industry that should generate high returns; low growth should not require high levels of investment. Businesses in the lower left should generate cash, while those in the upper left grow so rapidly that they require additional cash despite their presumably high profit margins. New ventures in the upper right may need additional cash to support fast growth on low margins.

If we think of a given portfolio of businesses, the scheme highlights the "mix" in terms of prospective growth, profitability, and cash flow. Of greater interest, however, is its dynamic aspect. A new product or business ideally moves from upper right to upper left to lower left over its life cycle. Cash from businesses in the lower left finances new entries in the upper right and likewise battles for market share and a hoped-for position in the upper left. Theoretically, a company balances the businesses in its portfolio by building some in the upper half, avoiding excess investment in the lower left, and considering disinvestment in the lower right (see Exhibit 3).

Exhibit 2. Growth-Share Matrix A

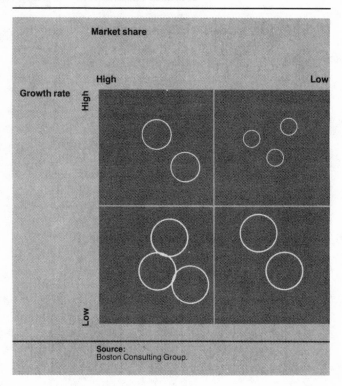

Source:
Boston Consulting Group.

Obviously, the growth-share concept has limits. First, strategies of technical and/or service differentiation do not fit in well. Second, low cost and rising share correlate, but the correlation may be either circular or even the reverse of the original hypothesis.[2] Third, there is a great deal more to running a business than managing a portfolio—that is, there are people, products, technologies, and so forth. Finally, a corporate strategy is more than simply the sum of the portfolio decisions affecting separate business ends; corporate strategy refers to the corporation as a whole.[3] If we keep these limitations in mind, however, we can use the growth-share matrix as a comprehensive way to think about industry dynamics and as a more appropriate framework for forging an industrial policy.

How Should We Think about Industrial Policy?

Industrial policy is only one element, however important, of a country's total economic strategy. A government must formulate and implement industrial policy through institutions that are competent, committed, and able to wield political clout. Otherwise the risk is high that the process will yield

Exhibit 3. Growth-Share Matrix B

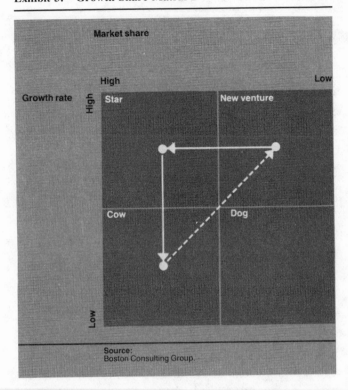

Source:
Boston Consulting Group.

a narrow technical exercise in portfolio analysis or, worse still, a new rationale for liberal bureaucrats to apply their noncompetitive values and theories.

With these caveats, let's look at a more general framework for industrial policy (see Exhibit 4), which would focus attention on opportunities to: (1) promote new undertakings in the upper right, (2) foster successful transitions in the upper left, (3) avoid excessive investment in the lower half (particularly the lower right quadrant), and (4) abandon businesses in the lower right unless special circumstances allow profitable operation. On the other hand, industrial policy should not attempt to do what it cannot: plan output and/or investment by sector.

1 Promoting Innovation

Government can promote innovation both by subsidizing R&D costs and by increasing the rewards for successful entrepreneurship. The Japanese give tax credits for *increases* in R&D, coupled with a limit on the total amount of credit. The French have used a variety of subsidies, some reimbursable if the project is commercially successful.

Exhibit 4. Competitive Position Matrix

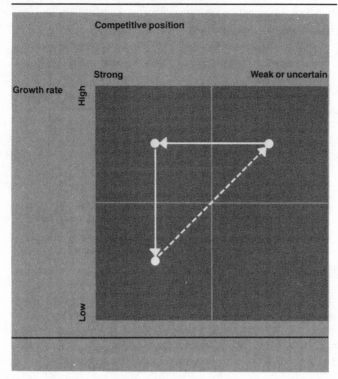

The capital gains tax affects the risk-reward ratio for the scientist or entrepreneur as well as the mobility of risk capital. A high tax reduces the rewards for those who succeed and forces an investor with a large capital gain in one venture to pay a severe penalty for transferring those funds to another venture. The Japanese have no capital gains tax. The Germans, however, tax capital gains as ordinary income. The French are particularly backward; a French inventor who receives stock in a new venture in recognition of the innovation must pay a tax on its nominal value at the time the stock is received rather than when the capital gains are realized.

The impact of the capital gains tax rate on the formation of new ventures in the United States has been analyzed in *America's Competitive Edge*.[4] The authors describe the decline in new ventures and in amounts of venture capital raised following the 1969 increases in the maximum rate on capital gains from 25% to 40%. They also note the dramatic increase in venture capital raised once the maximum rate was reduced to 25% in 1978.

Industrial policy can also promote new technologies within existing companies. While U.S. antitrust laws usually preclude joint ventures, the Japanese encourage them within an industry to solve major technical problems or to accelerate the development of prototypes. In numerous cases, the Japanese have made investment subsidies contingent on the formation of the joint venture. The participants are free to use the technological fruits of the venture in competition with one another as well as with foreign companies.

2 Encouraging "Winners"

With an adequate portfolio of new ventures and business development in established companies, government can help promote the growth of strong industries through foreign trade and investment policies. Japan, for example, restricted foreign imports and generally limited or prohibited foreign investment in new industries until Japanese entrants were established. While opening up its market in the 1970s, Japan has restricted the roles of foreign companies in those industries targeted for growth in the 1980s and 1990s, such as telecommunications, integrated circuits, and computers.

The European Common Market countries do not have this option. There is no European Community policy on restricting foreign investment, and internal trade restrictions are prohibited. The most a member country can do is discourage foreign takeovers and subsidize *selected* industries or companies. When the French tried to be quite restrictive, investors went to Belgium or Germany and exported to France.

The French government uses export subsidies to foster sales of capital equipment and weapons. Aiming to supply 20% of its energy needs by 1985 (compared with the 3% to 5% proportion of its neighbors), it also promotes the development of atomic power. But since the state, through the electricity monopoly, is the only buyer, this is not a model for the competitive sector.

In high-technology industries such as computers and space, the French have been less successful. The Plan Calcul was a costly failure, yet the takeover of Honeywell-Bull, plus subsidies for smaller companies, gives France a significant entry in mainframes and minis. Sponsorship by PTT (the French telephone company) of a "program télématique" based on subscriber telephones may give France a strong position, if not the lead, in a sector of telecommunications. Automobiles have been a consistently strong point among French exports, but both state-owned Renault and privately-owned Peugeot have operated like private-sector companies. Unless the EC follows the French and Italian lead in imposing quotas on auto imports, France's auto sector is vulnerable to Japanese competition and also to the French tendency to maintain an overvalued exchange rate. France has a decidedly mixed record in building its new state-sponsored projects into strong, competitive activities.

Germany has enjoyed remarkable industrial strength for the past 30 years, but it is concentrated in chemicals, metalworking, and mechanical equipment. Its position is not nearly as strong in electronics, computers, or telecommunications. Indeed, several careful observers point out that Germany not only lags behind the United States, Japan, and France in these growth areas but also has not launched a program to catch up. If Germany permits the renewal of its industrial portfolio to lag, it will have less capacity to carry the costs of its increasingly generous welfare state in the late 1980s and 1990s.

The United States has the world's largest economy and industrial portfolio, mostly the result of natural competitive development. Public policy has focused on the U.S. market and prevention of cooperation among participants in an industry. Until very recently, international competition has been ignored. It is as if our market were so large and our companies so strong that the government need not be concerned with promoting their performance. Neither the regulators nor the courts have given much weight to the impact of regulation on either domestic economic performance or international competition. Recent decisions by the Reagan administration and the Federal Trade Commission to dismiss the antitrust suits against IBM and the cereal manufacturers represent an important and promising policy reversal. And the proposed settlement of the AT&T case should liberate one of the most important sources of U.S. technical strength to compete both internationally and domestically.

3 Limiting Investment in Low-Growth Sectors

The economic case for limiting investment in low-growth sectors is obvious; countries, like companies, should try to redeploy their resources where the prospects are brighter. In most cases, however, governments do not intervene but rely on market forces. How well the market works depends on the strategy and structure of individual companies. Single-business companies in low-growth industries will continue to invest despite low returns because they know only one product or industry. Diversified companies can invest in higher-growth sectors within the organization.[5]

Government may implicitly encourage investment in low-growth areas by distorting prices or providing loan guarantees. Trade barriers foster higher prices and profits in protected sectors. Domestic subsidies also lead to overinvestment. For example, the U.S. government protected small banks by fixing prices on savings accounts; at the same time, it provided low-cost mortgage money that increased jobs in the building trades. Coupled with tax deductions for interest payments on home mortgages and massive spending on freeways, the government subsidized the development of suburbs and drew capital away from industry and into unnecessarily large, single-family dwellings.

The negative impact of tariffs and subsidies is well known and the subject of continuing attention by the public and government. But less well understood is the effect of wage and price controls, which may be worse. By setting uniform criteria for all industries, they implicitly favor the older, slow-growth industries. But controls work against high-growth industries, which generally have the most rapid productivity increases and the opportunity to reduce prices while giving above-average wage increases. In fact, higher wages are necessary to attract enough new employees to *sustain* productivity. A wage and price control system allows no credit for price cuts by high-tech companies and, at the same time, forbids them to use rising wages to bid for new employees.

4 Abandoning Losers

Political logic in a democracy works against accelerated abandonment of low-growth, low-profit industries. Winning, high-profit companies—and the new jobs they create—seldom get the headlines generated by potential job losses in declining industries. A job lost is more important politically than a job not created, as any government official knows. In most of the North Atlantic countries, government, not business, takes responsibility for unemployment. Government must choose to keep a losing company solvent or pay unemployment compensation and the other costs of a decline or shutdown. The Chrysler saga points up that continued operation, even with losses, may be less costly—at least in the short run.

Operating in private and without formal responsibility for job security, companies abandon losing ventures more rapidly than government does. Democratic governments, naturally concerned with jobs and votes, have a long record of retarding rather than facilitating the process. In the same way, private capital markets are more flexible and less politicized than public funding over the long run. When it comes to capital allocation, democratic governments will do worse than the market mechanism and much worse than well-managed diversified companies. If enacted, proposals to revive the Reconstruction Finance Corporation are likely to give government a more adroit mechanism for retarding rather than accelerating disinvestment—or, simply put, a better way of doing the wrong thing. The problem lies not so much with the concept as with the social and political context.

On the other hand, large private companies that take little or no responsibility for employment are a major cause of the government's active involvement in ill-advised rescue attempts. To the extent that senior executives think business leadership is the management of assets that are bought and sold to promote a higher share price for stockholders with little regard for the "investments" made by long-term employees, they abdicate a responsibility they should shoulder. The root of the problem lies in a short-sighted sense of business responsibility backed by equally narrow academic theories of corporate finance that force government to compensate. The recent contract revisions between Ford Motor Company and the United Auto Workers, with their emphasis on employment security and changes in corporate governance, point in a very positive direction. Unfortunately, it is unlikely that the concessions were nearly enough for industry to regain a sound competitive position in the near future.

5 Investment and Output Planning

Several governments have tried to plan investments and output. The most extensive experience was in France, where a process begun in 1945 was much heralded in the 1960s and abandoned in the 1970s—for pragmatic rather than ideological reasons. Bluntly put, it failed. Conceived in a closed economy where the choice was either to make or do without and where it worked well, the plan did not adapt to an open economy with imports, exports, and the critical choices of make or buy. Its focus remained domestic, leading France to overinvest in industries sheltered from foreign competition.[6]

In the 1950s and 1960s, the Japanese had a similar approach but abandoned it as their economy opened to world trade. At present only the Communist countries, in circumstances reminiscent of the closed economies of the 1950s, attempt to plan output and investments.

There is an obvious theoretical attraction to the involvement of government in planning; some economists note that because big business plans, government should do no less. However, they overlook the critical difference: business plans in private, while government—in a democratic society—inevitably plans in a quasi-public setting. Forcing a company to do its planning in public would yield a public relations document, not a plan. In the same way, the French government's industrial plans were essentially public relations documents by the 1960s and consequently of little value to either business or government.

A Cautionary Note

Sound industrial policy could aid the performance of all the industrial countries. But it is not a panacea and does not exist in a vacuum. By itself it cannot overcome the excessive costs and other competitive handicaps imposed by the welfare state, any more than it can offset the impact of a consistently overvalued currency.

In fact, much of the current enthusiasm for the notion of industrial policy hinges on the premise that better "portfolio management" by government is both necessary and sufficient to ease the growing industrial malaise.[7] This position has obvious attractions for liberal economists with a strong ideological commitment to the welfare state because it allows some of them to dismiss as unimportant the inadequate levels of corporate profitability and investment of recent years.

Exaggerated claims for industrial policy could lead to the same kind of unrealistic expectations as did the "fine tuning" of aggregate demand espoused by liberal economists in the 1960s. The claims could blind us to reforms needed to reverse the inadequate corporate profitability found in all the North Atlantic countries.

The idea of politicians and bureaucrats guiding business toward a better industrial portfolio is more or less reassuring depending on your view of their values, business savvy, and professional competence. Those who draw inspiration from Japanese experience overlook not only the productivity-oriented nature of the Japanese strategy but also the staffing of key ministries (MITI and Finance) by career civil servants of very high quality. The U.S. bureaucracy, conversely, is characterized by rapid turnover, uneven quality, and—at least historically—little understanding of or concern for the essentials of a productive, competitive industrial sector. These bureaucrats do not have the same capacity or motivation to take a sound, long-term view of business opportunities as do American business executives. And the adversary nature of U.S. business-government relations adds an additional hazard, for it is through this relationship that proposals would eventually be formulated and implemented.

Business—Government Relations

The four largest market economies have different records in this area. The French and Japanese promote industries most actively; the United States, least. In Germany the government has been less interventionist than in France or Japan, and Chancellor Schmidt's more activist ministers of science and technology offset free-market advocates in the ministry of economics. Despite their differences, France, Germany, and Japan believe that government is the senior member of the business–government partnership—in short, that it guides without enacting new laws or regulations. When the chips are down, business doesn't take government to court (as it does in the United States) but rather follows its advice.

In fact, we take for granted that business and government are natural adversaries in the United States. But it has not always been so. Alfred Chandler calls the 1890s the turning point for business–government relations here. While businessmen had always been active civic leaders prior to the Civil War, the public—through government—began to attack them before the end of the century. The reason was that big companies, particularly the railroads, came before big government. As Chandler notes, "In 1890 at least a dozen railroads employed over 100,000 workers, (while) the civilian working force in Washington numbered just over 20,000."[8]

The railroads enjoyed not only great size but near monopolies in many inland areas, with the power to make or break businesses or even towns by their rates. They also opened the way for national consumer-goods companies, such as the meat-packers or A&P, that displaced many small businesses—nearly 50% of the wholesalers between 1889 and 1929. Small business, not farmers or consumer groups, mounted the initial attack on big business and helped limit its powers.

In Europe and Japan, the national markets were much smaller and big government developed before big business. In addition, consumer-goods producers used wholesalers rather than displacing them through forward integration. Some of the largest companies were manufacturers of industrial goods and interested in export sales. Government was a natural ally; it was more of a senior partner to business than an adversary and sanctioned business federation as a practical mechanism for organized dialogue.

In each of these countries, business has developed a "peak federation" that serves not only as a legitimate interlocutor for business with government but also as a way of molding business consensus toward certain general, as opposed to company- or industry-specific, goals. While the United States has an established federation for labor, it has several for business—but not one that enjoys comparable standing to those in other industrial countries.

Lack of institutional mechanisms on the business side matches weak institutional links in the U.S. government. The Commerce Department, as spokesman for business interests, is still organized as a service bureau responsible for the census and weights and measures and not for an important policymaking role. Its voice has been fourth or fifth in economic policymaking, after the Treasury, State, and Justice departments, and the Council of Economic Advisers. Commerce has had very little power; the recent transfer of customs from Treasury to Commerce came not so much from a desire to give the department more power as from congressional frustration and anger that the Treasury could so easily flout legislative intent in the enforcement of antidumping statutes.

Adversary business–government relations, coupled with a consumer-oriented economic strategy, produce bizarre policy in the executive branch. For example, the government long considered imports of cheaper manufactured goods beneficial because they reduced costs for the consumer. That some imports might be favorably priced due to dumping—with the potential for destroying an American industry within a few years—concerned only those most directly affected, not the executive branch. Japanese television exports illustrate the problem. While Japanese companies cut prices and raised market share in the United States in the 1970s, their domestic market remained closed. Imports of color televisions into Japan from *all* foreign sources remained less than 0.5%.

First, the American television industry's claims of Japanese dumping produced four years of inaction, then a customs investigation that showed dumping approached 20% of invoice prices. The Treasury Department attempted to squelch the investigation, but Congress intervened on behalf of the industry. Finally, after most American companies were either forced or bought out, the importers pleaded no contest and paid $77 million in fines for dumping and filing fraudulent invoices. Of course, the $77 million went to the Treasury Department, not to the injured companies. By settling for no-contest pleas, the executive branch acceded to Japanese requests that there be no public record of the behavior of the exporters, importers, or their respective governments.[9] A recently released study of the machine tool industry indicates that the television case is not an isolated example.

High officials of the U.S. government describe the process as one where Treasury, State, Justice, and the CEA will take the consumer point of view and support foreign companies against a hopelessly outgunned Commerce Department. Departed officials of the Carter administration not only point to the low priority accorded the role of healthy, productive companies in building the U.S. standard of living but also describe how high officials of the Justice Department threatened other government officials with personal criminal prosecution if efforts to help American companies were viewed as restraint of trade.

Our economic strategy is half a strategy, to foster short-term consumer welfare. It is not the strategy that built our industrial base in earlier decades nor is it the one used by the Japanese to overtake us in the last 30 years. Both of those relied on investing in the future to build a rising standard of living through rising productivity. Passing the benefits along to consumers in the form of lower prices was part of the story, but only part.

This "half" strategy has also allowed big business to escape responsibility for the economic security of its employees. When Japanese companies shoulder that responsibility, employees have a long-term stake in the company, its products, and their own productivity. Americans have increasingly looked to the federal government for their economic security; product quality and productivity suffer as economic security becomes an entitlement rather than something the employee and the company produce together.

Implications for the United States

To the extent that damage to our economy is self-inflicted, we can correct it through an appropriate change in economic policy. A good example is the U.S. capital gains tax. Its increase in 1969 resulted in declining investment in new ventures, while its reduction in 1978 quickly brought on a surge of new investment. Recent acceleration of depreciation schedules will pump up cash flows and investment when the U.S. economy recovers. While helpful, the changes do not directly address the critical problem.

We cannot achieve long-term economic recovery as long as U.S. policy focuses on short-term consumer welfare and on the entitlements and subsidies of a welfare state. This policy has steadily shifted American economic incentives away from work, saving, and investment. Until the United States rebalances its priorities, its incentives, and its rhetoric, there is little chance we will become competitive with the productivity-oriented societies of East Asia.

The Europeans do not pose a similar competitive threat. If anything, they are in a weaker position than the United States because their priorities have become even more lopsided than our own.

Recently there has been much discussion of industrial policy and reindustrialization as well as a quickening of interest in improving the business–government relationship. While constructive steps can and should be taken, even the most favorable scenario for change does not nearly address the seriousness of the problem. For example, it is fantasy to hope that government aid in reallocating an inadequate level of saving and investment will turn the economy around.[10] In addition, real respect and constructive dialogue in business–government relations will require that both government and business see the need to balance short-term consumer welfare with the imperatives of investing to build long-term productivity.

The United States has few significant natural advantages to count on, except in agriculture. Our comparative advantage will depend more and more on the goals, policies, and institutions through which the American economy is organized. Over time, the United States and all the other welfare states of the North Atlantic area will be less competitive with the productivity-oriented societies. When we tinker with small issues, we overlook or deny the challenge. To address this fundamental problem, we must recognize that government, in assuming greatly increased responsibility for the economic security of the individual, has relieved the individual and the large business enterprise of that responsibility. The various security programs result in a double cost on business, first by taxing to finance welfare and economic security programs and second by reducing the responsibility, motivation, and mobility of labor. We cannot expect industrial performance to fundamentally improve until we reduce these costs.

What It Will Take

Industrial performance will improve when employees gain economic security through long-term commitments to productive, profitable companies. In turn, business must recognize this commitment and must adapt its strategies, organization, and personnel policies accordingly. Companies can no longer equate management with manipulation of the balance sheet, where divisions are bought and sold or plants closed and opened with little or no reference to the rights of those who work there. Management must adopt a measure of performance a good deal broader than the highly regarded "impact on the price per share." Unless management defines its role more broadly, government can hardly relinquish its responsibility for employment.

If business assumes more responsibility and government less, the two could then work toward a different kind of industrial policy. Achieving a better working relationship requires government to have a more knowledgeable, competent, and credible focal point for its contact with business. Antitrust laws that subject both business and government leaders to the threat of criminal prosecution should be substantially revised.

A New Federal Charter

To encourage big companies to accept greater responsibility for the interests of their employees, Congress should enact a new federal charter of incorporation, not to supersede state charters but to serve as an alternative. Incorporation under the new federal statute would require a formal commitment to the interests of both employees and shareholders. Specifically, companies would guarantee employment security for all employees with at least 10 years' service, subject to safeguards in case of gross negligence or misbehavior. In addition, companies would consult employees through their elected representatives, at various levels, including the shop floor, the plant or product division, and the corporate board of directors. While such a new law would allow companies to tailor their schemes of governance, the law would set certain standards and subject charters to challenge and adjudication in the courts. Charters would last for a finite term (say, 50 years) and would require periodic renewal.

As an incentive for management to accept these new responsibilities, a takeover of a federally chartered company would require an affirmative vote by employees as well as stockholders. In addition, the law would exempt the company from the treble-damage provision of the antitrust laws.

As an incentive for shareholders, the federal charter would permit creation of a reserve fund for employment stability. Annual payments would be tax deductible, and the fund would finance investments designed to enhance job security. Its use would require approval of employees as well as management. This special reserve for job security would enhance cash flows and strengthen the balance sheets of companies electing to adopt the new charter and thus enhance shareholder interests along with those of employees.

A New Mission for the Commerce Department

The government should make the Commerce Department the focal point for industrial policy, broaden its powers, and change its name. At present, the U.S. government has no such clear focal point. Trade policy, for example, is the mandate of the special trade representative (STR) in the White House. I suggest the merger of STR with the Commerce Department into a new Department of Industry, Trade, and Commerce (ITC). ITC should have primary responsibility for promotion of U.S. exports and the power to authorize joint ventures to promote research or accelerate the development of a new technology, ventures that would be exempt from the antitrust laws.

Since the business community is highly fragmented and has no central organization, the ITC should work with business to establish a more legitimate form of dialogue to identify and evaluate industrial problems of general interest to business. The secretary of the ITC should have statutory powers to protect both corporate and government participants in this dialogue from criminal antitrust liability. Congress should grant immunity from the sunshine provisions of the Advisory Committee Act, as it has for the committees that now advise the STR.

Review of Antitrust Laws

Antitrust laws should reflect the realities of international competition and the need for a less hostile relationship between business and government. Recent decisions, such as the dropping of the case against IBM, are important steps in the right direction. They do not, however, go far enough. It will be difficult for business and government to work toward a more rational economic strategy as long as the Justice Department has the legal basis to threaten either side with criminal prosecution whenever they discuss basic questions of economic strategy. In addition, American business needs some form of relief from the ever-increasing use of antitrust suits as a way to hold companies up for ransom. Such suits, when launched by lawyers working on a contingency-fee basis, have become a new frontier for entrepreneurially oriented lawyers, who know that it is usually cheaper to settle than to fight, even if the allegations are without merit. Provisions of the alternative charter provide one remedy; in its absence another is needed.

Industry probably *can* coexist with the welfare state. The reforms outlined here would enhance its chances of survival in the United States. By themselves they are not enough. Basic reform of the welfare state is also required.

Notes

1.   Edwin O. Reischauer, *The United States and Japan,* 3d ed. (New York, Viking, 1964), (original edition, Cambridge, Mass., Harvard University Press, 1950).

2.   Richard G. Hamermesh, "Administrative Issues Posed by Contemporary Approaches to Strategic Planning: The Case of the Dexter Corporation," Harvard Business School Working Paper (HBS 79–53, 1979).

3.   Richard J. Rumelt and Robin C. Wemsley, "In Search of the Market Share Effect," University of California at Los Angeles Working Paper (MGL-63; revised May 1, 1981).

4.   Richard Bolling and John Bowles, *America's Competitive Edge* (New York, McGraw-Hill, 1982).

5.   See my article, "The Industrial State: Old Myths and New Realities," *HBR*, March-April 1973, p. 133.

6.   See my article, "How Practical Is National Economic Planning?" *HBR*, March-April 1978, p. 131.

7.   See Ira Magaziner and Robert Reich, *Minding America's Business* (New York, Harcourt Brace Jovanovich, 1982); and the Boston Consulting Group, *A Framework for Swedish Industrial Policy* (Uberforlag, Sweden, 1978) for examples of sound analysis of industry coupled with a failure to analyze the impact of the welfare state on the competitive position of industry.

8.   For a contrary view see Robert B. Reich, "Why the U.S. Needs an Industrial Policy," *HBR*, January-February 1982, p. 74.

9.   Alfred D. Chandler, Jr., "Government versus Business: An American Phenomenon," *Business and Public Policy,* ed. John T. Dunlop (Boston, Division of Research, Graduate School of Business Administration, Harvard University, 1980), p. 3.

10.   See "Zenith v. U.S.A.," nos. 4-379-054 and 4-379-067, distributed by HBS Case Services, Soldiers Field, Boston, Mass. 02163; and John J. Nevin, "Can U.S. Business Survive Our Japanese Trade Policy?" *HBR*, September-October 1978, p. 165.

Appendix: Industrial Performance—Is There a Problem?

How severe are our alleged symptoms? In the last decade, we have become aware that a rising standard of living depends primarily on increasing productivity and secondarily on growth in the labor force. Table A shows productivity trends for selected countries in the 1970s: while *all* countries grew less rapidly than in the 1960s, U.S. productivity grew the slowest; that of the East Asians, the fastest.

Turning to employment, and particularly to industrial employment, the Europeans come in last (see Table B). In each major European country, industrial employment peaked around 1970, well before the first oil crisis. The United States, Japan, and Canada have been able to create or maintain jobs in manufacturing. Europe lost manufacturing jobs, and Japan saw employment concentration shift from manufacturing to services—while always maintaining full employment.

In Europe, investment stagnated in the 1970s, in dramatic contrast to the situation in East Asia (Table C). The breakdown of industrial investment in Germany is especially illuminating. By 1976, investment in capacity expansion had almost disappeared, while capital to rationalize operations and so reduce the labor force increased. With a rising exchange rate, companies found investment in Germany less attractive but put in capital to reduce wage costs through labor-saving equipment.

Small differences in growth rates make a big difference if they persist. While in 1960 the industrial countries had a higher share of per-capita GNP invested than the East Asians, by 1979 they were outstripped by the Japanese, who were investing more per capita in absolute terms.

A shift in income distribution preceded the stagnation of investment. Between 1965 and 1975 the share of income going to employees went up (see Table D), that to property and entrepreneurship down. The achievement of full employment in the 1960s increased the power of organized labor, and wage demands far exceeded productivity gains. Eventually corporate balance sheets deteriorated and companies had to trim their rates of investment. By 1973 even the communist leadership in Italy wanted to moderate wage demands in order to reestablish more normal profit margins, new investment, and, finally, new jobs. While data on East Asia are fragmentary, trends of income distribution seem quite different, with only Japan showing a higher share of income for employees.

Rising labor costs are only part of the problem, of course. The East Asians benefited from trade negotiations that opened the world economy, shipping costs that declined relative to product values, and licensing agreements that made most technologies available on easy terms. Under these circumstances more and more investment has moved offshore, and the East Asians have gained in relative position as the older industrial societies have declined.

Table A	Productivity trends In real gross domestic product per person employed				
	Compound growth rate				
	1960-70	1970-73	1973-75	1975-79	1970-79
North America					
Canada	3.8*†	3.1	−1.3	0.9	1.1
United States	2.7	1.9	−1.3	0.5	0.6
European Community					
Belgium	4.4	4.4	1.3	2.9	3.0
France	4.7	4.6	1.9	3.2	3.4
West Germany	3.8	4.6‡	2.1	3.8	3.4‡
Netherlands	4.1	4.5	1.5	3.8‡	3.3‡
United Kingdom	2.1*	3.8	−1.0	2.3	2.1
Scandinavia					
Norway	3.5	3.8‡	3.0	−	−
Sweden	3.8*	1.4	0.2	0.5	0.7
Asia					
Hong Kong	7.1†	7.5	−	4.0‡	−
Japan	9.6	7.0	0.9	4.7‡	4.2‡
Korea	6.2	5.1‡	5.0	6.7	5.9‡
Singapore	6.8	−	3.1	3.0	3.0‡

*New data series

†1963 to 1970

‡Column 2: the years are
1972-1973 for West Germany
and Norway.
1971-1973 for South Korea
Column 4: the years are
1975-1977 for the Netherlands
1976-1978 for Japan

Sources:
United Nations.
*Monthly Bulletin of
Statistics.*
March 1981. table 66.
International Labour Office.
*Yearbook of
Labour Studies.* 1980.
table 3.

Table B	Comparison of manufacturing or industrial employment in thousands

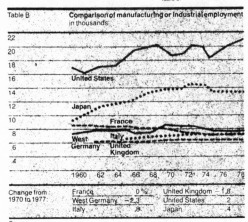

Change from 1970 to 1977:	France	0%	United Kingdom	−1.8
	West Germany	−2.3	United States	2
	Italy	.8	Japan	−.4

Source:
OECD data. courtesy of Data Resources
Corporation

Table C	Gross domestic investment compound annual growth rate		
		1960-1970	1970-1978
	West Germany	4.1	− 0.2
	France	7.3	1.7
	United Kingdom	5.0	1.5
	Italy	3.8	− 0.4
	Netherlands	6.8	− 0.1
	Sweden	5.0	− 1.3
	Belgium	6.0	1.9
	Switzerland	4.1	− 4.6
	Denmark	5.7	0.2
	United States	4.8	1.6
	Canada	5.8	4.7
	South Korea	23.6	13.7
	Taiwan	16.2	8.2
	Malaysia	7.2	10.2
	Hong Kong	7.4	10.2
	Singapore	20.5	5.5

Source:
NAE Research Associates, Inc.,
NAE Research
International Perspective.
March 1981.

Table D   **Labor's share of total domestic factor income**

Source:
Morgan Guaranty Trust Company
of New York,
World Financial Markets,
May 1982, p. 3.

National Strategy for Stronger U.S. Competitiveness

In the light of the current economic recovery in the United States, the cries of industrial policy advocates are falling on deaf ears. If there is no real economic problem, there is little reason to make major changes in the way economic policy is formulated, critics insist. This article points out, however, that the recovery, instead of signaling a long-lasting turnaround, seems best understood as a domestically oriented, consumer-led, ephemeral phenomenon. The problem of our declining competitiveness in manufacturing, which first manifested itself in the late 1960s, has not been solved. Our export position has continued to deteriorate across the board, even in high-technology.

In this follow-up to his McKinsey Award-winning HBR article, "Can Industry Survive the Welfare State?" (September-October 1982), Mr. Scott takes issue with mainstream economists who argue that our economic problems are manageable within the current policy framework. Part of the problem is the theoretical structure with which they view the economy. The theory of comparative advantage, for example, is based on a view of the world that is almost 200 years old. He argues that today's world requires that we turn the theory on its head (as the Japanese have done). He suggests how the United States might take a similar approach to creating and implementing an economic strategy.

No one can dispute that the United States has been losing its margin of economic leadership for more than 30 years—and that in the last 15 years the deterioration has become more widespread and severe. In 1950, the

Published 1984.

United States accounted for about 6% of the world's population, 40% of its GNP, and 20% of world trade. By 1980, we had 5% of the world's population, but only 21.5% of its GNP and 11% of its trade. Market share in volume terms of world trade was maintained in the 1970s thanks to a declining dollar (see Exhibit 1). After 1980, the dollar strengthened and the dollar share of exports rose—while the volume share decreased.

The declining dollar should have helped U.S. companies boost the profitability of their operations. It may have helped, but it was not enough. Since the mid-1960s, the profitability of U.S. companies has declined and for the last decade the return on manufacturing assets has hardly been above that of corporate bonds (see Exhibit 2). Loss of market share and profitability over a sustained period signal an unmistakable decline in competitiveness.

This decline has occurred just as the United States has become more integrated into the world economy. Manufactured exports now equal approximately 20% of domestic manufacturing output and provide the main impetus for export growth. Unfortunately, while we've become more dependent on trade in manufactured goods, we've steadily lost world market share in industrial exports. The loss is across the board, covering all major sectors, and is not the result of dramatic decline in one or two (see Exhibit 3).

Another critical indicator of decline is our trade balance. Positive from 1893 to 1970, it turned negative in 1971 and has generally continued downhill. Some forecasts call for a $100 billion trade deficit in 1984. Sharp changes in commodity prices affected the overall balance but, more important, the balance in manufactured goods swung from generally strong surpluses in the early 1960s to a hesitant equilibrium by the late 1970s.

While few dispute the declining margin of U.S. economic leadership, a national debate has risen concerning both the degree and meaning of the decline. Are the causes to be found in a noncompetitive set of policies and institutions, for example, or in mismanagement of monetary and fiscal policy which has led to record budget deficits, high interest rates, and an overvalued dollar? The appropriate diagnosis is important, because if the problems are not deep-seated and fundamental, there is little reason to change the way the government or companies deal with them. In particular, there is little reason to experiment with industrial policy when all but its most enthusiastic advocates understand that—in the present American context—industrial policy runs a substantial risk of making things worse rather than better.

Conventional Ideas

Many mainstream economists, including President Reagan's Council of Economic Advisers (CEA), believe that the decline in our share of free-world GNP and exports is a sign that conditions after World War II were unusual and that, except for an overvalued dollar, we have now returned to normal.

Exhibit 1. U.S. Share of Exports to the World

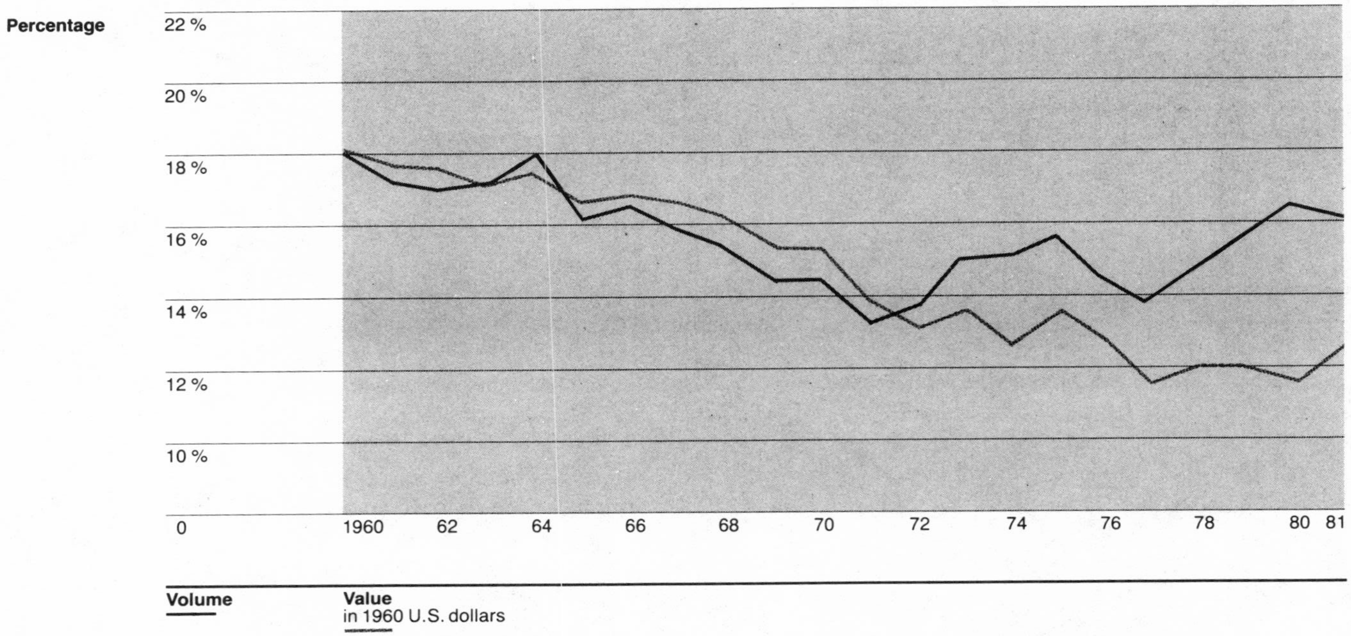

Percentage

22 %
20 %
18 %
16 %
14 %
12 %
10 %
0

1960 62 64 66 68 70 72 74 76 78 80 81

Volume

Value
in 1960 U.S. dollars

Source:
International Financial Statistics,
International Monetary Fund.

Exhibit 2. Rate of Return on Total Assets in Manufacturing, Corporate Bond Rate, and Prime Rate, 1960–1982

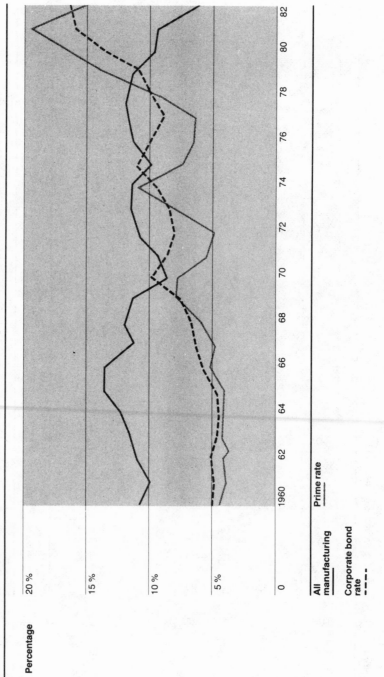

Exhibit 3. U.S. Share of World High-Technology Exports

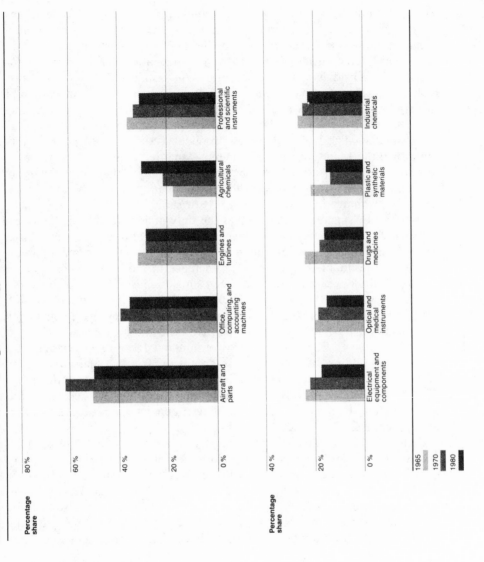

They point out that investment income continues to rise, reflecting earnings on foreign direct investment and foreign loans, and that net service income, a small item on our international balance sheet before 1980, is now substantial.

These economists believe that our trade outlook is not a cause for alarm, although adjustments are necessary. According to this view, you must look beyond the trade balance in manufactured goods to the composition of this trade in order to evaluate the true competitiveness of U.S. industry. This shows the United States increasing exports of products in which it has an advantage—like high-technology products, resource-intensive products other than fuels, and foreign investments—and decreasing exports of those industries in which it's at a disadvantage. In short, they argue that the economy is behaving as economic theory in general, and the theory of comparative advantage in particular, suggests it should (see Exhibit 4).

The CEA members believe that the only major difficulty is the overvalued dollar. High interest rates have indeed made the dollar more attractive and have driven up its price—much to the detriment of U.S. manufacturers. There is little doubt that the dollar's increase of more than 30% in three years on a trade-weighted basis has been a major cause of the growing trade deficits. In addition, the overvalued dollar handicaps us in pricing and profits, both at home and abroad, and hence reduces the corporate capacity for investments to sustain a future competitive base and create new jobs.

Correct as far as it goes, this line of thinking doesn't recognize the full scope of the competitive challenge. It ignores the fact that many symptoms of our economic malaise showed up between 1973 and 1979, when the dollar floated down and was considered undervalued. In addition, correcting the overvaluation requires a reduction of budget deficits via some combination of tax increases and spending restraint.

The budget problem is far more serious than implied by the term "mismanagement." For 20 years, the United States allocated a rising proportion of the budget to social programs while cutting defense; the defense share dropped from 50% in 1960 to below 25% in 1978 while entitlements grew by an almost offsetting amount. When military spending began to rise in 1978, social spending was not cut. As a result, we have a commitment to guns and butter which we are unwilling or unable to finance through taxes. Thus

Exhibit 4.   U.S. Trade Balances by Sector as Percentage of GDP

	Item	Percentage of GDP			Item	Percentage of GDP	
		1972	1979			1972	1979
U.S. comparative advantage	Research-intensive manufactures	0.93 %	1.63 %	U.S. comparative disadvantage	Non-research-intensive manufactures	−1.27 %	−1.44 %
	Resource-intensive products other than fuels	0.06 %	0.67 %		Fuels	−0.27 %	−2.41 %
	Invisibles (services and investment income)	0.40 %	1.44 %				

Source:
Economic Report of the
President, 1983, p. 58.

the exchange rate problem is really one of fundamental priorities, not easy to correct or solve, and not just the result of short-term mismanagement.

Another group of analysts takes issue with the administration economists and recognizes the deterioration in international competitiveness, but finds its source in microeconomic or industrial mismanagement. These analysts maintain that many leading corporations have become complacent, have paid inadequate attention to product quality and to product and process innovation, have overemphasized short-term earnings, and have produced a new school of management aptly labeled "paper entrepreneurship."[1] Systematic evidence to support these arguments is difficult to marshal. However, many senior corporate executives admit that their companies are guilty of some, if not all, of the charges, which shows that the reasoning is on solid ground. Most would also claim that their companies have intensified efforts to rectify the situation, beginning with the 1980–1981 recession.

This group believes that the responsibility for improved management of our industrial system lies with business managers. In a decentralized private enterprise economy it is up to individual companies to straighten things out in response to painful messages from the market.

Still other experts, however, see the problem as too serious, and the capacity of business managers as too uncertain, to rely on this time-honored solution. Instead, they call on the government to take on a new role as promoter of industrial adjustment using the vehicle of an industrial policy. These analysts argue that since companies and industries have failed to adjust to international competition, the government must act to reduce the frequency and cause of market failure and take a more constructive role in solving industrial problems.[2]

The industrial policy advocates distinguish two types of economic adjustment problems—those facing stagnant or declining industries on the one hand and those confronting new, generally high-technology industries on the other. In the former case, failure to adjust leads to highly visible difficulties, as companies and regions suffer. At the other end of the development cycle, U.S. high-tech companies, increasingly challenged by foreign competitors in areas that once seemed to be American territory, need government assistance.

These problems clearly exist. But many industrial policy proponents ignore the fact that our government has no mechanism to formulate an explicit industrial policy and no clearly accepted role other than that of referee of marketplace competition. Moreover, the remedy increasingly proposed—that the government target various industries for support—is not well understood. Some would like to use industrial targeting as the slogan for the protection of the entitlements of overpaid steel and auto employees (not only blue-collar employees but also white-collar and top management).

Stranger things have happened. Supply-side economics was the slogan behind which we enacted the largest consumer tax cut of the postwar era. In the heat of partisan debate both the virtues and vices of targeting are overstated, reflecting the reactions to a potential shift of power from business to government and, likewise, to a shift of costs and benefits among sectors of industry.

I believe experience will show that, in a democracy, targeting is the least important element of an industrial policy. Moreover, if targeting were undertaken as an "add on" to existing efforts, without first effecting a fundamental change in the goals and policies of the state, it would almost certainly do more harm than good. In the United States, it would probably become another "entitlement program," planned and managed by the same interest groups and bureaucrats who brought us the earlier entitlements. It would add to our competitive handicap rather than help reduce it.

On the other hand, I believe industrial policy advocates are on the right track when they claim that our economic malaise calls for a new, perhaps radical, cure. We suffer from a problem of national competitiveness that is distinct from both the overvalued dollar and out-of-date managerial practices and attitudes.

An appropriate solution can be found only if we recognize the crux of our problem to be our economic strategy in relation to the changing nature of international competition. Our competitiveness is not deteriorating vis-à-vis traditional rivals in the North Atlantic area. In fact, most West European countries suffer more acutely from economic maladjustment than do we. By and large, their experiments with industrial policy should serve as warnings of the consequences of trying to add on such a policy while preserving the priorities and policies of the welfare state.

To appreciate the competitive challenge of the 1970s and 1980s, we must focus on the industrial successes of a group of densely populated countries, mostly in East Asia. We must compare our performance with theirs, and we must recognize what that comparison says about the theory of comparative advantage on which our economic strategy is based. Once we understand both their outstanding performance and the theory on which it is founded, we will recognize that the United States needs more than better macro- or microeconomic management or an add-on industrial policy. It needs a national economic strategy that combines the best elements of all three camps.

The Root of the Problem

The malaise of North Atlantic industrial countries has four main causes: a less favorable world economic environment, new competition, the targeting policies of some governments, and the general anti-industrial bias of our present economic strategy.

Lower growth, successive oil price shocks, and the monetary squeeze from October 1979 through July–August 1982 are key elements of the present economic environment. The price shocks accentuated the need for rapid adjustment at a time when slower growth made adjustment more difficult. In a growing market, forecasts that lead to excess capacity, such as that which has developed in steel and petrochemicals in the United States and Western Europe, can be overcome in the short term. In a stagnant economy, the impact of surplus capacity does not go away; in a declining market, the problems become steadily more apparent.

New patterns of international competition contribute to our economic maladjustment. Declining trade barriers, shrinking transport costs, and improvements in communications have facilitated global competition and worldwide product sourcing. There are more competitors today, some with economic and social systems different from those of Western Europe and North America. While Japan is the most familiar example, the "new Japans" are vigorous global competitors. Although they were much later to industrialize and have roughly half Japan's population, Korea, Taiwan, Hong Kong, and Singapore now have half as large a trade surplus with the United States as Japan does, despite numerous import restrictions. More to the point, they export more manufactured goods to the United States than Britain does, almost twice as much as Germany, and four times as much as France. Their manufactured trade surplus with the United States is three times that of the entire European Community.

Industrial targeting as practiced by some nations poses the third threat to economic well-being. Working together much the way defense contractors might work with the Department of Defense to target key technologies, business and government in some countries collaborate to identify key industries or technologies for commercial purposes. The examples cited most often are France, Japan, and several of the newly industrialized countries. Some industrial policy enthusiasts argue that West Germany and Britain also follow this practice.

Targeting pits businesses in some countries against business and government in others and has been branded as the newest, potentially most significant unfair trade practice, notably by the United States and Britain. Foreign to our Anglo-Saxon tradition, targeting was not envisaged when the rules of the trade and monetary systems were established at the end of World War II. Postwar planners viewed companies as the principal economic players and governments as referees. But governments now function in some economic systems as partisans, coaches, managers, and even owners. They have game plans in which companies play cooperative roles, at least for some period of time.

In spite of the growing use of industrial policies elsewhere, the United States has had no explicit industrial policy except in areas deemed essential for national defense. The "invisible hand" operating through the market mechanism is seen as adequate, and indeed as the most effective adjustment mechanism in the world.

When faced with problems, such as in the auto and steel industries, government response has been limited to a series of short-sighted, incoherent, ad hoc decisions. Protectionist measures do not promote economic adjustment. But in the absence of an industrial policy, the United States, ignoring its role as "leader of the free trade camp," has increasingly practiced protectionism nonetheless.[3] Despite greater willingness to intervene in economic affairs, European governments such as those of France, Belgium, and Sweden have faced similar adjustment problems, and their responses have not been successful. By itself, targeting may be an "unfair" and unwanted element in the trading system, but as practiced by the traditional industrial states, it has not been of major significance. Only when coupled with an aggressive overall strategy, as in the case of Japan and Korea, has it had major economic importance. It is the strategy and the economic rationale behind it on which we need to focus and not on targeting per se.

Not Just Economic Adjustment

While the problems of certain industries are widely recognized, economists do not consider them serious enough to warrant basic changes in U.S. economic policy. They believe that as economic adjustments take place in line with the law of comparative advantage, the United States will gradually specialize in goods produced by industries in which we are strong, relative to international competition. Other industries will, by definition, lose market share.

Some of the available data seem to confirm this line of thinking. The United States appears to rapidly be increasing its net exports in high-technology sectors while giving ground in low-tech (Exhibit 5). But as the breakdown in Exhibit 3 of U.S. market share in the top 10 high-technology sectors shows, from 1970 to 1980 our share in 7 of the 10 categories dropped, with agricultural chemicals registering the only significant gain. U.S. exports grew rapidly in high-tech but world markets grew even faster and the United States lost market share.

Exhibit 6 shows U.S. trade data classified by level of technology, using R&D spending (excluding weapons and munitions) as a proxy for level of technology. In this grouping, made by Regina Kelly of the U.S. Department of Commerce, aircraft, with R&D spending in excess of 11% of sales, led the list, and wood and paper products, with R&D less than 0.5%, were at the bottom.[4]

The dotted line in Exhibit 6 represents average U.S. world market share in manufactured exports, and the solid line shows theoretical comparative advantage, including above-average share in high-tech and agribusiness and below-average share in other categories.

Using this classification scheme, we can compare actual U.S. performance with the theory, and also with the performance of other industrialized countries. Exhibit 7 shows reported U.S. comparative advantage for the manufacturirng sector as revealed by events and compares it with that of France, Germany, and Japan. At first glance, it looks as if we have exported from our technology strength. The top two categories have above-average share, as do categories 23, 24, and 25, which are in agribusiness. Categories 3, 4, 5, and 6 are weaker than might have been expected, while 8—agricultural chemicals—shows surprising strength. Category 11, radio and television, is surprisingly low, and the share of motor vehicles is on the wane.

It is important to note, however, that most sectors changed little between 1965 and 1980. This indicates that the United States was not shifting its comparative advantage toward high-technology areas in this period but building on advantages it had had for years.

Much the same holds true for West Germany and France. Neither of these countries has significantly improved its high-tech market share, as a task force of the EEC Commission recently confirmed, noting that the nine members "do not manifest market leadership in any sector" and that "the relatively small number and nature of the sectors in which the Community's shares are growing . . . is cause for some concern." Large European industrial countries' exports depend on corporate strategies on the one hand and on general cost levels on the other. France exports Peugeots—and West Germany, Mercedes—not because of great comparative advantages but because of the continuing creativity of managers and employees of the companies concerned, and fluctuations in prices and exchange rates.

The Japanese pattern reveals striking differences. The magnitude of the changes between 1965 and 1980 indicates much faster and farther-reaching adjustment, with Japan gaining share in high-technology areas and losing it in low-technology sectors.

The Japanese have shown that it is possible to upgrade a national industrial portfolio; it appears to be the only major industrial power to have done so. High-level Japanese officials explain the changes as the result of their rejection of the static theory of comparative advantage, so firmly entrenched in Western economic theory. In its place, they say, they have developed a notion of dynamic comparative advantage. Japan has shown not only that comparative advantage can be shifted but also that the shifts can be created and managed according to a pattern or plan.

Comparative Advantage: Static or Dynamic?

Many American economists claim that the Japanese are not doing anything different, and that Japan's export pattern agrees with the predictions of traditional economic theory that countries export commodities whose production requires intensive use of productive factors found locally in abundance. The theory assumes diminishing marginal returns and a law of increasing costs, as well as full employment, costless factor mobility, and universal access to production technologies. In any given country, productive factors are interchangeable and movable. If used at capacity, they are like land: additional production raises marginal costs.[5]

But the theory of comparative advantage was formulated almost 200

Exhibit 5.   U.S. Trade Balances in R&D-Intensive Manufactured Goods, Non–R&D-Intensive Manufactured Goods, and Transportation Equipment*

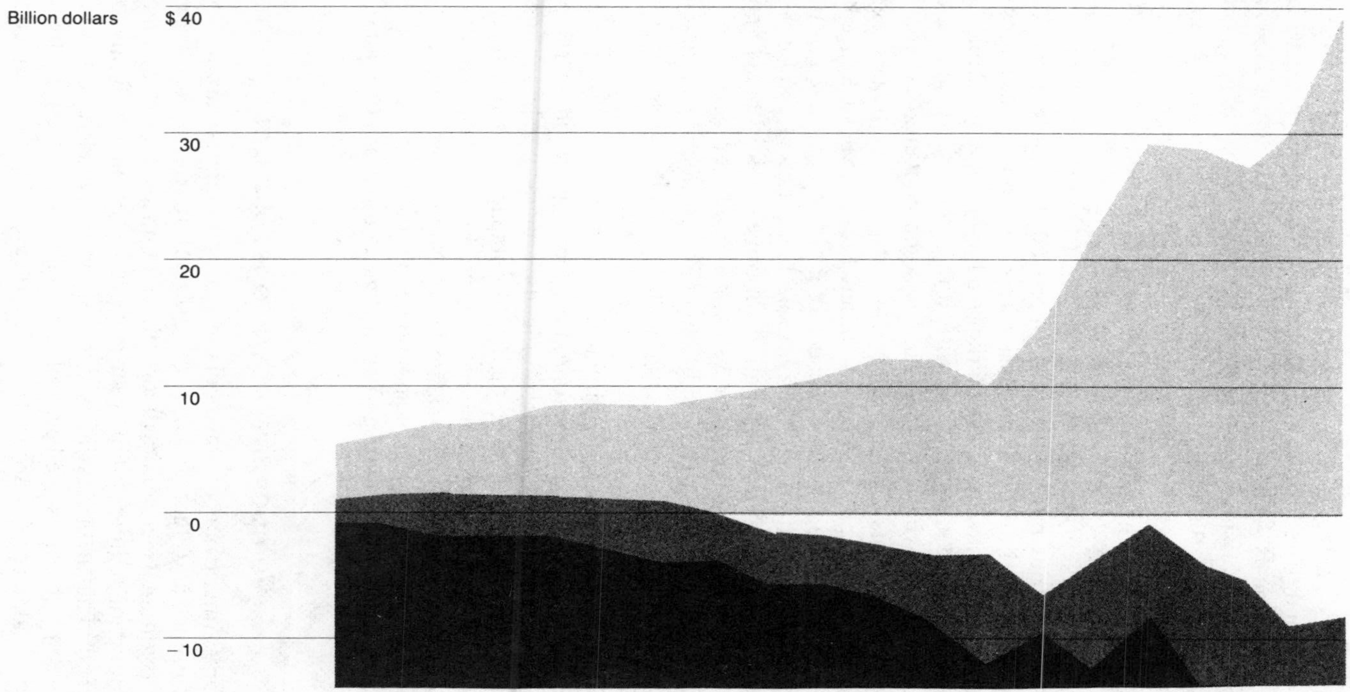

Billion dollars

$ 40

30

20

10

0

– 10

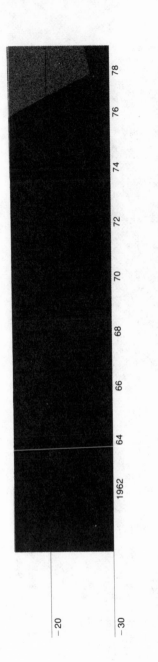

R&D-intensive manufactured goods

Transportation equipment

Non-R&D-intensive manufactured goods

1962 64 66 68 70 72 74 76 78

−20
−30

*R&D-intensive manufactured goods include chemicals, nonelectrical machinery, aircraft, professional and scientific instruments. Transportation equipment refers to motor vehicles and parts. Non-R&D-intensive manufactured goods include food products, metals and fabrication, other manufacturing.

Sources:
Science Indicators, 1978; U.S. Department of Commerce. Domestic and International Business Administration, *Overseas Business Reports*, August 1967, April 1972, April 1977, June 1978, August 1979.

Exhibit 6. Comparative Advantage of U.S. Manufactured Exports in Theory*

Industries ranked by level of technology*

Market share

		−2.0	1.0†	2.0	3.0	4.0

1 Aircraft

2 Office machines

3 Electrical equipment

4 Optical and medical instruments

5 Drugs

6 Plastic and synthetic materials

7 Engines and turbines

8 Agricultural chemicals

9 Professional and scientific instruments

10 Industrial chemicals

11 Radio and television

12 Road motor vehicles

13 Other chemicals

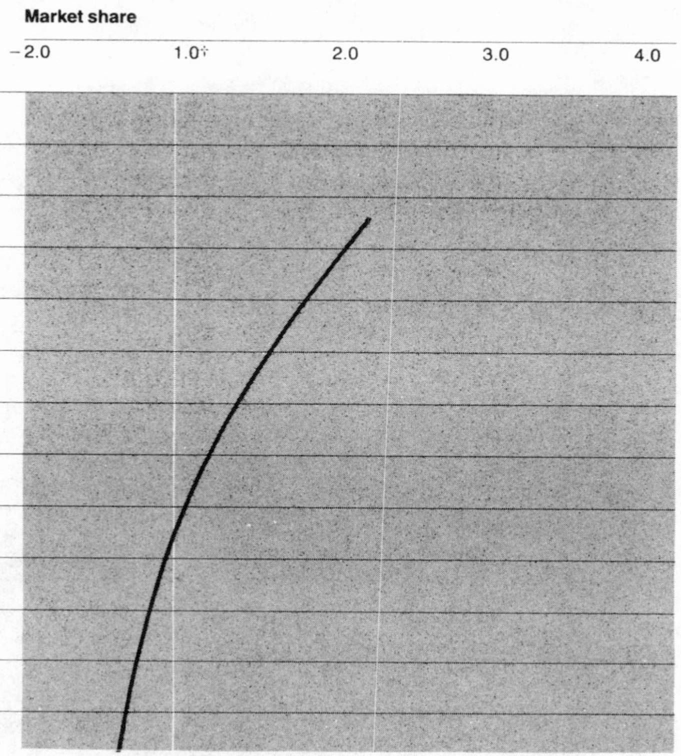

14 Electrical machinery

15 Other transportation equipment

16 Textile fibers, yarns, fabric

17 Nonelectrical machinery

18 Nonferrous metals

19 Miscellaneous manufacture

20 Fuels

21 Apparel and footwear

22 Iron and steel

23 Foods, beverages, tobacco

24 Leather and rubber products

25 Animal and vegetable oils, fats

26 Wood and paper products

*Industry rankings based on National
Science Foundation data, as compiled
by Regina Kelly, *The Impact of Technological Innovation on Trade Patterns,*
U.S. Department of Commerce, Bureau
of Economic Policy and Research,
ER-24, December 1977.

Exhibit 7.   Indexes of Revealed Comparative Advantage, 1965 and 1980

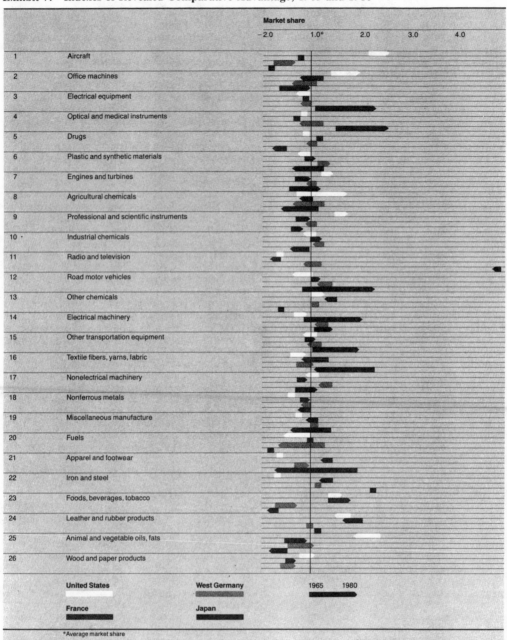

		Market share
		−2.0 1.0* 2.0 3.0 4.0

1 Aircraft
2 Office machines
3 Electrical equipment
4 Optical and medical instruments
5 Drugs
6 Plastic and synthetic materials
7 Engines and turbines
8 Agricultural chemicals
9 Professional and scientific instruments
10 Industrial chemicals
11 Radio and television
12 Road motor vehicles
13 Other chemicals
14 Electrical machinery
15 Other transportation equipment
16 Textile fibers, yarns, fabric
17 Nonelectrical machinery
18 Nonferrous metals
19 Miscellaneous manufacture
20 Fuels
21 Apparel and footwear
22 Iron and steel
23 Foods, beverages, tobacco
24 Leather and rubber products
25 Animal and vegetable oils, fats
26 Wood and paper products

United States   West Germany   1965   1980

France   Japan

*Average market share

114

years ago—we have to adjust it for the realities of the current real-world situation.

Being endowed with a natural resource, for example, does not necessarily benefit a country. The oil-exporting countries, particularly those in which oil plays an important role in foreign exchange earnings, have thus far been conspicuous failures as exporters of manufactured goods. Iran and Venezuela are striking examples of this. In both of these countries, large oil reserves, exploited for several decades, permitted a single industry to achieve abundant exports despite high exchange rates. But persistently high exchange rates have made it difficult for other industries within these countries to compete in world markets. Both Iran and Venezuela compensated for this problem by protecting the domestic market behind trade barriers. Venezuela, for example, still depends on oil and oil-related products for 95% of its exports.

Unemployment of more than 30 million people in the OECD countries alone should raise doubts about the idea of full employment and the possibility of free movement of labor. Aside from labor, other important economic variables lack mobility. Technologies are embodied in equipment, know-how, and patents; companies jealously guard them to develop competitive strengths. IBM and Digital Equipment have not been as willing to share patents and know-how with foreign companies as was RCA to share its TV patents, for example. Yet adopting new technologies helped the Japanese steel industry rise to market leadership while reluctance to change was a key factor in the decline of the U.S. steel industry.[6]

A more fundamental weakness of traditional economic theory is its belief in a law of rising costs, according to which increased use of limited resources brings diminishing returns and higher costs. While the proposition holds in the short run, abundant evidence indicates that in the long run costs decline indefinitely in real terms, partly from increasing returns to scale and partly because users learn to be more efficient.

High-technology seems most susceptible to rapid change and declining costs. Experience curves in the semiconductor industry, for example, show costs declining relentlessly by 30% annually. But diminishing costs show up elsewhere. When the Japanese began their drive to build a competitive export steel industry, their costs were more than 50% above American levels; now their industry is the world's most competitive.

Unfortunately, the experience curve so familiar to management consultants has not made its way into economic theory; it continues to treat evidence of the curve's existence as anecdotal and suspect. Economists rationalize the demise of U.S. industries such as TV and autos on the grounds that consumers will benefit from lower-cost imports. They assume that those who lose their jobs will automatically find equivalent work. With automatic adjustment, no strategy is needed. Thus the government continues to espouse the policy of free trade, with 10 million unemployed, while denying the need for domestic policy changes to speed the pace—or alter the pattern—of adjustment.

Testing the Theory

I do not want to imply that mainstream economists are unaware of the weaknesses in some of their assumptions. However, in general they view these weaknesses as exceptions to a basically sound theory; they continue to use it nonetheless. Their attachment to a static theory of comparative advantage, however, inhibits the nation's capacity to recognize and acknowledge the possibility of a national strategy to shape or create comparative advantage, or indeed of a substantive industrial strategy at all.

Japan's remarkable postwar economic growth is based, in considerable measure, on the Japanese government's rejection of static, conventional economic theories.[7] Japanese leaders recognized that Japan could create competitive advantages by mobilizing technology, capital, and skilled labor to attack problems or identify opportunities in selected sectors. They created a strategy of dynamic comparative advantage at the national level that parallels the strategy of a diversified company as it shifts resources from less promising to more promising areas. As a high-level MITI official explained in a 1970 OECD publication:

"Should Japan have entrusted its future, according to the theory of comparative advantage, to these industries characterized by intensive use of labor? [With a population of 100 million] had [Japan] chosen to specialize in this kind of industry, it would almost permanently have been unable to break away from the Asian pattern of stagnation and poverty. . . .

"The Ministry of International Trade and Industry decided to establish industries which require intensive employment of capital and technology, such as steel, oil refining, petrochemicals, automobiles, aircraft, industrial machinery of all sorts, and later electronics, including electronic computers. From a short-run, static viewpoint, encouragement of such industries would seem to conflict with economic rationalism. But, from a long-range point of view, these are precisely the industries where income elasticity of demand is high, technological progress is rapid, and labor productivity rises fast. It was clear that without these industries it would be difficult to raise [our] standard of living to that of Europe and America; whether right or wrong, Japan had to have these heavy and chemical industries."[8]

In other words, Japanese planners identified industries in which technical change and rising productivity could yield declining unit costs.

A good way to understand the significance of this policy is to think of it in terms of the classic example of Ricardo's theory of comparative advantage—that, in the eighteenth century, England and Portugal would each gain by specializing respectively in production of cloth and wine even though Portugal might produce both wine and cloth more cheaply than England. According to the static, resource-based theory, both countries would be better off by concentrating on those products in which they had an existing comparative advantage.

By following that path, however, the Portuguese sacrificed long-term growth for short-term gains. Had they used a dynamic theory of comparative advantage, they would have chosen to specialize in the growth industry of the day (cloth) and use the powers of government to supplement those of the market in marshaling resources necessary for entry and successful participation. Such a strategy would require Portugal to think in terms of acquiring or creating strength in promising sectors rather than simply accepting the existing mix of resources and exploiting the "endowment" as efficiently as possible.

Creating Comparative Advantage

Since costs will decline, a government can protect the domestic market during an initial period of relative high costs by providing low-cost, long-term finance to promote capital investment, and by controlling access of foreign technology. In addition, a government can push companies to accept the latest technologies and set minimum sizes on new plants, requiring them to be brought rapidly to world scale. It can avoid excess capacity by requiring companies to stagger the construction of new plants and requiring the first in the field to supply competitors until they have had an opportunity to build their own facilities.

The Japanese practice of nurturing new industries is reminiscent of the well-established infant industry paradigm, the notable case in which economic theory implicitly accepts declining costs. Traditionally, however, this practice seemed justified only for a limited number of import-substitution industries. Japan and other countries in East Asia have broadened their application to include creation and nurturing of a wide array of industries, particularly those which are export-oriented. The South Korean decision to build color television capacity from zero to four million units, targeted largely for the American market, is a case in point.

Japanese policies do not end—or begin—with targeting. They also promote savings and discourage consumer borrowing, thus increasing the supply of loanable funds and reducing demand. They help lower the cost of money, encourage investment, and accelerate the pace of change. Steady growth and controlled inflation provide a stable business environment conducive to long-term planning and sound business investment decisions.

A Different Role for Government
Of course, Japanese institutions and ideology differ from ours. In Japan, linking large industrial groups by shareholdings with banks creates a structure resistant to bankruptcies, facilitates great use of debt, and lowers the cost of capital. Companywide unions tie employee interests more closely to companies than industries. The business practice of paying large bonuses to permanent employees as a form of profit sharing means that labor costs adjust to changing circumstances. Bonuses encourage employees to relate

their prosperity to the company's performance and the company can cut them back to reduce labor costs in a recession.

The critical features of the Japanese system, according to Chalmers Johnson, are that:

☐ Government gives high priority to promoting development, or baking the pie before dividing and distributing the pie.

☐ Policy focuses on substance as much as, if not more than, on process.

☐ Policy is developed in a give-and-take dialogue between the business community and bureaucracy, with politicians and labor leaders normally playing secondary roles.

☐ The bureaucracy, by virtue of its selection, internally controlled assignment, and promotion process, shares both a long-term view and the competence to analyze industrial problems with the business community.

The difference between developmental and regulatory states, according to Johnson, is that a "regulatory, or market-rational, state concerns itself with forms and procedures—the rules, if you will, of economic competition—but it does not concern itself with substantive matters. The developmental, or plan-rational state, by contrast, has as its dominant feature precisely the setting of such substantive social and economic goals."[9]

A developmental state like Japan relates goals and policies to market realities rather than to ideological dogma, as does the Soviet Union. Japan and the new Japans aim to accelerate their development in order to catch up with more advanced countries and establish political equality, but they work through the marketplace rather than by pricing or quota systems; bottom-up planning by companies has a legitimate and at times decisive role to play.

A regulatory state like the United States, however, emphasizes the rules and procedures of competition, not substantive outcomes. Defense-related industries notwithstanding, regulatory states do not believe that government should promote the growth of one industry or abandon another. The fate of industries is left to the marketplace on the assumption that the invisible hand is the most effective manager of substantive outcomes. But for developmental states, substantive choices are matters of national concern, and rules of competition have lesser priority.

The distinction is not just one of economics; it concerns the political role and fundamental goals of the state. The philosophy of a developmental state differs markedly from a regulatory state's laissez-faire belief in the magic of the marketplace. For example, it probably requires a government that asks for short-term sacrifices in the standard of living to amass the savings necessary to finance needed investments, and a "MITI" to protect the home market while helping secure the necessary technologies.

Toward Economic Strategy

A government using a strategy of upgrading can promote individual companies through support for studies of proposed new sectors. It can reduce the risks involved in initiating change by targeting sectors for new or stepped-up activity by making resources available on favorable terms. It can, in effect, alter the risk-reward prospects by reducing the risks and increasing the rewards. In addition, it can offer negative incentives such as high-cost credit for investments in sectors it wants to discourage. With a national strategy of upgrading involving both macro- and microeconomic policies, a government can help some sectors more than it hurts others.

Dynamic comparative advantage requires strategic planning at the level of the company, the industry, and the national government. By focusing on new technologies and long-term returns, companies can establish themselves in one new sector after another. With the help of government they can move faster and with less risk. Over time, they can reshape the industrial profile of a country.

Strategy at the industry level will aim at managed, not maximum, competition. It will strive to avoid duplication of innovative effort through coordination of basic R&D, and also work to achieve agreements by companies on discontinuing marginal products. (A discontinuance agreement in the United States at the industry level is now a criminal offense. We still work with the notion that more competition is better—that five gas stations at an intersection are better than four.)

A national economic strategy will not fit neatly into the conventional distinction between macro- and microeconomics. It will encompass the structure and administration of important policy-making institutions, such as Treasury, Commerce, and the U.S. Trade Representative. The government will use the powers of state to promote the competitiveness of the economy in general and that of certain industries in particular.

Where We Go Right—And Wrong

In its broadest sense, national economic strategy involves the managed development of a nation's resources—plans to promote savings and investment, programs to develop education and infrastructure. The initiatives to develop canals, railroads, and the interstate highway networks are examples of national economic strategy. But penalty taxes on interest and dividends, which, coupled with interest deductions on personal income tax, penalize savings while subsidizing borrowing does not. U.S. government policy has been characteristically consumption-oriented and anti-industrial.[10]

One big step forward has been the development of market promotion policies where the government has intervened to improve the working of the market system.[11] This intervention differs from regulation because its purpose is to improve functioning in terms of substantive results through, for instance, retraining programs to increase labor mobility, loan guarantees to small businesses to offset distortions in private capital markets, and regional development schemes to counteract market imbalances or to promote a less-developed area. One recent, successful U.S. market-promotion policy involved reduction of the capital gains tax to free funds resulting from investments. This policy led to a revival of the venture capital market in 1978 and 1979, and helped spur price-earnings ratios, thus making equity capital cheaper for new ventures.

In theory, the U.S. government could take a more active role by supplementing the invisible hand with targeting. The Department of Defense has long practiced targeting, sometimes with important commercial spillover as in the cases of jet aircraft, computers, and semiconductors.

Of interest in this respect are the so-called related-diversified companies, characterized by a strong commitment to R&D, related core skills, and divisional structures.[12] Successful in-house ventures of these companies are shifted to the status of semi-autonomous profit centers to give them the benefits of contact with the market while still under the protective umbrella of the parent company. The capacity to nurture new ventures in-house appears to be a key reason that related-diversified companies have outperformed conglomerates with their financially based portfolio management programs.[13]

The government can accelerate the development of industries and projects that are too risky for the private sector. The eventual effect of a government's targeting is to alter the industrial mix and business portfolios faster and differently than would be the case if each company were allowed to follow its own investment plans. Government can assist companies to enter new areas more quickly because it can help reduce risks and mobilize resources that are beyond the capabilities of a single company; for the same reason, it can abruptly quit areas that fail to meet expected returns. Since the external challenge is mostly in trade of manufactured goods, a national strategy should be primarily concerned with the industrial sector.

The Problem of the Welfare State

Much of the current enthusiasm for industrial policy in the United States is based on the premise that we need new institutions to permit business, labor, and government to collaborate in sectoral targeting and restructuring, and that these can be easily added to the government structure. This, it is said, is what the Europeans have done.

Unfortunately, European successes with targeting have been exaggerated. As far as industrial employment, investment, and development of new high-technology sectors go, European countries are in worse shape than we are. France has had almost 30 years of experience with Japanese-type industrial strategy, and abandoned it once in the 1970s as a failure. The current revival by the socialist government has yet to show positive results.

The problem lies with adding industrial policy to an anti-industrial strategy without other more fundamental changes. It is like alcoholics believing they can deal with their problems by drinking coffee. The fundamental problem for all the North Atlantic countries lies in overindulgence in the welfare state, not underdevelopment of industrial policy.

The essential characteristic of the welfare state is the redefinition of economic security as a guaranteed right whose entitlement has no duties or performance requirements, rather than as an achievement based on work and saving. Two entitlement programs, pensions and medical care, now account for roughly 50% of public spending in most North Atlantic countries that continue to expand these programs, regardless of cost, despite more than a decade of stagflation and increased international competition. It is time to consider the cost of these entitlement programs and our ability to bear this cost.

The problem is not so much the concept or its implementation, but the amount of welfare relative to the productive capacity of a country. At some point benefits and the related costs become too high to permit an economy to function competitively. Jobs that can be transferred to a lower cost environment are moved. Employment falls.

The economic stagnation of the North Atlantic area over the last 10 years suggests that quite a few countries may have crossed the threshold of "too much." The growth that has occurred has been fueled by increased borrowing at home, abroad, or both. It is like taking more wine to recover from a hangover. And, unfortunately, most of the discussion of industrial policy thus far focuses on the coffee and ignores the dependence on wine.

Change the Process

For the United States to be internationally competitive it must shift basic priorities toward the promotion of national, corporate, and individual economic performance, and halt the growth of entitlements or reduce them. To accomplish a fundamental rebalancing of priorities requires that the United States change the process by which it deals with economic difficulties. Because it denies the existence of a problem, the present Council of Economic Advisers is an unlikely source of leadership. Solutions will not be found if bureaucrats attempt to manage the industrial portfolio or if we depend for a coherent response on our fragmented political process. Business and labor are more conscious of the competitive challenge, but they lack the credibility necessary to speak from a broad, national point of view.

The United States needs to establish a new process to build the broad consensus required to support remedial legislation, one that can benefit from the best possible analysis to clarify the nature of the problem (see the appendix for one suggestion).

The goals of proposals such as those for the creation of a national cooperation council are to shift the way we think about government and society and to ease government into the unfamiliar role of promoting economic competitiveness. Implicitly, they accept the notion that comparative advantage can be created as well as given. But such proposals are unlikely to receive serious consideration until we recognize that there is a problem of competitiveness and a need to shift national priorities to meet that challenge. Also, we must acknowledge the need for a broad educational campaign to stimulate national awareness.

It is not clear that this kind of proposal, if adopted, would yield the competitive national strategy we need. For, in addition, the United States must reduce the anti-industrial aspects of its cultural ethos, shift public attention toward competitiveness, and reduce the overemphasis on short-term consumer benefits and entitlements. The public has to understand that the nation must have the capacity to *earn* its standard of living. We must retreat from the spending and borrowing binges that characterize the strategies of so many older industrial states.

Changes are more apt to occur and will be more effective if business leaders recognize a broader concept of stewardship, one that pays more attention to the rights of employees and a good deal less to those of shareholders. By giving more Americans a greater stake in a growing pie, one might hope for added political support for the policies and institutions needed for prosperity.

We must begin to focus on the realities of trade with the new competitors of East Asia and change both the substance of U.S. economic policy and the process through which it is formulated and implemented. We must be willing to admit there's a problem and then take some risks in experimenting with a national strategy to avoid the even greater risk of continued decline.

Notes

1. See Robert H. Hayes and William J. Abernathy, "Managing Our Way to Economic Decline," *HBR*, July–August 1980, p. 67.

2. Ira C. Magaziner and Robert B. Reich, *Minding America's Business: The Decline and Rise of the American Economy* (New York, Harcourt Brace Jovanovich, 1982).

3. John Zysman and Laura Tyson, *American Industry in International Competition* (Ithaca, Cornell University Press, 1983), chapter 1.

4. Regina Kelly, *The Impact of Technological Innovation on Trade Patterns*, U.S. Department of Commerce, Bureau of International Economic Policy and Research, ER-24, December 1977.

5. Richard Caves and Ronald Jones, *World Trade and Payments*, 3d ed. (Boston, Little Brown, 1981), p. 115.

6. Michael Borrus, "The Politics of Competitive Erosion in the Steel Industry," in *American Industry in International Competition*.

7. Miyohei Shinohara, *Industrial Growth, Trade, and Dynamic Patterns in the Japanese Economy* (Tokyo, University of Tokyo Press, 1982), p. 24.

8. *The Industrial Policy of Japan* (Paris, Organization for Economic Cooperation and Development, 1972), p. 15.

9. Chalmers Johnson, *MITI and the Japanese Miracle* (Stanford, Stanford University Press, 1982), p. 18.

10. See my article, "Can Industry Survive the Welfare State?" *HBR*, September–October 1982, p. 70.

11. *American Industry in International Competition*, p. 21.

12. Leonard Wrigley, "Divisional Autonomy and Diversification," unpublished doctoral dissertation, Harvard Business School, 1970.

13. Richard R. Rumelt, *Strategy, Structure and Economic Performance* (Boston, Division of Research, Harvard Business School, 1974), and my article "The Industrial State, Old Myths and New Realities," *HBR*, March–April 1973, p. 133.

Appendix: A Sample Plan for the United States

Several bills introduced in the first session of the 98th Congress proposed a national cooperation council. Among those identified with this initiative were Congressmen Richard A. Gephardt, John J. La Falce, Stanley N. Lundine, and Timothy E. Wirth. Proposals, outlined in the Wirth bill (H.R. 3443), call on the United States:

1 To acknowledge that the restoration and expansion of America's economy is a national priority;

2 To create a forum or forums in which representatives of business, labor, and federal, state, and local governments will identify national economic problems, develop long-term strategies to address them, and create broad consensus in support of those strategies;

3 To establish sectoral councils of public and private leaders to develop similar long-term strategies for sectors and sub-sectors of the economy or particular regions of the country;

4 To report to the President and the Congress annually on the state of the economy.

By supplementing the Council of Economic Advisers (CEA) with a cooperation council whose members, representatives of business, labor, government, and the public, would have fixed terms of six years, the Wirth bill would amend the Employment Act of 1946.

The council would address problems on all levels, and its deliberations and recommendations would be confidential until they had been delivered to the President and/or the Congress. The provisions of the Federal Advisory Committee Act that requires all standing advisory committees to conduct open meetings that the press can attend would not apply.

The council would have the same status and independence as the Federal Reserve Board. It would analyze the problems facing the United States in an international perspective, an area in which the CEA has been notoriously weak and which it essentially ignored until 1971. The council would have powers broader than those of the CEA, notably to evaluate and propose remedies for specific sectoral problems.

An independent agency, the council would have a major responsibility to build consensus among the branches of government, including an increasingly fragmented Congress. A mechanism for sustained give-and-take among representatives of business, government, and labor through an economic bureaucracy not subject to presidential appointment, the council would offer a distinctive way to meet the competitive features of the Japanese system.

The council's most important innovative task would be to analyze desirable outcomes or developments and propose policies needed to achieve them. Just how this process would work in a society that ignores substantive issues but encourages special interest groups to vie with government on distribution is not easy to foresee. The mandate would be similar to that of the French National Planning Commission, although the council members would be more independent than the French commissioners because they would have term appointments and could pick their own staff director. Only time would tell, of course, whether the members could win broad public support and forge the necessary links with the executive branch to be effective.

While there are risks that such a council would generate more heat than light, the problems to be addressed are so important and the present institutions so inadequate that the risks and gains of creating another agency ought to be the object of careful study. Such research deserves the support of both business and labor.

PART TWO

RE-EXAMINING THE CONVENTIONAL WISDOM

AN OVERVIEW

In *A Life in Our Times*, John Kenneth Galbraith credits himself with coining the phrase "the conventional wisdom."[1] Galbraith reports he was looking for a phrase to capture "the beliefs that are at any time assiduously, solemnly and mindlessly traded between the pretentiously wise," a phrase "that was overtly respectful but with an undertone of disdain, even amusement. Something nicely balanced between approval and ridicule." The choice of words was a happy one and has served well. Applied to the practice of management, however, it loses its tone of gentle amusement. So great are the organizational stakes, so extensive the human costs, no hidebound allegiance to "what everybody knows" can absolve managers of their responsibility to question familiar assumptions when the conditions that gave rise to them have changed.

"An economy's performance," Lawrence Revsine reminds us in "Let's Stop Eating Our Seed Corn," "can be monitored intelligently only if policymakers and the public have a clear idea of what is happening to its long-term productive capability." So, too, at the level of the individual company, where the need for "accurate information about real underlying performance" is particularly acute. "Rather than haphazardly funding individual projects, management needs to determine which businesses have the strategic characteristics that make them good candidates for mechanization." Thus argues Bradley Gale in "Can More Capital Buy Higher Productivity?"

Together, Revsine and Gale, one concerned with accounting systems and the other with capital investment decisions, make a common point: the conventional wisdom no longer holds; the numbers in common use do not tell the truth; what often passes for management thinking is little better than a kind of disciplined sleepwalking.

The five articles in this section all have as their purpose the goal of waking up managers. Fresh thinking is the order of the day; the dangers of stale thought, all too obvious. As Gale notes, "Very frequently, not knowing the cause of the illness—in fact not even having correctly identified the patient—we prescribe medicine whose effects are at best dissipated and at worst cause havoc." It is time, then, to reexamine diagnostic skills and the assumptions on which they rest.

Notes

1. John Kenneth Galbraith, *A Life in Our Times* (Boston, Houghton Mifflin, 1981), p. 339.

7
The Industrial State
Old Myths and New Realities

BRUCE R. SCOTT

J.K. Galbraith in *The New Industrial State* has depicted modern industry as a collection of inflexible, self-satisfied colossi. Recent evidence, presented for the first time in this article, shows that Galbraith's analysis describes the "old" industrial state and not the new. Similarly this article demonstrates that the strong medicines he and his followers have prescribed to bring our large companies back "under control"—nationalization, price control, and the like—are irrelevant to the case. The author argues that these critics have misperceived the real trends in corporate evolution and that the remedies for our economic problems lie in quite a different direction from the one they have suggested. Competitive pressures are still the most potent forces governing corporate evolution, the author points out; and, if we really want to make the business community more responsive to public needs, what we ought to do is shape and enhance these pressures to encourage even greater market sensitivity and responsiveness among our industrial giants. The alternative—to govern industry through more direct regulation—places too much responsibility on the wisdom of the economists, some of the best of whom are unequal to the task. The author concludes by suggesting new policies for two areas that are of particular concern today—antitrust regulation and the social responsibility of corporations. He also notes some of the effects the Galbraith viewpoint has had on the economic evolution of less developed countries.

There is a sentiment in some quarters that the large corporations of the United States and of the highly industrialized countries of Europe are out of control. These institutions are criticized for manipulating markets rather than responding to them; for pursuing their own growth and aggrandizement instead of serving the true economic needs of today; and for an unfortunate, if perhaps unintentional, disregard of the public interest.

Published 1973.

This kind of criticism usually begins with the proposition that competition is a declining force in the marketplace, and that, therefore, there is no longer an effective market mechanism to shape corporate strategies and structures into useful members and servants of the economy and the public well-being. This kind of criticism usually ends with the recommendation—or the demand—that government exert itself to bring the corporations back under some semblance of control.

Probably the most notable spokesman for this viewpoint is J.K. Galbraith. In *The New Industrial State* he indicated that the direction of corporate evolution is inimical to the public well-being, and, on that justification, he has not hesitated to suggest such sharp remedies as nationalization and price controls.[1]

However, as his critics have suspected all along, Galbraith is mistaken about the direction in which corporations are evolving. Data on the large companies of the United States and Europe are now available that undercut his contention that the company is becoming a nonresponsive monolith, insulated from competitive forces. Instead, it appears, these forces are very much alive. They are effectively shaping corporate strategies and organizational forms, and shaping them in ways that are different from the ones Galbraith hypothesized.

The actual trends of corporate evolution have some remarkable implications for public policy in both the highly industrialized economies and in the developing countries. These implications are just as remarkable in their way as the drastic "remedies," such as nationalization, proposed by Galbraith. At the end of this article I shall talk a bit about these implications for two areas of domestic concern—antitrust regulation and pollution control—as well as for the directed growth of "basic industry" in less developed nations.

I should point out that Galbraith does not contend that top management has been mischievous, or that it has plotted to arrange such an outcome. Rather, in his view, top management has responded rationally to the uncertainties created by growing markets and advancing technology by building up strategies and structures for the corporation that insulate it from competitive market pressures. Nonetheless, he argues that since management has been so *successful* at winning independence from the market forces, new regulatory forces are needed, and it is the responsibility of government to supply the necessary regulation and control.

It is not surprising that Galbraith's viewpoint has found such favor with civil servants and government officials, as well as with those who are inclined to socialism. Nor is it surprising that it has found favor among professors of economics who serve as advisers to governments in matters of industrial policy. To each—the civil servant, the socialist, and the professor of economics—it is the call to the colors, each must move forward to help the public restore the public interest to its rightful place. And the solution, of course, is via more economic planning and public control.

Galbraith has stated that his basic purpose in *The New Industrial State* was to describe what exists; he is at work on another volume which will spell out the implications more fully.[2] However, in describing the status quo, he has not burdened his readers with supporting evidence. In particular, he offers no systematic evidence on the evolution of the large company. Instead, he offers an economic argument buttressed by anecdotes.

Therefore, before I discuss public policy implications, let me first give an analysis of the Galbraith viewpoint and the new data that bear on it, and try to diagnose how this erroneous, distorted perspective arose in the first place. It will then be all the clearer why the SOS sounded in *The New Industrial State* was a false alarm.

Call to the Colors

In the chapter titled "The Approved Contradiction," Galbraith makes his two basic points about the modern corporation, as he understands it. After recalling that shareholders have by and large lost control to management, he names two popular misconceptions about the corporate form:

1   Corporate strategy is no longer subordinate to market forces. Instead, the corporation now tends—successfully—to dominate, manipulate, and control its markets.

2   The corporation no longer tries to maximize its economic gains as its primary reason for being. Instead, management seeks some minimum acceptable level of economic performance, a level just adequate to satisfy the wants and technical interests of the "technostructure" within itself. On the individual plane, he makes the point that managerial salaries do not vary with profits, and hence professional managers—who constitute the vast majority—have no direct incentive to maximize profits.

As a result, he argues, the corporation is no longer subject to market forces, either in terms of external competitive pressure or in terms of internal motivation for high economic performance.

Thus Galbraith finds the corporation a growing center of autonomous power—one that is influencing government and public policy rather than the other way around. The corporations have become the masters rather than the servants of our market economy; and they have mastered it via strategies of market domination created by organizations of dedicated technocrats who no longer pursue profits beyond a certain acceptable level.

The Supporting Argument . . .

His argument goes somewhat as follows. The growing size of markets plus continual advances in technology permit continuously increasing *economies of scale*. As a result, large-scale enterprise is characterized by increasing *subdivision* of tasks, increasing *specialization* of labor and equipment, and an increasingly complex managerial job of *integrating* the various specialized subunits.

. . . Has Grains of Truth

This sounds familiar, though it would seem that the argument applies more readily to some industries than others—notably to heavy industry or those that involve particularly long sequences of operations, such as aircraft or automobile manufacture. It would also seem to apply more readily to some of our less-diversified large companies. Indeed, I believe Galbraith's argument has a validity, but one that is limited in a number of ways:

☐ Specialization and coordination *are* taking place at lower levels in most companies. These activities have been going on for at least 100 years. One also finds increasing integration at various levels within the company. At the *corporate* level, however, I question whether these are the *dominant* forces shaping the strategy of the corporation.

☐ I acknowledge that his argument is insightful for those areas where there is no real market mechanism, notably in the military-industrial complex. This area is of particular interest to him, and doubtless its dynamics have influenced his thinking. However, one must be extremely cautious in generalizing on the basis of this specialized sector.

The reason is that while the military-industrial complex involves considerable hardware, money, and people, there are *very* few major companies whose primary business is the supply of weapons and defense systems. No doubt Lockheed and Raytheon and a few others fit his description, but most big U.S. companies derive the major part of their business elsewhere. Hence it is reasonable to look elsewhere for the determinants of the corporate strategy of big business as a whole.

☐ His description of strategy and technostructure fits quite closely with a one-industry company managed through a functional organization, without product divisions, subunit profit centers—and so on. However, in an era of diversification, it is important to find out how many large companies are still wedded to a one-industry strategy.

What of Strategy and Structure?

Before Galbraith's viewpoint can be evaluated, then, one has to analyze the strategies and structures of our large companies, and in what directions they are evolving. In other words, the questions to study are these:

☐ How does one characterize the great body of our large corporations in terms of strategy and structure?

☐   What trends can one observe in the development of strategy and structure, once the categories have been established?

Galbraith has given these questions only the most summary and casual kind of treatment.

On the strategic side, he has noted that some companies have diversified so as to reduce market risk. "But," he says, "the more common strategies require that the market be replaced. . . ."[3] His general assertion is that strategies of market domination and control are a more characteristic way of dealing with uncertainty than strategies of diversification. He gives no evidence, either for the United States or any other country, but he makes this pivotal point nonetheless.

Galbraith has even less to say about organizational structures. He notes in Chapter 7 that all derive from the same legal framework and lets it go at that.

In short, Galbraith's argument on the rise of the new industrial state is based on the assertion that a new type of industrial corporation is arising— a corporation with a strategy of market dominance rather than diversified, competitive profit-seeking, whose managerial structure is dominated by technicians rather than profit-sensitive generalist managers. He mentions other possible strategies, such as diversification, but does not examine their relative importance among large companies. He does not even note the existence of any forms or styles of management other than the new technostructure.

He speaks as if U.S. Steel, Du Pont, and Textron were essentially similar to one another, and likewise to Lockheed and Raytheon.

He has also overlooked the fact that while salaries do not vary with profits, bonuses *do*.

Obviously, such oversimplification invites criticism, and criticism encourages revision; and Galbraith has made some revisions in his own views. But, as he himself has said, these revisions amount only to changes in emphasis, and they leave the basic thrust of his argument quite unchanged. Certainly, he has not enlarged his argument to include an adequate critique of the evolution of strategic and structural forms in our large corporations.

Even if one acknowledges that his argument seems true for some companies, then, these very serious difficulties remain:

First, one needs a scheme for classifying our large companies so those that closely fit Galbraith's thesis can be sorted out from those that do not. For example, this scheme must distinguish strategies of market dominance from those of diversification and distinguish the technostructures from the profit-hungry divisions of some of our highly diversified firms.

Second, there is the problem of empirical research. One needs data on trends to show which categories of strategies and structures are becoming more common and which less common.

Most of this article is devoted to reporting a research program that has been under way at the Harvard Business School for almost a decade and which has undertaken both the conceptual and the empirical chores. (A brief description of this project appears in the appendix.)

Trend to Diversification

In his pioneering work *Strategy and Structure,* Alfred D. Chandler analyzed the historical development of some 70 large U.S. companies and found that each of several characteristic strategies is associated with a particular type of structure. He also found that in many cases there is a characteristic developmental sequence.[4] For instance, the strategy of vertical integration managed through a centralized structure tends to be succeeded by a strategy of diversification managed by a decentralized structure. His work suggested a developmental model of the company, a model based not on hypothetical aspects of the corporation but on the two critical areas in which management exercises managerial choice: strategy and structure.

Since 1963 I have worked at formalizing and testing such a developmental concept. With the help of a number of colleagues, I have developed a three-stage model in which the stages follow one another in historical sequence.[5] Each stage has not only a distinctive set of managerial characteristics but also a distinctive "way of life." Exhibit 1 gives a recent version of this model.

A brief inspection reveals that the Stage II company fits Galbraith's analysis quite closely, while the Stage III company—with its diversified operation, its profit centers, and its variable compensation based on economic performance—does not.

Similarly, the transition from Stage II to State III does not fit his analysis of the way companies grow, since the critical variable is *not* continuing growth in size but a change in strategy—that is, from a strategy based on market position in one industry to a strategy based on market opportunities in several industries. Therefore we concluded that the three stages of company evolution are not *small, medium,* and *large,* as Galbraith implies, but *small, integrated,* and *diversified,* as the work of Chandler suggested years ago.

Research on the *Fortune* "500" in the late 1960s showed that most of these companies were in Stage III, and that none (obviously enough) were in Stage I. It was also clear that Stage III includes companies that are dissimilar both in type and in degree of diversification. As a result, Stage III was subdivided according to how and how much the company had diversified. The resulting classes were these:

Dominant business companies that derive 70%–95% of sales from a single business or a vertically integrated chain of businesses (for example, General Motors, IBM, Texaco, Scott Paper, U.S. Steel, and Xerox).

Related business companies that are diversified into related areas, where no single business accounts for more than 70% of sales (for example, Du Pont, Eastman Kodak, General Electric, and General Foods).

Exhibit 1. The Three Stages of Organizational Development

Company characteristics	Stage I	Stage II	Stage III
Product line	Single product or single line	Single product line	Multiple product lines
Distribution	One channel or set of channels	One set of channels	Multiple channels
Organization structure	Little or no formal structure; "one-man show"	Specialization based on function	Specialization based on product-market relationships
Product-service transactions	Not applicable	Integrated pattern of transactions $$A \to B \to C \to \text{Markets}$$	Nonintegrated pattern of transactions $$A \quad B \quad C \to \text{Markets} \leftarrow$$
R&D organization	Not institutionalized; guided by owner-manager	Increasingly institutionalized search for product or process improvements	Institutionalized search for *new* products as well as for improvements
Performance measurement	By personal contact and subjective criteria	Increasingly impersonal, using technical and/or cost criteria	Increasingly impersonal, using *market* criteria (return on investment and market share)
Rewards	Unsystematic and often paternalistic	Increasingly systematic, with emphasis on stability and service	Increasingly systematic, with variability related to performance
Control system	Personal control of both strategic and operating decisions	Personal control of strategic decisions, with increasing delegation of operating decisions through policy	Delegation of product-market decisions within existing businesses, with indirect control based on analysis of "results"
Strategic choices	Needs of owner versus needs of company	Degree of integration; market-share objective; breadth of product-line	Entry and exit from industries; allocation of resources by industry; rate of growth

Source: Bruce R. Scott, *Stages of Corporate Development* (Case Clearing House, Harvard Business School). Copyright © 1971 by the President and Fellows of Harvard College.

Unrelated business companies that have diversified without necessarily relating new business to old, and where no single business accounts for as much as 70% of sales (for example, Litton, LTV, North American Rockwell, Olin, and Textron).

(A *single* business here is defined as one that manufactures and distributes a single product, a line of products with variations in size and style, or a set of closely related products linked by technology or market structure. Corporate examples are Peabody Coal, American Motors, and several beer companies.)

Leonard Wrigley, who formulated these subclasses, discovered that dominant business companies are managed through a hybrid structure where top management directly controls the basic business through a functional structure while managing the remainder through product divisions.[6] Both the related and unrelated businesses were found to be managed by divisional structures.

Trend to Divisional Forms

Singling out the dominant business companies as a separate class turned out to be very important because this group includes many of the giants of U.S. industry, such as Exxon, GM, Ford, and U.S. Steel. It also includes many of the same companies about which Galbraith has written.

With this refined terminology, Wrigley analyzed a 20% sample of the *Fortune* "500." His findings, summarized in Exhibit 2, are briefly these:

☐ Almost all large U.S. companies had diversified by over 5% of sales.

☐ Some 80% of them had diversified by 30% of sales or more.

☐ The single businesses were organized functionally.

☐ The diversified businesses were, overwhelmingly, organized by divisions.

☐ By 1967 over 90% of the *Fortune* "500" were diversified to some extent, and over 80% were managed by the multidivisional form.

Subsequently, Richard Rumelt sampled 40% of the *Fortune* "500" and traced their evolution in strategy and structure using categories based on, but more refined than, Wrigley's (see Exhibit 3). His analysis, covering the period 1950–1970, confirmed what Wrigley's data has suggested—namely, increasing diversification and a trend away from single and even dominant businesses. It also demonstrated the decline of the functional organization and the dramatic rise of the form based on product divisions.

Rumelt also found that while geographic divisions were sometimes used, they were rarely used as the basic units of management of the large U.S. company. The holding company was likewise a rarity. The other form,

Exhibit 2. Strategy and Structure of the 1967 Fortune "500"

		Structure	
	Strategy	Functional	Divisional
Single business (no diversification)	6%	6%	0%
Dominant business	14	5	9
Related business	60	3	57
Unrelated business	20	0	20
Total	100%	14%	86%

Source: Leonard Wrigley, *Divisional Autonomy and Diversification* (unpublished DBA dissertation, Harvard Business School, 1970).

Exhibit 3.   Evolution of strategy and structure of the Fortune "500," 1950–1970

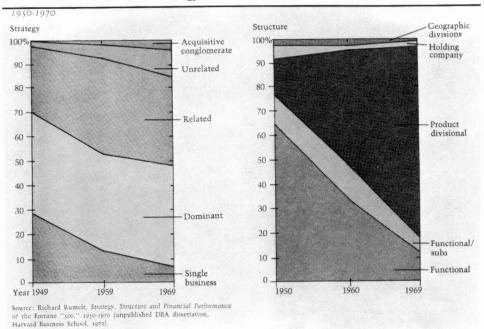

Source: Richard Rumelt, *Strategy, Structure and Financial Performance of the* Fortune *"500," 1950-1970* (unpublished DBA dissertation, Harvard Business School, 1972).

which Rumelt calls "functional/subs," is a hybrid wherein the principal business is directly managed by top management in the traditional functional form and the other, smaller, diversified businesses are managed as product divisions or subsidiaries. This form is, of course, quite common among companies with a dominant business.

Misperception of the Trend.   Thus the observable trend is quite different from that hypothesized by Galbraith. The companies that best fit Galbraith's description of the modern corporation are those with either a single business or a dominant business managed by either a functional structure or the function/sub hybrid form. *Yet these two groups constitute only about half the* Fortune *"500," and they are declining rather than increasing as a percentage of the total.* They are also growing less rapidly and hence are losing ground in relative size as well as in numbers.

On the other hand, *the two groups which have been increasing in importance are ignored in his analysis—both conceptually and empirically.* These groups comprise the companies with strategies of pursuing related and unrelated businesses.

Before I try to account for these discrepancies between the data and Galbraith's assertions, it will be useful to review the evolutionary trends of corporate strategy and structure in the major countries of Western Europe. Not only do these trends show a meaningful continuity and relationship with

Exhibit 4. Evolution of Strategy and Structure in the Four Major Western European Countries, 1950–1970

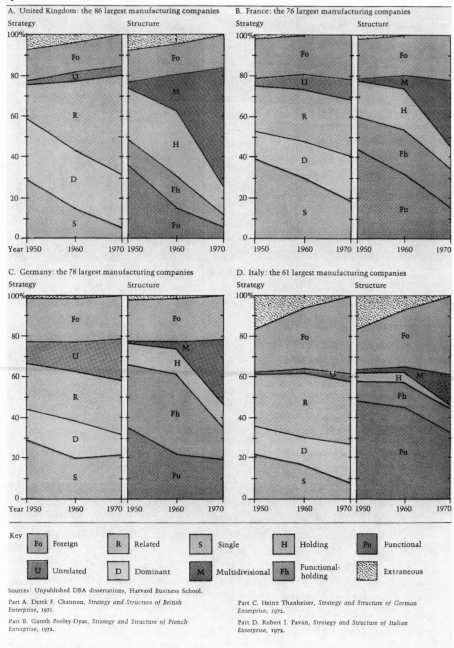

A. United Kingdom: the 86 largest manufacturing companies
B. France: the 76 largest manufacturing companies
C. Germany: the 78 largest manufacturing companies
D. Italy: the 61 largest manufacturing companies

Key
Fo Foreign   R Related   S Single   H Holding   Fu Functional
U Unrelated   D Dominant   M Multidivisional   Fh Functional-holding   Extraneous

Sources: Unpublished DBA dissertations, Harvard Business School.

Part A. Derek F. Channon, *Strategy and Structure of British Enterprise*, 1971.

Part B. Gareth Pooley-Dyas, *Strategy and Structure of French Enterprise*, 1972.

Part C. Heinz Thanheiser, *Strategy and Structure of German Enterprise*, 1972.

Part D. Robert J. Pavan, *Strategy and Structure of Italian Enterprise*, 1972.

the domestic trends I have just described; they also very dramatically illustrate the vital, essential ways in which competitive pressures continue to shape the modern corporation, Galbraith's contentions about the "insulation" of the corporation from competition notwithstanding.

European Parallels

Using the same concepts as Rumelt and Wrigley did, Derek F. Channon, Robert J. Pavan, Gareth Pooley-Dyas, Heinz Thanheiser, and I have analyzed the evolution of the top companies in the United Kingdom, France, Germany, and Italy. The results are shown in Exhibit 4, with the foreign companies segregated so as not to double count them.

These data demonstrate a trend toward diversification in each of these countries; they also show a decline in the proportion of companies in only one business. Actually the graphs *understate* this trend, because many companies which used to make hundreds of products now make thousands, and many companies which used to be in a few businesses are now in many. A still more striking trend is apparent in the rapid increase in the number of companies managed by product divisions.

The transition toward the diversified, multidivisional organization appears to have progressed farthest in the United Kingdom and least in Italy, but in all the countries the broad trends are similar. Overall, both in strategy and structure, the European companies appear headed the same way as their U.S. counterparts.

The major forces inducing this transition also appear to be similar in all five countries. Many traditional industries and markets have been experiencing slower growth rates. At the same time, R&D and rising consumer incomes have been generating new products and new markets. Alert managers have been diversifying into related areas to sustain the growth of their companies, rather than limiting themselves to the destinies of a single industry (such as coal, textiles, electric meters, or whatever).

In short, growth via diversification has become the most common strategy in Europe, as it has in the United States; increasing diversity plus competitive pressures seem to be forcing European companies to adopt the divisional structure, as they have the large companies in the United States.

Competitive Pressures

It is important to pause a moment to consider the role of competition in inducing this trend of structural change. Structural change is not a painless process; the change from the functional structure to the divisional can be very painful indeed, particularly for some of the high-status specialists in a company.

Since the divisional structure requires more generalists and more overhead, the transition to divisional structure is also likely to be costly. Given its costs in both human and financial terms, a company does not undertake such a transition lightly; in fact, it often refuses to undertake such a transition at all unless the pressures for change are overwhelming.

Furthermore, diversification alone and of itself does not appear to constitute adequate pressure for change to the divisional structure. Exhibit 4, clearly shows that diversification preceded divisionalization in all four European countries; one can note that in France, Germany, and Italy there were quite a few diversified companies in 1950, yet almost no divisional structures. In fact, there were many diversified companies in these countries in the 1930s and some even earlier, but the divisional form did not begin to spread rapidly until the 1960s.

In many cases, therefore, there was a time lag of 20 to 30 years or more between the change in strategy and the change in structure. The change in strategy appears to be a necessary condition for a company to change to the divisional structure. However, it is not in itself a sufficient condition. Companies that change to a strategy of diversification frequently continue to carry on with a functional structure for many years.

Growing knowledge about the divisional organization seems to have been an important element in the recent spread of this form in Europe. This knowledge has not always been readily available in Europe; in recent years it has come from a number of sources, notably U.S. companies and consulting firms.

However, our research suggests that one other critical element is competitive pressure—the pressure of competition in the marketplace. So long as competitive pressures are low or moderate, a strategy of diversification can be managed in a variety of ways. At an extreme, if there were not competition at all, any form of management structure would be adequate for operations of any degree of diversity. However, *the divisional structure appears to be the most effective way to manage the strategy of diversification under highly competitive conditions*. This observation receives strong support both from interviews with management and from the body of numerical data represented in Exhibits 3 and 4.

For example, the divisional form spread most rapidly in the United States, where antitrust legislation maintained the competitive concept even in the 1930s and with renewed vigor in the late 1940s and the 1950s. In addition, supply caught up with demand more rapidly in the United States than in Western Europe in the period after World War II, and as a result competitive pressures returned more rapidly in the United States than in Western Europe, where continuing shortages maintained sellers' markets in many areas well into the 1950s.

The trend to divisionalization came next in the United Kingdom, getting underway in the 1950s and sweeping rapidly in the 1960s. I believe this was due in part to the long-standing ties between the United Kingdom and the United States, but it was also due in part to British efforts to restore more competitive market conditions via a reduction in restrictive practices, beginning about 1956.[7]

On the Continent, divisionalization did not really make much headway until the 1960s. If one had data for each year, and not just 1960 and 1970, he would almost certainly see that it accelerated sharply as the decade went on. In other words, it would follow the rise in competitive pressures generated partly by the Common Market and partly by supply catching up with demand. Those pressures have been strong enough to uproot traditional structures even where there have been both strong personal and cultural barriers to organizational change.

On this point my argument is like that of a biologist. Where there is little competition, almost any species can survive. Where there is strong competition, there is pressure which eliminates the least fit. Before the European settlers introduced the weasel into New Zealand, even birds without wings could survive there because there were no predators. Once the weasel arrived, birds without wings, such as the kiwi, rapidly declined and are now almost extinct.

Something similar—though perhaps less dramatic—also appears to be happening in the population of large companies in the United States and Europe. In each country the divisional structure is gaining, and *all others* are declining. It appears that the strategy of diversification—under conditions of increasing competition—is leading top managers in all five countries to abandon other forms of organization in favor of the divisional form. And the overwhelming majority of these organizations are managed through *product* divisions.

Galbraith's Signal Omission

I am now in a position to explain the discrepancy between Galbraith's view of industrial evolution and the facts this research has uncovered. The error is this: his argument takes account of only one of the two technological trends which have been shaping corporate strategies.

Surely enough, he has taken account of the increasing economies of scale associated with higher volumes, more complex equipment, and larger plants—that is, with simple industrial growth. In other words, he has correctly analyzed the impact of technology on the production process within the company.

However, he has failed to consider the other aspect of modern technology which has influenced the corporation—namely, the development of new products via research. His analysis simply overlooks the impact of R&D on the creation of new products and new markets.

And it is R&D which has shaped the strategies of the largest group of companies—those which we call "related diversified." These are companies which have moved beyond dependence on a single market to multimarket strategies, both as a way to seek more rapid growth *and* as a way to balance the risks associated with any single business. They have chosen to manage their diversified operations by the divisional structure.

These companies are characterized by an institutionalized R&D effort, by the systematic search for new products, and by the exploitation of new developments within the structure of management by product divisions. In fact, one of the most important strengths associated with the divisional structure is management's ability to move rapidly into new areas via the establishment of new divisions. The divisional structure not only is elastic enough to accommodate new divisions, but it also has a built-in "school" for training managers at lower levels. Hence a divisionalized company has a pool of management talent on which to draw.

One should note that these are, essentially, *competitive* advantages and strengths. While Galbraith has hypothesized an end to competition, based in part on technological imperatives and in part on management's use of planning to replace the marketplace, the majority of large companies have faced up to the fact of increasing competitive pressures. They have done this through better planning, including planned diversification into new, attractive growth and profit opportunities which they identify through their R&D capability.

Position of the Dominants

On the other hand, there is an important group of companies to which Galbraith's analysis may indeed apply, though for different reasons from those which he hypothesized.

It would appear that his thesis fits many of the dominant-business companies, especially those characterized by heavy capital commitments in a single mass-production industry where specialization and integration are the keys to low-cost operations. These include the big oil companies, the steels, the meat packers, the pulp and paper companies—in fact, most of the major raw-materials processors and some of the mass-production assemblers of mechanical goods, such as the major automobile companies.

These are the types of companies which he uses as examples. They are very large and very important, as everyone knows. But he alleges that they are also the archetype of the "new industrial state." Are they?

Exhibits 3 and 4 show that the dominant-business companies are definitely not disappearing; they appear to retain a steady share of the population. And if one goes behind these figures to look at this particular subgroup, one of the striking features is the stability of its membership. In particular, the vertically integrated members of this group—the "dominant verticals" as Rumelt called them—included roughly 75 of the *Fortune* "500" in 1949, 1959, and 1969, and by and large these were the same companies in all three decades. Thus they had neither diversified out of this group nor declined in size so as to drop from the population.

In studying this group of companies, one notes at once that they are not the "new industrial state" in terms of new companies. Most of these companies were giants before World War II and some before 1920. Nor are they new in the sense of having new strategies; for many, the strategy of integration predated not just World War II but World War I. Nor, as we shall see, were these vertically integrated heavyweights "new" in the sense of providing leadership in terms of economic performance.

Comparative Economic Performance

The data on comparative performance by structure and strategy shown in Exhibit 5 were obtained from a computerized data bank of the financial performance of listed NYSE companies. While the results they suggest should not be considered definitive, they are indicative.

Exhibit 5 shows financial performance by type of structure for the period 1950–1970, reduced to annualized averages for the 20-year period. The first interesting point here is that product-divisional companies scored higher on *all* the conventional financial measures than either of the other two structural categories. Since the product-division form has become more popular during this period, as data presented earlier in this article show, it looks as if managements are moving toward the higher performance form of organization and abandoning the lower performance forms.

If one looks at the evidence by class of strategy, one finds that the comparisons are less clear-cut but still suggestive. From Exhibit 5 it seems clear that the diversified companies have done much better than the single or dominant companies, not only in growth in sales and growth in earnings, but also in growth in *earnings per share*. The companies with a single business are last by a wide margin. One can also note the relatively high performance of the companies that have diversified into *related* areas—high performance not only in growth, but also in return on capital and return on equity.

In Exhibit 6, Rumelt has taken the analysis another step by segregating some distinct subgroups within the categories. While the dominant business categories as a whole appear low, it is the dominant verticals which are particularly low.

Exhibit 5.   Financial Characteristics of the Strategic and Structural Categories, 1950–1970

(All values are percentages except for P/E, which is a ratio)

	Single business	Dominant	Related	Unrelated	Average	Functional	Functional/ subs	Product divisional	Average
			Strategy					Structure	
Sales growth	7.17	8.03	9.14	14.24	9.01	8.55	6.49	9.77	8.98
Earnings growth	4.81	7.95	9.39	13.86	8.72	6.76	9.57	10.66	9.17
EPS growth	3.92	5.99	7.64	7.92	6.57	5.08	8.32	8.63	7.37
P/E	14.60	15.74	19.21	15.75	17.02	14.86	16.60	18.73	17.21
ROI	10.81	9.64	11.49	9.49	10.52	10.28	9.49	10.75	10.43
ROE	13.20	11.64	13.55	11.92	12.64	12.28	11.09	12.90	12.45

Source: Richard Rumelt, *Strategy, Structure, and Financial Performance of the Fortune "500"* (unpublished DBA dissertation, Harvard Business School, Boston, 1972).

Exhibit 6. Financial Characteristics of the Strategic Subcategories, 1950–1970
(All values are percentages except for P/E, which is a ratio)

	Dominant			Related			Unrelate
	Vertically integrated	Closely related	Other	Closely related	Linked	Passive	Acquisiti Conglomerat
Sales growth	7.42	9.48	6.93	9.62	8.06	6.10	20.6
Earnings growth	7.34	9.08	8.10	10.39	7.15	7.78	18.6
EPS growth	5.14	7.60	6.11	8.56	5.57	5.96	9.4
P/E	15.68	15.92	15.41	19.19	19.27	13.77	17.4
ROI	8.24	12.71	8.69	11.97	10.43	9.40	9.5
ROE	10.18	14.91	10.28	14.11	12.28	10.38	13.1

Source: Richard Rumelt, *Strategy, Structure, and Financial Performance of the* Fortune "500" (unpublished DBA dissertation, Harvard Business School, Boston, 1972).

Companies in the second subgroup have a strategy of closely related, but not vertically integrated, diversification. These companies are approximately as numerous, and show above-average performance on all measures except the P/E ratio. In effect, this subgroup segregates the raw material processors from many of the mechanical equipment makers; the exhibit shows that the closely related subgroup has a much higher economic performance.

Examination of the dominant verticals strikingly reveals that on two of the key measures of economic performance, ROI and ROE, these giants are the *lowest of any group* or subgroup—they are below average by more than 2% per year in both categories. Since annual averages were used, their true performance lag would be the cumulative percentage calculated by compounding this 2% for the 20-year period. This is hardly the economic performance one would expect of the trail blazers for a "new industrial state."

Again, Exhibit 6 makes it clear that unrelated diversification is also a low-performance strategy. The figures for the unrelated passives make this point very strongly. And while the acquisitive conglomerates make a better showing, notably on earnings per share, the premise of this performance is continual acquisition. Were one to analyze this subcategory in light of the economic and market conditions of the 1970s, he would probably find the performance of the acquisitive conglomerates falling dramatically and approaching the performance of the bulk of unrelated diversifiers. As a whole, too, the unrelated diversifiers appear to be having digestion problems as a consequence of their earlier diversification moves.

It is important to note that there were exceptions to these general conclusions in the dominant-business category. Some companies did extremely well—in fact, their principal business did so well that they could hardly have found attractive options via diversification. Xerox and IBM are examples. But neither of these companies had much in common with the slow-moving giants in the vertically integrated group of raw-materials processors.

Low-Performance Syndrome

In the case of the dominant verticals, one is at once inclined to ask this question: How and why have they stayed so long with such low-performance strategies?

My guess is that most of these companies are aware that they have a low-performance strategy; but they have realized this too late, and they now find it extremely difficult to diversify. They have let themselves stay too long with the one-industry strategy and are now trapped by the results of it. If anything, their performance in the 1970s is likely to look even further below average than in the past.

Most of these companies are in mature industries, characterized by slow growth in demand, high economies of scale, chronic overcapacity, and low profits. Some, such as steel, were mature before World War II. Some of the newer materials processors joined the ranks of low performers more recently, such as the aluminum companies. All these industries are characterized by commodity products and sensitivity to price. Hence a low-cost position is vitally important.

In addition, marginal additions to plant appear attractive; these companies must invest in plant to stay in the game and to keep bringing costs down. This goes on until overcapacity and dumping bring down the earnings for the whole industry group.

At the same time, if the management of a dominant vertical tries to diversify, it faces a dilemma. It has little by way of transferable skills; hence any area is likely to be "new," and therefore difficult.

Further, a dominant vertical needs to make *big* commitments in new fields if it is to diversify as much as 30% of its sales. Yet any high-growth, high-profit industry is likely to be populated by higher-profit companies which command higher price/earnings ratios in the stock market. To acquire for stock would further dilute earnings. To acquire for cash would cause problems for the cash-hungry principal business of the company.

In short, these companies cannot move easily via either cash *or* stock acquisitions.

Thus these companies remain as they are, not from choice but because escape is difficult. Judging from our field research, and even from the annual reports we have read from these companies, my colleagues and I have concluded that a good many dominant-vertical managements realize their dilemma. They know they have a low-performance strategy, and they are trying to do something about it.

Galbraith in Perspective

This conclusion reinforces the general message uncovered by the data: *business executives in the highly industrialized countries of Europe and in the United States tend to move toward high-performance strategies and structures when competitive pressures induce them to do so.* Under the competitive pressures of the EEC, European companies seem to be rapidly moving in the same direction that the large U.S. companies have found so effective—namely, the divisionalized forms of diversified enterprise.

And it is well to remember that it is the impetus and shock of continual technological innovation that has promoted a new generation and a higher order of flexibility and responsiveness in the corporate forum. This is a far different conception from the one Galbraith advanced, that technology is creating a new state of industrial monoliths who are philosophically remote from the markets they enjoy and dominate.

Instead, it might seem that we have a new class of industries which are ready to join the ranks of the public utilities and of the regulated public servants. Certainly some of our vertically integrated giants have shown little more foresight than the railroad or coal companies of yesteryear. And perhaps those that remain as "one-eyed giants" deserve a fate similar to the coal companies or the railroads.

In summary, it appears to me that Galbraith has analyzed the strategies and structures that were new in the 1920s or earlier, and which characterized the population of companies that emerged from World War II. His is the *old* industrial state, and not the new.

The new is elsewhere—in the company that is market—and profit-oriented; in the diversified, divisional company that Galbraith omits from his analysis, but more recently has acknowledged to exist.

This new state presents its own challenges to public policy, and it is these challenges that I should like to discuss in conclusion.

Public Policy Implications

The basic theme of this article is that a majority of the largest companies in the industrialized West are behaving in a thoroughly market-oriented fashion. Far from "replacing" or dominating markets, they are becoming increasingly sensitive to new markets and are willing to shift resources from one market to another as opportunities develop.

Furthermore, in response to competitive pressures, the largest companies are moving spontaneously in the direction of the higher performance strategies and structures; in fact, they had begun to move in this direction long before most economists and public officials were aware of what they were doing. Thus, not only in serving their customers but also in shaping their own growth, the large companies remain oriented to market forces.

These conclusions have profound implications for public policies on business in this country. Within the scope of this article I can only indicate what these may be; but I feel it imperative to discuss the point briefly, if only to counterbalance the ill-conceived prescriptions for increasing the government's direct regulation of corporate enterprise that have been advanced by those economists who favor Galbraith's viewpoint.

The conclusions make it clear, for example, that the United States should *not* develop the same inclination to nationalize and over-regulate that some governments in industrialized Western Europe have developed. In Europe, and particularly in France, this inclination appears to be colliding with the natural direction of corporate evolution, and this collision has been unfortunate for all concerned.

It would be more than unfortunate if this country were to make this same mistake. If, for example, we were to follow the European inclination and confirm our vertical-dominant heavyweights in their present strategies by freezing them into nationalized or seminationalized entities, their performance level would probably remain abysmally low. Indeed, it might even sink to levels so low that these institutions would have to turn to the government for financial support, as more than one of our railroads have already had to do.

Even if they are not nationalized, but merely left to themselves, we can only expect the dominant heavyweights to turn in the lowest level of performance, and to continue to overinvest large amounts of capital which might be much better employed elsewhere.

Diversification through Antitrust
What I should like to suggest for these raw-materials processors is that the government, as a matter of public policy, encourage them to reach a higher level of performance. To do this, these companies must of course outgrow the one-industry mentality.

As I have previously pointed out, some are already beginning to do so. This promising development might be encouraged by offering these companies profit and growth opportunities in new areas, areas promising enough to compete with their perpetual need to keep on investing in their traditional areas to maintain their market positions. Further, as a matter of policy, the dominant verticals should be encouraged to avail themselves of these areas of possible diversification, by law and by incentives. Diversification could bring a new and more market-oriented way of life to these one-eyed giants.

Yet there are only three routes a dominant vertical can take toward diversification: internal diversification, acquisition, and absorption into another company. The first route is slow, because these companies have so few transferable skills to build on. The third is anathema, since it means loss of control.

The second, the acquisition route, is guarded if not blocked by the antitrust policy enforced by the Justice Department. Here, then, is an area where the Justice Department might well reconsider its policy and *encourage* some of our one-eyed giants to diversity (even by acquisition) so they do not wind up like the meat packers, the coal companies, the railroads, and the other lumbering colossi who have allowed themselves to be bypassed by the industrial system.

This suggestion may be unwelcome to the Justice Department. But if this country is not to add to its proportion of industrial dinosaurs—its inflexible, capital-hungry heavyweights—then public policy must offer the dominant vertical a new option; and perhaps the best one available is the option of diversifying by acquisition in return, say, for scrapping segments of existing capacity. This kind of quid pro quo would encourage competition and diversity of strategy in the broadest sense.

Diversification, however—even related diversification—is not a complete answer, by any means. In addition to encouraging diversification, we need to sharpen the market mechanism as it applies to these companies, and let that mechanism do the work of regulating and correcting their operations.

Under favorable conditions of this kind, the inner dynamics of the corporation will fall into line; for once a company has diversified into related and more profitable areas, it will face an *internal* competition for funds among its businesses, where the new, higher-profit activities compete with the old.

Environmental Control

The same general principle would work in other areas as well. Consider pollution control, for example. Companies that pollute the air, land, or water can be taxed "by the pound"; and if necessary the tax can be made progressive. Companies that generate garbage through their packaging could be made to pay a tax proportional to the difficulty of finally disposing of this packaging. For those producers whose products themselves become unsightly garbage, such as the automobile manufacturers, a sliding scale of taxes could be worked to favor those automobiles that last longer.

Thus there is indeed an alternative to nationalizing our large companies, or adding to the number of economists and government agencies already regulating them. My analysis suggests that we reshape some of the market forces to make better use of the skill, sensitivity, and flexibility of the large corporation in its diversified, divisionalized form. That way, public policy would be working *with* the natural evolution of the corporate form, not against it. Our industrial economists could perhaps render valuable service here by showing us how to make better use of those forces. This would at least give them a change of pace from prescribing bureaucratic rules and regulations, which, on some occasions, turn out to have remarkably little relevance to the problems at hand.

To recapitulate: while I believe that we ought to continue to take advantage of the market mechanism, I am far from regarding it as a cure-all in itself. As the U.S. economy becomes more and more complex, adjustments must be made so the market mechanism will function smoothly. Public values should be built into it through special taxation, for example, and some kinds of activity must be encouraged or discouraged. Otherwise, the modern industrial state cannot continue to harness effectively the energy of its leading corporations.

The alternative is to allow economists to substitute their energy and planning skills for those of the modern corporation. I question whether they are equal to this task. After all, the data presented in this article show that some of our illustrious economists are planning today for the industrial state of 30 years ago, rather than the new industrial state that is actually emerging.

New Dinosaurs in LDCs

If Galbraith's conclusions are out of date for the developed economies, they are still more unfortunate when applied in the less developed nations. In such countries they are frequently used as a rationale for heavy investments in prestige projects in basic industries such as steel and petrochemicals— the industries that give the lowest returns, not only in profitability but also in employment per dollar invested.

One can expect these investments to have a far lower economic return in most of these countries than in the United States—where they already enjoy the lowest level of any major group.

The economic performance of the dominant verticals in the United States is conditioned by the fact that most have a solid competitive position in a *very large home market*. Through long traditions of so-called industrial statesmanship, these companies' prices remain relatively stable even under conditions of overcapacity. In the steel industry, for example, prices increase regularly despite excess capacity. As a result, while already at the bottom, their economic performance would be still lower if prices more nearly reflected supply and demand conditions.

The less developed countries are characterized by small markets— small not only in terms of population but in terms of purchasing power. Yet to achieve the economies of scale so touted by economists and production managers, these same countries are and have been investing their scarce resources in very large projects in "basic industry." To utilize the new capacity at anything above nominal rates, they must sell a substantial share of the output in export markets. And here is the tragedy.

When selling this new production abroad, these countries must compete with the excess capacity dumped by others. Since the production is largely of a commodity nature, price competition is a critical element in making such sales. As a result, the developing countries often find a new project must dump, not its *marginal* output, but perhaps even half or more of total production, with the result that the project yields a very low return or even a sizable loss.

Some would argue that such projects earn foreign exchange. However, they do so in industries in which one can buy at favorable prices, thanks to dumping by others.

Some would also argue that these projects are valuable economically because they spawn other, smaller industry; they are often justified as a necessary backbone for a modern industrial state. No doubt there is some validity to this argument, but this validity lies essentially on the production side and ignores the context of the modern industrial state as a whole.

It ignores, for example, the fact that the developed nations have, by and large, the most equal distribution of income and hence the broadest public participation in the marketplace and the widest sharing of the fruits of economic progress. In the low-income economies (with the notable exception of Japan) large segments of the population characteristically are excluded from the money economy and barely share in the progress economists so crudely measure in units of "GNP per capita."

Partly as a consequence of the Galbraith viewpoint, one finds governments in the LDCs concentrating on large and showy, but very low-return, projects, while paying little attention to the distribution of income and other essential services necessary to the development of a healthy, stable society. Public officials enjoy the splendor of the new technology; misery and revolution breed in the countryside.

Let me conclude with these observations. The Galbraith viewpoint perceives the industrial state in terms of production concepts rather than marketing concepts, both for the major countries of the industrialized West and for the less developed countries. Hence it misunderstands the real dynamics of economic evolution. So far as the LDCs are concerned, its great shortcoming is that it retards true economic growth. For the developed economies, the prescriptions it offers have all the advantages of a "new" battle plan for winning World War I.

Notes

1. J. K. Galbraith, *The New Industrial State* (Boston, Houghton Mifflin), 1967.

2. Ibid., 2nd edition, pp. xxi–xxii.

3. Ibid., 1st edition, p. 38; 2nd edition, p. 26.

4. Alfred D. Chandler, *Strategy and Structure* (Cambridge, M.I.T. Press), 1962, Chapter 1.

5. See, for example, John McArthur and Bruce R. Scott, *Industrial Planning in France* (Division of Research, Harvard Business School, 1969), Chapter 4.

6. Leonard Wrigley, *Divisional Autonomy and Diversification* (unpublished DBA dissertation, Harvard Business School, 1970); see also Norman Berg's "Strategic Planning in Conglomerate Companies," *HBR*, May–June, 1965.

7. Derek F. Channon, *Strategy and Structure of British Enterprise* (unpublished DBA dissertation, Harvard Business School, 1971).

Appendix: Research on Industrial Development

This article represents a progress report on Industrial Development and Public Policy, a continuing research program of the Harvard Business School for which the author has direct responsibility. This program dates back roughly a decade, to the formulation of an explicit model of the stages of corporate development.

The program has used two basic methods:

1 Traditional case studies, based on intensive field research, to increase our understanding of the structural changes that are associated with growth and diversification.
2 Analyses of trends in the changes in the population of corporations, through both field and library research.

Both approaches were demonstrated simultaneously in a published study, *Industrial Planning in France,* which analyzed the strategies of some 50 French companies, as well as the industrial-development strategy of the French government.

Company case studies have been selected from France, Germany, Sweden, Switzerland, and the United Kingdom, as well as the United States. In addition, the case studies and writings of Professor Norman Berg have had an important role in this research, particularly in distinguishing among various classes of diversified companies.* The population studies include two analyses of the *Fortune* "500," one in 1969 by Leonard Wrigley and a second in 1972 by Richard Rumelt, each as the basis for a Doctor of Business Administration dissertation. In addition, they include studies of the top 100 companies in the United Kingdom, in France, in Germany, and in Italy, each also undertaken as DBA theses topics.

The present article presents findings based on the explicit analysis of strategy and structure of over 200 of the *Fortune* "500" industrials in the United States and over 300 of the largest industrials of Western Europe.

*See "Strategic Planning in Conglomerate Companies," *HBR*, May–June 1965, p. 79.

Let's Stop Eating Our Seed Corn

LAWRENCE REVSINE

In a world of economic uncertainty, there is a demand for bold solutions to complex problems. Once these solutions are put forth and endorsed by experts, the public tends simply to sit back and watch what happens. Little time is spent analyzing possible consequences.

One such solution is the FASB's approach to inflation accounting. While the author believes that the FASB's approach is a step in the right direction, he also argues that the latitude permitted by the FASB in defining and presenting inflation-adjusted income may have dangerous long-term consequences. He feels the FASB's approach does not necessarily stress maintenance of physical capacity. Because of this, even adjusted profits may appear "obscene" to the public. This perception may well influence legislation and regulation—with the result that corporations will not be able to husband enough resources for future development. The author believes his alternative could generate much better results in the long term.

Because of the prevailing gloom in current economic headlines, it is easy to forget that these same headlines portrayed 1979 as a year of record corporate profitability. And once a recovery gets under way, it should not be long before we are deluged by another flood of optimism.

But the optimism will be misplaced. Inflation renders much of the so-called profit heralded by the headlines nonexistent. Because past costs are much lower than current costs, the traditional historical cost assumption used by accountants creates the illusion of prosperity—particularly for capital-intensive companies with older assets.

For example, the Commerce Department estimates that profits reported in 1979 were overstated by approximately 50% due to inflation. In individual

Published 1981.

cases distortions can be even more extreme; after eliminating the effects of price increases, Southern New England Telephone's 1979 income from continuing operations was a full 92.4% less than the traditional profit number.

But it is the illusory profits that seem to have the greatest impact on the general public, legislators, and policymakers. In the words of SEC Chairman Harold Williams, this situation "leads . . . to [misguided] demands . . . to moderate these profits." Most important, since taxes are also based on the illusory figures, retained profits are already inadequate to maintain existing productive capability in certain industries.

As the 1979 annual report of the Dillingham Corporation points out: "Under present laws the effective tax rate has risen to confiscatory levels, resulting in after-tax earnings that are insufficient to replace assets, provide a positive return to shareowners and generate the cash required for growth. As the new methods of inflation accounting indicate . . . our 1979 effective tax rate rises from 46% in the conventional statement to . . . 89% using the current cost method." And the imposition of new taxes (like that on windfall oil profits) worsens the capital formation crisis and could threaten the very survival of essential business sectors.

Financial decision makers are trying to help alter this trend by providing Congress, policymakers, and the general public with more relevant accounting data; some even view the FASB's recent inflation accounting statement as a solution in itself.[1] But that oversimplifies matters. The many forms of inflation accounting do not necessarily highlight the real inflation-induced threat to productive capacity. Some systems even ignore the issue—and if used may make things worse by stimulating restrictive taxes and regulations.

This article evaluates the threat to business's survival when inappropriate inflation-adjusted income numbers are used as a basis for national policy decisions. It counters the mistaken impression that a simple move to inflation accounting protects business capacity. It also outlines features of a system designed both to forestall potentially dangerous legislative and regulatory actions and to provide a more realistic picture to policymakers.

Where to Begin?

Accounting statements are used as a basis for regulation and help shape the public's opinion about business. A good financial reporting system should give accurate data about the economic performance of individual companies, thus promoting economic strength. It should neither report illusory profits nor hide excessive returns.

To develop this type of system, the focus must shift from income to capital. This is not especially difficult, since any framework for accounting income is linked conceptually to maintenance of capital. For example, income is usually defined as the maximum amount of inflow during a period that can be consumed without dipping into the start-of-period capital. More succinctly, income is what remains after the company has set aside enough resources to preserve its starting capital position.

This immediately raises the question of how the starting capital position ought to be defined. In other words, what capital should we, as an economy, attempt to maintain? There are essentially two options: (1) maintenance of *physical* capital and (2) maintenance of *dollar* capital.

The choice between these two options is an important one since the alternatives lead back to profoundly different views of income—views that affect public policy in very different ways. Ideally, what we are looking for is a system that can adjust income for inflation at the same time that it stimulates the most desirable economic and social policy actions.

Physical Capital Maintenance

To understand the basic characteristics of the physical capital-maintenance approach, consider the following situation:

On January 1, 1980, a company owned two units of inventory with a total historical cost (and current value) of $40. It also had two fixed assets with a total historical cost book value (and current value) of $150. One fixed asset was new; the other, one year old. Each cost $100, had a two-year life, and experienced a straight-line decline in service potential. The company's balance sheet on that date is presented here. On January 2, 1980, the replacement costs of the fixed assets increased by 10%; the new asset then cost $110 and the one-year-old asset, $55. These new fixed asset prices remained in effect during 1980.

Assets			Equities	
Inventory		$ 40		
Fixed assets	$200			
Less: accumulated depreciation	(50)			
		150	Owners' equity	$190
		$190		$190

On December 31, 1980, the replacement cost of the inventory was $24 per unit. The company sold one unit of inventory on December 31, 1980, for $150—which was received in cash on that date.

We also assume that the company wished to distribute a cash dividend equal to 100% of its "income" (however defined).

Given these data, current cost financial statements that are prepared using the *physical* capital-maintenance assumption look like the statements in Exhibit 1.

Under the physical capital-maintenance approach to inflation accounting, income equals $16. This number, called "current cost income from continuing operations" is one of the disclosures now required by the FASB.[2]

Exhibit 1. Current Cost Financial Statements Physical capital maintenance

Statement of income and retained earnings
Year ended December 31, 1980

Sales revenues		$150
Current cost of goods sold	24	
Current cost depreciation expense ($110 ÷ 2) + 55]	110	134
Current cost income from continuing operations		16
Holding gain" (a direct credit to retained earnings – *not* income); inventory, $8 + fixed assets, $15		23
Dividend paid (100% of income from continuing operations)		(16)
Net addition to owners' equity		$ 23

Statement of financial position
December 31, 1980

Assets			Equities	
Cash		$134		
Inventory		24	Owners' equity:	
Fixed asset	$110		January 1, 1980 balance	$190
Less: accumulated depreciation	(55)	55	Addition during 1980	23
		$213		$213

To understand the physical capital-maintenance view, it is important to understand precisely why income is considered to be $16:

☐ The company started 1980 with two units of inventory and two fixed assets (one that is new and one that is one year old). Thus the starting capital position is defined in physical terms.

☐ Units of inventory cost $24 each on December 31, 1980; and, when new, fixed assets cost $110 each (they cost $55 after one year).

☐ If "income" of $16 is "consumed" (paid as a dividend), there is $134 left of the original inflow from sales revenues ($150 cash inflow minus the $16 dividend).

☐ The $134 retained is precisely equal to the amount needed to purchase another unit of inventory and another fixed asset (to replace the one asset that wore out during 1980): 24 + 110 = 134.

☐ If this is done, the company will once again have two units of inventory and two fixed assets (one that is new and one that is one year old). Notice that this is precisely equal to its start-of-period capital position expressed in physical terms.

☐ Thus a dividend of $16 (equal to 100% of current cost income from continuing operations) allows the company to begin its next year of operations at the same physical capital level as it did the year before.

Notice that here income exists only after a company generates sufficient resources to maintain the level of physical capacity at which it started.

Dollar Capital Maintenance

If we look at the previous example from the dollar capital-maintenance approach, current cost financial statements look like Exhibit 2.

In order to understand what capital is being preserved in the dollar capital-maintenance approach, it is necessary to explain why income is considered to be $39. The analysis proceeds as follows:

☐   The company started 1980 with assets that had an aggregate market value of $190. Thus, the starting capital position is defined in dollar (rather than physical) terms.

☐   If "income" of $39 is "consumed," this will retain $111 of the original inflow from sales revenues ($150 cash inflow minus the $39 dividend).

☐   The $111 holdback can then be used to purchase an additional $111 of assets (for example, one new fixed asset for $110 and 1/24th of a unit of inventory for $1). Asset purchases totaling $111 (in any configuration) would again leave the company with assets having an aggregate market value of $190 ($111 + 55 [fixed asset] + 24 [inventory]), which is precisely equal to its start-of-period market value of assets.

☐   Thus, a dividend of $39 (equal to 100% of total current cost income) allows the company to reestablish its start-of-period capital position, defined in dollar terms—that is, nominal dollar market value.

Exhibit 2.   Current Cost Financial Statements

Dollar capital maintenance

Statement of income and retained earnings
year ended December 31, 1980

Sales revenues		$150
Current cost of goods sold	24	
Current cost depreciation expense [($110 ÷ 2) + 55]	110	134
Current cost income from continuing operations		16
"Holding gain" (an income component in this concept); inventory, $8 + fixed assets, $15		23
Total current cost income		39
Dividend paid (100% of total current cost income)		(39)
Net addition to owners' equity		**$ 0**

Statement of financial position
December 31, 1980

Assets			Equities	
Cash		$111		
Inventory		24	Owners' equity:	
Fixed asset	$110		January 1, 1980 balance	$190
Less: accumulated depreciation	(55)	55	Addition during 1980	0
		$190		**$190**

Note: FASB Statement No. 33 computes the "holding gain" (which the FASB calls "increases or decreases in current cost amounts") net of overall inflation. For expository ease, I ignore this complication since it does not affect my analysis or conclusions. In Statement No. 33, this holding gain number is not directly added to current cost income from continuing operations, but the FASB does indicate that such cost changes are an element of income in a dollar capital-maintenance approach.

Consequences of the Alternatives

The choice of physical or dollar capital maintenance, as the example illustrates, determines what number one gets for current cost income ($16 or $39). In Statement No. 33, the FASB explicitly chose not to express a preference for either concept. Instead, companies are simply required to disclose holding gains on assets next to the figure for income from continuing operations. Whether these gains are to be included in total income (the dollar capital-maintenance approach) or excluded (the physical capital-maintenance approach) is left to the discretion of the reporting companies and the readers of their financial statements. This latitude may prove disastrous in the long term since the messages conveyed by each approach differ radically and could thus elicit divergent policy responses. To illustrate, consider what happens if the company in the example decides to distribute a $39 dividend—the amount of income shown in Exhibit 2 for the dollar capital-maintenance approach. After paying a $39 dividend:

☐ The amount of cash left over ($111) is only sufficient to buy, say, one new fixed asset and 1/24th of a unit of inventory at year-end prices.

☐ While the company has indeed maintained the market value of its assets at $190, in physical terms its assets have been reduced.

☐ This means that the remaining productive capacity is insufficient to maintain the previous level of physical operations.

Current cost income based on the dollar capital-maintenance concept could thus result in a level of consumption (not just dividends but also taxes and adverse regulatory decisions) that decreases the company's future capacity to produce real goods and services. This result arises because holding gains (increases in beginning-of-the-period market values) are treated as income in a dollar capital approach. But, as Exhibit 1 shows, holding gains cannot be consumed or taxed away without diminishing future productive capacity.

If the public believes that these holding gains constitute real income, legislative and regulatory pressures may be exerted to eliminate them; but confiscating these holding gains reduces the productive capacity of business. From a social standpoint, any payout of holding gains—as dividends, taxes, or whatever—is tantamount to eating our seed corn.

In contrast, current cost income based on a physical capital-maintenance concept considers income to exist only insofar as inflows exceed the amount needed to maintain physical productive capacity. This figure for current cost income is the more relevant yardstick for national policy decisions because only by maintaining existing production potential do we provide an undiminished opportunity for future inflows and future prosperity.

Windfall Profits Tax

Many recent taxation and regulatory debates reveal a widespread misunderstanding about the nature of holding gains. Consider the controversy about the windfall profits tax on oil. Part of the reason that the oil companies' profits appeared excessive to the public is because these profits were measured on a historical cost basis and are distorted by inflation.

Using our previous example, notice that historical cost profit would be $30 (revenues of $150 minus original costs of $20 for inventory and $100 for fixed assets) which is $14 greater than current cost income computed on a physical capital-maintenance basis. This $14 difference consists of realized holding gains. That is, the historical cost profit number includes $4 of realized holding gain on the unit of inventory actually sold during the period (the cost increased from $20 on January 1, 1980 to $24 on December 31, 1980) and $10 of realized holding gain on the two fixed assets. (The cost increase for fixed assets was $10 on the new asset and $5 on the old asset. Since the new asset was depleted by 50% and the old one totally "consumed," $10 of fixed asset holding gains are implicitly "realized" under traditional historical cost accounting.)

The historical cost method automatically includes realized holding gains on assets sold or used in the bottom-line number and does not differentiate between these "holding gains" and income from continuing operations.

The effect is anything but trivial. Here's an illustration: Mobil Corporation reported that in 1979 39% of its third quarter historical-cost earnings increase from foreign sources was attributable to holding gains on inventory. But that's not all. The cost of replacing fixed productive capacity also keeps increasing; and the impact is cumulative since fixed assets have long lives. Accurate adjustments for the additional overstatement due to fixed asset holding gains are harder to come by, but undoubtedly the distortion is considerable. For example, Shell Oil Company's 1979 ratio of income from continuing operations to shareholders' equity declined from 18.4% on a historical cost basis to 5.1% on a physical capital-maintenance basis (after eliminating illusory holding gains on both inventory and fixed assets).

As Exhibit 1 shows, holding gains must be retained within the company to maintain physical capital. If these "gains" are taxed away, Congress essentially confiscates a portion of productive capacity. Since remaining resources are insufficient to start the cycle again, a tax on holding gains—which is essentially what the windfall profits tax is—really represents a tax on capital. (The fact that the tax, as finally enacted, is an excise rather than an income tax makes this a little harder to see but does not change the ultimate economic effect.)

Is this tax consistent with the expressed policy of encouraging greater domestic energy investment? Clearly not. After paying the tax, companies that want to reestablish their previous level of operating capacity would require an infusion of new outside capital just to put themselves back where they started from. But new capital will be more expensive since the windfall profits tax reduces real profitability.[3]

Such legislation could easily worsen an already difficult energy situation. Furthermore, even a move to inflation accounting won't automatically solve the problem of oil companies' illusory profits. Only if inflation-adjusted income is based on a physical capital-maintenance concept will holding gains be excluded from income. Only then can legislators, regulators, and the general public get financial data that are relevant for evaluating social policy issues.

Far-Reaching Impact

The side effects of dollar capital maintenance afflict all U.S. enterprises, not just oil companies. Evidence raises the disturbing possibility that many capital-intensive companies may be dissipating productive capacity. For example, approximately one-third of the 30 Dow-Jones industrials are estimated to have paid dividends in excess of their current cost income from continuing operations in each of the years 1976, 1977, and 1978.[4]

The problem is reduced only slightly for less capital-intensive companies. For example, American Hospital Supply Corporation made the following disclosure in its 1979 annual report: "Cash dividends paid in 1979 were 26% of reported net earnings. The payout was . . . 81% of net earnings adjusted for changes in specific prices [that is, current cost income from continuing operations]." Thus, after adjustment for inflation, income holdbacks are far lower than the reassuringly comfortable percentages often cited.

Additional erosion of productive capacity occurs because of regular corporate income taxes as well. As Koppers noted in its 1979 annual report: "[Inflation accounting] does suggest the significant hidden impacts of income taxes in periods of high inflation and the adverse effects on a company's ability to retain earnings to meet the escalating cost of replacing and expanding its productive capacity. It therefore emphasizes the need to reconsider national tax policies in order to give recognition to the reality of inflation."

These adverse tax effects arise because the existing tax laws are based on historical cost income and thus automatically include realized holding gains in taxable income. Since "holding gains" must be retained within the company to maintain physical productive capacity, taxing any portion of these so-called gains runs the risk of reducing future productive capabilities. Furthermore, these effects do not fall equally on all. The real tax burden tends to be higher for capital-intensive companies with relatively older assets, raising the potential for subtle but significant redistributions in favor of service-oriented industries.

Physical capital maintenance is also an especially important concept in regulated industries where rates must be high enough to ensure continuation of the regulated service. But if regulators treat holding gains as income, then rate relief is less likely and long-term physical capital maintenance is endangered.

The Role of Debt

One frequently advanced argument is that companies benefit from having outstanding debt during inflation; thus some contend that a gain on debt must be included in the determination of inflation-adjusted income. Doing so offsets, to a degree, the adverse effects on profitability; when these gains on debt are added in, inflation appears much less damaging.

Because of this factor, some people have resisted accounting and tax reforms since "things aren't as bad as inflation accounting makes them appear to be." Nor has the FASB settled the issue. According to Statement No. 33, the gains on debt must be disclosed but do not have to be included in the determination of total income.

Our previous discussion helps to resolve the controversy over debt. The key question becomes: Is a business in a better physical capital position because it issued debt in a period of inflation? Clearly not. To see why, return to the example for which I drew up the statements in the exhibits.

Assume that all facts are the same but one. Assume that the company was financed with $100 of debt and $90 of equity on January 1, 1980. Further assume that overall inflation was 10% during 1980. Following FASB 33, we report a gain on debt of $10 ($100 of book value times 10% inflation) to reflect the fact that the debt will be paid back with "cheaper" dollars. What's important to understand, however, is that the so-called gain on debt simply doesn't exist under a physical capital-maintenance concept. That is, the $10 "gain" is not income in a physical capital view and cannot legitimately be added to the $16 of current cost income from continuing operations, as some would have us do.

The proof is straightforward. If we treated the so-called gain on debt as income, the new income figure would be $26—that is, $16 from Exhibit 1 plus $10 of "gain on debt." (For simplicity, interest on the debt is ignored. This simplification does not affect the conclusion.) Given our assumption of a 100% dividend payout, the ending cash balance would be $124. But since it now takes a total of $134 to replace the unit of inventory ($24) and one fixed asset ($110), a payout of $26 does not allow the firm to maintain its original physical capital.

The "shortage" is $10, precisely equal to the "gain on debt." In other words, this $10 cannot be income in a physical capital-maintenance sense. If we treat this item as income to the entity, we would face the risk of taxing away resources that are needed internally to maintain physical productive capacity.

(Some people might argue that this $10 of "extra" payout may be recouped by issuing additional debt. Unfortunately, this misses the entire point of physical capital maintenance. That is, amounts that are needed within the corporation in order to maintain productive potential shouldn't be taxed away in the first place! What is the rationale for instituting an income measure that could force companies to reshuffle their financing in order to stay even?)

To summarize, if the policy objective is to maintain physical capital, then there is no such thing as an inflation gain on debt. Those who argue otherwise are implicitly adopting a dollar capital-maintenance view of income, a view that could easily lead to decreases in productive capability.

The Downward Spiral

Given the enormous social impact of accounting numbers, there is some truth to the old adage that "accounting is far too important to be left solely in the hands of accountants." I feel we urgently need a reporting system that will provide accurate information about real underlying performance. Whether industry is maintaining its existing production capacity is crucially important to America's future.

Inflation accounting provides useful data for social policy decisions only if physical capital maintenance governs the preparation of reports. While the two options—"physical" and "dollar"—use the same measurement techniques, they classify certain items differently and result in different final income figures. Do not underestimate the importance of this difference. At stake is the entire question of how corporate performance is communicated to legislators, regulators, and to the public. How these groups see corporations' profit situations in turn influences whether they try to dampen or brighten the business climate.

If holding gains on assets or gains on debt are treated by accountants as an element of income, it is difficult for most people to see just how severely businesses are suffering from inflation. Under the dollar capital approach, we run the risk of taxing and otherwise distributing resources that must be retained within the business in order to maintain productive capacity.

The physical capital view considers maintenance of productive capacity to be of utmost importance. In this view, income exists only after continuation of physical capital is ensured; thus, neither asset-holding gains nor gains on debt are counted as income.

An economy's performance can be monitored intelligently only if policymakers and the public have a clear idea of what is happening to its long-term productive capability. When financial reports convey the message more accurately, a climate will be created in which the problem can be resolved. Then policymakers will be encouraged to formulate laws that allow the nation's economy to build for the future rather than to inadvertently consume existing capital.

Notes

1. Financial Accounting Standards Board, "Statement of Financial Accounting Standards No. 33: Financial Reporting and Changing Prices" (Stamford, Conn., September 1979).

2. Financial Accounting Standards Board Statement No. 33, 1979, p. 11; the physical capital-maintenance concept was also explored in a slightly different context by Richard F. Vancil, "Inflation Accounting—The Great Controversy," *HBR*, March–April 1976, p. 58; and in my book, *Replacement Cost Accounting* (Englewood Cliffs, N.J., Prentice-Hall, 1973).

3.   On this point also see Paul Craig Roberts, ''The Windfall Illusion,'' *Wall Street Journal*, November 28, 1979.

4.   These estimates are from Sidney Davidson and Roman L. Weil, ''Excerpts from Estimated Financial Statements Complying with FASB Statement No. 33 for the Dow-Jones Industrials'' (unpublished manuscript, University of Chicago, 1980).

9

Can More Capital Buy Higher Productivity?

BRADLEY T. GALE

By now, corporate managers may be tiring of the debate that has been swirling around the question of declining U.S. productivity, a debate that has generated much discussion but few practical or new suggestions for a turnaround. Often, companies have injected capital into declining industries to improve their own productivity levels without achieving any long-term, tangible objectives. According to the Strategic Planning Institute (SPI), part of the problem may be a lack of analytic tools available to top management. Instead of relegating improvement of productivity to line managers, SPI feels, top management must decide for itself where capital should be allocated. To that end, SPI is using its data base comprised of confidential information culled from more than 200 member companies to help solve the problem. In this article, the research director of SPI offers companies practical guidelines and formulas for more accurate productivity measurement and better linking of strategic planning to capital allocation.

Whether you are a manager or an economist, you know about the mounting evidence of declining productivity in the United States. In fact, signs suggest that the need for productivity improvement may be our most pressing domestic economic problem—and our most difficult to solve. But before we

Published 1980.

Editor's note: HBR readers have benefited from the SPI approach to management problems before. "Impact of Strategic Planning on Profit Performance," by Sidney Schoeffler, Robert D. Buzzell, and Donald F. Heany, was published in March–April 1974, p. 137; and "Market Share—A Key to Profitability," by Robert D. Buzzell, Bradley T. Gale, and Ralph G.M. Sultan, appeared in the January–February 1975 issue, p. 97.

can tackle it, we first need to find a useful way to measure operating effectiveness. If we can't accurately establish which businesses are falling behind and why, then we can't sensibly determine corrective actions.

Out of a desire to do something, business and government have promoted solutions: shop-level approaches that require cost cutting, efficiency experts, stringent controls, and behavior modification—or mechanization/automation programs aimed at increasing labor productivity, lowering costs, and boosting margins. Very frequently, not knowing the cause of the illness—in fact not even having correctly identified the patient—we prescribe medicine whose effects are at best dissipated and at worst cause havoc.

Rather than haphazardly funding individual projects, management needs to determine which businesses have the strategic characteristics that make them good candidates for mechanization. Even more important, management needs to know which businesses are poor candidates for mechanization. With appropriate measurement tools, strategic planning can be linked to the capital allocation process, and companies can avoid both unproductive investments and investments that gain output per employee but at excessive costs.

Many companies delegate the problem of productivity improvement to operating managers who are "close to the action." Although it is important to involve them, this focus is narrow; it misses the essential links among productivity improvement, strategic planning, and capital allocation. A broader approach involving key decision makers and long-term planning seems essential.

Rather than evaluating investment in new equipment as a simple choice between increased capital costs and reduced labor costs, management needs to consider the long-term consequences of mechanization. Increased investment always affects the competitive climate; in the short run, it almost invariably reduces ROI (return on net plant and equipment and working capital). But the long-run outcome depends on how a business is structured within its own economic environment.

The Strategic Planning Institute in Cambridge, Massachusetts, has used its data base to develop guidelines for businesses contemplating new investments to increase productivity (see the appendix). These guidelines offer managers some practical advice for their own businesses by focusing on the following key questions:

- [ ] Which businesses should be allowed to mechanize-automate?
- [ ] Is a business's output per employee above or below par?
- [ ] How is operating effectiveness best measured?
- [ ] When do shop-level approaches to labor productivity pay off?
- [ ] How can sound portfolio management improve capital and labor productivity?

Which Businesses Should Automate Further?

The SPI data base offers empirical support for the belief that labor output can be increased by investing more capital equipment per worker. But it also tells us that labor output is influenced by other factors: a high market share or a high level of capacity utilization helps to boost labor output; unionization and new product introduction, on the other hand, tend to reduce it.

To monitor and control productivity, we must first be able to measure it. But that is not simple. Different productivity measures are needed for different purposes. They range from engineering concepts of efficiency (physical units of output per physical unit of input) to financial concepts of profitability (total revenues to total costs). And between these extremes are measures such as unit labor costs (dollars of input per unit of output) and labor output (value added per unit of input).

Most managers are familiar with Murphy's law: "If it can go wrong, it will." When it comes to measuring productivity, a less-known corollary, Howe's law, is equally compelling: "Every man has a scheme that will not work." At SPI, we prefer to use the concept of value added, which represents the amount that purchased raw materials and components increase in value when they have been converted into the products of the business or—stated another way—a firm's sales minus its purchases. Dividing value added by the number of employees gives a measure of labor output that is comparable across businesses. In addition, it reflects both the physical output of each worker and the value of that output.

The concept of value added per employee is not designed to measure every aspect of productivity. But it *is* designed to enable multibusiness general managers to compare both the level and the rate of change in output per employee across their portfolios. The value-added concept is applied in a way that takes capital (as well as labor) inputs into account and also links productivity improvement to profitability through strategic planning and sound capital allocation.

The various businesses included in the SPI data base show a wide distribution of value added per employee. Across the large sample, businesses register from less than $10,000 to more than $60,000.

Productivity and Profitability

As might be expected, we have found that fixed investment increases labor output. Yet, even though investment in equipment to automate production does allow each worker to add greater amounts of value, mechanization is *not* an all-purpose panacea for problems in labor output. For most businesses, unfortunately, we have also found that increased investment intensity reduces profitability.

The explanation for this disquieting relationship is not merely arithmetic. There are several good reasons why investment intensity hurts ROI:

☐ Increasing investment can lead to aggressive competition, especially when economic conditions worsen and plant and equipment are only partially used. The resulting pressure to use capacity can explode into price and marketing wars.

☐ Heavy fixed investment acts as a barrier to *exit*. When the business cycle turns down or when the real growth rate of an industry declines, investment-intensive businesses are hurt the most. (Heavy investment intensity does not represent a barrier to *entry*, because investment is measured as a ratio to employees, not as an absolute amount of investment required.)

☐ Managers sometimes focus on a normal return on sales, forgetting the heavier than normal investment per dollar of sales required for some projects. A normal return on sales combined with a greater than normal amount of investment per dollar of sales yields a lower return on investment.

There are many examples of investment-intensive, low-profit businesses—commodity paper, chemical and steel products, to name a few. For the average business (neither a good nor a bad mechanization candidate), ROI will fall with increased investment in mechanization.

Even with this likelihood, such an investment may still be desirable. Those projects that indicate a negative net prospect for percentage ROI often promise a favorable one for dollar results because the lower percentage is applied to a larger investment base. In such cases, it seems that management faces a difficult decision: it must choose between increased sales and dollar profits on the one hand and a decreased rate of profitability on the other.

But our findings also show that certain conditions—a large market share, low rate of new product introduction, and good capacity utilization (see Exhibit 1)—enhance the benefits of investment intensity and alleviate the threats to profitability and thus help ease management's task.

Relative Market Share

Relative market share has a positive effect on value added per employee. A large share relative to competitors usually allows greater labor specialization and economies of scale within the business, resulting in increased efficiency. Large-share businesses also enjoy economies of cumulative volume, which reduce unit costs by the experience-curve effect and by spreading set-up costs over a longer production run.

At first glance, it seems that higher investment greatly helps value added per employee, regardless of whether market share is large or small (see Exhibit 2). For large-share businesses, the difference in value added

Exhibit 1. Some Businesses Are Good Candidates for Mechanization; Others Are Not

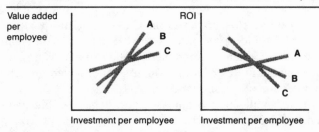

A: Good candidate for mechanization (high share, low rate of new product introduction, good capacity utilization, rapid real market growth, etc.)

B: Average business

C: Poor candidate (low share, high rate of new product introduction, low capacity utilization, negative real market growth, etc.)

Exhibit 2. (a) High-Share Businesses Get a Bigger Output Boost from Heavy Investment; (b) High-Share Businesses Are Better Able to Maintain ROI, No Matter How Investment Intensive

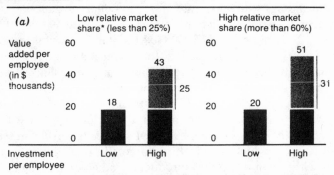

*Note: Relative market share is defined as a business's share of its served market divided by the combined shares of its three largest competitors.

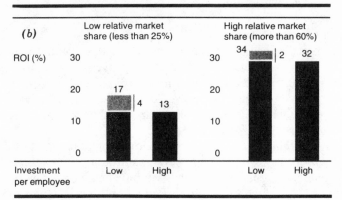

between high-investment and low-investment businesses ($51,000 minus $20,000) is $31,000. For small-share businesses the comparable difference is $25,000. However, closer inspection shows that the positive effect of investment on value added is greater when the market share is large. Moreover, this greater increment of value added allows large-share businesses to sustain their very high rates of return on investment even though they have much more investment per employee at stake.

In contrast, small-share businesses do not have a big enough value-added increment to prevent their already low rate of profit from being lowered further by investment intensity. The average ROI of small-share businesses that are investment intensive is about 25% lower than those that are not investment intensive—13% versus 17% (see Exhibit 2).

Rate of New Product Introduction

New product introduction is usually associated with a reduction in labor output and profits (Exhibit 3). Manufacturing a new product often requires reorganizing the production process. New methods of production must be perfected and learned by workers, so downtime and waste tend to be greater during the early life of a product.

For businesses with a low rate of new product introduction, the value-added differential between high-investment and low-investment businesses is $32,000, or $49,000 minus $17,000 (see Exhibit 3). For businesses with a high rate of new product introduction, the corresponding differential is only $21,000, probably because the effectiveness of a mechanized production system is disrupted by the continuous appearance of new products.

Even though they have more investment at stake, businesses with a low rate of new product introduction get a large enough boost from value added to allow them to sustain their ROI. In contrast, businesses with a high rate of new product introduction do not. In fact, the average ROI of businesses with a high rate of new product introduction and high investment per employee is about 30% lower than that of low-investment businesses—17% versus 24% (see Exhibit 3).

Other Influences

While the preceding variables may carry the greatest weight in determining a particular business's relative capacity to improve its productivity, other—perhaps less tangible—factors can affect its chance of success as well, including the degree of unionization, capacity utilization, real market growth, and the extent to which its product lines are standardized or made to order.

Heavy Unionization: This often leads to low profitability and labor output, perhaps by work rules that inhibit production and by impediments to the rate of technological change. Frequently, unions bargain for work rules that result in slower production or lower production quotas. Unions also resist

Exhibit 3. **(a) Businesses with a Low Rate of New Product Introduction Get a Bigger Output Boost from Heavy Investment; (b) Among Investments Intensive Businesses, Those with a Low Rate of New Product Introduction Are Better Able to Maintain ROI**

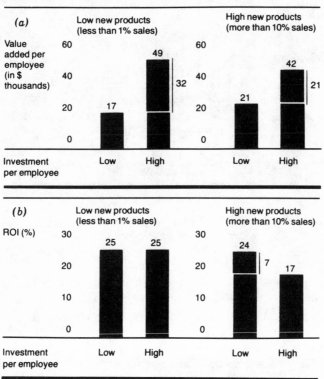

any reduction in the work force implied by an employer's move toward additional automation. Sometimes, unions bargain for a larger portion of value added as wages, thus leaving a smaller one for profits.

Even more significant, unions may actually reduce the amount of value added per employee available to be split between wages and profits (see Exhibit 4). Alternatively, perhaps businesses with a low level of labor output are more likely to become unionized, while those where morale is good and productivity high may be less susceptible to unionization.

Capacity Utilization: At high operating levels, fixed costs are spread over a large volume of output and usually reduce unit costs. High capacity utilization also tends to elevate selling prices and profit margins, considerably boosting ROI.

Surprisingly enough, however, capacity utilization has only a weak, though positive, impact on value added per employee, because marginal,

Exhibit 4. Businesses with a Low Degree of Unionization* Get a Bigger Output Boost from Heavy Investment

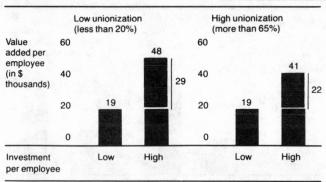

***Note:** Unionization is measured as the percentage of unionized employees in a business (managerial and nonmanagerial, salaried and hourly).

inexperienced employees are hired during peak operating times, while more experienced employees are retained at low ones. (For businesses with high fixed capital intensity, the positive effect is somewhat stronger.)

Real Market Growth: Real market growth helps value added per employee, especially when fixed capital intensity is high (see Exhibit 5). Slow growth rates may depress margins, particularly when growth is negative and plant and equipment cannot be liquidated easily. Rapid growth will tend to increase sales margins when the increase in demand is not fully anticipated and supply is short. Rapid growth does not increase ROI very much, because new plant and equipment are required, frequently at an inflated cost that has only partially been depreciated.

Exhibit 5. Businesses in Growing Markets Get a Bigger Output Boost from Heavy Fixed Investment

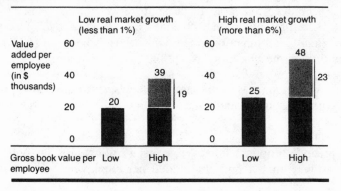

Standardized vs. Made to Order: Product differentiation tends to be more prevalent among businesses producing made-to-order goods. When a business carries a high level of investment per employee, product differentiation provides some insurance against price or marketing wars. By contrast, businesses that make nondifferentiated products are subject to severe price competition, especially when demand is slack and a lot of investment is at stake.

Scoring Your Mechanization Payoff

From our findings, profiles can be constructed that indicate the strength of a particular business as a candidate for increased mechanization (see Exhibit 6). Generally speaking, good candidates can be identified by high market share, low rate of new product introduction, nonunionization, high capacity utilization, rapid real market growth, and differentiated products.

If one of your businesses closely matches the profile of a good candidate, then mechanization could result in dramatic increases in its labor output with almost no injury to profitability. On the other hand, if a business looks like a poor candidate, automation is likely to seriously injure profits while only slightly increasing labor output.

You can score your own businesses on their potential mechanization payoffs by referring to the percentage ranking for good and poor candidates in Exhibit 6. Give a business 3 points for any attribute that puts it on the good-candidate list, 2 points for a percentage rank that puts it midway, and 1 point for an attribute that categorizes it as a poor candidate. Using this tabulation, you will see that the average business will receive 12 points; the range will be from 6 points for a particularly doubtful candidate to 18 points for an excellent candidate.

Some companies allocate resources for funding individual projects that are designed to carry them over a particular hurdle; more suitably, they should set business strategies and provide the required investment funds for

Exhibit 6.   Profiles of Good and Poor Candidates for Mechanization

Factor	Good candidate	Poor candidate
Relative market share	High (more than 60%)	Low (less than 25%)
Sales from new products	Low (less than 1%)	High (more than 10%)
Unionization	Low (less than 20%)	High (more than 65%)
Capacity utilization	High (more than 85%)	Low (less than 70%)
Real market growth	High (more than 6%)	Low (less than −1%)
Standardized (S) vs. produced to order (PTO)	PTO	S

the entire program. A narrow focus is frequently accompanied by optimistic financial projections that are not borne out by the realities of the business's strategic position. Companies that fund projects rather than business strategies should reconsider any mechanization projects approved for businesses with scores of 10 points or less.

Is Your Value Added per Employee Above or Below Par?

Can you judge whether your business is appropriately productive, given your amount of fixed investment? You can—if you use your fixed investment per employee as a measure. Suppose, for example, your business averages $35,000 of output per employee. If you compare this figure with the average for a business with your amount of investment per employee, you can judge how you are doing (see Exhibit 7).

Let's say your investment is between $7,000 and $12,000. Your business is doing very well indeed, because the average output for a business with this investment intensity is only $25,000. If your fixed investment is between $30,000 and $40,000, however, your value added level of $35,000 is well below the norm ($55,000) for businesses with this high a level of investment intensity. But if your fixed investment is between $17,000 and $27,000, you are right on target—you might reasonably expect a value added of about $35,000.

The basic tool we use is shown in Exhibit 7, which provides a benchmark for comparing productivity levels (value added) of businesses with different amounts of fixed investment. Here's how it works: (1) calculate

Exhibit 7. Setting Benchmarks for Value Added per Employee (based on a single factor)

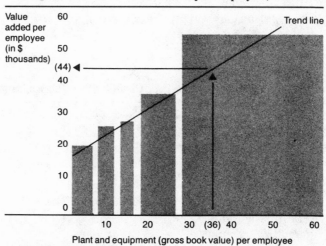

the dollar amount of plant and equipment per employee for your business, (2) position your business along the horizontal axis of Exhibit 7, and (3) use the trend line to find the level of value added per employee normally achieved by businesses with your amount of fixed investment. A business with $36,000 of fixed investment would have a value added norm of about $44,000. Check to see where your business falls in relation to the trend line.

So far, we have used fixed investment alone to establish a benchmark. However, suppose two businesses each have $36,000 of fixed investment per employee, but one is serving a rapid-growth market and the other, a declining market. If we look back at the findings about real market growth (Exhibit 5), we find that investment-intensive businesses in rapid-growth markets average $48,000 value added, while those in declining markets average $39,000. The norm of $44,000, based solely on fixed investment, can be refined, therefore, by incorporating information on the real market growth rate.

Since several other factors besides fixed investment influence value added per employee, it is possible to establish a more realistic benchmark or par by adjusting the norms from the trend line in Exhibit 7 up or down depending on a business's capacity utilization, market share, market growth rate, degree of unionization, and rate of new product introduction. The SPI data base has been used to develop a model that, when applied to data from different time periods, automatically makes adjustments for the effects of inflation. Factors included in the model are: (1) consistent with economic theory, (2) reasonable to knowledgeable businesspeople, (3) statistically significant, and (4) controllable by management. Once par has been established for each business, a manager can assess the actual value added of each business in the portfolio against par.

To illustrate this par concept, Exhibit 8 shows profiles of three businesses and indicates the par level of value added per employee for each.

Exhibit 8. Business Profiles and Corresponding Par Levels of Value Added per Employee

Businesses	A	B	C
Relative market share (%)	15%	130%	130%
Sales from new products	30	2	2
Unionization	85	0	0
Capacity utilization	60	90	90
Real market growth rate	1	8	8
Standardized (S) vs. produced to order (PTO)	S	PTO	PTO
Fixed investment per employee	$30,000	$30,000	$15,000
Par value added per employee	$24,000	$41,000	$30,000

Business A (par $24,000) and Business B (par $41,000) have the same fixed investment per employee. However, in contrast to Business B, Business A has a weak relative market share, is highly unionized, offers standardized products, and serves a slow-growth market. One might say A has a weaker strategic position and therefore a lower par.

By comparing Businesses B and C (par $30,000), you'll see they differ only in fixed investment per employee. Since Business B has a stronger strategic position than A and more investment than C, Business B has the highest par. Given the productivity-influencing characteristics of your business, you can estimate the level of value added per employee that is your par.

How Can You Measure Operating Effectiveness?

Differences between actual and par arise from factors not included in the model used to establish par, such as employee motivation and morale or management's organizational ability.

How should you interpret the difference from par? After taking into account the effects of key structural influences (e.g., fixed investment per employee), the deviation from par can be considered as a measure of *operating effectiveness* relative to other businesses. Its impact is positive and dramatic (as shown in Exhibit 9); moving a business from well below par to near par roughly doubles its ROI.

Separating actual value added into its par and deviation from par components helps to indicate the kind of action management should take to

Exhibit 9.   Operating Effectiveness Has a Dramatic Positive Effect on Profitability

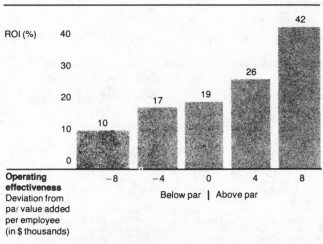

improve labor productivity. As we discuss in the following section, the appropriate action depends on whether the par for the business is low or the business itself is below par.

When Does Tradition Pay Off?

Managers responsible for a portfolio of businesses can rank those businesses according to their differences from par. Businesses that are below par need more traditional, shop-level productivity programs, such as those to improve either managerial effectiveness or worker motivation.

By contrast, consider one of your businesses that should have a very low par but is performing somewhat above par. Because it is already above par, its operating effectiveness has probably received management attention and is under control, so a shop-level program is less likely to succeed. The par/deviation from par framework indicates instead that the low level of output per employee is due to the production structure, market environment, and competitive position of the business (the low par).

Whether such a business is a good candidate for mechanization to increase value added per employee (without reducing ROI) can be analyzed by scoring the business's mechanization payoff potential. If the business has several structural characteristics that place it in the poor-candidate category, these weaknesses should be addressed before attempting a mechanization strategy.

How to Manage a Portfolio to Improve Productivity

In the past, most efforts to improve productivity were tactical actions at the shop level. However, beginning in the 1950s companies began to realize the importance of strategic planning. By the 1960s—and more prevalently in the 1970s—formal structures were brought to decisions that formerly had been made in a less desirable way. Companies began to accept the practice of performing a strategic audit to analyze the key profit-influencing characteristics of their business units.

Some of the companies that pioneered in strategic planning have already achieved impressive results. One such company is Mead, whose executives evolved a planning philosophy in the 1970s that blended their ideas with concepts and evidence advanced by SPI and the Boston Consulting Group.[1]

In 1972, Mead conducted an extensive review of its market segments and product lines. The major objective was to focus incremental capital on businesses where cost-effective leadership was possible. To implement this strategy, Mead concentrated on three factors: capital allocation, people management, and asset management. Specifically, Mead executives decided to:

☐ Eliminate low-growth businesses with low market share.

☐ Move emphasis from lower-priced, commodity-type businesses to higher-priced, value-added lines.

☐ Obtain market leadership if possible (e.g., in paperboard, focus on market share and specialty products; in paper, focus on product lines where technical capability exists).

☐ Monitor significant drifts toward investment intensity by individual businesses.

☐ Discourage investment-intensive solutions to business problems and encourage, through business planning and capital-project review, creative solutions that are not investment intensive.

Major divestitures made by Mead during the pasts few years include a pig iron business, two soil pipe plants, two container plants, a lime business, a cement business, an upholstery operation, a school and commercial supply business, a company making paper plates, a partnership in a Belgian paper mill, a ferroalloy business, a distribution chain for educational products, and a 50% interest in an asbestos and plastic pipe business. For the most part, these divested businesses produced commodity-type undifferentiated products, had small market shares, and their percentage in Mead's asset mix declined from 13% in 1972 to only 2% in 1976 (see Exhibit 10).

By contrast, the percentage of Mead's asset mix in businesses that had good strategies increased from 39% to 53%. In addition, about half of Mead's assets were tied up in businesses undergoing strategic changes in 1972. These businesses increased their return on net assets from 2.8% in 1972 to 11.8% in 1976. Thus, by shifting its asset mix toward more profitable businesses and improving the profit rate of businesses undergoing strategic change, Mead was able to achieve a dramatic increase in corporate profitability.

Mead also devoted a great deal of attention to people management in these five years. The company held a seminar for some 300 of its managers to familiarize them with the new approach to financial and strategic planning. In addition, Mead reorganized several businesses, made changes in man-

Exhibit 10.   Improvements in Mead Asset Mix and Return on Net Assets

	Asset mix		Return on net assets	
	1972	1976	1972	1976
Inappropriate businesses for Mead	13.2%	2.1%	2.4%	4.2%
Businesses with good strategies in place	38.5	53.4	8.8	9.6
Businesses undergoing strategic changes	48.3	44.5	2.8	11.8
Total corporate return on net assets			4.7%	10.4%

agement, and improved productivity by monitoring and reducing the number of employees per dollar of sales.

Mead's concentration on people and asset management achieved substantial results. Investment per employee between 1972 and 1976 measured in current dollars increased about 40%, or 7% at an annual rate, a slight decline in real terms. By contrast, value added per employee measured in current dollars increased by 80%, or about 12.5% per year. By improving its strategic position, Mead was thus able to increase its value added per employee without a corresponding increase in investment per employee. In addition, Mead's asset-management program resulted in an 18% reduction in investment per dollar of sales.

Taken together, the capital-allocation, people-management, and asset-management programs allowed Mead to more than double its return on total capital, from 4% in 1972 to 11.2% in 1976. In addition, Mead's standing in terms of return on total capital improved among the 16 largest forest products companies, from 12th in 1972 to 4th in 1976.

How These Comparisons Can Help

Investment in new plant and equipment is often evaluated in terms of increased capital and reduced labor costs. This conventional perspective is incomplete because it ignores key factors that affect capital and labor productivity. It is also misleading because no consideration is given to the way increased investment affects the competitive climate and, inevitably, selling-price levels in the industry.

Executives need an objective benchmark to help them evaluate actual versus potential levels of output per employee. The methods of comparison presented here allow them to pinpoint which businesses need which kinds of productivity-improvement programs. Those businesses that are below par for value added per employee probably need more traditional, shop-level productivity programs.

To balance capital and labor productivity, a business's production structure as well as its competitive position and market environment must be considered. The score for mechanization-payoff potential can help decision makers determine which businesses contemplating mechanization are likely to achieve anticipated cost reductions and avoid unanticipated price declines and, perhaps more important, which will be ineffective users of investment funds.

Notes

1. This section draws on two 1977 Mead Corporation booklets, "Why Strategic Planning?" and "Mead Executive Management Presentation to Paper and Forest Products Analysts." (Available from Mead World Headquarters, Courthouse Plaza Northeast, Dayton, Ohio 45463.)

Appendix: The Data Base Backup

This article is based on a study of more than 1,700 businesses included in the data base assembled by the Strategic Planning Institute (SPI), a non-profit, tax-exempt organization located in Cambridge, Massachusetts. Known as the PIMS (profit impact of market strategy) program, the data base includes the strategy experiences, both good and bad, of product and service businesses operated by the more than 200 member companies of all sizes located in North America, Europe, and Australia. Each "business" is a division, product line, or other profit center within its parent company, selling a distinct set of products or services to an identifiable group of customers, in competition with a well-defined set of companies. For each, a meaningful separation can be made of revenues, operating costs, investments, and strategic plans.

SPI disguises and summarizes the information in the data base before making it available to member companies. It documents the actions taken by each business, the market it serves, its competitive environment, and the financial results achieved. Included in the data are over 200 separate characteristics of each business experience, not only traditional balance sheet and income statement data but also information about market share, investment intensity, productivity, product quality, and unionization.

10 Is Vertical Integration Profitable?

ROBERT D. BUZZELL

On the face of it, vertical integration seems a sensible strategy. Managers can assume that their transaction costs will go down, that they will be guaranteed necessary supplies, that internal coordination will improve, and that they'll reap the benefits of the technological capabilities of other units. In a study of 1,649 manufacturing-processing units, the author of this article discovered, however, that in more cases than not, the minuses outweigh the pluses. Because vertical integration requires managers to pump quite a bit of capital into new operations, the strategy may not be worth it unless a company gains needed insurance as well as cost savings from the acquisition.

Vertical integration, or the lack of it, can have a significant impact on business performance. While some observers claim that adequate vertical integration can be crucial to survival, others blame excessive integration for causing corporate failure. Examples of the reasons behind moves toward integration and of their success or failure aren't hard to find:

☐ In mid-1981, Du Pont acquired Conoco Inc. in a $7.3 billion transaction. Edward Jefferson, chairman of Du Pont, stated that the merger would give the company "a captive hydrocarbon feedstock source" and would "reduce the exposure of the combined companies to fluctuations in the price of energy and hydrocarbons."[1]

Published 1983.

☐ In the early and mid-1970s, producers of integrated circuits and finished electronic product manufacturers made a flurry of vertical integration moves into each other's industries. Texas Instruments integrated forward into calculators, watches, and other products. Bowmar, the early leader in hand-held calculators, made a desperate effort to integrate backward into integrated circuit production. (The move ultimately failed, and Bowmar withdrew from the business.) The president of Commodore, another calculator producer, argued that backward integration was neither necessary nor desirable. "It's well worth it [to spend more for chips]," he claimed, "and to be able to get into and out of a technology when you want to."[2]

☐ Some observers have blamed the U.S. automobile industry's woes, in part, on excessive vertical integration. According to Robert H. Hayes and William J. Abernathy, "In deciding to integrate backward because of apparent short-term rewards, managers often restrict their ability to strike out in innovative directions in the future."[3]

As these cases illustrate, vertical integration moves sometimes involve big commitments of resources and can make or break the fortunes of even a large corporation. Managers of smaller businesses, too, often face "make versus buy" and "use versus sell" choices for certain materials, components, products, or services. Should a manufacturer operate a company-owned trucking fleet or use independent owner-operators? At what point can a small supermarket chain afford to own and operate its own warehouse? Is it wise for Coors to manufacture all of its own beer cans and bottles, or is Anheuser-Busch's approach—buying about half its requirements from suppliers—a better strategy?

These alternatives, and countless others that managers select affecting the vertical scope of a company's (or a business unit's) activities, define a business's vertical integration strategy.

Despite the importance of decisions about vertical integration, managers have few guidelines for this aspect of strategy. Consultants and academic authorities on strategic planning and management have offered numerous prescriptions for success in designing corporate portfolios and for market segmentation, pricing, and product development strategies. But beyond suggesting lists of possible advantages and risks, researchers have little to say about vertical integration. Nor does economic theory offer much in the way of guidance.

In this article I summarize the results of some analyses based on the PIMS (profit impact of market strategies) data base. I undertook the investigation to determine how vertical integration relates to business profitability. To shed some light on the following questions, I analyzed PIMS data for business units with varying degrees of vertical integration:

1 In general, are highly integrated businesses more or less profitable than those that are less integrated?

2 Under what conditions does a high or a low degree of vertical integration appear to be most beneficial?

Before presenting the results of the analyses, I want to give attention to the potential benefits and drawbacks of being vertically integrated that previous studies have identified.[4]

Pluses and Minuses

According to the traditional economic definition, vertical integration is the combination, under a single ownership, of two or more stages of production or distribution (or both) that are usually separate. In the oil industry, for example, the process that takes the oil from the well to the service station is divided into four stages—crude oil production, transportation, refining, and marketing. Some companies specialize in just one of these—Buckeye Pipe Line Company, for instance, focuses on the transportation stage. Other companies combine two or three stages, and the fully integrated major oil companies are involved in all four.

The Pluses

What are the benefits of vertical integration in the oil industry or in any industry that has several distinct production stages?

☐ *Transaction costs.* In many cases, a major objective of vertical integration is to eliminate, or at least greatly reduce, the buying and selling costs incurred when separate companies own two stages of production and perhaps the physical handling costs as well. Thus, a company that manufactures integrated circuits as well as finished products can operate with little or no sales force, advertising, sales promotion, or market research. Another producer selling to independent customers would need all these activities.

☐ *Supply assurance.* Vertical integration may also be essential to assure a supply of critical materials. Certainly, this aspect of vertical integration has been a major attraction of that strategy to the petroleum industry, both in its early days and more recently in the OPEC-dominated 1970s.[5] During the crisis of 1973–1974, with little warning, some companies found their supplies sharply reduced and prices doubling or tripling. Apart from the impact they have on materials costs, shortages of materials in industries with high fixed costs are extremely damaging because they lead to low usage of expensive facilities.

☐ *Improved coordination.* Even when supplies of materials are certain, vertical integration may permit cost reductions through improved coordination of production and inventory scheduling between stages. Some argue that an in-house supplier can schedule production more efficiently when it has firm commitments from a "downstream" manufacturing or distribution facility than when it deals with independent customers.

□ *Technological capabilities.* Some claim that, in general, businesses and companies that are vertically integrated, especially backward, are best equipped to innovate because they participate in many of the production and distribution activities in which change can occur. This argument rests in part on the notion that a critical requirement for successful innovation is adequate coordination of marketing and technical functions and that integration improves coordination.[6]

□ *Higher entry barriers.* The more vertically integrated a business, the greater the financial and managerial resources required to enter and compete in it. Established companies in an industry may combine their operations as a way of raising the stakes and discouraging potential new entrants. Of course, this gambit is effective only if vertical integration becomes necessary for competing.

The Minuses

If this strategy offers so many potential gains, why don't more managers employ it? Operating on an integrated basis brings offsetting costs and risks, the most important of which are increased capital requirements, unbalanced throughput, reduced flexibility, and loss of specialization.

□ *Capital requirements.* When a business integrates either backward or forward, it must provide the capital that the newly integrated operations require. Studies based on the PIMS data base and other evidence show that high investment intensity usually leads to low profitability.[7] The implication is that unless the operating cost savings of vertical integration are substantial, investment intensity will make integration strategies unprofitable.

□ *Unbalanced throughput.* A problem inherent in combining various stages of production or distribution is the varying scale of operation that each stage may require for efficient functioning. For example, to achieve costs competitive with those of independent suppliers, a manufacturer may have to produce integrated circuits at a very high volume. But if the manufacturer integrates forward into minicomputers, say, he would find that the "minimum efficient scale" of operation for integrated circuits may be much greater than the volume needed for efficient production of minicomputers. The fact that scale requirements differ among vertically linked activities suggests that integrated businesses must either operate on a scale large enough to satisfy the requirements of the most volume-dependent production stages or suffer the penalties of operating on inefficient scales at one or more stages. An implication of this line of reasoning is that vertical integration is probably more feasible for businesses with high market shares, which, relative to competitors in that market, involve large-scale operations. The experience of the automobile industry illustrates this point. According to one estimate, General Motors buys 10% to 15% of its standard components from outsiders, while Ford buys 40% to 50%.[8]

☐ *Reduced flexibility.* Because vertical integration implies commitment to a particular technology or way of operating, it can be an extremely risky strategy. If technology or market changes make the products or methods of one stage in a vertically integrated system obsolete, the integrated company may find adjusting very difficult. In the 1960s, Jonathan Logan, a women's apparel producer, committed itself to double-knit fabrics by investing in a textile mill. Later, when double-knits had gone out of fashion, Jonathan Logan continued to manufacture them, principally to accommodate the mill's production. In 1981, when it finally closed the mill, the company reported a $40 million write-off.

☐ *Loss of specialization.* A somewhat hard to pinpoint, but often important, danger of vertical integration is the very distinct managerial approaches that the various stages of production or distribution may require. For instance, retail or wholesale distribution operations seem to need forms of organization, control systems, and management styles that are quite different from those for manufacturing and processing. Up to the mid-1930s, the major U.S. oil companies were expanding their ownership of service stations. Then the companies began to phase out their ownership positions in favor of franchising. A prime reason for this shift was the inflexible way in which companies operated their service stations and priced their products.[9] This approach may work for manufacturing, but it doesn't for retailing.

Other industries have had problems similar to those of the oil refiners when they attempted to integrate forward into retailing. For instance, in the 1960s the inner-city stores owned and operated by the major tire producers suffered severely when mass merchants started competing with them and consumers moved to the suburbs. Integrated manufacturers such as Robert Hall and Bond, the men's clothing producers, and Sherwin-Williams, the paint producer, all had similar difficulties during the 1970s. While other reasons may also account for these companies' troubles, it appears that their efforts to run geographically dispersed retail chains were handicapped by a "manufacturing mentality."

Is It Profitable or Isn't It?

Since vertical integration entails both benefits and risks, it is reasonable to expect the payoff of a strategy of increased integration to vary according to the market and competitive conditions in which a business operates. To explore the profit impact of variations in vertical integration, I have used the PIMS data base.

The PIMS research program has been described in several published accounts.[10] Consequently, only a very brief discussion of this data base is necessary here.

The data used in the analysis are for "businesses," not companies. Each business is a subdivision of a company, usually a product division or a product line that is distinguished from other parts of the company by the customers it serves, the competitors it has, and the resources it employs. The use of business unit data is of particular importance in the analysis of vertical integration. A company can be vertically integrated and treat the linked segments either as a single, combined business or as separate units. The PIMS data include some measures of the extent of vertical integration that go beyond the business unit level. But profitability and other performance measures are confined to the reporting business units. Hence, the data base allows us to explore the effects of vertical integration strategies that are implemented *within* single business units. Only to a very limited extent, however, can we examine the impact at a company level.

As of early 1982, the PIMS data base contained financial, market, and strategic data on 1,742 business units over four or more years. In the analysis reported here, I have excluded service and distribution businesses both because the samples of these kinds of operations are small and because the meaning of vertical integration in service and distribution industries is less clear than in manufacturing. The sample used here therefore consists of 1,649 manufacturing-processing industry businesses. They cover consumer products, industrial goods and components, and raw and semi-finished materials. The data for each business unit are for four-year periods during the 1970s; only the most recent four years of this information are used.

PIMS Measures

The PIMS data base includes two types of vertical integration measures—absolute and relative. The absolute measure is value added as a percentage of sales for each business unit. *Value added* is defined as sales revenue minus all purchases (materials, components, supplies, energy, and services) by one business from other businesses. (Purchases from another business in the same parent corporation are treated as "outside" purchases.) Thus, value added as a percentage of sales is simply

$$\frac{\text{sales} - \text{purchases}}{\text{sales}} \times 100$$

To explore how differences in this ratio are related to profitability, one has to make an adjustment. Because each business unit's value-added measure includes net profit, increases in profitability arising from many sources other than vertical integration will also increase value added and thus create an apparent positive relationship between the two factors.

To eliminate the tautological relationship between the ratio of value added to sales ratio and profitability, I have constructed an adjusted ratio in which *reported* net profit is replaced by an *average* rate of return on each business unit's invested capital. The appendix shows the method of calculation used.

In the analysis that follows, I use adjusted value added as a percentage of adjusted sales (as defined in the appendix) as the primary measure of each business unit's degree of vertical integration (I use "VA/S" to refer to this measure). The businesses in the data base vary greatly in VA/S, from a low of around 20% to a high of 90%. The average for the 1,649 businesses is 56%, half of them being clustered between 45% and 65%.

Business units' VA/S differ, no doubt, because they operate in different industries or product markets, where norms vary. To supplement the VA/S measure of vertical integration, use an additional measure of *relative* vertical integration. This relative measure is based on PIMS participants' responses to the following question: In comparing the degree of backward vertical integration of this business with that of each of its leading competitors, do you find this business's less, about the same, or greater? Responses to this question indicate that more than 60% of the PIMS businesses integrated to about the same extent as their competitors.

Finally, the businesses reported whether their parent companies were vertically integrated (backward *and* forward) to a greater or lesser extent than others in the industry. Where a business was integrated to the same degree as competitors but the company was more (or less) so, either the company or one or more of its competitors had carried out a vertical integration strategy but organized the component activities into separate business units. While we can compare businesses that vary in terms of overall company vertical integration, our measures of performance, including profitability, are limited to those of the reporting business unit itself. Because transfer prices among vertically linked businesses may be distorted in one direction or another, performance at this level may or may not be a reliable indicator of the total effect of integration on the company.

To test the general propositions about vertical integration strategies listed earlier, then, we can compare the profit and other performance results that business units varying in degree of integration have achieved. As I indicated, I use both absolute and relative measures.

Vertical Integration and Profitability

Exhibit 1 shows average pretax profit margins, investment-to-sales ratios, and returns on investment for businesses with differing levels of vertical integrations as measured by VA/S percentages. As expected, profit margins expressed as percentages of sales rise as VA/S increases. The differences in profit margins are modest up to a VA/S of 60%, but from that point, profits rise consistently with increasing integration.

Investment intensity, however, rises along with VA/S over the whole

Exhibit 1.   Vertical Integration and Profitability

Vertical Integration Measured by Adjusted VA/S	Net Profit as Percentage of Sales	Investment as Percentage of Sales	Net Profit as Percentage of Investment (ROI)	Number of Businesses
Under 40%	8%	38%	26%	267
40–50%	8	45	22	341
50–60%	9	54	20	389
60–70%	10	56	22	338
Over 70%	12	65	24	314

range of the data. As a result, the pretax rate of return on investment declines up to the point where VA/S is between 50% and 60%. Beyond an integration level of 60%, investment intensity increases more slowly than profit margins, and ROI consequently rises with increasing vertical integration.

The "V-shaped" relationship between VA/S and ROI suggests that profitability is highest at the two opposite ends of the spectrum. Either a very low or a very high level of integration yields an above-average rate of return, while earnings are lowest in the middle. This pattern is identical to one reported by Edward Bowman in a study of minicomputer and computer peripherals manufacturers. Bowman interpreted the pattern to mean that a company "can do most of its work itself, such as research and development, production, and service, and be relatively successful. On the other hand, it can be low on value added, essentially a purchased-component assembler, and also successful. The middle ground is apparently a questionable strategy."[11]

The data in Exhibit 1 suggest that what Bowman found in a single industry also applies to manufacturers in general. (Supplementary analyses show the same V-shaped pattern for consumer and industrial products manufacturers. The only exceptions were producers of raw and semifinished materials, for which ROI declined consistently over the whole range from low to high VA/S.)

The figures in Exhibit 1 demonstrate clearly how rising investment requirements offset the higher profit margins associated with intensified vertical integration. If integration can somehow be achieved without the penalty of a proportionally higher investment base, then increasing vertical integration should be extremely beneficial. Exhibit 2 shows that this is, indeed, the case. Here the PIMS businesses are sorted into nine groups on the basis of both VA/S and investment intensity. The data indicate that when investment intensity is constant, ROI steadily increases as levels of VA/S rise.

The lesson seems clear: if a company's management can carry out a

Exhibit 2.   Vertical Integration, Investment Intensity, and Return on Investment

	Investment as Percentage of Sales		
	Under 40%	40–60%	Over 60%
Adjusted VA/S	Average ROI	Average ROI	Average ROI
Under 50%	31% (322)*	19% (196)	8% (90)
50–65%	35 (165)	19 (233)	10 (182)
Over 65%	38 (91)	26 (180)	12 (190)

*The number of businesses in each cell is shown in parentheses.

strategy of increasing integration without greater investment intensity, this strategy usually leads to higher profitability. But the data also show that the winning combination of high VA/S and low investment intensity is uncommon. Of the 461 businesses in the highest VA/S group (over 65%), fewer than one-fifth also had low levels of investment intensity.

Relative Vertical Integration and Profitability

As noted earlier, cross-sectional differences in the VA/S among businesses are mainly due to differences in the nature of the markets or industries in which they operate. To the extent that this is true, one might conclude that the main implication of the data in Exhibit 1 is that it pays to be in the kinds of businesses in which VA/S is inherently very low or very high. In many cases, however, managers have to make strategic choices about a business unit's relative degree of vertical integration. Is it profitable to be more highly integrated than the industry norm?

Exhibit 3 shows the average ROI performance for PIMS businesses whose relative vertical integrations varied. These data are given separately for consumer and industrial products businesses; as I mentioned earlier, the feasibility of forward integration, backward integration, or both depends on where a business is located in a production-distribution system. Exhibit 3 shows measures of relative integration at both the business unit level and the company level.

The data in Exhibit 3 suggest that for both consumer and industrial product manufacturers, backward vertical integration slightly enhances ROI. For consumer products manufacturers, ROI is also higher when the parent company is more forward integrated than competitors are. This result is somewhat surprising; forward integration in consumer goods industries presumably means, in most cases, operation of company-owned wholesale and retail distribution facilities or both, which (as I argued earlier) often require different management systems and styles than manufacturing does. The ROI figures shown in Exhibit 3 are of course for the manufacturing components of the companies involved. Possibly these businesses earn above-average rates of return at the expense of their captive downstream customers.

Exhibit 3.   Relative Vertical Integration and Profitability

Relative Vertical Integration[a]	Type of Business	
	Consumer Products Average ROI	Industrial Products Average ROI
At business unit level:		
Backward integration		
Less	20% (106)[b]	21% (316)
Same	22 (277)	22 (730)
More	23 (58)	26 (162)
At company level:		
Backward integration		
Less	23 (115)	20 (302)
Same	21 (255)	23 (678)
More	24 (71)	24 (228)
Forward integration		
Less	19 (64)	23 (208)
Same	22 (343)	22 (822)
More	27 (34)	22 (178)

[a]In each case, the degree of vertical integration in compared with that of leading competitors in the market that the business unit serves.
[b]The number of businesses is shown in parentheses.

Scale and Profitability

As I have said, large businesses should more often be able to use vertical integration strategies than their smaller competitors because large companies are more likely to be able to operate at efficient scales at each stage of activity. Of course, sometimes a company can integrate backward or forward on the basis of the shared requirements of two or more businesses that operate in separate product markets. For example, Texas Instruments produces semiconductors and other components that go into end products such as calculators, watches, and microcomputers. In other words, ways exist to achieve efficient scale other than by having a large share in a single market. Nevertheless, other things being equal, large market share businesses should derive greater benefit from increasing vertical integration.

Exhibit 4 shows that these effects do, indeed, depend on size. Here I've grouped the PIMS businesses according to relative market share, defined as the ratio of a business unit's market share to the combined shares of its three largest competitors. For businesses with small relative shares—less than 25% of those of their three largest competitors combined—ROI is significantly lower when a business is highly vertically integrated. This relationship applies both to the absolute level of integration, measured by VA/S, and to relative backward integration at the business unit level. For busi-

Exhibit 4.   Vertical Integration, Relative Market Share, and Profitability

Vertical Integration	Relative Market Share[a]		
	Under 25% Average ROI	25–60% Average ROI	Over 60% Average ROI
Adjusted VA/S			
Under 50%	14% (235)[b]	26% (202)	33% (171)
50–65%	14 (188)	19 (204)	29 (188)
Over 65%	9 (113)	22 (150)	31 (198)
Relative backward integration			
Less	14 (193)	24 (139)	30 (90)
Same	13 (293)	21 (351)	31 (363)
More	11 (50)	23 (66)	34 (104)
Relative forward integration at company level			
Less	14 (110)	27 (84)	29 (78)
Same	13 (361)	22 (396)	31 (408)
More	15 (65)	19 (76)	34 (71)

[a]Relative market share is a business unit's market share, expressed here as a percentage of the combined share of its three largest competitors.
[b]The number of businesses is shown in parentheses.

Note: The differences among the three market-share groups are statistically significant at the 99% probability level. In a multiple regression model that includes all major PIMS profit determinants, the coefficient of VA/S is negative but insignificant for small-share businesses. For businesses with relative shares above 25%, VA/S has a significant negative coefficient ($p > 0.99$) and $(VA/S)^2$ has a significant positive coefficient ($p > 0.99$).

nesses with relative market shares over 25%, ROI is highest for the high and low extremes of integration based on the VA/S measure. When relative share exceeds 60%, however, ROI rises consistently with increasing relative backward integration.

Relative forward integration is analyzed in Exhibit 4 on the basis of comparisons among each business unit's parent company and competing companies. The relationship between this kind of integration and ROI is irregular. For businesses with small market shares, the extent of forward integration seemingly makes no difference; for high-share businesses, operating in a vertically integrated company helps profitability. For those in between—namely, those with relative shares between 25% and 60%—ROI is highest when the parent company is less integrated than competitors.

The figures in Exhibit 4, then, provide some support for the idea that the net effects of vertical integration vary according to the size of the business unit. The data also show that competitors with large market shares are more likely to pursue vertical integration strategies. For instance, more than 35% of the businesses with relative shares greater than 60% reported VA/S over

65%, whereas just 20% of the business units with small market shares reported this figure.

Market Stability

To test the proposition that vertical integration strategies are more effective when market conditions and technology are stable, I compared the relationship between ROI and VA/S for businesses in very stable and not very stable conditions. I divided the data base according to high and low real-growth rates, maturity of markets, degree of technological change, and rates of new product introduction. None of these analyses showed significant differences in the impact of vertical integration on profit. Apparently, integration strategies can be successful in both stable and unsettled markets.

Materials Costs

As mentioned earlier, some observers have advanced the notion that companies make integration moves like the Du Pont-Conoco merger because they find integrated organizations less vulnerable to increases in raw materials costs. If this is a valid theory, then a high VA/S should have the biggest impact on profitability when materials costs are growing most rapidly. To test this hypothesis, I separated the PIMS businesses into groups with high and low inflation in materials costs and set the dividing line at 10% annual rate of increase (see Exhibit 5).

The results are the opposite of the prediction. Among businesses that experienced rapid materials-cost inflation, ROI was highest when vertical integration was low, and vice versa. Possibly this situation reflects the greater capital intensity and fixed costs of highly vertically integrated business units. Whatever the explanation, the data certainly cast doubt on the notion that integration provides insurance against the effects of inflation.

Product Innovation

The final hypothesis that I tested concerns the relationship between vertical integration and product innovation. Are highly integrated businesses more

Exhibit 5.   Vertical Integration, Cost Inflation, and Profitability

Rate of Inflation in Materials Costs	Adjusted VA/S		
	Under 50% Average ROI	50–65% Average ROI	Over 65% Average ROI
Under 10% per year	21%	21%	24%
Over 10% per year	27	21	20

Note: The difference between the two groups is statistically significant. In a multiple regression equation in which ROI was the dependent variable and all the major PIMS profit determinants were independent variables, the coefficient of VA/S was positive for businesses whose materials costs rose by less than 10% annually ($p > 0.97$). For businesses with cost growth above 10%, the coefficient was negative ($p > 0.975$).

Exhibit 6.   Vertical Integration and Product Innovation

	Adjusted VA/S	
	Under 50%	Over 50%
	Average percent of new products	
Product life cycle stage		
New and growing markets	16%	19%
Mature and declining markets	5	8
Recent technological change		
No	5	8
Yes	12	18
Market share		
Under 15%	8	12
15–30%	8	10
Over 30%	4	10

innovative? Exhibit 6 shows the percentages of sales that new products generated for businesses with low, medium, and high VA/S. (Here "new products" are items introduced during the preceding three years.) The exhibit shows separate figures for businesses competing in mature versus growth markets, for businesses in which major technological change had occurred recently versus those where it had not, and for businesses with small, medium, and large market shares.

The results indicate that highly integrated businesses do generate more new products. In Exhibit 6, I use a cutoff of 50% to separate high from low VA/S because the data were essentially the same for all businesses beyond the 50% level. In both mature and growing markets, high levels of integration correspond to high rates of new product introduction. The same pattern holds regardless of whether technology is changing or whether the business has small market share or a strong competitive position. Thus, the experience of the PIMS businesses lends support to the notion that vertical integration facilitates product innovation. In some instances, the need to innovate might justify a vertical integration strategy even if the move exacted some penalty in short-term profitability.

Evaluating Vertical Integration Strategies

Is vertical integration profitable? Sometimes yes, sometimes no. The statistical analyses reported here do not, of course, provide any formula for determining just how a particular integration strategy will affect performance. But the experiences of the PIMS businesses, together with other evidence drawn from various industries, do suggest some guidelines for evaluating the possible benefits and risks of integration.

1. *Beware heightened investment needs.*   When a high level of vertical integration hurts ROI, it is usually because investment intensity is rising. An ideal strategy is one in which value added increases but the investment base does not. No doubt, the best way to ensure the investment base is to develop proprietary products or processes whose value derives from superior performance rather than from extensive in-house manufacturing or processing. Successful producers of cosmetics and other personal care products, for example, often enjoy ratios of value added to sales of 70% or more without heavily investing in plant and equipment. In much the same way, some companies in the computer industry have modest in-house manufacturing operations but very high VA/S. These companies add value through technical skills in design and customer service or both, not through production of standarized components.

Unfortunately, far more often, rising capital requirements accompany rising vertical integration. Many businesses seem to follow the path from "northwest" to "southeast" in Exhibit 2. When they do, the return on investment tends to fall. Are most decisions to increase vertical integration, then, mistakes? No doubt many of them are. Managers probably often underestimate the investment needed to support moves into their suppliers' or customers' businesses.

They may also view vertical integration moves as a means of defending profitable core businesses. This reasoning is no doubt often valid, and accepting modest profits in one part of a business if it promises high rates of return elsewhere is perfectly sensible. The question is, how much is this kind of insurance worth? The data in Exhibit 2 indicate that the cost is often excessive.

2. *Consider alternatives to ownership.*   In the traditional sense of the term, vertical integration is an arrangement based on ownership of activities linked up and down. In some cases, at least, manufacturers can reap some of the benefits of integration without owning all the stages. A manufacturer might, for example, reduce transaction costs via long-term contracts with independent suppliers. This approach is apparently more common in Japanese than in American industry. Hayes and Abernathy say that "long-term contracts and long-term relationships with suppliers can achieve many of the same cost benefits as vertical integration without calling into question a company's ability to innovate or respond to innovation."[12]

3. *Avoid "part-way" integration.*   The V-shaped relationship between vertical integration and profitability (see Exhibit 1) suggests that some businesses may suffer because they don't carry their linking strategies far enough. Recall that the most profitable businesses are those at the extremes of the vertical integration spectrum. In general, the least profitable position is an intermediate one. The implication is that, on this dimension of strategy, a clearly defined position is most likely to succeed. In the vertical scope of a business, managers should be wary of taking gradual, piecemeal steps that can lead to the unrewarding middle ground.

4. *Carefully analyze scale requirements.* A significant risk in many vertical integration strategies is that a production or distribution stage has too small a scope to be run competitively against independent suppliers or customers. Presumably for this reason, the PIMS data show that integration is much more likely to pay off for businesses with quite large market shares.

Just what scale of operation makes a given integration strategy effective depends, of course, on the technologies available in the situation. The conclusion I draw from the statistical data, however, is that mistakes are fairly common. Quite a few small-share businesses are highly integrated and, on average, unsuccessful. Some of them, at least, suffer from what Peter Drucker calls "being the wrong size." Excessive vertical integration is not the only route to becoming wrong sized, but it may well be one of the usual ones.

5. *Be skeptical of claims that integration reduces raw materials costs.* Economists have long questioned the idea that vertically integrated businesses or companies are somehow insulated from fluctuations in the cost of key raw materials. Unless it monopolizes materials supply, they ask, why should a vertically integrated enterprise be able to supply itself at anything less than open market prices? The data in Exhibit 5 indicate that skepticism about cost advantages is often well-founded.

All of these guidelines may seem unduly negative. Each points to possible dangers or illusions associated with increased vertical integration. Given that integration strategies often involve big investments, caution does seem advisable. On the other side, however, vertical integration is often a highly successful strategy. Especially for businesses and companies that enjoy strong market positions, increased integration can pay off in both profitability and greater product innovation.

Notes

1. "Du Pont's Costly Bet on Conoco," *Business Week*, July 20, 1981, p. 52.

2. "Why They're Integrating into Integrated Circuits," *Business Week*, September 28, 1974, p. 55.

3. Robert H. Hayes and William J. Abernathy, "Managing Our Way to Economic Decline," *HBR*, July-August, 1980, p. 72.

4. For a more extensive discussion of the potential benefits and limitations of vertical integration, see Michael E. Porter, chap. 14, *Competitive Analysis* (New York, Free Press, 1980).

5. David J. Tecce, "Vertical Integration in the U.S. Oil Industry," in *Vertical Integration in the Oil Industry*, ed. Edward J. Mitchell (Washington, D.C., American Enterprise Institute, 1976), p. 105.

6. Edwin Mansfield and Samuel Wagner, "Organization and Strategic Factors with Proba-

bilities of Success in Industrial Research and Development," *Journal of Business*, April 1975, p. 180.

---

7. Bradley T. Gale, "Can More Capital Buy Higher Productivity?" *HBR*, July-August, 1980, p. 78.

---

8. Robert A. Leone, William J. Abernathy, Stephen P. Bradley, and Jeffrey Hunker, "Regulation and Technological Innovation in the Automobile Industry," report to the Office of Technology Assessment (Washington, D.C., July 1981), p. 43.

---

9. Gale, ibid.

---

10. See Sidney Schoeffler, Robert D. Buzzell, and Donald F. Heany, "Impact of Strategic Planning on Profit Performance," *HBR*, March-April, 1974, p. 137; and Robert D. Buzzell, Bradley T. Gale, and Ralph G.M. Sultan, "Market Share: A Key to Profitability," *HBR*, January-February 1975, p. 97.

---

11. Edward H. Bowman, "Strategy, Annual Reports, and Alchemy," *California Management Review*, Spring 1978, p. 70.

---

12. Hayes and Abernathy, p. 73.

Appendix: Adjustment of Ratio of Value Added to Sales as a Measure of Vertical Integration

Many companies use value added—or, specifically, its ratio to sales—as a measure of the extent of vertical integration. The logic of the measure is straightforward: the more that stages of production and distribution are combined within an enterprise, the higher the ratio of value added to sales. At the limit is the business that is completely self-contained—it makes no purchases from outside suppliers, and the ratio of value added to sales is 100%. At the opposite extreme is the business that performs only a single, narrowly defined function—for example, the broker who sells a commodity on a commission basis.

While the ratio of value added to sales (VA/S) clearly rises with increasing vertical integration, VA/S is not a good measure of vertical integration. As defined, value added includes a business unit's pretax profits. Suppose that profits increase for some reason totally unrelated to vertical integration. Then VA/S will also rise, but clearly it would be incorrect to treat such a change as an increase in vertical integration.

The same reasoning applies to differences among businesses. If businesses A and B are identical in all respects except that A has a profit of 20% of sales while B has one of only 10%, treating the resulting ten-point spread in their VA/S as a difference in degree of vertical integration would be inappropriate.

The fact that value added includes net profits poses an especially difficult problem for an analysis of the relationship between vertical integration and profitability. If no adjustment is made in the VA/S measure, then both

VA/S and measures of profitability such as ROI will reflect many things that affect profits. The result will inevitably be a high—but spurious—positive relationship between the two. Some way must therefore be found to adjust VA/S to eliminate, or at least minimize, the tautological relationship between it and profitability.

I derived the adjusted measure of VA/S used in this analysis as follows:

1 I subtracted net profit from each business unit's reported figures for value added. (For businesses reporting net losses, I do not add losses back to the reported value-added amount.) For businesses that earned positive profits, I also subtracted net profit from reported sales.

2 A "normal" profit, amounting to 20% of investment at book value, is added to value added and to sales. (The 20% figure is approximately the average pretax, preinterest rate of return for the businesses in the PIMS data base.)

3 The adjusted VA/S, used as a measure of vertical integration, is simply

$$\frac{\text{Value added } - \text{ net profits } + \text{ 20\% of investment}}{\text{Sales } - \text{ net profits } + \text{ 20\% of investment}}$$

11
Capacity Strategies for the 1980s

ROBERT A. LEONE and JOHN R. MEYER

The faltering competitiveness of American industry has now become a topic of broad national discussion. Out of that discussion has emerged a renewed awareness that sound production management is of crucial importance to our industrial health.

In this article the authors take a careful look at one strategic production issue: the decision to add new plant capacity. Whether the costs of new capacity are rising or falling, identifiable strategies exist for making profitable long-term decisions. Properly understood, today's competitive environment offers abundant opportunities for success, not merely survival. The trouble comes when managers attempt to make decisions about additions to capacity without first checking to see if their strategic assumptions are appropriate to the present economic climate.

It's 1960. You are the president of virtually any investor-owned electric utility in the United States. Your customers are happy with declining electricity prices. You and your fellow executives in the industry savor the prospect of all-electric living, for the commodity on which your business rests has a 40-year history of declining prices. Regulators are happy with your amenability to requests for lower rates. Environmentalists are happy with your increasing use of clean oil, natural gas, and—in time—nuclear power. Even your investors are happy. Why shouldn't they be? Your common stock is selling well above book value, your bond rating has never been higher, and you have just raised your dividend again.

Your capacity strategy? Expand as rapidly as possible. Preempt your competition by offering inducements to residential and industrial development. Price aggressively to encourage consumption. Construct large capital-intensive generating facilities to squeeze every last economy of scale out of

Published 1980.

new technology. And your strategy works. Declining costs keep prices down and customers and regulators happy. New technologies improve environmental quality and reward investors.

It's 1980. You are now chairman of the board of the same utility. Your customers are outraged at rising electricity prices. They have responded by sharply curtailing overall demand—but not, of course, during the peak times when electricity is most costly for you to generate. Regulators are outraged at the frequency of your requests for rate increases. Rates in the past 10 years have risen so rapidly that they have completely offset the 50 preceding years of rate decreases. Environmentalists are outraged at your increasing dependence on coal or nuclear power. Even your investors are outraged. And they are right to be. Your common stock is selling at less than 80% of book value, your bond rating was recently lowered, and you have even contemplated a reduction in dividends.

Your old capacity strategy will not work. Rapid expansion is neither politically possible nor economically attractive. Preemptive competitive moves merely increase the number of disgruntled customers. Even your intuition— conditioned by years of experience with strategic decisions and their consequences—is under challenge. To pursue economies of scale seems more like throwing good money after bad than the sound economics it once was. Conservation, perhaps the only strategy now palatable to all your constituencies, is at best a holding action. It's hard for you to believe, but even well-managed growth can be unprofitable.

The Lessons of U-Shaped Costs

Your dilemma is not unique. The circumstances just described are specific to the utility industry, but the problems they represent are not. In one industrial sector after another, costs that had been falling are now rising; once satisfied customers are now vocal in their criticism; communities that once sought an expanded economic base now erect barriers to industrial development. Strategies that worked in the 1960s will not work in the 1980s. Why?

In the past decade, the U.S. economy has run an uneasy course between excessive inflation and high levels of unemployment. It has experienced both the externally imposed shock of escalating energy costs and the internally imposed constraints on economic decision making associated with a regulatory boom. As a result, energy efficiency is now a top priority, daily attention to regulatory issues is commonplace, worker attitudes have changed as real incomes fail to keep up with expectations, and, as prices rise, the public is increasingly suspicious of business intentions. These changes in industrial economics need not by themselves invalidate existing strategies. Cumulatively, however, they have yielded another, virtually unnoticed economic change that does: in industry after industry, new production facilities no longer represent low-cost capacity. Thus U.S. industry enters the 1980s confronting an economic reality both unfamiliar and unwelcome, yet rife with profound implications for corporate strategy.

In a wide variety of industries, unit costs associated with capacity additions using the best most up-to-date technology have followed what we call a U-shaped cost-development pattern over time. Frequently in current dollars, and to a lesser extent in deflated dollars, production costs have first declined, then bottomed out, and finally risen over time in the manner stylized in Exhibit 1.

During the 1950s and early 1960s, productivity improvements associated with increasing volume, new technologies, learning curve effects, and the like commonly outpaced inflation or other cost increases. Computers and integrated circuits are only the most familiar examples of such declining-cost industries. There are many others: advances in oxygen technology helped keep steel costs in check for decades; economies of scale and improvements in distribution (e.g., in electricity generation) kept productivity up for many vital commodities; learning curve efficiencies along with advances in data processing yielded substantial productivity improvements in a variety of service industries from fast foods to banking.

These developments often resulted in a pattern of stable or even declining costs, creating the left-hand side (LHS) of the U-shaped pattern in Exhibit 1. In the late 1960s, however, this situation began to change. Many industries found it ever more expensive to replace or expand capacity. Productivity improvements no longer offset cost increases due to inflation, energy and capital costs, or regulatory constraints. Production costs associated with new installations tended to be higher than for existing capacity. Today, as a consequence, a growing number of industries are positioned on the right-hand side (RHS) or rising-cost portion of the U-shape.

Cost Advantages and Disadvantages

The LHS, so characteristic of many industries in the 1950s and 1960s, represents a situation in which the newest plant brought onstream typically has unit costs that are low for its industry. When an industry is on the LHS, new facilities are not severely handicapped by initial capital, environmental, or safety costs that are high relative to those of predecessors. In such circumstances, it is more profitable for management, say, to build a spanking new Burns Harbor facility than to rebuild older steel-making facilities in Bethlehem, Pennsylvania. It is more profitable to install a huge new thermal plant at Ravenswood, Queens, than to update old electricity-generating facilities around the periphery of Manhattan.

All of this changes dramatically, however, when management encounters rising costs with new capacity on the RHS. Here inflation or some other adverse development can so escalate the costs of even the least expensive

Exhibit 1. U-Shaped Cost-Development Pattern

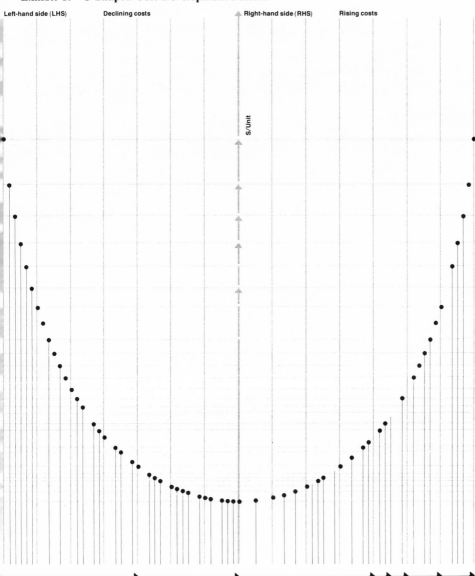

197

new plant that any efficiencies flowing from new technology may not be sufficient to create unit costs lower than those achieved by facilities already in place. When inflation is rampant, the technologies of older palnts, even if relatively inefficient, are often not so inefficient as to offset totally their historical or embedded capital cost advantage. Renovated buildings, for example, can rarely be made quite as energy efficient as their new counterparts, but this disadvantage can often be overcome by their lower embedded capital cost.

Moreover, when government-mandated "new source performance standards" for meeting various pollution and safety regulations are substantially more stringent for new than for old facilities, new plants can be even further disadvantaged. In such circumstances, cost increases can easily outpace technological improvement, and the total unit costs of production in new or replacement facilities are likely to be well above historical levels. In point of fact, this is what did occur in many U.S. industries during the 1970s.

Implications for Strategy

An industry's position on the U-shape has, therefore, significant implications for a number of key managerial decisions—especially those regarding the timing, scale, location, and technology of new production facilities. As summarized in Exhibit 2, these implications vary dramatically on the two sides of the curve. Consider first the declining-cost or LHS situation so familiar to business managers in the 1950s and 1960s.

The LHS Situation

Timing. From a strategic standpoint, a management confronted with LHS conditions will typically find it economically attractive to build capacity in anticipation of growth in demand. Building ahead of demand when on the LHS is, after all, a relatively inexpensive and risk-free means of preempting entry by others. Perhaps the most obvious example of this strategy in action is the aggressive expansion of the Japanese steel industry after World War II. Moreover, the surpluses accruing to such low-cost installations, over and above their unit cost advantage, provide enough of a cushion against adversity to make further investment attractive under a very wide set of future circumstances.

Under LHS conditions a tendency thus exists for industry capacity to lead industry growth. This explains, at least partially, the experience of paper and aluminum producers in the 1950s and 1960s for whom bouts with excess capacity were a recurrent problem.

Exhibit 2. Strategic Implications of U-Shaped Cost Patterns

Although there are no hard-and-fast rules for managers on either the LHS or RHS, tendencies are:

In Declining-Cost Situations to:	In Rising-Cost Situations to:
1 Build large scale	1 Build small scale
2 Build new or greenfield plants	2 Renovate existing facilities
3 Lead growth in demand with preemptive addition to capacity	3 Make more frequent addition to capacity to better track or even lag behind demand
4 Exploit economies of scale and compete on the basis of price	4 Avoid the risk associated with the exploitation of economies of scale and compete on the basis of service, quality, and other dimensions
5 Locate in developing areas and less-developed countries	5 Locate in developed areas with existing markets
6 Exploit operating leverage by choosing capital-intensive technologies	6 Avoid operating risk by choosing technologies with a high ratio of variable to total costs
7 Debt finance new facilities to exploit their favorable risk profiles	7 Debt finance existing facilities to exploit their favorable expectations for use
8 Forecast demand using relatively simple trend-projection methods	8 Forecast demand using sophisticated analytic methods
9 Expand by building new capacity	9 Expand by acquisition of existing capacity

Scale and Location. Not only will capacity tend to lead growth in demand under LHS conditions, new capacity will often be added in the form of large-scale production facilities. Such facilities are intended both to exploit the opportunities for cost reduction and to preempt entry by competitors. Since these large-scale facilities characteristically represent new or "greenfield" plants, management tends to locate them in developing regions where the best sites are not already occupied. By implication, then, the Sunbelt in particular and less-developed regions (or nations) in general become major beneficiaries of LHS industrial conditions. Should a recession take hold, the older regions with their higher-cost facilities will bear the primary burden of idle or underutilized capacity.

Technology. Since new capacity is low-cost capacity, its use is readily assured. In this situation, high operating leverage constitutes a less serious risk than it otherwise might. Hence, management will find it attractive to pursue the cost advantages that are often associated with capital-intensive (but high fixed-cost) technologies. Indeed, under LHS circumstances, a good deal of financial leverage is also justified. This fact helps explain, for example, the attractiveness of very high rates of debt financing in Japanese industries such as steel during their period of aggressive capacity expansion.

The RHS Situation

Scale and Timing. The strategic implications of RHS conditions are substantially more difficult for management to sort out. At the least, being on the right dictates a rather more conservative capacity investment policy than is appropriate to the LHS situation. Specifically, when an industry is on the RHS, capacity additions are closer to the margin of the industry's supply and, therefore, should be undertaken with more hesitancy, be smaller in scale, and occur more frequently. Put simply, RHS conditions make smaller increments of capacity attractive because they risk less and are relatively easily accommodated by market growth.

In practice, this phenomenon helps explain the current success of "minimills" in the steel industry—mills which, though not necessarily as cost-efficient as their larger counterparts when operating at full capacity, need only minimal capital commitments. As part of a strategy to "nibble" away at a growing steel market, they can effectively undercut the economic arguments for constructing large greenfield mills. Larger facilities, by virtue of their dependence on volume for operating economies, lack this strategic capability.

In an industry like steel that is marked by substantial scale economies, a continuing pattern of small increments to existing capacity can easily destroy those economies or, at best, postpone them. Thus, the dynamics of the RHS situation tend both to cause and to perpetuate a suboptimal scale of production—particularly in relatively competitive industries.

This phenomenon also helps explain the relative attractiveness in recent years of expanding capacity by acquisition. Such a strategy, for example, has allowed airlines to buy existing aircraft with low embedded costs. Expanding capacity with new equipment or construction is likely to incur to-day's high capital replacement costs at the same time that it creates the very conditions of excess supply that make high fixed-cost investments unprofitable in the first place.

Technology. In a rising-cost situation, management tends to adopt production methods with relatively high variable costs and low capital costs for the simple reason that facilities built to this rule tend to be smaller in scale and risk less capital. Management will find this risk-reducing strategy even more effective if the prices of raw materials swing with the market demand for the final product.

Consider, for example, the use of secondary fiber—that is, wastepaper—in paper-recycling facilities. The use of wastepaper as a resource successfully avoids many of the capital costs associated with a fully integrated pulp and paper facility. The price of wastepaper, moreover, is highly variable, shifting with the demand for the recycled product; this variability lessens profits in the upturns of the business cycle. More to the point, the converse is also true, since declining wastepaper prices stabilize profits on a downturn—a primary consideration under RHS conditions.

The same arguments apply, of course, to minimills in the steel industry or reprocessing facilities in the aluminum industry, which rely on metal scrap as a major raw material. In RHS situations, these small-scale facilities have a double advantage: (1) they have few economies of scale to lose in a downturn, and (2) their raw material inputs tend to fall in price as demand slackens.

Increased Importance of Demand Forecasting. When the costs of significant new capacity are high and rising, management has no easy rationale for undertaking capacity expansion. Even building for replacement, often a standard justification under LHS conditions, is extremely difficult. Both new and replacement capacity will have costs that are high relative to the facilities already in place or to be replaced. In such circumstances, demand takes on a magnified importance in any strategic capacity decision. Management must be able to analyze demand carefully and forecast it accurately.

On the RHS, simple extrapolation, a method of forecasting historic demand trends sufficient to LHS conditions, is likely to prove seriously inadequate. Thus, a more sophisticated method of demand forecasting, one closely tied to the microeconomists' notion of price elasticity, becomes necessary. Just as the electric utilities gave demand forecasting a low priority in their planning when the industry faced LHS conditions, they must emphasize sophisticated demand analysis now that costs are rising.

This phenomenon is by no means limited to electric or other utilities. Any management facing rising costs and a stable or declining business—whether in steel, black-and-white TVs, or even public school enrollments—must base all capacity decisions on a very close analysis of demand. Under these conditions, accurate forecasting is not just helpful; it is absolutely essential.

Plan to Exploit the RHS Situation

Faced with the complex, confusing, and often counterintuitive facts of business life on the RHS, a good number of managers have been sorely tempted to resign themselves to a capacity strategy designed merely to keep their heads above water.

This is unnecessary and unwarranted defeatism. Of course, the RHS situation is unpleasant—it goes deeply against the grain and violates the familiar dictates of common sense. But it is not so unpleasant nor disturbing nor inexplicable that sound management cannot turn it to strategic advantage.

It may, for instance, seem counterintuitive that the economic advantages of new large-scale capacity can be *less* attractive strategically in an RHS than in an LHS situation. There are, however, two straightforward reasons for this. First, in a rising-cost situation, the cost advantages of scale may be more than offset by the added risk associated with the operation of facilities that are high cost relative to existing facilities. Even though a large-scale fully integrated petrochemical facility may produce chemicals at a lower unit cost than a small-scale facility, if demand cannot sustain the profitable use of the larger capacity, its cost advantage is not worth very much.

Second, since rising costs make it very difficult for new installations to compete on price, the basis of competition for new capacity often shifts to such nonprice dimensions as service or quality. The operators of minimills in the steel industry have successfully employed service and delivery times as competitive weapons. Even the management of new entrants into the fast-food industry, as the industry reached market saturation and found profitable new sites increasingly costly, turned toward competition based on service, larger portions, and variety—factors that minimized an established competitor's embedded cost advantage. Price, after all, is not the only basis for competition.

The Virtues of "Lagging"

Some will argue, of course, that inflation is here to stay and that building ahead of demand, even in rising-cost circumstances, is better than building tomorrow at inflated prices. However appealing, this can be a dangerous path of action. For one thing, if very many competitors choose it, excess supply will make the strategy unattractive for all—even if inflation persists. Furthermore, a disciplined competitor who avoids the temptation to over-build will not be saddled with the high embedded costs of new facilities if inflation subsides or other competitors overexpand. When and if additional demand actually materializes, the disciplined competitor will still have the option to compete for that market as then-current prices and costs dictate.

The point is that there is limited risk to a lagging capacity strategy in RHS circumstances and much real economic risk to a more aggressive strategic posture. To illustrate, many of the domestic airlines, tempted by the deregulation of the industry, expanded aggressively into new markets only to discover that unanticipated increases in the cost of jet fuel made their preemptive demand-leading strategies highly unprofitable.

The most commonly successful strategies for preempting tomorrow's inflation by investing today have been in the real estate market—particularly the market for single-family residential dwellings. Remember, however, that such investment has been accomplished more often by acquisition than by expansion. The most frequent success stories in real estate involve the appreciation of existing dwellings with their low embedded capital costs. Speculative gains to new high-cost housing have been more elusive and far less spectacular. And this is precisely what one would expect in RHS conditions.

Success, Not Survival

Overall, the most troublesome reaction among managers to the strategic implications of rising costs is the pervasive feeling that the only tenable blueprint is for survival, not for profitability. Not so. We cannot stress enough that quite the opposite is true.

In the steel industry, for example, which is unquestionably facing rising costs, competitors with traditional strategies based on large-scale, capital-intensive production methods are in serious financial difficulty. By contrast, the profitable performers are those using small-scale facilities to compete on the basis of specialty products or service in regional markets. The profits of these companies are typically high not only for the steel industry but for the manufacturing sector as a whole.

Similarly, among electric utilities the small-scale producers using agricultural wastes, process steam from manufacturing, or low-head hydro power are outperforming their more traditional competitors. Of equal importance, they are doing so by earning a return on their investment well above the norm for American industry generally.

These examples underscore our basic proposition: just as there are strategies that can successfully exploit the opportunities created by declining costs, there are strategies that can successfully exploit the opportunities created by rising costs. The challenge for management is, as always, to recognize the specific economic reality with which it must deal and to adapt capacity strategies accordingly.

Public Policy Issues

There is nothing inevitable about this pattern of U-shaped costs. It represents an empirical fact for several industries at the present time and may or may not persist. Nevertheless, given that RHS conditions are fairly widespread today and given as well their relevance to capacity strategies in the private sector, it is appropriate to ask what effect the phenomenon may have on the broader issues of public policy. Stated somewhat differently, policy analysts and economists frequently advise managers about the implications of public policy for corporate strategy. Our discussion of capacity strategies in LHS and RHS situations suggests turning the tables for a moment. Let us ask instead what these changes in business policies might mean for public policy.

Pricing Policy

Government regulatory agencies frequently establish prices on the basis of embedded average costs. This, of course, avoids the creation of visible "windfalls" for industry and tends to keep overall price levels stable. In LHS situations, this practice keeps customers, politicians, and investors happy since declining costs keep rates down, avoid political confrontations, and yet leave room for profitable investment in new and still lower-cost facilities.

In RHS situations, however, using historical costs to set prices retains its political appeal but at the expense of discouraging investment in new facilities. Indeed, such regulatory pricing policies have in recent years discouraged investment in new energy-efficient manufacturing technologies, retarded the nation's conversion to coal, and inhibited numerous other productivity-enhancing capital investments.

"Grandfather Exceptions"

A common regulatory practice exempts existing facilities from costly environmental and safety regulations and imposes relatively more stringent standards on new facilities. The apparent rationale is to protect established jobs and communities. Clearly, though, such exemptions also discourage investment, as the embedded capital cost advantages of existing facilities will be enhanced, not reduced, by a grandfather regulatory advantage.

Timing

One of the more predictable consequences of government regulation is that it almost inevitably extends the planning horizon imposed on business. In RHS circumstances, short planning horizons facilitate strategies aimed at matching investment in new facilities as closely as possible with growth in demand. This delicate balancing act risks, however, a perpetuation of suboptimal manufacturing scales and capabilities. On the other hand, longer planning horizons, by frustrating small-scale capacity additions, may help bring new large-scale facilities on stream.

Though we believe that the exploitation of such subtle distinctions in timing is presently beyond the state of bureaucratic art, we would note that questions of timing are being addressed by some policy-makers in their discussion of sophisticated "industrial policies" and economic planning.

Macroeconomic Policy

When the economy is generally experiencing declining costs, macroeconomic policy choices are relatively painless. Stimulation to move out of a recession is not quickly dissipated in higher prices; deflationary policies to avoid "over-heating" at the peak of the cycle will not totally abort management's rationale for productive plant and equipment investment.

Under RHS conditions, by contrast, stimulating demand (say, in a period of so-called stagflation) will drive prices up to the replacement cost levels necessary to justify further investment but will also intensify any inflationary tendencies in the economy. Suppressing demand when the economy becomes overheated runs the risk of lowering productivity growth (to the extent this is reliant on investment), again intensifying inflationary tendencies. At a minimum, supply bottlenecks should appear rather more quickly in an RHS upturn than has historically been the case under LHS conditions.

In general, RHS conditions simply do not admit of easy or painless public policy choices. The appropriate public policy actions may be hard not only for regulators to swallow, but for politicians, the public, and business as well.

☐ Pricing at current replacement costs will mean that windfalls will be created, which in turn could encourage further political intrusion into the affairs of business.

☐ Abandoning grandfather regulatory clauses will stimulate investment in new plant and equipment, but it will also drive up the costs of maintaining existing facilities and increase problems of economic dislocation as old facilities are forced to close.

☐ Shorter lead times in planning will mean that new smaller-scale facilities can be brought on-line less expensively, but this may preclude exploitation in the long term of the economies inherent in new large-scale productive facilities.

☐ A less-stringent monetary policy will necessitate more responsible fiscal policy controls, but fiscal policy offers no painless alternatives for business, government, or the general public.

A Concluding Thought

In the private sector, the high production costs of new capacity overthrow a host of familiar strategic assumptions, assumptions that came into vogue during a prolonged era of LHS conditions. The RHS world of today necessitates different, more conservative investment strategies. It also requires facilities of different scale, geographic location, and technical configuration.

Here lies the central challenge for management, both public and private. The RHS situation will not likely change soon. Its consequences will persist just as long as new capacity experiences total unit costs of production that are high relative to the total costs of existing facilities. This is an inescapable reality—until and unless inflation is contained or technology provides breakthroughs that greatly accelerate productive efficiency. It will be a mark of good management, again both public and private, to turn this reality to advantage.

PART THREE

MANAGING THE MATURE COMPANY

AN OVERVIEW

At the heart of this volume lies the issue of maturity, to which the six articles in this section address themselves. Though quite different in approach, these articles show there are ways to manage such businesses, as well as strategies to guide them, toward decent and, perhaps, even outstanding levels of performance. As always, the challenge is to make creative adjustments to demanding competitive circumstances and not to give in, as Hamermesh and Silk put it, to "glib recommendations that companies either divest these businesses or 'harvest' them as 'cash cows'." Especially so, when "to harvest" so very readily translates into "to abandon." After all, research shows that "it is quite possible to compete successfully and to earn high returns in these industries."

It may ease the managerial conscience to divest a troublesome division, and there are many situations in which the decision to get out is perfectly in order. But—and this is an important "but"—the wish to escape to seemingly greener pastures ought not lead to immediate action as if by conditioned reflex. Instead, it should occasion some hard-headed strategic thought. Getting out too early is a far more common—and avoidable—danger than is staying in too late. It was General Grant who, deep in the toils of the Civil War, confessed his intention to fight it out on the lines he then occupied if it took all summer. Taken to an extreme, this is rank stubbornness. In the right measure and in support of a carefully wrought strategic plan, it is the stuff of which great managers are made.

Diseases That Make Whole Industries Sick

LOUIS E. NEWMAN

In established industries where too much capacity chases after too little demand, cut-throat price competition often makes it impossible for many, if not most, of the companies involved to earn an acceptable profit. The reason? Not, as many observers might suppose, a set of inescapable economic forces but rather a set of misguided managerial beliefs. As the author makes clear, managers in such industries often treat price-sensitive businesses as if they were volume sensitive, reward sales volume rather than the quality of sales, and base prices on cost accounting systems not comparable to those in use by the rest of the industry. Paying attention to these beliefs may not return every industry to economic health, but it will certainly help an industry avoid becoming unnecessarily sick.

☐ The president of an industrial company doing an annual business of $7 million told me that he needed to expand, that his present plant was working around the clock, and that his company was one of the fastest growing in the industry. His only complaint was that the company was barely breaking even from a profit standpoint—barely breaking even while operating at capacity!

☐ The sales manager of a company which competes with the rapidly growing company just mentioned told me that his firm was losing money. Competitive prices were "terrible"; more than three quarters of all business being booked was accepted at large discounts from catalog prices. He went on further to explain the efforts his company was making to upgrade its sales force. He was proud of the fact that his sales staff was being paid what was one of the highest commission

Published 1961.

rates in the industry, a flat 10% whether the order was taken at the catalog price or at a discounted price.

☐ About the same time the general manager of another company in the same industry as the first two companies lamented that his competitors did not know their costs. "If they did," he compained, "they never could be selling at the murderously low prices they are quoting!" He went on further to explain that his company used a very accurate system for determining costs and one particularly well suited to his plant. In fact, it was a system he himself had devised.

All three of the men depicted in these real cases were frustrated by the fact that, though they were operating in a growing industry, even in these "good times" they could not earn a profit that justified the capital tied up in their businesses. It seemed to them that they were operating their plants economically; they felt their competitors were able and honest; and obviously business was plentiful. Why, then, were prices so low, and profits so hard to earn?

The fact is that each of these men had widely held but highly erroneous beliefs—beliefs that can and do make industries sick. One such belief can hurt, but all acting together can make an entire industry operate at a loss.

What are these beliefs that do such damage?

☐ The first occurs when managements erroneously consider their business to be "volume-sensitive," when, in fact, it is "price-sensitive."

☐ The second takes place when companies feel that salespeople should be paid on a basis that rewards only the "volume" of their sales instead of on a basis that recognizes also the "quality" of the sales job done.

☐ The third is the fond delusion that manufacturers can set prices based on cost accounting systems of their individual choice rather than on an industry-wide, uniform system of accounting.

Each of these beliefs, when it becomes a business practice, results in conduct that tends to depress prices. Even when only a handful of manufacturers follow such practices, prices can be depressed across an entire industry.

What happens? Certain manufacturers cut their prices in the sincere belief that they are better off by doing so. Other manufacturers may subsequently feel that taking business at the cut prices is a losing proposition, but not to take business at all is even more costly. The result is almost tragic. Manufacturers fight like cats and dogs for business that will lose money for all of them. A vicious circle is kept in motion by managers who believe they are acting wisely. They feel as though they are slowly bleeding to death. All they can hope for is to prolong their corporate life by slowing the bleeding.

But, while it is easy enough, perhaps, to see what others are doing wrong, understanding why they are making such serious mistakes and recommending what they can do about this—that is another matter entirely. If I may, I'd like to recommend—or, at least, suggest—some practices that may serve to remedy these ills that beset entire industries.

Delusions of Volume

The first form of corporate sickness is characterized by the delusion that volume increases will cure the profit problems of any company. Actually, increases in volume will *only* cure the ills of a company whose products are *volume-sensitive*. Therefore, I recommend that each product in a business be examined to see if it is price-sensitive or volume-sensitive; and that plans be made to handle price-sensitive products differently from volume-sensitive products.

By "volume sensitive," I am referring to a business where earnings are so sensitive to changes in volume that sizable reductions in price can be made profitably if volume increases are enough to offset the price reduction. This might occur in a paper mill with its relatively high investment and high fixed costs, and its low material, labor, and other variable costs.

In the volume-sensitive industries, successful managers have developed certain rules of thumb which take into consideration these truisms:

☐ Price reductions can often be much more than compensated for by the resulting volume increase.

☐ Holding down hourly rates for labor is far less important than ensuring that no plant shutdown occurs.

☐ Purchasing raw materials on the basis of cost is often not as important as assurance of delivery.

☐ Multishift operations permit increases in plant output at very low incremental costs.

These beliefs may be well and good in the volume-sensitive industries. However, when the same practices are carried over into a price-sensitive industry, serious losses can result. By "price-sensitive" I mean a business where earnings are so sensitive to changes in price that sizable increases in volume will not profitably offset even a minor decrease in price.

An example of this might well be the paint business which has very high material costs—high variable costs, but relatively low fixed costs. In the paint business, for instance, it is entirely possible that no amount of added volume could compensate for a general price cut of 10%, regardless of the capacity at which the plant is operating.

In certain types of companies in the paper business, on the other hand, a 10% price decrease that resulted in 20% more volume might shift a non-profitable operation into the "black"—even if the plant was operating at about its break-even point.

Effect of Price Changes

A very useful tool with which to examine a business to see whether it is especially sensitive to price change or volume change is the break-even chart. Three of these charts are shown in Exhibit 1.

Figure A is a typical break-even chart for a manufacturer of fluorescent lighting fixtures. Such a manufacturer would have a material cost in the range of 45% to 55% of selling price, and a total variable cost in the range of 65% to 80%. (Probably Figure A is typical of a great many small- and medium-size plants in the metal fabricating industry.)

The importance of price level to the business can be seen by raising or lowering the level of prices. In Figure B, the price level has been raised 10%. Note that this increase dropped the break-even point from 70% to 50% of capacity—roughly a 30% drop compared with a 10% rise, or a 3 to 1 ratio. Stated another way, this manufacturer could *still break even with almost a third less business* at a 10% higher price level.

The effect of a smaller price change would be directly proportional to that of the 10% price change. For example, a 5% price increase would move the break-even point down from 70% to 60%—roughly a 15% drop compared with the 5% price rise, again a 3 to 1 ratio. What is the obvious conclusion from all this? The particular business is three times as sensitive to price change as it is to volume change.

Figure C illustrates what happens in the same business when the price level is dropped by 10%. The break-even point, you will notice, has now moved from 70% of capacity to 100% of capacity. In this case *no amount of volume increase* can make the business profitable after a 10% price drop. Moreover, we would find that if the company is operated above its 100% capacity point—by overtime, extra shifts, outside help, or other devices—the cost line will bend upward with the extra costs. This upward turn will further push up the break-even point, possibly so much that the company will actually lose money although it is booming with business.

Exhibit 1.   What Happens to Break-Even Point when Price Is Raised or Lowered?

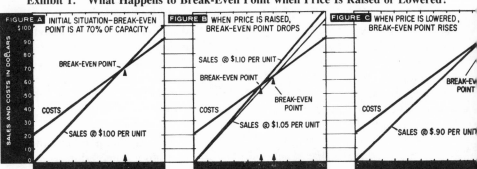

To keep this and the succeeding examples simple we have talked in terms of units of output and dollars of sales and costs. We could have used percentages instead; thus, we can read 100% capacity for 100 units, and 100% sales volume (or, for the other line, 100% costs) for $100; all other figures then are in ratio to 100%. Thus, in the event of a price increase of 10%, as in B, sales volume at 100% capacity would of course be 110% of sales volume at the original price, and the break-even point drops from 70% to 50% of capacity; and, similarly in C, after a 10% decrease in price, sales volume at 100% capacity is 90% of sales volume at the original price, and the break-even point rises from 70% to 100% of capacity.

Differences in Costs

Exhibit 2 compares the break-even points of two different businesses. A paint manufacturing company (A) has high variable but low-fixed costs. A paper producer (B) has low variable but high-fixed costs. In the initial situation depicted in Exhibit 2, both companies are producing 60 units and selling them at $1 each, which is also their break-even point. Now, suppose both companies, being unsatisfied with this unprofitable condition, wish to determine what will happen if they either increase or decrease their prices by 10%.

Exhibit 2.   What Happens to Break-Even Point with Different Mixes of Fixed and Variable Costs?

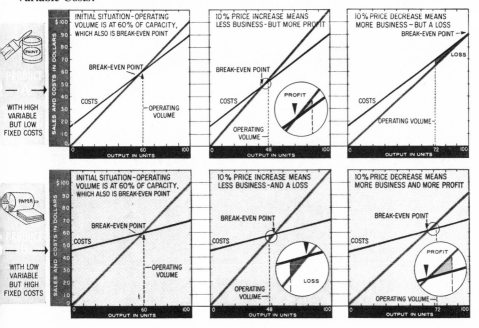

In this illustration, the assumption is made that a 10% price increase will result for both companies in 20% less business (48 units @ $1.10, or $52.80 sales); and a 10% price decrease will result in 20% more business (72 units @ $0.90, or $64.80 sales). This assumption may or may not be wholly valid, but it helps to show that with the same change in price and volume for *both* companies, a price increase may improve the profit position of Company A, while causing a poorer earning position for Company B; and that, again, the converse results from a price decrease. The same picture would show up if we used percentages of capacity instead of units, and percentages of sales volume instead of dollars, as stated in the preceding section.

It should be emphasized that all products, or models, in a given manufacturer's plant cannot always be covered by a single break-even chart. For example, a plant manufacturing insulating materials might find that its insulating varnishes had a material cost in the order of 60% of selling price, while certain of its insulating sheets might have material costs more nearly in the order of 30%. Thus, even though the two products were made in the same plant, and sold by the same sales organization, the varnish line would be price-sensitive while certain sheet insulation might be volume-sensitive. Usually, products will not be found this dissimilar in a single product line, but it is not a safe practice to generalize.

Miscompensated Sales Force

To remedy the troublesome malady known as epidemic price cutting, I suggest that managements should pay salespeople on a basis that recognizes not only volume of sales but also the price level at which these sales are made.

Many sales managers and company presidents I have talked with vigorously agree with the principle of recognizing and rewarding good performance on the part of their sales forces. They are just as emphatic in their avowal that we should all recognize poor performance and penalize it severely. But the discrepancy between what they practice and what they preach is often vast.

In 1959 I made a survey of the field sales compensation practices of the ten leaders in an intensely competitive industry. The results of this survey are condensed in Exhibit 3.

The significant fact revealed by this survey was the close correlation between the method of paying the sales force and the portion of sales that was secured at the catalog price. The same survey examined the extent to which catalog prices were maintained when the authority for cutting prices was reserved entirely to the factory organization and was not delegated, in whole or in part, to the field sales force. It was found that withholding price-

Exhibit 3.   Field Sales Compensation of Different Manufacturers in a Highly Competitive Industry

Selling Price as Percent of Catalog Price	Manufacturers				
	A	B	C	D	All Others
	Commission as percent of selling price				
100%	7.5%	7.5%	7.0%	7.5%	7.0% – 10.0%
95	5.0	6.0	5.0	7.0	7.0 – 10.0
90	2.5	4.0	5.0	6.5	7.0 – 10.0
	Portion of sales at 100% catalog price				
	85%	60%	55%	50%	33%

cutting authority from the field sales organization helped decrease the portion of business taken at cut price. But, even so, the correlation was not clearly as well defined as that indicated by the payment plans shown in the table.

It should be borne in mind that Exhibit 3 examines the field sales compensation plans in a price-sensitive industry. In such an industry you would expect that the manufacturers would realize the great personal value of encouraging their sales force to sell at catalog prices. You would expect special premiums, perhaps, to the salespeople who sold at catalog prices, and, conversely, heavy penalties to the salespeople who got business at cut prices.

Instead, as Exhibit 3 shows, several of the leading manufacturers pay their sales force substantially the same rate for business taken at sharply cut prices as they pay for business taken at the catalog price. The result is that the entire industry is struggling to keep quality up in the face of competition that is made singularly vicious because some companies are rewarding their sales forces equally well for poor jobs of selling as they are for good jobs. And in a normally competitive system, the practices of just a few companies can raise havoc with an entire industry.

One of the problems in correcting such a situation is the difficulty of determining when a good job or a poor job is being done. In the case of the ten companies surveyed in Exhibit 3, most set their territory sales quotas on the basis of history and experience. What is wrong with that? Simply this: it is my belief that *each salesperson should be held accountable for getting a certain percentage of the available business in his or her territory, at competitive prices*. The salespeople must then be guided as to whether it is better, from the company's standpoint, for them to exert their efforts toward getting a better price for a smaller volume, or more volume at a lower price.

The best way to guide the sales force is by means of a compensation plan that rewards them most when they do what is best for the company. The difficulty comes in determining in an objective manner how much business is available, territory by territory. These data may not be known exactly, but usually there are ways by which they can be approximated. In any case, some such approximation must be made in order to identify a good job so that the effective salesperson can be rewarded, and to identify a poor job so that the weaker salesperson can be penalized.

Thus, while the volume part of the sales staff's pay is often difficult to determine, the price level part is usually not so difficult to ascertain. Most manufacturers are fed a continuous flow of competitive price information from contacts with customers, dealers, and published information. Here again, though, the sales staff's compensation should be geared to the prices they receive in order to encourage them to spend the effort necessary to get full payment for features of value to the customer.

Capricious Costing

To remedy the industry-wide disease which reaches its climax in a disastrous price war, I suggest that uniform accounting systems are needed throughout the industry.

A "rose is a rose is a rose" (á la Gertrude Stein) may be true, but certainly the same could not be said of a cost. An identical product, made on an identical machine, with identical direct material and labor costs, may have a very different cost according to two managers who use different systems of costing. The fact is that costing systems try to spread the indirect costs (or overhead) equitably across the product line. The best these systems can hope to accomplish is to "average out" costs correctly. This would, of course, be all right if every competing manufacturer used the same basic costing system. If they do not, however, then the price level in the industry is likely to sink to the lowest common denominator of the various systems. The more systems in use, the more "ridiculously low" the prices that result will be. This can be shown in a short series of examples that, while oversimplified, are nevertheless realistic. Suppose that overheads in three companies are applied on the following basis:

Company A   100% of direct labor cost.
Company B   100% of material cost.
Company C   50% of the sum of direct labor and material.

Now let us work through several examples where Companies A, B, and C are manufacturing products that are identical, and see what differences the three overhead methods cause. In the case of one product let us assume a direct labor cost of $5 and a material cost of $5. The cost work-up then is:

	Company A	Company B	Company C
Direct Labor	$ 5	$ 5	$ 5
Material	5	5	5
Overhead	5	5	5
Total	$15	$15	$15

That example works out fine. The total direct labor and material in the product is $10, the overhead is $5, and all three systems result in a total cost of $15.

The picture changes with a different mix of costs. Suppose the direct labor and material still total $10, but in the case of this product direct labor is $2 and material is $8. Our example now works out like this:

	Company A	Company B	Company C
Direct labor	$ 2	$ 2	$ 2
Material	8	8	8
Overhead	2	8	5
Total	$12	$18	$15

At this point, Manufacturer B is apt to wonder how it is possible for Manufacturer A to be eager to sell at prices so far below cost.

Now here is a third example. Again $10 is the total cost of direct labor and material, but in this case $8 goes for direct labor and $2 for material. Our example becomes:

	Company A	Company B	Company C
Direct Labor	$ 8	$ 8	$ 8
Material	2	2	2
Overhead	8	2	5
Total	$18	$12	$15

Now it is Manufacturer A's turn to wonder how Manufacturer B can sell this model at such a low price.

The fact is, as in all three examples, that *the market price level of the product will tend to be set largely by the lowest cost arrived at by the different systems of overhead.*

If, instead of three manufacturers with three different costing systems, there were several hundred manufacturers, and, instead of three costing systems, there were many more, the result would be a general depression in the price level for all products in an entire industry. This depression would be caused by various managers believing different models were different in cost when in fact they were not. Moreover, it is entirely possible that one

Exhibit 4.   How Industry Price Levels Are Driven Down by Different Costing Systems

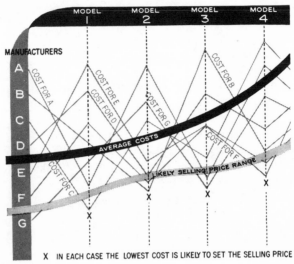

X IN EACH CASE THE LOWEST COST IS LIKELY TO SET THE SELLING PRICE

system would show a lower total cost than another, even if both its direct labor and its material costs were higher than the other system's.

Suppose 10 manufacturers producing the same line of models each had the same *average* costs for all the models. Even so, the difference in their costs for the *individual* models might result in all of them selling *all* of their models at below-average costs. Exhibit 4 gives a rough picture of such a possible situation. Fortunately the picture is not usually quite that extreme, but even a smaller variety in costing systems can and does bring a chaotic situation in the market place.

The only cure for such a situation lies in industry-wide adoption of common accounting procedures. Many industries already have these common accounting systems available for use, but the members fail to see the values inherent in their wide adoption. A case in point is the uniform accounting system developed by the National Electrical Manufacturers Association.

Conclusion

Industries become highly competitive when demand is appreciably below the capacity of the industry to satisfy the demand. But there is less likelihood of prices being depressed below the levels at which the industry can support itself if certain bad practices are recognized and corrected. The cure is not through collusive agreements; rather it depends on managers recognizing three simple maxims:

1 Each product must be examined to see if it is price-sensitive or
   volume-sensitive. Price-sensitive products deserve more sales effort
   to support prices than do volume-sensitive products.

2 Sales compensation plans in price-sensitive industries should especially reward the field sales force for success in holding the catalog
   price level.

3 Uniform accounting systems should be adopted to lessen the likelihood of different manufacturers believing that cost differences
   exist when in fact they do not.

13

Survival Strategies in a Hostile Environment

WILLIAM K. HALL

How are such domestic manufacturing industries as steel, tire and rubber, auto-motive, heavy-duty truck and construction equipment, home appliance, beer, and cigarette evolving in the face of today's adverse external pressures? Given the lower growth, inflationary, regulatory, and competitive impacts, what business strategies are appropriate? Which strategic choices offer the best chances for survival, growth, and ROI in a hostile environment? This author investigates these issues and presents some preliminary findings from an ongoing research project which explores the strategic and structural changes that took place in the 1970s and that are expected to continue into the 1980s.

As economists, managers, and industry analysts pause to look back on the past decade, there remains little doubt that the business environment in the United States grew increasingly hostile during the 1970s. More important, there is now little doubt that this hostile environment will continue (and perhaps even worsen) during the decade ahead, reflecting the combined effects of:

☐ Slow erratic growth in domestic and world markets.

☐ Intensified inflationary pressures on manufacturing and distribution costs.

☐ Intensified regulatory pressures on business conduct and investment decisions.

☐ Intensified competition, both from traditional domestic competitors and also from the new wave of foreign competitors entering U.S. markets with different objectives and frequently lower ROI expectations.

Published 1980.

As a result of these growing pressures, large U.S. manufacturing corporations are witnessing a major evolution in industry structures and competitive behaviors. Many structures that were stable and highly profitable during the "go-go" decade of the 1960s are now moving toward instability and marginal profitability.

Moreover, the broad range of corporate strategies and business "success formulas" which brought prosperity in those earlier years are no longer working. Instead, these are being replaced with a much narrower range of strategic choices that are becoming essential to survive in the hostile environment ahead.

The purpose of this article is to present some preliminary findings from an ongoing research project that my colleagues and I are conducting to explore these strategic and structural changes in more depth. This project is focusing on these broad questions:

1 How are industry structures in the mature markets evolving in the face of the adverse external pressures of the late 1970s?
2 Given this evolution, what business strategies are appropriate? Which strategic choices give the best chances for survival, growth, and return in the hostile environment ahead?

In-Depth Investigation

To examine these issues, I selected eight major domestic manufacturing industries for comprehensive study because of their importance to national and/or regional economic development and also because the adverse external trends of the 1970s have been especially severe in their impact on them. As a result, during the 1970s, all eight industries underwent a significant structural change which is expected to continue into the 1980s. Within these industries, I examined the strategies and evolving competitive positions of the 64 largest companies by using a combination of public data sources and field interviews.

In examining the impact of external pressures on these companies, I found that the eight industries either matured during the 1970s or will mature in the 1980s, resulting in lower growth records and growth expectations as shown in Exhibit 1. Although the industries (on average) exceeded national economic growth rates in the 1950s and 1960s, they grew only slightly faster than the GNP in the 1970s, and they are projected to grow significantly more slowly than the U.S. economy in the 1980s.

During this maturation period, these eight industries, which are capital, raw material, and labor intensive, have been subjected to heavy inflationary pressures that cannot easily be price recovered. All are being forced by regulatory agencies to make major investments to comply with new occu-

Exhibit 1.   Compound Annual Real Growth Rates in Demand—United States (eight basic industries)

	1950–1970	1971–1980	1980 Forecast[a]
Industrial goods			
Primary products			
Steel	4.0%	2.2%	1.5%-2.5%
Tire and rubber	4.2	1.4	1.0-1.5
Intermediate products			
Heavy-duty trucks	7.0	2.8	2.5
Construction and materials handling equipment	7.8	3.6	2.3
Consumer goods			
Durable products			
Automotive	4.8	3.5	2.0-3.0
Major home appliances	6.2	2.9	2.3-2.8
Nondurable products			
Beer	3.1	2.5	2.3
Cigarettes	1.6	1.0	0
Average growth rates— eight industries	**4.8%**	**2.4%**	**1.9%**
Average growth rates— U.S. GNP	**3.7%**	**2.3%**	**2.5%**

[a]Based on economic forecasts and industry projections.

pational safety and health regulations and with new product safety, performance, and environmental protection standards.

In addition to the domestic pressures, foreign competition has been harsh in the eight basic industries selected for study. Foreign competitors have achieved significant market shares in three of the industries—steel, tire and rubber, and automotive; moderate shares in two—heavy-duty trucks and construction and materials handling equipment; and entry positions in the other three—major home appliances, beer, and cigarettes.

Because many of these foreign competitors are either nationalized, quasinationalized, or highly salient in their own countries, they are frequently willing to accept lower returns in U.S. markets, offsetting these lower returns against unemployment, balance of payments, and capital gains at home. Although these foreign approaches have been criticized as unfair, the results have altered U.S. domestic industry structures in all eight cases.

Needless to say, the net effect of these adverse trends has made life anything but pleasant for managers and companies in these basic industries.

Profitability and sales growth levels have generally fallen to or below the average manufacturing returns in the U.S. economy (Exhibit 2). And industry spokesmen frequently speak out, urging either public assistance or some type of return to the simpler, less painful world of the 1960s.

As one senior executive I interviewed commented: "Maybe I should have accepted that job as an IBM systems engineer after graduation from college. It sure would be fun to look forward to going to work in the morning." Despite the outcries, the adverse external trends haven't gone away, and structural evolution continues at a slow, but inevitable, pace.

The heavy-duty truck manufacturing industry provides an excellent example of this evolution. In the early 1960s, spurred by rapid growth in the economy and by the completion of the U.S. interstate highway system, the industry grew at more than 8% per year. Eight major manufacturers—International Harvester, General Motors, Ford, Mack, White Motor, Diamond Reo, Chrysler, and Paccar—participated fairly equally in this growth, producing 60 truck models to serve the rapidly growing light-heavy and heavy-duty segments (19,000 pounds and greater gross vehicle weight).

However, by the late 1970s, annual growth had slowed to less than 3%. Emission regulations and inflation had raised unit costs. Investments for new truck model development had slowed to the extent that the number of models had dropped from 60 to 35 by 1979.

As a result of this movement toward a hostile environment, Chrysler

Exhibit 2. Financial Returns and Revenue Growth Rates, 1975–1979 (eight basic industries)

	Return on Equity	Return on Capital	EPS Growth	Revenue Growth
Steel	7.1%	5.7%	5.5%	10.4%
Tire and rubber	7.4	5.9	3.9	9.6
Heavy-duty trucks[a]	15.4	11.6	13.8	13.8
Construction and materials handling equipment	15.4	10.7	16.8	13.0
Automotive[a]	15.4	11.6	13.8	13.8
Major home appliances	10.1	9.0	3.2	6.8
Beer	14.1	10.2	6.2	12.4
Cigarettes	18.2	10.5	8.9	12.2
Average—eight industries	**12.9%**	**9.4%**	**9.0%**	**11.5%**
Average *Fortune* "1,000" company	**15.1%**	**11.0%**	**13.1%**	**13.1%**

[a]All vehicle manufacturers.

closed its heavy-duty truck manufacturing operation, Diamond Reo was in bankruptcy, and White lingered near receivership. Both Mack and International Harvester had lost significant market share and were searching for foreign assistance or major cost-cutting programs to maintain their viability. Of the eight healthy domestic competitors in the early 1960s, only three—General Motors, Ford, and Paccar—maintained free-standing, vibrant, competitive positions as they entered the decade of the 1980s.

Similar moves toward lower profitability and consolidation occurred in all eight industries as the hostile environment took its evolutionary toll. In steel, Bethlehem announced in 1977 the largest corporate quarterly loss in U.S. history up to that time (exceeded by Chrysler two years later and U.S. Steel in late 1979), Jones & Laughlin and Youngstown merged under the failing firm provision of U.S. antitrust laws in 1978, and Kaiser tried to sell its steel-making operation to the Japanese in 1979. In rubber, industry analysts waited impatiently for Uniroyal to exit the industry; and in automotive, Chrysler made front-page headlines in its race against time to achieve federal loan assistance. Words like "dinosaur" and "dog" were coined by industry observers to describe the evolving competitive profiles in all eight industries.

However, the profiles of basic industry problems and corporate failures tell only part of the story. These "disaster" tales need to be juxtaposed against some success stories to see how some companies have survived and even prospered in the same hostile environment. The resulting comparisons provide important insights into survival strategies and industry dynamics not only for general managers in the eight industries under study but also for managers in other industries as they lead their companies into the new decade. For example, a careful comparison of success and problem strategies in the eight industries in this study demonstrates that:

☐ Great success is possible, even in a hostile environment.

☐ Strategies leading to success share common characteristics.

☐ Successful strategies come from purposeful moves toward a leadership position.

☐ Problems come from failure to gain or defend a leadership position.

☐ For a deteriorating position, diversity may not be the proper recovery approach.

☐ Structural evolution moves toward a dynamic equilibrium as basic industries face a hostile environment.

I will amplify and discuss each of these insights in subsequent sections of this article.

Great success is possible, even in a hostile environment

When one looks at the eight industries in this study, as well as at other basic manufacturing industries facing the hostile environment of the 1980s, it is easy to slip into generalizations by extrapolating from aggregate industry problems to the individual companies within the industry.

Recent articles in the business press, asking "What Killed the U.S. Steel Industry?," "Is Chrysler the Prototype?," or proclaiming "Tire Industry Goes Flat" or "Last Chances for Cigarette Producers," are typical of those that tend to project adverse trends uniformly onto all competitors in the industry. In fact, however, nothing could be further from the truth. Some of the most vibrant successful companies in the world reside and prosper in these seemingly hostile industry environments.

If one eliminates from my eight-industry sample of 64 companies all competitors who gain a majority of revenues and profits from diversification efforts outside their basic industry (e.g., Armco Steel and General Tire), then the most profitable remaining competitors (the industry leaders) in terms of corporate return on equity are those shown in Exhibit 3.

While some variation in returns exists among these leading competitors (Goodyear and Inland had significantly lower returns and growth rates than the other six), the corporate average return on equity earned over the last

Exhibit 3. Financial Returns and Growth Rates, 1975–1979 (leading companies in eight basic industries)[a]

	Average Return on Equity	Average Return on Capital	Annual Revenue Growth Rate
Goodyear	9.2%	7.0%	10.0%
Inland Steel	10.9	7.9	11.4
Paccar	22.8	20.9	14.9
Caterpillar	23.5	17.3	17.2
General Motors	19.8	18.0	13.2
Maytag	27.2	26.5	9.1
G. Heileman Brewing	25.8	18.9	21.4
Philip Morris	22.7	13.5	20.1
Average	**20.2%**	**16.3%**	**14.7%**
Median *Fortune* "1,000" company (same time period)	**15.1%**	**11.0%**	**13.1%**

[a]Excluding those companies that gained a majority of their returns from diversification efforts.

half of the 1970s easily places these companies in the top 20% of the *Fortune* "1,000" industrials and well ahead of the median *Fortune* company on return on capital and annual growth rate.

Moreover, the average returns on both equity and capital in my sample of industry leaders are well ahead of those earned by the leading international oil company (Phillips Petroleum). These average returns are also well ahead of those earned by companies heralded by the business community as technology leaders (Xerox, Eastman Kodak, Texas Instruments, and Digital Equipment), and these returns are likewise well ahead of those earned by corporations singled out as models of progressive diversification and acquisition planning (General Electric and United Technologies).

In fact, as Exhibit 4 shows, the industry leaders shown in Exhibit 3 outperformed all of the highly touted companies during the most recent five years. In addition, the industry leaders grew faster than premier corporations

Exhibit 4. Financial Returns and Growth Rates, 1975–1979 (leading companies in other and more rapidly growing industries)

	Average Return on Equity	Average Return on Capital	Annual Revenue Growth Rate
International oil			
Phillips Petroleum	19.5%	14.7%	16.6%
Technology leaders			
Xerox	17.8	14.4	15.5
Eastman Kodak	18.8	17.7	11.8
Texas Instruments	17.2	16.3	14.6
Digital Equipment	17.0	15.5	37.4
Diversification leaders			
General Electric	19.4	16.9	10.5
United Technologies	18.3	12.6	19.0
Average of these "high performance" leaders	**18.3%**	**15.4%**	**17.9%**
Average (leading companies in basic industries from Exhibit 3)	**20.2%**	**16.3%**	**14.7%**
"Blue chip" competitors			
IBM	21.9	21.2	13.5
3M	20.7	17.7	13.1

like 3M and IBM, and they returned only slightly less to their shareholders and capital investors than these same "blue chip" competitors in high-growth industries.

In retrospect, perhaps the much publicized article, "TI Shows U.S. Industry How to Compete in the 1980s,"[1] should have been written about one of the leading companies in my sample instead of about Texas Instruments, because 75% of the leaders in the basic industries I studied outperformed TI during the latter half of the 1970s. Moreover, they outperformed TI in industries that averaged only 2.4% real growth during the past decade, significantly less than the 15% to 20% compound growth rates of the semiconductor industry during this same period.

Thus even a cursory analysis of leading companies in the eight basic industries leads to an important observation: survival and prosperity are possible even when the business environment turns hostile and industry trends change from favorable to unfavorable. In this regard, the casual advice frequently offered to competitors in basic industries—that is, diversify, dissolve, or be prepared for below-average returns[2]—seems oversimplified and even erroneous. A hostile environment offers an excellent basic investment opportunity and reinvestment climate, at least for the industry leaders insightful enough to capitalize on their positions.

Strategies leading to success share common characteristics

A more detailed examination of the business strategies employed by the top two performing (nondiversified) companies in each of the eight industries sampled reveals that these success strategies share strong common characteristics, irrespective of the particular industry. Indeed, throughout their modern history, all 16 of these leading companies have demonstrated a continuous, single-minded determination to achieve one or both of the following competitive positions within their respective industries:

☐ Achieve the lowest delivered cost position relative to competition, coupled with both an acceptable delivered quality and a pricing policy to gain profitable volume and market share growth.

☐ Achieve the highest product/service/quality differentiated position relative to competition, coupled with both an acceptable delivered cost structure and a pricing policy to gain margins sufficient to fund reinvestment in product/service differentiation.

A rough categorization of the strategies employed by these 16 companies, based on selective field studies and observed behavior over time, is shown in Exhibit 5. In most cases, the industry growth and profit leaders chose only one of the two strategic approaches, on the basis that the skills and resources necessary to invest in a low-cost position are insufficient or incompatible with those needed to invest simultaneously in a strongly differentiated position.

The rudiments of this strategic trade-off can be found as early as the 1920s in Alfred P. Sloan's statements regarding General Motors' selection of a cost-reduced strategy:

> Management should now direct its energies toward increasing earning power through increased effectiveness and reduced expense. . . . Efforts that have been so lavishly expended on expansion and development should now be directed at economy in operation. . . . This policy is valid if our cars are at least equal to the best of our competitors in a grade, so that it is not necessary to lead in design.[3]

However, in at least three cases, the leading companies in my sample chose to combine the two approaches, and each has had spectacular success.

Caterpillar has combined lowest cost manufacturing with higher cost but truly outstanding distribution and after-market support to differentiate

Exhibit 5. Competitive Strategies Employed by Leading Companies (eight basic industries)

Industry	Achieved Low Delivered Cost Position	Achieved "Meaningful" Differentiation	Simultaneous Employment of Both Strategies
Steel	Inland Steel	National	
Tire and rubber	Goodyear	Michelin (French)	
Heavy-duty trucks	Ford	Paccar	
Construction and materials handling equipment		John Deere	Caterpillar
Automotive	General Motors	Daimler Benz (German)	
Major home appliances	Whirlpool	Maytag	
Beer	Miller	G. Heileman Brewing	
Cigarettes	R.J. Reynolds		Philip Morris

its line of construction equipment. As a result, Caterpillar, ranking as the 24th largest and 39th most profitable company in the United States, is well ahead of its competitors and most of the *Fortune* "500" glamour companies.

Similarly, the U.S. cigarette division of Philip Morris combines the lowest cost fully automated cigarette manufacturing operation in the world with highest cost focused branding and promotion to gain industry profit leadership, even without the benefit of either the largest unit volume or segment market share in both domestic and international markets.

And finally, Daimler Benz operates with elements of both strategies but in different segments, coupling the lowest cost position in heavy-duty truck manufacturing in Western Europe with an exceptionally high quality feature-differentiated car line for European and North American export markets.

A more complete picture of the strategic and performance profiles of all major competitors in these eight hostile environments can be obtained by positioning on a matrix those businesses whose axes reflect the relative delivered cost position and the relative product/service differentiation with respect to other competition. The result is a conceptual diagram like that shown in Exhibit 6.

Although the quantification of competitive profiles in this format is typically inexact—because of the proprietary nature of relevant cost, sector, and performance data—a qualitative attempt to perform this analysis for the heavy-duty truck manufacturing industry is presented in Exhibit 7. This representation, based on an analysis of industry interviews and public records, is imprecise, yet it correlates perfectly with the industry performance profiles over time.

For example, from Exhibit 8, it is clear why Ford and Paccar continually lead the heavy-duty truck industry in growth and financial performance. It is equally clear why White lingers near bankruptcy and also why Freightliner and International Harvester are rethinking their strategies for heavy-duty trucks. (Freightliner entered into a distribution agreement with Volvo in an attempt to differentiate its distribution system in the light-heavy segment, and International Harvester initiated a major cost-reduction effort in truck design and manufacturing in an attempt to improve its weak relative cost position.)

A similar analysis of business-level returns for all 16 leading competitors in the eight industries (Exhibit 8) indicates some interesting aspects of the respective strategies, as the following comparison reveals:

☐ The *lowest delivered cost* leader typically grows more slowly, holding price increases and operating margins down to gain volume, fixed-cost reductions, and improved asset turnover. In addition, this competitor will typically have a lower sales turnover than the differentiated

Exhibit 6.   Strategic Profile Analysis (basic mature industries)

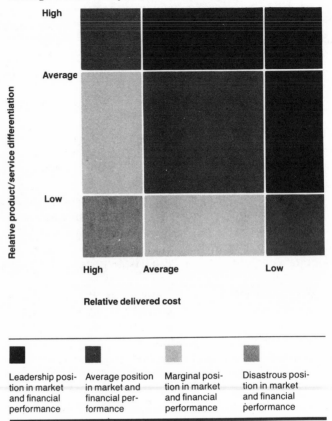

producer, reflecting the higher asset intensity necessary to gain cost reductions in production and distribution.

☐   The *differentiated position* leader typically grows faster, with higher prices and operating margins to cover promotional, research, and other product/service costs. At the same time, this competitor typically operates with lower asset intensity (higher sales turnover), reflecting both higher prices and a lower cost "flexible" asset base.

Successful strategies come from purposeful moves toward a leadership position

In examining the business strategies and subsequent performance of the leading competitors, it becomes clear that purposeful movement toward and defense of a "winning" strategic position—either lowest cost and/or superior

Exhibit 7.   Strategic Profiles in U.S. Heavy-Duty Truck Manufacturing

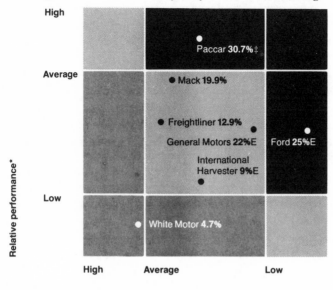

price-justified differentiation—has been the fundamental long-term objective of all 16 high performance companies. There is little doubt that consistency and clarity of purpose have helped to mobilize and coordinate internal resources in gaining and defending a leadership position.

It is important to note that the time-phased pattern of investment decisions used to attain and hold these winning positions was based on "doing the right things" to gain leadership in lowest costs and/or differentiation. As a result, all the high performers in my sample used careful strategic analysis to guide their investments, avoiding simplistic adherence to doctrinaire approaches toward strategy formulation which come from the naive application of tools such as:

☐   *Share/growth matrices.*   Planning models that suggest that mature market segments should be "milked" or "harvested" for cash flows.

Exhibit 8.   Business Level Returns and Revenue Growth Rates

	Operating Margins	Sales Turnover	Operating ROA	Revenue Growth Rates, 1975–1979
Leading Industrial Goods Producers[a] 1978				
Steel				
Inland Steel	8.3%	1.3	10.8%	11.4%
National	12.0	1.5	18.0	12.0
Tire and rubber				
Goodyear	8.6	1.5	12.9	10.5
Michelin	10.0 (est.)	N.A.	N.A.	N.A.
Heavy-duty trucks				
Ford	11.0 (est.)	2.3	25.0 (est.)	12.7
Paccar	12.7	2.4	30.5	15.5
Construction and materials handling equipment				
Caterpillar	15.5	1.8	27.9	14.9
John Deere	10.0	1.3	13.0	17.5
Leading Consumer Goods Producers[a] 1978				
Automotive				
General Motors	9.6%	2.0	19.2%	13.2%
Daimler Benz (automotive)	11.0	2.4	26.4	15.1
Major home appliances				
Whirlpool	8.4	1.0	8.4	5.3
Maytag	21.8	1.8	39.2	9.1
Brewing				
Miller	8.2	1.5	12.3	29.2
G. Heileman Brewing	9.5	3.5	33.3	32.2
Cigarettes				
R.J. Reynolds	17.1	2.3	39.3	15.0
Philip Morris	17.7	1.4	24.8	20.1

[a]Lowest delivered cost producer listed first, followed by most differentiated producer.

☐ *Experience curves and PIMS.*[4] Planning models that suggest that high market share and/or lowest cost vertically integrated production are keys to success in mature markets.

Instead, based on a case-by-case analysis, the performance leaders made investment decisions that frequently conflicted with these doctrinaire theories:

1. The leadership positions in mature markets were not being milked by any of the 16 competitors, contrary to the advice of consultants who emphasize the portfolio approach to asset management. In fact, the top managers in two of the leading companies I interviewed laughed when they discussed this concept. They pointed out that their future success and growth opportunities were far greater if they aggressively reinvested in their base business than if they redeployed assets into other (diversified) industries.

2. Low-cost production is not essential to prosper in mature markets, contrary to the belief of strong proponents of the experience curve. Instead, high sustainable returns also come from reinvesting in an average cost, highly differentiated position, as the data of the previous section and Exhibit 8 demonstrate, and as the ongoing track records of companies like Paccar and Maytag clearly illustrate.

3. High market share and accumulated experience are not essential for cost leadership in a mature market, as indicated by proponents of the experience curve and some large-sample empirical studies like PIMS. In fact, four of the eight low-cost producers in this study—Inland Steel, Whirlpool, Miller, and Philip Morris—have achieved their lowest cost positions without the benefit of high relative market shares.

Rather, these producers have focused their plants by emphasizing modern automated process technology, and they have heavily invested in their distribution systems to gain scale economies and other cost reductions in their delivery systems.

4. Vertical integration is not necessary to exploit cost leadership in mature markets, as suggested by a number of empirical and economic studies. In fact, all of the low-cost producers in the industries under study were less vertically integrated into upstream and downstream activities than at least one other major competitor in their industry.

Instead of emphasizing vertical integration as a policy, all looked for selective integration into high value-added, proprietary componentry, following the type of integration policy first delineated by General Motors in the 1920s of "not investing in general industries of which a comparatively small part of the product is consumed in the manufacture of cars."

Instead of fully integrating, the low-cost leaders invested to have the most efficient process technology in at least one selective stage of the vertical chain. Consider, for example, Ford in truck assembly and Inland in order entry-distribution. The result in all cases is focus—the ability to orient management attention to gain low costs in a partially integrated operation. As one of Ford's major competitors observed:

> Ford is the least integrated of any of the high-volume heavy-duty truck manufacturers in the world, yet it is still the low-cost producer and gains one of the highest ROIs in the industry. In retrospect, Ford's strategy was brilliant; they let the rest of us learn to manufacture componentry while they learned to manufacture profits.

Problems come from failure to gain or defend a leadership position

A more detailed examination of the marginal or failing competitors in each of the eight basic industries (Exhibit 9) also reveals some interesting observations:

1. The historical strategies and policies pursued by these companies have placed them in an unstable position. All are the high-cost producers in their segments, and all have a product that not only is largely undifferentiated in any meaningful sense but also in many cases is below average in quality and performance.

2. The external pressures that these companies complain about—unwarranted regulation and unfair foreign competition—are simply the final blows, sealing a fate that was predestined by improper strategic positioning or repositioning in the 1950s and 1960s, a period when there was still growth and time to maneuver.

3. Many of these marginal producers held low-cost or differentiated positions in these earlier years, and made strategic errors in their reinvestment decisions which contributed to their marginal or failing positions today, as the following examples show.

International Harvester. Led the U.S. heavy-duty truck manufacturing industry in 1965 with a market share of 30%. However, over the next decade, IH failed to reduce costs as rapidly as Ford and GM. As a result, the IH truck division is now a high-cost low-margin producer.

White Motor. A strong number-two truck producer in the mid-1960s, invested in backward integration into cabs, frames, axles, and engine manufacturing, assuming that this would reduce costs. Unfortunately, these investments, all made at suboptimal capacities for efficient scale economies,

Exhibit 9. Marginal or Failing Companies in U.S. Markets

Steel	J&L-Youngstown
	Kaiser
Tire and rubber	Uniroyal
	Mohawk
	Cooper
Heavy-duty trucks	White Motor
Construction and materials handling	Massey Ferguson
equipment	Allis Chalmers
Automotive	Chrysler
Major home appliances	Tappan
Beer	Most regional breweries
	Schlitz
Cigarettes	Liggett & Myers

resulted in a relative high-cost position, adding momentum to White's deteriorating situation.

Tappan.   The technology leader in ranges in the early 1960s, chose to broaden that product line, to diversify, to reduce R&D expenditures, and to outsource certain key engineering activities. As a result, it failed to gain the low-cost position in ranges (today held by GE). And by failing to reinvest in technology, it lost its differentiated position in ranges to Caloric (gas), Jenn-Air (electric), and Raytheon (microwave).

Chrysler.   The technology leader in the U.S. automotive market in the early 1950s with a 25% market share, chose to make questionable international expansion decisions while adopting a "me too" participatory strategy in the domestic market. The subsequent decline in Chrysler's position and returns was predictable, and this disaster trajectory was certainly accelerated in the early 1970s when its management team announced a revised (but highly inappropriate) strategy to "try to be a General Motors in whatever segments of the market we choose to compete in."

> *For a deteriorating position, diversity may not be the proper recovery approach*

Over the past several years, it has become fashionable to recommend product/market diversification as a way out of an unstable or failing position for mature companies in hostile environments. Unfortunately, in the 64 companies I examined in this research, diversification has "helped" overcome major competitive/performance problems in only three—B.F. Goodrich, General Tire, and Armco Steel (now Armco Group). These three competitors recognized the tenuous nature of their positions early in the maturity cycle and took steps to resegment their base businesses into more advantageous positions by redeploying assets in carefully chosen diversification moves.

Goodrich moved into high-margin, specialty segments of the tire industry while diversifying to attain a low-cost position in PVC and other basic chemicals.

General shifted into low-cost production of tires for commercial vehicles while diversifying to attain a participatory position in very high-growth, fragmented industries such as communications and aerospace.

Armco proceeded into low-cost steel production in selected regional segments like oil country pipe, while diversifying into high-growth markets like oilfield equipment, oil and gas exploration, and financial services. (A recent public relations release from Armco announced that most of its new capital investment would go toward growing these diversification ventures, while maintaining only current capacity levels in steel making.)

These early efforts to resegment and to gain meaningful diversification have paid off. General and Armco lead all competitors in the rubber and steel industries in return on capital and growth, while Goodrich has moved into a stable third place among the surviving tire and rubber producers.

On the other hand, efforts to gain meaningful economic diversification have eluded most of the other problem competitors in the eight industries. By waiting too long to begin diversification efforts, most lack the capital and managerial skills to enter new markets and/or to grow businesses successfully in these markets. Thus their diversification efforts to date have been too small or have been managed in too conservative a fashion to obtain sustainable performance improvements, as witnessed by the very minor performance contribution of U.S. Steel's diversification program into chemicals and the continuing problems of Liggett & Myers despite a 43% diversification program out of the tobacco industry.

As a result of these modest participatory efforts, some of the marginal performers in the eight industries have even divested diversified assets to gain capital and "hang on" for a few more years in the base business. Two notable examples are White Motor's recent sale of its construction equipment operation and Uniroyal's sale of its consumer goods division.

On the whole, it would appear that diversification comes too little and too late for most companies caught in a hostile environment. However, for a courageous few, continued managerial commitment and refocus on the base business to provide a steady flow of capital for promoting meaningful positions in diversified businesses may work to ensure ongoing growth and vitality.

Exhibit 10. Strategic and Performance Subgroups (basic industries)

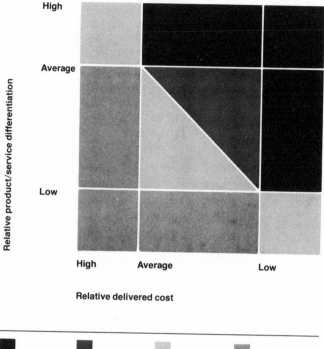

Structural evolution moves toward a dynamic equilibrium as basic industries face a hostile environment

A summary of the underlying data in my study suggests that basic industries in mature hostile environments are moving through a structural evolution, leading ultimately to four industry and performance subgroups (Exhibit 10):

1. *Leadership position.* Competitors who achieve the lowest delivered cost and/or the highest differentiated position. These positions are gained either on a full product line (Caterpillar) or on an economically viable segment (Whirlpool in washers and dryers). At maturity these competitors will

have the highest growth rates and returns in the industry, the best reinvestment prospects, and they should be able to prosper and coexist in dynamic equilibrium even though external pressures continue.

2. *Next best position.* Competitors who attain the second best position in either cost or differentiation (again on either a full or partial line basis). These companies will have moderate but generally acceptable growth rates and returns, and reinvestments can (and will typically) be made at return levels slightly above the cost of capital. For these companies, vulnerability to strategic and performance deterioration occurs mainly when the industry leaders or a set of externally subsidized competitors choose to attack aggressively. (For example, the recent problems of Ford in the U.S. automotive market can be directly traced to GM's more aggressive market share strategy, coupled with the European and Japanese attacks on U.S. small car markets.)

3. *Next worst position.* Competitors who finish in third place as the industry matures. Given a hostile environment, growth rates and return prospects for these companies are bleak unless they resegment into uncovered niches and gain a sustainable leadership position in these segments (AMC in utility vehicles, Goodrich in performance tires), or unless they can make major asset redeployment into meaningful diversified markets (like Armco and General). Without the ability to resegment or diversify, competitors in this class ultimately will move toward a marginal or failing position. (Chrysler in automotive, Uniroyal in tires, and Schlitz in brewing are examples of companies currently going through such a transition.)

4. *Marginal or failing position.* Competitors who end up last in mature hostile environments ultimately must fail or be subsidized, either through government ownership or aid (Chrysler) or through cash infusions from a diversified parent (Kaiser in steel, Allis Chalmers in construction equipment). Despite efforts to use such subsidies to resegment and refocus their operations, the survey data shows no successful efforts in such turnaround attempts among the 64 competitors in the eight basic industries, raising a fundamental question as to whether there is any real possibility of strategic turnaround. Consequently, a society or a company subsidizing this type of marginal competitor should expect the worst—perpetual subsidies, perhaps slightly offset by infrequent operating returns during high peaks in basic economic cycles.

In Summary

The strategic and performance data from this eight-industry study suggest that both great successes and failures are occurring as basic mature industries move into a hostile business environment created by slower growth, higher inflation, more regulation, and intensified competition. Uniformly, the successes come to those companies that achieve either the lowest cost or most differentiated position. Simultaneously, survival is possible for those companies that have the foresight to downsize their asset commitments into niches in their basic industry and to use their incremental capital for meaningful diversification moves. For the weaker companies, the inability to achieve a lowest cost or most differentiated position results in high vulnerability and ultimate failure or perpetual subsidy.

For general managers guiding their companies into the economic environment of the 1980s, the implications of these findings are clear. The laws of the jungle change as maturity comes and hostility intensifies. In such a jungle, the range of strategic options narrows, requiring both an early warning of the coming hostility and an early strategic repositioning for a company to survive and prosper.

Hence intensified efforts must be made to create internal administrative structures and mechanisms to recognize and efficiently manage this repositioning. (GM's effective organizational restructuring in the early 1970s to respond to the down-sizing imperative stands as a brilliant case study in the use of such an administrative effort to create strategic change.)

For public policymakers monitoring and attempting to influence the business environment, these results suggest that failures will be inevitable as industry structures evolve in the face of maturity and hostility. The currently popular attempts at forced consolidation and subsidies are one way of dealing with these failures. However, these actions should be taken with full knowledge that they will not stop the driving market forces.

The question that remains in the decade ahead is whether the short-run employment, balance of payments, and fiscal stability provided by such public policy actions is worth the long-run cost of maintaining an inefficient industry structure that conflicts with the driving market forces created by a hostile environment.

Notes

1. *Business Week*, September 18, 1978, p. 66.

2. See, e.g., Theodore Levitt, "Dinosaurs among the Bears and Bulls," *HBR*, January–February 1975, p. 41; also the section on basic industries in Richard P. Rumelt, *Strategy, Structure, and Economic Performance* (Boston: Division of Research, Harvard Business School, 1974), pp. 128–139.

3. Alfred P. Sloan, Jr., *My Years with General Motors* (New York, Doubleday, 1964), pp. 65–66, 172.

4. PIMS (Profit Impact of Market Strategies) is a multiple regression model which relates profitability to a number of associative variables. See Sidney Schoeffler, Robert D. Buzzell, and Donald F. Heany, "Impact of Strategic Planning on Profit Performance," *HBR*, March–April 1974, p. 137.

14

The Surprising Case for Low Market Share

CAROLYN Y. WOO and ARNOLD C. COOPER

Conventional wisdom has it that companies with low market shares are doomed to marginal profits, at best, while market-share leaders show the best returns on investment. If the conventional wisdom is correct, though, most companies would be candidates for harvesting or liquidation. However, many companies with low market shares survive and even prosper. What characteristics enable the highly profitable low-share company to succeed? The authors contend that companies in industries with slow growth and few product changes and those that make frequently bought items are among businesses that prosper with low market share. Similarly, low-share businesses that pursue a specific focused competitive strategy, often emphasizing quality and cost, seem to do best.

Can businesses with small market shares be successful? If so, what strategies characterize such businesses? This article seeks to answer these questions by using research on 126 businesses, 40 of which have demonstrated superior performance despite low market shares.

Strategists tend to place much importance on having high-market-share positions. Bruce Henderson of the Boston Consulting Group observed, "In a competitive business, it [market share] determines relative profitability. When it does not seem to do so, it is nearly always because the relevant product market sector is misdefined or the leader is mismanaged."[1] One study, based on analysis of data at the Strategic Planning Institute in Cambridge, Massachusetts, concluded that "a difference of ten percentage points

---

Published 1982.

in market share is accompanied by a difference of about five points in pretax ROI."[2]

High market share is frequently seen as offering businesses a number of attendant advantages, including economies of scale, brand-name dominance, and greater bargaining power with suppliers, distributors, and customers.

These correlations have often been interpreted to mean that businesses with low market shares inevitably have poor long-term prospects. Accordingly, analysts usually advise such businesses to build market share or reposition themselves so that they dominate some market segment. And, they contend, if neither action is feasible, the small-share business should be harvested or divested. Since only a few businesses are market-share leaders, presumably such dismal prognoses apply to most companies.

Each of these alternatives can cause serious problems. Building market share is a risky, costly activity that can ignite retaliatory actions by competitors. For low-share businesses in particular, share building may not even be possible because of limitations of resources or market influence. To reposition in an effort to dominate a market segment, a company must have product- and market-development capabilities. Harvesting or divestiture may be especially difficult in the multibusiness corporation because facilities, distribution channels, or customers are shared with other units in the company. Legal or social pressures may make it difficult to leave a business, and finally, those companies that lack attractive investment alternatives may realize little benefit from harvesting funds.

All of these concerns suggest that simple prescriptions do not apply to low-share businesses. Moreover, recent research suggests that pessimism about the prospects of low-share businesses is not always warranted. In 1978, Richard G. Hamermesh and associates reported on three companies they had studied—Burroughs, Union Camp, and Crown Cork & Seal—which had all been highly successful despite low-share positions.[3] They concluded that the strategies of these companies were characterized by the following: creative market segmentation, efficient research and development expenditures, controlled growth, and strong leadership. A subsequent study by William K. Hall identified companies in eight mature industries that had exhibited outstanding performance despite nonleadership positions.[4] The experiences of these companies demonstrate that market leadership is not always necessary to attain the lowest cost position. They also show that the lowest cost position is not required to achieve high margins.

Both studies show that long-run competitive success is feasible despite low-market-share position.

A New Approach

This article reports findings from a research project that examines a much larger number of businesses than the studies just mentioned and that looks at a number of factors associated with strategy.We have focused on two sets of broad questions, both relating to high-performing, low-share companies:

1 What kinds of industry settings do these businesses enter? What types of products do they offer?
2 How do these businesses compete? Do they allocate resources in distinctive ways to achieve a competitive advantage?

For a given business, performance might be expected to depend both on the product, market, and industry characteristics that determine its competitive environment and on its business strategy, that is, the way it competes within that environment.

The businesses in this sample were chosen from the PIMS data base.[5] Each business is defined as "a division, product line or other profit center within its parent company, selling a distinct set of products or services to an identifiable group or groups of customers, in competition with a well-defined set of competitors." We studied a total of 649 domestic manufacturing companies for the period 1972 through 1975. From this group, we sought to identify low-share businesses that achieved superior returns without diminishing their market shares. To qualify, businesses had to show a pretax return on investment of at least 20%. Their market shares could not exceed 20% of the combined share of their three largest competitors. Of the 649 businesses, 40 met these requirements.

It should be noted that the managements of these businesses estimated their own market shares, defining the market in terms of the customers they sought to serve. It is clear that the market definitions used directly affect a company's market share; however, these are the market definitions used by managements in their own planning. It should also be noted that, because of the nature of the PIMS data base, most of these were divisions of large corporations, not free-standing small businesses.

For contrast, we compared these high-performing businesses with two control groups: effective high-share businesses and ineffective low-share businesses. The definitions of those groups and the number of businesses in each category are shown in the ruled insert.

The Best Circumstances

For proprietary reasons, the names of the companies or the industry segments they serve are not given in the data base. However, we do know the characteristics of their industries, as reflected by 13 different factors. These factors are the nature of the product, the degree of product standardization, the importance of auxiliary services, the stage of product life cycle, purchase frequency by both immediate and end users, geographic scope, industry value added, industry concentration, number of competitors, industry growth, market growth, and frequency of product changes (see Exhibit 1). In ex-

Exhibit 1. Dimensions of Market Environment and Competitive Strategy

Market
environment:

Elements of
a competitive
strategy:

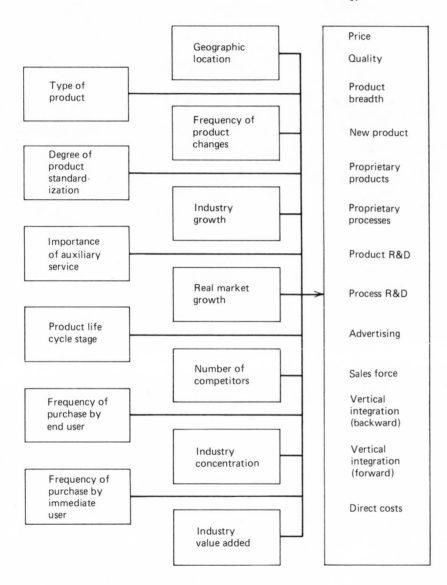

amining these environmental characteristics, we can determine whether high-performing, low-market-share businesses sell in markets with distinctive characteristics.

Using a statistical technique called "cluster analysis," we could classify the environments of the 126 businesses into six groups.[6] These six groups, shown in Exhibit 2, differ in a number of dimensions but particularly in the nature of the products and their market growth rates. These six groups do not describe all possible environments but do include the settings of the 126 businesses we studied. Bear in mind that businesses within a group do not necessarily compete with each other; rather, they compete in environments with common characteristics.

The distribution of effective low-share businesses and the two control samples in these six groups is displayed in Exhibit 3. Most of the effective low-share businesses are found in three environments: those designated as groups three, four, and six. Group four contains almost 50% of these high performers; this is an environment characterized by businesses offering standardized industrial components and supplies in low-growth markets.

Exhibit 2.   Characteristics and Composition of Market Groups

Group one	Group two
3 businesses	11 businesses
Consumer nondurable and industrial components	Consumer nondurable and industrial components
Very high-growth market	Declining market
Regular product changes	Frequent product changes
Nonstandardized products	Standardized products
High degree of auxiliary services	Low degree of auxiliary services
Purchased moderately often	Purchased often
Low value added	High value added

Exhibit 2. *(Continued)*

	Group three	Group four	Group five	Group six
	19 businesses	42 businesses	14 businesses	36 businesses
	Consumer durable and capital goods	Industrial components and supplies	Capital goods and industrial components and supplies	Industrial components and supplies
	Declining market	Low-growth market	High-growth market	Low-growth market
	Frequent product changes	Infrequent product changes	Some product changes	Periodic product changes
	Standardized products	Standardized products	Mainly standardized products	Nonstandardized products
	Low to moderate degree of auxiliary services	Low degree of auxiliary services	High degree of auxiliary services	High degree of auxiliary services
	Not purchased often	Purchased often	Not purchased often	Purchased moderately often
	Moderate value added	High value added	High value added	High value added

☐ Effective low-share businesses

☐ Ineffective low-share businesses

▨ Effective high-share businesses

245

Exhibit 3.   Distribution of Effective Low-Share Businesses and Two Control Groups across Six Market Groups

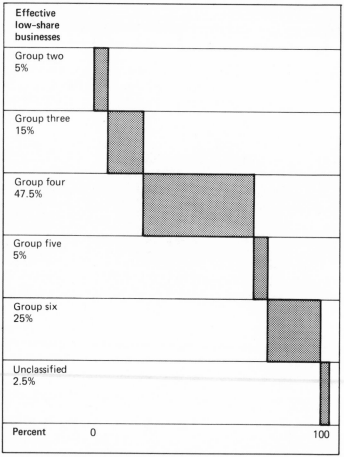

Another 25% are included in group six, an enviroment also characterized by slow market growth but which has industrial components that are less standardized and that are experiencing some product changes. Group three, which contains 15% of these high-performing businesses, includes mature consumer durables and capital goods in slow-growth markets.

The environments where we found most of the high-performing, low-share businesses share certain characteristics, some of which are very different from the environmental characteristics often thought to be most promising for smaller businesses:

1. *Profitable low-market-share businesses exist in low-growth markets.* Groups four and six, which account for 72.5% of profitable low-share businesses, are characterized by real (inflation adjusted) growth rates of zero to 1%. This may seem surprising because limited opportunities and low

Exhibit 3. *(Continued)*

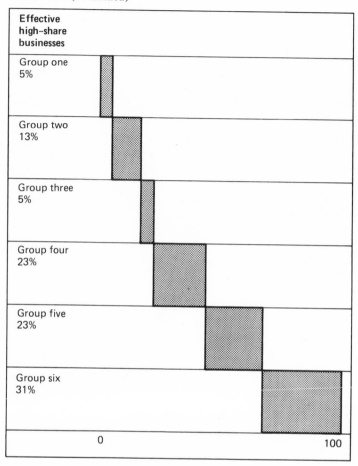

profits are often thought to be associated with low-growth markets. High-growth markets, however, are turbulent arenas where competitors try to grab share leadership before the market stabilizes. During this period, competition can be intense. Rapid product and process changes add to the uncertainty. Often a shakeout period follows, when weak competitors are forced to exit. This turbulence is repeated when the market reaches a stage of negative growth.

Profitable low-share businesses thrive between these two stages. Most of them seek mature though nondeclining markets with low real growth. Such markets seem to provide a more stable environment, in which there is less elbowing to gain market share. Hence, this structure makes it easy for all players to define and protect their positions.

2. *Their products don't change often.* The mature markets mentioned previously also have low levels of product and process change. The concentration of profitable low-share businesses in this environment is sur-

Exhibit 3. *(Continued)*

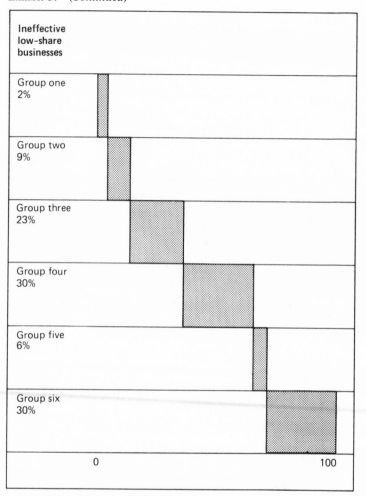

prising. High rates of change benefit companies that can move quickly, as well as those seeking product differentiation opportunities. Low-market-share companies are often expected to benefit from such environmental changes.

Frequent changes may, however, force all members of an industry to spend heavily on product introduction as well as on research and development, which is difficult for smaller businesses that have less revenue to support these activities. High rates of change may also force smaller producers to scrap production tools and dies before their useful lives run out. By contrast, the greater production volumes of businesses with large market shares may mean that tools and dies are depreciated and ready for replacement sooner. Moreover, frequent changes also reduce the stability of markets and may be a reflection of greater competitive intensity.

3. *Most of their products are standardized and they provide few extra services.* Smaller businesses are often viewed as having the flexibility that permits them to cater to customers' special needs. They might be expected to avoid direct competition with large corporations' standardized products. They are often advised to choose fields in which competition is based on custom products or auxiliary services such as engineering consultation, frequent on-site visits, or maintenance and repair.

Contrary to expectations, 72.5% of successful low-share performers competed in markets characterized by standard products (groups two, three, four, and five). Moreover, the markets were not heavily supported by auxiliary services.

Competing in such markets permits focused strategies, in which companies need not incur the costs of providing custom products or special services. These market characteristics may stem from the nature of industrial components and supplies, which (as we discuss next) are the main products of successful low-share businsses. These products often require little subsequent servicing or technical support.

4. *Most of them make industrial components or supplies.* All businesses in groups four and six and some in two and five manufacture industrial components and supplies. These represent 70% to 80% of successful low-share performers in our sample. Purchase decisions for industrial products are based largely on performance, service, and cost. In industrial markets, it may be possible for small-share businesses to develop strong relationships with selected customers through emphasis on performance variables important to them. Advertising, normally thought to have high economies of scale, is usually less important for industrial products; therefore, small-share businesses are at only a minor competitive disadvantage.

In addition, purchases of industrial products are frequently governed by contracts. This guarantee of a market puts the sellers in a better position to project sales volume, capital spending, and costs.

5. *These products and supplies are purchased frequently.* Market share appears to be less important for products that need to be bought often. More than half the low-share businesses studied produced such items (groups two and four). For such products, customers tend to rely more on experience and less on the brand name of market leaders for indications of reliability and performance. Thus, the share advantage of market leaders is less pronounced in these markets.

In addition, the rate of product purchases is likely to affect the requirement for working capital. High purchase frequency usually leads to faster turnover of inventory and receivables, allowing for quicker recovery of capital. Indeed, in our study, businesses making frequently purchased products had lower working-capital ratios than others.[7]

6. *Profitable low-share businesses are in industries with high value added.* Companies in these industries often enjoy margins wide enough

to absorb cost increases from suppliers or price declines in the markets they serve. High-value-added industries are less likely to invite forward integration by suppliers or backward integration by customers. When the value-added factor is high, many opportunities exist for differentiation according to product characteristics and cost structures. In this study, 82.5% of successful low-share businesses are in such industries (groups two, four, five, and six).

Which Strategies Work Best?

How do high-performing, low-share businesses compete in particular environments? Competitive strategy is reflected by the emphasis organizations place on such variables as relative prices, quality, product-line breadth, emphasis on new products, and advertising and selling efforts. (A more complete listing of factors comprising competitive strategy is contained in Exhibit 1.)

Examining market groups three, four, and six, where nearly 90% of these successful low-share businesses are clustered, we find distinctive patterns of competitive strategy in each environment:

1. *A strong focus tailored to environmental differences.* These successful businesses are distinguished by highly focused strategies. They do not try to do everything. They compete in carefully selected ways with the competitive emphasis differing according to the market environment.

Effective low-share businesses had similar strategies in groups four and six, both of which involve the sale of components and supplies. In group four, where products are standardized and undergo little change, successful low-share businesses are distinguished from the two control groups by their orientation toward low costs, low prices, and high quality. Though these characteristics are also present in group six, the high-performing, low-share businesses in this group are notable for their lower product R & D allocations and lower levels of backward integration. Products in group six undergo frequent changes. Hence, careful monitoring of product R & D is important to achieve a balance between long-term competitive position and short-term profitability.

In this market environment, we found that successful low-share businesses adopted a very conservative posture toward R & D spending yet achieved ROIs exceeding 20% over four years. Though the long-term success of this approach has not been proved, a lower R & D emphasis did not reduce the competitiveness of these businesses in the four-year period we observed. The lower vertical integration policy also contributed to success by providing these low-share businesses with greater flexibility to respond to changes, which minimized the disadvantage of their lower volumes.

In the mature consumer durables and capital goods area (group three), which contains 15% of our sample, effective low-share businesses adopt an aggressive marketing strategy and place less emphasis on quality, competitive prices, or research and development. The heavy emphasis given to marketing, particularly in the use of their sales forces, compensates for the other shortcomings of these businesses. Their reputations for quality were lower than competitors', and their product lines were not as broad. Yet these businesses command high prices. They sustain higher direct costs and have less forward and backward integration than do competitors. Despite weaker positions in cost, quality, and product value, a targeted marketing focus enables these businesses to derive rather strong margins from a low-share position in a declining market environment.

2. *A reputation for high quality.* Except for those businesses in group three, effective low-share performers consistently turned out high-quality products. Superior performance and reliability may be particularly important competitive weapons in the sale of industrial components and supplies. Knowledgeable buyers and frequent use lead to constant evaluation of tangible product characteristics.

3. *Medium to low relative prices complementing high quality.* The majority of successful low-share performers had lower prices than competitors (72.5% in groups four and six). Like product quality, competitive prices are particularly important in the environments in which these businesses compete. Buyers of industrial products are well informed and often enjoy strong bargaining positions in dealing with suppliers. When switching costs are low, buyers can solicit bids from eager suppliers. Within these mature, technologically stable markets, price might be expected to be an important consideration in purchase decisions. Note that the combination of high product quality and lower price means that these businesses offer their customers exceptionally good value.

4. *Low total cost.* Relatively low costs presumably permit low-share businesses to offer high-quality products at low prices and still show high profits. It follows that effective low-share businesses have lower unit costs than do ineffective low-share businesses. How do they achieve low costs? (After all, they do have higher unit costs than the market-share leaders because of smaller production volumes and less vertical integration.) In part, by concentrating on a narrow line of standardized products. These high-performing, low-share businesses also spend less on product R&D, advertising, promotion, sales force support, and new product introduction.

Strategies of Poor Performers

Interestingly, there are no substantial differences in the environments chosen by effective and ineffective low-share businesses. Both have more than 80% of their businesses in groups three, four, and six. The differences between these two groups of companies relate more to how they compete in each environment.

By contrast, low-performing, low-share businesses compete aggressively along many fronts; they might emphasize broad product lines, advertising, selling expenses, product R&D, and process R&D. They also have considerable vertical integration, which requires still more resources. Their price-quality performance is below that of their competitors. We observed the absence of a clear focus in all three market groups (three, four, and six) where we compared these low-performing, low-share businesses with high-performing, low-share businesses.

In general, the resource allocation patterns of ineffective low-share performers are similar to those of effective large-share businesses. The latter offer a broad line of products complemented by aggressive marketing, selling R&D, and new product introduction. They are also highly integrated vertically. While both groups emphasize a large number of competitive weapons, small-share businesses lack the sales volume to support such broad-scale aggressive strategies.

The 126 Companies We Studied

Type of Business	Pretax Return on Investment	Relative Market Share	Number of Businesses
Effective low-share	20% or higher	20% or lower	40
Effective high-share	20% or higher	125% or higher	39
Ineffective low-share	5% or lower	20% or lower	47

Implications for Success

First, low market share does not inevitably lead to low profitability. Despite the well-accepted correlation between market share and profitability, market share is not a necessary condition for profitability. The dismal prospects often foreseen for low-share businesses do not always come to pass—certainly not to this sample of 40 businesses, all very profitable despite low-share positions.

Since these businesses have low market shares and are positioned in low-growth markets, they would usually be classified as candidates for harvesting or divestiture. The performance of these 40 businesses demonstrates that such blanket recommendations should be considered with care.

Second, a stable market environment contributes to low-share success. The performance of effective low-share businesses depends on both the characteristics of their industry settings and their business strategies. The successful businesses tend to concentrate in competitive environments somewhat different from those of effective large-share businesses but similar to those of ineffective low-share performers. These environments are not characterized by an absence of large-market-share businesses, as might be expected if "niche" strategies were followed. Rather, the overriding feature is stability. Low market growth, infrequent product and process changes, high value added, and high purchase frequency all contribute to more predictable and less turbulent environments. These markets are unlikely to attract new competitors, but they may be viewed as unexciting by existing competitors. As such, competitors' divisions may receive less top management attention and staff support, and they may be staffed by less able and creative managers.

Third, selectivity is a key to low-market-share success. Effective low-share businesses compete in distinctive ways. They normally offer superior products at prices lower than competitors. This supports the traditional wisdom that success in any business ultimately depends on the benefits provided customers.

The most distinctive feature of these strategies is selective focus. They do not copy the strategies of market leaders (unlike ineffective low-share businesses). These high-performing, low-share businesses choose particular bases of competition, such as product quality and price. They then limit their expenditures in other areas of competition, such as product R&D, product-line breadth, or marketing expenditures, so that they can achieve high performance despite relatively limited sales volume.

The specific strategy of any business must be tailored to its capabilities and the requirements of its competitive environment. Small-share businesses clearly vary widely in their possibilities. But the experience of these 40 companies demonstrates that success is possible for well-positioned and well-managed small-share businesses.

Notes

1. Bruce D. Henderson, *Henderson on Corporate Strategy* (Cambridge, Mass., Abt Books, 1979), p. 94.

2. Robert D. Buzzell, Bradley T. Gale, and Ralph G.M. Sultan, "Market Share—A Key to Profitability," *HBR*, January-February 1975, p. 97.

3. Richard G. Hamermesh, M. Jack Anderson, Jr., and J. Elizabeth Harris, "Strategies for Low Market Share Businesses," *HBR*, May-June 1978, p. 95.

4. William K. Hall, "Survival Strategies in a Hostile Environment," *HBR*, September-October 1980, p. 75.

5. PIMS (Profit Impact of Market Strategy) is a research program sponsored by the Strategic Planning Institute in Cambridge, Massachusetts and includes more than 1,000 member businesses.

6. For a detailed discussion of the methodology, refer to Carolyn Y. Woo and Arnold C. Cooper, ''Strategies of Effective Low Share Businesses,'' *Strategic Management Journal*, July-September 1981, p. 301.

7. A correlation coefficient of + .26 was obtained between purchase frequency and working-capital-to-revenue. Based on the definition of the purchase frequency variable, the coefficient indicated that longer time periods between purchases (infrequently purchased products) were correlated with higher working-capital-to-revenues ratios.

15

Strategies for Low Market-Share Businesses

RICHARD G. HAMERMESH, M. JACK ANDERSON, JR.,
and J. ELIZABETH HARRIS

What do the Burroughs Corporation, Crown Cork & Seal Co., Inc., and the Union Camp Corporation have in common? Although none of them enjoys a dominant market share, all three earn quite respectable returns on their equity, have healthy profit margins, and continue to maintain strong sales growth year after year. In this article, the authors identify and analyze four characteristics that help explain their success: they compete only in areas where their particular strengths are most highly valued, make efficient use of limited research and development budgets, eschew growth for growth's sake, and have leaders who are willing to question conventional wisdom.

During the past several years, a great deal of research on profitability and market share has uncovered a positive correlation between the two. One study shows that "on the average, a difference of ten percentage points in market share is accompanied by a difference of about five points in pretax ROI."[1] Although in general market share and return on investment do go hand in hand, many of the inferences that both managers and consultants have been drawing from this finding are erroneous and misleading.

One of the most dangerous inferences drawn from this generality is that a low market-share business faces only two strategic options: fight to increase its share or withdraw from the industry. These prescriptions completely overlook the fact that, in many industries, companies having a low market share consistently outperform their larger rivals and show very little inclination to either expand their share or withdraw from the fight. Perhaps

---

Published 1978.

the best example of this situation is the steel industry, where producers such as Armco Steel, Inland Steel, and Kaiser Steel have consistently earned a higher return on equity than their much larger competitors, United States Steel and Bethlehem Steel.

Often, planning systems that are based on this generality also have serious flaws. Most of these systems place a business in one of four categories, according to its market share and the industry's growth rate.[2] Depending on the category a business falls in, a strategy is automatically prescribed. Low market-share businesses in low-growth industries should be divested; high market-share businesses in low-growth industries should be "milked" or "harvested" for cash; high market-share businesses in high-growth industries should maintain their growth; and low market-share businesses in high-growth industries should increase their market share.

Although each classification system has its own nuances, all such systems share the same shortcoming: they define strategy at such a high level of abstraction that it becomes meaningless. A successful business strategy must be specific, precise, and far-ranging. It should state the markets in which a business will compete, the products that will be sold, their performance and price characteristics, the way in which they will be produced and distributed, and the method of financing. By taking the attention of corporation executives away from these essential details and instead focusing their attention on abstractions, many planning systems do a great disservice.

Finally, such sweeping generalities offer little consolation to those businesses that, for one reason or another, find themselves in a poor market position. Since only one competitor enjoys the highest share of any given market, most businesses must face the disadvantage of not having the highest market share. They must devise a specific strategy that will lead to the best possible performance, regardless of their position.

During the past several months, we have been studying businesses that have outperformed other much larger companies in their industries. We have identified four important characteristics that most of these successful businesses share. In this article, we shall discuss these characteristics.

Indications of Performance

Although there are numerous ways to define successful performance and low market share, we have chosen two straightforward definitions. Low market share is less than half the industry leader's share, and successful companies are those whose five-year average return on equity surpasses the industry median. Applying these criteria to the over 900 businesses in 30 major industries listed in *Forbes Annual Report on American Industry* revealed numerous successful low share businesses. From a list of these companies, we chose three—Burroughs Corporation, Crown Cork & Seal Co., Inc., and Union Camp Corporation—for close study. These three companies have surpassed not only their industries' average return on equity but have actually led their industries in several important performance categories.

Consider Burroughs. During the mid-1960s, many analysts predicted that the corporation, with its narrow line of computers, aging accounting machines, and market share of less than 3%, would soon withdraw from the main-frame computer market. Today, Burroughs competes more effectively with IBM than does any other computer company. Its market share is still dwarfed by that of IBM, but during the past five years, its sales and earnings per share have grown faster than IBM's. And although Burroughs's net profit margin and return on equity trail IBM's, they exceed those of NCR, Sperry Rand, Honeywell, and Control Data by a substantial margin.

It is significant that results by line of business, which are reported in 10-K statements and which distinguish businesses such as Control Data's finance and insurance lines and Honeywell's controls line, also indicate that on a return-on-sales basis, Burroughs's computer line greatly outdistances that of all its rivals except IBM. (See Exhibit 1 for detailed comparisons of the financial positions of main-frame computer manufacturers.)

Crown Cork & Seal is another successful low share company. In fact, as Exhibit 2 shows, its financial performance over the past decade has consistently been the highest of the major metal can manufacturers. Yet Crown Cork & Seal has not always enjoyed such success. In early 1957, the company was near bankruptcy, and with sales of $115 million in 1956, it had to compete with American Can (1956 sales of $772 million) and Continental Can (1956 sales of $1 billion).

Today, Crown Cork & Seal is still much smaller than its two giant rivals, but with profits of $46 million (15.8% return on equity), the prospect of bankruptcy has long since passed. Although Crown Cork & Seal's com-

Exhibit 1. Comparative Performance of Major Main-Frame Computer Manufacturers Through 1976

Company	Total Sales (in millions of dollars)	Net Profit Margin	Return on Equity (five-year average)	Annual Sales Growth (five-year average)	Earnings per Share Growth (five-year average)
IBM	$16,304	14.7%	20.5%	12.8%	14.1%
Burroughs	1,871	9.9	14.3	14.5	17.1
Sperry Rand	3,203	4.8	13.1	11.1	12.9
NCR	2,312	5.0	11.8	9.6	46.0
Honeywell	2,495	4.5	9.7	8.5	5.1
Control Data	1,331	2.5	4.7	12.4	−0.1

Source: Annual reports of the above companies and *Forbes,* January 9, 1978.

Exhibit 2.   Comparative Performance of Major Metal Can Manufacturers Through 1976

Company	Net Sales (in millions of dollars)	Net Profit Margin	Return on Equity (five-year average)	Annual Sales Growth (five-year average)	Earnings per Share Growth (five-year average)
Crown Cork & Seal	$ 910	5.1%	16.2%	14.7%	14.5%
Continental	3,458	3.8	14.1	10.5	14.3
National Can	917	2.5	12.2	16.5	5.9
American Can	3,143	3.3	12.0	9.2	16.9

Source: Annual reports of the above companies and *Forbes*, January 9, 1978.

petitors have all diversified, an analysis of 10-K statements for 1976 shows that the pretax returns on sales of their metal packaging businesses were all below 6%; Crown Cork & Seal's pretax return on sales was nearly 10%.[3]

Our third company, Union Camp, competes in the extremely competitive, highly fragmented forest products industry. Over 3,000 companies have major product lines in this industry, and it has been highly volatile and plagued with overcapacity, depressed prices, pollution control problems, and high construction costs.

Despite these problems, Union Camp's earnings per share have increased by almost 27% annually over the past five years, and average return on equity has been over 20%. As the ninth largest company in its industry, Union Camp competes with such giants as International Paper and Weyerhaeuser, which are three and a half and two and a half times larger than Union Camp. As shown in Exhibit 3, Union Camp's weak market position

Exhibit 3.   Comparative Performance of Major Forest Products Companies Through 1976

Company	Sales (in millions of dollars)	Net Profit Margin	Return on Equity (five-year average)	Annual Sales Growth (five-year average)	Earnings per Share Growth (five-year average)
Union Camp	$1,003	11.1%	21.7%	13.6%	24.9%
Weyerhaeuser	2,868	10.2	19.5	15.4	18.1
Mead	1,599	5.6	17.4	7.5	31.7
International Paper	3,540	6.0	16.2	11.0	21.5
Boise Cascade	1,932	5.2	12.0	1.2	Not applicable

Source: Annual reports of the above companies and *Forbes*, January 9, 1978.

has not prevented the company from outperforming its larger competitors. Comparisons of the pretax return on 1976 sales of the paper and paperboard portions of these companies show that Union Camp leads the pack with a 28% return. The next highest rate was posted by Boise Cascade's paper operations.

Elements of Strategy

Except for their low market-share positions and exceptional performances, Burroughs, Crown Cork & Seal, and Union Camp seem to have little in common. Certainly their competitive environments are extremely different. Computer main-frames constitute a highly technological, rapidly growing industry that is dominated by one company. The metal container industry is extremely mature and, with only four major competitors, is a classic oligopoly. The forest products industry is also mature, but it is very fragmented.

Given these rather substantial differences in industry settings, are there any common strategies that these three successful low share companies have implemented to yield profits? Our research suggests four characteristics that these companies share: they carefully segment their markets, they use research and development funds efficiently, they think small, and their chief executives' influence is pervasive.

Segment, Segment, Segment

First, to be successful, most businesses must compete in a limited number of segments within their industry, and they must choose these segments carefully. Thinking in broader terms than only the range of products offered and the types of customers served, most successful companies define market segments in unique and creative ways. For example, besides products and customers, a market can also be segmented by level of customer service, stage of production, price performance characteristics, credit arrangements with customers, location of plants, characteristics of manufacturing equipment, channels of distribution, and financial policies.

The point is an important one. To be successful, a low share company must compete in the segments where its own strengths will be most highly valued and where its large competitors will be most unlikely to compete. Whether that strength is in the type and range of products offered, the method by which the product is produced, the cost and speed of distribution, or the credit and service arrangements is irrelevant. The important thing is that management spend its time identifying and exploiting unique segments rather than making broad assaults on entire industries.

Aerosol and Beverage Cans.   Although the metal container industry sells to numerous industries and faces competition from glass, aluminum, fiberfoil, and plastic containers, Crown Cork & Seal has elected to concentrate on two product segments: (1) metal cans for hard-to-hold products such as beer and soft drinks and (2) aerosol cans. In an industry where transportation costs represent a large proportion of total costs, Crown Cork & Seal has built small single-product plants close to its customers instead of large and possibly more efficient multiproduct plants located at some distance from its customers.

The two market segments Crown Cork & Seal serves have both grown more rapidly than the total industry, but they also require expert skills in container design and manufacturing. The company has a particular advantage over competitors in the soft drink and brewing industries because it is the largest supplier of filling equipment to these companies. Thus Crown Cork & Seal has segmented its market by products, customers, customer service, and plant location. It is significant that the company sells to growth segments in which it has special expertise.

Four Large Paper Mills. In the forest products industry, Union Camp has had to overcome the disadvantages of having a relatively small timberland holding—only 1.6 million acres—in contrast to International Paper's 23.7 million acres and Weyerhaeuser's 16.7 million acres. Although this difference makes Union Camp's raw material prices higher, the company has achieved consistently lower operating costs than its large rivals. Since the location of plants is important, Union Camp, like Crown Cork & Seal, operates only four very large mills, strategically situated in deep water ports close to both Union Camp's southern timberlands and its eastern customers.

For example, at its Franklin, Virginia plant, Union Camp operates the largest fine-paper machine in the world. As a low-cost producer of paper products, this corporation produces large volumes of only a limited number of paper products, and in bleached paper, Union Camp is not fully integrated. Instead, it sells most of its output to end-product converting companies. By selling to a rather small number of paper converters, the corporation has established a superior service record.

Thus Union Camp has segmented its market by stage of production, manufacturing policies, prices, products, customers, and services.

Three Distinct Computer Lines. Unlike Union Camp and Crown Cork & Seal, which do not offer complete lines in their industries, Burroughs offers a full line of computers. But in developing its full product line, the corporation has taken advantage of historical ties to the financial community, where it has been a major supplier of accounting machines for decades. Today, Burroughs possesses an 18% share of the banking segment, almost three times its overall market share.

In designing its large computers, the B5000 series, Burroughs has emphasized ease and flexibility of programming at the expense of efficient use of main memory. This form of segmentation has been justified by the tenfold decrease in memory costs since 1964, while talented programmers have become both scarce and expensive.

In medium-size computers, Burroughs has chosen to imitate IBM's design and to compete on price. The company has reportedly underbid IBM by considerable amounts on some large government contracts. In the small-computer market, Burroughs has continued to upgrade its electronic accounting machines and has given them the capability to serve as either terminals to a larger computer or as free-standing accounting machines.

Thus, although Burroughs offers a full line of main-frame computers, within each line it has segmented the market to capitalize on its particular skills and resources.

That Crown Cork & Seal, Union Camp, and Burroughs have had to compete in unique market segments in order to attain their success should not be surprising. But what these three companies reveal is that the opportunities to segment an industry are enormous and extend to every facet of a business. When a business segments its markets in unique and creative ways, it can far surpass the performance of its larger competitors. The marketing vice president of one high market-share business once commented:

> For years, we have been unable to understand why our profits have been mediocre despite our strong market position. The expert planners at corporate staff have been of little help. About a year ago, we decided to do a detailed study of our industry. We found that, although we had the highest market share, in all of the important and more profitable market segments, we were taking a beating. We were leading the pack, however, in the unappealing segments of the markets.

Use R&D Efficiently

Although low market-share companies can improve their performance by pursuing narrow market segments, their larger rivals still seem to have a tremendous advantage, because of their size, in research and development. Our research suggests that smaller companies seldom win R&D battles but that they can channel their R&D spending into areas that are the most likely ones to produce the greatest benefits for them.

Lower Process Costs.   At both Crown Cork & Seal and Union Camp, for example, R&D is focused on process improvements aimed at lowering costs. A Crown Cork & Seal executive has noted:

> We are not truly pioneers. Our philosophy is not to spend a great deal of money for basic research. However, we do have tremendous skills in die forming and metal fabrication, and we can move to adapt to the customer's needs faster than anyone else in the industry.[4]

Alexander Calder, Jr., Union Camp's chairman, has adopted a similar R&D strategy:

> We are known to be very strong in process and in the manufacturing of industrial products. . . . We do little basic research like Du Pont. But

we are good at improving processes, developing improved and some new products, and helping to build new manufacturing capabilities.[5]

Another R&D strategy Union Camp and Crown Cork & Seal have developed is to work closely or jointly with their largest customers on major developments. For example, Crown Cork worked closely with large breweries in the development of the drawn-and-ironed cans for the beverage industry. As a result, the company beat all three of its major competitors in equipment conversion for the introduction of this new product.

Concentrate on Innovations. For Burroughs, the problem of developing an R&D strategy is much more difficult and crucial than for the other two companies because of the rapid changes and high technology in the computer industry. Although Burroughs spends 6% of its sales on R&D compared with IBM's 7.5%, in dollar terms the difference is staggering—$112 million versus $1.2 billion. To compensate, Burroughs runs an extremely efficient R&D operation and concentrates on truly innovative products. And because of its low share position, these products are able to attract enough new customers to more than offset the trading up by Burroughs's existing customers.

IBM, on the other hand, has paced its innovations because, whenever it introduces a new system, a significant amount of its leased equipment is exchanged for the new system. As a result, Burroughs is recognized as one of the technological leaders in the computer industry.

Burroughs also runs an extremely efficient R&D operation. Its chairman, Ray Macdonald, spends a great deal of time at his R&D center and exerts tremendous pressure on his engineers.

Think Small

Another characteristic of successful low market-share companies is that they are content to remain small.[6] Most of them emphasize profits rather than sales growth or market share, and specialization rather than diversification.

Limit Growth. Macdonald limits Burroughs's growth in the rapidly growing computer industry to 15% per year because he maintains that fast growth does not allow for the proper training of people and the development of a management structure. And in an industry where giants such as General Electric and RCA have faltered because they have found the pursuit of market share to be too costly, Burroughs has been consistently profitable despite only slow and modest gains in market share. Macdonald notes:

> There are two theories of growth in this industry. One is ours, where you plan to grow at a sustainable and affordable rate and put market share low on the list of objectives. Then there are others who thought that this rate was inadequate and took risky measures to increase their growth and market share. They were moths around a candle on that one.[7]

Union Camp and Crown Cork & Seal have also emphasized profits rather than size. At Crown Cork & Seal, management decided not to continue to compete in the oil can market even though the company had a 50% share of this segment. Despite the loss of sales, management decided that it had other more profitable opportunities and that new materials such as fiberfoil provided too great a threat in the motor oil can business.

During the 1973–1975 recession, Union Camp's management resisted customer pressure to produce a broad line of white papers. To Union Camp, the extra sales could not be justified by the added production costs.

Diversify Cautiously. Unlike many of their larger competitors, most successful low market-share companies are not diversified. For example, both Continental Can and American Can have diversified widely, while Crown Cork & Seal has continued to concentrate on making metal cans. When successful low market-share companies do diversify, they tend to enter closely related areas. For example, Union Camp has diversified into wood-based chemicals and retail distribution of building materials. Union Camp's vice chairman, Samuel Kinney, Jr., explained another element of Union Camp's diversification strategy:

> You must have someone in the parent organization who really understands the [new] business before it gets heavy. Other paper companies have had troubles along these lines. They had these MBAs who, I am sure, were intelligent. But once they failed, there wasn't a damn thing anyone could do back at headquarters. They didn't know the business, and they were completely out on a limb.[8]

Ubiquitous Chief Executive

The final characteristic of these companies we found striking is the pervasive influence of the chief executive. John Connelly of Crown Cork & Seal, Alexander Calder of Union Camp, and Ray Macdonald of Burroughs have all been described as extremely strong-willed individuals who are involved in almost all aspects of company operations.

To a large extent, it is understandable that leaders of low market-share companies are dynamic, tough people who see obstacles as challenges and enjoy competing in unorthodox ways. It may simply take a strong-willed leader to convince and inspire an organization to "beat the odds."

This is not to imply that the chief executives of large share companies are not also strong-willed, dynamic, and tough. But most often these executives work with teams of other senior managers and limit their responsibilities to a few key areas. In successful low share companies, the influence of the chief executive often extends beyond formulating and communicating an ingenious strategy to actually having a deep involvement in the daily activities of the business.

At Union Camp, for example, Calder still retains responsibility for sales and marketing. Macdonald of Burroughs is deeply involved in both the development and the marketing of new products.

Of course, the pervasive influence of the chief executive in low market-share business makes the problem of management succession an extremely difficult one. Connelly, now 72, has yet to retire or to pick a successor. While Macdonald retired in December 1977, he has retained the position of executive committee chairman, and analysts are already questioning Burroughs's prospects without him. Though reports differ about what the actual situations are, only Union Camp's Calder seems to have been able to delegate significant responsibilities and to practice a more participatory style of leadership than the others have.

Alternative to Growth

Although this article has an optimistic tone, we must acknowledge that there are some serious obstacles a low market-share business must overcome. These usually include small research budgets, few economies of scale in manufacturing, little opportunity to distribute products directly, little public and customer recognition, and difficulties in attracting capital and ambitious employees. Moreover, previous research indicates that, on the average, the return on investment of low share businesses is significantly less than that of businesses with high market shares.

We have made no attempt to refute these research findings or to deny the obstacles facing low share businesses. But we have sought to demonstrate that many of the inferences being drawn from these findings are simplistic and misleading. Simply put, not all low share businesses are "dogs."

Rather, we have found that a small market share is not necessarily a handicap; it can be a significant advantage that enables a company to compete in ways that are unavailable to its larger rivals. We believe that these findings are significant.

For the independent low share company, these findings represent an alternative to bankruptcy and the high costs and risks associated with efforts to increase market share.

To the large diversified company, the findings suggest that formal planning systems must go beyond simply placing each division in one of several categories. Categorization schemes can provide a useful conceptual handle for top executives, but the best planning systems are those which encourage and enable a division to seek the best fit between the opportunities in the competitive environment and the particular skills, strengths, and resources each division possesses.

In sum, our findings indicate that, in a division or in an independent company, management's first objective should be to earn the maximum return on invested capital rather than to achieve the highest possible market share.

Notes

1. Robert D. Buzzell, Bradley T. Gale, and Ralph G.M. Sultan, "Market Share—A Key to Profitability," *HBR*, January–February 1975, p. 97.

2. See *Perspectives on Experience* (Boston, Boston Consulting Group, Inc., 1968 and 1970) for a description of a typical classification system.

3. For a more comprehensive description of Crown Cork & Seal, see E. Raymond Corey, "Key Options in Market Selection and Product Planning," *HBR*, September-October 1975, p. 119.

4. "Crown Cork & Seal and the Metal Container Industry," Harvard Business School case study, ICCH No. 6–373–077 (Boston; Intercollegiate Case Clearinghouse, 1973), p. 30.

5. "Union Camp Corporation," Harvard Business School case study, ICCH No. 9–372–198 (Boston, Intercollegiate Case Clearinghouse, 1972), p. 6.

6. For an excellent discussion of the risks of attempting to build market share, see William E. Fruhan, Jr., "Pyrrhic Victories in Fights for Market Share," *HBR*, September-October 1972, p. 100 (Chapter 8 in this text).

7. "How Ray Macdonald's Growth Theory Created IBM's Toughest Competition," *Fortune*, January 1977, p. 98.

8. "New Growth at Union Camp," *Dun's Review*, March 1975, p. 43.

Appendix: Implications for Diversified Companies

While low market-share divisions of large diversified companies face many of the problems we have encountered in our research, it is important to note that their status creates additional problems as well as some opportunities.

An obvious advantage is that many of the more established diversified companies maintain large, centralized research and development centers. One successful division we studied had few funds itself for new product development. But when a competitor developed a product that was based on a new technology, those at corporate headquarters had their R&D center imitate the development in accordance with a one-time request from the division.

On the negative side, most large companies place great emphasis on growth and reward those division managers whose units grow the fastest. This philosophy runs counter to the needs of many divisions to segment and think small. Many large companies also use formal planning techniques that categorize their divisions. The division managers then must convince their top managers that, despite the dismal projections and warnings of statistically oriented planners, their divisions do face a bright future.

An example illustrates these problems and the ways in which they can be overcome. Consolidated Businesses is a typical diversified company op-

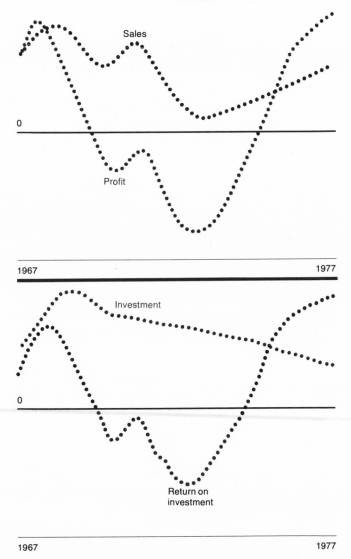

erating in 65 businesses ranging from air conditioners to automobile parts.*
Dedicated to continuous increases in sales and earnings, its semiconductor
division produced a full line of sophisticated devices and had grown quite
rapidly prior to a sudden sharp decline in its sales and profits. After a number
of management changes, a new division team and executives from the group
vice president's staff undertook a complete review of the division and its

*This disguised example was also reported on in Richard Hamermesh's article, "Responding
to Divisional Profit Crises," *HBR*, March-April 1977, p. 124.

industry. They determined that the division could only succeed by concentrating on serving a distinct group of industrial customers.

By doing this, the semiconductor division has recorded the highest ROI in its history; in fact, it enjoys one of the highest ROIs within Consolidated Businesses (see the accompanying table). Even though the division's sales are lower than they were ten years ago and its profits are at about the same level, Consolidated Businesses' top executives understand that the high return it is earning on shareholders' investment more than compensates for these facts. They have also promoted many of the semiconductor division's managers for their performance.

16
How to Compete in Stagnant Industries

RICHARD G. HAMERMESH AND STEVEN B. SILK

As more and more industries decline or increase only modestly, the need for competent managers in stagnant industries will grow. Instead of following the often-
heard advice to harvest such businesses, managers should understand the characteristics of their markets and build strategy accordingly. On the basis of their study
of a number of declining industries, these authors identify some consistent characteristics in companies that have competed successfully.

From 1950 to 1973, the U.S. economy enjoyed record prosperity. Gross
national product and per capita disposable income, measured in real terms,
grew at annual rates of 3.7% and 2.4%, respectively. Among the many
consequences of this growth has been an attitude among managers that
growth is beneficial and will continue and an assumption that the most
talented and aggressive managers should lead rapidly growing divisions.
Slowly growing or declining divisions have been left to the less aggressive
or over-the-hill managers.

Such attitudes and assumptions may have made sense when growth
seemed unlimited. Since 1973, however, economic growth has slowed, with
real GNP and real per capita disposable income rising very slowly. And the
limited supply of natural resources has led most economic observers to
forecast a prolonged period of slower growth. Thus, in the future, more
industries will experience declines or only modest increases in the demand
for their products. This situation will create a tremendous need for managers
who can effectively lead businesses that compete in stagnant industries.

Despite the increasing need for competent management in stagnant
industries, little research has been conducted on what strategies make the
most sense in such industries. Existing theory offers little sound advice.

Published 1979.

Instead it offers the glib recommendations that companies either divest these businesses or "harvest" them as "cash cows." Unfortunately, harvesting can often become synonymous with abandonment. Moreover, the difficulty of finding a buyer often makes divestment impossible, and liquidation is often impractical. One experienced division manager commented on the problem in the following way:

> Recently our corporate planning people studied our division and determined that we should drop certain product lines because they were in tough, slowly growing markets. But that isn't so easy. Without those sales, we'd no longer be covering our plant overhead and most of our other products would become unprofitable.

In our study of possible approaches to competing in stagnant industries, we first defined stagnant industries as those whose total unit demand over a ten-year period had either declined or increased at less than half the rate of real GNP. After identifying 12 industries which met our criteria, we then looked carefully at those companies that were notably successful or unsuccessful in order to determine what competitive strategies were most likely to succeed or fail in such industries. Finally, through interviews with managers in many of these companies, we were able to gain a better understanding of the administrative problems of managing a stagnant industry.

Our research shows that it is possible to compete successfully and to earn high returns in these industries. More specifically, it reveals some important characteristics of the strategies of the successful businesses. Equally important, our work also indicates that the way top management interacts with and administers its stagnant businesses often has a substantial impact on their performance.

Harsh Realities

Before turning to the most promising strategies, it is necessary to examine the difficult realities of life in a stagnant market. An appreciation of these realities is critical because, as we shall see, strategies that run counter to them nearly always fail, while the successful strategies are consistent with market conditions.

Perhaps the most difficult reality to accept is that rapid growth probably will not return to a stagnant industry. Consider the coffee industry. Between 1960 and 1975, total consumption of coffee fell 3.2%. Admittedly, in certain years demand has increased and in others price increases have led to pronounced declines. But over a long period of time, the overall trend has been a slow decline. The fact that consumption per person has fallen even more rapidly suggests that this trend will continue.

The point is an important one. In a declining or slowly growing industry, there may be some years when demand is buoyant. But it is essential for managers not to let wishful thinking color their views. Instead, they must accurately assess the long-range prospects and face the problems of competing in a stagnant marketplace. Management's acceptance of the reality of a continuing slow demand is a prerequisite for developing successful strategies.

For example, at one company we visited, we were told about the shaky relationship between the corporate office and a division that competed in a declining market. Corporate management was dissatisfied with the division's performance, while the division was upset that none of its capital requests had been approved in the past four years. Closer examination revealed that, although top management did not want to commit additional resources to the division, it was still pressuring the division to grow. The division's response was to develop plans for growth that required additional capital investment.

When both division and corporate management confronted the reality of declining demand in a series of strategy-setting meetings, the problem was eventually resolved. The division then adopted a set of goals consistent with its market opportunities, and corporate management began to measure divisional performance on the basis of cash flow and return on investment.

The next unpleasant reality is that competition is usually more intense in stagnant markets than in those that are growing rapidly.[1] A company can substantially increase its sales in a rapidly growing industry without taking market share from competitors. In fact, often it takes all of a company's managerial and financial resources just to meet growing demand. The major problem is expansion, not competition. When industry growth slows, however, company growth can be achieved only at the expense of others, and competition increases.

As competition intensifies, the number of companies competing in the industry usually declines, and the market shares of the largest companies increase. For example, in the cigar industry, where unit demand has been declining by 5% a year for 15 years, the number of manufacturers declined from 283 in 1958 to 132 in 1972. In the coffee industry, not only has the number of companies declined but the combined market shares of the three largest corporations increased from 47% in 1960 to 67% in 1976.

A final reality, and one that is often overlooked, is that changes in products, technology, production process, and distribution still occur in stagnant industries. In fact, research by William J. Abernathy and James M. Utterback has shown that some innovations, notably in the manufacturing process, tend to occur more frequently as a market matures.[2] For example, improvements in cigar-forming equipment have changed the industry from a "craftsman" business to an automated one. As we shall discuss later, improvements by the Japanese in the manufacturing process of motorcycles made possible the development of the recreational motorcycle market. Stagnant demand, then, does not prevent significant changes.

Failure to recognize these realities can lead to competitive strategies that seem logical but are seldom successful. This is most likely to occur when stagnant sales are viewed as "a marketing problem" instead of as a fact of life. Rather than increasing total demand, typical marketing solutions such as brand proliferation and heavy advertising usually result in higher inventory investment, higher manufacturing costs, and lower profitability. Other research has shown that, although increased advertising tends to benefit businesses in their introduction or growth phases, it is seldom useful for declining businesses.[3]

Strategies for Success

Given these realities, are there any approaches that not only avoid the possibility of extinction but that also offer hope for a reasonable return on investment in stagnant industries? Our research uncovered three common characteristics of the strategies of businesses that have succeeded in stagnant industries: they identify, create, and exploit growth segments within their industries; they emphasize product quality and innovative product improvement; and they systematically and consistently improve the efficiency of their production and distribution systems.

Growth Segments

Perhaps the best way to avoid some of the unpleasant realities in a stagnant industry is to concentrate on growth segments. A classic example is the strategy followed by General Cinema Corporation.

Over the past 30 years, the number of motion picture theaters in the United States has declined by almost 20%. As late as 1946, movie admissions accounted for $1 out of every $5 spent on recreational items versus $1 out of every $40 today. During this extended period of decline and stagnation, one market segment—the shopping center theater—has been growing at an impressive rate. And General Cinema Corporation has been the leader in recognizing this opportunity and in concentrating its resources in this growth segment. Today General Cinema has about 700 shopping center theaters, usually with multiple auditoriums (Cinema I and II theaters). In a declining total industry, General Cinema has been able to maintain average earnings increases of over 20% during the past 10 years and a return on equity of 20%.

Of course, it can be argued that by competing in growth segments a company has merely figured out how to avoid competing in a stagnant industry. And this is precisely the point. Choosing what business to compete in is at the very heart of the strategy formulation problem, and the best strategists spend considerable time analyzing their industries in an effort to identify emerging or growth segments. Admittedly, there are some industries for which it is virtually impossible to identify growth segments, but in most industries opportunities do exist. As the chairman of a $300 million specialty paper and chemical company recently told us, "There is a high-growth segment in every industry you can think of."

Another example illustrates how imaginative thinking can uncover growth opportunities, even within a sluggish capital goods industry. Since the Arab oil embargo in 1973, demand for electrical power in the United States has hardly risen, leading to a major reduction in orders for new power-generating equipment. Westinghouse Electric's Power Systems Company has not been able to avoid this dearth of new orders, but it has compensated for these lost sales by expanding its service business.[4] As customers have postponed or canceled new purchases, demand for repair and maintenance work has surged. Not only is Westinghouse filling this demand, but it is also actively developing new products and concepts that should enable the company to exploit this growth segment.

For example, replacement parts are being developed that improve the efficiency of existing systems, and a portable precision machine shop allows technicians to machine heavy rotors on location. As a result of these efforts, during the past six years service volume has tripled, enabling the Power Systems Company to show steady gains in sales and earnings.

Since the identification of growth segments usually requires considerable insight and creativity, it is difficult to prescribe a set of procedures that will lead to their identification. Nevertheless, there probably is a way to think about an industry that should help identify growth segments. The key is to recognize that, on close examination, most industries are composed of numerous segments and subsegments. And these can be defined along a variety of dimensions: customer group, price, product characteristics, product use, geography, service, and technology.

Merely listing and thinking about segments, however, is not enough, for detailed breakdowns of industry statistics along the relevant dimensions are also required. This information is seldom publicly available and requires a research investment to collect and analyze it. For example, just considering customer grouping, simply to obtain a breakdown by age, sex, geographic location, economic status, and buying motivation may involve considerable effort. In some of the companies we visited, it was not unusual for one or two staff people to work full time at collecting and analyzing such data. Thus a creative management that is willing to view its stagnant industries as being composed of smaller segments and to collect and analyze detailed industry data is much more likely to identify segments with growth potential.

Innovation and Quality

Another characteristic of successful strategies in stagnant industries is the pursuit of high-quality, innovative products. Such products allow the company to avoid some of the price competition that often typifies stagnant markets. Product innovations have the further advantage of being difficult and expensive for competitors to imitate.

An example of a high-quality innovative product is General Foods's freeze-dried instant coffee, which offers better-tasting instant coffee. For almost ten years, it has grown rapidly and achieved the highest margin of all coffee products. The freeze-dry technology is also more expensive than traditional technologies. Most coffee producers—with the notable exception of Nestlé—have been unwilling or unable to invest in either the research or the capital equipment necessary to compete in this segment. Thus this innovation has provided high margins in a segment with few competitors.

Further evidence that high quality and innovation are particularly important in stagnant industries comes from analysis of the 1,000 businesses in the PIMS (profit impact of market strategies) data base.[5] For all these businesses, higher product quality is associated with a larger return on investment, but the relationship appears to be most significant in stagnant markets (see Exhibit 1). Also striking are the relationships among ROI, market growth, and expenditures for research and development (see Exhibit 2). For moderate and rapid-growth markets, the PIMS data indicate no benefits to ROI from increased spending on R&D. However, in the stagnant markets, high rates of R&D spending correlate with higher ROIs.

The association between ROI and R&D spending in stagnant industries may indicate that, in addition to the benefits from a major new product innovation, in many cases there is also a payoff from consistently higher levels of spending on research that produces a steady stream of higher-quality products. The group vice-president in charge of the fastener divisions in a large corporation explained:

> Our business is a mature one, and in some divisions unit demand is actually declining. But because of the nature of our business and our own efforts, each year 20% of our products are new ones designed for the new models in the appliance, clothing, auto industry, and so on. Thus there would be a danger in reducing our spending on R&D. By designing innovative new products we not only maintain our volume but also avoid competing in commodity items.

One result of this strategy was that the fastener group's return on assets was among the highest in the corporation.

Exhibit 1. Return on Investment as a Function of Market Growth and Product Quality (in Percentages)

Market Growth	Product Quality		
	Low	Medium	High
Low	15	14	31
Medium	16	22	29
High	21	23	28

Source: Based on data from PIMS companies in *The Limited Information Report,* distributed by the Strategic Planning Institute (Cambridge, Mass., 1977), p. 16.

Exhibit 2.   Return on Investment as a Function of Market Growth and Research and Development Expenditures (in Percentages)

Market Growth	R&D Sales		
	Low	Medium	High
Low	14	21	19
Medium	22	19	15
High	21	20	12

Source: Based on data from PIMS companies in *The Limited Information Report,* distributed by the Strategic Planning Institute (Cambridge, Mass., 1977), p. 16.

Operating Efficiencies

Another characteristic of the successful stagnant industry businesses we studied was their constant attention to cost reduction. The most common way to achieve lower costs seems to be by improving the manufacturing process. Often these improvements stem from constant and systematic attention to efficiency. For example, Samuel Hollander has shown that more than half of the reduction in rayon costs at Du Pont has resulted from gradual improvements rather than from major investments and programs.[6]

A dramatic example of the power of process innovations is the Japanese approach to the motorcycle industry. During the 1950s, demand for motorcycles declined as fewer people used them as a primary mode of transportation. Rather than exit from this sick industry, the major Japanese manufacturers embarked on an ambitious program to lower their costs and to concentrate on smaller motorcycles (under 750 cc). High degrees of specialization and automation have been the hallmarks of the approach. One Honda plant, for example, makes only engines. Both Suzuki and Yamaha have plants almost entirely dedicated to the manufacture of specialized machine tools. As the Japanese lowered their costs and broke price barriers, they were able to create a new growth segment in the industry—the recreational bike.

Although improvements in the manufacturing process are the most common way of lowering costs, other efficiencies can be achieved. For example, the orderly and planned consolidation of production facilities can have a dramatic impact on ROI. In the previously mentioned fasteners group, one division's ROI was less than 10%. Consolidation of its manufacturing facilities with those of other divisions has helped to lift its ROI to 35%.

The important point, however, is not only that facility consolidations lead to higher rates of return; it is also that by accepting the realities of stagnant demand, management can plan for the orderly consolidation of manufacturing facilities. For example, the division manager of a business that supplies materials to U.S. shoe manufacturers determined that over a three-year period his need for two manufacturing plants would disappear.

He used this time to identify another division in the company that needed manufacturing capacity. The shift from a two- to a one-factory operation has enabled the division to operate at high levels of efficiency, and the changeover was implemented with a minimum of disruption.

A final form of operating efficiency is possible through broad and efficient distribution, which is especially important in stagnant industries requiring high volumes for efficient manufacturing operations. For example, Whirlpool's appliance business is concentrated in the stagnant washer, dryer, and refrigerator segments. To ensure the volume needed to manufacture at efficient scale, Whirlpool has used Sears as the distribution outlet for 60% of its production. Indeed, private labeling is a common way of achieving broad and efficient distribution in stagnant industries.

It should be noted that the three characteristics we have identified of the strategies of the successful businesses often reinforce each other. In both the motorcycle and the appliance industries, attention to operating efficiencies led to concentration on growth segments. And in the motorcycle industry, the smaller, cheaper recreational bikes were high-quality product improvements. Clearly, the successful companies differ in the degree to which they emphasize the three strategies, but most of them exploit elements of each.

Top Management's Role

When we began this study, our objective was to identify the characteristics of successful strategies for competing in stagnant industries. In talking with managers in these businesses, however, it quickly became apparent that the nature of top management's involvement and its choice of general managers for these businesses were also critical determinants of their success.

In most large, diversified corporations, it is beyond the scope of corporate management to set strategy for individual business units. Nevertheless, top managers do influence business unit strategy through the reporting system, compensation system, planning system, organizational arrangements, and personnel selection. Obviously, corporate managers attempt to establish systems and an organizational context that facilitate the business units' efforts to compete successfully. For business units that compete in stagnant industries, corporate-level managers can accomplish this by not labeling the status of these business units, by not mandating "milking" strategies, and by assigning talented general managers to run these businesses.

Avoiding Labels

Throughout this article, we have pointed to the payoffs of accepting and dealing with slowing sales as a reality of life. Although it is essential that top management consider this reality when developing business plans, it is also important not to assign pejorative labels to these businesses.

One label sometimes used for low-growth businesses is "dog." Such a characterization can have a debilitating effect on morale within the division, and it suggests that not much attention needs to be given to these businesses. But, as we have seen, competition in stagnant industries is usually intense, and success is dependent on creative strategies and skilled implementation. A group vice president of a large industrial company explained his experiences as follows:

> Two of the divisions that report to me are in very sluggish industries. In one case, we have been able to develop more original strategies, have the employees all fired up, and are making a good return. But I have had to fight to keep the corporate planners from giving their view of the situation. In the other division, the notion that they have a dog has been allowed to permeate from the top. I feel there are some original things we could do there, but it's impossible to get anyone at the division very excited to try something new. Eventually we'll probably sell or liquidate the division.

The point is a simple one. Top managers do have the responsibility to make sure that the business unit accepts stagnant industry demand as fact. But, as we have shown, stagnation does not mean that successful ways of competing do not exist. Successful strategies are more likely to be adopted when the stagnant condition is accepted as a fact of life rather than labeled as a dreaded condition.

Avoiding Milking

Another inappropriate top management response is to require these businesses to adopt milking, or harvesting, strategies automatically. The overwhelming defect of these strategies is that they are internally oriented, ignoring events in the external environment and assuming a lack of change within the industry. This attitude is often reflected by attempts to milk the businesses for cash and thus to minimize investments in research and engineering. Unfortunately, there is often a thin line between managing a business in this way as a cash cow and abandoning it.

When Alcoa and Reynolds Aluminum developed a process to produce two-piece cans, their intentions reportedly were to make the process available to can manufacturers in order to increase their raw material sales. However, the two largest can producers, American Can and Continental Group, were reluctant to incur the costs involved in line changeovers at a time when they were diversifying into growth businesses and de-emphasizing their slowly growing can operations.

The result was that Alcoa and Reynolds began to build their own can lines and that two smaller producers, National Can and Crown Cork & Seal, also invested heavily in new two-piece can lines. Because the new cans have proved very popular and offer important manufacturing benefits, the companies that were willing to invest in the new process have gained market share at the expense of their larger competitors, who assumed a static situation and were harvesting their can manufacturing businesses.

The penalties for adopting milking strategies that assume a static competitive and technological situation can be severe. The director of corporate planning at one of the widely diversified companies we visited explained:

> If one of our high-growth divisions misses or is late on an innovation, it is not that serious, because in a few months they will have another chance to be first on the next set of innovations. But in slowly growing divisions, change is less frequent. And if you miss a change, the next one may not come for another five to ten years. By that time, you could be out of business.

Admittedly, many successful businesses that compete in stagnant industries do generate more cash than they consume and in this sense could be considered cash cows. But there is an important distinction between generating positive cash flows as the result of strategic actions aimed at improving a business's competitive position and making positive cash flows the major objective of a business.

In the former approach, a business develops its strategy after assessing conditions and changes in the external environment and relates these to internal competence. After management formulates a strategy, it applies financial tests such as ROI, cash flow, or rate of growth and makes a decision whether to adopt the proposed strategy. Conversely, the milking approach leads to a strategy that is consistent with a certain set of cash flows. In our view, this approach is much less likely to produce creative strategies that will be successful over a long period of time.

Choosing Managers

Earlier in this article, we noted the historical tendency of most top managements to assign their most talented and aggressive managers to their rapidly growing divisions while leaving their stagnant divisions to less aggressive and competent managers. Keeping in mind that competition in stagnant industries is usually more intense than in growth situations, it is easy to see the problems that arise when less competent managers are assigned to these businesses.

Choosing appropriate general managers for low-growth businesses, then, is a major challenge. For example, selecting "marketing men" who only focus on increasing sales is likely to lead to strategies that are inappropriate in these industries. Our observation has been that it is crucial for an experienced general manager to be assigned to run one of these businesses and that his or her future promotions be tied to success with these divisions. A group vice president at an industrial company explained:

> I try to assign these [stagnant] businesses to people who are ready for their second or third general management job. These are real good positions to test the flexibility of these people. Also, I think by assigning

talented people we get a leg up on our competitors who may be down-playing these businesses.

Of course, choosing good people becomes a hollow gesture if it is not backed up with bonuses and promotions for outstanding performance. And here it is important to remember that success will usually not manifest itself in high rates of sales growth but rather in high levels of ROI. Nothing signals top management's expectations more clearly than the promotion of general managers who have competed successfully in a stagnant marketplace.

In Summary

We have tried to address one of the most difficult strategic problems that managers face, a problem we think will proliferate in the future. Despite our recommendations regarding successful strategies and management's involvement, it should be apparent that competing in these industries will always be difficult. We can then ask: Why bother? Why not diversify into higher-growth businesses and simply divest low-growth businesses?

In answering these questions, it is important to recognize that, from the corporate perspective, diversification is often an effective way to deal with these problems. In fact, one of the major roles of top management in a diversified company is to ensure that growth businesses will be maintained within the corporation. But it is a rare company that competes only in rapidly growing industries. Thus corporations must eventually address problems of competing in slower industries.

There are other reasons why diversification is not a panacea for the problems of competing in stagnant industries. In some companies, these businesses are simply too large to be disposed of or liquidated. For example, even though the coffee industry is declining, General Foods still derives 40% of its sales and one-third of its earnings from its coffee business. It has no choice but to compete vigorously and effectively in the coffee industry.

In other circumstances, divestment is simply impossible. Who would want to buy one of these businesses? So, in many cases, management cannot avoid the problems of competing in stagnant industries. Indeed, as we pointed out earlier, accepting and dealing directly with the problem is usually the first step in adopting and implementing a successful strategy.

The next step is to choose a strategy and stick with it. In several of the situations we studied, divisional management kept wavering among a broad range of strategies. One month management proposed a series of product-line extensions, while the following month simplifying distribution would be the fad. This lack of consistency not only wastes valuable time and fails to produce results for the division but also confuses the corporate managers who are trying to understand and help the divisions.

Competing in stagnant industries requires adoption of clear strategies that emphasize growth segments, innovative products, and production efficiencies. At the same time, top managers must avoid the tendency to label these businesses pejoratively, to require them to implement harvesting strategies, and to assign them to weak managers.

When these guidelines are followed, competing in these industries can be profitable and slow growth can become an ally. As competitors stumble into the ever-present pitfalls, a tremendous opportunity is created for companies that are willing to compete aggressively and imaginatively. For them, competition in these industries is by no means dull; rather, it is exciting and profitable.

Notes

1. See Michael E. Porter, "How Competitive Forces Shape Strategy," *HBR*, March–April 1979, p. 137.

2. See James M. Utterback and William J. Abernathy, "A Dynamic Model of Process and Product Innovation," *Omega,* 3, no. 6 (1975), p. 639.

3. See Paul W. Farris and Robert D. Buzzell, *Relationships Between Changes in Industrial Advertising and Promotion Expenditures and Changes in Market Share,* Marketing Science Institute Working Paper No. 76–119 (Cambridge, Mass, December 1976).

4. See "More Manufacturers Are Selling Services to Increase Returns and Smooth Cycles," *Wall Street Journal,* December 26, 1978, p. 24.

5. For a more complete description of the PIMS project, see Robert D. Buzzell, Bradley T. Gale, and Ralph G.M. Sultan, "Market Share—A Key to Profitability," *HBR*, January–February 1975, p. 97.

6. See William J. Abernathy and James M. Utterback, "Patterns of Industrial Innovation," *Technology Review,* June–July 1978, p. 3.

17

End-game Strategies for Declining Industries

KATHRYN RUDIE HARRIGAN and MICHAEL E. PORTER

During the last year or so you watched the demand for one of your business's products decline and noted that the same decline hit your competitors. Searching for a reason, you realize that your product may be becoming technologically obsolete. It looks as if it's just a question of time. Can you be profitable if you stay in and invest? What should your end-game strategy be?

Kathryn Harrigan and Michael Porter have studied the strategies of over 95 companies that confronted declining markets. They found that end games can sometimes be very profitable and that companies successful in end games ask themselves some crucial questions about the nature of the industry—what exit barriers face each competitor, how the pattern of decline will affect competition, and whether their relative strengths match the remaining pockets of demand. The authors discuss the factors that determine the profitability of remaining in a declining industry as well as the strategic alternatives, and offer guidelines for choosing an end-game strategy.

> End game *n* 1: the last stage (as the last three tricks) in playing a bridge hand 2: the final phase of a board game; specifically the stage of a chess game following serious reduction of forces.[1]

As early as 1948, when researchers discovered the "transistor effect," it was evident that vacuum tubes in television sets had become technologically obsolete. Within a few years, transistor manufacturers were predicting that by 1961 half the television sets then in use would employ transistors instead of vacuum tubes.

Published 1983.

Since the 1950s, manufacturers of vacuum tubes have been engaged in the industry's end game. Like other end games, this one is played in an environment of declining product demand where conditions make it very unlikely that all the plant capacity and competitors put in place during the industry's heyday will ever be needed. In today's world of little or no economic growth and rapid technological change, more and more companies are being faced with the need to cope with an end game.

Because of its musical chair character, the end game can be brutal. Consider the bloodbath in U.S. gasoline marketing today. Between 1973 and 1983, in response to high crude oil prices and conservation efforts by consumers, the output from petroleum refineries declined precipitately. Uncertainty concerning supply and demand for refined products has made predicting the speed and extent of decline difficult, and an industry consensus has never evolved. Moreover, the competitors in this end game are very diverse in their outlooks and in the tactics they use to cope with the erratic nature of decline.

As in the baby food industry's end game, where a ten-year price war raged until demand plateaued, gasoline marketers and refiners are fighting to hold market shares of a shrinking pie. As industry capacity is painfully rationalized and companies dig in for the lean years ahead in their end game, a long period of low profits is inevitable.

In the vacuum tube industry, however, the end game was starkly different. Commercialization of solid-state devices progressed more slowly than the transistor manufacturers forecast. The last television set containing vacuum tubes was produced in 1974, and a vast population of electronic products requiring replacement tubes guaranteed a sizable market of relatively price-insensitive demand for some years. In 1983, several plants still produce tubes. Where obsolescence was a certainty and the decline rate slow, the six leading vacuum tube manufacturers were able to shut down excess plant capacity while keeping supply in line with demand. Price wars never ruined the profitability of their end game, and the companies that managed well during the decline earned satisfactorily high returns, particularly for declining businesses.

To recoup the maximum return on their investments, managers of some declining businesses are turning with considerable success to strategies that they had used only when demand was growing. In the past, the accepted prescription for a business on the wane has been a "harvest" strategy— eliminate investment, generate maximum cash flow, and eventually divest. The strategic portfolio models managers commonly use for planning yield this advice on declining industries: do not invest in low- or negative-growth markets; pull cash out instead.

Our study of declining industries suggests, however, that the nature of competition during a decline and the strategic alternatives available for coping with it are complex (see the appendix). The experiences of industries that have suffered an absolute decline in unit sales over a sustained period

differ markedly. Some industries, like vacuum receiving tubes, age gracefully, and profitability for remaining competitors has been extremely high.
Others, like rayon, decline amid bitter warfare, prolonged excess capacity,
and heavy operating losses.

The stories of companies that have successfully coped with decline
vary just as widely. Some companies, like GTE Sylvania, reaped high returns
by making heavy investments in a declining industry that made their businesses better sources of cash later. By selling out before their competitors
generally recognized the decline, and not harvesting, other companies, like
Raytheon and DuPont, avoided losses that competitors subsequently bore.

In this article we discuss the strategic problems that declining demand
poses, where decline is a painful reality and not a function of the business
cycle or other short-term discontinuities. Sometimes, of course, innovations,
cost reductions, and shifts in other circumstances may reverse a decline.[2]
Our focus here, however, is on industries in which available remedies have
been exhausted and the strategic problem is coping with decline. When
decline is beyond the control of incumbent companies, managers need to
develop end-game strategies.

First, we sketch the structural conditions that determine if the environment of a declining industry is hospitable, particularly as these affect
competition. Second, we discuss the generic end-game strategy alternatives
available to companies in decline. We conclude with some principles for
choosing an end-game strategy.

What Determines the Competition?

Shrinking industry sales make the decline phase volatile. The extent to which
escalating competitive pressures erode profitability during decline, however,
depends on how readily industry participants pull out and how fiercely the
companies that remain try to contain their shrinking sales.

Conditions of Demand

Demand in an industry declines for a number of reasons. Technological
advances foster substitute products (electronic calculators for slide rules)
often at lower cost or higher quality (synthetics for leather). Sometimes the
customer group shrinks (baby foods) or buyers slide into trouble (railroads).
Changes in lifestyle, buyers' needs, or tastes can also cause demand to
decline (cigars and hatmaking equipment). Finally, the cost of inputs or
complementary products may rise and shrink demand (recreational vehicles).
The cause of decline helps determine how companies will perceive both
future demand and the profitability of serving the diminished market.

Companies' expectations concerning demand will substantially affect
the type of competitive environment that develops in an end game. The
process by which demand in an industry declines and the characteristics of

those market segments that remain also have a great influence on competition during the decline phase.

Uncertainty.   Correct or not, competitors' perceptions of demand in a declining industry potently affect how they play out their end-game strategies. If managers in the industry believe that demand will revitalize or level off, they will probably try to hold onto their positions. As the baby food industry examples shows, efforts to maintain position despite shrinking sales will probably lead to warfare. On the other hand, if, as was the case of synthetic sodium carbonate (soda ash), managers in different companies are all certain that industry demand will continue to decline, reduction of capacity is more likely to be orderly.

Companies may well differ in their perceptions of future demand, with those that foresee revitalization persevering. A company's perception of the likelihood of decline is influenced by its position in the industry and its difficulty in getting out. The stronger its stake or the higher its exit barriers, the more optimistic a company's forecast of demand is likely to be.

Rate and Pattern of Decline.   Rapid and erratic decline greatly exacerbate the volatility of competition. How fast the industry collapses depends partly on the way in which companies withdraw capacity. In industrial businesses (such as the synthesis of soda ash) where the product is very important to customers but where a substitute is available, demand can fall drastically if one or two major producers decide to retire and customers doubt the continued availability of the original product. Announcements of early departure can give great impetus to the decline. Because shrinking volume raises costs and often prices, the decline rate tends to accelerate as time passes.

Structure of Remaining Demand Pockets.   In a shrinking market, the nature of the demand pockets that remain plays a major role in determining the remaining competitors' profitability. The remaining pocket in cigars has been premium-quality cigars, for example, while in vacuum tubes it has been replacement and military tubes.

If the remaining pocket has favorable structure, decline can be profitable for well-positioned competitors. For example, demand for premium-quality cigars is price insensitive: customers are immune to substitute products and very brand loyal. Thus, even as the industry declines, companies that offer branded, premium cigars are earning above-average returns. For the same reasons, upholstery leathers are a profitable market segment in the leather industry.

On the other hand, in the acetylene industry, ethylene has already replaced acetylene in some market segments and other substitutes threaten the remaining pockets. In those pockets, acetylene is a commodity product that, because of its high fixed manufacturing costs, is subject to price warfare. The potential for profit for its remaining manufacturers is dismal.

In general, if the buyers in the remaining demand pockets are price insensitive, for example, buyers of replacement vacuum tubes for television receivers, or have little bargaining power, survivors can profit. Price insensitivity is important because shrinking sales imply that companies must raise prices to maintain profitability in the face of fixed overhead.

The profit potential of remaining demand pockets will also depend on whether companies that serve them have mobility barriers that protect them from attack by companies seeking to replace lost sales.

Exit Barriers

Just as companies have to overcome barriers in entering a market, they meet exit barriers in leaving it. These barriers can be insurmountable even when a company is earning subnormal returns on its investment. The higher the exit barriers, the less hospitable the industry is during the industry's decline. A number of basic aspects of a business can become exit barriers.

Durable and Specialized Assets. If the assets, either fixed or working capital or both, are specialized to the business, company, or location in which they are being used, their diminished liquidation value creates exit barriers. A company with specialized assets such as sole-leather tanneries must either sell them to someone who intends to use them in the same business, usually in the same location, or scrap them. Naturally, few buyers wish to use the assets of a declining business.

Once the acetylene and rayon industries started to contract, for example, potential buyers for plants were few or nonexistent; companies sold plants at enormous discounts from book value to speculators or desperate employee groups. Particularly if it represents a large part of assets and normally turns over very slowly, specialized inventory may also be worth very little in these circumstances. The problem of specialized assets is more acute where a company must make an all-or-nothing exit decision (e.g., continuous process plants) versus a decision to reduce the number of sites or close down lines.

If the liquidation value of the assets is low, it is possible for a company to show a loss on the books but earn discounted cash flows that exceed the value that could be realized if management sold the business. When several companies perform this same analysis and choose to remain in a declining industry, excess capacity grows and profit margins are usually depressed.

By expanding their search for buyers, managers can lower exit barriers arising from specialized assets. Sometimes assets find a market overseas even though they have little value in the home country. But as the industry decline becomes increasingly clear, the value of specialized assets will usually diminish. For example, when Raytheon sold its vacuum tube-making assets in the early 1960s while tube demand was strong for color TV sets, it recovered a much higher liquidation than companies that tried to unload their vacuum tube facilities in the early 1970s, when the industry was clearly in its twilight years.

High Costs of Exit. Large fixed costs—labor settlements, contingent liabilities for land use, or costs of dismantling facilities—associated with leaving a business elevate exit barriers. Sometimes even after a company leaves, it will have to supply spare parts to past customers or resettle employees. A company may also have to break long-term contracts, which, if they can be abrogated at all, may involve severe cancellation penalties. In many cases, the company will have to pay the cost of having another company fulfill such contracts.

On the other hand, companies can sometimes avoid making fixed investments such as for pollution control equipment, alternative fuel systems, or maintenance expenditures by abandoning a business. These requirements promote getting out because they increase investment without raising profits, and improve prospects for decline.

Strategic Considerations. A diversified company may decide to remain in a declining industry for strategic reasons even if the barriers just described are low. These reasons include:

☐ *Interrelatedness.* A business may be part of a strategy that involves a group of businesses, such as whiskey and other distilled liquors, and dropping it would diminish overall corporate strategy. Or a business may be central to a company's identity or image, as in the case of General Cigar and Allied Leather, and leaving could hurt the company's relationships with key distribution channels and customers or lower the company's purchasing clout. Moreover, depending on the company's ability to transfer assets to new markets, quitting the industry may make shared plants or other assets idle.

☐ *Access to financial markets.* Leaving an industry may reduce a company's financial credibility and lessen its attractiveness to acquisition candidates or buyers. If the divested business is large relative to the total, divestment may hurt earnings growth or in some way raise the cost of capital, even if the write-off is economically justified. The financial market is likely to ignore small operating losses over a period of years buried among other profitable businesses while it will react strongly to a single large loss. While a diversified company may be able to use the tax loss from a write-off to mitigate the negative cash flow impact of exit decisions, the write-off will typically still have an effect on financial markets. Recently the markets have looked favorably on companies who take their losses on businesses with little future, an encouraging sign.

☐ *Vertical integration.* When companies are vertically integrated, barriers to exit will depend on whether the cause of decline touches the entire chain or just one link. In the case of acetylene, obsolescence made downstream chemical businesses, using acetylene as a feedstock, redundant; a company's decision whether to stay or go had to encompass the whole chain. In contrast, if a downstream unit depended on a feedstock that a substitute product had made obsolete, it would be strongly motivated to find an outside supplier of the substitute. In this case, the company's forward integration might hasten the decision to abandon the upstream unit because it had become a strategic liability to the whole company. In our study of end-game strategies, we found that most vertically integrated companies "deintegrated" before facing the final go/no go decision.

Information Gaps.   The more a business is related to others in the company, and especially when it shares assets or has a buyer-seller relationship, the more difficult it can be for management to get reliable information about its performance. For example, a failing coffee percolator unit may be part of a profit center with other small electrical housewares that sell well, and the company might not see the percolator unit's performance accurately and thus fail to consider abandoning the business.

Managerial Resistance.   Although the exit barriers we've described are based on rational calculations, or the inability to make them because of failures in information, the difficulties of leaving a business extend well beyond the purely economic. Manager's emotional attachments and commitments to a business—coupled with pride in their accomplishments and fears about their own futures—create emotional exit barriers. In a single-business company, quitting the business costs managers their jobs and creates personal problems for them such as a blow to their pride, the stigma of having "given up," severance of an identification that may have been longstanding, and a signal of failure that reduces job mobility.

It is difficult for managers of a sick division in a diversified company to propose divestment, so the burden of deciding when to quit usually falls on top management. But loyalty can be strong even at that level, particularly if the sick division is part of the historical core of the company or was started or acquired by the current CEO. For example, General Mills's decision to divest its original business, flour, was an agonizing choice that took management many years to make. And the suggestion that Sunbeam stop producing electric percolator coffee makers and waffle irons met stiff resistance in the boardroom.

In some cases, even though unsatisfactory performance is chronic, managerial exit barriers can be so strong that divestments are not made until top management changes.[3] Divestments are probably the most unpalatable decisions managers have to make.[4]

Personal experience with abandoning businesses, however, can reduce managers' reluctance to get out of an industry. In an industry such as chemicals where technological failure and product substitution are common, in industries where product lives are historically short, or in high-technology companies where new businesses continually replace old ones, executives can become used to distancing themselves from emotional considerations and making sound divestment decisions.

Social Barriers. Because government concern for jobs is high and the price of divestiture may be concessions from other businesses in the company or other prohibitive terms, closing down a business can often be next to impossible, especially in foreign countries. Divestiture often means putting people out of work, and managers understandably feel concern for their employees. Workers who have produced vacuum tubes for 30 years may have little understanding of solid-state manufacturing techniques. Divestiture can also mean crippling a local economy. In the depressed Canadian pulp industry, closing down mills means closing down whole towns.[5]

Asset Disposition. The manner in which companies dispose of assets can strongly influence the profitability of a declining industry and create or destroy exit barriers for competitors. If a company doesn't retire a large plant but sells it to a group of entrepreneurs at a low price, the industry capacity does not change but the competition does. The new entity can make pricing decisions and take other actions that are rational for it but cripple the competition. Thus if the owners of a plant don't retire assets but sell out instead, the remaining competitors can suffer more than if the original owners had stayed on.

Volatility of End Game

Because of falling sales and excess capacity, competitors fighting in an end game are likely to resort to fierce price warfare. Aggression is especially likely if the industry has maverick competitors with diverse goals and outlooks and high exit barriers, or if the market is very inhospitable (see Exhibit 1).

As an industry declines, it can become less important to suppliers (which raises costs or diminishes service) while the power of distributors increases. In the cigar business, for example, because cigars are an impulse item, shelf positioning is crucial to success, and it's the distributor who deals with the retailer. In the whiskey trade too, distillers hotly compete for the best wholesalers. Decline has led to substantial price pressures from these powerful middlemen that have reduced profitability. On the other hand, if the industry is a key customer, suppliers may attempt to help fight off decline as, for example, pulp producers helped the rayon industry fight cotton.

Perhaps the worst kind of waning-industry environment occurs when one or more weakened companies with significant corporate resources are committed to stay in the business. Their weakness forces them to use desperate actions, such as cutting prices, and their staying power forces other companies to respond likewise.

Strategic Alternatives for Declining Businesses

Discussions of strategy for shrinking industries usually focus on divestment or harvest strategies, but managers should consider two other alternatives as well—leadership and niche. These four strategies for decline vary greatly,

Exhibit 1.   Structural Factors That Influence the Attractiveness of Declining Industry Environments

Structural Factors	Environmental Attractiveness	
	Hospitable	Inhospitable
Conditions of demand		
Speed of decline	Very slow	Rapid or erratic
Certainty of decline	100% certain predictable patterns	Great uncertainty, erratic patterns
Pockets of enduring demand	Several or major ones	No niches
Product differentiation	Brand loyalty	Commodity-like products
Price stability	Stable, price premiums attainable	Very unstable, pricing below costs
Exit barriers		
Reinvestment requirements	None	High, often mandatory and involving capital assets
Excess capacity	Little	Substantial
Asset age	Mostly old assets	Sizable new assets and old ones not retired
Resale markets for assets	Easy to convert or sell	No markets available, substantial costs to retire
Shared facilities	Few free-standing plants	Substantial and interconnected with important businesses
Vertical integration	Little	Substantial
"Single product" competitors	None	Several large companies
Rivalry determinants		
Customer industries	Fragmented, weak	Strong bargaining power
Customer switching costs	High	Minimal
Diseconomies of scale	None	Substantial penalty
Dissimilar strategic groups	Few	Several in same target markets

not only in their goals but also in their implications for investment, and managers can pursue them individually or, in some cases, sequentially:

☐ *Leadership.* A company following the market-share leadership strategy tries to reap above-average profitability by becoming one of the few companies remaining in a declining industry. Once a company attains this position, depending on the subsequent pattern of industry sales, it usually switches to a holding position or controlled harvest strategy. The underlying premise is that by achieving leadership the company can be more profitable (taking the investment into account) because it can exert more control over the process of decline and avoid destabilizing price competition. Investing in a slow or diminishing market is risky because capital may be frozen and resistant to retrieval through profits or liquidation. Under this strategy, however, the company's dominant position in the industry should give it cost leadership or differentiation that allows recovery of assets even if it reinvests during the decline period.

Managers can achieve a leadership position via several tactical maneuvers:

Ensure that other companies rapidly retire from the industry. H. J. Heinz and Gerber Products took aggressive competitive actions in pricing, marketing, and other areas that built market share and dispelled competitors' dreams of battling it out.

Reduce competitors' exit barriers. GTE Sylvania built market share by acquiring competitors' product lines at prices above the going rate. American Viscose purchased—and retired—competitors' capacity. (Taking this step ensures that others within the industry do not buy the capacity.) General Electric manufactured spare parts for competitors' products. Rohm & Hass took over competitors' long-term contracts in the acetylene industry. Proctor-Silex produced private-label goods for competitors so that they could stop their manufacturing operations.

Develop and disclose credible market information. Reinforcing other managers' certainty about the inevitability of decline makes it less likely that competitors will overestimate the prospects for the industry and remain in it.

Raise the stakes. Precipitating the need of other competitors to reinvest in new products or process improvements makes it more costly for them to stay in the business.

☐ *Niche.* The objective of this focus strategy is to identify a segment of the declining industry that will either maintain stable demand or decay slowly, and that has structural characteristics allowing high returns. A company then moves preemptively to gain a strong position in this segment while disinvesting from other segments. Armira followed a niche strategy in leather tanning, as Courtaulds did in rayon. To reduce either competitors' exit barriers from the chosen segment or their uncertainty about the segment's profitability, management might decide to take some of the actions listed under the leadership strategy.

☐ *Harvest.* In the harvest strategy, undergoing a controlled disinvestment, management seeks to get the most cash flow it can from the business. DuPont followed this course with its rayon business and BASF Wyandotte did the same in soda ash. To increase cash flow, management eliminates or severely curtails new investment, cuts maintenance of facilities, and reduces advertising and research while reaping the benefits of past goodwill. Other common harvest tactics include reducing the number of models produced; cutting the number of distribution channels; eliminating small customers; and eroding service in terms of delivery time (and thus reducing inventory), speed of repair, or sales assistance.

Companies following a harvest strategy often have difficulty maintaining suppliers' and customers' confidence, however, and thus some businesses cannot be fully harvested. Moreover, harvesting tests managers' skills as administrators because it creates problems in retaining and motivating employees. These considerations make harvest a risky option and far from the universal cure-all that it is sometimes purported to be.

Ultimately, managers following a harvest strategy will sell or liquidate the business.

☐ *Quick divestment.* Executives employing this strategy assume that the company can recover more of its investments from the business by selling it in the early stages of the decline, as Raytheon did, than by harvesting and selling it later or by following one of the other courses of action. The earlier the business is sold, the greater is potential buyers' uncertainty about a future slide in demand and thus the more likely that management will find buyers either at home or in foreign countries for the assets.

In some situations it may be desirable to divest the business before decline or, as DuPont did with its acetylene business, in the maturity phase. Once it's clear that the industry is waning, buyers for the assets will be in a strong bargaining position. On the other hand, a company that sells early runs the risk that its forecast will prove incorrect, as did RCA's judgment of the future of vacuum tubes.

Divesting quickly will force the company to confront its own exit barriers, such as its customer relationships and corporate interdependencies. Planning for an early departure can help managers mitigate the effect of these factors to some extent, however. For example, a company can arrange for remaining competitors to sell its products if it is necessary to continue to supply replacements, as Westinghouse Electric did for vacuum tubes.

Choosing a Strategy for Decline

With an understanding of the characteristics that shape competition in a declining industry and the different strategies they might use, managers can now ask themselves what their position should be:

☐ Can the structure of the industry support a hospitable, potentially profitable, decline phase (see Exhibit 1)?

☐ What are the exit barriers that each significant competitor faces? Who will exit quickly and who will remain?

☐ Do your company's strengths fit the remaining pockets of demand?

☐ What are your competitors' strengths in these pockets? How can their exit barriers be overcome?

In selecting a strategy, managers need to match the remaining opportunities in the industry with their companies' positions. The strengths and weaknesses that helped and hindered a company during the industry's development are not necessarily those that will count during the end game, where success will depend on the requirements to serve the pockets of demand that persist and the competition for this demand.

Exhibit 2 displays, albeit crudely, the strategic options open to a company in decline. When, because of low uncertainty, low exit barriers, and so forth, the industry structure is likely to go through an orderly decline phase, strong companies can either seek leadership or defend a niche, depending on the value to them of remaining market segments. When a company has no outstanding strengths for the remaining segments, it should either harvest or divest early. The choice depends, of course, on the feasibility of harvesting and the opportunities for selling the business.

When high uncertainty, high exit barriers, or conditions leading to volatile end-game rivalry make the industry environment hostile, investing to achieve leadership is not likely to yield rewards. If the company has strengths in the market segments that will persist, it can try either shrinking into a protected niche, or harvesting, or both. Otherwise, it is well advised to get out as quickly as its exit barriers permit. If it tries to hang on, other companies with high exit barriers and greater strengths will probably attack its position.

This simple framework must be supplemented by a third dimension of this problem—that is to say, a company's strategic need to remain in the business. For example, cash flow requirements may skew a decision toward harvest or early sale even though other factors point to leadership, as interrelationships with other units may suggest a more aggressive stance than otherwise. To determine the correct strategy a company should assess its

Exhibit 2.   Strategies for Declining Businesses

	Has competitive strengths for remaining demand pockets	Lacks competitive strengths for remaining demand pockets
Favorable industry structure for decline	Leadership or niche	Harvest or divest quickly
Unfavorable industry structure for decline	Niche or harvest	Divest quickly

strategic needs vis-à-vis the business and modify its end-game strategy accordingly.

Usually it is advantageous to make an early commitment to one end-game strategy or another. For instance, if a company lets competitors know from the outset that it is bent on a leadership position, it may not only encourage other companies to quit the business but also gain more time to establish its leadership. However, sometimes companies may want to bide their time by harvesting until indecisive competitors make up their minds. Until the situation is clear, a company may want to make preparations to invest should the leader go, and have plans to harvest or divest immediately should the leader stay. In any case, however, successful companies should *choose* an end-game strategy rather than let one be chosen for them.

The best course, naturally, is anticipation of the decline. If a company can forecast industry conditions, it may be able to improve its end-game position by taking steps during the maturity phase (sometimes such moves cost little in strategic position at the time):

☐ Minimize investments or other actions that will raise exit barriers unless clearly beneficial to overall corporate strategy.

☐ Increase the flexibility of assets so that they can accept different raw materials or produce related products.

☐ Place strategic emphasis on market segments that can be expected to endure when the industry is in a state of decline.

☐ Create customer-switching costs in these segments.

Avoiding Checkmate

Finding your company's position in Exhibit 2 requires a great deal of subtle analysis that is often shortchanged in the face of severe operating problems during decline. Many managers overlook the need to make strategy in decline consistent with industry structure because decline is viewed as somehow different. Our study of declining industries revealed other factors common to profitable players:

☐ *They recognize decline.* With hindsight, it is all too easy to admonish companies for being over-optimistic about the prospects for their declining industries' revitalization. Nevertheless, some executives, such as those of U.S. oil refineries, fail to look objectively at the prospects of decline. Either their identification with an industry is too great or their perception of substitute products is too narrow. The presence of high exit barriers may also subtly affect how managers perceive their environment; because bad omens are so painful to recognize, people understandably look for good signs.

Our examination of many declining industries indicates that the companies that are most objective about managing the decline process are also participants in the substitute industry. They have a clearer perception concerning the prospects of the substitute product and the reality of decline.

☐ *They avoid wars of attrition.* Warfare among competitors that have high exit barriers, such as the leather tanning companies, usually leads to disaster. Competitors are forced to respond vigorously to others' moves and cannot yield position without a big investment loss.

☐ *They don't harvest without definite strengths.* Unless the industry's structure is very favorable during the decline phase, companies that try to harvest without definite strengths usually collapse. Once marketing or service deteriorates or a company raises its prices, customers quickly take their business elsewhere. In the process of harvesting, the resale value of the business may also dissipate. Because of the competitive and administrative risks of harvesting, managers need a clear justification to choose this strategy.

☐ *They view decline as a potential opportunity.* Declining industries can sometimes be extraordinarily profitable for the well-positioned players, as GE and Raytheon have discovered in vacuum tubes. Companies that can view an industry's decline as an opportunity rather than just a problem, and make objective decisions, can reap handsome rewards.

Notes

1. *Webster's Third New International Dictionary* (Springfield, Mass., G. & C. Merriam, 1976). The term has also been used for an existentialist play by Samuel Beckett.

2. See Michael E. Porter, *Competitive Strategy* (New York, Free Press, 1980), Chapter 8. The book also contains a treatment of exit barriers and other industry and competitor characteristics discussed in this article.

3. See, for example, Stuart C. Gilmour, "The Divestment Decision Process," DBA dissertation, Harvard Graduate School of Business Administration, 1973; and Kathryn Rudie Harrigan, *Strategies for Declining Businesses* (Lexington, Mass., D.C. Heath, 1980).

4. See Michael E. Porter, *Interbrand Choice, Strategy and Bilateral Market Power* (Cambridge, Harvard University Press, 1976).

5. See Nitin T. Mehta, "Policy Formulation in a Declining Industry: The Case of the Canadian Dissolving Pulp Industry," DBA dissertation, Harvard Graduate School of Business Administration, 1978.

Appendix: Study of Strategies for Declining Businesses

Compiling 20-year histories of industry competition and company departures, we studied the strategies of 61 companies in eight declining industries.* We interviewed key competitors in the rayon and acetate, cigar, baby food, electric percolator coffee maker, electronic vacuum receiving tube, acetylene, synthetic soda ash, and U.S. leather tanning industries. (Follow-up studies examined the petroleum refining and whiskey distilling industries and attained consistent results.) Leaving their industries, 42 companies were profitable or did not suffer significant losses, while 19 were unprofitable or suffered sizable losses. Thirty-nine of the 42 successful companies followed the prescriptions of the strategy matrix shown in Exhibit 2. Sixteen of the 19 unsuccessful companies acted contrary to the recommendations of the strategy matrix. In short, if companies followed the matrix recommendations, their chances for success were better than 92%, while if they did not follow them, their chances of success were about 15%.

*See Kathyrn Rudie Harrigan's *Strategies for Declining Businesses* (Lexington, Mass, D.C. Heath, 1980).

PART FOUR
GETTING OUT, BUYING IN

AN OVERVIEW

It does happen, of course, that competitive circumstances do from time to time call for a redeployment of assets. To criticize these divestitures or acquisitions or whatever as being wrong in principle is as much an error as to applaud them merely for the size of the transactions completed. As with every significant managerial decision, the value of such transactions must stand or fall on the degree to which they help or hinder a company's strategic objectives. When they take on a life of their own, when they are thought to confer merit on their participants simply because they *are* participants, then matters have gotten out of hand. What results, as Robert Reich has argued, is an unfortunate explosion in the population of "paper entrepreneurs," who spend their time and talents

> establishing joint ventures, consortiums, holding companies, mutual funds; finding companies to acquire, "white knights" to be acquired by . . . engaging in proxy fights, tender splits, spinoffs, divestitures . . . going private, going public, going bankrupt.

The nine articles in this section add a note of sanity and calm reason to this financial cacophony by, first, defining the measures by which managers can calculate the value and appropriateness of such activities and, second, by holding up the lessons of past experience as a guide.

How to Redeploy Assets

RICHARD H. HILLMAN

Companies often place too much blind faith in the maxim that "integration is a good thing," the author argues; they are quick to dismiss any notion of redeploying assets wherever it might mean a diminished level of integration. Thus, they forgo the long- and short-term gains redeployment can bring to a business whose markets have shifted, say, or whose "integrated" position has been undermined by new industrial developments upstream or downstream. The author goes on to sketch a scheme for charting out the redeployment options available to a company and for evaluating each one before selecting or rejecting.

Asset redeployment is very much in vogue—companies today seem more and more willing to divest themselves of low-return operations and apply the assets thus liberated to areas that promise a better return.

In part, this trend can be explained by the present scarcity of cash, which has forced many companies to redeploy assets they might otherwise have left where they were. A second factor is the current pressure to increase profitability, which has made companies try to beef up their higher-profit operations at the expense of thinning down those that are less profitable in the short run.

Thus far, however—with certain significant exceptions—companies have limited their divestments to "independent" operations (i.e., operations that are not integrated with the activities of the parent company to any significant extent). In other words, while companies are willing to buoy up their integrated operations by liquidating the distant cousins of the family, by and large they seem not to have realized that the technique of asset redeployment can be extremely useful *within* a block of integrated operations.

Published 1971.

Managers naturally balk at the idea of selling off an integrated division, or even a part thereof, holding to the very sensible philosophy that "integration is protection." Integration does indeed protect a company; it lends stability, which is especially appreciated during periods of market fluctuation. But integration can be overdone; it is possible to elevate it, as a concept, above the realities of a business situation.

Where integration is viewed uncritically, or as an end in itself, profitability is likely to be undermined. Equally, on the other hand, a company that is courageous enough to reexamine the pattern of integration it has been developing, and to change that pattern where it ought to be changed, can wind up with higher profits and still maintain an effective and integrated operational design. For example:

☐ Several years ago Getty Oil Co. and some other companies in the oil industry began to divest themselves of sizable percentages of their gas stations. Since these retail outlets were providing relatively unsatisfactory returns, the companies considered, their assets should be shifted to the exploration and production end of the business, where the payoff was much greater.

Thus, in 1966, Getty sold off all of its marketing and refining operations in the western United States to Phillips Petroleum Company and reinvested most of the proceeds in its exploration and production segments. To increase short-term profitability, in effect, Getty substantially altered the balance of its assets within its industry segments.

To maintain an integrated structure, however, the company retained its refining and retailing operations in the eastern United States. The company was satisfied that these operations would give it sufficient stability—that is, a sufficient level of integration.

☐ Similar redeployments have occurred in integrated mining companies. Since returns are typically higher in the primary-metal area than in the area of fabricating, some companies have shifted assets out of fabricating and into primary production.

The decision to redeploy among integrated segments is a difficult one; and before any such decision can be reached, company management must examine each segment of its operations separately and then judge whether, if any segment is found to be carrying less than its share of the profit load, its assets should be liquidated and reapplied where they can earn a better return. If the company does decide to redeploy for faster profit, it runs some risk of weakened integration. How can it weigh the two and reach a decision?

A Question of Balance

In brief, to manage integrated assets successfully, a company must achieve a balance of assets among its operating segments that maximizes short-term profits but does not sacrifice its long-term stability. To do this, it must retain whatever part of its low-return segments it needs to protect itself from potential market fluctuations while applying as many of its assets as possible in high-profit leverage operations.

To find such a balance, the company must examine three factors and their interrelationships:

1　The economics of each operating segment and the interdependency of these economics on the economics of the other segments.
2　The market fluctuations that affect each segment—and, more explicitly, the ranges of these fluctuations and the probabilities that they will occur.
3　The attitude of its own management toward risk.

In this article I want to show how these factors can be sorted out. But first, to understand where such an analysis ought to be applied, it will be helpful to take a brief look at how imbalance comes about in the first place. It has its roots, most often, in the poorly managed expansion of a business.

Water Seeks Its Level

Over the years, many a company has expanded its operations forward toward its consumers or backward toward its raw materials without ever considering *explicitly* the balance it was striking between short-term profitability and the long-term stability of the organization, so far as asset distribution is concerned.

Instead, management often has simply allowed the asset balance between divisions to seek its own level, like water. The level of assets allocated to each division is determined de facto by the volume of through-put it receives from or passes on to the other segments of the business.

To put the matter another way: what frequently happens is that top management, in the name of integration, allows assets to gravitate to the segments of the company that have the greatest mass and activity, and hence the greatest attractive power. Over time, other areas will suffer from shortages of assets; and these are likely to be the less-developed segments of the company. These very segments may be the ones that have the greatest profit potential, especially over the short term; and they tend to remain in a semistarved and neglected condition.

Imbalance is also likely to occur as a company's market environment changes over time—when the relative profitability of the segments of a business shifts, for example, or when a maturing market or life cycle diminishes the risk of market fluctuations.

Ideally, as such shifts occur, a company should alter its asset distribution to reflect its new market environment. However, such market changes often evolve subtly over time, and a company does not recognize them until a significant imbalance is manifest.

Once imbalance has occurred, the financial benefits of shifting—either forward or backward—may sustantially outweigh the risks. Thus:

☐ In soft goods, the primary profit leverage comes most often from the marketing area, with manufacturing returning value that is low in comparison. Companies like Mattel, Inc., have therefore subcontracted a large part of their integral manufacturing, which they had formerly performed themselves, and applied the assets thus liberated in the more profitable retailing segment.

☐ Dart Industries, on the other hand, sold the Rexall drugstores, which for decades had been the very heart and identity of the company. "It was a bit like selling Mother," said Justin Dart. However, since these retail stores were providing an unsatisfactory return on the company's investment, Dart Industries decided to liquidate them and put the assets into the ethical drug manufacturing segment of the business, which was more profitable.

To find out whether such a shift is desirable, a company must quantify all the potential benefits and risks it faces. This means breaking its operations into separate segments and calculating the relative profitability of each, on the one hand, and the contribution each makes to the long-run stability of the company, on the other. With this information in hand, company management is in a position to assess the range of redeployment opportunities, making a cost/benefit analysis of each of the redeployment alternatives.

Identifying Opportunities

In exploring the possibilities of asset redeployment, the first decision a company must make is how it will measure the relative profitability of its various business segments. (This may not be as simple as one might think.) These segments must then be separated by revenue, costs, assets, and any other measures needed to calculate their relative profitabilities. This calculation will provide the basis for assessing the range of opportunities for asset redeployment.

Measuring the ROI
While the best means for measuring ROI varies between industries, *profits realized on operating assets employed* is considered most representative for many integrated manufacturing operations:

$$\text{ROI} = \frac{\text{profitability}}{\text{operating assets}}$$

If a company chooses this measure, "profits" and "operating assets employed" must of course be explicitly defined to calculate the return.

Profits on the Top.   For the profitability measure, or numerator, companies often choose operating profits before extraordinary items and before taxes.

First of all, the present and future earning power of a segment can generally be calculated from a single year's returns, since even in cyclical industries, short-term relative profitability remains approximately constant regardless of how total sales and earnings fluctuate.

Second, obviously, extraordinary items could give a misleading picture of the earning power of the assets; and companies prefer before-tax figures because it is simpler to ignore all the tax effects as long as they apply to all business segments.

However, if different segments receive different tax treatment, after-tax figures may be more appropriate. For example, in the exploration and production segment of the oil industry, such tax advantages as immediate full expensing of intangible drilling costs and depletion allowance deductions provide additional profitability that other segments of the industry—transportation, refining, and marketing—do not enjoy.

Nor will profits always be the best measure of "profitability." Sometimes, as in real estate operations, where investments are based on cash flows rather than on profits, cash-flow figures are more appropriate.

Assets on the Bottom.   The measure selected should be the one that represents the company's investments most realistically. The choice is usually among these:

- [ ] Net or gross fixed assets.
- [ ] Net or gross fixed assets, plus working capital.
- [ ] Book value of total assets.
- [ ] Market value of total assets or fixed assets.

Since the company wants to compare the return on assets as currently deployed with what they might earn if they were invested differently, market value is generally the most appropriate measure.

But since market-value figures are not easily available, and since it is sometimes costly to determine this value from independent appraisals, many companies choose one of the more accessible measures, at least as the basis for a first analysis. A measure will serve adequately for a first analysis if it is close enough to market value to calculate the *relative* profitability of the segments. Once this relative profitability is known, the company can decide whether it is worth spending money on appraisals for a finer view of one or more segments.

The Manufacturing Company

To see how this process works, let us discuss it in more detail in conjunction with an actual case history. As I describe this history, the reader may find

Exhibit 1. Potential Pitfalls in the Seven-Step Process to Asset Redeployment

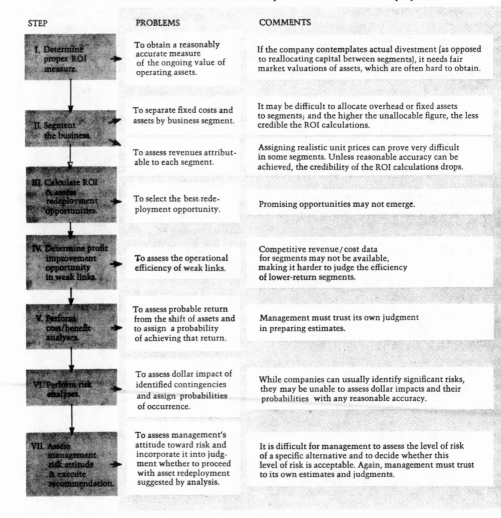

STEP	PROBLEMS	COMMENTS
I. Determine proper ROI measure.	To obtain a reasonably accurate measure of the ongoing value of operating assets.	If the company contemplates actual divestment (as opposed to reallocating capital between segments), it needs fair market valuations of assets, which are often hard to obtain.
II. Segment the business.	To separate fixed costs and assets by business segment.	It may be difficult to allocate overhead or fixed assets to segments; and the higher the unallocable figure, the less credible the ROI calculations.
	To assess revenues attributable to each segment.	Assigning realistic unit prices can prove very difficult in some segments. Unless reasonable accuracy can be achieved, the credibility of the ROI calculations drops.
III. Calculate ROI & assess redeployment opportunities.	To select the best redeployment opportunity.	Promising opportunities may not emerge.
IV. Determine profit improvement opportunity in weak links.	To assess the operational efficiency of weak links.	Competitive revenue/cost data for segments may not be available, making it harder to judge the efficiency of lower-return segments.
V. Perform cost/benefit analyses.	To assess probable return from the shift of assets and to assign a probability of achieving that return.	Management must trust its own judgment in preparing estimates.
VI. Perform risk analyses.	To assess dollar impact of identified contingencies and assign probabilities of occurrence.	While companies can usually identify significant risks, they may be unable to assess dollar impacts and their probabilities with any reasonable accuracy.
VII. Assess management risk attitude & execute recommendation.	To assess management's attitude toward risk and incorporate it into judgment whether to proceed with asset redeployment suggested by analysis.	It is difficult for management to assess the level of risk of a specific alternative and to decide whether this level of risk is acceptable. Again, management must trust to its own estimates and judgments.

it helpful to refer occasionally to Exhibit 1, which displays the steps a company should go through in making a redeployment analysis.

A medium-sized, integrated manufacturer of soft goods, which I shall call simply The Manufacturing Company (TMC), selected fixed assets plus working capital as its most appropriate measure of operating assets.

TMC was uncertain whether to use net or gross fixed assets, but reached its decision as follows: the company had taken a lot of depreciation on its manufacturing plants and other buildings, but since the buildings could easily be converted to new uses, the depreciated value shown on the books could not be said to represent their market value accurately. Therefore, rather than use the *net* figure, which reflected the depreciation, the company should use *gross* fixed assets.

TMC added working capital to its asset measure since capital, quite simply, made up a significant portion of the company's assets.

It thus calculated the relative profitability of its business segments by the equation:

$$\text{ROI} = \frac{\text{operating profits before taxes and extraordinary items}}{\text{gross fixed assets} + \text{working capital}}$$

A formulation of this kind is sufficient for an initial analysis, but, we should note, gross fixed assets are not necessarily an accurate measure of actual market value.

If a company reaches the point where it contemplates actual divestment in the near future, it may need professional appraisals of the fair market value of its fixed assets. Of course, if the company is only considering a rebalancing of assets over a period of years and does not plan an immediate and outright sale, such costly appraisals may not be a consideration.

Segmenting the Business

A company's most difficult task is determining the ROI of its segments: separating out the revenues, costs, and assets attributable to each. It must go through this breakdown process, of course, before it can compute the profitability or the assets of its individual segments.

A company organized, like TMC, on a profit- or cost-center concept obviously has an initial advantage here, since its ordinary reporting systems will provide most of the data needed for the analysis. But even when many of the financial facts are on hand, there are often some revenue, cost, or asset data not easily separable into the different segments.

In such cases it is best to identify some logical allocation factor in assigning the charges. To take a simple example, if sales and manufacturing both occupy the same building, the costs and assets of the building might be allocated by the number of square feet each operation uses. Where there is no such reasonable basis for allocation, the data should not be incorporated into the analysis to avoid biasing the results.

As Exhibit 2 shows, TMC's segments are raw materials, manufacturing, wholesale, and retail operations.

Once the segments have been defined and the assets of each have been determined, the company must next investigate the costs and revenues of each segment and then use these figures to calculate that segment's profitabilty.

Costs. Costs are a relatively simple matter. For each segment, the company requests the direct cost per item produced from the accounting office or seeks estimates from operating personnel. TMC fortunately had the data at hand.

Exhibit 2.   TMC's Business Segmented on a Per-Unit Basis

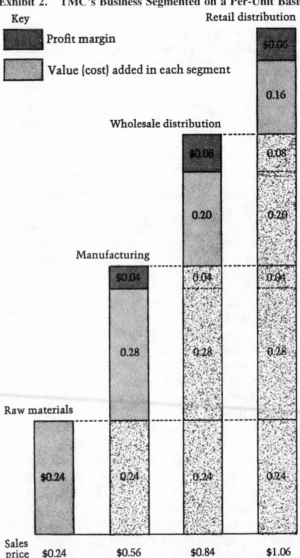

Revenues.   Revenues are more difficult to pinpoint. Except in the last segment, where a sale is made to an outside user, the sales price of a unit is
likely to be merely an internal transfer price, set for accounting purposes,
that does not necessarily reflect the true market value of the item produced.

The true market price is, of course, the figure that the company wants,
because it represents the true earning power of the segment's assets. To get
a true market figure for the value added per unit manufactured, for example,

TMC resorted to this simple device: it requested bids for subcontracts of its manufacturing operations from other companies. The figure thus obtained, together with the company's own cost and transfer-price data, enabled it to set a reasonably accurate figure for the per-unit revenue of its manufacturing operation.

In some other industries, I might note, published data on comparable products or services may ease the problem of setting unit prices. But where competitive information is not available, management may be reduced to its own best estimates.

Once the per-unit cost and price is known at each segment, the company can calculate the per-unit profit of the segment by subtracting. The appropriate figures for TMC's four segments are also presented in Exhibit 2.

By multiplying the unit cost and price data by the volume the segment produces, the company can, finally, determine the total direct revenues and costs per unit for each operation. It then gathers fixed-cost figures for each segment from accounting, allocating overhead on some reasonable basis where required.

Profitability and ROI.   With these figures at hand, the company can calculate the profitability of each business segment—the numerator of the ROI equation.

The denominator has already been obtained by breaking down the assets by individual operation, either directly or by allocation. All that remains to the ROI calculation for each segment is a simple division.

Assessing Opportunities . . .

In TMC's case, as we can see from Exhibit 3, the ROI calculations show that profit leverage is greatest in the wholesale distribution segment, which has fewest assets. Conversely, the least profitable operation, manufacturing, has the most assets employed. It looks as though TMC should consider the possibility of shifting some of its assets from manufacturing to the wholesale operation.

Before proceeding with a cost/benefit analysis of asset redeployment, of course, any sensible management will first determine whether there is some way to improve the profitability of the manufacturing operation so as to eliminate the occasion for redeployment.

. . . and Cost/Benefit Analysis

If the lower returns of a given business segment turn out to be a "fact of life," or if the possible profit improvement is so marginal that redeployment cannot be ruled out, a cost/benefit analysis of the alternatives is needed to spell out the profitability of the shift and the risk the company runs in making it.

Initially, management should take a close look at the "receiving" segment to find out whether it can absorb the new assets, and, if it can absorb

Exhibit 3.   TMC's Profitability, Calculated by Segments (in millions of dollars)

	Manufacturing	Wholesale distribution	Retail distribution
Revenues	$35.0	$55.0	$70.0
Costs			
Fixed	12.0	30.0	23.3
Variable	20.5	20.5	43.2
Total costs	32.5	50.5	66.5
Pretax operating profits	2.5	4.5	3.5
Assets			
Gross fixed assets	18.0	6.0	14.0
Working capital	6.0	14.0	8.0
Total	24.0	20.0	22.0
Pretax ROI	10.4%	22.5%	15.9%

Note: Some figures do not add to consolidated figures because of intracompany transactions.

them, what return it can expect from making the shift. In other words, it must ask:

☐ Is the market demand great enough to absorb the increased volume that the receiver could produce?

☐ Will the increased volume require additional fixed investments or cause any increases in the variable costs?

☐ Is the increased volume likely to cause overall price reductions?

These questions, and many others that may be appropriate to the individual circumstances, lead to the one big question: What return can be expected from redeploying assets from segment x to segment y?

To answer this question, management must identify the possible benefits, examine the costs or risks involved, determine the potential dollar impact of each benefit or risk, and then assign the probability (or, more likely, a range of probabilities) of each benefit or risk occurring.

The Gains.   For example, TMC believed that if it divested itself of one of its three manufacturing plants, it could free approximately $6 million for investment in its wholesale operation. Based on a historical wholesale-volume/asset ratio of 2.75, management estimated that the volume of the wholesale segment could be increased by $16.5 million, or 30%, without increased investment. Also, using historical profit margins, management estimated that pretax profits could be increased by approximately $680,000, with the probability of realizing that amount pegged at about .8. In other words, TMC's management decided that there was a .8 chance of achieving the $680,000 potential, or a probable benefit of $544,000.

The Risks. As I have already implied, the biggest risk in any significant shift of assets ordinarily is the loss of protection that full integration affords.

How can a company be sure, for instance, of getting sufficient raw materials at reasonable cost, or of having sufficient marketing outlets for its products, if it gives up some or all control of these parts of its business? While the risks will vary with the individual company, usually there are a few key ones. For example:

☐ An oil company divesting itself of retail outlets probably has two primary concerns: (a) that the supply-and-demand balance will continue to favor the exploration and production segment, so that crude oil prices continue to encourage good profit margins; and (b) that the growth in demand will continue to provide outlets for crude oil even though the company no longer controis as many (or any) outlets itself.

☐ When the Studebaker Corporation disposed of its automobile manufacturing and selling interests in 1963, it was doubtless concerned with whether demand for its automotive products would continue at reasonable profit margins without a captive car-manufacturing operation.

To wrestle with problems like these management must:

☐ Identify the kinds of contingencies against which it wants protection.

☐ Assess the probabilities that each of these contingencies may develop.

☐ Assess the potential dollar impact of each contingency. (Often a range of probabilities or "dollar impacts" is more appropriate than a single probability, since it is difficult to assess probabilities of uncertain events in the future.)

Before it began its analysis, TMC's management had already decided it did not wish to risk divesting itself of more than one of the company's three manufacturing plants, which represented approximately 30% of its manufacturing capability. This divestiture would free up about $6 million for investment in the wholesale operation, and the 30% of its manufacturing requirements could easily be subcontracted to outside manufacturers who had already submitted bids.

In considering these subcontracting arrangements, TMC decided that the primary risk factor was the future availability of a supply of manufactured product at an acceptable price. A sudden failure in outside supply, it feared, might cause lost sales opportunities until a new source geared up to fill the void.

However, a little research around the industry suggested that this was really not a very big risk, since several alternative sources could supply the company's needs within a reasonable time. Furthermore, short-term needs could be satisfied either through increased production in the two remaining plants or through the maintenance of a higher level of inventory against just such a contingency.

Decision to Proceed

The potential costs of these contingencies as well as the probability of their occurrence, as estimated by TMC's management, are shown in Exhibit 4. If we subtract the total estimated cost figure of $129,000 from the estimated benefit figure of $544,000, we get a probable annual increase in pretax profits of $415,000, in addition to the one-time-only capital gain that would be realized on the sale of the plant.

The data in Exhibit 4 show only those costs and benefits that management identified as having a substantial impact on profits. Many lesser concerns, as well as some qualitative risks which could not be quantified, were also considered in management's final deliberations on the question of whether to proceed with the suggested redeployment.

However, management was fairly confident of its assessments of dollar impacts as well as their assigned probabilities of occurrence. Consequently, it felt that the potential benefits sufficiently outweighed the potential risks to proceed with the asset redeployment. Although the final accounting is not yet in, there are enough positive concrete results to date to confirm the wisdom of this decision.

Divestment for Diversification.   It is worth pointing out that a company may decide to divest itself of an integrated asset even if it plans to apply the proceeds outside its central, integrated structure. For example, when Stu-

Exhibit 4.   Summary of TMC's Cost/Benefit Analysis

Item	Potential annual dollar impact on pretax profits	Probability of occurrence	Probable annual dollar impact on pretax profit
Benefits to TMC			
Divestiture of one plant and investment of proceeds in wholesale operations	$ 680,000	.8	$544,000
Costs to TMC			
Potential loss of supply resulting in lost sales opportunities	sales—$4,000,000 profit—$ 320,000	.2	$ 64,000
Possible increased cost of outside supply	$ 200,000	.2	$ 40,000
Increased inventory carrying costs	$ 25,000	1.0	$ 25,000
Total costs			$129,000
Probable net benefit (cost) on pretax profits			$415,000

debaker Corporation disposed of its automobile interests in 1963, it reinvested most of its new moneys in diversification—notably in its merger with Worthington Corporation, a heavy machinery and pump manufacturer. The lesson is this: if a company is considering redeployment at all, it should consider divestment of both integrated and nonintegrated assets and reinvestment both in its central operations and in diversified areas as well.

Conclusion

This sketch only hints at the amount of thought and discussion management must engage in to determine the key assumptions and to perform a thorough analysis. And, indeed, one of the most important benefits of any such analysis is that it forces management to think through explicitly many issues that previously had been dealt with only in generalities.

In the process of quantifying the risks of asset redeployment, the managers of TMC found to their surprise that dependence on outside subcontractors was not nearly as high a risk as they had always believed. In fact, some managers concluded that the overall risk might even be *decreased* if TMC had ready access to another manufacturing source in case of a strike at the company's plants.

TMC further benefited from its efforts by making this type of analysis an ongoing part of its annual capital budgeting process. Capital allocations could thus be budgeted with an eye on key profit leverage points in the business.

Of course, an analysis will not always be as straightforward as it was in TMC's case. The relatively clean-cut TMC analysis belies the difficulties that can arise along the way in this type of examination.

To summarize, because of the prevalence of the "integration is protection" attitude, many companies may be overlooking the major opportunities for profit improvement which they can achieve by changing the asset balance in their integrated operations. The key to success in such maneuvers, as we have seen, is to achieve a balance which maximizes short-term profitability while not sacrificing long-term profit stability. This means applying as many assets as possible in the high-profit, high-leverage segments while maintaining an acceptable lower level in the less profitable operations to minimize the risk of market fluctuations.

Once this asset balance has been achieved, an annual analysis like the one I described can and should be made a part of the yearly capital budgeting process. Shifts in the market environment or in the costs of doing business may in turn shift profit leverage in the various operations; and subsequent capital budgeting decisions should reflect this fact.

19

Strategy for Divestments

ARTHUR BETTAUER

At a time when managers are actively rearranging corporate assets as if the divisions or subsidiaries in question were but so many pieces on an industrial chessboard, it is particularly useful to remember that the selling of a division involves not just a strategic decision but also a complex marketing effort. In this early overview of the managerial challenges posed by divestment, the author lays out a series of guidelines to help managers plan—and execute—that marketing effort.

One of the most agonizing problems for top management is deciding whether and how to dispose of part of the organization. Very little has been published to provide guidance on the many factors involved. We do know, though, that some companies have wastefully tied up executive talent and capital in efforts to turn sick operations around. Others have realized far too little for units sold because the dispositions were not properly planned and executed.

Interest in the question of divestment seems to be increasing. One indirect source of pressure is the Securities and Exchange Commission, which is supporting divisional reporting of operating results by conglomerate companies. Chairman Manuel F. Cohen has observed:

> There may be diversified companies which are maintaining low-profit or money-losing operations for reasons which would not be persuasive to stockholders or financial analysts, and requiring separate disclosure might well result in the improvement or elimination of the substandard operation to the ultimate benefit of the stockholders and of the economy generally.[1]

What strategic and operational factors should management consider during the three basic stages of deciding on, planning, and carrying out a divest-

Published 1967.

ment? I shall describe these factors in this article, drawing on the divestment experiences of a good many companies with which I am familiar. From cases of successful as well as unsuccessful divestment operations, an executive can, I believe, learn some helpful lessons covering such matters as:

☐ The costs and repercussions as well as potential gains of disposing of a division.

☐ The importance of planning a disposal as a major marketing operation that requires many talents.

☐ The technique of selling parts of a division instead of the whole.

☐ The role of special methods like the spin-off.

☐ The need for swift progress in negotiations with carefully selected prospects, once a disposal has been definitely planned.

For the sake of convenience, subsidiary companies, divisions, and branches will all be referred to as "divisions" in this discussion.

Is Disposal Desirable?

The question of possible disposal may arise for such varied reasons as unsatisfactory performance, expansion needs which the parent is unable to fulfill, management personality conflicts, activities not in harmony with the rest of the organization, receipt of an attractive offer, or a government decree. While there are some executives who feel that selling a significant division represents a public confession of failure, a number of companies, including Congoleum-Nairn, Inc. and Studebaker Corporation, have made impressive progress after facing up to needs for major divestments. The two named organizations gave the following reasons:

☐ *Congoleum-Nairn.* "While our major effort continues to be the building of our sales volume, realistic forecasts do not indicate a projected sales level adequate to provide a satisfactory net return to our Company on the basis of its present physical structure. . . . Accordingly, a plan for a major realignment of the Company's functions and facilities was developed by the management." (1960)

☐ *Studebaker.* "The basic difficulty in South Bend was insufficient volume of sales. Our facilities there were such that there was no way to reduce our costs so that a profit could be made upon such volume." (1963)

During the initial phase of top-level consideration, the question of divestment may already be a subject of open discussion inside and outside the company, or, conversely, no hint of it may have arisen. In either case, top management must weigh the possible adverse effects of premature disclosure of its deliberations against its needs for special information. Some of the means of obtaining necessary data without compromising secrecy beyond acceptable limits include a study of the division in question that emphasizes additional *investment* possibilities, studies of *all* divisions, and consultation with independent professional advisers (certified public accountants, bankers, counsel, and so forth) known to maintain confidences. During this stage it is important for top management to see that the division does not make new long-term commitments.

Unless the division is incurring unbearable losses, top management will probably be concerned primarily with the effects of disposal on the remaining organization rather than with the mathematics of alternative investment possibilities for the capital involved. Possible repercussions on marketing, personnel, and community relations are extremely difficult to quantify; yet the impact on such activities of a withdrawal may be quite significant both in the near future and in the long run.

Among the stated reasons given for divestments (usually in somewhat stuffy but revealing corporate prose) are unsatisfactory profit performance, debt reduction, desire for diversification, lack of top management knowledge in a narrow line of business, and high-cost, badly located operations. Here is a sampling of statements from annual reports:

☐ *Unexcelled Chemical Corporation*: ". . . Colgate, with its established distributorship organization, is in a position to develop and realize upon the potential of the Division and hence was willing to acquire all the assets of the Division at a price so attractive that your management and directors felt it could not be refused." (1960)

☐ *Telautograph Corporation*: "The product is good, but the continuing need to spend large sums on development and exploitation is beyond our means." (1960) The divison in question was sold to Westinghouse Electric Corporation.

☐ *Walworth Company*: "We have eliminated . . . items which did not lend themselves to sale through our nationwide distributor network and, therefore, were imcompatible and conflicted with our new sales division's policy of distributor selling." (1961)

☐ *W. R. Grace & Co.*: ". . . moving away from businesses which, in the judgment of management and the Directors, do not have a logical place in the Company's future plans." (1965) The disposals included Grace National Bank of New York.

Estimating Proceeds and Costs

Once top management decides, with the approval of the board of directors, that the company is willing to consider disposing of part of the business, the specific division in question can be dealt with. The division's future potential and requirements must be carefully and thoroughly analyzed. The estimated net proceeds of eliminating the division, and various alternative investment opportunities, should be compared with the alternatives of continuing the status quo or investing more in the division. Such a comparison might involve something between a complex mathematical exercise and an obvious answer based on the amounts involved. Unfortunately, it is frequently quite difficult to estimate the costs of disposal and the price a buyer might pay until some detailed planning of the proposed transaction has been completed.

In some instances, sick divisions in an otherwise profitable company have seriously impaired earnings for the entire corporation. More than once, in fact, a sick division has depressed the market price of a corporation's stock to levels below book value. When this happens, management should consider divesting the company of low-profit units which can be sold approximately at book value and, in the absence of more favorable investment opportunities, using the proceeds to acquire treasury stock. This will have the effect of increasing earnings on the remaining outstanding shares as well as improving book value per share. It will also give management an opportunity to concentrate more attention on areas where it has a record of success. The hypothetical example in Exhibit 1 illustrates in a grossly exaggerated fashion the financial effect of disposing of a low-profit division.

Among the possible costs that should be considered in connection with a divestment are:

☐ Severance compensation, vacation accruals, and formal and informal pension provisions.

☐ Possible demands of key personnel whose continued employment in the division in question may be considered essential by prospective purchasers.

Exhibit 1. Financial Impact of Sale of Sick Divisions (data other than per-share amounts in thousands)

	Sick divisions	Healthy divisions	Total corporation
BEFORE DIVESTMENT			
Net income	o	$1,000	$1,000
Book value	$10,000	$10,000	$20,000
Number of shares outstanding			1,000
Book value per share			$20
Earnings per share			$1
Market value per share (10 times earnings)			$10
AFTER DIVESTMENT			
(Assuming that $10,000 proceeds are invested in 667 treasury shares at $15 per share)			
Net income			$1,000
Book value			$10,000
Number of shares			333
Book value per share			$30
Earnings per share			$3
Potential market value per share (10 times earnings)			$30

NOTE: The assumed sale of nonearning assets at book value is, of course, dependent on factors related to alternative uses, such as appreciated real estate values.

- ☐ Termination or transfer of leases and other commitments.
- ☐ Precipitation of tax obligations.
- ☐ Legal and accounting services.
- ☐ Appraisals.
- ☐ Finders' fees.
- ☐ Executive time.
- ☐ Loss of initiative, momentum, and sales during the negotiation period.

Obviously these items will depend on the type of transaction ultimately undertaken, and some may be subjects for negotiation. For example, a buyer may have little concern for the welfare of noncontractual pensioners and therefore be unwilling to continue making voluntary payments without gaining offsetting concessions.

Key personnel of the division to be sold can be expected to shift loyalties to their new top management at some stage in the proceedings. Although initially helpful in discussions leading to the sale, the division manager may turn around and provide the purchaser with information damaging to the seller's negotiating position as a means of ingratiating himself with his new boss. Being forewarned is an advantage, but there is no standard solution for this type of problem. In general, if key personnel are left with the feeling that the seller has taken them into his confidence and considered their future and their special services, there is less likelihood of the problem arising.

Planning the Disposal

It is essential that the disposal be planned as a major marketing operation requiring many talents. Marketing, legal, financial, tax, accounting, production, industrial relations, public relations, and other special skills will all be needed. A weak approach, such as delegating to a moderately effective middle echelon executive the task of selling a divison for "as near book value as possible," will inevitably achieve a weak result.

Sales should be made to the purchasers who can make the best economic use of the properties at prices based on value received. The degree of secrecy required in this stage should be decided on the basis of real needs and should not be overdone.

Selling the Parts

Probably the most common mistake in dispositions is the assumption that an entire division must be sold in a single transaction. Where a division is to be sold on the basis of its earning power, extra assets—such as unused real estate, warehouses, and equipment—can frequently be sold *separately* rather than thrown in free. Sometimes these extra assets command prices well in excess of book value, particularly where the right buyer is found. Further, where earnings on profitable products have been off-set by losses on other products, if may be possible to segregate the profitable part of the business for sale on an earning power basis and the balance for sale on a specific asset basis, thereby increasing total realization significantly. Thus:

Division A has a net book value of $1,000,000 and annual net earnings of $100,000. An estimated sales price might be $1,000,000 at ten times earnings. However, when uneconomic and unessential operations are segregated, it is found that net earnings of the profitable operation amount to $150,000 a year. At the same time, this segregation makes available for separate disposal excess assets with a book value of $300,000.

Now the estimated sales price might be $1,500,000 for the profitable operation plus whatever could be realized separately on the $300,000 of excess assets. Under such circumstances, the analysis might result in a decision to retain the profitable part of the division and dispose only of the excess.

More than one seller has learned the art of such a breakdown too late—and learned from the person or group he sold to. Consider the chagrin of the former owners of a small two-plant manufacturer when they learned, after selling out, that the buyer had in effect financed the acquisition out of the business itself. The significant steps involved were: selling one of the two plants for a noncompeting use, consolidating all operations in the other plant, and obtaining substantial financing by means of (a) a loan on receivables and (b) the sale and lease-back of machinery and vehicles. Although financing costs were heavy, the buyer was able to run the operation on an increasingly profitable basis and eventually to sell out at a handsome price. This price was based on the earnings potential that was in the business all the time.

Awkward complexity can usually be overcome by segregating certain components of the operation and dealing with them separately. The components must be ones that can logically be separated from other parts of the property. This method also has the helpful effect of reducing the size of individual transactions—although, of course, it cannot be extended to the point of splitting what a buyer would consider a viable unit. Here is an interesting case:

In 1965 Countrywide Realty Inc. (formerly The Kratter Corporation) sold primarily the marketing and distribution portion of the Jacob Ruppert beer business to another brewery. Countrywide Realty retained the New York City brewery property. Thus a marketing operation was sold for its value to a brewery with available production capacity, while the land and buildings were held for a different use. The Boston Celtics basketball team, owned by Ruppert, also was not included in the sale.

Other means of reducing the size of individual transactions in order to facilitate disposal include reducing inventory in advance of the disposal, financing receivables, mortgaging or arranging sale and leaseback of properties, and transferring useful equipment, tools, vehicles, and so forth to remaining units of the organization on a selective basis. These moves help make sales possible to small buyers.

It is important to be optimistic when setting a price on the components to be sold. The purchaser will be buying the division's future, not its past. The items to evaluate from a buyer's viewpoint are potential earnings and growth, appraisals in excess of book value, cost savings which the purchaser might realize, abilities of key personnel, fear that a competitor might buy the division, and matters of a similar nature. Often the main reason for a surprisingly high price on an acquisition is that the seller had the courage to ask for it.

Varying Forms of Payment

A willingness to accept considerations other than cash may provide the flexibility needed for maximum realization on the disposal. In view of the many alternatives, a careful analysis of financial, accounting, and tax considerations is obviously desirable.

Take the question of "goodwill," for example. If a division is sold at a price in excess of book value, the excess may be entered as goodwill on the buyer's balance sheet. But certain buyers balk at having to do this. What alternatives are possible?

Sometimes the buyer can allocate the whole selling price to specific tangible assets, with some valued at more than book value if justified by current values. If it is not appropriate for the buyer to do this, another course may be open. If the seller is willing to accept voting stock of the buyer as payment, holding it as an investment, and if other conditions are met, the transaction may be classified as a "pooling of interests." This generally results in a more advantageous accounting treatment from the buyer's viewpoint. Of course, if such an approach looks feasible to managers in the selling company, they should review the possibilities with company accounting executives and independent certified public accountants in order to fully understand the effects and implications.

The report of The Superior Oil Company for the four months ending December 31, 1963, stated: "In January 1964, the capital stock and advances account of The Superior Oil Company of Venezuela was traded to Texaco Inc. for 1,804,317 shares of the capital stock of Texaco." The financial statements of Texaco Inc. for 1964 indicated that the exchange of shares was considered a "pooling of interests."

Notes, mortgages, and portions of future profits are among the various means whereby the seller can help finance the purchaser's acquisition. If 30% or less of a fixed sales price is realized in cash in the year of sale, the installment method may be used for federal income taxes, with the gross profit prorated over the period in which payments are received.

While a higher price can often be obtained by selling on extended terms, care should be taken to ensure that the additional risk is justified by the credit worthiness of the buyer. Several sad cases, best unnamed, could be cited where payments due on mortgage notes were not met, so that the sellers had the unpleasant task of trying to dispose of divisions a second time and at sharply reduced prices.

Where a significant question exists as to the future potential of an operation, it may be possible to set a price on the basis of a fixed amount plus contingent payments related to sales or earnings.

The Spin-Off Method

A form of divestment which should be considered if the circumstances are appropriate is the spin-off. This involves: (1) creating a subsidiary, if it does not already exist, to own the division or properties involved; and (2) distributing the shares of the subsidiary proportionately to stockholders of the parent company.

Although stockholders seem to gain the impression that they receive something extra in a spin-off, they initially have two pieces of paper instead of one representing the same underlying entities. If the spun-off company is able to attract sufficient market interest on its own and to achieve better earnings through new management autonomy, despite higher administrative costs, the stockholders will probably find their impression justified.

Spin-offs were used by Standard Oil of New Jersey after the courts ordered divestment of many subsidiaries in 1911 under the antitrust laws. In 1943 the same company spun off Consolidated Natural Gas Company in order to avoid regulation as a utility holding company. In another case, the Bank Holding Company Act of 1956 confronted Transamerica Corporation, the huge western holding company, with a choice of dropping its banking interests or its other interests. As a result, in 1958 the company formed and spun off Western Bancorporation (formerly Firstamerica Corporation), the country's largest bank holding company, and concentrated on the development of its insurance and other interests.

While the spin-off has been used most frequently in the case of court-ordered divestments, it lends itself to the disposal of any subsidiary capable of operating on its own. In 1954 United Aircraft spun off its Chance Vought division with the statement that "Chance Vought is in the airframe business and thus competes with customers of the engine and propeller divisions of United, a situation which has proved awkward." However, by 1961 Chance Vought Corporation decided to give up its separate existence and sold its assets to the company now known as Ling-Temco-Vought, Inc.

Facing Up to Liquidation

Sometimes a division has such poor prospects of survival as an economic entity that liquidation is the only logical alternative. A few such cases were described as follows by the managements in charge:

□ *Burlington Industries, Inc.*: ". . . we finally realized that some operations required radical changes to be competitive and to stop losses. The most serious problem of this sort was at Peerless Woolen Mills, when we were finally forced by continuing substantial losses to make a liquidation decision. This step was taken only after making every possible effort to sell at $2 million less than estimated liquidation values." (1961)

□ *Fibreboard Paper Products Corporation*: "Liquidation of the Company's unprofitable linoleum and felt base floor covering business at Emeryville started April 1, 1961 and was completed during the year. All transactions related to the liquidation, including the sale of inventories, cost of closing down the manufacturing facilities, termination allowances, and losses on the sale or abandonment of machinery, equipment and buildings, were recorded through a liquidation account and charged directly to surplus." (1961)

□ *General Mills, Inc.*: "For the past few years, the Feed Division has been a substantial drain on earnings. . . . management could not see how it was possible to make a satisfactory return on investment in the future. Therefore, . . . the decision was made to withdraw from the feed business through an orderly liquidation which is now in progress." (1962)

□ *General Mills, Inc.*: "At the close of the year, management, with the approval of the Board of Directors, adopted a plan to reduce the company's domestic milling capacity about 55%. Nine of our 17 mills are being closed, freeing financial and human resources for business offering greater opportunity for growth." (1965)

In all of these cases, the losses on liquidation were reduced significantly by resultant reductions in federal income taxes.

Effects of such liquidations on communities may be mitigated to some extent by giving the local political, financial, and business leaders sufficient notice to persuade other businesses to use the facilities or secure federal or state area redevelopment aid. Transfer and retraining are means of helping employees to withstand the impact.

Approving the Plan

When sufficient analysis has been accomplished, a report should be presented to top management outlining:

1 The recommended form of disposal and alternatives.
2 The amount and type of consideration which might be expected, and the related tax effect.
3 Likely purchasers — either described or identified.
4 The anticipated impact on the company's financial statements.

Generally, some communication with experts or others outside the company is required in order to develop adequate information for such a report. At this point it is up to top management to adopt a general plan setting forth limits for negotiation, obtain board of director approval, and assign responsibility for handling the transaction.

Making the Sale

Essentially the task of the seller's team is to identify the best potential buyers; negotiate a fair price; resolve legal, financial, tax, accounting, and other problems; and close the sale.

The best planning can easily be wrecked by faulty execution. If time is wasted in extended discussions with shoppers and would-be brokers without clients, rumors begin to spread, employee morale deteriorates, key personnel leave, competitors become more aggressive, and customers grow nervous. The result may well be a painful deal with the junkman.

Once the plan has been adopted, in other words, it must be pursued vigorously and swiftly. Generally the potential gains or losses are sufficiently large to warrant the time of some of the company's outstanding talent.

Identifying Prospects

Unless certain candidates are obvious, it might be well to start by eliminating the types of companies that management would like to avoid. These may include competitors of the company as it will operate after the divestment, industry leaders with antitrust problems, companies with insufficient resources where the seller requires cash, unlisted companies considered unattractive to key personnel of the division, and others. Occasionally there is a newspaper account of a proposed merger which is dropped in its late stages because of questions raised by the Federal Trade Commission or Justice Department, and one wonders whether time and expense might not have been saved by more advance consideration of the antitrust problem.

The simplest and least time-consuming approach to a logical prospect is a letter or telephone call by the president of the seller to the president or chief executive of the potential buyer. The company's counsel should be asked to review the contents of any offering. A letter might simply set forth a reason for selling, a brief description of the business to be sold, a comment that a usual type of contract would be involved affording adequate protection to buyer and seller, and a statement that the two companies are acting as principals with no brokers involved and that no obligation is assumed by the offering company merely because the recipient of the letter looks at the situation. The seller might enclose or offer to furnish on request financial statements, appraisals, credit agreements, and so forth.

If the recipient of the letter has any interest at all, he or she will probably call to inquire about the approximate price range involved, ask for additional data, and request time to consult with other officials of his or her company.

If it is considered necessary to deal with outside sources in order to locate or contact prospective buyers, it is important that there be clear understanding regarding "finders' fees" so that unexpected claims can be avoided. Certain types of organizations generally do not accept such fees; it may be best to ascertain in advance whether or not this is the practice. Among the possible sources of information regarding prospective buyers are the following:

1 Business reference services (particularly listings showing companies active in making acquisitions).
2 Industry associations.
3 Bankers.
4 Certified public accountants and lawyers.
5 Investment bankers, business consultants, and brokers.
6 Management officials (particularly of the division involved) and members of the board of directors.
7 Suppliers and customers of the division.

Common Tax Problems

While tax problems can be quite varied due to special circumstances, certain types of federal income tax considerations appear to recur frequently in sales of divisions.

In general, buyers desire the maximum basis for income tax purposes in assets they acquire for use in the regular course of business—inventory, supplies, buildings, and so on—or for immediate resale. They are somewhat less interested in the tax basis of assets which will presumably remain unchanged for many years (e.g., land, investments) and are generally unhappy about acquiring assets (e.g., goodwill) which cannot be written off for tax purposes.

The sellers generally want to avoid having their gains taxed at ordinary income tax rates, as might result from recapture of depreciation after 1961 on sale of depreciable assets. (The phrase "recapture of depreciation" refers mainly to gains on the disposition of machinery and equipment. The Internal Revenue Code makes the gains taxable as ordinary income to the extent of depreciation and amortization deducted after 1961. A portion of the gains realized on buildings sold since 1963 may also be taxable as ordinary income if accelerated depreciation was used.) They prefer capital gain treatment for the gain and often are happiest with a tax-free exchange. Tax-free treatment is available under specified conditions in an exchange of stock for substantially all of an existing subsidiary's assets or for an interest in the subsidiary's stock resulting in 80% control.

Reconciling the tax preferences of buyer and seller may involve offsetting price or other concessions. For example:

> *It is generally preferable from the seller's viewpoint to sell stock in a subsidiary, rather than sell assets, in order to avoid the recapture of depreciation. If the buyer desires to maximize the asset basis of the acquired business, he or she will prefer buying physical facilities rather than stock. In the event that the stock is bought and the company later liquidated, the buyer will have to pay the income tax arising from the recapture of depreciation subsequent to 1961. The solution to this problem is a matter of bargaining.*

Since tax considerations usually represent such important issues in the transaction, it is advisable to have a tax specialist review the proposed contract before it becomes final.

Accounting and Finance

Buyers will require current financial statements of the unit involved and may also want these audited either by their own independent public accountants or the sellers' or both. Sellers should understand that they bear the primary responsibility for the accuracy of the financial statements they furnish and that the opinion of the independent public accountants represents an additional check. Buyers may, in addition, require representations or warranties with respect to specific items such as tax provisions, liabilities, receivables, and inventories.

The seller should review the division's financial statements and underlying records carefully for items which would affect the buyer's comparisons of past results with future projections. For example, head office charges by the parent company, interdivisional transactions, use of accelerated depreciation, LIFO inventory pricing, excess tax reserves, and matters of that kind should be called to the attention of the buyer. If appropriate, pro forma statements should be prepared separately to show what the results would have been after elimination of such items (which presumably will not recur in the future).

Since balance sheets of going concerns necessarily include some estimates (e.g., anticipated bad debt losses, legal damages, expense accruals), allowance should be made in negotiations for minor variations arising in the normal course of business. However, a limitation should be specified in order to be sure that both parties agree on the dividing line between material and immaterial variations.

As previously mentioned, the buyer may desire a particular form of transaction depending on whether he believes it advantageous to apply "pooling of interests" or "purchase" accounting. However, "pooling of interests" accounting is out of the question if the seller refuses to accept voting stock in settlement.

The degree to which the seller is willing to finance the transaction through acceptance of notes or stock is a matter for negotiation in each case, depending largely on the type of buyer being dealt with and the seller's financial requirements.

Negotiations and Settlement

Once initial discussions have proceeded to a stage indicating that serious negotiations can be started, executives of the buying and selling companies should arrange to meet. At the meeting each company will be represented by a team of negotiators. The size of the respective teams may be decided jointly or separately. Presumably a lawyer will be included on each team, since the expected result of the negotiation will be the preparation of a contract. Accountants, tax experts, and other specialists should be asked to keep themselves available to respond to telephone calls from the negotiators or to make special presentations at the sessions.

The seller must be alert to the problems of the buyer and eager to help solve them. This requires that he be capable of evaluating quickly the effects of various alternatives. An apparently minor concession can have a significant effect on price as well as on taxes.

The drafting of agreements is a legal matter and should be left to the lawyers. However, it is imperative that there be clear understanding between the principals and counsel and that the language of the agreement be understood by the laymen. If some delay is expected in the drafting of a formal agreement, the lawyers may prepare a letter or memorandum of intent which sets forth the basic terms and conditions but which is not binding on the parties.

When the parties have reached substantial agreement and when the appropriate management or board approvals have been obtained, officials of the buyer and seller should talk to key employees involved and should prepare announcements for release to their employees and to the public. The timing and the content of these announcements are matters of importance since employee morale as well as the stock prices of the companies involved may be affected. Both the Securities and Exchange Commission and the New York Stock Exchange have emphasized the need for timely disclosure of important information of this nature.[2]

At the conclusion of successful negotiations, prices and terms are frequently settled tentatively by executives of the buyer and seller on the basis of preliminary interim financial statements or estimates of current performance. At this point, lawyers draw up the contracts which will make the agreement legally binding. A safeguard frequently employed is to make the price subject to results shown by audited financial statements as of the closing date, with provisions for delaying settlement until such statements are available and for resolving any disputes as to accounting matters. The independent accountants for the two parties should be asked to clear any references to work they will be required to perform. Restraints are generally placed on the activities of the division in question during this period to ensure that it does not incur major indebtedness, dispose of significant assets, or take actions other than those usually taken in the ordinary course of business.

It is at this time that a certain amount of petty wrangling usually arises. The buyer's middle- and lower-echelon personnel begin to interpret the details of the contract and figures. They may ask whether interim accruals of expenses are consistent with year-end practices; whether pension, bonus, and vacation accruals are adequate; whether book inventories are accurate; whether provisions should be made for sales returns and allowances, maintenance, and commitments; and so on. The legal and tax departments or advisers of the respective entities raise points which they consider advantageous to their side. In addition, outside factors such as a sharp decline in stock market prices may result in either revision or cancellation of the transaction.

In short, the lull between negotiations and final signing of the contract is a period of anxiety for sellers since the buyers are trying to uncover any unpleasant surprises before it is too late. They may be raising extraneous questions as well as pertinent ones. The seller's proper role at this time calls for cooperation, frankness, and patience.

Conclusion

If corporate experiences with divestment were to be summarized in terms of guides for management actions, 10 rules would stand out.

1. *The decision to divest must be timely.* Management should face up to the problem and prepare to act before employees and outsiders view the decision as inevitable and overdue.

2. *Top executives must consider a broad range of factors.* The mere fact that the investment in a division can achieve a better return elsewhere does not mean that instant disposal is needed. The effects of divestment on the remaining organization and its marketing, personnel, and community relations are important considerations.

3. *The disposal of a division is a major marketing operation.* Management must marshal as much talent and enthusiasm as if it were planning the launching of a new product.

4. *The sum of a division's parts may be greater in value than the whole.* Components which can be sold as units on the basis of asset value should be evaluated separately from those which can be sold on the basis of earning power.

5. *Simple components of a division may be sold more easily than the whole complex division itself.* What is more, disposal of unnecessary appendages may make the remainder of the division sufficiently attractive to keep rather than sell.

6. *Planning should include an evaluation from the viewpoint of potential buyers.* To be able to negotiate effectively, the seller should understand the buyer's concerns in the transaction. These concerns include financing, taxes, and accounting, as well as management, marketing, production, earning power, and so forth. Naturally, all potential variations cannot be anticipated, and there will have to be some give and take when negotiations begin.

7. *Key personnel of the division may present an important problem.* They may or may not be wanted by the buyer. If they are vital to the transaction, their loyalties may shift to the buyer before the settlement, with adverse effects on the seller's position.

8. *A spin-off should be considered if the division has sufficient size and potential to be a publicly owned company.* Unless an adequate price can be obtained for the division's future potential, the stockholders may be better off retaining their interest in the form of ownership of a separate company.

9. *The negotiators must maintain communication with the planning technicians.* What may appear to be a minor tax concession may have a major impact. Technical aspects require adequate evaluation at a distance from the bargaining table.

10. *The fact that a sales agreement is drawn up and signed is not an appropriate signal that the seller's team can relax.* There can be many a slip between the agreement and the settlement. The buyer's representatives will be questioning details in the sales terms until the final settlement is signed.

Notes

1. Address before the American Institute of Certified Public Accountants, October 5, 1966, Boston, as reprinted in *The Journal of Accountancy*, December 1966, p. 56.

2. See Arthur Fleischer, Jr., "Corporate Disclosure/Insider Trading," *HBR*, January-February 1967, p. 129.

20

New Emphasis on Divestment Opportunities

ROBERT H. HAYES

Now that the great acquisition movement of the 1960s has passed into history, some experts think that a significant movement toward divestiture has begun. Since every acquisition implies a divestiture, and vice versa, any "movement toward divestiture" would represent a change primarily in market emphasis and atittudes, rather than a change in the volume of acquisition/divestiture transactions. The author explains why he thinks this reversal in emphasis is likely to occur, and suggests that the rules by which the game is played, as well as just its name, are also going to change. He then characterizes the ways companies have approached divestiture in the past— as the "unpleasant underside" of acquisition, as it were—and goes on to describe the new character we can expect divestiture to assume in the coming years. Perhaps his most important conclusions are that companies will come to regard divestment as a useful and legitimate tool of corporate planning and strategy, and that they will approach it far more calmly, deliberately, and rationally than they have done heretofore. In analyzing the historical patterns of divestiture and projecting what the new emphasis on divestiture will mean, the author has drawn on his experience in a long-continuing research project on the nature of the divestment process, supported by the Harvard Business School's Division of Research. While working on this project, he has had the opportunity to study divestiture in some 18 companies. He concludes the article with recommendations as to how companies might begin to rationalize their approaches to divestment opportunities.

"If the 1960s qualified as the Age of Acquisition, then the 1970s promise to be the Decade of Divestiture." This prediction crops up again and again in my conversations with businessmen and in the financial press.

Published 1972.

If the next few years do become known as the Decade of Divestiture, however, it is not necessarily because there will be more divestitures in total than there were in the 1960s, and certainly not because there will be more divestitures than acquisitions. There will always be just as many of one as the other, since, at least to my knowledge, nobody has yet made an acquisition without somebody else making a divestiture.

What *will* be different is the nature of the market for companies and/ or divisions—the seller's market of the 1960s will be replaced by a buyer's market in the 1970s. Business attitudes and procedures will change, too, in reflection of this new market emphasis.

In this article I shall explore some of the kinds of changes that will be required and the reasons behind them.

The New Market

A variety of forces are behind these changes, but two stand out. First, companies will be more interested in making "fractional" divestments (that is, the sale of a subsidiary, division, or part of a division). Second, they will be making these divestments at a rather inopportune time:

☐ Profit margins have dropped about 20% since the mid-1960s, when they averaged almost 6% for all manufacturing companies. They now seem entrenched in the 4%–5% range, and will probably continue under pressure. (This pressure is increasing, in fact, because of recent actions of the Price Commission.)

☐ Price/earnings ratios, which averaged over 19 to 1 in the years 1961–1965, have also settled into a new track, lower by over 15%. Few predict that they will rise to their former levels in the near future.

☐ Interest rates will continue high, probably above 6%.

In such an environment, with both stock and debt more costly and risky, potential buyers are likely to be more concerned with value for their money than with maintaining a particular growth rate or P/E ratio. Companies are likely to base their decisions more on a payback criterion than on ROI, and to discount heavily returns more than five years into the future. While the number of potential sellers will probably increase, the number of potential buyers will probably decrease. The divestor will become the seeker, not the sought.

It will also be a different market in the sense that companies will increasingly accept divestment as a valid element of corporate planning and strategy, rather than simply as a last resort. The stigma that is now attached to divestment will fade over time, and a new breed of companies will be willing to enter the market as sellers. Sellers, as a whole, will be much more deliberate in their approach to divestiture decisions and negotiations, to match the deliberate approach of the buyers.

To fully understand these and other changes that are coming, we must first examine the divestment process as it exists today. I shall then trace out the new patterns we can expect to see in the marketplace as a whole and recommend a general approach that a divestment-minded company might consider adopting.

Divesting is Different

There is a popular misconception about divestitures that runs something like this: because acquisition and divestiture are two sides of the same coin, with a divestiture simply being a "reverse" acquisition, a company can somehow rotate the procedures it uses in making acquisitions through 180° and use them for making divestitures.

Acquisition and divestiture *are* two sides of the same coin, to be sure; but they are *opposite* sides. While they share certain characteristics, their differences are both numerous and crucial, and they require different approaches, different kinds of information, different methods of analysis, and different management practices.

Moreover, they are negotiated in a completely different psychological atmosphere. For one thing, unlike an acquisition, *a divestiture always hurts.* It hurts financially, because the divesting company is essentially penalizing its income statement to strengthen its balance sheets, which are usually less visible to the investing public. It hurts emotionally, because a divestiture almost invariably reflects a mistake in judgment, a broken commitment, or incompetence on somebody's part. A divestiture is an expression of failure; and, as a result, individuals are likely to be hurt in the course of it.

Second, *a divestiture is for keeps.* The divestiture decision is one of the least reversible decisions that an executive might make. An acquiring company, on the other hand, has at least some time and space for maneuver, and can take a variety of actions that will enhance the future profitability of an acquisition. Moreover, an acquirer often has the final option of bailing out if things do not progress as expected, losing only a little cash and pride in the process. Unfortunately, as any parachutist knows, you cannot bail back in.

Third, *the risks and rewards in a divestiture are different*, in kind as well as in degree. An acquisition usually represents an exchange of something having a (relatively) certain value for something with less certain value— the buyers take risks, in the expectation that they can get more out of their purchases than they paid for them. They may be looking for complementary product lines, new markets, operating economies of scale, particular kinds of skills, particular kinds of people, or just increased income flow. It is an aggressive, confident step, taken rationally and with knowledge of the opportunities involved.

The sellers, on the other hand, mainly want liquidity—usually cash or something close to it. They want to reduce operating losses, reduce implicit opportunity losses, reduce investment requirements . . . *and reduce their risk*. They want *out*, and their major concern is how to get out as gracefully as possible. They are moving away from a situation they dislike or mistrust, rather than toward a situation they wish to exploit.

Companies Divest . . .

The atmosphere of suppressed emotionalism pervading divestiture negotiations has fostered a group of management practices that is considerably different from those associated with acquisition proceedings.

. . . in Secrecy

Most conspicuous, of course, is the intense concern with secrecy. Managers give different reasons for this concern. In part it reflects the fact that divestitures historically have been implicit admissions of failure, and managers planning a divestiture move delicately to protect the rather fragile egos of those involved. Another reason is that, should negotiations with the first potential buyer break down, the divestor wants this fact kept secret from a second potential acquirer, to protect the market "image" of the unit being divested. (See the appendix for a discussion of scarcity of information.)

For the most part, however, this secrecy reflects the fear of the adverse effect that knowledge of the divestment proceedings might have on the morale and efficiency of the personnel associated with the unit being divested. People like to buy; they do not like to be sold.

This tradition of secrecy is now breaking down, to some extent, because of the influence of new full-disclosure regulations, and it will continue to break down as divestiture becomes a more common and acceptable practice among well-managed companies. This relaxation of secrecy will have a certain impact on the divestment process, which I shall discuss later.

. . . with Little Expertise

While much of the initial screening and intensive analysis of potential acquisitions (and, often, acquisition negotiations themselves) are carried out or supervised by specialized staff personnel, most divestitures are still conducted almost entirely by a small group of top management personnel. This practice promotes speed and favors secrecy, but it has two signal drawbacks:

1. Since most companies divest rather infrequently, divestment analyses and negotiations are often the responsibility of top managers who have little experience in such matters. Equally, these managers seldom have the time to carry out the kind of thorough background analyses that an experienced acquisition analyst would be expected to provide.

2. Whereas an acquiring company will often be evaluating or negotiating with several possible acquisition candidates at the same time, di-

vesting companies generally deal only with a single potential buyer at a time. Again, this is partly caused by the desire to preserve secrecy and to protect the ultimate purchaser by limiting the dispersion of confidential information. But it is also a practice the divesting group is forced to adopt in order to avoid spreading its very limited time and resources too thin.

Hence, rather than look at a number of possible acquirers and develop an explicit "approach strategy," most divesting companies must be content to identify single potential buyers through the friendly auspices of a discrete intermediary—a close acquaintance of the group, an outside member of the board, an investment banker, or a consultant.

. . . under Strong Time Pressure

Not only does this practice tend to limit the search process unnecessarily; it adds considerable pressure of time to the negotiations once they begin, for several reasons:

☐ The longer negotiations proceed, the more likely it is that secrecy will break down.

☐ The divesting company wants to avoid the "wallflower" image that might develop if a unit it is selling remains on the block too long.

☐ The company may also be under some pressure from the intermediary who brought it together with the prospective acquirer.

☐ The divestor often needs the money or at least needs to reduce operating losses.

As a result, an agreement is generally concluded with the first potential buyer, often at some sacrifice for the divesting company. Should the initial negotiations break down, of course, the would-be divestor will approach a second potential buyer in a bargaining position that is even weaker, psychologically and strategically.

Plans to Divest . . .

One might suspect that the importance and irrevocability of divestiture decisions, the inexperience and limited time of the executives usually called on to make them, and the relative availability of skilled intermediaries and consultants would have led divestment-minded companies to develop sophisticated procedures for approaching these decisions. The preceding discussion of the psychological issues and management practices associated with divestiture decisions suggests that this is not the case. Indeed, once the decision to seek divestiture has been made, there is generally little attempt at careful analysis.

. . . Ignore Capital-Budgeting Effects

Despite the fact that divestitures are usually undertaken and negotiated by the same executives who make a company's major capital-budgeting decisions, these executives seldom attempt to apply the company's normal captial-budgeting processes to a divestment proposal. They seldom order special studies to be undertaken. They seldom attempt to anticipate the possible uses of the funds that will be made available, or even to evaluate the changes in net cash flow that are likely to occur. They appear to make their divestiture decisions largely on an ad hoc basis.

Indeed, in a surprising number of decisions, financial factors are given little weight. The decisions hinge, rather, on such qualitative judgements as "that business is a drag—let's get out" or "it's not worth the time we spend on it," and the asking price they set simply reflects book value plus or minus some premium.

Essentially, then, divestors conduct a forced sale and content themselves with getting whatever they can from it. So great is the emotionalism—accentuated by the secrecy, time pressures, and small-group dynamics—surrounding the proceedings that the tendency is to "get it over with"; and the negotiated price in this climate is then justified on the basis that "it was better than nothing" and "now, at least, we're rid of it." In such an atmosphere, the buyer clearly has the upper hand.

New Patterns in the Market

How will the future be different? I foresee several major, interrelated changes:

- ☐ There will be more fractional divestments.
- ☐ There will be an increase in the divestments companies' conduct in a given period.
- ☐ There will be a change in the kind of companies making divestments.

These changes represent the natural aftermath of the merger fever of the 1960s. They also represent the revolution in management information and control systems that occurred during the same interval, and the economic slowdown and liquidity crunch that marked its end.

More Fractional Divestments

Over the next few years, it appears, a major portion of the operating units divested will be ones that have been acquired within the past ten years. Figures provided by W. T. Grimm & Company show that the number of fractional divestments has risen from under 700 in 1968 to 1,400 in 1970, and to over 1,900 in 1971. During the same period the total annual number of divestments has remained generally in the 4,500–5,000 range, except for a peak of over 6,000 in 1969.

Many of these fractional divestments have represented simply the merger "aftermarket"—the market in those operating units or divisions which are part of an acquired company but do not fit the strategy and structure of the acquiring company. (This aftermarket will probably tend to decline in importance during the next year or so.) Others represent the effects of government pressure; LTV and ITT are recent dramatic examples.

Reevaluation of Acquisitions.   A growing number of fractional divestments, however, will result from corporations' reevaluations of their overall strategies—often forced on them by economic necessity. Such a divestment will represent more than simply a single executive's or group's failure to select an appropriate acquisition or to manage its assets effectively, but will call into question the company's whole strategy for growth. As a result, a number of companies will swallow their pride and disgorge a number of unpromising operations over the next few years. For example:

☐ Conglomerate A, after making over 100 acquisitions in the past decade, is planning to sell off almost one fifth of them. "We're short of cash, and they simply don't fit the framework we see for ourselves now," company officials privately admit.

☐ Company B did not intend to become a conglomerate. It started as a diversified company and, in the words of an executive, "got sucked into the 'growth equals glamor' philosophy in the late 1960s. Now we've come to our senses." The company is quietly looking for oportunities to sell almost half the acquisitions it made during that period.

Other companies that picked up what they thought were "bargains" several years ago are beginning to realize that, to keep these businesses healthy and growing, they must continue to pump funds into them—often at the expense of projects that they feel to be more a part of the "real" business or which promise a much higher ROI.

☐ A "high flyer" bought a subsidiary in the mid-1960s at a price which promised a 20% return on investment, based on the projected cash flows over the first seven years, and which promised an immediate EPS improvement. In attempting to turn it around, however, the acquiring company suddenly came to realize that it "couldn't afford to succeed in that business"—that every additional investment in plant would only promise a 7% ROI.

Reconsideration of "Competence."   Underlying these companies' primary concern—the necessity to disengage themselves from unprofitable activities and to improve corporate liquidity—I see a rather fundamental change in management philosophy taking place. "Synergy," the buzzword of the Decade of Acquisition, is now used, more often than not, with a rather derisive connotation. Executives today talk instead of "focus," "organizational competences," and "technical (or market) expertise."

It appears to me that the recent recession, coupled with the spectacular collapse of several of the "go-go" companies and their preoccupation with pyramidal growth, is encouraging a transfer of power back to managers whose strengths are in operations and financial control.

These executives, who often have risen through the ranks of line management, tend to view the once-popular notion that "a good manager can manage any kind of business" with a healthy distrust. They believe, rather, that individuals and companies can do only certain things well—well enough, that is, to compete in the marketplace. As one such executive has recently phrased it, "We can't do everything, and we will have to be considerably more selective in our choice of activities."

Moreover, these managers often either did not participate in the original decision to acquire a unit that is being considered for divestiture or argued against the acquisition at the time it was made; therefore, they have little vested interest to defend when the possibility of divestment is raised. They tend to view divestiture objectively, as simply another potentially useful tactic: "We didn't use to even consider divestment as being a possible solution to a divisional problem," states one manager, "now it's always in the backs of our minds."

Growth of the Portfolio Concept.   Increasingly, financial managers are looking at the company as a portfolio of assets that must be continually reviewed, augmented, and pruned. "We have several businesses that are doing fairly well, but we wouldn't hesitate to sell any one of them if the right offer came along," is a typical comment. The growing emphasis on ROI, both as a measure of success and as a basis for executive compensation, strengthens this attitude. Moreover, the use of sophisticated management information systems that permit not only frequent and timely performance reviews, but projections of future performance as well, makes it possible to translate this attitude into action more easily. For example:

☐   Avco Corp., W. R. Grace & Co., Monsanto Company, and Union Carbide Corp., companies that are neither short of cash nor restructuring their corporate strategy, publicly admit their intent to continually reassess the performance of their divisions, and to dispose of those that do not measure up.

In short, rather than waiting until the issue has been forced, more and more companies are looking ahead and developing relatively sophisticated rationales for divestiture. Aside from the traditional rationales, such as "losing money," "marginal operations," and "doesn't fit," they refer increasingly to an inadequate earnings potential that is occasioned by "a coming overcapacity in the industry," "an uneconomic scale of operations," or "a marketing region too dispersed to permit economic distribution and sales effort."

More Frequent Divestments

This increased emphasis on corporate consolidation, occasioned and encouraged by post-merger spin-offs, strategy reevaluations, and a renewed concern with internal control, will mean that many multidivisional companies are likely to undertake a series of divestitures over the next few years.

It will be almost impossible for any company to carry out such a sequence of divestitures if it follows the traditional procedures—that is, with a small group of very senior executives working at high pressure in complete secrecy. First of all, these executives simply won't have the time. Second, there probably will not be as much concern with secrecy as heretofore, partly because divestments will be forced on the company by visible economic conditions and strategic responses thereto, and partly because of the increasingly stringent enforcement of full-disclosure regulations.

The inevitable consequence of these changes will be the enlargement of the divestiture function and a transferral of much of its activity to staff personnel. Often these staff personnel will be drawn from the same group that is or has been concerned with acquisition identification and analysis.

A Stable, Careful Divestor

Thus the nature of the "typical" divestor is almost certain to change in the following ways:

☐ More multidivisional companies will become divestors.

☐ These companies will be likely to make multiple divestments.

☐ Divestors will be more sophisticated—many will be companies that have survived the financial wizardries of the 1960s which, in some instances, they may have been instrumental in creating.

☐ They will have competent staffs available for researching and evaluating proposals—in many cases, staffs that have gained valuable experience during the acquisition period of the 1960s.

☐ Divestors are likely to be more healthy—they will have stronger financial bases, and they will be able to play a longer game than their predecessors.

☐ They will be unhurried—they will take (or make) time for adequate staff analysis and the development of explicit divestment strategies.

Furthermore, the factors that motivate companies to divest will change, and this will mean a change in the nature of the units offered for sale. A unit slotted for divestiture will no longer necessarily be a money loser; it may merely be a unit that its parent considers to have low potential as a continuing member of the family. In my opinion, therefore, larger numbers of viable operating units are likely to be brought to market in the 1970s.

An Open Market.   In the context of the buyer's market which will prevail, it will be absolutely necessary for divestors to make analyses and to formulate strategies with care. However, they will no longer need to place heavy emphasis on secrecy, both for the reasons already given and because, as more and more well-managed companies make policy-motivated divestitures, there will be less and less stigma attached to them in the marketplace.

Moreover, as an increasing number of divestments are generated by sophisticated control systems that regularly cull operations which do not measure up to standard, buyers will develop an appropriate wariness, the greater number of viable offerings notwithstanding. One executive has remarked: "When somebody tells me that his company wants to sell a subsidiary which 'doesn't fit into the new corporate strategy,' what I say to myself is 'another rathole up for grabs.'"

To explain what forms of analysis might be appropriate for a divestor in this more stringent environment, let us first look at the other side of the coin—the forms of analysis that an acquirer generally uses in evaluating a potential acquisition.

Value: Differing Views

Today, a company usually goes through a certain sequence of steps when it considers an acquisition.

First, it attempts to project the candidate's earnings and cash throwoffs for at least three to five years into the future—often it looks as far as ten years ahead. It also tries to determine the candidate's potential cash needs (for modernization, capacity expansion, working capital increases, debt refunding, and so on) over the same period.

In addition, since its explicit cash flow projections only look a few years into the future, it sometimes assesses the candidate's "value" at the end of that period (the "investment horizon"). This "terminal value" is generally a quick-and-dirty approximation based on some percentage of the candidate's projected assets at that time, or on its projected earnings at that date times some assumed P/E multiple.

These net cash flows are then translated into a current dollar value— that is, the sum that the candidate is worth *now* to the prospective acquirer. Usually, this translation is accomplished by a discounted-present-value method or average-ROI criterion that explicitly takes into account what the acquiring company could earn on alternative investments.

Finally, this monetary value, or base-line figure, is then adjusted for a variety of other considerations. These include its impact on the purchaser's earnings, P/E multiple, and debt capacity; the possible synergistic effects (complementary product lines, sales patterns, or distribution facilities); the perceived value of the personnel to be acquired with the company; and also, some measure of the uncertainty surrounding the purchaser's valuations of these elements.

The divesting company can, and should, go through a similar analysis before it negotiates the sale of a unit (or other asset). But, for the divestor, the adjusted base-line figure represents the value of this asset *only if it is not sold*. Therefore, this figure should not be regarded as a fair selling price, *but as the minimum acceptable price*. The difference here is the difference between what something is worth to a buyer and what the seller can get for it. In this sense, selling a company is less like buying a company than it is like selling a house.

The key factor distinguishing these prices is the way each reflects uncertainty:

☐ There will usually be considerable uncertainty in the acquirer's mind as to the real value of the company she is considering purchasing. Although this uncertainty represents an important consideration, in most cases it is of secondary importance to her.

☐ For the divestor, on the other hand, the uncertainty surrounding the price he will get is considerably greater, despite the fact that he generally has better forecasts of its future earnings than any potential buyer would have.

Exploiting Uncertainty

In some cases, in fact, the assessment of the uncertainty surrounding the purchase price is sufficiently important to dominate any other consideration in the divestor's mind.

That this is so has been demonstrated by several fairly recent examinations of the divestiture process, and I shall shortly explain why. But what is rather surprising to me, and to many others who have been scrutinizing divestors, is that this central fact is generally not properly taken into account and *exploited* by those who make the final divestment deal.

Basically, the divestor has to deal with more uncertainty than the acquirer, because the acquirer must only decide the personal value of a prospective acquisition, whereas the divestor must decide its value to *somebody else*—in fact, many "somebody elses."

In other words, when the seller puts his company on the market, he lacks precise knowledge about who the ultimate purchaser will be and the basis on which she will make her decision to buy. Two prospective acquirers, of course, will tend to look at more different factors than would a single company; and, more importantly, two prospective acquirers looking at the same factors will arrive at different assessments of the unit's value. This will be true even of a factor as unambiguous as a cash flow projection; the values of a stream of periodic cash flows depend on who is looking at them and what his alternatives are. For example, in simplified terms:

☐ Suppose Company A is considering purchasing Unit X. It projects that Unit X's cash flows will be between $800,000 and $1,200,000 per year over a long period of time, averaging $1,000,000 annually. If Company A wants a 15% return on its investment, it should be willing to pay between

$$\$800,000/.15 = \$5,330,000 \qquad \text{and}$$
$$\$1,200,000/.15 = \$8,000,000 \qquad \text{for Unit X}$$

☐ Company B, on the other hand, estimates that Unit X's cash flows will be $1,100,000 per year, but it feels that this estimate may be in error by as much as $220,000 in either direction—that is, the flows may drop to $880,000 or rise to $1,320,000. Since Company B demands a 10% ROI, it should be willing to pay between

$$\$880,000/.10 = \quad \$8,800,000 \qquad \text{and}$$
$$\$1,320,000/.10 = \$13,200,000 \qquad \text{for these returns}$$

Note, from the figures, that both Company A and Company B would assess their uncertainty regarding the appropriate purchase price at plus or minus 20%. To the divesting company, however, these figures imply a conceivable range of offers from $5,330,000 to $13,200,000—or plus or minus 43% around the midpoint.

Each additional factor that is taken into consideration and each additional company that becomes a potential purchaser will extend and complicate this frame of uncertainty.

The crucial, and often unappreciated, implication of this uncertainty is that it represents an opportunity rather than a threat to the divestor, *provided that he can afford to say "no."* If he can afford to wait, he does not have to accept low offers—hence his upside potential is greater, other things being equal, than his downside risk. Uncertainty implies opportunity, then, for the divestor; his strategic difficulty is knowing how long he ought to wait for the right opportunity to appear.

In acquiring, a company's basic strategy hinges on two estimates: what it thinks the asset is worth, and what it thinks it can buy it for. In divestiture, however, once an offer has been received, the divestor's decision hinges on (a) an estimate of the probability of receiving a better offer in the future, and (b) the cost of delaying the decision. In essence, the divestor must weigh the weather forecast against the sailing plans.

The Waiting Game

To apply this technique to help decide whether it should accept a current offer or wait, management needs to estimate the following factors:

☐   How long will it take to generate a second offer?

☐   How high might this offer be? How low?

☐   What are the relative likelihoods of various offers in this range?

☐   What is the cost of waiting until that offer comes through? (This requires estimates of the losses, or profits, that will be generated by the operating unit in that interval, and the opportunity cost associated with delaying acceptance of the current offer.)

Given this information it is possible to calculate a cut-off price that represents the *most* that the divestor can expect to gain by waiting. If the current bid is above that cut-off value, management should accept it; otherwise, it should reject it.

For example, suppose a would-be divestor estimates that the next offer to be received is just as likely to be above $12 million as below; just as likely to be in the $10.5–$13.5 million range as outside that range; and almost certain not to be greater than $18 million or smaller than $5 million. He believes that such a bid can be obtained in three month's time, and that, in that interval, the unit to be divested will generate a net cash flow of $300,000. The funds received from the offer, if accepted, would be used to reduce short-term indebtedness on which the divestor is paying 1% per month simple interest. Finally, let us make the assumption that the divestor can wait as long as he wants for the offer he thinks is "right."

On the basis of this information, the divestor's cut-off price should be about $15 million (see Appendix B for an explanation of this calculation). This may look too high—and, indeed, there is only about one chance in ten of getting a bid that high—but it is appropriate for a situation where the seller can afford to wait as long as necessary, and where the only cost of delay is the cost represented by the interest payments that could have been avoided.

This cut-off value would drop, clearly, if the unit to be divested were earning less than it is (or consuming cash rather than providing it); or if the alternative investment opportunities available to the company promised higher rates of return than 1% per month; or if it were necessary to accomplish the divestment within a specified time interval. It would tend to rise under contrary assumptions.

Revising Estimates over Time

Usually, of course, a seller will have established some informal time limit on her search, such as a year or two. Given such a limit, the cut-off value I have described will slightly overstate the true value. The appropriate downward adjustment is relatively easy to make; the divestor need only supply some additional information about the length of time she is willing to wait and what she will do if this time runs out and the unit still has not been sold.

Even this corrected value, however, is not a sufficient guide, because it is going to change as time passes—as the company gets closer to its maximum waiting time.

In fact, the whole probability distribution of bid prices may be expected to change as time passes. This change may occur in a predictable manner. If, for example, divestors are able to predict in advance the likely magnitudes of the offers they would receive from different potential buyers, and if they approach the buyers according to the descending order of magnitude, then the probability distribution of the "next bid" will move toward lower values as time progresses.

It is more likely, however, that the bid probabilities will change unpredictably, as the sellers are continually revising them to reflect new information as they obtain it. (The offers themselves will probably be the most influential kind of such information, incidentally. There are circumstances in which the seller would *never* accept the first offer received, since the size of the offer will affect the assessment of the probability distribution of future bids so greatly that the seller will prefer to adopt a "wait-and-see" attitude.)

In either case, the calculation procedure is simple enough so that it can be repeated to reflect and incorporate such changes.

Concluding Note

My purpose in the preceding discussion is not to champion the technique itself, but to point out the fact that a technique does exist which can assist managerial decision-making in the divestment area.

The potential value of such a methodical technique—applied in situations that have been dealt with in the past largely "by guess and by golly," in an atmosphere of pressure (and some desperation) that discourages careful analysis—is enormous. It can provide the sellers with a measure of value and an explicit strategy to guide their steps. It puts them back in the driver's seat, where they have to be if the road to market in the 1970s turns out to be as rocky as it looks from here.

Appendix A: Scarcity of Information

Investigating the decision processes used by divesting companies is both difficult and frustrating. Because of the aura of failure that has surrounded divestment proceedings in the past, it is extremely hard to get top managers to talk about divestments they have made, even though these divestments were consummated several years previously.

Moreover, it is rare to find any written documents pertaining to divestitures. This is partly because the decision to divest, and the ensuing negotiations, have generally been confined to a handful of top people in a company. Hence there has been less need for the kind of internal correspondence that serves to keep a large group abreast of developments in an acquisition. This scarcity of documentation is also due to the intense concern for secrecy that has marked divestment proceedings in the past. Another contributing factor is this: whereas an acquiring company essentially has to educate itself about the proposed acquisition, and generates mountains of information and analyses in the process, divestors are generally intimately familiar with what they are selling and carries most of the relevant information in his head.

If it is hard to get a company to talk about long-past divestments, it is even harder to get one to talk about a divestment that is contemplated or actually going forward. But even though most investigators have been forced to rely on relatively sketchy, after-the-fact reports, orally transmitted by individuals whose objectivity is suspect and unsupported by written documents, the distinctive atmosphere of pressured secrecy and the almost amateurish character of many divestment proceedings have manifested themselves clearly.

Appendix B: Calculating the Minimum Acceptable Price

The idea behind this calculation is a very simple one. At base, the decision whether or not to accept any particular offer for a unit will represent a trade-off between such estimates as:

☐   The value of the proceeds of the divestment. (If, in the example described in the text, the divestor accepts the current bid, he will have the purchase price plus 3% in the coffers after three months have elapsed.)

☐   The probability that he will receive a better offer in the future.

☐   The costs associated with waiting until he receives an acceptable offer.

In making this trade-off, the divestor should begin by estimating the value of the unit to be sold immediately prior to his receiving an offer for it. Then he should estimate how this value would be affected if he decides to reject that offer and wait for the next one to come along (in three months, in the example given in the text).

Now suppose he sees equally balanced scales. That is, suppose he sees no particular advantage to accepting the present offer (except increased liquidity), and he sees no particular drawback to rejecting it and waiting for the next one; however, because the offer is available, he thinks he might as well take it for the sake of gaining the ready cash. Under these circumstances, the present offer would be defined as the *minimum acceptable price*, or the cut-off price.

In the example given in the text, one way to describe this cut-off price is this: it is the value of the proceeds plus 3% interest on the proceeds. Another way to describe it is as $300,000 plus the value of the unit (to the divestor) in three months' time. Thus the calculation is:

$$1.03 \times \text{cut-off} = \$300,000 + \text{value of unit after three months}$$

This equivalence is not as simple as it looks, because the "value after three months" will vary with the cut-off price that the divestor sets three months hence, assuming he rejects the present offer and waits for the next one.

That fact notwithstanding, there is a mathematical procedure by which the divestor can isolate the one value in the range of possible offers (that is, $5 million to $18 million) that makes this equation balance. That value is roughly $15 million. To verify this, just plug $15 million into the equation just displayed in place of the cut-off *and* the value of the unit after three months—the two sides of the equation will be roughly equal.

Of course, if the divestor *knew* what the future value would be, he could calculate the cut-off for present bids from the relationship just displayed:

$$\text{cut-off} = (\$300,00 + \text{future value})/1.03$$

Unfortunately, he doesn't. Hence, to get a handle on the present and future value of the unit before any offers for it are made, the divestor must do one or more of three things:

1. Estimate his present cut-off, weigh this figure against the relative likelihoods that he will get a particular range of offers now, and then adjust his estimate accordingly. He then can plug this estimated cut-off into the first equation and get a figure for the minimal value of the unit three months hence.
2. He can estimate the unit's value three months hence and work back to its present value.*
3. He can estimate the present value of the unit and assume that the future value will be just the same. (This is an unrealistic assumption, usually, but it is often convenient to think the divestment problem through from this viewpoint as well.) He can then work back, from this postulated future value, to the present cut-off.

Once he has established the present and future cut-offs he feels are correct, the divestor will be in a position to evaluate a present offer (or offers) and weigh it against future possibilites.

---

*See my article, "Optimal Strategies for Divestiture," *Operations Research*, March-April 1969, p. 292 (reprints available from the author).

Diversification via Acquisition

Creating Value

MALCOLM S. SALTER and WOLF A. WEINHOLD

When debating whether to try to acquire a business that will take their company into either a related or an unrelated field, top corporate officers must answer this vital question: Will it create value for our shareholders? The interest of top management is in improving operating results, which, it hopes, will eventually be reflected in a higher value for the company's stock. Unless management has good reason to believe that the transaction can produce a market value higher than investors could obtain themselves by diversifying their own portfolio, the company should not make the acquisition. The authors discuss the misconceptions that maintain the popularity of corporate diversification programs (many of them unsuccessful) and then outline ways in which a merger can create value for stockholders.

During the past 25 years an increasing proportion of U.S. companies have seen wisdom in pursuing a strategy of diversification. Between 1950 and 1970, for example, single-business companies comprising the *Fortune* "500" declined from 30% to 8% of the total. Acquisition has become a standard approach to diversification.

In recent years the productivity of capital of many multibusiness companies has lagged behind the economy. Nevertheless, diversification through acquisition remains popular; between 1970 and 1975, acquired assets of large manufacturing and mining companies averaged slightly more than 11% of total new investment in those companies, and most of that activity was diversifying acquisition.[1] In the past few years the pace of activity has been slower than in the hectic 1967–1969 period, but the combination of high corporate liquidity, depressed stock prices, and slow economic growth has

Published 1978.

meant that for many companies acquisitions are among the most attractive investment alternatives. Since mid-1977, hardly a week has gone by without at least one major acquisition being announced by a diversifying corporation.

In light of this continuing interest and the apparent economic risks in following such a strategy, we present a review of the theory of corporate diversification. We begin by discussing seven common misconceptions about diversification through acquisition. We then turn to the basic question facing companies wanting to adopt the strategy: How can a company create value for its shareholders through diversification?

Our consideration of value creation leads to an examination of the potential benefits of the alternatives available—related-business diversification and unrelated-business diversification. Businesses are related if they (1) serve similar markets and use similar distribution systems, (2) employ similar production technologies, or (3) exploit similar science-based research.[2]

Common Misconceptions

There are seven common misconceptions about diversification through acquisition that we can usefully highlight in the context of recent history. They relate to the economic rationale of this strategy and to the management of a successful diversification program.

1. *Acquisitive diversifiers generate larger returns (through increased earnings and capital appreciation) for their shareholders than nondiversifiers do.* This notion gained a certain currency during the 1960s, in part because of the enormous emphasis that securities analysts and corporate executives placed on growth in earnings per share (EPS). Acquisitive diversifiers that did not collapse at once from ingesting too many businesses often sustained high levels of EPS growth.

However, once it became apparent that a large proportion of this growth was an accounting mirage and that capital productivity was a better indicator of management's performance and a business's economic strength, the market value of many acquisitive companies plunged.

Many widely diversified companies have had low capital productivity in recent years. Exhibit 1 shows the performance of a sample originally selected by the Federal Trade Commission in 1969 as representative of companies pursuing strategies of diversification and not classifiable in standard industrial categories. Although the average return on equity of the sample was 20% higher than the average of the *Fortune* "500" in 1967, it was 18% below the *Fortune* average in 1975. Even the surge in profits in 1976 and 1977 and the impact of nonoperating, accounting profits in several corporations failed to bring the sample average up to the *Fortune* average. What is even more telling than the return on equity figures is that the sample's return on assets was 20% or more below the *Fortune* "500" average throughout the 10-year period.

Thus it is not surprising that acquisitive diversifiers have had low price-earnings ratios. On December 31, 1977, the average P/E of the sample, which includes many busy diversifiers, was 30% below that of the New York Stock Exchange stocks as a whole. This discount has changed little over several years. Even high return-on-equity performers like Northwest Industries, Teledyne, and Textron have P/Es well below the market's average.

Such low market values imply great uncertainty about the size and variability of future cash flows. And when they are uncertain about a company's cash flow, investors and stock analysts view them as less valuable than reliable and predictable earnings streams, so they are inclined to discount the company's future earnings heavily. The high discount rates of acquisitive diversifiers produce growth with less capital appreciation than that of nondiversifiers whose earnings streams appear to be more predictable. What will create value is growing cash flows with little uncertainty about their size or variability.

2. *Unrelated diversification offers shareholders a superior means of reducing their investment risk.* Unrelated diversification may be attractive from an investor's point of view—its use is frequently offered to justify or defend conglomerate mergers—but it is not a superior means of reducing investment risk. (By *investment risk* we mean the variability of returns over time, *returns* being defined as capital appreciation plus dividends paid to investors.)

According to contemporary financial theory, a security's risk and return can be decomposed into two elements: (1) what is specific to each company and called "unsystematic" because it can be diversified away and (2) what is "systematic" because it is common to all securities (the securities market) and hence nondiversifiable.[3] Since the unsystematic risk of any security can be eliminated through simple portfolio diversification, the investor does not need widely diversified companies like Litton Industries and Gulf & Western Industries to eliminate the risk for him.

Contemporary financial economists believe that prices of securities reflect the consensus of many knowledgeable buyers and sellers concerning a company's prospects. This consensus leads to an efficient capital market, where the investor finds it extremely difficult to consistently make risk-adjusted profits in excess of those the market realizes as a whole. Although it does not claim that the price of every security always accurately reflects its underlying (systematic) risk, the theory does suggest that when one views all securities over time, the "overvaluations" and "undervaluations" by the market balance out.[4]

Several researchers have extended this efficient capital market concept to the analysis of conglomerate mergers. Their studies suggest that unrelated corporate diversification has little to offer investors with respect to risk reduction over a diversified portfolio of comparable securities.

They also suggest that if diversified companies cannot increase returns or reduce risks more than comparable portfolios do, these companies can

Exhibit 1. Performance Data of 36 Diversified Manufacturers (1967, 1973, 1975, 1977)

Company	1967 Year-End Total Assets (in millions of dollars)	Return on Assets	Return on Equity	1973 Year-End Total Assets (in millions of dollars)	Return on Assets	Return on Equity
Avco	$1,618.5	3.4%	14.7%	$ 1,412.2	(1.3)%	(3.6)%
Bangor Punta	144.4	4.0	13.6	328.1	0.5	1.3
Bendix	833.4	5.5	11.3	1,427.0	4.1	11.1
Boise Cascade	865.2	3.3	11.3	1,585.4	9.0[a]	21.1[a]
City Investing	338.9	4.0	18.5	3,622.8	2.0	10.3
Colt Industries	197.1	6.1	16.7	266.0	4.0	10.0
FMC	931.8	6.6	13.6	680.5	5.7	11.6
GAF	473.5	4.1	6.9	627.0	4.6	8.7
General Tire	741.7	4.1	8.4	1,233.9	6.2	12.9
W.R. Grace	1,578.4	3.4	8.6	2,003.8	4.2	11.3
Gulf & Western	749.4	6.4	26.8	2,364.1	3.8	13.4
ICI	865.5	2.3	4.0	1,736.6	3.0	6.0
ITT	2,961.2	4.0	11.4	10,133.0	5.2	14.1
Walter Kidde	253.1	7.0	14.7	739.5	5.1	12.5
Koppers	326.5	4.3	7.7	520.3	5.7	11.2
LTV	845.1	4.8	18.3	1,829.1	2.7[a]	23.7[a]
Litton	945.0	7.4	19.0	2,116.2	2.0	5.2
Martin Marietta	527.2	7.0	11.9	1,074.0	5.3	11.4
3M	1,034.7	14.2	19.9	2,280.9	13.0	20.6
NL Industries	576.4	8.9	13.4	987.8	4.8	10.9
Northwest Industries	1,286.3	3.0	6.0	964.8	5.9[a]	13.4[a]
Norton Simon	463.8	3.3	6.7	1,120.0	7.0	15.5
Ogden	381.7	5.3	14.1	713.6	3.7	12.9
Rapid-American	337.8	4.8	14.9	1,755.5	1.7	13.7
SCM	451.4	5.6	19.7	552.7	3.3	7.8
Signal	1,090.3	4.5	9.1	1,378.1	4.2	8.7
Singer	1,049.2	4.8	11.1	1,897.0	5.0	11.9
Sperry Rand	1,095.2	5.9	11.9	1,840.6	4.9	10.6
Studebaker-Worthington	561.0	5.9	12.1	995.1	3.3	10.5
TRW	710.9	7.6	17.3	1,446.1	6.6	15.1
Teledyne	337.7	6.4	15.8	1,229.6	5.3	12.6
Tenneco	3,589.3	4.1	11.8	5,127.3	4.5	12.3
Textron	669.7	9.2	20.4	1,310.4	7.7	16.1
U.S. Industries	162.3	7.4	20.5	1,033.5	6.5	12.7
White Consolidated	277.3	3.8	14.7	597.4	5.9	15.1
Whittaker	118.0	7.4	29.3	589.4	(1.0)[a]	(3.3)[a]
Sample average		5.3	13.9		4.0	12.2
Fortune "500"		7.8	11.7		5.0	12.4

Criteria for the selection of companies in the Federal Trade Commission sample:
1. Each company in 1969 had total assets of $250 million or more.
2. Each company had 50% or more of its total sales derived from manufactured products.

344

1975			1977			
Year-End Total Assets (in millions of dollars)	Return on Assets	Return on Equity	Year-End Total Assets (in millions of dollars)	Return on Assets	Return on Equity	EPS Growth Rate (1967– 1977)
$ 1,250.4	4.9%[a]	12.1%[a]	$ 4,125.6	2.8%[a]	18.6%[a]	3.6%
234.9	3.6	8.7	395.4	4.6	13.9	2.1
1,567.6	5.1	11.1	1,810.6	6.5	14.1	7.7
1,569.5	4.1	7.5	1,799.0	6.4	12.1	7.8
3,938.0	0.8	5.0	4,721.0	1.8	10.2	14.7
866.3	6.0	14.8	1,112.2	6.3	13.8	9.3
1,843.9	5.9	13.7	2,141.5	5.6	12.7	6.8
705.4	4.4	8.4	762.4	(6.2)	(14.2)	—
1,427.3	4.4	9.1	1,587.3	7.3	13.3	12.9
2,523.8	6.6	18.8	2,941.0	4.8	11.4	3.0
3,305.7	4.2	17.5	4,159.1	3.6	12.2	8.0
2,241.7	2.2	5.3	2,613.2	3.0	7.1	6.5
10,408.0	3.8	9.6	12,285.5	4.5	10.7	4.8
854.9	5.1	12.3	1,107.2	5.1	11.0	3.2
679.7	8.9	17.6	851.9	7.8	14.1	14.2
1,962.8	0.7	3.9	2,067.0	(1.9)[a]	(10.1)[a]	—
2,185.7	1.6	4.4	2,063.8	2.7	6.5	(4.1)
1,139.0	4.9	9.4	1,376.8	7.4	14.1	8.5
3,016.8	8.7	15.0	3,529.6	11.7	18.2	10.0
1,059.5	4.3	9.1	1,325.8	5.0	9.4	(1.2)
1,184.1	8.6	18.6	1,764.6	7.3	18.2	13.4
1,355.7	6.1	11.9	1,487.2	6.9	12.4	12.9
926.0	5.1	14.8	1,021.7	4.9	15.4	6.1
1,481.0	(0.6)	(4.9)	1,485.3	3.2[a]	22.5[a]	7.8
704.1	4.0	10.1	767.9	4.9	10.9	0.0
1,866.8	2.2	5.3	2,152.8	4.7	11.6	6.0
1,797.1	(25.2)	(96.0)	1,461.9	6.5[a]	20.6[a]	0.8
2,533.1	5.2	12.9	2,841.5	5.5	12.1	10.1
883.6	3.4	9.1	915.2	7.6	15.5	12.1
1,686.5	6.2	14.1	2,056.7	7.5	16.7	8.0
1,141.9	8.9	20.5	1,420.1	13.7	28.4	32.3
6,584.2	5.2	15.0	8,278.3	5.2	13.9	8.4
1,433.3	6.7	13.1	1,738.3	7.9	14.8	5.5
941.7	1.1	2.1	837.4	5.1	8.4	(3.8)
858.2	5.5	16.0	934.2	5.9	15.5	13.1
508.9	0.6	1.6	481.2	3.3	9.7	1.6
	3.6	9.5		5.3	12.4	
	5.7	11.6		6.5	13.3	

3. Each company had less than 50% of its total sales in any one industry and was engaged in three or more product lines.

[a]Extraordinary items included.

at best offer the investor only value comparable to that of a mutual fund. Indeed, widely diversified companies with systematic risks and returns equivalent to those of a mutual fund may actually be *less* attractive investment vehicles because of their higher management costs and their inability to move into or out of assets as quickly and as cheaply as mutual funds do.[5] For a specific case involving systematic risk, see the Appendix comparing Gulf & Western Industries with a portfolio having like assets.

3. *Adding countercyclical businesses to a company's portfolio leads to a stabilized earnings stream and a heightened valuation by the marketplace.* This misconception is an extension of the previous one. For decades, proponents of unrelated or conglomerate diversification have argued that when a company diversifies into an industry with a business cycle or a set of economic risks different from its own, it enhances the "safety" of its income stream. In essence, this sense of safety is a very simple form of the "risk pooling" concept underlying insurance.

In light of the poor performance of many diversified companies, it should be obvious that safety is difficult to attain. Because of the complex interactions of the United States and other nations' economies, finding genuinely countercyclical businesses is very hard. At the most, there are industry cycles that either lead or lag behind the general economy (e.g., housing and capital goods, respectively) or that are less cyclical than the general economy (e.g., consumer goods and tobacco products).

Even if diversifying companies can identify the countercyclical businesses, diversifiers find it difficult to construct balanced portfolios of businesses whose variable returns balance one another. Moreover, inasmuch as businesses grow at various rates, widely diversified companies face the continual challenge of rebalancing their business portfolios through very selective acquisitions.

Quite apart from this argument, the low stock market values of widely diversified companies during the past eight years indicate that the marketplace has heavily discounted the future cash returns to investors in companies consisting of purportedly countercyclical businesses. Although there are undoubtedly many reasons for this situation, it suggests that the market may be more interested in growth and the productivity of invested capital than in earnings stability per se. In addition, investors have little incentive to bid up the prices of diversified companies because an investor can obtain the benefits of stabilizing an income stream through simple portfolio diversification.

4. *Related diversification is always safer than unrelated diversification.* This misconception rests on the notion of corporate executives that they reduce their operating risks when they stick to buying businesses they think they understand. They want to limit their diversification to businesses with similar marketing and distribution characteristics, similar production technologies, or similar science-based R&D efforts.

Although this presumption often has merit, making related acquisitions does not guarantee results superior to those stemming from unrelated diversification. For example, Xerox's entry into data processing via its acquisition of Scientific Data Systems, which Xerox justified on the ground of technological, marketing, and manufacturing compatibility, led to a great drain on earnings for years. The management of Singer decided to take advantage of the company's competence in electromechanical manufacturing as the basis for its diversification program. The result was dramatic failure, leading to a $500 million write-off of assets.

A close reading of the Xerox and Singer cases suggests that successful related diversification depends on both the quality of the acquired business and the organizational integration required to achieve the possible benefits of companies exchanging their skills and resources. Such exchange has been called *synergy*.

Even more important, the perceived relatedness must be real, and the merger must give the partners a competitive advantage. Unless these conditions are met, related diversification cannot be justified as superior or even comparable to unrelated diversification as a means of reducing operating risks or increasing earnings.

5. *A strong management team at the acquired company ensures realization of the potential benefits of diversification.* Many companies try to limit their pool of acquisition candidates to well-managed companies. This policy is rarely the necessary condition for gaining the potential benefits of diversification.

As we shall stress later in this article, the potential benefits of related diversification stem from augmenting the effective use of the surviving company's core skills and resources. Usually such improvement requires an exchange of core skills and resources among the partners. The benefits of unrelated diversification are rooted in two conditions: (1) increased efficiency in cash management and in allocation of investment capital; and (2) the capability to call on profitable, low-growth businesses to provide the cash flow for high-growth businesses that require significant infusions of cash.

Whether pursuing related or unrelated diversification, it is often the acquiring company's management skills and resources—not those of the acquired company—that are critical to achieving the potential benefits of diversification. Indeed, if the acquired company is well managed and priced accordingly by the capital market, the acquirer must exploit the potential synergies with the acquiree to make the transaction economically justifiable.

6. *The diversified company is uniquely qualified to improve the performance of acquired businesses.* During the height of the merger and acquisition activity of the 1960s, executives of conglomerates often argued that they could improve the profitability of acquired companies by "modernizing" administrative practices and exerting more operating discipline than that demanded by the marketplace.

Consider the testimony of Harold S. Geneen, then chairman and president of International Telephone & Telegraph Corporation, at a government hearing concerning how ITT provided "constructive bases for merger."

"We can afford to price fairly," Geneen said, "and to exchange our own equity stocks with the shareholders of an incoming company. We can improve operating efficiencies and profits sufficiently to make this valuation worthwhile to both sets of shareholders." In a document outlining ITT's acquisition philosophy and submitted to the hearing, Geneen wrote that from 1960 to 1965 the company had "developed the ability through management skills, routines, and techniques to set and progressively meet higher competitive standards and achieve them in practically every line and product that we have undertaken."[6]

The claims that Geneen and many other successful diversifiers have invoked are not benefits of diversification per se but simply the benefits of that nebulous factor, "good management." Single-business companies pursuing vertical integration or horizontal expansion through acquisition can achieve identical results. To gain the benefits Geneen claimed, a company needs only to allow managers with the requisite skills to implement their desired improvements in the organization.

Rarely, it may be argued, does an organization willingly take steps that could alter its traditional administrative and managerial practices. Under these circumstances, change will occur only when forced from the outside, and diversifying companies often represent such a force. Nevertheless, the benefits achieved are not, strictly speaking, benefits of diversification.

7. *Great deals are made by professional "deal makers."* The most potentially dangerous misconception on our list is the one that credits the imaginative work of investment bankers and other brokers with the success of a diversifying acquisition. The investment banker's role is to provide attractive ideas, but it is the company's role to select the ideas that have the greatest strategic and economic value.

This role involves developing diversification objectives and acquisition guidelines that fit a carefully prepared concept of the corporation. It also involves the company's ability to recognize and exploit the potential for creating value through diversifying acquisitions. Every experienced corporate diversifier has learned, often painfully, that he must live with an acquisition long after it has ceased being a "great deal."

Ways to Create Value

A company following a diversification strategy can create value for its shareholders only when the combination of the skills and resources of the two businesses satisfies at least one of the following conditions:

☐   An income stream greater than what could be realized from a portfolio investment in the two companies.

☐   A reduction in the variability of the income stream greater than what could be realized from a portfolio investment in the two businesses—that is, reduced systematic risk.

Included in both conditions is explicit comparison of corporate diversification on the shareholder's behalf with independent portfolio diversification on the investor's part. This comparison deserves comment.

Most benefits derived from reducing unsystematic corporate risk through diversification are, of course, equally available to the individual investor. Diversified companies can achieve trade-offs between total risk and return that are superior to the trade-offs available to single-business companies. Diversified companies cannot create value for their stockholders merely by diversifying away unsystematic risk.

Inasmuch as investors can diversify away unsystematic risk themselves, in efficient capital markets unsystematic risk is irrelevant in the equity valuation process. A diversifying company can create value for its shareholders only when its risk-return trade-offs include benefits unavailable through simple portfolio diversification.

There are seven principal ways in which acquisition-minded companies can obtain returns greater than those obtainable from simple portfolio diversification. The first four are particularly relevant to related diversification, whereas the last three are more relevant to unrelated diversification.

1.   *A diversifying acquisition can raise the productivity of capital when the particular skills and one merger partner's knowledge of the industry are applied to the competitive problems and opportunities facing the other partner.*   When the reinforcement of skills and resources critical to the success of a business within the combined company leads to higher profitability, value is created for its shareholders. This reinforcement is the realization of synergy.

The acquisition by Heublein, Inc. of United Vintners in 1968 is a good case in point. Heublein's strategy during the 1960s was to obtain high margins in marketing liquor and specialty food products through intensive, innovative advertising. At the time, Heublein stood out in this respect because the industry was production- and distribution-oriented. The company's liquor products division accounted for more than 80% of 1965 sales. Its principal product was the premium-priced Smirnoff vodka, the fourth largest and fastest growing liquor brand in the United States.

The 1968 acquisition of United Vintners, the marketing arm of a large grape growers' cooperative that owned two of California's best-known wine brands, gave Heublein the opportunity to raise its investment in an industry where it had some experience (it was the U.S. distributor for Lancers wine) and to extend the application of its proven skills in promoting specialty products. By identifying and then exploiting an emerging consumer preference for lighter-bodied, often slightly flavored products, Heublein helped

United Vintners launch two new products—Cold Duck (a champagne-sparkling burgundy combination) and Bali Hai (a fruit-flavored wine).

By the end of 1969, one year after its acquisition of United Vintners, Heublein had increased sales by over 2.5 million cases and augmented the subsidiary's profitability. Heublein's marketing strategy was so successful that during the 1960s and early 1970s its return on equity averaged over 30% and the marketplace valued Heublein at over 35 times its earnings. Heublein discovered in its diversification efforts, however, that its strategy of aggressive advertising was not the key success factor in either brewing (Hamm's beer) or fast foods (Kentucky Fried Chicken), and its market valuation suffered accordingly. By 1977, Heublein had seen its P/E fall to 10 and its stock price to one-third of its previous high.

2. *Investments in markets closely related to current fields of operation can reduce long-run average costs.* A reduction in average costs can accrue from scale effects, rationalization of production and other managerial efforts, and technological innovation. For example, a marketing department's budget as a percent of sales will decline if existing resources can be used to market new or related products. Similarly, a large company like Procter & Gamble can expect its per-unit distribution costs to decline when it augments the use of its existing distribution system to move products to the marketplace. This notion has been the basis of many acquisitions made by consumer products companies.

3. *Business expansion in an area of competence can lead to the generation of a "critical mass" of resources necessary to outperform the competition.* In many industries, companies have to achieve a certain size, or critical mass, before they can compete effectively with their competitors.

For example, the principal way many small laboratory instrumentation companies hope to offer sustained competition against such entrenched companies as Hewlett-Packard, Tektronix, Beckman Instruments, and Technicon is to attain a size giving them sufficient cash flow to underwrite competitive research and development programs. One way to reach this size is to make closely related diversifying acquisitions.

4. *Diversification into related product markets can enable a company to reduce systematic risks.* Many of the possibilities for reducing risk through diversification are implicit in the previous three ways to increase returns because risk and return are closely related measurements. However, diversifying by acquiring a company in a related product market can enable a company to reduce its technological, production, or marketing risks. If these reduced business risks can be translated into a less variable income stream for the company, value is created.

Although there is no evidence that General Motors's strategy was developed with this notion in mind, an important result of GM's diversification within the motor vehicle industry has been its ability to easily absorb changes in demand for any one automotive product. GM's extensive related-product line reduces the company's marketing risk and enables GM's managers to concentrate on production efficiencies. As a result, GM's income stream tends to be less volatile than those of its competitors and of portfolios of discrete investments in unassociated, although automotive-related, companies.

5. *The diversified company can route cash from units operating with a surplus to units operating with a deficit and can thereby reduce the need of individual businesses to purchase working capital funds from outside sources.* Through centralizing cash balances, corporate headquarters can act as the banker for its operating subsidiaries and thus can balance the cyclical working capital requirements of its divisions as the economy progresses through a business cycle or as its divisions experience seasonal fluctuations. This type of working capital management is, of course, an operating benefit completely separate from the recycling of cash on an investment basis.

6. *Managers of a diversified company can direct its currently high net cash flow businesses to transfer investment funds to the businesses in which net cash flow is zero or negative but in which management expects positive cash flow to develop. The aim is to improve the long-run profitability of the corporation.* This potential benefit is a by-product of the U.S. tax code, which imposes double taxation of dividends—once via corporate profits taxes and once via personal income taxes. By reinvesting its surplus cash flow, the company defers taxes that stockholders otherwise would have to pay on the company's dividends.

In November 1975, Genstar, Ltd. of Canada justified this way of creating value in a submission to the Royal Commission on Corporate Concentration. There Genstar argued that the well-managed, widely diversified company can call on its low-growth businesses to maximize net cash flow and profits in order to enable it to reallocate funds to the high-growth businesses needing investment. By so doing, the company will eventually reap benefits via a higher ROI and the public will benefit via lower costs and, presumably, via lower prices.

As Exhibit 2 shows, two of Genstar's major business areas—cement as well as chemicals and fertilizers—used far less cash (for working capital and reinvestment) in 1971–1974 than they generated (*cash generated* being defined as net income after taxes plus depreciation and deferred taxes). Genstar recycled the excess cash flow into its housing and land development, construction, and marine activities. So Genstar was able not only to employ its assets more productively than before, but also to reap economic benefits beyond those possible from a comparable securities portfolio.

Genstar's argument for cross-subsidization has an important extension. Diversified companies have access to information that is often unavailable

**Exhibit 2.   Relationship between Cash Used and Cash Generated
by Business Areas of Genstar, 1971–1974**

Area	Cash Use Ratio[a]
Building supplies	1.01
Cement	.31
Housing and land development	1.72
Construction	1.67
Chemicals and fertilizers	.38
Marine activities	1.87
Imports and exports	.46
Investments	.52
Total for the company	1.02

[a]The cash use ratio is cash used divided by cash generated. A business
area's cash use ratio is determined by comparing its cash used with its cash
generated. A cash use ratio higher than 1 indicates that the business area
is a net cash user, while a ratio of less than 1 indicates a net cash generator.
Cash generated is defined as net income after tax plus depreciation and
deferred tax.

to the investment community. This information is the internally generated
market data about each industry in which it operates, data that include
information about the competitive position and potential of each company
in the industry.

With this inside information, diversified enterprises can enjoy a significantly better position in assessing the investment merits of particular
projects and entire industries than individual investors can. Such access
enables the companies to choose the most attractive projects and thereby
to allocate capital among "their" industries more efficiently than the capital
markets can.

7.   *Through risk pooling, the diversified company can lower its cost
of debt and leverage itself more than its nondiversified equivalent. The
company's total cost of capital thereby goes down and provides stockholders
with returns in excess of those available from a comparable portfolio of
securities.*   As the number of businesses in the portfolio of an unrelated
diversifier grows and the overall variability of its operating income or cash
flow declines, its standing as a credit risk should rise. Because the company
pools its own divisions' risks and supports any component threatened with
bankruptcy, theoretically (at least) the company should have a somewhat
lower cost of debt than that of companies unable to pool their risks. More
importantly, the reduced variability of the diversified company's cash flow
improves its ability to borrow.

This superior financial leverage enables the corporation's shareholders to shift some risk to government and thereby reduce the company's total cost of capital. (Since interest, in contrast to dividends, is tax deductible, the government shoulders part of the cost of debt capitalization in a business venture.) These benefits become significant, however, only when the enterprise aggressively manages its financial risks by employing a high debt-equity ratio or by operating several very risky, unrelated projects in its portfolio of businesses.

Although this type of company can enjoy a lower cost of capital than a less diversified company of comparable size, it can also have a higher cost of *equity* capital than the other type. This possibility stems from the fact that part of the financial risk of debt capitalization is borne by the equity owners. In addition, investors' perceptions of risk are not solely conditioned by the degree of diversification in corporate assets. Indeed, the professional investor may be unwilling to lower the rate of return on equity capital just because a company has acquired a well-balanced or purportedly counter-cyclical collection of businesses.

The risks and opportunities the investors perceive for a company greatly depend on the amount and clarity of information that they can effectively process. As a company becomes more diversified, its business can become less clearly defined and its investors' uncertainty about its risks and opportunities can rise. The greater this uncertainty, of course, the higher the risk premium the equity investor demands and the higher the company's cost of equity capital becomes.

Diversification Strategies

An unrelated-business diversifier is a company pursuing growth in product markets where the main success factors are unrelated to each other. Such a company, whether a conglomerate or simply a holding company, expects little or no transfer of functional skills among its various businesses. In contrast, a related-business diversifier uses its skills in a specific functional activity or product market as a basis for branching out.

The most significant benefits to the stockholder occur in related diversification when the special skills and industry knowledge of one merger partner apply to the competitive problems and opportunities facing the other. Shareholders' benefits from unrelated or conglomerate diversification can occur where more efficient capital and asset management leads to a better return for investors than that available from a diversified portfolio of securities of comparable systematic risk. Exhibit 3 summarizes the benefits that are attainable from the two types of diversification.

Unfortunately, the benefits that offer the greatest potential are usually the ones least likely to be implemented. Of the synergies usually identified to justify an acquisition, financial synergies are often unnoted, whereas op-

Exhibit 3. Potential Benefits of Diversification

	Related-Business Diversification	Unrelated-Business Diversification
Product-market orientation	Diversification into business with similar marketing and distribution characteristics, similar production technologies, or similar science-based research activities.	Diversification into product markets with key success variables unrelated to the key success variables of the acquirer's principal business.
Transferable resources	Operating and/or functional skills; excess capacity in distribution systems, production facilities, or research operations.	General management skills; surplus financial resources.
Nature of potential benefits	Increased productivity of corporate resources through operating synergy, improved competitive position accruing from greater size of business and lower long-run average costs, all leading to reduction in the variability of the income stream and/or a larger income stream than that available from simple portfolio diversification.	Efficient cash management and allocation of investment capital, reduced cost of debt capital, and growth in profits through cross-subsidization, all leading to a larger income stream than that available from simple portfolio diversification; unlikely reduction of systematic (market-related) risk.
Relative ease of achieving potential benefits	Difficult because of organizational problems associated with integrating formerly self-sufficient companies into the acquiring company.	Easy-to-achieve capital efficiencies and benefits from cross-subsidization.

erating synergies are widely trumpeted. Yet our experience has been that the benefits most commonly achieved are those in the financial area.

It is not hard to understand why. Most managers would agree that the greatest impediment to change is the inflexibility of the organization. The realization of operating benefits accompanying diversification usually requires significant changes in the company's format and administrative behavior. These changes are usually slow to come, and so are the accompanying benefits.

Nevertheless, diversification does offer potentially significant benefits to the corporation and its shareholders. When a company has the ability to export or import surplus skills or resources useful in its competitive environment, related diversification is an attractive strategic option. When a company possesses the skills and resources to analyze and manage the strategies of widely different businesses, unrelated diversification can be the best strategic option. Finally, when a diversifying company has both of these abilities, choosing a workable strategy will depend on the personal skills and inclinations of its top managers.

Notes

1. Bureau of Economics, Federal Trade Commission, *Statistical Report on Mergers and Acquisitions* (Washington, D.C., November 1976), p. 93.

2. Richard P. Rumelt first articulated this useful definition in his *Strategy, Structure, and Economic Performance* (Boston, Division of Research, Harvard Business School, 1974).

3. William F. Sharpe, *Portfolio Theory and Capital Markets* (New York, McGraw-Hill, 1970), p. 96.

4. For summaries of empirical evidence supporting the efficient market theory, see Eugene F. Fama, "Efficient Capital Markets: A Review of Theory and Empirical Work," *Journal of Finance*, May 1970, p. 383; and Michael C. Jensen, "Capital Markets: Theory and Evidence," *Bell Journal of Economics and Management Science*, Autumn 1972, p. 35.

5. See Keith V. Smith and John C. Shreiner, "A Portfolio Analysis of Conglomerate Diversification," *Journal of Finance*, June 1969, p. 413; J. Fred Weston and Surenda K. Mansinghka, "Tests of Efficiency Performance of Conglomerate Firms," *Journal of Finance*, September 1971, p. 919; and R. Hal Mason and Maurice B. Gondzwaard, "Performance of Conglomerate Firms: A Portfolio Approach," *Journal of Finance*, March 1976, p. 39.

6. Hearings before the Antitrust Subcommittee of the Committee of the Judiciary, U.S. House of Representatives, November 20, 1969.

7. A more thorough presentation of this method of making a comparative risk analysis is available from the authors at Harvard Business School, Soldiers Field, Boston, Mass. 02163.

Appendix. Analysis of Systematic Risk

Since portfolio theory tells us that reducing systematic risk is impossible through portfolio diversification, let us analyze a portfolio of assets against a diversified company's assets similar in size and allocation. This risk analysis requires three kinds of information: (1) the investment composition, by industry, of the diversified company; (2) the size of the investment the company has made in each industry; and (3) the systematic risk of each of those industries.

Summing the industries' systematic risks, weighted by their relative size in the portfolio, results in a measure of the portfolio's systematic risk. The last step before comparing the portfolio's systematic risk with the diversified company's systematic risk is to adjust for differences in financial risk. Once this is done, the analyst can determine, within statistical limits, whether the diversifying corporation has reduced its systematic risk.

The results of a risk analysis of Gulf & Western Industries, a high return-on-equity performer for over a decade, are presented in Table A. An analysis of a comparable portfolio for G&W is given in Table B. Both tables reflect a five-year period ending in July 1975. The businesses of G&W's eight divisions overlap very little. Grouping these divisions with Gulf & Western's investment portfolio produces a well-diversified comparable portfolio.

As Table A indicates, Gulf & Western's systematic risk, adjusted for financial leverage, differs insignificantly from that of a comparable portfolio. All three systematic risk measurements are within one standard deviation of each other. Whatever benefits Gulf & Western provides its shareholders, reduction of investment risk apparently is not one of them.[7]

Table A.   Portfolio Comparison

	Systematic Risk (beta)	Standard Deviation
Gulf & Western's portfolio statistics		
Leverage = .37[a]		
Systematic risk (according to Merrill Lynch, Pierce, Fenner & Smith)	1.15	.20
Systematic risk (according to Value Line)	1.35	.20
Comparison portfolio's statistics		
Weighted average leverage = .30[b]		
Weighted average systematic risk[b]	1.15	
Systematic risk when leverage = .37	1.26	.15

[a]Market value of debt divided by the sum of the market values of debt and equity.

[b]Taken from Table B.

Table B. Systematic Risk Analysis of a Portfolio Similar to That of Gulf & Western Industries (dollars in millions)

Group	Standard & Poor's Industry Category	Industry Average: Sales/Assets	Industry Average: Debt/Assets	G&W's 1974 Sales	Assets of a Company Comparable to G&W Group	Debt of a Company Comparable to G&W Group	Comparable Company's Assets as Percentage of Portfolio's Assets	Industry's Systematic Risk	Weighted Systematic Risk of Comparable Companies in Portfolio
Food and agricultural products	Sugar	2.1	.45	$ 175	$ 85	$ 37	4.3%	.6	.026
Natural resources	Lead and zinc	1.2	.1	178	150	15	7.5	.72	.054
Paper and building products	Paper	2.1	.4	405	190	75	9.5	.9	.085
Financial services	Small loan finance	.6	.15	494	446	70	22.4	1.35	.302
Leisure time	Movies	1.8	.3	298	165	50	8.3	1.65	.137
Automotive replacement and parts	Automotive replacement and parts	3.0	.1	225	75	7	3.8	1.7	.063

Table B. (*Continued*)

Group	Standard & Poor's Industry Category	Industry Average: Sales/ Assets	Industry Average: Debt/ Assets	G&W's 1974 Sales	Assets of a Company Comparable to G&W Group	Debt of a Company Comparable to G&W Group	Comparable Company's Assets as Percentage of Portfolio's Assets	Industry's Systematic Risk	Weighted Systematic Risk of Comparable Companies in Portfolio
Consumer products	Tobacco	2.1	.3	212	100	30	5.0	.85	.042
Manufacturing Automotive OEM		2.3	.3	327	140	45	7.0	1.25	.104
	Capital goods: machinery	1.8	.25	285	160	40	8.0	1.3	.068
	Electrical	2.0	.2	195	100	20	5.0	1.3	.088
Operating group's total				$2,794	$1,611	$389	80.8%		.969
Intangibles					100		5.0	.969[a]	.048
Investments					284	211	14.2	.95	.135
Total					$1,995[b]	$600	100.0%		1.15

[a]Intangibles arise from an excess investment over the equity acquired. Its risk matches that of the underlying assets (operating portfolio).

[b]G&W's 1974 annual report listed this investment as $1,983 million (within 1% of the comparison portfolio).

358

22
Choosing Compatible Acquisitions

MALCOLM S. SALTER and WOLF A. WEINHOLD

In today's low-growth yet volatile environment, many companies choose to diversify through acquisition. An acquisition candidate with high potential will be one that can create economic value by leading to a free cash flow for the combined company that is either larger or less risky than that of a comparable investment portfolio. Candidates with the greatest promise for value creation will be those offering a good fit with the acquirer's unique set of skills and resources. The authors examine how an assessment of these skills and resources can help companies decide (1) whether related or unrelated acquisitions make sense, (2) which economic, strategic, and managerial variables should be stressed in evaluating an acquisition candidate's risk-return profile, and (3) what potential exits for successful integration with the acquiring company.

Although some view large-scale acquisitions primarily as the province of adventurous conglomerates, in fact many old-line conservative giants are actively involved in such activities. General Electric, for instance, paid $2 billion in stock for Utah International, Exxon paid $1.2 billion in cash for Reliance Electric, and Allied Chemical and Kennecott Copper each paid more than $500 million for their respective acquisitions of Eltra and Carborundum.

When such corporate acquisitions succeed, it is often because the acquirers have a mechanism for identifying candidates that offer the greatest potential for creating value for the company's shareholders. In a previous article, we pointed out that value is created when diversifying acquisitions lead to a free cash flow for the combined company (1) that is greater than could be realized from a portfolio investment in the two companies or (2) whose variability is smaller than it would be with a portfolio investment in the two companies. (See Article 21 by us.)

Published 1981.

Effective systems for identifying and screening acquisitions have four important properties. First, they must provide means of evaluating a candidate's potential for creating value for the acquirer's shareholders. Second, they must be able to reflect the special needs of each company using the system. Relying on checklists or priorities with supposed universal applicability is the surest possible way of placing an entire acquisition program in jeopardy. Third, they must be easy to use—but not overly rigid. Because most structured frameworks of analysis run the risk of promoting mechanical solutions to complicated policy issues, formal screening and evaluation procedures must not be allowed to crowd out more informal, spontaneous contributions to the decision-making process.

Fourth, and perhaps most important, an effective acquisition screening system must serve as a mechanism for communicating corporate goals and personal knowledge among the parties involved. The analytic concepts and language inherent in such a system can significantly aid managers in implementing an acquisition program that is conceptually sound, internally consistent, and economically justifiable.

This article will focus on guidelines for screening acquisitions that diversify the acquirer's operations. Our interest in such acquisitions is prompted by two considerations.

First, in today's low-growth yet volatile environment, most companies with high-growth goals or an imbalanced portfolio of businesses find diversification necessary. Only a few companies have both the organizational and the technological traits for successful diversification through internal development and thus acquisition becomes the only alternative.

Second, large companies seeking expansion opportunities often find significant antitrust barriers in their pursuit of those acquisition candidates that make the greatest strategic and business sense. These high-potential acquisitions are companies closely related to existing businesses. However, the company that reaches for the benefits of scale economies, production efficiencies, or market rationalizations will, in many cases, run afoul of antitrust legislation.

Acquisitions for diversification can be related or unrelated to the original business. Each type has important variants.

Related acquisitions that might be called "supplementary" involve entry into new product markets where a company can use its existing functional skills or resources. Such acquisitions are typically most valuable to companies with a strong competitive position and a desire to extend their corporate competence to new areas of opportunity. The base on which this form of diversifying acquisition is built can either be a proprietary functional skill, as is the case for many of the major pharmaceutical and chemical companies, or a more general corporate capability, such as Gillette showed in disposable consumer products or United Technologies in capital goods.

Related acquisitions that are "complementary" rather than supplementary involve adding functional skills or resources to the company's existing distinctive competence while leaving its product-market commitment relatively unchanged. This type of acquisition is most valuable to companies in attractive industries whose competitive or strategic position could be strengthened by changing (or adding to) their value-added position in the commercial chain.

A classic example would be an original-equipment automotive parts manufacturer expanding into the distribution of replacement parts to secure a more stable, controllable market. Such a strategy often leads to a form of vertical integration as these new functional skills and/or resources are more closely linked to the diversifying company's core businesses. The acquisitions of American Television and Communications by Time, Inc. or Cardiac Pacemakers by Eli Lilly represent this complementary type of strategy.

Unrelated acquisitions involve entry into businesses with product markets or key success factors unrelated to existing corporate activities. These unrelated businesses can be managed either actively or passively. In active management, the corporate office becomes heavily involved in evaluating the new division's objectives and in establishing a highly competitive internal market for capital funds. Conglomerates such as Teledyne, Gulf & Western, and International Telephone and Telegraph typify companies pursuing this approach. In passive management, corporate headquarters usually limits its involvement to investment reviews, but there may be a centralized financing or banking function. The recent U.S. acquisitions by Thomas Tilling, Thyssen, and the Flick Group are all examples of this strategy. Diversified U.S. companies like U.S. Industries, IU International, and Alco Standard have historically followed this strategy, although recent economic events have forced the corporate office in each of these instances to take a more active management role.

The choice of a particular acquisition strategy largely depends on identifying the route that best uses the company's existing asset base and special resources. When a company can export (or import) surplus functional skills and resources relevant to its industrial or commercial setting, it should consider related acquisitions as an attractive strategic option. On the other hand, a company that has a special capacity to (1) analyze the strategies and financial requirements of a wide range of businesses, (2) tolerate—and even encourage—a lack of uniformity in the organization's structure, and (3) transfer surplus financial resources and general management skills among subsidiaries when necessary can exploit the potential benefits of unrelated acquisitions.

Acquisition Guidelines

The decision to pursue a specific type of diversifying acquisition provides the context for drawing up precise guidelines. Although every acquisition-minded company should undertake an audit of corporate strengths and weaknesses as well as an analysis of its risk-return profile and cash flow characteristics, the process of developing acquisition guidelines for related diversification should differ in focus and in content from what is used for unrelated diversification.

Related Diversification

The most significant shareholder benefits from related acquisitions accrue when the special skills and industry knowledge of one merger partner can help improve the competitive position of the other. It is worth stressing again that not only must these special skills and resources exist in one of the two partners, but they must also be transferable to the other. Thus, acquisition guidelines would describe those companies with functional skills and resources that would either add to or benefit from the company's resource package.

Lest such identification appear too obvious or elementary, consider the dilemma that Ciba-Geigy Corporation faced in its 1974 acquisition of Airwick Industries. Ciba-Geigy's products were almost entirely specialty chemicals and pharmaceuticals. Its corporate objectives were to continue to improve its long-term profits through new products derived from its extensive research program and from acquisitions in related fields. An attractive acquisition, according to Ciba-Geigy's acquisition task force, should:

☐ Participate in growing markets.

☐ Have a proprietary position in its markets.

☐ Have operations likely to be favorably affected by Ciba-Geigy's know-how in both research and development and the manufacture and marketing of complex synthetic organic chemicals.

☐ Be product rather than service oriented.

☐ Have sales of $50 million or more.

☐ Earn a good gross profit margin on sales.

☐ Have the potential for a return on investment of 10% or more.

☐ Be involved in such activities as specialty chemicals; proprietary pharmaceuticals; cosmetic and toiletry products; animal health products; proprietary household and garden products; medical supplies; products and services related to air, liquid, and solid waste treatment; or photochemicals and related products.

The search—a model of intelligent acquisition behavior—involved reviewing more than 18,000 companies in-house, along with an outside computer review. In addition, the company circulated the acquisition criteria among commercial and investment banking firms for their suggestions, and the task force worked with the company's divisions to identify attractive candidates. All told, about 100 companies came through this screen and were scrutinized more closely. Among these was Airwick Industries.

Airwick had 1973 sales of $33.5 million, net earnings of $2.7 million, and a return on shareholders' investment of 22.5%. The company's principal products were air fresheners and a full line of sanitary maintenance items (such as disinfectants, cleansers, insecticides with odor-counteracting features, and some swimming pool products). Over the previous five years, the rapidly growing air freshener market had become extremely competitive. Bristol-Myers, American Home Products, and S. C. Johnson had all entered the market. Although Airwick's financial performance had been good, it was clearly facing financial pressures in meeting the marketing onslaught of these major consumer products companies.

After several weeks of extensive interviews and analysis, Ciba-Geigy's task force concluded that Airwick was a sound company that had numerous potential synergies with Ciba-Geigy. The task force reported that acquisition of Airwick would be an attractive way of entering the household products business, if Ciba-Geigy had a strategic interest in this area. The tentativeness of this conclusion suggests that the acquisition guidelines failed to provide sufficient criteria for a final choice of the acquisition candidate.

Related diversification requires that new businesses or activities have a coherence or "fit" with the existing businesses of the acquirer. Achieving this fit involves exploring a range of possible choices. A quick review of Ciba-Geigy's eight acquisition guidelines finds only two that express any notion of strategic fit (third and fourth). The company's distinctive skills lay in its sophisticated research in organic chemicals and its technologically advanced production skills. Relative to many other companies, Ciba-Geigy did not require nor perhaps encourage an advanced marketing program.

If Ciba-Geigy's objectives were to build on these skills and talents a strategy of related-supplementary diversification, attractive acquisition candidates would have similar critical success variables. Specifically, such businesses would:

1   Require high levels of chemically based research and development skills.
2   Manufacture products by chemical processes requiring a high degree of engineering or technical know-how.
3   Sell principal products on technically based performance specifications.
4   Not require heavy advertising or expensive distribution systems that would take resources away from the maintenance of distinctive R&D and manufacturing capabilities.

Ciba-Geigy would have steered away from businesses that were either marketing intensive or involved in the production of commodity chemicals, including many of those businesses it had targeted.

Alternatively, if Ciba-Geigy had wished to add important skills and resources in new functional activities—a related-complementary diversification strategy—attractive acquisition candidates would have experience in large-scale manufacturing, marketing, and distribution of chemically based products. They would be businesses:

1 Whose resource inputs could include Ciba-Geigy's specialty chemicals.
2 Whose success depends highly on chemical usage or application.
3 Whose production and/or distribution involve chemically based products.
4 Whose key success factor is marketing oriented. This may include, but is not limited to, companies with extensive distribution systems, well-known brand names, and/or a tradition of customer acceptance.

These quite different sets of acquisition guidelines, although both seeking related diversification, help explain the task force's dilemma with Airwick. Lacking precise diversification objectives and acquisition guidelines, the task force analyzed Airwick according to related-supplementary criteria, which required skills similar to those of Ciba-Geigy. However, Airwick's key success factors were quite different from Ciba-Geigy's, and Ciba-Geigy's functional strengths were largely irrelevant to Airwick's future. Naturally, the task force felt the need to hedge its recommendations until it had more meaningful acquisition guidelines for marketing-oriented companies.

The lesson of this case is simple but fundamental. Companies pursuing a strategy of growth into related fields must decide whether to expand existing skills and resources into new product markets or whether to add new functional skills and resources.

Unrelated Diversification

The principal benefits for companies pursuing unrelated acquisitions stem from improved corporate management of working capital, resource allocation, or capital financing and lead to a cash flow for the combined company that is either larger or less risky than its component parts. A company pursuing unrelated acquisitions therefore can usefully focus its acquisition criteria on the size and riskiness of a business's cash flow and the compatibility of this cash flow pattern with its own cash flow profile. Once again, lest this appear too obvious, consider the uncertainty faced by General Cinema Corporation.

General Cinema, the nation's largest operator of multiple-auditorium theater complexes and largest soft drink bottler, has compiled an enviable financial record. Both return-on-equity and earnings growth have exceeded 20% for the last decade. By the mid-1970s, the company had reduced the large amount of debt it had incurred while actively acquiring soft drink bottlers. It then began an acquisition search for a "third leg of the stool."

General Cinema's acquisition guidelines indicated a preference for well-run small- to medium-sized companies ($5 million to $20 million in pretax earnings) whose consumer- or leisure-oriented products had unique characteristics that protected them against competition. Senior managers spoke of using the company's competence in any new acquisition. All this suggests some very general related-diversification strategy.

General Cinema's actions suggest, however, that this strategy was not followed. Its soft drink bottling business is not closely related to the multiple-auditorium theater business in either a product-market or a functional skill sense, nor were several of its previous diversification attempts, which involved bowling alleys, FM radio stations, and furniture retailing.

Thus, in General Cinema's case, the difference between the company's espoused theory of diversification and its actual behavior is clear. Assuming, therefore, it had a realistic interest in unrelated diversification, what additional acquisition guidelines could usefully structure General Cinema's search for an attractive unrelated acquisition candidate?

Turning first to General Cinema's risk profile, one finds a high level of risk at the corporate level (its stock had a beta in excess of 1.8) but relatively low levels of risk at the operating subsidiary level. This divergence in risk levels was due to management's policy of aggressive financial leverage with a debt-to-equity ratio (including capitalized leases) exceeding 3 to 1. By incurring high levels of financial leverage to increase its risk level, rather than assuming either operating or competitive risk, General Cinema was creating value for its shareholders.

A cash flow analysis of General Cinema's product-market portfolio reinforces these conclusions. All of General Cinema's divisions were classic cash cows—the largest competitors in mature, low-growth industries. In addition, the competitive positions of both the theater and bottling divisions were especially strong due to the franchise nature of both markets. Because both movie theaters and bottling operations are capital-intensive businesses, their cash flows, relative to many industries, were high. General Cinema's cash flow strength was likely to increase as continued growth in revenues and financial leverage interacted to generate an increasing surplus of cash funds.

In short, General Cinema showed many of the characteristics of a well-managed, unrelated diversifier. In fact, the distinctive competence General Cinema's senior managers often referred to consisted of well-developed planning and control skills in the corporate office, a key success variable for many such companies. Thus, additional acquisition guidelines for General Cinema, reflecting an unrelated-active strategy, could be as follows:

1 The acquisition candidate should be asset intensive. The assets could either be fixed, such as buildings and equipment, or intangible, such as trademarks, franchises, or goodwill. In either case, they should be well established with significant on-going value in order to be "bankable."

2   Since high levels of debt would be used, the acquisition's assets should create high barriers to entry. This implies products relatively immune to technological obsolescence or markets not exposed to significant levels of internal competition or external pressure.

3   Since General Cinema's surplus cash flow is increasing, an attractive acquisition should have significant growth potential over an extended period of time.

4   The acquisition candidate may have a low pretax return on invested capital (say 16%). However, total invested capital (debt, leases, and equity) should be at least three times the equity investment. Reflecting this (potential) leverage, the pretax return on equity should be high (at least 30%).

5   The requirements for relative immunity to market change and a high growth rate imply that the acquisition would be service oriented rather than technology based.

6   For senior managers to feel comfortable with the acquisition, they should market or distribute products or services to the consuming public.

7   Because General Cinema lacks surplus general managers, the acquisition should have good operating managers. Successful integration into General Cinema requires that the acquisition be adaptable to intensive planning and financial controls.

Most of the guidelines are as applicable to companies managing unrelated acquisitions passively as to companies operating actively. However, the criteria requiring integration into an intensive planning and financial control system and a corporate-managed resource allocation process embody those elements found in most actively managed portfolios of unrelated businesses.

The Ciba-Geigy and General Cinema cases clearly show how closely tied acquisition guidelines should be to overall corporate strategy. Effective acquisition guidelines must reflect carefully thought-out corporate objectives. In situations where the objectives (and especially diversification objectives) lack specificity or relevance, acquisition guidelines will be vague and have limited use in structuring a process for productive acquisition search and screening.

Screening the Candidates

Once an acquisition-minded company has established detailed and comprehensive guidelines, it can develop its own system for identifying promising candidates. This screening system should identify candidates with the greatest potential of creating value for the acquiring company's shareholders.

As we said earlier, economic value is created only when diversifying acquisitions lead to a free cash flow for the combined company (1) that is greater than could be realized from a portfolio investment in the two companies or (2) whose variability is smaller than would occur from a portfolio investment in the two companies.

We have identified eight principal ways in which one or both of these conditions can be met through diversifying acquisitions as well as several additional ways that are not, strictly speaking, due to diversification.[1] Each involves the way in which the two companies' resource structures can be successfully integrated to form a more efficient business unit.

The following list briefly outlines those economic, strategic, and managerial variables that have the greatest potential impact on value creation. These variables can be divided into two broad categories—those dealing with the candidate's risk-return profile and those dealing with the candidate's integration potential.

Risk-Return Variables

Return characteristics principally concern the size and timing of an acquisition's prospective cash flows. Although such characteristics are often thought of as company specific, many industries show readily identifiable cash flow patterns over their business cycles and/or their life cycles.

Size and Period of Cash Flow. These variables focus on the pattern of free cash flows into and out of the acquisition over time. Generally, a period of investment (negative cash flow) during industry growth is followed by a period of return (positive cash flow) during maturity. A specific acquisition's cash flow pattern will reflect its capital intensity, profitability, growth rate, and stage of maturity.

Noncapitalized Strategic Investments. These are investments in assets that are not reflected on the company's balance sheet, but are nevertheless important to its competitive success. Such assets as R&D skills, production technology, and market power (through advertising or distribution presence) are typically highly illiquid, but are often the most effective competitive weapons and market entry barriers a company has.

Returns Due to Unique Characteristics. Returns from the intangible assets developed through "strategic expenses" are often high, because along with specialized management skills they usually represent a company's distinctive competence. Alternatively, high returns may reflect entrepreneurial talents or access to one-of-a-kind sources of supply. Care should be given to distinguishing between company characteristics that can be developed and unique characteristics such as entrepreneurial talent, government franchises, or access to low-cost natural resources.

Investment Liquidity. Liquidity primarily depends on the marketability of the investment's underlying assets. Generally, the less risky an asset and the higher its collateral value, the easier it is to convert into cash. Highly liquid assets seldom provide distinct competitive advantages, however, or yield high rates of return.

Every return (or cash flow) has some level of risk; normally, the greater the potential returns, the greater the risks. A critical part of management's job is to control these risks so that the risk-return trade-off becomes more attractive than otherwise.

Vulnerability to Exogenous Changes in Supply or Demand. These risks arise from exposure to changes outside the company's control or, alternatively, the inability of managers to influence their business environment. The risks faced by a company depend on how critical a specific environmental factor is to the company, how readily available substitutes are, and how specialized the company's internal resources are. The greater the company's ability to lay off or pass on these environmental risks in the marketplace, the more stable its cash flow and the lower its risk.

Ease of Market Entry and Exit. Generally, the easier market entry or exit is, the more likely it is that industry rates of return will be driven toward normal or risk-adjusted levels. Entry-exit barriers can include capital requirements, specialized skills and resources, market presence, and government licenses or permits. Michael E. Porter described how knowledge about and use of entry and exit barriers can be critical in corporate strategy and competitive rivalry.[2]

Excess Productive Capacity. The risk of excess capacity is directly linked to market growth and the nature of capital investment to meet that growth. If it is most efficient to add new productive capacity in large increments of fixed investment (with corresponding sunk costs) and if these assets are long-lived (or with similar technological efficiencies), significant incentives to maintain volume through price cutting will exist whenever one competitor's relative demand falls off. Where market demand is relatively price inelastic, everyone in the industry will suffer revenue losses and reduced profitability.

Gross Margin Stability. This is closely related to production capacity risks and the ease of market entry and exit. Gross margins are good indicators of profitability and the availability of cash flow to support the development of more competitive technological, marketing, or administrative systems. The stability of gross margins also indicates the relative attractiveness of increasing operating leverage by substituting capital investment (with its fixed costs) for variable costs in the production process.

Competitive Strength. This depends on market share position, vulnerability to external forces in the marketplace, and position vis-à-vis suppliers and purchasers. Substantial evidence shows that in many industries companies with high market share have higher cash flows and higher returns on investment than those with low market share. If, however, a high market share position requires large investments in relatively specialized assets (fixed or intangible), these companies may also be highly vulnerable to major changes in the marketplace. Such external market risks include technological obsolescence, swift changes in consumption patterns, and new distribution or marketing systems accompanying changing demographics or technology. Finally, shifts in the bargaining strengths, or competitive positions, of suppliers or purchasers may substantially alter the costs or benefits of internal market share positions.

Societal Liabilities. The increasing legislation concerning social issues and the public welfare has altered the costs and rates of returns of many companies. Driving forces behind this legislation include environmental concerns, consumer protectionism, and employee safety and benefits.

Political Risk. Many companies have discovered that political and environmental risks may be significantly greater than the strategic, competitive, or technological risks faced in day-to-day business. The Mideast crisis and the continued turbulence in much of the Third World are only the most obvious instances. Unstable economic and monetary policy in the United States and trade policy in Japan are other, equally important, facets. Failure to assess and manage these risks correctly may render an otherwise successful corporate strategy irrelevant.

Each of these risk measures reflects one particular aspect of an asset's or a company's risk profile. How managers handle these risks as well as the inherent economic characteristics of the asset can be summarized through the following two capital market risk measures:

☐ *Financial risk.* This refers to the burden of fixed contractual payments incurred to own an asset. The greater this fixed burden (usually through debt or lease payments), the greater the financial risk. Skilled managers often use financial risk as an integral part of corporate strategy.

☐ *Systematic and unsystematic risk.* These measure the volatility (or the riskiness) of the returns of an asset or a business relative to the returns of all other assets in the marketplace. Systematic or market-related risk, which is most relevant to equity investors because it directly influences market value, reflects a company's inherent cash flow volatility and financial risk relative to the volatility of the economy in general. Unsystematic risk measures the risk specific to a particular company or asset. It can be reduced or eliminated by investors through portfolio diversification.

Integration Potential

The second set of criteria a diversifying company should consider in developing its screening program concerns the acquisition's potential for successful integration. Such criteria are often much more important for a related diversifier than for an unrelated diversifier. In fact, a related diversifier may well focus most of its efforts in this area, because its corporate strategy and business commitments will render many risk-return criteria meaningless. Nevertheless, issues of organizational compatibility and the availability of general management skills are critical to the success of all diversifying companies.

Supplementary Skills and Resources. These criteria principally reflect a related-supplementary diversification strategy. Consequently, they focus on a company's ability to transfer and effectively use the skills and resources of one partner to the competitive advantage of the other. Generally, the potential benefits of this type of merger increase as the shared skills and resources constitute an increasingly larger element in the cost of doing business.

Complementary Skills and Resources. These criteria reflect a related-complementary diversification strategy. They focus on improving the competitive position of the business by adding new functional skills and resources to the existing resource base.

Financial Fit-Risk Pooling Benefits. These criteria are more important in unrelated than in related diversification. They focus on developing an internal capital market that is more efficient than the external capital marketplace. These benefits can arise out of improved working capital (cash) management, improved investment management (cross-subsidization), improved resource allocation, or more aggressive financial leverage.

Availability of General Management Skills. Talented general managers are essential whenever value creation depends on the revitalization of underused assets. A surplus of general management resources in either partner must always be considered an extremely positive feature.

Organizational Compatibility. As any experienced diversifier will know, this is a critical issue. All of the previous criteria identify the potential for value creation, which can be realized only by an organization that can effectively exploit this potential and thereby create a more competitive enterprise.

Meeting Individual Corporate Needs

An acquisition screening system should reflect a company's specific objectives. For example, a currently cash-rich company expecting to face substantial capital investment demands in five years might articulate its size and period of investment criteria as: "The most favorable investment pattern (purchase price plus subsequent infusion of funds into the acquisition) is a maximum of $100 million over the next three-year period. The acquired company should become financially self-sufficient by the end of the third year and generate surplus cash flow by the fifth year.''

By composing such statements, a company can tailor generic guidelines often found in acquisition screening grids to its own unique needs. Where guidelines or screening criteria are complex or especially important to the acquiring company, any particular measure may require more than one statement. Similarly, the desired characteristics of industries and companies may be expressed in either positive or negative terms depending on the acquiring company's resources and objectives.

Developing these criteria should involve all members of the group or task force responsible for formulating and implementing the acquisition program. Each should generate descriptive statements based on one's understanding of the company's objectives and needs. Subsequent discussions among these persons can then lead to a single set of generally accepted and explicit screening criteria.

Once formal statements or criteria have been developed, it is sometimes useful to establish weightings or scoring ranges for each measure. These scoring ranges will reflect the importance of each item to the acquiring company.[3] Specific designation of the value of each measure forces managers to discuss the entire acquisition in terms of corporate objectives, resources, and skills.

Such a discussion also ensures internal consistency of the program. Wide discrepancies may signal that managers differ in their perceptions of the company's objectives, strategy, or distinctive competence or, alternatively, that they have either overlooked or understood only implicitly key elements in the diversification strategy.

As the acquisition task force screens industries, industry subgroups, and individual companies, the process will typically be iterative, reducing the potential acquisition universe to a smaller and smaller size. Industry subgroups (companies sharing the same key success factor or similar products and/or markets) will replace industries, and companies will replace industry subgroups until a limited set of candidates exists.

At each step in the screening process, the managers involved should individually evaluate the potential candidates and then meet to analyze their evaluations and discuss any major differences. Managers should ask: Do the results make intuitive sense? Why is there such a wide (or narrow) spread in the point scores? Has some critical element been overlooked?

As the screening process develops, company strategists should modify both the explicit screening criteria and their scoring ranges as new information about the potential acquisition and/or the environment emerge. Some diversifiers may also be useful to make the statements more detailed as the screening process narrows attention to fewer candidates or to eliminate certain criteria altogether. Generally, the need to revise statements will be less for related diversifiers than for unrelated diversifiers, since the former typically have a smaller universe of candidates to choose from. Clear communication of objectives and differences of opinion is particularly important since, once an acquisition decision has been made, a company can reverse itself only with very high financial and organizational costs.

This procedure should stimulate the flow of information and judgments among those responsible for the acquisition program and lead to a questioning of assumptions, provide a critical analysis of differences of opinion, and improve the consistency between corporate objectives and resources. Just as the capital budget or the operating budget can be used as a communications tool, so too can the acquisition screening grid serve an important communications function.

Potential for Value Creation

The last step in the screening process is determination of the candidate's potential for value creation for the shareholders of the acquiring company. This potential should then be compared to the cost of the acquisition as well as to the company's other investment opportunities (including the repurchase of its own stock).

In many ways, this procedure is similar to capital budgeting exercises that use the notion of net present value or discounted cash flow, but the analysis of a potential acquisition is significantly more complex than most capital budgeting decisions. Whereas the typical investment project involves assets with risks reasonably similar to those already in the company's portfolio and under the control of familiar managers, this is not the case with many acquisition candidates. Not only may the acquired asset's risks be different but the managers of an acquired company are often of unknown quality. Even where some familiarity exits, the managers' attitudes and motivation can change radically after the acquisition is consummated.

Another significant difference between an acquisition and the typical investment project is that the capital marketplace acts as a pricing mechanism to equate the value of a company with its risk-return characteristics. A lucky acquirer may well find a bargain or, more precisely, a company whose intrinsic value is greater than its market value plus the transaction costs necessary to acquire it.

Much more likely, however, is the case where an acquisition candidate is not undervalued relative to its existing level of cash flow and risk but rather is underusing its asset base. In this case, the acquirer will have to make extensive changes in the acquired company's management and/or use of assets for the acquisition to be economically justifiable. These changes will result typically in a company whose risk and expected cash flow are vastly different from what they previously were. Historic measures of this asset's performance may well be useless in the evaluation of future prospects.

The specific mechanics of net present value (or the discounted cash flow valuation process) appear in almost any financial handbook and are in the repertoire of most investment bankers or management consultants. (For a good summary of this evaluation process, see Article 23 in this book by Alfred Rappaport.) For discounted cash flow to be useful in acquisition analysis, it should be readily adaptable in the following three areas:

1 Developing detailed cash flow projections (including additional capital investments) over the acquired company's period of ownership.
2 Establishing relevant rates of return for the acquired company (and its constituent parts) based on its prospective risk characteristics and its capital structure.
3 Performing sensitivity analyses under the various economic, operating, and financial scenarios likely to be faced.

While this approach seems straightforward and objective, it is in practice much more complex and intuitive. Wherever operating, financial, or strategic changes are to be made in the acquired company's businesses, simple extrapolation or projection of current performance is, at best, risky. Similarly, if integration with the acquirer is to occur, as in related diversification, managers must evaluate changes in the cash flows and risk levels of both acquirer and acquired. Virtually every attempt to achieve one of the several potential benefits of diversification will lead to subtle yet important changes in the combined company's cash flow and risk characteristics. Careful use and a thorough understanding of the valuation process are of paramount importance, for slight errors in estimating these cash flows or risk levels can lead to valuation prices that differ by 30% or 40%.

Nevertheless, a careful application of the method we have outlined will force a company to be as concrete as possible in its assessment of future risks and returns. No one formula or method, least of all a simplified discounted cash flow analysis, should be expected to reveal by itself the best option or decision. The worth of any screening and evaluation system will vary according to both the quality of information used and the ability of managers to use this tool without crowding out important intuitive judgments about the compatibility of corporate cultures, the quality of an acquisition candidate's management, and the long-term strength of a candidate's competitive position.

The room for error in making these judgments is considerable. The anticipated benefits of an acquisition are often greater than those finally realized. Reaping benefits that stem from operating synergies requires considerable time and management effort. The knowledge of which benefits are achievable and at what costs comes from both prior experience and a strong sense of administrative feasibility. These personal characteristics of decision makers, along with the ability to value future returns accurately, lie at the base of a successful acquisition screening system.

Preparing the Ground

Executives often ask why they should have elaborate acquisition guidelines when such decisions must often be made without sufficient time for detailed, comprehensive analysis or when candidates best suited to their company's needs are not available. To summarize, formal acquisition guidelines can help companies prepare themselves for swift action in three ways:

First, working through a formal process in periods of relative calm tends to reinforce a broad understanding among executives of the company's objectives. Given the complexities of organizational life in the modern corporation, this benefit is not trivial.

Second, experience with a structured process, such as articulating acquisition guidelines or writing specific screening criteria, leads to widely shared assumptions about the company's strengths and weaknesses and its special needs and to a general agreement on what is most important for future profitability and corporate development.

Third, working within a formal system develops a common language or set of concepts relevant to the acquisition decision. This language system and the analytic framework it represents serve to ensure that key decision makers follow similar logic when acquisition opportunities suddenly appear and quick decisions are necessary.

The issue concerning the availability of acquisition candidates is often overemphasized. Most companies, especially those that are publicly owned, are available at a price. In the capital markets, where there is a continual auction of corporate securities, companies change hands every day. The real question is not whether attractive candidates are available but whether the company's potential to create value for the acquirer's shareholders is sufficient to justify the purchase price.

Notes

1. See our book, *Diversification Through Acquisition: Strategies for Creating Economic Value* (New York, Free Press, 1979).

2. Michael E. Porter, "How Competitive Forces Shape Strategy," *HBR*, March–April 1979, p. 137.

3. See our book, *Diversification Through Acquisition*, p. 194, for a detailed explanation of how to develop a weighting system.

23

Strategic Analysis for More Profitable Acquisitions

ALFRED RAPPAPORT

As more and more corporations see acquisitions and mergers as an important part of their growth strategy, the acquisitions market has become intensely competitive, and buyers are paying a substantial premium for target companies. This author describes a framework for acquisitions analysis that evaluates both the buying and the selling company and helps the buyer decide, among other things, the maximum price the buyer should pay for a particular company as well as the best way to finance the acquisition.

Less than a decade after the frantic merger activity of the late 1960s, we are again in the midst of a major wave of corporate acquisitions. In contrast to the 1960s, when acquirers were mainly freewheeling conglomerates, the merger movement in the 1970s includes such long-established giants of U.S. industry as General Electric, Gulf Oil, and Kennecott Copper. Because of the decline in the value of the dollar and the greater political stability of the United States, foreign companies also have become increasingly active buyers of U.S. companies during the past few years.

Most acquisitions are accomplished with cash today, rather than with packages of securities as was common in the 1960s. Finally, the current merger movement involves the frequent use of tender offers that often lead to contested bids and to the payment of substantial premiums above the premerger market value of the target company. In 1978, cash tender offer premiums averaged more than 70% above premerger market values.

The popular explanation for the recent merger rage is that the market is "undervaluing" many solid companies, thus making it substantially cheaper

Published 1979.

to buy rather than to build. Couple this belief with the fact that many corporations are enjoying relatively strong cash positions and the widely held view that government regulation and increased uncertainty about the economy make internal growth strategies relatively unattractive, and we see why mergers and acquisitions have become an increasingly important part of corporate growth strategy.

Despite all of the foregoing rationale, more than a few of the recent acquisitions will fail to create value for the acquirer's shareholders. After all, shareholder value depends not on premerger market valuation of the target company but on the actual acquisition price the acquiring company pays compared with the selling company's cash flow contribution to the combined company.

Only a limited supply of acquisition candidates is available at the price that enables the acquirer to earn an acceptable return on investment. A well-conceived financial evaluation program that minimizes the risk of buying an economically unattractive company or paying too much for an attractive one is particularly important in today's seller's market. The dramatic increase in premiums that must be paid by a company bidding successfully calls for more careful analysis by buyers than ever before.

Because of the competitive nature of the acquisition market, companies not only need to respond wisely, but often must respond quickly as well. The growing independence of corporate boards and their demand for better information to support strategic decisions such as acquisitions have raised the general standard for acquisition analysis. Finally, sound analysis convincingly communicated can yield substantial benefits in negotiating with the target company's management or, in the case of tender offers, its stockholders.

Malcolm S. Salter and Wolf A. Weinhold outlined seven principal ways in which companies can create value for their shareholders via acquisition in Article 22. In my article, I will show how management can estimate how much value a prospective acquisition will in fact create. In brief, I will present a comprehensive framework for acquisition analysis based on contemporary financial theory—an approach that has been profitably employed in practice. The analysis provides management and the board of the acquiring company with information both to make a decision on the candidate and to formulate an effective negotiating strategy for the acquisition.

Steps in the Analysis

The process of analyzing acquisitions falls broadly into three stages: planning, search and screen, and financial evaluation.

The acquisition planning process begins with a review of corporate objectives and product-market strategies for various strategic business units. The acquiring company should define its potential directions for corporate growth and diversification in terms of corporate strengths and weaknesses and an assessment of the company's social, economic, political, and technological environment. This analysis produces a set of acquisition objectives and criteria.

Specified criteria often include statements about industry parameters, such as projected market growth rate, degree of regulation, ease of entry, and capital versus labor intensity. Company criteria for quality of management, share of market, profitability, size, and capital structure also commonly appear in acquisition criteria lists.

The search and screen process is a systematic approach to compiling a list of good acquisition prospects. The search focuses on how and where to look for candidates, and the screening process selects a few of the best candidates from literally thousands of possibilities according to objectives and criteria developed in the planning phase.

Finally comes the financial evaluation process, which is the focus of this article. A good analysis should enable management to answer such questions as:

☐ What is the maximum price that should be paid for the target company?

☐ What are the principal areas of risk?

☐ What are the earnings, cash flow, and balance sheet implications of the acquisition?

☐ What is the best way of financing the acquisition?

Corporate Self-Evaluation

The financial evaluation process involves both a self-evaluation by the acquiring company and the evaluation of the candidate for acquisition. Although it is possible to conduct an evaluation of the target company without an in-depth self-evaluation first, in general this is the most advantageous approach.[1] The scope and detail of corporate self-evaluation will necessarily vary according to the needs of each company.

Two fundamental questions posed by a self-evaluation are: (1) How much is my company worth? (2) How would its value be affected by each of several scenarios? The first question involves generating a "most likely" estimate of the company's value based on management's detailed assessment of its objectives, strategies, and plans. The second question calls for an assessment of value based on the range of plausible scenarios that enable management to test the joint effect of hypothesized combinations of product-market strategies and environmental forces.

Corporate self-evaluation viewed as an economic assessment of the value created for shareholders by various strategic planning options promises potential benefits for all companies. In the context of the acquisition market, self-evaluation takes on special significance.

First, although a company might view itself as an acquirer, few companies are totally exempt from a possible takeover. During 1978 alone, 80 acquisitions exceeding $100 million were announced. The recent roster of acquired companies includes such names as Anaconda, Utah International, Babcock & Wilcox, Seven Up, Pet, Carborundum, and Del Monte. Self-evaluation provides management and the board with a continuing basis for responding to tender offers or acquisition inquiries responsibly and quickly. Second, the self-evaluation process might well call attention to strategic divestment opportunities. Finally, self-evaluation provides acquisition-minded companies a basis for assessing the comparative advantages of a cash versus an exchange-of-shares offer.

Acquiring companies commonly value the purchase price for an acquisition at the market value of the shares exchanged. This practice is not economically sound and could be misleading and costly to the acquiring company. A well-conceived analysis for an exchange-of-shares acquisition requires sound valuations of *both* buying and selling companies. If the acquirer's management believes the market is undervaluing its shares, then valuing the purchase price at market might well induce the company to overpay for the acquisition or to earn less than the minimum acceptable rate of return.

Conversely, if management believes the market is overvaluing its shares, then valuing the purchase price at market obscures the opportunity of offering the seller's shareholders additional shares while still achieving the minimum acceptable return.

Valuation of Acquisitions

Recently *Business Week* reported that as many as half of the major acquisition-minded companies are relying extensively on the discounted cash flow (DCF) technique to analyze acquisitions.[2] Although mergers and acquisitions involve a considerably more complex set of managerial problems than the purchase of an ordinary asset such as a machine or a plant, the economic substance of these transactions is the same. In each case, there is a current outlay made in anticipation of a stream of future cash flows.

Thus the DCF criterion applies not only to internal-growth investments, such as additions to existing capacity, but equally to external-growth investments, such as acquisitions. An essential feature of the DCF technique is that it explicitly takes into account that a dollar of cash received today is worth more than a dollar received a year from now, because today's dollar can be invested to earn a return during the intervening time.

To establish the maximum acceptable acquisition price under the DCF approach, estimates are needed for (1) the incremental cash flows expected to be generated because of the acquisition and (2) the cost of capital—that is, the minimum acceptable rate of return required by the market for new investments by the company.

In projecting the cash flow stream of a prospective acquisition, what should be taken into account is the cash flow contribution the candidate is expected to make to the acquiring company. The results of this projection may well differ from a projection of the candidate's cash flow as an independent company. This is so because the acquirer may be able to achieve operating economies not available to the selling company alone. Furthermore, acquisitions generally provide new postacquisition investment opportunities whose initial outlays and subsequent benefits also need to be incorporated in the cash flow schedule. Cash flow is defined as

(earnings before interest and taxes [EBIT]) × (1-income tax rate) + depreciation and other noncash charges − capital expenditures − cash required for increase in net working capital

In developing the cash flow schedule, two additional issues need to be considered: (1) What is the basis for setting the horizon date—that is, the date beyond which the cash flows associated with the acquisition are not specifically projected? (2) How is the residual value of the acquisition established at the horizon date?

A common practice is to forecast cash flows period by period until the level of uncertainty makes management too "uncomfortable" to go any farther. Although practice varies with industry setting, management policy, and the special circumstances of the acquisition, 5 or 10 years appear to be an arbitrarily set forecasting duration used in many situations. A better approach suggests that the forecast duration for cash flows should continue only as long as the expected rate of return on incremental investment required to support forecasted sales growth exceeds the cost-of-capital rate.

If for subsequent periods one assumes that the company's return on incremental investment equals the cost-of-capital rate, then the market would be indifferent whether management invests earnings in expansion projects or pays cash dividends that shareholders can in turn invest in identically risky opportunities yielding an identical rate of return. In other words, the value of the company is unaffected by growth when the company is investing in projects earning at the cost of capital or at the minimum acceptable risk-adjusted rate of return required by the market.

Thus, for purposes of simplification, we can assume a 100% payout of earnings after the horizon date or, equivalently, a zero growth rate without affecting the valuation of the company. (An implied assumption of this model is that the depreciation tax shield can be invested to maintain the company's productive capacity.) The residual value is then the present value of the resulting cash flow perpetuity beginning one year after the horizon date. Of course, if after the horizon date the return on investment is expected to decline below the cost-of-capital rate, this factor can be incorporated in the calculation.

When the acquisition candidate's risk is judged to be the same as the acquirer's overall risk, the appropriate rate for discounting the candidate's cash flow stream is the acquirer's cost of capital. The cost of capital or the minimum acceptable rate of return on new investments is based on the rate investors can expect to earn by investing in alternative, identically risky securities.

The cost of capital is calculated as the weighted average of the costs of debt and equity capital. For example, suppose a company's aftertax cost of debt is 5% and it estimates its cost of equity to be 15%. Furthermore, it plans to raise future capital in the following proportions: 20% by way of debt and 80% by equity. Exhibit 1 shows how to compute the company's average cost.

It is important to emphasize that the acquiring company's use of its own cost of capital to discount the target's projected cash flows is appropriate only when it can be safely assumed that the acquisition will not affect the riskiness of the acquirer. The specific riskiness of each prospective candidate should be taken into account in setting the discount rate, with higher rates used for more risky investments.

If a single discount rate is used for all acquisitions, then those with the highest risk will seem most attractive. Because the weighted average risk of its component segments determines the company's cost of capital, these high-risk acquisitions will increase a company's cost of capital and thereby decrease the value of its stock.

Case of Alcar Corporation

As an illustration of the recommended approach to acquisition analysis, consider the case of Alcar Corporation's interest in acquiring Rano Products. Alcar is a leading manufacturer and distributor in the industrial packaging and materials handling market. Sales in 1978 totaled $600 million. Alcar's acquisition strategy is geared toward buying companies with either similar marketing and distribution characteristics, similar production technologies, or a similar research and development orientation. Rano Products, a $50 million sales organization with an impressive new-product development record in industrial packaging, fits Alcar's general acquisition criteria particularly well. Premerger financial statements for Alcar and Rano are shown in Exhibit 2.

Exhibit 1. One Company's Average Cost of Capital

	Weight	Cost	Weighted Cost
Debt	.20	.05	.01
Equity	.80	.15	.12
Average cost of capital			.13

Exhibit 2.   Premerger Financial Statements for Alcar and Rano (in millions of dollars)

	Alcar	Rano
Statement of income (year ended December 31)		
Sales	$600.00	$50.00
Operating expenses	522.00	42.50
EBIT	78.00	7.50
Interest on debt	4.50	.40
Earnings before taxes	73.50	7.10
Income taxes	36.00	3.55
Net income	$37.50	$ 3.55
Number of common shares outstanding (in millions)	10.00	1.11
Earnings per share	$3.75	$3.20
Dividends per share	1.30	.64
Statement of financial position (at year-end)		
Net working capital	$180.00	$7.50
Temporary investments	25.00	1.00
Other assets	2.00	1.60
Fixed assets	216.00	20.00
Less accumulated depreciation	(95.00)	(8.00)
Total	$328.00	$22.10
Interest-bearing debt	$56.00	$5.10
Shareholders' equity	272.00	17.00
Total	$328.00	$22.10

Acquisition for Cash

The interactive computer model for corporate planning and acquisition analysis used in the Alcar evaluation to follow generates a comprehensive analysis for acquisitions financed by cash, stock, or any combination of cash, debt, preferred stock, and common stock. In this article, the analysis will concern only the cash and exchange-of-shares cases. In the cash acquisition case, the analysis follows six essential steps:

☐   Develop estimates needed to project Rano's cash flow contribution for various growth and profitability scenarios.

  ☐   Estimate the minimum acceptable rate of return for acquisition of Rano.

  ☐   Compute the maximum acceptable cash price to be paid for Rano under various scenarios and minimum acceptable rates of return.

  ☐   Compute the rate of return that Alcar will earn for a range of price offers and for various growth and profitability scenarios.

  ☐   Analyze the feasibility of a cash purchase in light of Alcar's current liquidity and target debt-to-equity ratio.

  ☐   Evaluate the impact of the acquisition on the earnings per share and capital structure of Alcar.

Step 1. Cash Flow Projections.   The cash flow formula presented earlier may be restated in equivalent form as

$$CF_t = S_{t-1}(1+g_t)(p_t)(1-T_t) - (S_t - S_{t-1})(f_t + w_t)$$

where:

CF = cash flow.

 S = sales.

 g = annual growth rate in sales.

 p = EBIT as a percentage of sales.

 T = income tax rate.

 f = capital investment required (i.e., total capital investment net of replacement of existing capacity estimated by depreciation) per dollar of sales increase.

 w = cash required for net working capital per dollar of sales increase.

Once estimates are provided for five variables, g, p, T, f, and w, it is possible to project cash flow.

    Exhibit 3 shows Alcar management's "most likely" estimates for Rano's operations, assuming Alcar control; Exhibit 4 shows a complete projected 10-year cash flow statement for Rano.

    Before developing additional scenarios for Rano, I should make some brief comments on how to estimate some of the cash flow variables. The income tax rate is the effective cash rate rather than a rate based on the accountant's income tax expense, which often includes a portion that is deferred. For some companies, a direct projection of capital investment requirements per dollar of sales increase will prove a difficult task.

    To gain an estimate of the recent value of this coefficient, simply take the sum of all capital investments less depreciation over the past 5 or 10 years and divide this total by the sales increase from the beginning to the end of the period. With this approach, the resulting coefficient not only represents the capital investment historically required per dollar of sales increase, but also impounds any cost increases for replacement of existing capacity.

Exhibit 3. Most Likely Estimates for Rano's Operations under Alcar Control

	Years		
	1–5	6–7	8–10
Sales growth rate (g)	.15	.12	.12
EBIT as a percentage of sales (p)	.18	.15	.12
Income tax rate (T)	.46	.46	.46
Capital investment per dollar of sales increase (f)	.20	.20	.20
Working capital per dollar of sales increase (w)	.15	.15	.15

Employing the cash flow formula for year 1:
$CF_1 = 50(1+.15)(.18)(1-.46) - (57.5-50)(.20+.15) = 2.96$

One should estimate changes in net working capital requirements with care. Actual year-to-year balance sheet changes in net working capital may not provide a good measure of the rise or decline in funds required. There are two main reasons for this: (1) the year-end balance sheet figures may not reflect the average or normal needs of the business during the year; and (2) both the accounts receivable and inventory accounts may overstate the magnitude of the funds committed by the company.

To estimate the additional cash requirements, the increased inventory investment should be measured by the variable costs for any additional units of inventory required and by the receivable investment in terms of the variable costs of the product delivered to generate the receivable rather than the absolute dollar amount of the receivable. (For an illustration of this calculation, see my Article 8.)

In addition to its most likely estimate for Rano, Alcar's management developed two additional (conservative and optimistic) scenarios for sales growth and EBIT-sales ratio. Exhibit 5 gives a summary of all three scenarios. Alcar's management may also wish to examine additional cases to test the effect of alternative assumptions about the income tax rate and capital investment and working capital requirements per dollar of sales increase.

Recall that cash flows should be forecast only for the period when the expected rate of return on incremental investment exceeds the minimum acceptable rate of return for the acquisition. It is possible to determine this in a simple yet analytical, nonarbitrary, fashion. To do so, we compute the minimum pretax return on sales (P_{min}) needed to earn the minimum acceptable rate of return on the acquisition (k) given the investment requirements for working capital (w) and fixed assets (f) for each additional dollar of sales and given a projected tax rate (T). The formula for P_{min} is:

$$P_{min} = \frac{(f+w)\,k}{(1-T)\,(1+k)}$$

Exhibit 4. Projected 10-Year Cash Flow Statement for Rano (in millions of dollars)

	Years									
	1	2	3	4	5	6	7	8	9	10
Sales	$57.50	$66.12	$76.04	$87.45	$100.57	$112.64	$126.15	$141.29	$158.25	$177.23
Operating expenses	47.15	54.22	62.36	71.71	82.47	95.74	107.23	124.34	139.26	155.97
EBIT	$10.35	$11.90	$13.69	$15.74	$18.10	$16.90	$18.92	$16.95	$18.99	$21.27
Income taxes on EBIT	4.76	5.48	6.30	7.24	8.33	7.77	8.70	7.80	8.74	9.78
Operating earnings after taxes	$5.59	$6.43	$7.39	$8.50	$9.78	$9.12	$10.22	$9.16	$10.25	$11.48
Depreciation	1.60	1.85	2.13	2.46	2.84	3.28	3.74	4.25	4.83	5.49
Less capital expenditures	(3.10)	(3.57)	(4.12)	(4.74)	(5.47)	(5.69)	(6.44)	(7.28)	(8.22)	(9.29)
Less increase in working capital	(1.13)	(1.29)	(1.49)	(1.71)	(1.97)	(1.81)	(2.03)	(2.27)	(2.54)	(2.85)
Cash flow	$2.96	$3.41	$3.92	$4.51	$5.18	$4.90	$5.49	3.86	$4.32	$4.84

Exhibit 5. Additional Scenarios for Sales Growth and EBIT/Sales

	Sales Growth			EBIT/Sales		
Scenario	Years 1–5	6–7	8–10	Years 1–5	6–7	8–10
1. Conservative	.14	.12	.10	.17	.14	.11
2. Most likely	.15	.12	.12	.18	.15	.12
3. Optimistic	.18	.15	.12	.20	.16	.12

Alcar's management believes that when Rano's growth begins to slow down, its working capital requirements per dollar of additional sales will increase from .15 to about .20 and its effective tax rate will increase from .46 to .50. As will be shown in the next section, the minimum acceptable rate of return on the Rano acquisition is 13%. Thus:

$$P_{min} = \frac{(.20 + .20)\,(.13)}{(1 - .50)\,(1 + .13)}$$
$$= .092.$$

Alcar's management has enough confidence to forecast pretax sales returns above 9.2% for only the next 10 years, and thus the forecast duration for the Rano acquisition is limited to that period.

Step 2. Estimate Minimum Acceptable Rate of Return for Acquisition. In developing a company's average cost of capital, measuring the aftertax cost of debt is relatively straightforward. The cost of equity capital, however, is more difficult to estimate.

Rational, risk-averse investors expect to earn a rate of return that will compensate them for accepting greater investment risk. Thus, in assessing the company's cost of equity capital or the minimum expected return that will induce investors to buy the company's shares, it is reasonable to assume that they will demand the risk-free rate as reflected in the current yields available in government bonds plus a premium for accepting equity risk.

Recently, the risk-free rate on government bonds has been in the neighborhood of 8.8%. By investing in a portfolio broadly representative of the overall equity market, it is possible to diversify away substantially all of the unsystematic risk—that is, risk specific to individual companies. Therefore, securities are likely to be priced at levels that reward investors only for the nondiversifiable market risk—that is, the systematic risk in movements in the overall market.

The risk premium for the overall market is the excess of the expected return on a representative market index such as the Standard & Poor's 500-stock index over the risk-free return. Empirical studies have estimated this market risk premium (representative market index minus risk-free rate) to average historically about 5 to 5.5%.[3] I will use a 5.2% premium in subsequent calculations.

Investing in an individual security generally involves more or less risk than investing in a broad market portfolio; thus one must adjust the market risk premium appropriately in estimating the cost of equity for an individual security. The risk premium for a security is the product of the market risk premium times the individual security's systematic risk, as measured by its beta coefficient.

The rate of return from dividends and capital appreciation on a market portfolio will, by definition, fluctuate identically with the market, and therefore its beta is equal to 1.0. A beta for an individual security is an index of its risk expressed as its volatility of return in relation to that of a market portfolio.[4] Securities with betas greater than 1.0 are more volatile than the market and thus would be expected to have a risk premium greater than the overall market risk premium or the average-risk stock with a beta of 1.0.

For example, if a stock moves 1.5% when the market moves 1%, the stock would have a beta of 1.5. Securities with betas less than 1.0 are less volatile than the market and would thus command risk premiums less than the market risk premium. In summary, the cost of equity capital may be calculated by the following equation:

$$k_E = R_F + B_j (R_M - R_F)$$

where:

k_E = cost of equity capital.
R_F = risk-free rate.
B_j = the beta coefficient.
R_M = representative market index.

The acquiring company, Alcar, with a beta of 1.0, estimated its cost of equity as 14% with the foregoing equation:

$$k_E = .088 + 1.0 (.052)$$
$$= \underline{.140}$$

Since interest on debt is tax deductible, the rate of return that must be earned on the debt portion of the company's capital structure to maintain the earnings available to common shareholders is the aftertax cost of debt. The aftertax cost of borrowed capital is Alcar's current beforetax interest rate (9.5%) times one minus its effective tax rate of 46%, which is equal to 5.1%. Alcar's target debt-to-equity ratio is .30, or, equivalently, debt is targeted at 23% and equity at 77% of its overall capitalization as Exhibit 6 shows Alcar's weighted average cost of capital. The appropriate rate for discounting Alcar cash flows to establish its estimated value is then 12%.

For new capital projects, including acquisitions, that are deemed to have about the same risk as the overall company, Alcar can use its 12%

Exhibit 6. Alcar's Weighted Average Cost of Capital

	Weight	Cost	Weighted Cost
Debt	.23	.051	.012
Equity	.77	.140	.108
Average cost of capital			.120

cost-of-capital rate as the appropriate discount rate. Because the company's cost of capital is determined by the weighted average risk of its component segments, the specific risk of each prospective acquisition should be estimated in order to arrive at the discount rate to apply to the candidate's cash flows.

Rano, with a beta coefficient of 1.25, is more risky than Alcar, with a beta of 1.0. Employing the formula for cost of equity capital for Rano:

$$k_E = .088 + 1.25 (.052)$$
$$= \underline{.153}$$

On this basis, the risk-adjusted cost of capital for the Rano acquisition is as shown in Exhibit 7.

Step 3. Compute Maximum Acceptable Cash Price. This step involves taking the cash flow projections developed in Step 1 and discounting them at the rate developed in Step 2. Exhibit 8 shows the computation of the maximum acceptable cash price for the most likely scenario. The maximum price of $44.51 million, or $40.10 per share, for Rano compares with a $25 current market price for Rano shares. Thus, for the most likely case, Alcar can pay up to $15 per share, or a 60% premium over current market, and still achieve its minimum acceptable 13% return on the acquisition.

Exhibit 9 shows the maximum acceptable cash price for each of the three scenarios for a range of discount rates. To earn a 13% rate of return, Alcar can pay at maximum $38 million ($34.25 per share), assuming the conservative scenario, and up to $53 million ($47.80 per share), assuming

Exhibit 7. Risk-Adjusted Cost of Capital for Rano Acquisition

	Weight	Cost	Weighted Cost
Debt	.23	.054[a]	.012
Equity	.77	.153	.118
Average risk-adjusted cost of capital			.130

[a]Beforetax debt rate of 10% times one minus the estimated tax rate of 46%.

Exhibit 8.   Maximum Acceptable Cash Price for Rano—Most Likely Scenario, with a Discount Rate of .130 (in millions of dollars)

Year	Cash Flow	Present Value	Cumulative Present Value
1	$ 2.96	$ 2.62	$ 2.62
2	3.41	2.67	5.29
3	3.92	2.72	8.01
4	4.51	2.76	10.77
5	5.13	2.81	13.59
6	4.90	2.35	15.94
7	5.49	2.33	18.27
8	3.86	1.45	19.72
9	4.32	1.44	21.16
10	4.84	1.43	22.59
Residual value	11.48	26.02[a]	48.61
Plus temporary investments not required for current operations			1.00
Less debt assumed			5.10
Maximum acceptable cash price			$44.51
Maximum acceptable cash price per share			$40.10

[a] $\dfrac{\text{Year 10 operating earnings after taxes}}{\text{Discount rate}} \times \text{year 10 discount factor} = \dfrac{11.48}{.13} \times .2946 = 26.02$

the optimistic scenario. Note that as Alcar demands a greater return on its investment, the maximum price it can pay decreases. The reverse is, of course, true as well. For example, for the most likely scenario, the maximum price decreases from $44.51 million to $39.67 million as the return requirement goes from 13% to 14%.

Step 4. Compute Rate of Return for Various Offering Prices and Scenarios.   Alcar management believes that the absolute minimum successful bid for Rano would be $35 million, or $31.50 per share. Alcar's investment bankers estimated that it may take a bid of as high as $45 million, or $40.50 per share, to gain control of Rano shares. Exhibit 10 presents the rates of return that will be earned for four different offering prices, ranging from $35 million to $45 million for each of the three scenarios.

Under the optimistic scenario, Alcar could expect a return of 14.4% if it were to pay $45 million. For the most likely case, an offer of $45 million would yield a 12.9% return, or just under the minimum acceptable rate of 13%. This is as expected, since the maximum acceptable cash price as calculated in Exhibit 8 is $44.51 million, or just under the $45 million offer.

Exhibit 9. Maximum Acceptable Cash Price for Three Scenarios and a Range of Discount Rates

Scenarios	Discount Rates				
	.11	.12	.13	.14	.15
1. Conservative					
Total price ($ millions)	$48.84	$42.91	$38.02	$33.93	$30.47
Per share price	44.00	38.66	34.25	30.57	27.45
2. Most likely					
Total price ($ millions)	57.35	50.31	44.51	39.67	35.58
Per share price	51.67	45.33	40.10	35.74	32.05
3. Optimistic					
Total price ($ millions)	68.37	59.97	53.05	47.28	42.41
Per share price	61.59	54.03	47.80	42.59	38.21

If Alcar attaches a relatively high probability to the conservative scenario, the risk associated with offers exceeding $38 million becomes apparent.

Step 5. Analyze Feasibility of Cash Purchase.   Although Alcar management views the relevant purchase price range for Rano as somewhere between $35 and $45 million, it must also establish whether an all-cash deal is feasible in light of Alcar's current liquidity and target debt-to-equity ratio. The maximum funds available for the purchase of Rano equal the postmerger debt capacity of the combined company less the combined premerger debt of the two companies plus the combined premerger temporary investments of the two companies. (Net working capital not required for everyday operations of the business is classified as "temporary investment.")

In an all-cash transaction governed by purchase accounting, the acquirer's shareholders' equity is unchanged. The postmerger debt capacity is then Alcar's shareholders' equity of $272 million times the targeted debt-to-equity ratio of .30, or $81.6 million. Alcar and Rano have premerger debt

Exhibit 10. Rate of Return for Various Offering Prices and Scenarios

		Offering Price			
	Total ($ millions)	$35.00	$38.00	$40.00	$45.00
Scenarios	Per share	$31.53	$34.23	$36.04	$40.54
1. Conservative		.137	.130	.126	.116
2. Most likely		.152	.144	.139	.129
3. Optimistic		.169	.161	.156	.144

balances of $56 million and $5.1 million, respectively, for a total of $61.1 million.

The unused debt capacity is thus $81.6 million minus $61.1 million, or $20.5 million. Add to this the combined temporary investments of Alcar and Rano of $26 million, and the maximum funds available for the cash purchase of Rano will be $46.5 million. A cash purchase is therefore feasible within the tentative price range of $35 to $45 million.

Step 6. Evaluate Impact of Acquisition on Alcar's EPS and Capital Structure. Because reported earnings per share (EPS) continue to be of great interest to the financial community, a complete acquisition analysis should include a comparison of projected EPS both with and without the acquisition. Exhibit 11 contains this comparative projection. The EPS stream with the acquisition of Rano is systematically greater than the stream without acquisition. The EPS standard, and particularly a short-term EPS standard, is not, however, a reliable basis for assessing whether the acquisition will in fact create value for shareholders.[5]

Several problems arise when EPS is used as a standard for evaluating acquisitions. First, because of accounting measurement problems, the EPS figure can be determined by alternative, equally acceptable methods—for example, LIFO versus FIFO. Second, the EPS standard ignores the time value of money. Third, it does not take into account the risk of the EPS stream. Risk is conditioned not only by the nature of the investment projects a company undertakes, but also by the relative proportions of debt and equity used to finance those investments.

A company can increase EPS by increasing leverage as long as the marginal return on investment is greater than the interest rate on the new debt. However, if the marginal return on investment is less than the risk-adjusted cost of capital or if the increased leverage leads to an increased cost of capital, then the value of the company could decline despite rising EPS.

Primarily because the acquisition of Rano requires that Alcar partially finance the purchase price with bank borrowing, the debt-to-equity ratios with the acquisition are greater than those without the acquisition (see Exhibit 11). Note that even without the Rano acquisition, Alcar is in danger of violating its target debt-to-equity ratio of .30 by the ninth year. The acquisition of Rano accelerates the problem to the fifth year. Whether Alcar purchases Rano or not, management must now be alert to the financing problem, which may force it to issue additional shares or reevaluate its present capital structure policy.

Acquisition for Stock

The first two steps in the acquisition-for-stock analysis, projecting Rano cash flows and setting the discount rate, have already been completed in connection with the acquisition-for-cash analysis developed in the previous section. The remaining steps of the acquisition-for-stock analysis are:

Exhibit 11. Alcar's Projected EPS, Debt-to-Equity Ratio, and Unused Debt Capacity—without and with Rano Acquisition

Year	EPS Without	EPS With	Debt/equity Without	Debt/equity With	Unused Debt Capacity (in millions of dollars) Without	Unused Debt Capacity (in millions of dollars) With
0	$ 3.75	$ 4.10	.21	.26	$25.60	$20.50
1	4.53	4.89	.19	.27	34.44	9.42
2	5.09	5.51	.17	.28	44.22	7.00
3	5.71	6.20	.19	.29	40.26	4.20
4	6.38	6.99	.21	.30	35.45	.98
5	7.14	7.87	.24	.31	29.67	-2.71
6	7.62	8.29	.26	.31	22.69	-7.77
7	8.49	9.27	.27	.32	14.49	-13.64
8	9.46	10.14	.29	.33	4.91	-22.34
9	10.55	11.33	.31	.34	-6.23	-32.36
10	11.76	12.66	.32	.35	-19.16	-43.88

Note: Assumed cash purchase price for Rano is $35 million.

☐ Estimate the value of Alcar shares.

☐ Compute the maximum number of shares that Alcar can exchange to acquire Rano under various scenarios and minimum acceptable rates of return.

☐ Evaluate the impact of the acquisition on the earnings per share and capital structure of Alcar.

Step 1. Estimate Value of Alcar Shares. Alcar conducted a comprehensive corporate self-evaluation that included an assessment of its estimated present value based on a range of scenarios. In the interest of brevity, I will consider here only its most likely scenario.

Management made most likely projections for its operations, as shown in Exhibit 12. Again using the equation for the cost of equity capital, the minimum EBIT as a percentage of sales needed to earn at Alcar's 12% cost of capital is 10.9%. Since management can confidently forecast pretax return on sales returns above 10.9% for only the next 10 years, the cash flow projections will be limited to that period.

Exhibit 13 presents the computation of the value of Alcar's equity. Its estimated value of $36.80 per share contrasts with its currently depressed market value of $22 per share. Because Alcar management believes its shares to be substantially undervalued by the market, in the absence of other compelling factors it will be reluctant to acquire Rano by means of an exchange of shares.

Exhibit 12. Most Likely Estimates for Alcar Operations without Acquisition

	Years		
	1–5	6–7	8–10
Sales growth rate	.125	.120	.120
EBIT as a percentage of sales	.130	.125	.125
Income tax rate	.460	.460	.460
Capital investment per dollar of sales increase	.250	.250	.250
Working capital per dollar of sales increase	.300	.300	.300

Exhibit 13. Estimated Present Value of Alcar Equity—Most Likely Scenario, with a Discount Rate of .120 (in millions of dollars)

Year	Cash Flow	Present Value	Cumulative Present Value
1	$ 6.13	$ 5.48	$ 5.48
2	6.90	5.50	10.98
3	7.76	5.53	16.51
4	8.74	5.55	22.06
5	9.83	5.58	27.63
6	10.38	5.26	32.89
7	11.63	5.26	38.15
8	13.02	5.26	43.41
9	14.58	5.26	48.67
10	16.33	5.26	53.93
Residual value	128.62	345.10[a]	399.03
Plus temporary investments not required for current operations			25.00
Less debt outstanding			56.00
Present value of Alcar equity			$368.03
Present value per share of Alcar equity			$ 36.80

$$[a] \frac{\text{Year 10 operating earnings after taxes}}{\text{Discount rate}} \times \text{year 10 discount factor} =$$

$$\frac{128.62}{.12} \times .32197 \qquad = 345.10$$

Exhibit 14. Calculation of Loss by Alcar Shareholders (in millions of dollars)

Alcar receives 86.27% of Rano's present value of $44.51 million (see Exhibit 8)	$38.4
Alcar gives up 13.73% of its present value of $368.03 million (see Exhibit 13)	(50.5)
Dilution of Alcar shareholders' value	$12.1

To illustrate, suppose that Alcar were to offer $35 million in cash for Rano. Assume the most likely case, that the maximum acceptable cash price is $44.51 million (see Exhibit 8); thus the acquisition would create about $9.5 million in value for Alcar shareholders. Now assume that instead Alcar agrees to exchange $35 million in market value of its shares in order to acquire Rano. In contrast with the cash case, in the exchange-of-shares case Alcar shareholders can expect to be worse off by $12.1 million.

With Alcar shares selling at $22, the company must exchange 1.59 million shares to meet the $35 million offer for Rano. There are currently 10 million Alcar shares outstanding. After the merger, the combined company will be owned 86.27%—that is, (10.00)/(10.00 + 1.59)—by current Alcar shareholders and 13.73% by Rano shareholders. The $12.1 million loss by Alcar shareholders can then be calculated as shown in Exhibit 14.

Step 2. Compute Maximum Number of Shares Alcar Can Exchange. The maximum acceptable number of shares to exchange for each of the three scenarios and for a range of discount rates appears in Exhibit 15. To earn a 13% rate of return, Alcar can exchange no more than 1.033, 1.210, and 1.442 million shares, assuming the conservative, most likely, and optimistic scenarios, respectively. Consider, for a moment, the most likely case. At a market value per share of $22, the 1.21 million Alcar shares exchanged would have a total value of $26.62 million, which is less than Rano's current market

Exhibit 15. Maximum Acceptable Shares to Exchange for Three Scenarios and a Range of Discount Rates (in millions)

Scenarios	Discount Rates				
	.11	.12	.13	.14	.15
1. Conservative	1.327	1.166	1.033	0.922	0.828
2. Most likely	1.558	1.367	1.210	1.078	0.967
3. Optimistic	1.858	1.630	1.442	1.285	1.152

value of $27.75 million—that is, 1.11 million shares at $25 per share. Because of the market's apparent undervaluation of Alcar's shares, an exchange ratio likely to be acceptable to Rano will be clearly unattractive to Alcar.

Step 3. Evaluate Impact of Acquisition on Alcar's EPS and Capital Structure. The $35 million purchase price is just under 10 times Rano's most recent year's earnings of $3.55 million. At its current market price per share of $22, Alcar is selling at about six times its most recent earnings. The acquiring company will always suffer immediate EPS dilution whenever the price-earnings ratio paid for the selling company is greater than its own. Alcar would suffer immediate dilution from $3.75 to $3.54 in the current year. A comparison of EPS for cash versus an exchange-of-shares transaction appears as part of Exhibit 16. As expected, the EPS projections for a cash deal are consistently higher than those for an exchange of shares.

However, the acquisition of Rano for shares rather than cash would remove, at least for now, Alcar's projected financing problem. In contrast with a cash acquisition, an exchange of shares enables Alcar to have unused debt capacity at its disposal throughout the 10-year forecast period. Despite the relative attractiveness of this financing flexibility, Alcar management recognized that it could not expect a reasonable rate of return by offering an exchange of shares to Rano.

Exhibit 16.   Alcar's Projected EPS, Debt-to-Equity Ratio, and Unused Debt Capacity—Cash vs. Exchange of Shares

Year	EPS		Debt/Equity		Unused Debt Capacity (in millions of dollars)	
	Cash	Stock	Cash	Stock	Cash	Stock
0	$ 4.10	$ 3.54	.26	.21	$20.50	$25.60
1	4.89	4.37	.27	.19	9.42	35.46
2	5.51	4.93	.28	.17	7.00	46.62
3	6.20	5.55	.29	.18	4.20	48.04
4	6.99	6.23	.30	.20	0.98	46.37
5	7.87	7.00	.31	.21	− 2.71	44.29
6	8.29	7.37	.31	.23	− 7.77	40.90
7	9.27	8.22	.32	.24	− 13.64	36.78
8	10.14	8.98	.33	.26	− 22.34	29.90
9	11.33	10.01	.34	.27	− 32.86	21.79
10	12.66	11.17	.35	.29	− 43.88	12.29

Note: Assumed purchase price for Rano is $35 million.

Conclusion

The experience of companies that have implemented the approach to acquisition analysis described in this article indicates that it is not only an effective way of evaluating a prospective acquisition candidate, but it also serves as a catalyst for reevaluating a ccmpany's overall strategic plans. The results also enable management to justify acquisition recommendations to the board of directors in an economically sound, convincing fashion.

Various companies have used this approach for evaluation of serious candidates as well as for initial screening of potential candidates. In the latter case, initial input estimates are quickly generated to establish whether the range of maximum acceptable prices is greater than the current market price of the target companies. With the aid of a computer model, this can be accomplished quickly and at relatively low cost.

Whether companies are seeking acquisitions or are acquisition targets, it is increasingly clear that they must provide better information to enable top management and boards to make well-conceived, timely decisions. Use of the approach outlined here should improve the prospects of creating value for shareholders by acquisitions.

Notes

1. For a more detailed description on how to conduct a corporate self-evaluation, see my article, "Do You Know the Value of Your Company?", *Mergers and Acquisitions*, Spring 1979.

2. "The Cash-Flow Takeover Formula," *Business Week*, December 18, 1978, p. 86.

3. For example, see Roger G. Ibbotson and Rex A. Sinquefield, *Stocks, Bonds, Bills, and Inflation: The Past (1926–1976) and the Future (1977–2000)* (New York, Financial Analysts Research Foundation, 1977), p. 57. They forecast that returns on common stocks will exceed those on long-term government bonds by 5.4%.

4. For a discussion of some of the problems in estimating beta as a measure of risk, see Eugene F. Brigham, *Financial Management: Theory and Practice* (Hinsdale, Ill., The Dryden Press, 1977), p. 666.

5. See William W. Alberts and James M. McTaggart, "The Short-Term Earnings Per Share Standard for Evaluating Prospective Acquisitions," *Mergers and Acquisitions*, Winter 1978, p. 4; and Joel M. Stern, "Earnings Per Share Don't Count," *Financial Analysts Journal*, July–August 1974, p. 39.

24

Venturing Corporations

Think Small to Stay Strong

MACK HANAN

To sustain their strength, corporations must adapt to changing business conditions. Acquisition has long been a popular adjustment. But diversifying externally has been a disastrous experience for many companies, and antitrust legislation has precluded it for others. What means of maintaining corporate vitality remain? By choice or default, the author contends, the best strategy for profitable growth today is developing new ventures within the corporation. Corporate venturing, however, has a sorry track record. Only a few of the major corporations that have tried it over the past ten years have anything to show. Most have quit cold after their failure rates became insupportable or have cleaned out nearly all their venture activities, along with some presidents. Do small business strategies have some connection with success? The author believes that they do and that large corporations can learn something from comparing their ventures with the way small businesses develop. He outlines small venture policies that large companies can use, warns that there are several pitfalls to watch for, and concludes with four standards for evaluating a venture's organization and operations.

> "With all our resources, talent, and money, how is it that we have failed when small companies have succeeded? Every day successful businesses are started up on a shoestring by people who couldn't even get jobs in our shipping room!"

Published 1976.

Several large corporations whose new ventures failed in the 1960s are wondering why.

A failure list would read like a compendium of the blue chips of American business. It would include airlines that failed in establishing computerized reservation services for passengers or land-sea-air distribution services for shippers; brewers who failed in diversifying into other alcoholic beverages; soft-drink manufacturers who failed in creating solid or semisolid snack foods, and snack food processors who failed in producing soft drinks; publishers who failed in launching profitable multimedia systems and other communications companies that failed in penetrating the entertainment business or in combining general learning services with entertainment; pulp and paper processors who failed in commercializing land development businesses in their forests; convenience food processors who failed in starting cosmetic ventures and cosmetic manufacturers who failed in marketing personal accessories; accessory manufacturers who failed in selling wearables; and woven wearables manufacturers who were unable to convert their marketing capability as easily as their manufacturing facilities to establish a business in nonwoven garments and accessories.

"We went right down the line," the president of one large corporation said. "We faced up to the crucial venture considerations. We created a corporate growth policy, set annually compounded growth objectives at twice the rate of climb of the gross national product, and agreed on basic growth strategies. We chose market intensification instead of diversification and stayed within our range of technical capabilities. We positioned our top management group correctly, I believe—as bankers and as business development consultants to our ventures. We had our patience money set aside, and it included secondary financing. We even put together a fail-safe control system.

"Yet we came out with a dozen gross failures and only one salable business concept. I'd like to know where we went wrong."

One thing such corporate soul-searching has made clear is that new business ventures are best treated as small start-up businesses, not as large businesses in miniature. They may appear to be frisky young colts out of the same stable, but they are really horses of different breeds. Usually, large companies lack the entrepreneurial workforce, the practical experience of carrying a new enterprise from conception through market entry, and the philosophical climate for managing small businesses. Applying large-company organization and operating methods to small businesses stifles them. If business ventures are to be brought to full term within a large corporation, they must be managed by applying small business strategies.

Strategies for Healthy Growth

Having drawn this conclusion, a few major corporations have tried out small business strategies on their new ventures and found five that bring success.

They are positioning an entrepreneurial leader as a venture manager, concentrating a venture's resources on a minimum number of functions, maintaining a flexible operating style, minimizing cost burden, and generating quick cash flow by providing a service or an additional product along with the venture product.

Entrepreneurial Management

In setting up a venture, a corporation must first concern itself with finding a venture manager, which is always a difficult task. It's impossible, however, until a company knows what kind of manager it needs.

Little or no correlation has been found between running an established business for marginally incremental annual profit and starting up a new big-winner organization from scratch. An established business generally requires a marginally innovative caretaker. A new organization, on the other hand, needs the high risk/reward orientation of an entrepreneur.

Major corporations are not natural habitats for entrepreneurial business creators. They must either be brought in from smaller companies or painstakingly developed from within the corporation.

If there is any conclusion that has surfaced about corporate business building, it is that product or brand managers, and even market managers, are not born venture managers. Neither will they become good venture managers by merely taking on new descriptions of their positions.

Some companies have a simple way of finding a venture leader. "I have an unfailing test for identifying entrepreneurial types," one corporate president says. "I throw every candidate right in with the alligators. The establishment man complains he can't farm alligators in a swamp. The entrepreneur farms 60% of the alligators, markets another 30% for everything but their squeal, drains their part of the swamp, and leases the land for an amusement park overlooking 'Alligatorland.' The other 10% of the alligators? That's his delayed compensation."

Other companies are trying to develop their own venture leaders. In analyzing what makes a good venture leader, these companies have zeroed in on three traits they suspect are basic.

One is a highly personal leadership style. Entrepreneurs make a memorable impact on business. Although they don't try to do everything, they are careful to project themselves into any situation where problem solving by persuasion is needed to get things unstuck and going again, motivation and morale building are critical, and risky decisions must be made. They are not everywhere in the company, but they *are* where the action is.

A second trait found in successful entrepreneurs is the ability to be comfortable in the presence of a high risk/reward ratio and, conversely, to be extremely uncomfortable without it. Both the risk and the reward must be high. Entrepreneurs climb the walls whenever there is too much reward for too little risk.

A third entrepreneurial characteristic is the tendency to conceive of a three- to five-year business plan as being only a rather loose envelope into which a manager can insert any number of short-term strategies. The short-ness of the term depends on business circumstance and managerial prefer-ence. As well as advancing toward an objective, each short-term strategy maintains a venture's management style, its market position, and its general image. The sum of all the short-term strategies amounts to the venture's long-term objective, represented by the envelope.

Some short-term strategies may have only a 30-day time frame. Others will net out in 90 to 100 days, which is about the maximum. Only a certain type of manager can feel stimulated as well as secure while generating a continual mix of miniplans that may frequently overlap and require a good deal of hands-on control. The kind of manager who can cope with all this is the entrepreneur.

Suitable Obsessions

Many large companies take commendable pride in "doing things right." As a result, they style their new business ventures as embryonic multinational organizations, which faithfully reproduce every functional cost center of their parent organizations.

Doing things this way works directly against a venture's need to con-centrate its scarce and expensive resources where they will do the most good, as a small business would. One of the surprising discoveries successful venturing companies have made is that a new business does not have to do everything "right" in order to survive and prosper. It can be wrong in some areas and even remiss in a few aspects of management as long as its manager hits the mark where it counts. This statement should not be construed as tolerance of sloppy management but rather as a directive to adopt small-company concentration on the minimum number of functions that can pro-vide the maximum amount of leverage for getting a venture off the ground.

Industry requirements vary so widely that practically every venture is subject to unique demands on its talent and financial resources. Nonetheless, three areas of concentration are assuming major importance as targets for large companies starting new ventures. They are marketing, consultative selling, and constant appraisal of commercial potential.

Market Penetration. From the start, market penetration should be one of a venture's major obsessions. Each commitment of business resources ought to be made according to how much it will speed up and safeguard annual sales growth. Companies that have ventured successfully or analyzed their unsuccessful ventures carefully have adopted a policy of generating new businesses "backwards." Their market penetration scenarios are written well before instead of just prior to commercial entry. The scenario then becomes the controlling script for determining who does what throughout the business gestation period. With eventual marketing as the venture's goal, all decisions can be biased toward market acceptance. One decision should be to select venture managers for their superior marketing skills rather than for other talents or experience. Another decision should be to place deliberate emphasis on producing a winning marketing plan, even at the expense of other functional plans.

Appraisal of Market Potential. The second management strategy for concentration is constant appraisal of the venture's commercial potential. Managers are forming the habit of asking, "What are we buying in return for our investment?" at each step of the venture's development. Some of them have identified three factors to evaluate—return on investment, sales (expressed in both units and dollars), and percentage share of the market. These, along with the operating ratio of profits to sales, of sales to sales cost, and of dollar sales value to market share percent provide supportive data.

Consultative Selling. A cornerstone of the marketing plan that seems to contribute significantly to success is preparing the venture's sales force to perform consultative selling, that is, to show customers how the venture's products and services can increase their profits. Under this strategy, one sales force, at a processed foods company, is training to help supermarket chain managers, their buying committees, store owners, and section managers find ways to reduce supermarket costs through innovative inventory control for the venture product. The trainees will help generate new sales revenue through related item displays or new stocking and shelving ideas. Another sales force, at an industrial manufacturer, consults with customers' technical, sales, and financial managers as well as their design engineers and purchasing agents. Together, they find ways to cut customer product costs or to improve sales with better engineering and marketing creativity.

Looseleaf Operating Plan

In creating new ventures in their own image, major corporations have often endowed the new management with an overly formalized operating style and a rigid organizational format. The master organization chart has simply been shrunk and imposed on the venture. No business has a greater need to stay loose organizationally and operationally than a small, new company. It must make up in flexibility what it lacks in numbers of people or in specialization. Attempts to introduce parent company specialists into a venture's operations often turn out poorly because the specialists bring with them the red tape, the protocol, and the structural uptightness of their establishment background.

No matter how difficult it is to permit their venture offspring to operate in a more flexible style than they themselves do, corporations should realize that flexibility may well be a necessary requirement for success. Because a venture's workforce must be small, it should be multifunctional. Everybody should have a specific job. Yet a "that's not *my* job" attitude should not be allowed to prevail when tasks that fall in the cracks between specific roles must be carried out. If roles cannot be interchanged, at least they can be shared.

At the same time, however, while managers in large companies spend most of their time seeking agreement from each other, venture leaders cannot afford to be so flexible as to share their roles as decision makers. They can't manage by consensus. Agreement is always desirable, but venture managers must practice persuasive leadership. They may have to be directive at times, even authoritarian. But they will most frequently be orchestrating ongoing dialogues among fellow venturers to hear their best thinking while, at the very same time, they may be implementing it as they go.

Nor can they be so flexible as to neglect the usual rules of operation. It does mean, though, that the book must be considerably smaller than usual in a large company and its pages loose-leaved for rewriting, replacement, and occasional rearrangement.

Venturing corporations are loosening up their business development style by staffing new enterprise teams with what one company calls "generalized specialists," people who are proficient in a recognized specialty but who have a general knowledge of one or more other specialities as well. In one company, management commented, "These are our very best people. How can we afford to assign them to growth?" A division president answered, "How can we afford *not* to?"

Some corporations are encouraging their ventures to charter eclectic organization formats, one of which centers a development group's activities on its market's needs rather than on a linear relation to internal capabilities.[1]

Functional overlap of marketing, technical, and financial people has advantages. Bringing marketing and technology closely together makes it feasible to insist that market needs be used to set priorities for just what new products to develop first and what benefits to expect from them. Competitive product analysis can also be easily interpreted for management in users' terms so that comparative benefits stand out, not just construction characteristics or ingredients. Then, when some marketing and financial functions are also blended in, still other advantages can be gained. For example, the marginal profit contribution of each product line can be regularly analyzed. Winners can be concentrated on and losers beefed up or dropped. Make-or-buy decisions about product components are most likely to be made on a short-term, repetitive basis in keeping with changes in cost and supplies.

Finally, as financial and technical functions come in for sharing, new product concepts can be strengthened. From the outset, they can be studied on a cost/benefit basis so that concepts that appear to be more costly than beneficial can be discontinued while still in idea form. It is, of course, quite true to say that all of these activities should be carried out in every company as a matter of good management practice. It is also true to say that they are not always carried out, and thus overlapping can help ensure good management practice at the very least and, at best, make it richly productive.

Garage Genesis

It is probably no accident that so many businesses have originated in garages. To minimize a venture's cost burden and endow it with the character of a small business, large companies have often rented space for their venture teams in such places. Center-city lofts and warehouses as well as rural farmhouses have also made good places to start. In one case, a successful venture began in a trailer. Another team, calling itself the Brick Church Ventures Group, worked in the vestry of a suburban church. These locations got them out of the mainstream of the parent companies' business, made it difficult for head-office people to poke around, and—at least in the case of the church—put them in a future-oriented environment.

A garage is an ideal spawning ground. It offers low rent and the kind of austere work environment that imbues the new team with the incentive to succeed. The only way out is up. Small businesses instinctively seek the low overhead of this type of location. After smothering many of their new ventures with overburdened cost structures and overengineered operating procedures, large companies have discovered that simplicity is an important business development strategy.

Attempts to approximate a truly independent business environment with a low overhead cost structure often lead to positioning a venture as if it were a spin-out of its parent company. Lockheed Aircraft Corporation's "skunk works" is an example of this kind of highly productive approach. It originated in the corporation's Advanced Development Projects Division as a small team of dedicated specialists who formed an implicit partnership to do a job defined only in general terms. Such a team can be directed to do something like "penetrate the optoelectronics business" and then go off by itself to operate with a relatively free hand. The venture manager is delegated practically complete authority for the program. The company's main control consists of a monthly cost-and-progress review. Innovation is expected, not suprisingly, and achievement is acknowledged immediately with generous financial rewards.

One company that runs business development this way has three rules. The first is to have "skinny" staffing. The body count is always one or two persons fewer than a parent company organization chart would call for. Either in spite of this or because of it, work-hour productivity has been 20% higher than the parent company average.

The second rule is to work within bare walls. The environment must be designed to convey the message that initial financing is finite. New businesses that dissipate their going-in funds on nonprofit-making expenditures will run into serious, perhaps fatal, trouble after the interior decoration stage of their growth when secondary capital is required. Before a dollar is spent, a skunk-works staff is indoctrinated to ask, "Will it contribute to short-range profit?" If so, they go on to further questions: "Can less be spent and the same profits still earned?" "Will an equal expenditure for something else contribute even more?"

The final rule is to provide "just enough" quality. It is designed to prevent overengineering. The two most prevalent reasons for venture failure are the absence of a market and overspending in the perfection of a product. The more technical the venture, the more susceptible it is to being saddled by unrecoverable sunk costs—unrecoverable because the level of performance that they were intended to achieve later turns out to exceed the market's value-to-price acceptance.

The alternative to a quest for the perfect product is not shoddy goods. It is a policy of matching the product to the market, which means two things: First, a venture product should be designed to meet but not exceed the benefits a market desires. Second, a market's perception of the product's value must exceed the product's price. When the products generated by a new business meet these criteria, they have the best chance of embodying just enough quality to ensure high margins.

Tandem Output

Cash flow is the life blood of a venture business. The first rule of all start-up businesses is to ensure a stream of earnings as quickly as possible in the venture's life cycle. By venturing on a two-track basis, some companies have been able to bring earnings on-stream earlier than if they had developed just one product at a time. Like many small companies, they assign the development of "early earners" (rapid payback products or services) to an express track. This decision buys time to subsidize the creation of slower but heavier earners on a second track.

The early earner is usually a product whose added value, easily perceived by its market, can be convincingly demonstrated by sales and advertising and requires little or no customer education. Drawing on proven technology, existing channels of distribution, and validated market acceptance, it carries a good margin because its investment base is comparatively small.

Razor and Blades. Another two-product system to develop cash flow is the time-honored "razor and blades" approach. One product, which acts as the razor, is manufactured and marketed as a relatively low-priced utilitarian commodity. It is designed to stimulate mass repeat sales for a second product, which is marketed as a branded specialty item like razor blades. The razor is the durable. The blades are the consumables, which carry a high price, command a strong margin, and, because of their rapid turnover, generate recurrent profits.

Belt and Suspenders. Successful small companies have frequently regarded offering a product by itself as taking an unacceptable risk. They have learned to diminish risk and buttress product acceptance by marketing related services. Marketing services with products can help hold a venture together with both "belt and suspenders."

This approach gives a venture business two potential profit centers instead of one. In the history of these systems, it is usually the product concept that is developed first. As its benefits are matched against customers' needs, the true service nature of what has been regarded only as product hardware often becomes evident. At this point, it is natural to ask whether an out-and-out service could make a significant contribution in addition to the service derived from the product.

Successful companion services may evolve through this type of hindsight. Once market penetration has begun, it usually becomes impossible to tell whether such a service is acting as the system's belt or as its suspenders. An ideal product and service system is really a unit of sale. Their benefits and packaging are so complementary that they are mutually supportive.

The two most typical services that large companies supply with products are financial support and a combination of customer consultation and education. The purpose of financial services is to enable customers to acquire and utilize venture products through progressive payments or leasing. Consultation and education services help customers make the most cost-effective applications of a venture's products after they have been acquired.

Consultation and education services are based on information about market needs and life-styles. Small businesses have usually been close to their market's needs. Since all new enterprises must collect and evaluate market information, commercializing it when the venture goes on-stream is a means of recovering costs as well as generating incremental profit. By holding information out for sale through consultation, a venture helps ensure its own success by maintaining its principal resource. The Ansul Company, a fire protection supplier, uses hazard control planning and firefighting education services to bolster new equipment sales and follows them with process monitoring services after installation.

Consultation services need not be rendered personally, however. Applications advice, for instance, can be given in guidebooks sold along with products. In consumer industries, food processors can publish newsletters or magazines for inclusion with their products in much the same way that premiums are merchandised. Ingersoll-Rand and some other industrial manufacturers regularly publish magazines showing customers how to use their equipment so that the perceived value of the ventures' products is enhanced.

Pitfalls to Watch For

Murphy's Law—"Anything that can go wrong will go wrong"—applies with a vengeance to adapting small business strategies for corporate growth. An entrepreneur who turns sour in a big-company climate, or who alienates its resource people to the point where they sour on him, can doom a venture, no matter how able a business developer he may be. Nor is the entrepreneur the sole potential risk. Carried to an extreme, flexibility can become chaos and everybody's business turns out to be nobody's business. A flexible organization style can be a virtue for a new enterprise, but if everybody tries to do everything, nobody may be able to do anything.

Experience shows that new ventures frequently encounter at least four other pitfalls, especially those ventures which incorrectly apply a razor-and-blades strategy or a belt-and-suspenders approach.

Branding the Razor

The most prevalent pitfall in a razor-and-blades system is to brand the product that acts as the razor. The razor may receive an excess of innovative technology and thereby incur a high-cost overlay, which is then passed along to the market in the form of a premium price. If the price reflects such an overlay, the company does not really understand the role of the razor.

If the market perceives the razor as too complicated or too expensive, or both, the blades will not sell and the system as a whole will never get off the shelf. The Polaroid SX-70 system illustrates this point. Although its introduction had been hobbled by the film's short retail shelf life, the original model was positioned at the highest price ever asked for a camera intended for a mass market. From the manufacturer's point of view, the price was justifiable because of the camera's exclusive combination of mechanical, chemical, and optoelectronic technologies. But from the consumer's point of view, the price was a violation of the rule of thumb that says, "Sell the razor at cost if necessary, even give it away to make a market for the blades." Polaroid's experience validates this dictum. Only when new models were introduced at about half the cost of the deluxe original along with a moderately priced model did the SX-70 line begin to move.

Failing to Brand the Blades

Next to failing to make the razor a commodity, a second common pitfall of systems marketing is neglecting to make the blades truly proprietary and therefore brandable. The more easily the blades can be knocked off by imitation, the more short-lived the system will be.

If the blades themselves are not unique, which is the case with most data-processing peripheral equipment and software, then their prescription, application, or maintenance must be individualized, as IBM's have been. Many IBM clients have penetrated behind the company's system and believe that it is IBM's industry data banks which support each system's cost-efficiency performance and serve as its true blades.

Creating Unrelated Services

Because product manufacturers are usually not sophisticated in service marketing, they are likely to come up with services that are only poorly related to their products. This is a major problem for consumer packaged goods processors, whose traditional concept of customer service may extend only as far as providing free menu suggestions or low-cost premiums.

For any service to make a joint contribution to product sales, it must bear a demonstrable profit-improvement value. It must be able to cut the customer's cost of using its companion product by reducing waste, loss, or spoilage, or it must be able to add importantly to his sales revenues or other benefits of product use. A service that can be promoted for these virtues may become the principal reason that consumers purchase the venture product. Eventually, the benefits of the service may pull the product through to the end user. When this occurs, the service can become the product's means of personification, implying its benefit the way Betty Crocker's multiple homemaker services symbolize General Mills products and AT&T Communications Consultants personify the profit improvement potential of telephone systems.

Giving One Product Second-Class Status

Management must also be careful not to promote a product that cannot stand on its own feet as a second line. Neither the belt nor the suspenders can afford to be casually treated as second rate. Yet many ventures break apart into two camps, the belt fanciers and the suspender fanciers. Each wants to allocate the greater share of venture resources to its own product. This kind of civil war wears down any insurance value that one product line can offer the other.

The pitfalls in managing the razor-and-blades or the belt-and-suspenders approach confront all companies, no matter what their size or sophistication. Just as Polaroid has had trouble with its razor and blades, so General Mills came a cropper in dealing with its belt and suspenders when it failed to make its computerized meal planning service a profitable adjunct to its food products.

It should not be assumed, however, that small companies, merely because they are small, are infallible. They make their own mistakes. But they operate so close to the edge, and they know so well how fatal a single fall can be that they take heroic measures to avoid one.

A small, personal estate-planning company accurately applied belt-and-suspenders thinking when it created an instructional service for insurance salesmen to teach them how to "push" its financial plans. Then it developed another teaching service so that the sales staff's clients could learn how to "pull" added use out of their salespeople in order to obtain improved benefits.

Christine Valmy, Inc., a small skin-care product manufacturer, recognized the interplay between service and product right from the start. One of the first things it did was to set up a school to train professional skin-care consultants. After graduation, they become purveyors as well as proponents of Valmy products. Within the company itself, salon treatments generate new customers for Valmy skin-care products.

Standards for Organizing Growth

Any organized effort to grow businesses from within large companies must have individual criteria for evaluation. Performance yardsticks will not only help professionalize the growth of a new enterprise and rescue it from amateurism but will also upgrade growth as an ongoing corporate commitment. In this way, a venture will be more than just a spasmodic excursion into the unknown. The new entity will have the status of the other management processes, where performance standards are commonplace.

At least four components of the venture business process should have standards. One is how well the venture manager achieves the venture's objectives by means of short-term strategy making within a three-to-five-year envelope type of plan.

A second standard is how well the venture has minimized its staff and facilities and made lean running its fundamental operating style. An initial staff can often be limited to a full-time venture manager and a sales or marketing manager supplemented with part-time resource managers in finance and technology. A major requirement for each staff member should be the ability to operate in one other area of expertise on an intermittent basis.

A third standard would be to ascertain how well venture products fit market needs and establish high value-to-price ratios. Product benefits should equal but not exceed minimum standards of market acceptance. Value should be perceived as exceeding price so that the venture product will be seen as a bargain, no matter how high the price. Furthermore, major products should be accompanied by companion services of a consultative or educational nature or a service that offers financial support to venture customers.

A final standard would be establishing an early onset of positive cash flow. In most cases, it should be on-stream no later than the end of the venture's first year of commercialization.

If a large corporation adopts standards of performance like these to regularize its growth, if it takes pains to avoid the most predictable problems, and if it organizes its internal development around small business-building strategies, what then? Is profitable growth ensured?

Apparently not. No matter how painstaking a venturing corporation may be in its analysis, all of its careful planning must ultimately hinge on the attitudes and the drive of the entrepreneur it places in charge. It is essentially in the entrepreneur's constant striving, telescoped time frame for getting things done, and sense of urgency that make ventures happen. Running scared, the entrepreneur has the compulsion to seek new sources of sustenance for the venture. No wonder that the primary rule of business venturing is "Find the manager."

If there is anything remotely resembling a formula for maintaining corporate vitality through new business ventures, the companies that have done their soul-searching would express it this way: Only when growth becomes the venture's overriding objective, as it is with a small business, can a corporation succeed in diversifying and expanding.

Notes

1. See my article, "Reorganize Your Company Around Its Markets," *HBR*, November-December 1974, p. 63.

25

The Risky Business of Diversification

RALPH BIGGADIKE

On the basis of a sample from the top 200 of the *Fortune* "500" and data from the PIMS (Profit Impact of Market Strategies) project, this author gives some guidelines for established companies on what to expect from new ventures. He points out that it takes an average of 10 to 12 years before the ROI of ventures equals that of mature businesses. He advocates rapid share building despite the adverse effect that this apparently has on current financial performance and thus advises large-scale entry for the company that wants to grow through the addition of a new business.

One way companies grow is to launch new businesses into product markets where they have not previously competed. For example, GE, starting with an incandescent lamp business, has moved to businesses covering more than 700 product markets. Recent examples of corporate diversification include the entries of Gillette into manufacture of felt-tip pens, John Deere into snowmobiles, and Texas Instruments into pocket calculators.

    Corporate growth through the addition of new businesses has received further impetus from the "product portfolio" concept, which argues that if a company is both to grow and to allocate resources wisely it must mix established with new businesses. Growth and a balanced portfolio are attractive objectives, but, for some companies, their pursuit has produced big problems. NCR reported losses of $60 million in 1972, primarily because of its entry into the computer field. General Foods took a $39 million write-off in 1972 on its entry into the business of fast food chains. Rohr Industries, Inc. announced a $59.9 million write-off in 1976 on its mass transit venture.

Published 1979.

Author's note. Parts of this article are drawn from my previous research reported in *Corporate Diversification* (Boston, Division of Research, Harvard Business School, forthcoming).

Results such as these suggest that launching new businesses is risky. Achieving a balanced product portfolio appears to be more difficult in practice than in theory. Articles on the product portfolio concept reinforce this perception of risk by referring to new businesses as "wildcats," "sweepstakes," or "question marks"—hardly the most reassuring of terms. From this viewpoint, corporate diversification resembles Russian roulette.

Conversely, some executives and economists argue that big losses are rare events. Venturing by established companies, they suggest, is much less risky than venturing by individuals. Some of the problems of individual ventures, such as acquiring capital, a brand reputation, and economies of scale, are less severe for established companies.

Another question concerning negative results is, "How long do we have to put up with losses?" Although most managers do not expect immediate profits, few accept several years of losses. Indeed, any corporate venture that promises losses for a period longer than the job horizon of most managers seems unlikely to survive. One company has a firm rule: "Kill new businesses if they are not profitable at the end of year 3."

The problem is that, with current knowledge of corporate ventures, one just does not know whether large losses for several years are the common experience or the exception. There is no known rationale for saying that new ventures should be profitable at the end of three years. In addition, it is not clear how much cash, on the average, a wildcat business will demand and over what time period.

This article deals with these issues. First, I present data on the performance of a sample of corporate new ventures. I seek to evaluate their initial performances and to determine the average length of time needed to achieve profitability. Second, I will address the question, "How might performance be improved?" and suggest some guidelines for future management of corporate ventures.

The Sample

The data in this article are from a sample of corporate ventures launched in the United States by the top 200 companies in the *Fortune* "500" and a sample of established businesses in the PIMS project.[1] A corporate venture is defined as a business marketing a product or service that the parent company has not previously marketed and that requires the parent company to obtain new equipment or new people or new knowledge. A business is defined as a division, product line, or other profit center within its parent company selling a distinct set of products or services to an identifiable group or groups of customers in competition with a well-defined set of competitors. Corporate acquisitions were included in the venture sample only if the acquiring company had committed significant resources to the business and altered its strategy after purchase.

The sample included 68 ventures launched by 35 companies that supplied data on their first two years of operations. Of these ventures, 47 had been operating for four years, allowing analysis of the second two-year period of operation as well. The sample consisted mainly of industrial goods businesses. Data were provided by managers of the parent company and of the venture and were disguised by the managers, thus limiting analysis to ratios only, not absolute dollar values.

All these ventures entered existing markets. Markets were defined at a segment level, a more narrowly defined market than those identified by, say, the Bureau of the Census. Thus the data used to measure market size and growth rates cover only the specific products or services, customer types, and geographic areas in which each corporate venture actually operates.

The population from which this sample was derived can be summarized as surviving corporate ventures, launched in the late 1960s and early 1970s by a subset of the *Fortune* top 200 companies mentioned earlier and characterized by a high degree of diversification. These results probably do not apply to ventures that individuals launched or that had to create entirely new markets (e.g., the first business to introduce penicillin).

The data base does, however, embrace entrants that entered existing markets with incremental innovations (e.g., the first business to introduce electronic calculators) and that had a "me too" technology. It also includes entrants to concentrated and fragmented markets and entrants to rapid growth and mature markets. Participating executives describe the ventures as typical examples of the new businesses that their parent companies have launched.

Financial Performance

The sample indicates that corporate ventures, on average, suffer severe losses through their first four years of operations. Exhibit 1 shows that the ROI for the median business was − 40% in the first two years and − 14% in the second two years.

A few businesses achieved profits in the first two years—specifically, 12 out of 68, or 18% of the sample. The most profitable venture recorded an ROI of + 80%; the lowest ROI was − 442%. By the end of year four, of the 47 ventures with four years of data, 18, or 38%, had made a profit. These 18 do not include seven of the 12 businesses profitable in year two. Early profitability in a venture, therefore, does not necessarily guarantee continued profitability.

One can now more precisely assess new businesses' appetite for cash. The ratio of cash flow to investment was − 80% in the first two years and − 29% in the second two years. No business had a positive cash flow in the first two years; six businesses had a positive cash flow in the second two years.

The ratio of gross margin to sales revenue showed the most favorable

Exhibit 1.   Financial Performance in the First Four Years of Operations

Performance Ratio	Median Value[a]	
	Years 1 and 2	Years 3 and 4
Return on investment[b]	− 40%	− 14%
Cash flow—investment[c]	− 80	− 29
Pretax profit—sales	− 39	− 10
Gross margin—sales[d]	+ 15	+ 28
Number of businesses	68	47

[a]I show performance of the median business because the sample performance was spread over a wide range. The median is not affected by extreme cases and therefore is less likely to mislead.

[b]The ratio of net pretax income to average investment. Income is calculated after deduction of corporate expenses but prior to interest charges. Investment is calculated as working capital plus fixed capital (valued at net book value).

[c]Cash generated by aftertax earnings *minus* cash absorbed by increased working capital and increased *net* investment in plant and equipment.

[d]Sales revenues *minus* purchases, manufacturing, and depreciation as a ratio to sales revenues.

picture. Of the 68 ventures, 48, or 70%, reported a positive gross margin in their first two years, which points to marketing and R&D expense as contributors to the negative income statements. Exhibit 2 shows that the median marketing expense to sales revenue ratio, at 38%, was the second highest operating ratio in the first two years; R&D expense to sales revenue ratio was a hefty 19%.

Most operating and capital ratios showed some improvement in the second two years. For example, Exhibit 2 shows that marketing-sales rev-

Exhibit 2.   Operating and Capital Ratios in the First Four Years of Operations

Operating Ratios	Median Value	
	Years 1 and 2	Years 3 and 4
Purchase—sales	46%	44%
Manufacturing—sales	28	25
Marketing—sales	38	22
R&D—sales	19	8
Capital Ratios		
Inventory—sales	24	22
Receivables—sales	16	12
Investment—sales	98	73
Number of businesses	68	47

enue ratio improved to 22% and investment-sales revenue ratio improved from 98% to 73%. However, these ratios did not improve because of any declining outlays on operating and capital items. In fact, outlays continued to rise in the second two years. Rather, growth in sales revenues—at 45% per year for the median venture—rose faster than outlays.

The key to improving financial statements, then, is to obtain rapid sales growth with a less than proportionate increase in outlays. Although not surprising, this perspective is in contrast to the common approach of forecasting improvement because of declines in initial launch outlays. According to this sample, both expenses and capital items go only one way—up.

Another common view, that the problem with new businesses is that initial returns are low because of high capital requirements, is also wide of the mark. Rather, in this sample the problem is that there is no return at all—net income is negative. The appellations "wildcats" or "sweepstakes" thus appear uncomfortably accurate descriptions of corporate new ventures.

Losses for How Long?

Severe losses over the first four years of operations raise the question, "How long, on the average, do corporate new ventures take to improve performance?" I estimated an answer to this question by extracting from the PIMS data base two groups of businesses in more advanced stages of development. One group of businesses, termed "adolescents," had data on their fifth through their eighth year of operations. The other group of businesses are, on average, 18 years old and describe their product or service as mature; these businesses can be regarded as established and were called "mature." These groups allow us to compare performance over three stages of business development: start-up, adolescence, and maturity.

It appears that new ventures need, on the average, eight years before they reach profitability. Note in Exhibit 3 that ROI did not become positive until the seventh and eighth years, with the median business earning 7%. However, the adolescents still have some way to go before attaining the 17% reported by mature businesses. In fact, a simple time projection of the results in the first eight years suggests that 10 to 12 years elapse before the ROI of ventures equals that of mature businesses.

Figures drawn from this comparison must be regarded as estimates because we cannot be sure that the businesses in the adolescent and mature samples were, in *their* first four years, structurally similar to the businesses in the venture sample. However, even if we limit accuracy to plus or minus two to three years, this length of time to reach profitability is not encouraging.

Cash flow does not become positive for the median business in the first eight years. A similar time projection suggests that 12 years are needed before ventures generate cash flow ratios similar to those of mature businesses.

Some executives previewing these results were initially astonished. This reaction led them, and me, to review personal experiences with cor-

Exhibit 3.   Median Performance in Start-Up, Adolescent, and Mature Stages

	Start-Up		Adolescence		Maturity
Performance Ratio	Years 1 and 2	Years 3 and 4	Years 5 and 6	Years 7 and 8[a]	Average Age about 18 Years
Return on investment	−40%	−14%	−8%	+7%	·17%
Cash flow—sales	−90	−29	−5	−4	+ 3
Pretax profit—sales	−39	−10	−5	−4	+ 9
Gross margin—sales	+15	+28	+19	+22	+26
Number of businesses	68	47	61	61	454

[a]Profit to sales is negative while ROI is positive because these averages are medians, not means (mean ROI is +5% and mean profit to sales is +1%).

porate ventures. The overriding question was, "Could the financial results be that bad for that long?" Managers found that the sample data were so provocative that they had to test them against their own venture experiences.

Although these personal recollections cannot be used analytically, the executives eventually concluded that the sample results squared with many of their companies' venture experiences. I cannot reveal these recollections, but I can cite examples from the public domain:

☐ Around 1970, Xerox started work on two new businesses—duplicators and electronic typing systems. In 1977, both were still unprofitable, although reports suggested that profitability was near.

☐ Singer tried to build a business machines venture for 10 years, but finally quit in 1975. The venture was still unprofitable.

☐ GE tried for 13 years, from 1957 to 1970, to establish its computer venture. The company's nuclear venture took about 15 years to reach profitability.[2]

Market Performance

Although the median corporate venture in the first four years increased sales revenues at 45% per year, this sales growth did not lead to a strong market position. The median venture achieved 7% share in the first two years and 10% in the second two years. Relative share (defined as the venture share divided by the combined share of the three largest competitors) is a more relevant measure of competitive position. The medium corporate venture held 11% and 13% in the first and second two-year periods, respectively.

Although the low initial share level might be expected for a new business, the apparent difficulty in improving share is disturbing. Although 39 of the 47 businesses with four years of share data gained share in the second two years, one-third gained less than a single point and only one-quarter gained more than four points. The impressive sales revenue growth for many ventures was negligible in the context of a market growing slightly faster and a starting position of zero share.

Market Share and Financial Performance

Persuasive theoretical arguments and a good deal of concrete evidence suggest that high market share improves financial performance.[3] Although this previous research was done on established businesses, it seems likely that share will similarly benefit new businesses. However, few researchers have discussed the financial impact of building share. One can argue from common sense that building share should damage financial performance in the same time period.

Building share can require higher quality, broader marketing, lower prices, and extended capacity—all expensive items that damage both income statements and balance sheets. Furthermore, some rapid share builders are starting from both a low share position and an inferior cost position. Their financial results will thus experience a "double whammy."

Earlier research leads one to expect a positive relationship between financial performance and share for new ventures. Conversely, in the same time period, a negative relationship between financial performance and share building should be expected. Although the small sample size and the wide variability in the data prevent rigorous testing of these relationships, one can say that the evidence of this sample supports them.

Effect of Market Share

To get the data on these relationships, I divided the venture sample into three approximately equal-sized groups—low, medium, and high relative market share ventures in their first and second two years. Exhibit 4 shows data on the first relationship: businesses with low relative share reported— 93% ROI, and businesses with high relative share reported −21% ROI in the first two years—a difference of 72 points. The impact of relative share on profit margin and cash flow/investment was similar. The advantages of high relative share continued in the second two years of operations. The benefits of share are similar to those cited for established businesses: profit margin increases sharply, and the purchases-to-sales and marketing-to-sales ratios decline.[4]

Effect of Building Share

Having share and building it produce quite different effects on financial performance. Exhibit 5 shows that the greater the rate of gain in relative share, the poorer the financial performance. Rapid share builders reported a median ROI of −20% for the first four years of operations compared to −4% ROI for those who were not building share. That is to say, a strategy

Exhibit 4. Relationship between Financial and Market Performance

Performance Ratio	First Two Years Median Value Relative Share[a]			Second Two Years Median Value Relative Share[a]		
	Low (below 4%)	Medium (4% to 42%)	High (over 42%)	Low (below 7%)	Medium (8% to 33%)	High (over 50%)
Return on investment	−93%	−40%	−21%	−20%	−5%	−6%
Cash flow—investment	−110	−67	−74	−39	−22	−23
Pretax profit—sales	−95	−35	−21	−29	−2	−5

[a]Relative share is the venture share divided by the combined share of the three largest competitors.

Exhibit 5. Financial Performance and Change in Relative Share, First Four Years

	Median Value		
Performance Ratio	Rapid Share Builders	Moderate Share Builders	Holders or Losers of Share
Return on investment	-20%	-10%	-4%
Cash flow—investment	-58	-20	-19
Pretax profit—sales	-24	-6	-2

of rapid relative share building carried a short-term penalty of 16 percentage points in ROI over the alternative of holding relative share.

As might be expected, the penalty on the cash flow-to-investment ratio was even more severe. Rapid relative share builders reported a median cash flow—investment ratio of -58%, whereas share holders reported -19%, a difference of 30 points.

On the average, the market share of rapid share builders was lower than that of the shareholders throughout the first four years of operations. Gaining share from a low share base was doubly handicapping. Rapid share builders, on the average, had price-cost margins worse than those of the shareholders. That is, they charged lower prices and carried higher direct costs than did their competitors. To gain share from a low share position, several ventures had to offer customers a better bargain, at the same time bearing the financial disadvantages of low share. This combination is surely the quintessence of the "double whammy."

Share Before Profits

The foregoing findings demonstrate that ventures cannot report both good financial and good market performance in the same time period: These two aspects of performance conflict. But we know from other studies that the highest ROI for established businesses goes to the highest market shareholder. If a business can have both good financial and good market performance only when share is established, the management implication is clear: a venture's objective for its early years should be to build share, regardless of short-run financial performance.

If we accept this objective, it follows that corporate ventures should enter on a large scale for the best results. Obviously, only a business with a large capacity relative to the size of the market has the potential to gain a large market share. This approach is often referred to as building capacity ahead of demand. But it is a controversial strategy and, some executives have argued, counterintuitive, because it raises the required investment and therefore the risk. Yet my findings here suggest the opposite: Perhaps the biggest risk is entering too small. It may be true, in corporate venturing as in love, that faint heart never won fair lady.

Entry Scale

To obtain further evidence for the idea that to enter on a large scale is the best strategy, I analyzed these ventures according to the size of their entry. I used two measures of scale: production and market scales. Production scale is defined as the initial production capacity of the business, expressed as a percentage of the market size. Market scale is defined as the number of customers served and the breadth of product line offered by the venture, relative to its competitors. Production and market scale together represent the maximum potential share a business can obtain. We need both measures of scale because economies of a large plant can be realized only if the output is continuously sold.

Exhibit 6 shows the distribution of this sample on these measures. Just over half the sample, 37 businesses, entered with a capacity less than 20% of the size of the market. Similarly, about half the sample offered product lines less broad than their competitors'; more than one-third served fewer customers than did their competitors. Thus, on the average, our sample consists of small-scale entrants.

When we look at performance by different sizes of entry scale, we see that the small-scale strategy failed to reduce losses. And neither did it build share. Exhibit 7 shows performance in the first two years by an index of entry scale, which is simply production and market scales combined. The big losers were those ventures with the smallest entry scale: These had a median ROI of −41%, compared with −24% for those with the largest entry scale. The second two years showed similar performances.

Exhibit 7 also returns us to relative share: The large-scale entrants achieved the highest relative share as well as the least negative financial performance. For a few businesses, therefore, the conflict between financial and market performance was less severe. Although these ventures still sustained losses, they were at least building market position.

These findings provide persuasive support for the argument that entering on a large scale is likely to lead to better financial results earlier than does the intuitively obvious approach, that is, entering on a small scale. In fact, small-scale entries are doubly handicapped. Their immediate financial performance is terrible, and satisfactory market position remains undeveloped.

Managers' Intentions

I asked managers whether they had deliberately chosen the small-scale entry strategy. Most venture managers had indeed targeted a low initial market

Exhibit 6.   Distribution of Sample on Entry Scale, First Two Years

Production scale:		
capacity as percentage of market size		
Less than 10%	21	31%
10%–19%	16	24
20%–29%	5	7
30%–39%	4	6
40%–49%	4	6
50%–59%	2	3
60%+	15	22
	67	99%
Median = 19%		
Marketing scale product line breadth		
Less broad[a]	44	65%
Same breadth	13	19
Broader	11	16
	68	100%
Segment size		
Fewer customers[a]	25	37%
About the same	36	54
More customers	6	9
	67	100%

[a]Relative to competitors

share. Exhibit 8 shows that 34 entrants, half the sample, set for the first two years a market share objective below 10%. Therefore, I judge that the poor performance of this sample was largely self-inflicted. In effect, these entrants obtained the market share they deserved, and this share in turn contributed to their financial losses. They could not generate enough revenue to cover their entry costs and to overcome their relative direct cost disadvantage.

An important management question here is, "Why would executives seek a low share?" At least four explanations come to mind:

1.   Perhaps there is still a widespread lack of awareness of the relationship between profitability and share. I suggest this explanation because, if executives were aware of this relationship, they would realize that they must build share in the start-up phase of a venture—ideally, reaching the number one position.

Exhibit 7.   Performance by Index of Entry Scale, First Two Years

	Median Value		
	Small Scale	Medium Scale	Large Scale
Return on investment	−41	−47	−24
Relative share	1	12	64

2.   Perhaps middle managers (presumably the proposers of new businesses) fear that, if they ask for too much capital and launching expenses, their idea will not be approved by top management. Thus they plan a small-scale entry to minimize their financial demands. Maybe capital-budgeting criteria emphasize financial results prematurely, thus fostering the practice of taking several small dips at the corporate well rather than one large scoop.

3.   Venture managers probably expect to be evaluated more on their own goals than on the long-run success of the particular venture. Therefore, they project a small share because they are more likely to attain it.

Iroquois Brands Ltd. seems to have deliberately overturned such standard capital-budgeting and evaluation criteria when it introduced a revolving venture capital fund. Iroquois hopes to encourage a long-term focus:

> Neither short-term earnings nor executive bonuses are penalized when the new ventures are started up. . . . The fund supplies 75% of the cost of approved projects, with the subsidiary putting up the remaining 25%. . . . Repayment, plus a 10% charge, starts one year after the new product goes to market or becomes profitable.[5]

4.   Another explanation could be that executives believe that starting small is prudent. After all, seeking high share requires larger investment for capacity and more marketing expenses to generate the sales to fill that capacity—all for a new business in an unknown, often still-evolving market. As one executive put it, "Far better to enter small, learn as you go, and expand with experience."

Exhibit 8.   Market Share Objectives, First Two Years

Share Objective	Businesses	Percentage
5% or less	24	36% ⎫ 51%
6%–10%	10	15 ⎭
11%–15%	8	12
16%–20%	8	12
20% +	17	25
	67[a]	100%

[a]One venture did not provide data.

If the small-scale approach were to work, it would seem most appropriate to the electronics industry—surely one of the most uncertain industries in the economy. Often, strategists cannot even be sure which of several competing production technologies is most efficient or profitable. Yet electronics executives argue strongly that "if you're going to get into a market, you'd better do it big." One of the major reasons for this view is an experience curve in which costs drop 15 to 30% each time accumulated volume doubles. In the face of such a cost-volume relationship, it is foolhardy to enter small, because the inevitable result must be an inferior relative cost position.

Not just in fast-growth markets do we hear executives saying, "Do it big." John A. Murphy, president and chief executive officer of Miller Brewing Company, said recently, "Ours is a simple objective; it is to become Number One."[6] Pursuing this objective, Miller and its owner since 1970, Philip Morris, have invested $500 million to increase capacity from about 5 million barrels to 34.8 million (in an industry growing at about 3% per year) and have spent $3 per barrel on advertising, almost three times the industry average. The results of Miller's strategy are shown in Exhibit 9.

One might argue that it is too early to evaluate the financial success of Miller's strategy. And, of course, the strategy has not been fully implemented. Miller spent $250 million in 1978 to add more capacity. But one cannot deny that Miller and its parent company have built a strong market position in an industry that is likely to enjoy many more years of life.

Management Implications

The clearest recommendation from this study is the need for large-scale entry. Such a recommendation might appear foolhardy in view of the financial results of this sample. Recall from Exhibit 7, however, that large-scale entrants reported the least negative results. I suggest that the eight years, on average, taken to reach positive net income would be reduced if higher relative share were achieved in the early years. Larger-scale entries might require less managerial patience.

Exhibit 9. One Company's Results with Large-Scale Entry

	1970	1971	1972	1973	1974	1975	1976	1977
Sales (in millions of dollars)	$198	$204	$210	$276	$404	$658	$983	$1,323
Profit (in millions of dollars)	$11.4	$1.3	$0.2	$(2.4)	$6.3	$28.6	$76.1	$106.5
Share	4%	4%	4%	5%	6%	9%	12%	15%
Market position	7	7	7	5	5	4	3	2

Source: Business Week, New York Times, and annual reports.

One might argue that market segmentation would allow profitable small-scale entries. However, as I explained while describing the sample, markets for the PIMS program are defined narrowly, at least compared with census definitions. Segmentation, therefore, has already occurred. We have been examining the performance of corporate ventures into parts of industries, rather than into entire industries. To illustrate this point, a venture marketing hospital pharmacy equipment confined the definition of its market to pharmacy equipment only, not to all types of hospital equipment. Therefore, its market share was its share of pharmacy equipment sales, not of hospital equipment sales.

I do not, however, recommend large spending on every opportunity in sight. Corporate diversification should not be played like Russian roulette. I do recommend that fewer ventures be launched, so that each can have the advantage of adequate resources to achieve a good market position, right from year one. Starting too many ventures at the same time diffuses the company's effort.

The recommendation for fewer ventures leads to another: One should back a new business and its managers as long as they continue to build share. Similarly, one should withdraw resources from a profitable venture if profits have been gained at the cost of share. It may be hard to realize in the heat of today's decisions, but a profitable corporate venture sitting on a low share is in fact tomorrow's dog. Conversely, the unprofitable venture gaining share and demanding ever more cash is tomorrow's winner.

The recommendation to enter on a large scale means that middle-level managers should "call it as they see it." I have seen too many corporate venture plans with, for example, marketing-sales ratios only slightly higher than those for established businesses and profits forecast for the second year. According to this sample, such a corporate venture rarely exists.

Middle-level executives must estimate what it will take to build a successful business and see that top executives know what they are getting into. This sample tells us that share points are gained only slowly and after the commitment of substantial resources. Middle managers should study the most recent venture pro forma they have been working on. If its operating and capital ratios are better than those shown in Exhibit 2, they should ask themselves, "Why will *this* venture outperform the median venture in a sample of corporate ventures?"

Similarly, if profits are forecast early in the life of the venture, they should ask, "What is relative market share in the first year of profitability?" It is quite probable that early profitability has been forecast at the expense of a long-term market position.

Conclusion

The data in this article tell us, more precisely than we knew before, about the risks in corporate ventures. The odds are unattractive. Indeed, many managers will find them daunting. But, at the same time, managers know that they have to build a balanced corporate product portfolio. I believe that the way to improve the odds and build the portfolio is to commit substantial resources to each venture and to defer immediate financial performance in favor of market position. Launching new businesses takes large scale entry and continual commitment; it is not an activity for the impatient or for the fainthearted.

Notes

1. See Sidney Schoeffler, Robert D. Buzzell, and Donald F. Heany, "Impact of Strategic Planning on Profit Performance," *HBR*, March–April 1974, p. 137; and Robert D. Buzzell, Bradley T. Gale, and Ralph G.M. Sultan, "Market Share—A Key to Profitability," *HBR*, January—February 1975, p. 97.

2. "GE's New Strategy for Faster Growth," *Business Week*, July 8, 1972, p. 52.

3. See Buzzell, Gale, and Sultan, "Market Share—A Key to Profitability."

4. Ibid., p. 99.

5. "Iroquois Brands: An Aggressive Search for the Unique," *Business Week*, February 27, 1978, p. 112.

6. *Milwaukee Journal*, September 22, 1977.

26

New Ventures for Corporate Growth

EDWARD B. ROBERTS

As the traditional avenues of corporate growth become less attractive, many companies find the appeal of new venture strategies harder to resist. Though difficult to implement and often slow to repay investments, these strategies do offer the promise of facilitating entry into new business areas with innovative, usually technology-based products. And for large companies with many layers of management and detailed control systems, ventures offer the special promise of recapturing some vital spark of entrepreneurial energy.

The author of this article discusses the growing appeal of new venture strategies and the particular kinds of needs that they meet. Then, drawing on his extensive research into venture organizations, he outlines in some detail the various major types of ventures, pinpointing the virtues and defects of each. He concludes with a few pieces of general advice about venturing.

To meet ambitious plans for growth and diversification, corporations are turning in increasing numbers to new venture strategies. However, most new ventures fail. And even when they do succeed, they often take ten years or more to generate substantial returns on the initial investment of capital and management attention. The question is obvious: Given its uncertain promise, why is corporate venturing proving so attractive?

The odds against its success are enormous. The push toward a venture strategy usually comes when a company, wishing to address customer needs it has not previously served, seeks either to enter new markets or to sell dramatically different products in its existing markets. Second, most ventures involve a new technology—whether that technology is new to the world or only to the company. Third, almost every corporation undertaking a

---

Published 1980.

venture has found it both necessary and desirable to establish for it a structure quite different from that in use throughout the rest of the organization.

Entering unfamiliar markets, employing unfamiliar technology, and implementing an unfamiliar organizational structure—even taken separately, each of these presents a troublesome challenge. Put all three together in a single new venture organization, and it is no wonder that their joint probability of success is rather small.

Nonetheless, venture strategies are increasingly attractive to many companies. My purpose in this article is, first of all, to consider just why this should be so. I then examine and evaluate the various options available to companies embarking on a venture strategy. Finally, I discuss what companies can do to improve the likelihood of venture success.

Though I address all three points, my focus will primarily be on two of the options: the large and small company joint venture, which has the principal virtue of speed of market impact, and the internal venture organization, which is best illustrated by Minnesota Mining and Manufacturing Company (3M) with its long-term record of success in venturing.

Why Establish a Venture Organization?

If the odds against a new venture strategy are high, what makes it so very appealing? The answer is really quite simple: the alternatives are no better. No other strategy for enhancing growth in size or profitability currently offers a higher probability of success. Consider:

☐ When it was still easy to identify unmet needs in the marketplace, companies could launch products to meet them with every expectation that the markets thus defined would continue to grow and to support continued company growth. Today, however, many such traditional markets have become saturated, incapable of additional sustained growth.

☐ When there were still few large companies in the developed world and little technological competition among them, a company could apply its R&D capacities to develop new products, which it could then sustain relatively easily by ongoing efforts at incremental innovation. Today, with technological sophistication diffused throughout the world, for a company to remain competitive—especially with mature high-volume products—requires far more than the uneven performance of traditional R&D.

☐ When untapped foreign markets were still plentiful, it was a simple matter to enter them. Today, the overwhelming likelihood is that those markets have long since been populated both by domestic competitors and by native companies.

☐ When interest rates were lower, price/earnings ratios higher, and antitrust regulation less strictly enforced, companies could readily grow and diversify by acquiring other companies. Today, an acquisitions strategy can rarely be pursued on such advantageous terms.

In short, the most common growth strategies of an earlier era are no longer so easy to follow or so likely to succeed. Consequently, venture strategies, even with their low probability of success, have begun to look much better.

The Spectrum of Venture Strategies

Exhibit 1 displays the range of alternative strategies for launching new ventures. At one end are those approaches that feature essentially low company involvement; at the other, approaches that demand high levels of commitment both in dollars and in management time.

Venture Capital

At the far left of the spectrum is venture capital, the investment of money in the stock of one company by another. During the mid- to late 1960s many major corporations decided to secure entry into new technologies by taking investment positions in young high-technology enterprises. Major companies in a variety of industries—companies such as DuPont, Exxon, Ford, General Electric, and Singer—sought out a "window" on promising technologies through the venture capital route, but few of them have been able to make the venture capital approach by itself an important stimulus of corporate growth or profitability.

Venture Nurturing

Second along the spectrum, venture nurturing involves more than just capital investment. Here the investing company also gives managerial assistance to the nurtured enterprise in such areas as marketing, manufacturing, and research. Though perhaps a more sensible approach to diversification than just the arm's-length provision of funds, venture nurturing is still unlikely to have a significant impact on the investor's sales or profits. Cabot Corporation, for example, tried this approach but gave up after two years of frustrating experience with several start-up companies.

Exhibit 1.   Spectrum of Venture Strategies

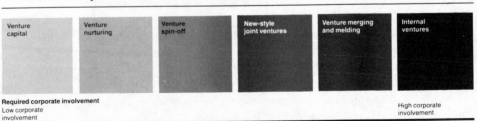

| Venture capital | Venture nurturing | Venture spin-off | New-style joint ventures | Venture merging and melding | Internal ventures |

Required corporate involvement
Low corporate involvement   High corporate involvement

Venture Spin-Off

As a by-product of its R&D efforts, a corporation may develop an idea or technology that does not fit its mainstream interest, that may entail substantial risks to the parent, or that may be better developed on an independent basis outside the company. The originating company will then spin off the new business as a separate corporation, either seeking to gain market and operational experience in a new field, as Exxon Enterprises did temporarily with its Solar Power Corporation, or to attract outside growth capital, as General Electric did with its formation of Nuclepore and other companies.[1] Venture spin-off may be a good way to hold on to an internal entrepreneur or to exploit a by-product technology, but the limited involvement it allows still promises only limited returns to the parent company.

New-Style Joint Ventures

Because I think this approach of particular importance, I will discuss it in more detail later on. Here large and small companies enter jointly into new ventures. The small companies provide entrepreneurial enthusiasm, vigor, flexibility, and advanced technology; the large ones, capital and, perhaps more important, worldwide channels of marketing, distribution, and service. This combination allows for the rapid diffusion of technology-based product innovations into large national and international markets.[2]

Venture Merging and Melding

Toward the right side of Exhibit 1 is an approach that I call, for lack of a better name, venture merging and melding. This is what Exxon Enterprises is attempting by deliberately piecing together all the various forms of technologically oriented venturing shown in Exhibit 1 into a critical mass of marketing and technological strengths. In turn, these strengths have allowed Exxon to transform itself from a huge—though unglamorous—one-product, narrow-technology oil company to an exciting company that is expanding into computers and communications, advanced composite materials, and alternative energy devices.[3]

Internal Ventures

Finally, on the far right are internal ventures, those situations in which a company sets up a separate entity within itself—an entirely separate division or group—for the purpose of entering different markets or developing radically different products. This approach has great potential but a mixed record to date. Du Pont, for instance, has had a spotty record in internal corporate-level venturing for nearly two decades.[4] Ralston Purina, however, has done reasonably well. For the record, the most consistently effective performance with internal ventures I know of is that of 3M, whose philosophy and methods I will describe in some detail later in this article.

Teaming the Large with the Small

Let us now examine in depth an approach to venturing that has shown itself to be relatively "quick and dirty" and adaptable: the new-style joint venture. You will recall that new-style ventures are those in which large and small companies join forces to create a new entry in the marketplace. The idea here is quite simple. The large company usually provides access to capital and to channels of distribution, sales, and service otherwise unavailable to the small company; in return, the small company provides advanced technology and a degree of entrepreneurial commitment the larger one often lacks. Together the strengths of both add up to a distinct competitive advantage.

Numerous studies on the process of innovation have shown time and again that small companies and individual inventors account for a disproportionate share of commercially successful, technologically based innovations.[5] Whether the explanation lies in their superior commitment, drive, freedom from constraint, flexibility, or closeness to the market, the facts themselves are quite clear. Small entrepreneurially minded companies have been unusually able to come up with technological advances that are competitive in the marketplace.

Balancing Needs with Strengths

But the small company has an obvious problem: its size. It has neither extensive market coverage nor an extensive sales force. It is usually not even a national company. Young entrepreneurial companies are often regional at best, and the obstacles they face—organizational and financial—in becoming national or international are tremendous. The great success stories of corporations such as Polaroid, Xerox, or Digital Equipment are clear exceptions to the rule.[6] In the vast majority of cases, the small technology-based company simply cannot grow from within to large-scale size with the time and resources available to it.

By contrast, a large company has relatively easy access to capital markets as well as significant capital availability within itself. Moreover, it not only has large sales but a large establishment overall. It has ample manufacturing capacity located near its various national and international markets. It has a distribution and marketing organization that covers all its relevant market territory. It can service its products on a national and international basis.

Competitive Advantage

Now, if the entrepreneurial commitment, innovative behavior, and advanced technological products of the small company were combined with the capital availability, marketing strength, and distribution channels of the large, it stands to reason that the synthesis might well create significant competitive advantage. Indeed, many pairs of differently sized companies have entered into just this kind of venture arrangement. Exhibit 2 lists but a few of the attempts in the Boston area alone.

Exhibit 2. Examples of Large/Small Company Joint Ventures

Large company	Small company	Area of joint venture
American Broadcasting Co.	Technical Operations	Black-and-white film transmitted for color TV viewing
American District Telegraph	Solid State Technology	Industrial security systems
Bell & Howell	Microx	Microfilm readers
Bravo	Anti-Pollution Systems	Molten-salt pollution control systems
Elliott (division of Carrier)	Mechanical Technology	High-speed centrifugal compressors
Exxon Nuclear (division of Exxon)	Avco Everett Research Laboratory	High-energy laser uranium isotope separation and enrichment
Ford Motor	Thermo Electron	Steam engines for automobiles
General Electric	Bolt Beranek & Newman	Hospital computer systems
Johnson & Johnson	Damon	Automated clinical laboratory systems
3M	Energy Devices	Updatable microfilm systems
Mobil	Tyco Laboratories	Long-crystal silicon solar conversion technology
Pitney Bowes	Alpex Computer	Electronic "point of sale" checkout systems
Roche Electronics (division of Hoffmann-La Roche)	Avco Everett Research Laboratory	Inflatable balloon heart assist systems
Wyeth Laboratories (division of American Home Products)	Survival Technology	Self-administered heart attack drug and injection systems

A typical example of a successful arrangement is the joint venture between Roche Electronics, a division of Hoffmann-La Roche, and the Avco Everett Research Laboratory. Their venture was to produce an inflatable balloon heart assist pump, and it has been both technically and commercially successful. The development of the product came from a combination of the electronics technology and materials capability of Avco Everett with the marketing, distribution, and field service capability of Roche. More recently, Avco Everett has taken over the entire venture as part of its own diversification movement into the medical field.

Characteristic Difficulties

However, no matter how appealing the prospect, the problems with this new-style approach are significant and troubling. Consider, for example, Johnson & Johnson's joint effort with Damon Corporation to develop automated clinical laboratory equipment.

At the time of the joint venture, Johnson & Johnson had annual sales of roughly $3 billion. By contrast, Damon, a spin-off from the MIT Research Laboratory for Electronics, had only $3 million in sales when it started negotiations with Johnson & Johnson and $30 million by the time it successfully concluded negotiations to initiate the joint venture three years later. The intended product was to sell at prices of $100,000 or more to large hospitals for doing clinical analyses of patient fluids.

Though a partial technical success, the product was a commercial failure. Why? Because two kinds of problems often confront new-style ventures.

Misreading. Often both partners misread the appropriateness of the large company's channels of marketing and distribution. It is all too easy for a large company to think that it can sell almost anything through its vast field sales and service organization.

In the Johnson & Johnson–Damon case, Johnson & Johnson could correctly say that it had salespeople regularly calling on every major hospital in the free world. Therefore, it might well have felt it had the representation necessary to sell a Damon-developed clinical laboratory system. But Johnson & Johnson sold largely disposable medical products such as Band-Aids; the people to whom it sold were reorder clerks, inventory supervisors, or head nurses; and the basis on which it sold was a combination of product quality and volume discounts.

To whom, however, does one sell a $100,000 piece of clinical laboratory equipment? Certainly not reorder clerks or inventory supervisors. The director of the hospital's clinical laboratories will be involved, as will the hospital's chief administrator. And in all but the largest hospitals, so will the board of trustees. It is too much to expect that sales personnel used to selling Band-Aids to reorder clerks can switch overnight to such a different level of responsibility and remain effective.

In addition, a major piece of clinical apparatus requires a special level of field service. With its different experience, Johnson & Johnson simply did not have that kind of field operation in place. To be fair, Johnson & Johnson had also been selling small medical instruments, but even this had not prepared it for the service requirements of a clinical laboratory analyzer.

Though it is easy to misread at first glance the appropriateness of a large company's marketing channels, a little careful thought and common sense are often all that are needed. The central question is clear: Do the company's sales and service organizations meet the particular requirements of the new product? If not, can they be made appropriate with only slight modifications—say, expanding an existing service capability or adding a specialty salesperson to an existing field office? Incremental change of this sort, if a realistic alternative, is almost always less expensive than starting from scratch and trying to build a whole new organization.

Impedance Mismatch. This is more of a generic problem of new-style ventures than the misreading just discussed. Differently sized companies tend to breathe, play, and act on very different frequencies. They have very different ways of managing themselves and their decision processes. David Kosowsky, the president of Damon, is quoted as saying that he would come to a negotiating session with Johnson & Johnson prepared to bet his company, ready to make decisions as needed. Yet he saw the Johnson & Johnson people as coming to the same meetings prepared to listen, absorb, report, and carry information back to their superiors for further consideration.

The small company entrepreneur is often ready to make a decision based on gut feelings and to commit on the spot whatever is necessary to implement the decision. The large corporation's time scale for making decisions extends for months and sometimes years.

In general, the behavior of a large company is very different from that of a small one. The large company does basic research. The small company does technical problem solving. The large company does market research.

The small company executive talks to a few friends in other organizations to get a feeling for how they view a potential product. Such differences in organizational temperament can easily produce strains and misunderstandings.

Despite these various difficulties, I believe that the promise of new-style joint ventures is quite high. More than any other form of venturing, they offer the possibility of reasonably quick market impact and profitability, for they seek to build on competitive strengths already in place.

Internal Venturing at 3M

For over 30 years, 3M has primarily based its steady growth in size and profitability on new businesses developed through internal ventures. More than most other major corporations, it has thoroughly organized itself to encourage and support them. Its long-term record of success—ROI increasing at approximately 16% compounded annually—speaks for itself, but we may legitimately ask just how 3M goes about venturing so successfully.

What Is a New Business?
To look at 3M's organization on paper (see Exhibit 3) is initially to see a rather ordinary structure. Near the top of the organization are two divisions

Exhibit 3.   3M Structure for New Ventures

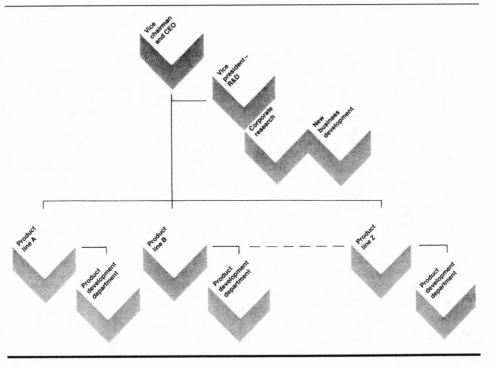

that report to the vice president of research and development: the Corporate Research Laboratory and the New Business Development Division. The latter, however, has quite a different charter than that of comparable units in most other companies. Here is where the real distinctions begin.

In 3M, a new business is defined behaviorally as one that has not yet reached critical mass in the marketplace, although it has perhaps as much as $20 million in annual sales. This means that the corporate New Business Development Division is charged with the responsibility of evolving, nurturing, and maintaining diverse business activities at various stages of development. It is an internal venture nurturing organization, an operation that not only gives birth but also support and sustenance. When new products are big enough to be self-sustaining, it spins them down the organizational chart as part of an existing division or as a new product line division.

Product Development

The second point worth noting about 3M's structure is that it is for the most part built on product line organizations, which have doubled in number since 1970, each with its own product development department. By itself this structure is not unusual. What is unusual is the charter of the product development departments. Each of them is charged with assisting the division that it serves by coming up with new products for that division's present line of business, with incremental improvements in old products, and with useful process changes. All of this is conventional. What is unconventional is that each of the product development departments is also charged with the responsibility for new venture development—new ventures without product line or business area constraints.

It is perfectly acceptable for any of these departments to develop products in any line of business, even if the new product competes with the output of another product division. Put simply, the 3M philosophy is, "We would rather have one of our own new products competing with an existing product line of 3M than have a competitor's new product competing." To the argument, "Surely that creates dissent and competition; isn't that bad?" 3M responds, "No, not from our way of thinking. We think that it can be good."

Does this philosophy create duplication of resources? Of course it does. Does it create efficiently used resources? I suspect that it does because the model of efficient competition is applied not just to the external but also to the internal marketplace. Competition for money, ideas, people, and market dominance keeps all participants in fighting trim.

The Eleventh Commandment

From top to bottom 3M's management provides active, spirited encouragement for new venture generation. Many at the company even speak of a special eleventh commandment: "Thou shalt not kill a new product idea." And they follow it seriously in practice. Contrary to the situation in many other companies, those in 3M who want to stop the development of a new product are saddled with the burden of proof. Benefit of the doubt goes right to those who propose projects, not those who oppose them.

Of course, pushing a new product idea does not immediately throw open an endless bank account, but it does guarantee a chance to succeed. With the burden of proof on those who wish to kill ideas, the work environment within the company is distinctly favorable to entrepreneurial activity. In part this environment is the result of promoting top management from within, frequently from successes in venture management. But it is everywhere reinforced. As one longtime observer has remarked, "You can't even talk for ten minutes to a janitor at 3M without the conversation turning to new products."

Sources of Funding

Another important kind of support for new ventures is the multiple sources of venture capital within the company. Corporate groups can provide funding for new ventures without regard to source, and each product line department can provide funding for its employee's ideas no matter what market they are aimed at.

Say someone engaged in product development or marketing approaches her boss with an idea for a new product. If, despite all of the pressures on the boss to be supportive, he still answers, "We really don't have the money; we can't afford to handle it; we can't support your activity," the proposer is not then shut off permanently inside 3M. She is free to go elsewhere in the company to seek support for her idea, and a real market exists for the potential support of these ideas.

Moreover, if she can convince someone else to support her idea, then her idea does not go alone; she goes with it. The individual must be able to move with her idea and to join with her sponsor in undertaking the product development work. Then she and her sponsor quite properly share the blame if it fails and the benefits if it succeeds.

Product Teams

3M also gives special attention to the formation of product teams, entrepreneurial minibusiness groups that 3M calls business development units. At an early stage of developing a new product idea, 3M tries to recruit individuals from marketing, the technical area, finance, and manufacturing to come together as a team, each member of which is committed to the further development and movement of this particular product into the market.

To make the team more effective, 3M does not *assign* people to such activities; the team members are recruited. This makes a very big difference in results. In most companies, a marketing person assigned to evaluate a technical person's idea can get off the hook most easily by saying that the idea is poor and by pointing out all of its deficiencies, its inadequate justification, and its lack of a market. Given the usual incentive systems, why should the marketing person share the risk? But instead of assigning him or her to evaluate the idea, 3M approaches Marketing and says, "Is anyone here interested in working on this?"

Here is a good instant test of a new product idea. If no one in the organization wants to join the new team, the idea behind it may not be very good. More important, whoever says, "I want in," becomes a partner, not a subordinate. He or she shares both in the risk and in the commitment and enthusiasm that go along with it. Team members are not likely to say, "This cannot be produced. It can never break even. It will never sell." They are involved as a team because they want to be, and they have a lot invested in making the idea work.

3M then supports its teams by saying to them in effect, "We are committed to you as a group. You will move forward with your product into the marketplace and benefit from its growth. But we cannot promise to keep you together forever as a new venture team. We will do our best to keep the team going so long as you meet our standard financial measures of performance throughout the life cycle of the product. If you fail, we will give you a backup commitment of job security at the level of job you left to join the venture. We cannot promise any specific job. But if you try hard and work diligently and simply fail, then we will at least guarantee you a backup job."

And some 3M ventures do get cancelled. Although the company will not reveal is success/failure data, it has said that its ratio of success is comparable to that of other organizations. The key difference, of course, is that 3M starts many more new ventures.

Measures of Performance

The financial measures that 3M applies to new ventures are simple and to the point: ROI, profit margin, and sales growth rate. Only if a product team meets these criteria will the company make every effort to keep it going. These measures are straightforward and objective. What sets 3M's standards apart, however, is what they do *not* include. First, they do not require a minimum "promised" size in sales volume for any given product idea. Instead, 3M says something like this to its product teams:

"Our experience tells us that prior to its entry into the market, we do not really know how to anticipate the sales growth of a new product. Consequently, we will make market forecasts that stick after you have entered the market, not before. We will listen to your ideas, argue with them, and do all kinds of analyses and estimates, but we will not say at the outset, 'The idea must be capable of generating $50 million or $100 million per year in sales.' Of course, we prefer larger businesses, but we will accept smaller businesses as entries into new fields."

Further, 3M's standards do not place area-of-business constraints on the generation of new product ideas. Unlike most other companies, it does not say to its teams, "Whatever ideas you come up with are fine, so long as they fall within business areas where we are strong." Nor does it say, "We want your new ideas—provided, of course, that the resulting products can be manufactured in our existing plants out of our existing stocks of raw materials and can be sold through our existing sales and distribution channels."

Reward Systems

The final element of 3M's approach to new ventures is its handling of rewards. All individuals involved in a new venture will have more or less automatic changes in their employment and compensation categories as a function of the sales growth of their product. Moreover, because the stimulation and sponsorship of new products is a responsibility of management at all levels, 3M has established special compensation incentives for those managers who are able to "breed" new ventures or departments.

Key Lessons from Venture Studies

I can make with confidence only three summary generalizations about successful new venture strategies.

□ *They require long-term persistence.* How long is long-term? At the bare minimum, if a corporation is not willing to commit itself to a five- to seven-year involvement, then it should not even think of undertaking new ventures. What is needed is "patient money"—money in the hands of an executive group that is centrally concerned with the future growth and development of the company, money that need not generate payoffs in the next few years. In fact, ten to twelve years is a more reasonable time span.

□ *They depend on entrepreneurial behavior.* The basis of every venture strategy is the attempt by a large company either to link up with or to emulate a small entrepreneurial company. In a sense this is surprising because it violates many of the textbook arguments for economies of scale. Yet in increasing numbers multimillion- and multibillion-dollar corporations are trying to scale down their manner of operating when they want to enter new business areas. They have rediscovered the special virtues of building an entrepreneurial organization and of harnessing entrepreneurial energy.

□ *No single strategy works for all.* What works for 3M will not necessarily work for every company. There are no magic formulas, and it is dangerously misleading to mimic the particular success of others. The current state of knowledge about venturing supports a far more modest conclusion: a variety of possible venture strategies is available, and it is up to each company's management to assess its own special needs, abilities, and personnel. This is simple common sense, but—like much sound managerial wisdom—it is all too often forgotten.

Notes

1. Sharon Sabin, "At Nuclepore, They Don't Work for G.E. Anymore," *Fortune*, December 1973, p. 145.

2. James D. Hlavacek, Brian H. Dovey, and John J. Biondo, "Tie Small Business Technology to Marketing Power," *HBR*, January-February 1977, p. 119.

3. "Exxon's Next Prey: IBM and Xerox," *Business Week*, April 28, 1980, p. 92.

4. Russell W. Peterson, "New Venture Management in a Large Company," *HBR*, May-June 1967, p. 68.

5. Five of these studies are referenced in my article, "Technology Strategy for the European Firm," *Industrial Marketing Management*, August 1975, p. 193.

6. See my article, "Entrepreneurship and Technology," *Research Management*, vol. XI, no. 4, 1968, p. 249.

PART FIVE

MANAGING THE GROWTH COMPANY

AN OVERVIEW

If this generation of managers has an idealized role model, it would not be the flannel-suited "organization man" of the early postwar years but, rather, the tieless and coatless entrepreneur of a high-technology growth company along Route 128 in Massachusetts or in California's Silicon Valley. The mystique of guiding a start-up venture through a period of astronomic growth into the ranks of the *Fortune* "500"—and, of course, becoming fabulously wealthy in the process—has taken hold in the managerial imagination. Even in the more sedate environment of established companies, the bonuses, the promotions, and the glory seek out those responsible for high-growth business lines or divisions. Maintaining solid profitability in slowly expanding enterprises, absorbing low current returns in order to revitalize a sluggish business—these, for the most part, are less attractive and less well rewarded assignments.

What often gets lost in this individual as well as corporate idealization of the booming success are the very real managerial problems such companies face. The six articles in this final section take a hard look at the costs, anticipated or otherwise, of fast-track expansion—not least, the stresses such expansion places on scarce managerial and financial resources. Equally important, they raise pointed questions about the advisability of growth- or share-driven strategies for every business. It is not always the case that more is better, even if more can be afforded and managed.

Growth Pains of the Threshold Company

DONALD K. CLIFFORD, JR.

The companies lying just beneath the *Fortune* "500" are large enough to expand dynamically and dramatically, but they are not yet large enough to enjoy the great power and inner strengths of the largest corporations. They rarely have the financial resources and flexibilities of the leaders; and their management groups usually lack the depth and skills needed to govern rapid growth successfully. The top management of a company moving toward the threshold of leadership must reckon with these two facts: it must bring about a series of major changes in organization, staffing, and management processes as the company grows through each stage of product/ market complexity and, at the same time, deal with the economic realities that make the life of the smaller company more difficult than that of the larger company. The responsibility for making these changes falls most heavily on the CEO, who must manage the company with the utmost skill and sensitivity. This article outlines the specific economic and management challenges that the CEO and the company must meet before it finally passes the threshold of full maturity as an industry leader.

Small and medium-sized companies—the ones with less than $20 million in sales—are usually managed and controlled personally by one or two entrepreneur/executives. The products and markets of these companies tend to be relatively simple and well-defined, and there is little need for formal management structures and processes.

In contrast, few companies with over $200 million in sales are able to operate informally. These are the leading industrials of the *Fortune* "500," companies whose complex and diverse operations call for specialized skills, formal structures, and carefully designed management processes.

Hence the company that moves from a $20 million- to a $200 million-level of annual sales must pass through a management metamorphosis; its

Published 1973.

top management must effect a transition from the simplicity of the entrepreneurial enterprise to the formality and sophistication of the giant.

Companies in the process of making this transition I label the *threshold
companies*. This particular group has hitherto received little attention, for
an understandable reason: they are, in one sense, a new breed. Fifteen years
ago the companies lying just below the giant industrials of the "500" had
relatively simple product lines, and their markets were virtually restricted
to the domestic United States. Today the companies in this group are multiproduct, multimarket entities, operating over the broad spread of the economy. Their high complexity demands sophisticated management, which is
rendered the more difficult because these companies do not enjoy the economic and market advantages of industry leadership.

The mixed performance of this group reflects the extraordinary demands placed on the managements and on the limited resources of these
companies. In the past three years, about 100 companies have succeeded in
passing over the threshold into the $200 million plus category, but hundreds
of others have declined both in profits and in sales volumes.

To gain an understanding of the dynamics of success and failure in this
group, my colleagues and I examined in some depth a sample of 795 threshold
companies, operating in many industries. We found the successful threshold
company is distinguishable by the skill with which it takes certain economic
and management hurdles that it must jump before it becomes a giant
corporation.

Three Economic Hurdles

Threshold companies consistently exhibit specific economic characteristics
that distinguish them from the giants, characteristics with which their managers must deal effectively if these companies are to join the ranks of the
largest corporations:

☐ Threshold companies have a significantly greater growth potential
and downside risk than the largest corporations.

☐ Their profit margins tend to be lower than those of their giant
competitors. Equally important, those margins are presently declining,
making the effectiveness of corporate strategy, marketing strategy, and
profit improvement highly critical.

☐ Financially, they are more sensitive. Their balance sheets show
more highly leveraged positions, and money costs them more than it
does their giant competitors.

Growth Potential and Downside Risk

Growth, as measured by earnings-per-share performance, varies far more
widely among threshold companies than among the giants. Some 44% of the

profitable threshold companies grew at a compound rate of more than 10% annually between 1965 and 1970; only 23% of the "500" grew at such rates. At the other end of the scale, 24% of the threshold companies showed an EPS that declined by more than 10% over this period; the corresponding figure in the "500" class is only 17%. Further, some 18% of the threshold companies actually lost money in 1970, compared with only 7% of the "500."

This general pattern is evident in most industry segments. For instance, in the sample of 24 food and beverage companies my colleagues and I studied, the corporations with the best showings on EPS outperformed the *Fortune* "500" on this measure, almost without exception. Similarly, the worst performers on this measure among the threshold group consistently performed at a lower EPS level than the "500."

But in individual companies the year-to-year volatility of earnings was also greater for the threshold corporation than for the giant. There seem to be several primary reasons for this difference:

☐ The threshold company is less diversified and hence is more strongly affected by industry cycles.

☐ It is less conservatively financed and hence is more readily influenced by economic and commercial developments.

☐ It is less powerful and has a weaker market position.

Importance of Profit Margins

Operating margins in the sample of 795 threshold companies are lower than they are among the giants, by 2% to 4% of sales. This disadvantage of the threshold companies is magnified by the fact that margin levels are declining for both groups of companies.

To get a more precise feel for the importance of margin maintenance to earnings results among the thresholds, my colleagues and I analyzed the best and worst performers in the eight industries listed in Exhibit 1. We found the following to be true:

☐ Sales growth is important, but does not guarantee EPS growth. Exhibit 1 shows that the sales growth of the best and worst performers was roughly the same in each of four industries—printing and publishing, building products, chemicals, and computer software and leasing. Yet, in these same industries, the spread of EPS growth was still dramatic.

☐ The best performers have high operating profit margins. This is true for each of these industries except electrical machinery and computer software and leasing. On the average, margins for the best EPS performers were 6.4% higher than those of the poor performers—a tremendous economic advantage.

☐ The study also made it clear that *in every instance* the top EPS performers succeeded in either maintaining or increasing their margin

Exhibit 1.   Financial Performance of Threshold Companies by Industry

| | Annual growth rates, 1966-1970 | | | |
| | EPS | | Sales | |
Industry	Best EPS performers	Worst EPS performers	Best EPS performers	Worst EPS performers
Fabricated metal products	11.9%	−14.2%	17.3%	6.3%
Printing and publishing	11.7	− 6.4	13.2	9.8
Building products	17.3	− 8.4	13.3	12.1
Chemical companies	11.9	−12.2	13.5	9.5
Nonelectrical machinery	9.6	−19.4	16.3	2.7
Food and beverage	13.8	−14.2	20.1	5.3
Electrical machinery	12.4	−20.7	14.9	3.2
Computer software and leasing	38.9	−19.5	56.4	72.8

| | Operating margin, 1970 | | Annual change in operating margin, 1966-1970 | |
Industry	Best EPS performers	Worst EPS performers	Best EPS performers	Worst EPS performers
Fabricated metal products	14.9%	8.0%	4.8%	− 5.5%
Printing and publishing	19.7	10.4	2.1	− 2.6
Building products	19.1	14.0	− .1	− 8.7
Chemical companies	22.9	7.5	− .3	−14.9
Nonelectrical machinery	13.4	7.6	− .7	− 8.5
Food and beverage	17.6	9.3	− 2.3	−10.4
Electrical machinery	3.6	7.7	− 2.8	−14.8
Computer software and leasing	18.9	47.5	− 4.8	−10.0

levels or holding margin deterioration to a minimum. (Notably, this occurred while the margins of U.S. corporations at large were declining sharply.)

Hence maintenance of operating profit margins appears to be a key—probably *the* key—to EPS growth in a threshold company. Management clearly needs the flexibility and resilience that extra margin brings.

Financial Sensitivity

Because their products and markets are growing in complexity, threshold companies often become preoccupied with operating performance at the expense of financial condition. This is a hazardous course for a company that has not yet achieved the financial resources or the financial stability of the giants.

To quantify the financial sensitivity of these companies, we created a "Threshold Company Dow Jones Average," using 30 threshold companies in the same industries as those in the real Dow Jones Average (see Exhibit 2). In comparing the financial structures and the performance of the two groups, we found that the companies in this Threshold Dow—

☐ . . . *have grown much faster.* Consequently their relative need for new capital was far greater.

☐ . . . *have used capital more efficiently.* However, because of

Exhibit 2.   The "Threshold Dow Jones"

A. *Comparative financial performance*

	Threshold company Dow Jones Average		Real Dow Jones Average	
	1966	1970	1966	1970
Sales volume	100%	189%	100%	123%
Total capital turnover	0.91	0.96	0.90	0.81
Long-term debt/equity ratio	0.46	0.56	0.24	0.34
Operating profit margin	16.40	14.60	20.80	16.80
After-tax profit	6.70	5.60	8.90	6.80

B. *Comparative financial profiles, 1970*

	Threshold company Dow Jones Average	Real Dow Jones Average
Debt/equity ratio	0.56	0.34
Debt-service coverage*	4.68	7.31
Average interest cost on total loans	6.97	5.97
Working capital turnover	4.58	7.49

* Debt/equity ratio times interest paid.

their rapid increase in volume, this increased turnover contributed little toward meeting new capital requirements.

☐ . . . *have continued to be more highly leveraged.*   (I might note that using increased debt to expand assets may be sound financial management up to a point, but this practice cannot be continued indefinitely.)

☐ . . . *have had to fight declining margins.*   As a result, future growth has had to be financed increasingly from external sources, barring major increases in capital turnover.

□ . . . *have had less conservative financial profiles.*   Not only were the Threshold Dow companies more highly leveraged, they also paid substantially higher interest rates, had lower debt-service coverage, and made less efficient use of working capital.

These distinctive and tougher economic characteristics make compelling demands on the management of threshold companies. At the same time, however, the top management of a threshold company faces an even greater challenge: it must adapt every phase of its management—structures, processes, and people—to the new demands of a shifting and increasingly complex product/market profile.

The Management Hurdles

Because threshold companies are changing more rapidly than companies of other sizes, the pace of their management adaptation must be greater. The kinds of changes management must make in order to keep the company under control can be discussed in five sequential steps:

1   As a threshold company grows, it almost inevitably attempts to serve an increasing number of markets with a wide range of products. Expanding product/market complexity dramatically compounds the number and intricacy of management's decisions and activities.
2   New skills must be introduced to handle these decisions and activities.
3   Changes in organization structure and management processes must be introduced to harness this broader range of skills—that is, to control and allocate resources to diverse products, markets, and technologies.
4   Changes in structure, management processes, and skills require the company to face up to difficult people problems—retraining, recycling, and replacing executives.
5   The entire change process depends on whether chief executives can radically alter their own roles in running the business as it grows. Of all the five changes that must be made, this one is frequently the most difficult of all to achieve.

Product/Market Complexity

Almost without exception, business corporations start off life with a single product line of reasonably simple design. This line is typically sold in limited geographic markets through relatively few channels to a few customer groups. As companies grow, however, change comes rapidly in the following areas:

1 *Products*
  Number and diversity of products.
  Complexity of individual products.
  Degree of forward/backward integration.
  Rate of product innovation.
2 *Markets*
  Geographic scope.
  Number and character of the distribution channels.
  Number and diversity of customer groups.
3 *Environment*
  Intensity of competition in pricing, products, and marketing.
  Economic, social, governmental, and labor pressures.

Exhibit 3 shows how one particular company evolved in a variety of these areas between 1968, when its sales amounted to $9.8 million, and 1972, when its sales amounted to $100.1 million.

Although each company one might analyze would show its own distinct evolutionary profile, change along these general lines is virtually inevitable. Most products generate no more than a few million dollars in annual sales; consequently, many new products must be added as a company moves through the $20 million–$200 million range. This product innovation, with its concomitant market extension, leads naturally to greater complexity in all the areas I have listed. (True, a few single-product companies, such as Polaroid and Wrigley, have achieved sales of several hundred million dollars, but cases of this kind are rare.)

In addition, many threshold companies enter new fields to create opportunities and excitement for their promising executives; in the minds of many chief executives, this is an objective which ranks close in importance to growth in earnings per share.

The result of this increasing activity is a geometric increase in the number and intricacy of decisions and activities management must undertake. The dollar impact of major decisions also increases with size. Yet, at the same time, top management's familiarity and direct contact with the details of the business necessarily diminish.

Fortunately, the top management of a threshold company can govern the rate of increase of complexity so that impossible demands are not placed on corporate capabilities. The majority of successful threshold companies follow strategies that build on key corporate strengths in products, technologies, and marketing, and they deliberately moderate the rate of increase in product/market complexity.

For an instructive contrast, one might look at the aggressive conglomerate strategy that caused growth explosions in a number of well-known companies in the last dozen years:

☐ One high-technology company that received a great deal of attention in the past year expanded to 24 divisions in a matter of a few

Exhibit 3. The Growth of Product/Market Complexity in a High Technology Company, 1968–1972

Degree of complexity   ◔ 1968   ● 1972

Dimensions of change	Low	Moderate	Substantial	High
A. Products				
Number and diversity of products	Single line	Several related	Several related, some unrelated	Diverse and complex
Complexity of individual products	Simple design	Multiple components	Highly intricate, technically sensitive	Technical and systematic
Degree of forward/ backward integration	None	Partial one-step	Extensive, multiple-step	Highly integrated
Rate of product innovation	Slow	Slow to moderate	Moderate to rapid	Rapid
B. Markets				
Geographic scope	Regional	National	National, significant export	Inter-national
Distribution channels	Single	Few	Several	Multiple, complex
Customer groups	Single, well-defined	Few	Several, distinct	Multiple, diverse
C. Environment				
Competitive intensity (price, product, marketing)	Low	Low to moderate	Moderate to intense	Very intense
External pressures (economic, governmental, social, labor)	Stable	Stable to moderate	Moderate to intense	Highly volatile, very intense

years, with sales volume still under $60 million. This company shortly found itself on the brink of bankruptcy.

☐ Another, in the consumer goods field, ballooned its product line by a series of acquisitions until it had over 10,000 items sold through multiple channels. This company also found itself in serious trouble.

Few companies can manage such an explosion in product/market complexity successfully. The ones that *have* followed the conglomerate strategy with good results have built on three key strengths:

1 A team of strong, proven operating managers with experience in larger, highly disciplined organizations.
2 A tight budgeting and control process.
3 Periodic, targeted profit improvement efforts designed to retain profit margins across a wide range of diverse fields.

These are strengths that any threshold company, conglomerate or otherwise, must have if it is to manage expanding markets and expanding complexity successfully.

Ideally, to gain an objective reading on the rapidity with which it is changing, a company should develop a profile of its complexity of three to five years ago, evaluate its position today, and then define and limit the level of complexity it chooses to reach three to five years in the future. (The kind of analysis shown in Exhibit 3 may be most helpful.) It should then weigh its strengths and decide whether they will be adequate to the scale of change it is contemplating.

Although this exercise depends as heavily on judgment as it does on specific factors (industry growth rates and the like), the results will help a threshold company understand the probable scope of changes needed in its management structures and processes, and may forestall a strategic mistake that would carry the company beyond its ability to manage effectively.

New Skills

The new skills required as product/market complexity increases depend on a company's industry mix and product mix, and also on the capabilities of present management. Broadly speaking, these skill requirements will fall into two classes:

1 Specialized or functional skills to meet the demand for new knowledge in specific areas.
2 General management skills to lead the overall development of a product line or market segment.

For example, during 1970 and 1971, one threshold company added six new products to its line, four of them highly technical. Among the skills it had to acquire were these:

- [ ] Functional skills in product and market forecasting.
- [ ] Functional skills in measurement and control of product profitability.
- [ ] Skills in production scheduling and inventory control.
- [ ] Technical-service capabilities and a new, technically trained sales force.
- [ ] General management skills to manage geographic profit centers.

Exhibit 4 shows how skill needs for financial and new-product management build up in an industrial products company. Similar changes take place for all other functions.

Identifying new and needed skills seems simple on the surface, but the experience of many companies shows that deciding which skills to add, and how to add them economically, requires careful planning. Otherwise, the company opens itself up to unnecessary cost, internal conflict, and confusion.

Most successful threshold companies find it necessary to "go outside" for some of the new skills that they need. It is not always easy for companies to make up their minds to do this. Aside from the expense involved, companies are understandably sensitive to the feelings of their long-term but inadequately prepared executives who have grown up with the company and now may become subordinate to a newcomer. However, the statement of one chief executive captured the essence of our observations:

Exhibit 4.   Management Requirements That Come with Increasing Complexity

	Degree of complexity		
	Low	Moderate to substantial	High
Financial management	Maintain sufficient control over capital to grow with minimum dilution.	Manage fixed and working capital effectively in several businesses.	Manage diverse, complex fixed and working capital effectively in many countries and businesses.
	Minimize cost of funds.	Cultivate commercial and investment bankers.	Cultivate financial community at the highest levels.
		Negotiate and finance acquisitions.	Negotiate and finance major acquisitions.
		Design public offerings and new financings.	Design public offerings and major financings.
			Manage complex tax and insurance problems.
New-product strategy	Make occasional product improvements.	Develop and/or introduce new products.	Introduce steady flow of new and diverse products into diverse markets through research, acquisitions, formal capital allocation, and formal planning.
	Pursue related markets with similar economic structures.	Enter new markets regularly.	
		Acquire small and medium-sized companies.	
		Plan capital allocations more carefully.	

"At $10 million you can't afford top people and you have to do the job yourself. But at $200 million, you can attract the best talent—and you'd better do it in the interests of both company growth and personal survival!" Going outside for new skills triggers the need for other changes:

☐ *New forms of compensation.* Since specialized and general management skills are most often found in large, stable, and secure corporations, the threshold company must devise special incentives to attract those skills to its seemingly less secure organization. Outsiders who come in at high levels usually do so because the threshold company offers not only opportunity for greater responsibility, but also financial incentives and opportunities for building capital that the giant corporation may no longer be able to match.

☐ *A more formal compensation plan.* As the company becomes more complex, top management loses its close touch with employees and can no longer make individual judgments on compensation. Since it cannot base compensation decisions on direct knowledge of an employee's performance, top management needs equitable, competitive salary ranges, uniform standards of evaluation, and mechanisms to ensure periodic review and modification of its cash compensation plan to keep it competitive with the market.

New Structures and Processes

Some threshold companies find it hard to face up to the fact that growing complexity, changes in skill mix, and the introduction of new people demand changes in organization structure. They make the mistake of trying to accommodate new skills and functions in the old, comfortable, entrepreneurial framework. Then they have to play catch-up ball.

In my view, there is no pat answer to "what should my structure be" at any given stage of corporate development. While there are some interesting theories of organizational evolution, virtually every structural form has been used successfully and unsuccessfully by companies in the same industry and with roughly the same product/market configurations. Restructuring requires individual tailoring to particular companies and individual top-management styles. However, some general tenets are valid for threshold companies as a group.

The "Right" Structure for a Company at Any Point in Time Depends Mainly on Five Determinants. In a threshold company, the relative importance of these five determinants often shifts so rapidly with growth that frequent reorganization becomes necessary, and the restructuring process itself comes to consume a substantial portion of the chief executive's time. These determinants are as follows:

1. *Corporate objectives, plans, and time horizons.*

2. *The number of distinct businesses making up the company.* The more homogeneous the product lines, the more likely it is that the company will lend itself to a functional organization. The more diverse the product lines, the more likely it is that the company is better suited to a profit-center structure of groups or divisions.

3. *The key factors for success in each major line of business.* Ultimately, market and economic success hinge on a very few critical decisions and activities—the "leverage points" of each business. Determining what these are requires intensive economic, product, and market analysis. In toys and proprietary drugs, for example, new-product introduction and advertising will get emphasis; in industrial machinery, sales and technical service are critical.

4. *Organization Principles.* Scores of principles have been offered up over the years as guides to good organization planning; for example: constraints on span of control, distinctions between line and staff responsibility, distinctions between line and functional authority, and many more. All have been successfully violated at one time or another, and their validity should be tested in each instance before they are accepted. However, organization principles do provide a checklist management can use to challenge a tentative structure.

5. *Managers' capabilities, styles, and personalities.* To be successful, a company must bend its structure to the realities of people, after a tough-minded assessment of their strengths and weaknesses. If the amount of bending from the "ideal" structure is too great, then another alternative should be considered—changing the people.

In Determining Structure, Asking a Few Key Questions Can Often Set the Threshold Company on the Right Path. For example, a company should ask when and under what conditions it may need to add a new division or group, an executive vice president, a chief operating officer to share the president's burden, or an "office of the president."

With respect to staff structure, it should ask what new functions should be added internally and what new functions should be filled by outside counsel and services. For both kinds of functions, it should ask where these functions ought to be positioned—that is, at corporate, group, or division level or at some combination of levels.

Further, it should ask how individual staff functions ought to be grouped. That is, should planning and diversification personnel report to a single executive? Should management information and data processing be placed under a vice president of finance, or should they report directly to the chief executive? And so forth.

Asking such questions as these led a specialty chemical company to a series of sound organization changes (see Exhibit 5). Like many growing threshold companies, this one began to broaden its base by diversifying— in its case, into the grocery field. Then, to expand the volume of its core product lines, it began to move through multiple channels to a wider range of customers with different marketing characteristics. Simultaneously, competition in several of its markets became more severe.

To respond to these changes, the company decided to abandon its simple functional structure; it divisionalized and strengthened staff support (Stage 2). This enabled it to focus general management skills on developing each major business; it also freed the chief executive for strategic planning and the development of key staff.

At yet a later phase (Stage 3), the company added more diversified-product divisions, and the president again found himself too caught up in operations. Hence a third form of organization was needed. The company decided to divide operations among four senior vice presidents—for chemical marketing divisions, for other industrial markets, for consumer markets, and for expanded administration responsibility. This move gave the company a corporate structure that was responsive to its needs.

Programming the Installation of Organizational Change Is as Important as the Choice of Structural Form. Threshold companies that carefully plan each step in implementing structural change consistently find that the new structure is better received by the organization. Plans for changeover can take a variety of forms. One company, for example, developed a highly detailed, four-month plan that included these elements:

☐ A comprehensive training and communications program for executives, which explained why change was vital and what the substance of the change was.

☐ Well-defined personal objectives and programs for each manager to ensure that his attitude and job focus would match his or her new responsibilities and title.

☐ A project team to work out the communications program, detailed written job descriptions, organization charts, organization policy statements, and standards for evaluating the success of change after six months of operation.

Other companies have used employee attitude surveys taken before and after the organization change to guide them in installation and to measure effectiveness after the fact.

A concern for execution and a recognition that it is an essential ingredient to effective change are particularly important in the threshold company, which is often less accustomed to a formal structure and requires fundamental change more frequently than the large corporation.

Supporting Management Processes Must Be Modified to Serve the New Structure. A threshold company operating within a new and more complex structure runs two kinds of risks: (a) using its resources ineffectively owing

Exhibit 5. Structural Evolution in a Chemical Company

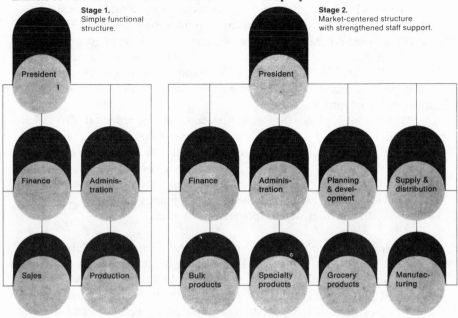

Stage 1.
Simple functional
structure.

Stage 2.
Market-centered structure
with strengthened staff support.

452

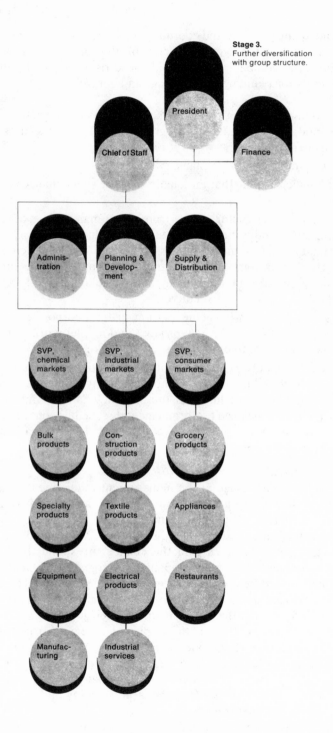

Stage 3.
Further diversification
with group structure.

President

Chief of Staff

Finance

Administration

Planning & Development

Supply & Distribution

SVP, chemical markets

SVP, industrial markets

SVP, consumer markets

Bulk products

Construction products

Grocery products

Specialty products

Textile products

Appliances

Equipment

Electrical products

Restaurants

Manufacturing

Industrial services

to lack of adequate planning and coordination; and (b) allowing staff functions to proliferate and costs to get out of control, thus endangering earnings per share. Threshold companies that avoid these risks frequently employ the following tools for planning, monitoring, and control:

☐ Annual operating plans that spell out revenue objective, cost budgets, and supporting action programs for all business units and staff departments.

☐ Capital expenditure plans.

☐ Financial plans that anticipate balance sheet changes and related financial needs.

☐ Periodic key-factor reports from senior managers on developments in important industries, markets, and products. Some CEOs find it more important to monitor their companies through such qualitative reports than through financial controls. Many chief executives make effective use of a monthly (sometimes weekly) status letter from division heads and staff executives.

☐ Strategic plans for achieving longer-term corporate objectives in sales and profit growth, new-product and market entries, deployment of cash and executive resources, and the like.

☐ Schedules of key meetings of top executives to review operations and strategy. While some threshold company executives complain of "meeting-itis," most find that the tendency can be controlled. Also, they recognize the need for formal meeting schedules once the company has grown so large that informal get-togethers cannot be easily arranged.

People Issues

The changes that take place in the management requirements of threshold companies as they grow can have both a positive and a negative impact on personnel and morale. CEOs talk enthusiastically about the new opportunities and executive motivation created by growth. Many middle- and upper-level management executives gain the chance to expand their skills and compensation potential as their company gets larger and branches into new fields. Others are left behind. Almost without exception, the threshold companies have to face up to replacing or building around certain executives who can no longer meet the requirements of their jobs.

The consensus of CEOs is that replacing a below-par performer is at once one of the toughest and one of the wisest steps a threshold company chief executive can take. And the higher the position in the organization, the tougher the decision. In fairness to the company, and to the individual, wisdom dictates that the CEO face the issue squarely and replace an individual, if that is what is necessary.

It is not always necessary, however, to let executives go when the company outstrips their abilities. I have seen many instances, and been told about others, in which executives have been successfully demoted, retrained, or recycled within the company. Some companies arrange for formal retraining, in company or academic settings, to "bootstrap" marginal performers up to the expected level of competence. Many have had good results from bringing in educators and consultants to help their people brush up on management skills.

Recycling is a special form of relocation that has worked well for some of the CEOs I have talked to. An executive who has proved strong in entrepreneurial start-up operations can sometimes be moved out of the mainstream of the business into a smaller division or new-product area where he can use his entrepreneurial skills.

Changing Role of the CEO

One of the most difficult, yet often the most important, requirements imposed by growth is to ensure that the role played by the CEO (or the top two or three executives) evolves to meet the new complexity of the company. Although the nature of this role change depends on several factors—the individual style and ability of the chief executive, industry requirements, the rate at which complexity increases—I can trace some general patterns.

When complexity is low, the chief executive typically knows all the details of the business and spends most of his or her time carrying out major functions: selling to key accounts, raising capital, thinking up new products, and hiring and training people. As complexity increases, however, the number of decisions and activities outstrips the time available, and the chief executive must rely increasingly on other executives to perform the major functions.

At this point, major shifts in emphasis begin to occur:

☐ The CEO must spend more time selecting, motivating, allocating, and evaluating key executive talent.

☐ He or she must devote a large share of time to strategic planning to ensure that new products are developed and that old products and markets are trimmed off, if they are unprofitable or take a disproportionate share of management time.

☐ And, almost inevitably, he or she must take on a host of other activities, such as dealing with the government, meeting with security analysts, serving on corporate boards, and participating in industry associations.

All too frequently, however, the chief executive finds it impossible to change. Many founder chiefs remain fundamentally entrepreneurs, preferring to make the operating decisions and carry out the major mainstream activities on their own. It is not surprising to find executives who build their companies to $10 million or $20 million in annual volume, then sell out to larger corporations and start over again.

Other executives stay with their companies but fail to change. In these instances, the dominant patterns seem to be that either the company stagnates or it gets into such serious financial trouble that the board of directors must step in to remove the chief. One finding of our study is that relatively few chief executives of threshold companies have been in their present positions since the company's entrepreneurial days.

The chief executives who make the change successfully may do so through formal retraining, counseling with experienced outsiders, or sheer determination. More often than not, however, their best course is to govern change by modifying the basic corporate structure of their companies in a carefully planned way. In company after company, we found this to be true: the CEOs who succeed in reallocating their time effectively and in developing the strong, diverse executive team needed by a complex company do so through major structural change.

Final Word

Threshold companies play a vital and distinctive role in U.S. business. An elite group that has moved far beyond the mass of smaller companies and is positioned on the threshold of leadership, these companies provide a unique competitive drive and vitality to the upper ranks of business.

Yet the 3,000 threshold companies in this country operate in a demanding management environment. Our analysis shows that, while many of them are growing much faster than the giants, their performance is far more volatile, their operating profit margins are lower and under pressure, and they are more highly leveraged and pay more for their debt.

The real keys to negotiating the passage to leadership are for the threshold company to recognize that it is passing through a period of rapidly compounding product/market complexity, to define the degree of that complexity, and to identify the changes its management must make.

The design and sequencing of organizational change depend on industry economics and conditions as well as on top-executive style. No amount of management effort can bring run-away success in a depressed industry. By the same token, mistakes that might be serious in the average company can often be tolerated in a company that has a unique product line or is operating in a fast-growing market.

However, I find that one generalization holds consistently: Threshold companies that *consciously* manage change fare better than those that do not. The companies that get into trouble are frequently those that allow product/market complexity to outstrip their managerial talent and processes. To put the point another way: the need to continually reshape the way a company is managed is the primary common thread that runs through the fabric of the threshold companies. Those with the motivation and discipline to effect and manage continuing change substantially increase their odds of becoming tomorrow's leaders.

28
How Fast Should Your Company Grow?

WILLIAM E. FRUHAN, JR.

Despite repeated calls to focus on product quality or on improving employee motivation, many American corporate executives continue to be obsessed with the financial growth of their companies. After all, making money is the one concrete way the world tells a company whether it's doing things right. Moreover, if a company stops making money, it may stop altogether.

But how do managers define growth? In what terms? For whom are profits important? In this article, William Fruhan examines the question of corporate growth and how it relates to the market value of a company's stock. Based on the fundamental assumption that a company is in business to create value for its shareholders, the author's ideas offer a provocative answer to the question the title asks. He explains the seemingly irrational behavior of the stock market over the past two decades and shows how a company's record of growth affects the fortunes of its stockholders. He then offers a sound rationale for choosing faster growth, negative growth, or divestment.

The phrase "fast growth" conjures up a picture of a high-technology company serving markets that have seemingly inexhaustible appetites for its products. Panting investors and rising stock prices are generally part of the image. A typical example of such a high-growth company is Tandy Corporation, owner of the Radio Shack chain and manufacturer of the TRS-80 microcomputer. At the other end of the growth spectrum are companies whose markets shrink due to declining demand and/or foreign competition and whose stock prices fall. These companies are typified by National Steel

Published 1984.

Exhibit 1. Relative Price Performance of Tandy Corporation and National Steel Corporation Common Stocks and the Dow Jones Industrial Average

Relative price
1972 = 100

1900

1700

1500

1300

1100

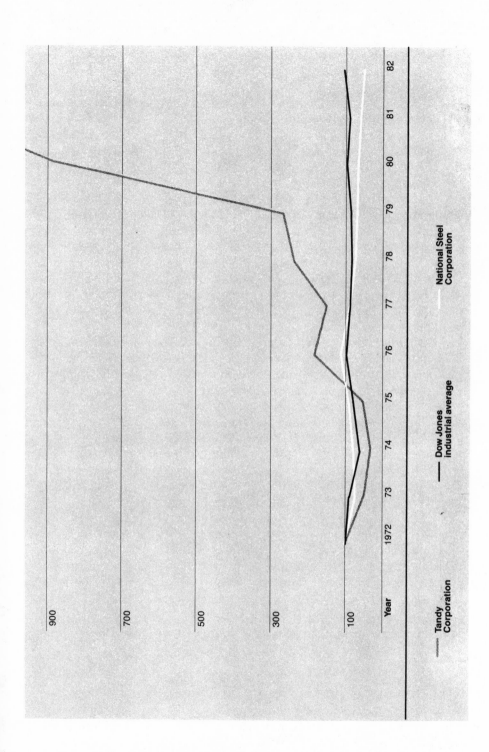

900

700

500

300

100

Year

1972 73 74 75 76 77 78 79 80 81 82

Tandy
Corporation

Dow Jones
industrial average

National Steel
Corporation

459

Corporation. (National Steel recently formed a holding company and adopted a new corporate name, National Intergroup, Inc.) Exhibit 1 shows the performances of Tandy and National Steel.

Obviously, some companies lack the financial resources to fully exploit available product-market growth opportunities. Others don't have opportunities adequate to match their financial capacity. Financial resources and product-market opportunity help determine how fast a company *can* grow, but given those two ingredients, how fast *should* a company grow? Is growth always so important?

Shareholders think growth desirable if it adds to the value of their common stock. Economists believe that addition of value to corporate common stock indicates the most efficient allocation of resources. Producers and consumers benefit under the direction of Adam Smith's invisible hand.

But the cases of Tandy and National Steel raise interesting questions: Under what circumstances does growth add value for a company's shareholders? To answer, you first must examine the interaction among inflation, capital costs, profitability, growth, and the market value of a company's common stock.

(National Steel has proven well aware of the implications of its situation. In the 1981 annual report to stockholders, the company announced that its "existing lines of business will be managed to provide a competitive return on their invested capital. Those businesses will be expanded that have good prospects for contributing to National's financial mission. Conversely, those businesses that cannot demonstrate either cash-generating capabilities or solid growth prospects will be reduced or divested." The implementation of this strategy as reflected in the imaginative form of the divestiture of the Weirton Division, a facility that accounted for one-third of steel production in 1981 and 1982, should be a major assist to National's efforts to return the company to adequate levels of profitability.)

The illustration of interrelationships in Exhibit 2 helps explain the peculiar behavior of stock market prices over the past two decades. The road map can guide us in solving the growth-rate puzzle. Exhibit 3 shows how both earnings and book value per share for the Dow Jones industrial stocks more than doubled from 1965 to 1981—while the market value actually

Exhibit 2. A Profitability Road Map

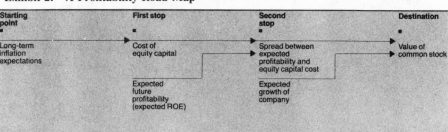

Exhibit 3. Financial Statistics of the 30 Dow Jones Industrial Stocks, 1965–1982

	Column							
	1	2	3	4	5	6	7	8
Year	Earnings per Share	Book Value	Market Value	Price-Earnings Ratio	Market to Book Value Ratio	Return on Equity	Annual Inflation Rate	Ten-Year Treasury Bond Rate[a]
1965	$ 53.67	$453	$ 969	18.1	2.1	11.8	1.7%	4.3%
1970	$ 51.02	$573	$ 839	16.4	1.5	8.9	5.9%	7.2%
1975	$ 75.66	$784	$ 852	11.3	1.1	9.7	9.1%	7.4%
1980	$121.86	$929	$ 964	7.9	1.0	13.1	13.5%	11.8%
1981	$113.71	$976	$ 875	7.7	.9	11.5	8.9%	16.4%
1982	$ 9.15	$882	$1,047	114.4	1.2	.1	3.9%	13.5%

[a]Average rate for the year. At December 31, 1982. the Treasury bond rate was 11%.

declined. The price-earnings ratio and the ratio of market to book value fell more than 60%. By contrast, earnings per share for the Dow Jones industrials collapsed in 1982 at the same time their market value rose almost 20%.

Observing this stock price schizophrenia, many executives first comment that the stock market is crazy, that investors move in response to the phases of the moon. Being rational, however, on further reflection the same executives come up with straight-forward answers anchored in economics: if, during a period of rising inflation, the increase in business profitability doesn't offset the impact of inflation on capital costs, then common stock values must decline. Similarly, when inflation is expected to decline, stock prices rise unless future business profitability (return on equity, or ROE) is expected to decline as rapidly as inflation.

Expecting Inflation

As the road map shows, the impact of inflation is important. Let's assume that the expected inflation rate is only 1%, for example, and investors demand a 9% real return on a stock investment. A company that expects to earn a 10% ROE on an equity base of $100 should find its equity capital valued in the market at $100. Because equity returns and equity costs are exactly equal, the market value represents 100% of book value. If long-term inflation expectations rise from 1% to 11% and the company's anticipated ROE stays at 10%, how can investors achieve adequate returns? Only by driving down the equity value to $50, or 50% of book value, as shown in Exhibit 4.

Seen in this light, the Dow Jones performance between 1965 and 1981 is not crazy. Inflation expectations increased dramatically between those years. This is reflected in the escalation in the annual rate of inflation actually experienced as well as in the yields of long-term Treasury bonds (see Exhibit 3). To maintain real returns at 9%, nominal return requirements for equity capital had to double between 1965 and 1981. Because the book value of the Dow Jones stocks also doubled, their market value should have been—and was— about the same in that period.

In 1982, the picture changed. Extraordinary write-offs at a few of the 30 Dow Jones industrials forced a profit collapse. Observers looked to full recovery of ROE in the near future. At the same time, inflation was expected to drop. The combination of these two factors would push up common stock prices sharply, reversing the result shown in Exhibit 4.

Inflation directly affects the cost of equity capital. Investors act to protect the purchasing power of their assets by pricing securities at levels that will cover inflation and produce a real return consistent with the risk assumed in owning a share of common stock.

The second stop on our road map consists of two components: a forecast of future inflation and a return requirement for accepting a specific level of risk. The mean annual real rates of return (before personal income taxes) investors earned on various kinds of financial assets over the 51-year period

Exhibit 4. The Price Impact of Changed Inflation Expectations

Item		Long-Term Inflation Expectations	
		1%	11%
A	Real return requirement for equity capital	9%	9%
B	Cost of equity capital (item A + inflation expectation)	10%	20%
C	Profits	$ 10	$ 10
D	Book value of equity	$100	$100
E	Company's ROE (item C/item D)	10%	10%
F	Market value of equity (item C/item B)	$100	$ 50
G	Market value to book value (item F/item D)	1.0	.5
H	ROE of equity owner (item C/item F)	10%	20%
I	Real ROE to equity owner (item H—inflation)	9%	9%

1926–1976 are as follows: U.S. Treasury bills, 0%; long-term government bonds, 1.1%; long-term corporate bonds, 1.8%; and common stock, 9.2%.[1] With long-term Treasury bonds yielding a nominal return of 11%, this suggests that investors harbor long-term inflation expectations of close to 10% (11% minus 1.1%). Taking this into account, the cost of equity capital for common stock of average risk ought to be roughly 19% or 20% (equal to an expected inflation rate of 10% plus a risk premium of 9%).

Growth and Profitability

Let's examine four hypothetical companies growing just fast enough to stay even with inflation. In nominal terms they grow annually at 10%, but they do not grow at all in real terms. Their profitability differs considerably, from an expected ROE of 25% to one of only 10% (see Exhibit 5). Each has a whimsical name that reflects its particular kind of investment opportunity.

My Cup Runneth Over, Inc.
Let's assume we invest $100 in a business that offers a 25% ROE (see Exhibit 6). Our profit yield is thus $25. If there is no opportunity for real growth, we would have to reinvest $10 to support a 10% nominal growth during times

Exhibit 5. Rates of Growth, Profitability, and Market to Book Value Ratios for Four Hypothetical Companies

Company	ROE	Rate of Growth in Nominal Sales	Earnings Retention Ratio	Market to Book Value Ratio
My Cup Runneth Over, Inc.	.25	.10	.40	1.29
Much Ado About Nothing Company	.20	.10	.50	1.00
Things Are Not Always What They Seem Corporation	.15	.10	.67	.71
Exit, Pursued By A Bear & Associates	.10	.10	1.00	.42

of 10% inflation. (Although there is considerable controversy about the impact of inflation on real sustainable rates of growth, a company's real sustainable rate of growth can be approximated by simply subtracting the rate of inflation from the nominal sustainable growth rate.)[2] That allows $15 in dividends.

We continue this process for ten years at which point returns no longer exceed the equity capital cost of 20%. We liquidate and return the accumulated book value (grown to $259.37 at the end of ten years) to the investors. When we calculate the present value of the annual dividends and final liquidation payment, the result is $129.05, or $29.05 more than the initial $100 investment.

Because the company earns a rate of return that exceeds its equity capital cost, every dollar of equity capital initially invested in this particular business is worth $1.29 in market value for shareholders. The company is aptly named, the shareholder's cup does run over.

Exit, Pursued By a Bear

At the other end of the investment spectrum is a business offering only a 10% ROE on a $100 investment (see Exhibit 6). Assuming no growth opportunity in real terms, we need to reinvest all of our $10 profit to support nominal growth in an environment of 10% inflation. No dividends are possible since financing the inflation-induced growth absorbs all profit. We continue this reinvestment process for ten years before liquidation. We return the accumulated book value of the investment (grown to $259.37 at the end of ten years) to our investors. When we calculate the present value of the annual dividends (there were none) and the final liquidating payment, the result is $41.89, or $58.11 less than the $100 investment.

Because the company earned a rate of return far below the cost of equity capital, every shareholder dollar initially invested in the business is now worth only 42 cents. The company may describe its 10% sales growth as progress, but in fact it is entirely due to inflation. The need to retain and invest capital has destroyed shareholder value.

The Middle of the Spectrum

Between these extremes on the profitability spectrum lie companies whose future ROEs are expected to be 20% to 15%. A business with a 20% ROE, which we'll call the Much Ado About Nothing Company, should enjoy a market value that exactly equals book value because capital costs exactly equal anticipated rates of return. Unless profitability exceeds equity capital costs, growth creates no value for shareholders.

Another type of company, Things Are Not Always What They Seem Corporation, expects an ROE of 15% and enjoys a market value equal to only 71% of book value. A decade ago the annual reports of these kinds of companies featured statements setting 15% as an ROE target, thought then to be a stellar achievement. Some companies continue to operate with this objective even though inflationary expectations and alternative Treasury bond investments have made a 15% return totally inadequate. Most depressing, the average profitability of the Dow Jones industrials has never reached even 15%.

Exhibit 7 shows the ratio between a company's market value and book value for various growth rates, as defined by the fraction of earnings reinvested annually. It is a richer profile of the interrelationships between profitability, growth, and value than that shown in Exhibit 5 because growth is not fixed. The exhibit shows that growth boosts value dramatically when profitability is expected to be high and destroys it when profitability is inadequate.

When a company with a 25% ROE grows fast enough to absorb two times its profits annually, its common stock value is 2.4 times its book value. (To reinvest at this rate, the company would have to sell annually an amount of new equity equal in value to the year's net income.) Similarly, if the company enjoys only a 10% ROE and chooses to reinvest two times its profits annually, its common stock ought to be valued at only .2 times book value. (These examples assume a ten-year reinvestment horizon. A different time horizon would greatly alter these values.)

Valuation Versus Profitability and Growth

A look at the 1966 to 1975 average rate of profitability and reinvestment by more than 1,400 U.S. industrial companies shows that nearly one-third earned an average ROE of 7.9% or less (Exhibit 8). Slightly more than 1% earned an average ROE of 25% and over in that decade.

Poor performers tended to have high reinvestment rates, to issue stock to finance acquisitions (often aimed at diversification), or to fund attempts to enhance the profitability of existing businesses. At the other end of the

Exhibit 6. Economically Rational Market Value of Two Hypothetical Companies' Equity

My Cup Runneth Over, Inc.: The company faces investment opportunities with 25% returns on equity in amounts sufficient to produce a 10% per year sustainable growth rate in sales for ten years. The company has a 20% cost of equity capital.

				Column			
1	2	3	4	5	6	7	8
Start of Year	Book Value of Share-holder's Investment	ROE Achieved	Profit after Tax	Earnings Retention Rate	Earnings Retained	Cash Return to Share-holders from Divi-dends and/or Sale of Stock at Book Value	Present Value Factor at 20% Dis-count Rate	Present Value of Column 6
1	$100.00	25%	$25.00	40%[a]	$10.00	$ 15.00	.833	$ 12.50
2	$110.00	25%	$27.50	40%[a]	$11.00	$ 16.50	.694	$ 11.46
3	$121.00	25%	$30.25	40%[a]	$12.10	$ 18.15	.579	$ 10.50
4	$133.10	25%	$33.28	40%[a]	$13.31	$ 19.97	.482	$ 9.83
5	$146.41	25%	$36.30	40%[a]	$14.64	$ 21.96	.402	$ 8.83
6	$161.05	25%	$40.26	40%[a]	$16.11	$ 24.25	.335	$ 8.09
7	$177.16	25%	$44.29	40%[a]	$17.72	$ 26.57	.279	$ 7.42
8	$194.87	25%	$48.72	40%[a]	$19.49	$ 29.23	.232	$ 6.80
9	$214.36	25%	$53.39	40%[a]	$21.44	$ 32.15	.194	$ 6.23
10	$235.79	25%	$58.95	40%[a]	$23.58	$ 35.37	.162	$ 5.71
11	$259.37					$259.37[b]	.162	$ 41.88
							Total present value	$129.05

$$\frac{\text{Economic value}}{\text{Book value}} = 1.29$$

Exit, Pursued By A Bear & Associates: The company faces investment opportunities with 10% returns on equity in amounts sufficient to produce a 10% per year sustainable growth rate in sales for ten years. The company has a 20% cost of equity capital.

1	$100.00	10%	$10.00	100%[a]	$10.00	$ 0	.833	$ 0
2	$110.00	10%	$11.00	100%[a]	$11.00	$ 0	.694	$ 0
3	$121.00	10%	$12.10	100%[a]	$12.10	$ 0	.579	$ 0
4	$133.10	10%	$13.31	100%[a]	$13.31	$ 0	.482	$ 0
5	$146.41	10%	$14.64	100%[a]	$14.64	$ 0	.402	$ 0
6	$161.05	10%	$16.11	100%[a]	$16.11	$ 0	.335	$ 0
7	$177.16	10%	$17.72	100%[a]	$17.72	$ 0	.279	$ 0
8	$194.87	10%	$19.49	100%[a]	$19.49	$ 0	.232	$ 0
9	$214.36	10%	$21.44	100%[a]	$21.44	$ 0	.194	$ 0
10	$235.79	10%	$23.58	100%[a]	$23.58	$ 0	.162	$ 0
11	$259.37					$259.37[c]	.162	$ 41.89
							Total present value	$ 41.89

$$\frac{\text{Economic value}}{\text{Book value}} = .42$$

[a] A 10% sustainable rate of growth in net worth (and sales) would require a 40% retention rate if the company earns an ROE of 25%.
[b] It is assumed that the stock will be sold at book value at the end of year ten, when future ROEs will equal the company's assumed cost of equity of 20%.
[c] A 10% sustainable rate of growth in sales would require a 100% retention rate if the company earns an ROE of 10%.

467

Exhibit 7.   Market to Book Value Ratios for Common Stock Based on a 20% Cost of Equity and a Ten-Year Horizon

Fraction of Earnings Reinvested Each Year	Expected Future Return on Book Equity			
	10%	15%	20%	25%
30%	.5	.8	1.0	1.3
70%	.5	.7	1.0	1.4
100%	.4	.7	1.0	1.5
200%	.2	.4	1.0	2.4

ROE spectrum, where high rates of reinvestment would have added greatly to shareholder value, the reinvestment rate is more restrained. In short, high-return opportunities are not as abundant as are the resources to pursue them.

It is surprising how close the theoretically determined market to book value ratios are to those based on actual data (see Exhibit 9). Refining the assumptions helps bring the two even closer together. To do this:

☐   Use data for individual rather than aggregate companies.

☐   Make more precise estimates of ROE and equity capital costs in both nominal and real terms.

☐   In determining the book value of common equity, use replacement cost values for assets rather than historic cost values.

With these refinements it is not even necessary to forecast growth rates to get a reasonable valuation fit between the theoretical and the actual market to book value ratios. Exhibit 10 demonstrates this fact.

What Price Growth?

Both theory and evidence demonstrate just how profitability and growth open up a gap between market and book value of a share of common stock. Exhibit 11 gives data on the evolution of that gap for three companies— Tandy Corporation, Xerox, and National Steel. The present value of expected excess returns on existing corporate investments, as well as all future corporate investment opportunities, is represented by the gap, stated in dollars per common share outstanding as well as in billions of dollars for the sum of the company's outstanding shares.

We can imagine that the financial histories of these companies represent the categories of rising star, fallen angel, and corporate clinker, respectively. Investor expectations of future profitability (expected ROE) would place these companies in the categories represented by My Cup Runneth Over, Things Are Not Always What They Seem, and Exit, Pursued By A Bear.

Exhibit 8. Profitability vs. Reinvestment Rate Profile of 1,448 Companies, 1966–1975

	Average Rate of Return on Common Equity					
Percent of Earnings Reinvested	7.9% or less	8.0% to 11.9%	12.0% to 17.9%	18.0% to 24.9%	25% and Over	Total
19% and less	5.1%	0.6%	0.5%	0.3%	0.1%	6.6%
20% to 39%	2.3	1.9	1.3	0.2	0.3	6.0
40% to 59%	3.1	6.4	5.2	1.2	0.5	16.4
60% to 79%	3.3	8.2	9.2	2.4	0.2	23.3
80% to 119%	4.7	9.9	10.6	2.0	0.1	27.4
120% to 159%	4.4	4.8	2.8	0.5	0.0	12.5
160% and over	6.5	.9	.4	0.0	0.0	7.8
Total	29.4%	32.7%	30.1%	6.6%	1.2%	100.0%

Exhibit 9. Market to Book Value Ratios of 1,448 Companies, 1966–1975

Percent of Earnings Reinvested	Average Rate of Return on Common Equity				
	2.0% to 7.9%	8.0% to 11.9%	12% to 17.9%	18% to 24.9%	25% and Over
19% or less	0.4	0.4	1.2	1.4	—[a]
20% to 39%	0.3	0.7	1.0	—[a]	3.7
40% to 59%	0.4	0.7	1.1	2.2	4.6
60% to 79%	0.4	0.7	1.0	1.9	—[a]
80% to 119%	0.4	0.7	1.0	2.1	—[a]
120% to 159%	0.4	0.7	1.5	3.0	—[a]
160% and over	0.4	0.6	1.9	—[a]	—[a]

[a]Not a meaningful figure.

Exhibit 10. Rank-Ordered Market to Book Value Ratios and Spreads Between Profitability and Equity Capital Cost for Large Grocery Chains, 1980

	Historic Cost Accounting			Replacement Cost Accounting	
Company	Market value[a] / Book value	ROE— Cost of equity	Company	Market value[a] / Book value[b]	ROE— Cost of equity[c]
Dillon Companies	2.25	.021	Weis Markets	1.61	.037
Cullum	1.93	.062	Dillon Companies	1.45	.024
Weis Markets	1.88	.037	Albertsons	.80	(.030)
Albertsons	1.73	.047	Cullum	.79	(.023)
Jewel	1.22	(.050)	Jewel	.68	(.066)
American Stores	1.08	(.015)	American Stores	.59	(.067)
Supermarkets General	1.06	.009	Kroger	.51	(.055)
Kroger	1.02	(.027)	Giant Foods	.43	(.064)
Fisher Foods	.89	(.135)	Supermarkets General	.41	(.098)
Safeway Stores	.81	(.044)	Fisher Foods	.40	(.150)
Giant Foods	.78	(.051)	Safeway Stores	.35	(.081)
Stop & Shop	.70	(.097)	Stop & Shop	.33	(.104)
Waldbaums	.51	(.037)	Waldbaums	.27	(.065)
A&P	.51	(.312)	A&P	.25	(.224)
Borman's	.35	(.255)	Borman's	.16	(.185)

[a]As of June 12, 1981.

[b]Under replacement cost accounting, the book value of the company's common equity is increased by the amount of the LIFO valuation reserve and by the difference between the net fixed assets at replacement cost and the net fixed assets at historic cost.

[c]Under replacement cost accounting, ROE is reduced as a result of higher depreciation charges due to the higher replacement cost of net fixed assets and the cost of equity capital is reduced by the expected rate of inflation.

Exhibit 11.   Common Stock Market Value, Book Value, and Corporate Profitability (ROE) for Three Companies

Tandy Corporation 1972-1982

Value per share: $ 75, $ 50, $ 25

Year	1972	1973	1974	1975	1976	1977	1978	1979	1980	1981	1982
Total company market value less book value in $ billions	$0.3	$0	$(.1)	$0	$0.5	$0.4	$0.5	$0.5	$1.9	$2.9	$4.5
ROE	.095	.109	.107	.176	.334	.373	.436	.479	.456	.400	.324

Xerox Corporation 1964-1982

Value per share: $ 150, $ 100, $ 50

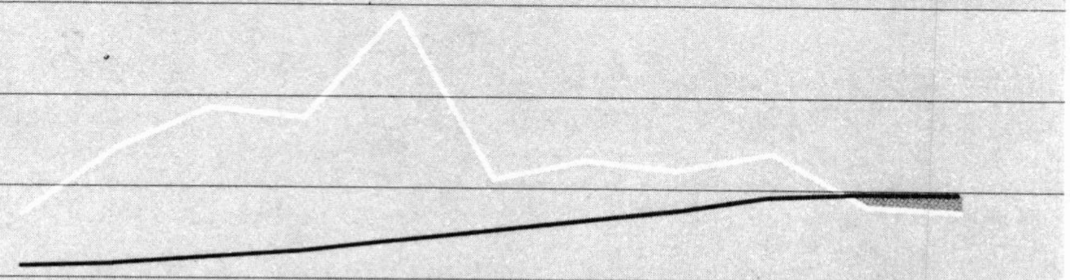

Year	1964	1966	1968	1970	1972	1974	1976	1978	1980	1981	1982
Total company market value less book value in $ billions	$ 1.9	$ 3.9	$ 5.5	$ 5.9	$ 10.5	$ 2.3	$ 2.5	$ 1.5	$ 1.4	$ (.3)	$ (.6)
ROE	.36	.33	.25	.23	.22	.20	.18	.18	.18	.16	.11

National Steel Corporation
1972-1982

Value per share

$ 150

$ 100

$ 50

Year	1972	1973	1974	1975	1976	1977	1978	1979	1980	1981	1982
Total company market value less book value in $ billions	$ (.3)	$ (.5)	$ (.6)	$ (.5)	$ (.4)	$ (.6)	$ (.8)	$ (.9)	$ (1.0)	$(1.1)	$ (.7)
ROE	.071	.094	.156	.048	.069	.047	.086	.092	.059	.059	deficit

—— Book value

—— Market value

Since 1976, investors in Tandy Corporation have been rewarded with truly remarkable levels of company profitability and growth (see Exhibit 11). They have responded by opening up a gap of $4.5 billion between the market value and the book value of the company's outstanding shares.

Xerox presents a picture of dramatically altered investor expectations. In 1972 the total market value of Xerox's common equity was $10.5 billion higher than the book value of that equity. By 1982 Xerox's star had fallen so low that the book value of Xerox's common equity was $550 million higher than its market value. In 1982 investors evidently believed that Xerox could not in the future achieve an ROE equal to its cost of equity capital. Why the bleak picture? During the 1970s, Xerox's highly profitable franchise in the copier market came under attack from the U.S. General Trade Commission, IBM, and Japanese competitors. The erosion of profitability in the basic copier business, exacerbated by a disastrous history of acquisition, shoved the market to book value ratio of Xerox's common stock below the level of an average industrial in 1982.

The National Steel data in Exhibit 11 show the consequences of earning ROEs that fall behind escalating equity capital costs. As inflation pushed National's equity cost higher during the decade, its nominal ROE declined. In spite of earnings retentions of nearly $25 per share over the decade ending 1981, the market price of National Steel's stock was $22.75 per share lower at the end of 1982 than at the end of 1972. In aggregate terms, National had reinvested close to $500 million in new equity capital, but over ten years the total value of the company's common equity had declined by $400 million. Such performance was common to many of the Dow Jones industrials. Because National Steel earned far less than its cost of equity capital, the more aggressively the company reinvested, the less the stock was worth on the market.

To Grow or Not to Grow?

The Tandy Corporation and National Steel examples provide a useful basis for reexamining our opening questions: How fast should a company grow, and under what circumstances does growth add value for shareholders? The answers to both hang on whether future profitability (ROE) exceeds or falls short of the cost of equity capital. If ROE is expected to exceed the cost of equity capital, the more growth the better. But inadequate profitability, coupled with a need to do nothing more than finance inflation-induced sales growth, can be disastrous for the company's valuation. If they cannot improve profitability, companies in such a position should consider a policy of rapid negative growth. National Steel has adopted just such a strategy, as the Weirton divestiture demonstrates.

In short, the key to value is profitability. If you've got it, flaunt it. If you haven't got it, try to get it. If you can't get it, get out.

Notes

1. Roger G. Ibbotson and Rex A. Sinquefield, "Stocks, Bonds, Bills, and Inflation: the Past (1926–1976) and Future (1977–2000)," 2d ed. (Charlottesville, Virginia, Financial Analysts Research Foundation, 1979).

2. For additional insights into real sustainable growth rates, see Robert C. Higgins, "How Much Growth Can a Firm Afford?" *Financial Management*, Fall 1977, p. 7, Dana J. Johnson "The Behavior of Financial Structure and Sustainable Growth in an Inflationary Environment," *Financial Management*, Fall 1981, p. 30, and Robert C. Higgins, "Sustainable Growth Under Inflation" *Financial Management*, Fall 1981, p 36.

29

Measuring Company Growth Capacity During Inflation

ALFRED RAPPAPORT

A financial statement based on historical costs does not, of course, provide an adequate economic picture of a business during a time of inflation. But neither does the replacement cost information recently prescribed by the SEC, the author of this article asserts. He advocates the use of a distributable funds measure for more effective management control systems. "Distributable funds" is defined as the maximum amount that the company can pay out to its stockholders during the fiscal period without impairing its business capability. Distributable funds thus represent the total amount made available during the period for dividends and expansion of business capacity. The components of distributable funds are aftertax income during the fiscal period, a cost increase provision for productive capacity, any change in working capital required, and any change in debt capacity. A company's distributable funds depend on return on sales, growth in sales, net working capital requirements, the rate of cost increases in productive capacity, dividend payout percentage, and the company's target debt-equity ratio. The recommended approach enables management to assess the effects of its operating, investment, financing, and dividend decisions on corporate performance.

> The failure of conventional financial reporting to reflect the impact of inflation on corporate earnings . . . obscures the fact that business is simply not accumulating and retaining the resources required to meet the challenges facing it. Put differently, it contributes to misleading the American public into believing that corporate earnings are so thoroughly

Published 1979.

Author's note. I gratefully acknowledge the helpful comments of a number of people, particularly John C. Burton. This article was written during my tenure as the 1977–1978 Coopers & Lybrand Research Fellow at the Graduate School of Management, Northwestern University.

476

adequate for all legitimate corporate purposes as to justify substantial additional reallocation of a portion of those earnings to social purposes.. . .

The economic reality is that American business overall is not generating and retaining funds adequate even to replace existing capacity and continue operations at present levels; on the contrary, some businesses may actually be distributing their capital and be in the process of unconscious liquidation.

So said Harold M. Williams, chairman of the Securities and Exchange Commission, in a speech to The Conference Board.[1] My purpose in this article is to introduce a performance measurement approach that enables top management to obtain a better understanding of its performance in an inflationary environment as well as in an environment of price stability. This measurement establishes a sound basis for assessing whether a business is in fact distributing its capital and unconsciously liquidating.

I shall show that this distributable funds approach gives insights into the current economics of a business not provided by either historical-cost financial statements or the recent SEC-mandated replacement-cost disclosure. Although the Financial Accounting Standards Board (FASB) and the SEC might wish to assess the merits of the statement of distributable funds as a supplementary disclosure for external reporting purposes, any such consideration should be preceded by a period of experimentation and by careful evaluation of the expected benefits compared with the costs of compliance.

Physical Capital Approach

The recent SEC ruling on disclosure of the estimated cost of replacing inventories and productive capacity at the end of the fiscal year, as well as the cost of sales and depreciation expense computed on the basis of estimated replacement cost during the year, is based on the physical capital concept of capital maintenance. This concept holds that a business earns no income until it makes provision to replace the productive capacity of existing assets. According to the FASB, "The general procedure to maintain physical capital is to value assets, such as inventories, property, plant, equipment, and some intangibles, at their current replacement costs and to deduct expenses, such as cost of goods sold, depreciation, and the like, valued at replacement cost from revenues to measure periodic earnings."[2]

Although this approach deals with the problems of "inventory profits" (i.e., increases in costs between the acquisition and the sale of inventory) and underdepreciation encountered under conventional reporting, replacement-cost income calculated under the physical capital approach suffers as a measure of distributable funds because:

☐   It is based on the assumption that maintaining existing productive capacity is the appropriate corporate objective. In an economy characterized by increasing product turnover and corporate diversification, maintaining existing productive capacity is rarely the optimal way of preserving and enhancing the earning power of the business. Enlightened executives continually seek opportunities to redeploy capital from unsatisfactorily profitable existing operations to more promising investment opportunities.

☐ It neglects working capital, which is an essential element of the company's continuing capacity to produce goods and services.

☐ It fails to account for debt, which generally is used to finance part of productive capacity.

The distributable funds approach addresses each of these limitations as well as the shortcomings of conventional historical-cost statements. To accomplish this, I introduce the concept of business capacity maintenance. This concept is based on the idea that a going concern has distributable funds available only after it makes provision to maintain that portion of its operating capability financed by equity. Distributable funds represent the maximum amount that the company can distribute to its stockholders during a period without impairing its business capacity.

In contrast with physical or productive capacity, business capacity includes not only productive facilities, but also the company's net working capital requirements as an essential element of its ability to make and sell a certain volume of products and services. The business capacity maintenance concept also recognizes that going concerns frequently discontinue some products while introducing new products and expanding into new markets. Because the price changes for depreciable assets may differ, separate provision must be made for productive capacity that management plans to replace and for capacity not expected to be replaced at the end of its economic life. Finally, the business capacity concept recognizes that part of a company's operating capability is ordinarily financed by debt.

In brief, the distributable funds approach accounts for the higher cost of conducting business, the funds required to operate at a larger sales volume than last period, and the possibility of financing a portion of the company's needs via debt.

Business capacity is the foundation for future earning power. Calculation of the distributable funds can provide managers and investors with a sound basis for assessing the future earning and dividend potential of the company.

Case of GSM Corporation

The amount of distributable funds made available during the period is affected not only by the profitability of operations, but also by whether the company (1) is operating in an inflationary environment, (2) plans to replace all its existing productive capacity or partially redeploy its capital to other product-market sectors, (3) is experiencing sales growth and therefore needs more working capital, and (4) has undergone a change in debt capacity.

To see how a statement of distributable funds is developed, consider the case of GSM Corporation, which is based on a composite of capital-intensive manufacturers.

GSM's statement of income (Exhibit 1) reports a 10% growth in sales and net income for 1978 over 1977. The aftertax return on sales for both years was 6%. The statement of financial position (Exhibit 2) reflects a rather strong current position and a debt-equity ratio of .50, which is average for GSM's industry. GSM's return on equity for both years was 18%. The statement of changes in financial position (Exhibit 3) shows that operations, coupled with an increase in long-term debt, provided sufficient financial resources for the company's expanded working capital needs, a dividend payout of 50% of net income, and capital expenditures substantially greater than depreciation.

A review limited to GSM's financial statements might lead an investor or securities analyst to believe that the company is growing and enjoying economic vitality. In fact, however, GSM is distributing its capital, not growing. The statement of distributable funds (Exhibit 4) discloses that its distributable funds deficits for 1978 and 1977 were $2,247,500 and $1.85 million, respectively. To illustrate how the distributable funds amount is determined, I shall review each item in Exhibit 4 in turn.

Exhibit 1. Statement of Income (year ended December 31)

	1978	1977
Sales	**$110,000,000**	$100,000,000
Costs and other expenses		
Costs of goods sold (exclusive of depreciation)	79,950,000	72,600,000
Selling, general, and administrative expenses	6,550,000	6,000,000
Depreciation	7,700,000	7,000,000
State, local, and miscellaneous taxes	1,100,000	1,000,000
Interest and other expenses on debt	1,500,000	1,400,000
Total	$ 96,800,000	$ 88,000,000
Income before taxes	**$ 13,200,000**	12,000,000
Provision for taxes on income	6,600,000	6,000,000
Net income	**$ 6,600,000**	$ 6,000,000
Cash dividends	**$ 3,300,000**	$ 3,000,000

Exhibit 2.   Statement of Financial Position (at year-end)

	1978	1977
Current assets		
Cash	$ 1,100,000	$ 1,000,000
Receivables, less allowance for losses	16,500,000	15,000,000
Inventories	26,400,000	24,000,000
Total	$44,000,000	$40,000,000
Current liabilities	11,000,000	10,000,000
Net working capital	33,000,000	30,000,000
Property, plant, and equipment—net[a]	22,000,000	20,000,000
Total	$55,000,000	$50,000,000
Long-term debt	$18,400,000	$16,700,000
Stockholders' equity	36,600,000	33,300,000
Total	$55,000,000	$50,000,000

[a]Gross amounts are $44,000,000 and $40,000,000 for 1978 and 1977, respectively.

Exhibit 3.   Statement of Changes in Financial Position

	1978	1977
Financial resources were provided		
From operations		
Net income	$ 6,600,000	$ 6,000,000
Depreciation	7,700,000	7,000,000
Total	$14,300,000	$13,000,000
From other sources		
Increase in long-term debt	1,700,000	1,500,000
Total	$16,000,000	$14,500,000
Financial resources were used for		
Capital expenditures	$ 9,700,000	$ 8,800,000
Dividends	3,300,000	3,000,000
Increase in net working capital	3,000,000	2,700,000
Total	$16,000,000	$14,500,000

Exhibit 4. Statement of Distributable Funds

	1978			1977		
Net income after taxes			$6,600,000			$6,000,000
Funds required for increases in costs of productive capacity						
Depreciation expense (at current replacement cost) for productive capacity expected to be replaced (see Exhibit 5)	$11,550,000			$10,500,000		
Less historical-cost depreciation	5,775,000			5,250,000		
Additional depreciation		$5,775,000			$5,250,000	
Depreciation expense (at current price levels) for productive capacity not expected to be replaced (see Exhibit 6)	$ 5,197,500			$ 4,550,000		
Less historical-cost depreciation	1,925,000			1,750,000		
Additional depreciation		$3,272,500			$2,800,000	
Total		$9,047,500			$8,050,000	
Funds required for increase in net working capital		2,300,000			1,600,000	
Less funds available via increased debt capacity		2,500,000			1,800,000	
Total			$ 8,847,500			$ 7,850,000
Distributable funds			$(2,247,500)			$(1,850,000)
Distributable funds			$(2,247,500)			$(1,850,000)
Less dividends			3,300,000			3,000,000
Funds available for expansion			$(5,547,500)			$(4,850,000)

The statement begins with net income after taxes, to which should be added deferred income taxes, if any, since they are treated as an increase in distributable funds. Net income is followed by the "funds required for increases in costs of productive capacity" section, which considers the impact of cost increases on cost of goods sold and on depreciation.

The "inventory profits" amount is already part of the SEC disclosure requirement. This figure represents an inflation adjustment to the cost of goods sold while the increase in required working capital adjusts for required increases in inventory levels –that is, cost of goods *not* sold. I make this distinction to show the reader that there is no "double counting" in making provision for changes in both required working capital and inventory profit.

For companies using either the first-in, first-out (FIFO) or the average-cost method of inventory costing, inventory profit can be estimated by taking the difference between the historical cost and the replacement cost of inventory at the time it is sold. Companies using the last-in, first-out (LIFO) method of inventory costing charge the most recent costs incurred to cost of goods sold, thereby in most cases reducing the amount and significance of inventory profits. GSM uses LIFO and reported no inventory profit for 1978 and 1977.

The depreciation expense (at current replacement cost) for productive capacity expected to be replaced is shown in Exhibit 5. At the end of 1978, GSM management estimated that of its gross fixed assets of $44 million, it expected that $33 million would be replaced.

The 1978 depreciation expense on the facilities expected to be replaced amounted to $5.775 million on a historical-cost basis. (For ease of exposition, I have assumed that the guideline lives used to calculate depreciation expense, which the Internal Revenue Service prescribes, closely approximate the assets' economic life as estimated by GSM management. In some industries, the estimated economic life is considerably greater than guideline life. When this is the case, the historical-cost depreciation should be calculated on the basis of estimated economic lives, rather than guideline lives, before multiplying it by the ratio of replacement cost to historical cost.)

GSM estimated its ratio of replacement cost (with current technology) to historical cost to be 2.0, thus yielding a replacement-cost depreciation expense of $11.55 million, or a provision of $5.775 million above historical-cost depreciation. This is a reasonable figure for a capital-intensive company. In an analysis of 10-K replacement-cost numbers of 175 companies in 21 industries, Arthur Young & Co. reported an average ratio of 1.68. The steel industry had a ratio of 2.21, metal manufacturing 1.98, petroleum refining 2.08, utilities 2.16, heavy equipment 1.59, soaps and cosmetics 1.46, beverages 1.64, airlines 1.54, and retailers 1.33.[3]

Any such ratio estimate necessarily is subjective, but it should be based on the least expensive approach consistent with minimum reliability standards.[4] In many companies, this may call for a combination of methods including indexing, appraisals, and direct pricing.

Exhibit 5. Depreciation Expense (at current replacement cost) for Productive Capacity Expected to be Replaced

	1978	1977
Facilities expected to be replaced	**$33,000,000**	$30,000,000
Facilities not expected to be replaced	**11,000,000**	10,000,000
Property, plant, and equipment—gross	**$44,000,000**	$40,000,000
Depreciation expense on facilities expected to be replaced	**$ 5,775,000**	$ 5,250,000
Multiplied by ratio of replacement cost to historical cost	**× 2.0**	× 2.0
Equals depreciation expense for productive capacity expected to be replaced	**$11,550,000**	$10,500,000

In developing a distributable funds statement, a company must make provision not only for cost increases in productive capacity it expects to replace, but also for that part of its capacity it will not replace, as explained earlier. This is necessary because during inflationary periods the purchasing power of a company's investment dollar is eroding, albeit at different rates that depend on the industrial sectors in which management contemplates redeploying its investment. If management is uncertain about where to deploy its investment in productive capacity, a "total economy" index such as the GNP price deflator can serve as the price change index. If it has more concrete investment plans, of course, a more specific index would be appropriate.

GSM management estimates that 25% of its 1978 gross fixed assets, or $11 million, will not be replaced. The 1978 depreciation expense on these facilities was $1.925 million. GSM plans to remain in the manufacturing sector and has chosen an industrial plant and equipment price change index.

The calculation of depreciation expense for productive capacity not expected to be replaced appears in Exhibit 6. Of the $11 million of facilities not expected to be replaced as of the end of 1978, assume that $6 million was purchased in 1955, when the industrial plant and equipment index was 100, and $5 million was acquired in 1960, when the index was 120. Adjustment of these historical costs to the 1978 index level yields a total index-adjusted cost of $29 million. This amount divided by the total acquisition cost ($11 million) of retained facilities establishes GSM's price change index to be 2.7.

This index is then applied to the historical depreciation expense of these facilities to obtain the depreciation expense at current price levels of $5,197,500. The additional $3,272,500 of depreciation is recorded in the state-

Exhibit 6.   Depreciation Expense (at current price levels) for Productive Capacity Not Expected to Be Replaced

1. Acquisition Date	2. Industrial Plant and Equipment Index	3. Acquisition Cost	4. Ratio of 1978 to Year-of-Acquisition Index	5. Index-Adjusted Cost (3 × 4)
1955	100	$ 6,000,000	290/100	$17,400,000
1960	120	5,000,000	290/120	12,100,000
1978	290			
		$11,000,000		$29,500,000

$$\text{Price change index} = \frac{\text{Index-adjusted cost}}{\text{Acquisition cost}} = \frac{\$29,500,000}{\$11,000,000} = \underline{\underline{2.7}}$$

	1978	1977
Depreciation expense on facilities not expected to be replaced	**$1,925,000**	$1,750,000
Multiplied by price change index for industrial plant and equipment	**× 2.7**	× 2.6
Equals depreciation expense (at current price levels) for productive capacity not expected to be replaced	**$5,197,500**	$4,550,000

ment of distributable funds as part of the funds required for increases in costs of productive capacity.

As a business expands or otherwise changes its operations, adequate working capital is no less an integral part of its capacity than is physical capacity. So any increases in net working capital requirements must be deducted in arriving at the distributable funds figure.

To demonstrate this point, assume that a company is at its target capital structure and that there is no change in debt capacity during the period; it is operating in a noninflationary environment, it plans to replace all of its existing productive capacity, and it distributes all its earnings as dividends. If the company's required working capital level has increased during the past year, it does not have the resources to sustain operations at current levels because it has paid out its entire earnings as dividends. To raise working capital to the level required by the most recent period's operations, the company is compelled to either increase its debt beyond the stipulated target level, thereby taking on more financial risk, or issue additional stock.

Working capital requirements may rise from one period to the next for a number of reasons, including higher sales volume, a change in the product mix, or changes in credit and inventory policies. Care is necessary in trying to measure changes in net working capital requirements; the actual change in net working capital from last year to this year ($3 million at GSM) may not yield a good measure of the rise or decline in the funds required.

There are two reasons for this. First, the end-of-the-year balance sheet figures may not reflect the average or normal needs of the business during the year. Second, both the accounts receivable and inventory balance sheet amounts may overstate the magnitude of the funds committed by the business. To estimate the additional funds required, two items should be considered: (1) an increased inventory investment in variable cost terms; and (2) a receivable investment in terms of the variable cost of the product delivered to generate the receivable rather than the absolute dollar amount of the receivable.

In each case, the amount reflects what the company must disburse in cash to carry these items.

For purposes of simplification let us assume that GSM's year-end working capital levels are normal for the year. Then I calculate the $2.3 million required for the 1978 increase in net working capital. To calculate the funds required for the increase in inventory level, multiply the increase in units of inventory by the current variable manufacturing cost. The 1978 variable cost of goods sold, $79.95 million (see Exhibit 1), is derived in Exhibit 7. During 1978 there was an increase of 1,400,000 units of inventory with a variable manufacturing cost of $1.50 per unit, yielding required funds of $2,100,000.

The amount of funds required for the increase in accounts receivable is calculated as:

Exhibit 7. Calculation of Variable Cost of Goods Sold in 1978

Beginning inventory, LIFO (variable manufacturing component)—22 million units @ $1.00	$ 22,000,000
Variable manufacturing costs of goods produced—54.7 million @ $1.50	82,050,000
Total goods available—76.7 million units	$104,050,000
Less ending inventory, LIFO (variable manufacturing component)— 22 million units @ $1.00 = $22,000,000 + 1.4 million units @ $1.50 = $2,100,000	24,100,000
Variable cost of goods sold—53.3 million units @ $1.50	$ 79,950,000

$$\text{Increase in accounts receivable} \times \frac{\text{Variable cost of goods sold}}{\text{Sales}}$$

$$= \$1,500,000 \times \frac{\$\ 79,950,000}{\$110,000,000} = \$1,100,000$$

The $2,300,000 increase in funds required in net working capital can then be summarized as:

Cash	$ 100,000
Accounts receivable	1,100,000
Inventories	2,100,000
Current liabilities	(1,000,000)
	$2,300,000

In GSM's case, each dollar of higher sales requires approximately 23 cents of funds for net working capital, or $2.3 million in 1978 for the $10 million sales increase over 1977.

Considering Debt Capacity

Most companies in part finance their operations with debt capital, and this, of course, must be taken into account in determining the distributable funds. Distributable funds become available only after business capacity has been maintained. The maintenance of business capacity, in turn, includes establishing a target level of financial risk, that is, the risk associated with financing the company's operations.

Estimating a company's debt capacity at some target level of financial risk involves an element of subjectivity. Debt capacity is not only related to debt-equity ratios, but may well be conditioned by interest coverage, cash flow to total debt ratios, strength of collateral, industry outlook, company operating characteristics, and company management. Nonetheless, financial executives should be able to estimate within a reasonable range how much more debt the company can incur without jeopardizing either its borrowing rate or its bond rating.

It is important to recognize that the funds available via increased debt capacity represent the change in that capacity during the fiscal period while the company kept the target level of financial risk constant. This means that the year-to-year change in the actual level of long-term debt is a good measure of funds available only if the company is operating at its target debt level at the end of each year.

Based on debt-equity ratios, cash flow, and value of collateral considerations, as well as discussions with the principal bond-rating services, GSM figured that the funds available via increased debt capacity were $2.5 million and $1.8 million for 1978 and 1977, respectively. The company increased its long-term debt in 1978 to $1.7 million; thus of the $2.5 million increase in funds available, $1.7 million had been used by the end of 1978 and $800,000 remained available.

Even after taking into account the increase in debt capacity, GSM reported deficits for distributable funds—$1.85 million in 1977 and $2,247,500 in 1978. Clearly the company was paying dividends at the risk of liquidating its business capacity. In 1978 GSM paid out $3.3 million from a $2,247,500 deficit in distributable funds, thus causing a shortfall of $5,547,500 in funds available for expansion of business capacity.

The GSM example clearly demonstrates that neither earnings growth nor additions to fixed assets give compelling evidence that a company has maintained its business capacity during the year. GSM's higher costs of productive capacity, coupled with an increase in its working capital requirements, have led it into partial liquidation of its business capacity.

Interdependent Elements

Why should management concern itself with and monitor distributable funds? The distributable funds approach provides a sound approximation of the total dollar amount made available during the period for dividends and expansion of business capacity. Business capacity, in turn, provides the basis for future earning power and hence returns to stockholders. Although periodic fluctuations in business capacity can be expected, of course, large or frequent distributable funds deficits could signal an erosion of business capacity and threaten the company's earning power—if not its very survival.

The distributable funds analysis presented here is no substitute for a well-conceived strategic plan; it serves as a supplement and a check for economic reasonableness on the company's various product-market strategies and its strategic plan. Moreover, it provides a check on the internal consistency of the company's operating, investment, financing, and dividend plans.

The distributable funds (DF) measurement is defined as:

$$DF = P(S + \Delta S) - (C - 1)(N)(S + \Delta S)$$
$$- W\Delta S + P(S + \Delta S)(1 - D)L$$

where P = net income after taxes as a percent of sales
     S = total sales of last period
   ΔS = increase in this period's sales over last period
    W = rate of additional net working capital required for each additional dollar of sales
    C = inflation-adjusted productive capacity to historical-cost productive capacity
    N = rate of historical-cost depreciation per dollar of sales
    D = target dividend payout percentage
    L = target debt-to-equity percentage

The four terms on the right-hand side of the equation are, respectively, net income after taxes, the cost increase provision for productive capacity, the change in working capital required, and the change in debt capacity. (Inventory profits may be incorporated in the working capital coefficient, W, and C represents the weighted average or composite inflation coefficient for all productive capacity, whether or not it is to be replaced.)

The company's distributable funds therefore depend on return on sales, sales growth, net working capital requirements, the rate of cost increases in productive capacity, the historical-cost depreciation per dollar of sales, the target dividend payout percentage, and the target debt-equity ratio. Because the rate of cost increase in productive capacity and depreciation per dollar of sales presumably are elements over which management can exercise little control, the company's distributable funds depend on how management decisions and policies affect the remaining five variables.

The four graphs in Exhibit 8 show how these variables are interdependent. In each graph, sales growth, aftertax profit to sales, and the inflation coefficient are treated as variables. The historical-cost depreciation per dollar of sales (N) in all cases is 5%. Each graph shows the range of the composite inflation coefficient (C) from 1.0 to 2.4.

These graphs enable the managers to assess (1) the likelihood, in light of the operating, investment, financing, and dividend assumptions imbedded in the corporate plan, that the company will generate distributable funds; and (2) the sensitivity of distributable funds to changes in operating, investment, financing, and dividend policies.

Consider Graph A. Suppose the company's plans call for a 50% dividend payout rate (D) and a debt-equity ratio (L) of .5. Working capital requirements are projected at 30 cents per dollar of increased sales (W), and the composite inflation coefficient (C) is projected to continue at about 2.2, the level of the recent past.

At a projected aftertax return on sales of 6% and a sales growth rate of 10%, the company's plan has, no doubt unknowingly, set the forces in place for generating distributable funds deficits. Graph A shows that for an assumed inflation coefficient of 2.2 and a 6% return on sales, the maximum affordable sales growth to achieve a distributable funds breakeven point is 5%. As another way of looking at it, if the company wants to grow at 10%, to avoid distributable funds deficits it must increase its return on sales to 7%. This kind of graph enables management to assess the trade-offs between sales growth and profitability on sales.

In addition, the sensitivity of distributable funds to cost increases in productive capacity can be easily tested. For example, if the inflation coefficient were reduced from 2.2 to 1.8, at a 6% return on sales the company could grow at a rate of 13% instead of 5%.

Graph B shows the sensitivity of a distributable funds breakeven to changes in working capital requirements. This graph is identical to Graph A except that working capital requirements are projected at only 20 cents

Exhibit 8. Interaction of Variables in Measuring Distributable Funds

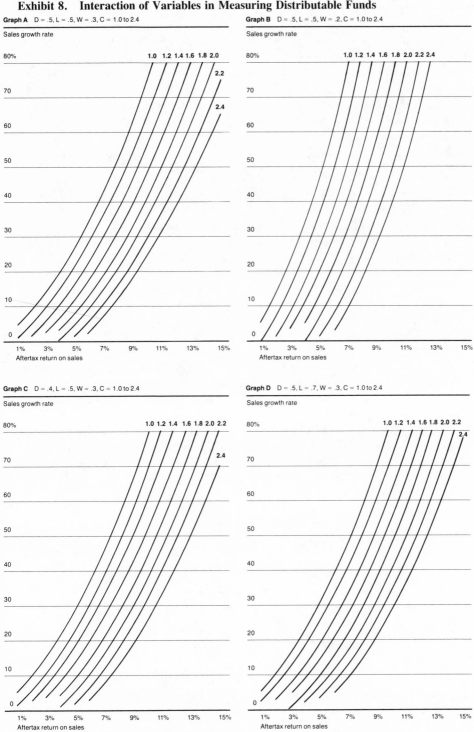

Graph A D = .5, L = .5, W = .3, C = 1.0 to 2.4

Sales growth rate

80%

1.0 1.2 1.4 1.6 1.8 2.0

2.2

70

2.4

60

50

40

30

20

10

0

1% 3% 5% 7% 9% 11% 13% 15%
Aftertax return on sales

Graph B D = .5, L = .5, W = .2, C = 1.0 to 2.4

Sales growth rate

80%

1.0 1.2 1.4 1.6 1.8 2.0 2.2 2.4

70

60

50

40

30

20

10

0

1% 3% 5% 7% 9% 11% 13% 15%
Aftertax return on sales

Graph C D = .4, L = .5, W = .3, C = 1.0 to 2.4

Sales growth rate

80%

1.0 1.2 1.4 1.6 1.8 2.0 2.2

70

2.4

60

50

40

30

20

10

0

1% 3% 5% 7% 9% 11% 13% 15%
Aftertax return on sales

Graph D D = .5, L = .7, W = .3, C = 1.0 to 2.4

Sales growth rate

80%

1.0 1.2 1.4 1.6 1.8 2.0 2.2

2.4

70

60

50

40

30

20

10

0

1% 3% 5% 7% 9% 11% 13% 15%
Aftertax return on sales

489

per dollar of added sales. The benefit of effective working capital management is quite apparent. By reducing the needed working capital requirements 10 cents per dollar of sales, the company boosts affordable sales growth rate from a modest 5% to more than 8%.

Graph C departs from the base case in only one respect—the dividend payout ratio is reduced from .5 to .4. Graph D increases the debt-equity ratio from .5 to .7. Managers may wish to test for themselves the sensitivity of the distributable funds breakeven point to these changes in dividend and financing policies.

Better Financial Control

It is essential that corporate management, as well as investors and the government, understand the effects of inflation on the capital invested in a business and on its earning power. Managers and investors need this information in their respective resource allocation roles; government needs the information to assure itself that its taxation policies do not tax at levels that impair capital formation and discourage investment. The task of developing useful and reliable measurements of the effects of inflation is extraordinarily complex, but it must be accomplished if we are to be well-informed decision makers.

The distributable funds approach I have presented enables management to assess the effects of its operating, investment, financing, and dividend decisions on corporate performance. It enables management to see which business units provide distributable funds and which use them. It is also a particularly useful statement for the outside director who wants to know whether the company is really growing. The concept of distributable funds is compatible with the strategic planning approach of most companies. Moreover, the cost of developing distributable funds statements is minimal for companies already subject to the SEC's replacement-cost disclosure rules.

For all of these reasons the distributable funds approach should prove to be a useful addition to more effective financial control systems.

Notes

1. Harold M. Williams, "Inflation, Corporate Financial Reporting and Economic Reality," New York, December 13, 1977.

2. *An Analysis of Issues Related to Conceptual Framework for Financial Accounting and Reporting: Elements of Financial Statements and Their Measurement,* FASB Discussion Memorandum, December 2, 1976 (Stamford, Conn., Financial Accounting Standards Board), p. 134.

3. "Inflation Accounting Is Here to Stay," *Business Week,* December 26, 1977, p. 109.

4. For a discussion of whether companies should add a "catch-up" depreciation charge to replace underdepreciated assets during inflation, see Richard F. Vancil and Roman L. Weil, "Current Replacement Cost Accounting, Depreciable Assets, and Distributable Income," *Financial Analysts Journal,* July-August 1976, p. 39.

30
Cash Flow Analysis
More Important Than Ever

BRADLEY T. GALE and BEN BRANCH

You won't find many executives arguing the importance of cash flow to the future success of their businesses, especially as inflation increases the already high cost of capital. Most will admit, however, that they tend only to monitor their cash—that they have few ideas about how to control it or use it to their strategic advantage.

Based on information culled from their extensive data base, Bradley Gale and Ben Branch of the Strategic Planning Institute have found that cash flow can be manipulated and can serve as an effective tool in business strategies. In this article, they demonstrate that a business's competitive position, the growth rate of its market, and its current strategic moves have a predictable effect on cash flow. By understanding how these factors impinge on cash supplies, the manager of a single business unit can evaluate the trade-offs among alternative strategies that use cash. Also, managers of groups of businesses can improve their ability to allocate cash supplies among their individual businesses.

Managers sometimes think that their strategies are tied to the tail of a very erratic cash kite and that fluctuations in cash supplies are too irregular and unpredictable to manage properly.

In fact, the reverse is true. Cash flow is predictable and manageable. A company's strategy and market position directly affect it. The recognition

Published 1981.

Authors' note. We gratefully acknowledge the contribution of colleagues at the Strategic Planning Institute—Mark Chussil, Donald F. Heany, Sidney Schoeffler, and Donald J. Swire—to the research for this article, and we thank Ruth G. Newman for her editorial guidance.

of this fact is as calming as it is essential—not only to the manager of a single business unit but also to a CEO or group vice-president.

The single business unit needs cash to grow, modernize, and finance normal day-to-day operations. But managers must analyze the cash potential of each business unit in order to decide which can be relied on as cash sources and which require heavy investment to grow.

In the 1980s, companies face increasing requirements for funds even as they deplete their resources by allocating more to energy conservation and environmental protection (so-called unproductive uses of cash). Moreover, skyrocketing inflation menaces their cash supplies. And lagging U.S. productivity compounds the problem of cash availability because it underscores the need for many businesses to reindustrialize at great expense.

We have used the PIMS data base (see Appendix A for a more detailed description of PIMS) to discover some important facts about cash generation and cash use, about how companies use and abuse this vital resource, and about ways in which they can restructure cash flow.

☐ *Growth drains cash.*   Being in a strong market is exciting, but keeping up with the fast pace requires cash. Even when real market growth is zero, inflation drains cash.

☐ *A high relative market share generates cash.*   But building a future market position requires large expenditures for marketing programs or new product development.

☐ *Aggressive asset management is vital to ensure sufficient cash.*   Increased investment relative to sales can be threatening because it always strains cash supply.

In this article, we examine these findings and their implications for all companies.

Cash Producers versus Cash Users

A large percentage of the businesses we studied consume more cash than they generate; in fact, more than a third have a negative operating cash flow before interest expenses (see Exhibit 1). After we subtract interest expenses and dividend payments from cash flow, about two-thirds of the businesses are cash drains.

That so many businesses are cash drains suggests that control is a slippery and complex problem. There are wide differences in the *rate* at which particular businesses use or generate cash. For example, 26% generate cash at a yearly rate above 10% of investment. On the other hand, nearly 15% of them *consume* cash at the 10% rate or beyond. Since businesses may show such divergent cash flow results, it is rational to assume that successful cash control demands systematic study and the careful attention of senior management.

Exhibit 1.   Cash Flow Level of PIMS Businesses, 1970–1979

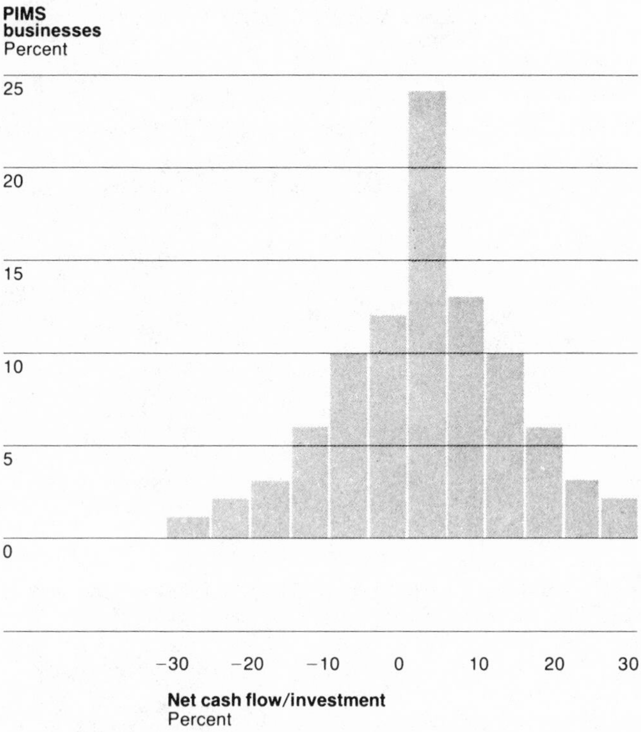

**PIMS
businesses**
Percent

Net cash flow/investment
Percent

Note:
8% of all PIMS businesses are beyond these bounds.

Businesses in fast-growth markets usually absorb cash unless corporate policy directs that they break even; businesses in slow-growth markets usually throw off cash unless they are allowed to keep and reinvest it.

Cash flow is lowest when sales growth (in current dollars) is rapid (see Exhibit 2A). When growth is slow or negative, cash flow is very positive. In fact, at a moderate growth rate, all a company needs is an average ROI to generate positive cash flow (before dividend or interest payments). At rapid growth rates, however, average ROI no longer suffices.

The algebraic relationship between growth and ROI needed to generate a break-even cash flow is positive and dramatic. But the correlation between growth and *actual* ROI is only moderate. When actual ROI exceeds that required to break even (growth rate below 15%), cash flow is positive. When it falls short, cash flow is negative. (Exhibit 2B shows ROI needed for a business to finance break-even cash flow at various rates of growth.)

We have observed how cash flow decreases with growth in current dollar sales. Such a decrease depends on growth in real market and selling price, as well as basic market share strategy.

Exhibit 2A. Rapid Growth Drains Cash

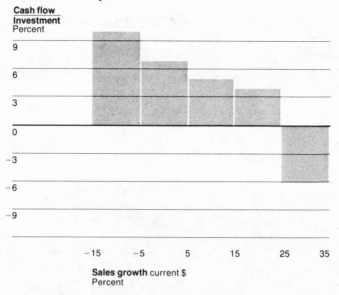

Cash flow
Investment
Percent

Sales growth current $
Percent

Exhibit 2B. ROI for Break-Even Cash Flow Increases with Sales Growth

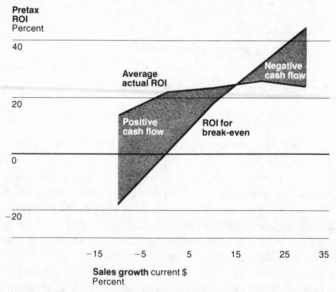

Pretax
ROI
Percent

Average
actual ROI

Negative
cash flow

Positive
cash flow

ROI for
break-even

Sales growth current $
Percent

Note: Break-even ROI (pretax, preinterest) $= 2g/(1 + g)$, where g is the rate of growth expressed as a decimal. If $g = .10$, ROI for break-even cash flow rate $= .2/1.1 = 18\%$. See S.J.Q. Robinson, "What Growth Rate Can You Achieve?" *Long-Range Planning,* August 1979. Also, readers will note that the crossover points between positive and negative cash flow rates shown in Exhibits 2A and 2B differ. The ROI for the break-even rate assumes that investment will grow at the same rate as sales over-time. But during the 1970s the ratio of investment to sales declined. Because investment did not keep pace with sales, the ROI actually needed to break even during the 1970s was less than that shown in Exhibit 2B.

When real market growth is rapid, maintaining share may require considerable cash for working capital and for additional plant and equipment.

Inflation also takes its toll. Although one might expect that a rise in the selling price would generate cash, it generally does not. Indeed, a company finds its cash depleted as rising prices are either accompanied by (or are prompted by) rising costs. In addition, as prices rise, the need of most companies to tie up larger amounts of money in inventory and accounts receivable exacerbates cash requirements.

Thus cash flow varies *inversely* with both the real market growth rate and the rate of increase in selling prices. Our data base shows that businesses with slow rates of selling price and real market growth generate an average cash flow rate of 6%, whereas those with the highest growth in both average only 2%.

One caveat: A low rate of cash flow year after year does not carry the same stigma as recurrent low ROI. Even negative cash flow is not necessarily a serious problem. As long as a business establishes the strategic position required to earn an attractive return, it generates cash when the market ultimately slows down. But, while rapid growth continues, the company may still require additional resources (see Exhibit 3).

If your business is in a slow-growth market, chances are you find it relatively easy to generate enough cash to meet your needs. But whether your market grows, shrinks, or stands still, a large relative share produces cash.

Large-share businesses in slow-growth markets (called "cash cows" in terminology coined by the Boston Consulting Group) have the highest cash flow, whereas small-share businesses in rapidly growing markets have the lowest. In our data base, the former generates an average positive cash flow of 9%, whereas the latter generates a negative 3%. Exhibit 4 shows cash flow contour lines emanating from an empirical model that captures the joint impact of real market growth and relative market share on cash flow.

These contour lines are smooth and systematic because they represent the *average* cash flow rate for a locus of growth/share positions. But we need to remember that growth and share together account for only about one-tenth of the dispersion in cash flow rates illustrated in Exhibit 1. An individual business may be above or below the cash flow value on its contour line because several key factors other than growth and share also affect its cash flow rate. Exhibit 5 presents some of the key factors that affect cash generation and cash use. They are selected from a cash flow model that explains about two-thirds of the dispersion in cash flow rates among business units.

In addition to market growth and share, a change in either market share or investment intensity can affect cash *flow* by influencing cash *use*. As we have seen, businesses often consume cash when attempting to maintain share in a growing market. Gaining or attempting to build share can also be expensive.

Exhibit 3. Cash Needs Are Determined by Environment and Strategy

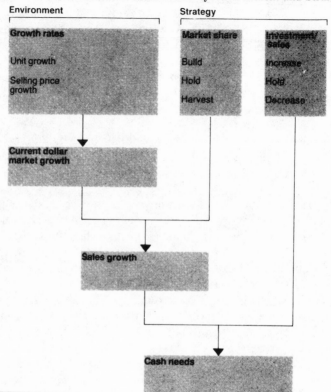

In addition to the normal jockeying for market share against domestic competitors, businesses also endure the pressures of world-class competition. Confrontations lead to shakeouts and fewer competitors. By definition, the survivors realize a net gain in share and a drain on their cash supplies.

Whether management decides to build share or capitalize on the business's present position, the decision should be based on the conscious realization of the impact of the decision on cash flow. If a company wishes to strengthen its future market position by increasing marketing expenditures or introducing new products, it will have to withstand higher costs in the short run.

Similarly, managers can generate cash by harvesting the business's present market position, reducing marketing expenditures, and withholding introduction of new products. Those businesses in our data base that aggressively put out a lot of new products and increase marketing expense show a negative cash flow of 4%, compared with a positive 5% for less aggressive companies.

Companies that increase investment intensity usually face a dramatic

Exhibit 4. Cash-flow-rate Contour Lines for the Growth-Share Matrix

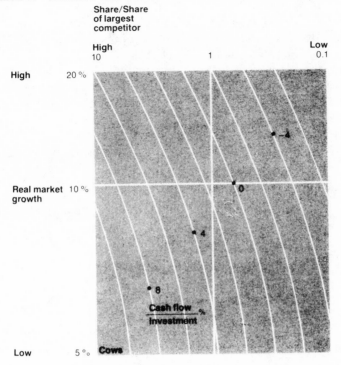

Exhibit 5. Summary of Factors Affecting Cash Generation and Use

Cash Generation		Cash Use	
Factor	Impact	Factor	Impact
Long-run		Real market growth	−
Market share	+	Selling price growth	−
Investment intensity	−	Percentage change in share	−
Short-run			
Rate of new product introductions	−	Point change in investment/sales	−
Marketing expense growth	−		

reduction in their cash flow. For example, management may decide to boost investment relative to sales and value added in order to push capacity ahead of the market, increase inventories, or liberalize receivables policy. This tactic may be sound, but it will cut into profits and increase the rate of investment buildup, thus reducing cash flow.

More serious may be circumstantial shifts, such as an unplanned rise in inventories or accounts receivable, the need to replace quickly plant and equipment at inflated costs, or a sales slump that reduces capacity utilization.

Although it is difficult to predict when circumstances will force a business to consume cash, world-class competition certainly acts as a catalyst. Foreign competitors with up-to-date technology, plant, and equipment put pressure on executives to reindustrialize, and soaring construction costs hike up the price tag of reindustrialization. Because the stakes are usually high, a miscalculation in the attempt to rebuild a single business unit can cripple an entire company. Without rigorous asset management, the equity built up over 40 or 50 years can dissipate in two or three years.

Aggressive asset management has two principal goals:

1 Reduce the amount of cash required to keep pace with growth.
2 Reduce excess capital and thereby improve profits.

Managers *can* reduce investment relative to sales without harming (and in fact they may *enhance*) the business's competitive position, but success requires careful strategic planning.

Cash Allocation and Portfolio Balance

A business unit's market environment, competitive position, and strategy all affect its rate of cash flow. In a portfolio context, the multibusiness general manager will want to turn the relationship around to focus on the effects of cash allocation on the strategy of individual business units.

The manager can find the ratio of cash reinvestment by dividing cash used (increase in gross plant and equipment plus increase in net working capital) by cash generated (aftertax income plus depreciation). Businesses with a cash flow rate of zero reinvest as much cash as they generate—that is, a cash reinvestment ratio of one.

Businesses in rapidly growing markets usually have cash reinvestment ratios greater than one, whereas those in declining or slow-growth markets have ratios much less than one.

The portfolio of an entire company will balance if the cash used by rapidly growing businesses roughly equals the cash generated by businesses with declining or slow growth. The same balancing effect can be achieved if the company requires each business unit to have a cash reinvestment ratio of one (see Exhibit 5).

This second balancing act may backfire. A business in a rapidly growing market may not keep pace and may be strangled. Its share of the market slips, and it cannot generate cash. If the cash generated by a business supplying a slow-growth market is not invested elsewhere, that business may overinvest in its basic product line. Such a business does not compensate for the cash flow needs of the company's high-growth businesses. Instead it becomes investment intensive; profits fall, as does its ability to generate cash.

By understanding that the welfare of the portfolio depends as much on capital allocation among businesses as on project selection within business units, managers can guarantee a more profitable equilibrium between present needs and long-term goals and begin to allocate assets strategically across the portfolio. With the increasing demands of high inflation, lagging productivity, and the need to reindustrialize, only astute companies that understand the link between strategy and cash will survive and prosper.

Appendix A. What Is PIMS?

The empirical evidence supporting our findings comes from the data base assembled by the Strategic Planning Institute (SPI), a nonprofit, tax-exempt organization in Cambridge, Massachusetts.

Called PIMS (profit impact of market strategy), the data base includes the business experiences, both good and bad, of more than 1,700 product and service businesses operated by SPI's more than 200 member companies in North America, Europe, and Australia. Each business is defined as a division, product line, or other profit center within its parent company, selling a distinct set of products or services to an identifiable group of customers in competition with a well-defined set of companies.

For each business, the data separate revenues, operating costs, investments, and strategic plans. Before making information in the data base available to member companies, SPI disguises and summarizes the collected data.

SPI collects data not only on traditional balance sheets and income statements, but also on each company's market share, investment intensity, productivity, product quality, and unionization. The data base describes more than 200 such characteristics for each business and, in addition, documents its actions, the market it serves, its competitive environment, and its financial results.

Appendix B. Alternative Measures of Net Cash Flow Rates

So far, we assume that interest expenses are zero. Typically, interest expenses are about 4% of investment (say, the ratio of debt to investment equals .4 and the interest rate equals 10%). Interest expenses are subtracted before taxes. Assuming the tax rate is 50%, we need to adjust our cash flow figures by 2% (.5 of 4%) to reflect interest expenses. Since the average net cash flow rate (preinterest expense) is 4%, the average cash flow rate after interest and taxes (but before dividend payments) would be about 2%.

If dividend payments are about 5% of investment (say ROI after interest expenses and taxes equals 10%, and half of profits is paid out as dividends), the average net cash flow rate after dividend payments will be about −3%.

The PIMS average for different measures of net cash flow (NCF) rates can be summarized as follows:

NCF Measure	PIMS Average, 1970–1979	Percentage of PIMS Business with Negative NCF Rates
(a) NCF rate, assuming interest expense = 0	4%	33%
(b) NCF rate, assuming interest expense = 4% of investment	2%	50%
(c) NCF rate, after interest expenses and assuming dividends = 5% of investment	−3%	67%

The exhibit shows NCF rates based on measure (a). To obtain rough NCF rates that reflect interest expenses (b), subtract 2 points from the NCF figures shown in the exhibit.

Simply subtracting an additional five points from after-interest cash flow rates will not yield a good approximation of the true after-dividend NCF rates. The dividend payout ratio usually declines as growth increases, and most of the exhibit shows the effects of growth-related factors. In very rapid growth situations, the additional subtraction could be as low as 0 to 2 points. In slow growth or declining environments, it could be as much as 8 to 9 points.

31
Strategies for High Market-Share Companies

PAUL N. BLOOM and PHILIP KOTLER

In recent years, a growing number of business practitioners and theorists have postulated that one way for a company to increase its return is by increasing its market share, and studies appear to have confirmed this relationship. But the authors of this article refuse to accept the blanket inference that "more" is necessarily always going to mean "better." A large market share, they point out, can spell more trouble as well as more profit for a company; a given project promising higher returns than others will surely entail greater risks as well. Given this direct link between profit and risk, it behooves companies to manage their market shares with the same diligence as they would manage any other facet of their businesses. This concept of managing market shares leads to some intriguing possibilities. Although most companies can profit by attempting to increase their market shares, some may conclude that they are at (or possibly beyond) the point at which expected costs and risks outweigh expected gains. The authors suggest various strategies that these companies might consider in attempting to manage their market shares.

Capturing a dominant share of a market is likely to mean enjoying the highest profits of any of the companies serving that market.[1] It can also mean winning the leadership, power, and glory that go with such dominance.

But high market share can also mean headaches. Companies possessing it are tempting targets for actual and potential competitors, consumer or-

Published 1975.

Authors' note: The authors would like to thank Warren Greenberg, Charles W. Hofer, Daniel Nimer, and Louis W. Stern for their very helpful comments and suggestions.

ganizations, and government agencies. IBM, General Motors, Campbell's, Coca-Cola, Kellogg, and Caterpillar are cases in point. Their market shares have been their blessing and their curse—their curse because they must make their decisions and manage their operations with much more care than do their competitors. These companies cannot aggressively seek larger shares because further gains may break the dam and let the waters of antitrust action pour in. In some cases, these companies may even have to give up some shares in order to stem the tide.

The company that acquires a very high market share exposes itself to a number of risks that its smaller competitors do not encounter. Competitors, consumers, and governmental authorities are more likely to take certain actions against high-share companies than against small-share ones.

Smaller competitors, for example, can direct certain types of attack against larger organizations, attacks that would not work as well against companies of equal or smaller size. One type of attack has been to file private antitrust suits in an attempt to demonstrate that the larger competitor has violated antitrust laws while amassing its dominant share. In one of these suits, a court recently ordered IBM to pay Telex $259.5 million (this was later reversed by an appeals court). Eastman Kodak, Xerox, Anheuser-Busch, Gillette, and General Foods are currently involved in other private antitrust actions.[2] Another type of attack involves the use of comparative advertising. Avis, B.F. Goodrich, Seven-Up, and others have found it profitable to mention or picture the products of their large competitors in their ads, and then to suggest the superiority of their own products.

Potential competitors also present problems because they may see the company with the largest share as the only competitor stopping them from capturing a portion of the profits being earned in a particular industry. Clearly, some large multiproduct companies have had considerable success in entering lucrative markets previously dominated by one or a few organizations. Procter & Gamble, for example, has recently entered several markets (potato chips, tampons, deodorant sprays, and toilet paper) with noteworthy results.

Yet another risk is posed by consumer or public-interest organizations. A larger market share usually means greater public visibility; consumer groups may choose the more visible companies as the targets of their complaints, demonstrations, and lawsuits. Campaign GM—the proxy battle to force General Motors to take a number of actions believed to be in the public interest—was conducted against the largest and most visible auto manufacturer. Similarly, SOUP—Students Opposed to Unfair Practices—was originally formed to fight the use of alleged deceptive practices in the advertising of Campbell Soup, the leader in the soup industry. Eastman Kodak, First National City Bank of New York, and DuPont are three other dominant market-share companies that have been singled out by consumer or public-interest organizations. Such attack by a consumer group can, of course, create ill will for the organization, as well as involve it in costly litigation.

The high market-share company also has to cope with antitrust initiatives taken by the government. The Justice Department and the Federal Trade Commission are placing a renewed emphasis on the "structural" characteristics of markets. Rather than wait for conclusive evidence that the conduct within an industry has been anticompetitive (that is, predatory or collusive), these agencies have taken action primarily because noncompetitive market structures have allegedly existed.

Recent suits have been filed against IBM, Xerox, the eight major oil companies, the four major cereal manufacturers, and ReaLemon; in all of these suits the government has emphasized that these companies' market shares are so large that their competition has virtually disappeared. One might say that these companies are now being penalized for their success. In any case, they are all involved in expensive legal battles, and they all face the prospect of being broken up or required to drastically alter their ways of doing business.

More high market-share companies can expect antitrust suits when the FTC begins to exercise its newly won authority to require line-of-business reporting from major corporations. With such attention focused on their daily operations, multiproduct companies will find it harder to disguise their dominance of a particular market, although they may be able to disguise its profitability through arbitrary allocations of fixed overhead. Congressional pressure to fight inflation through stepped-up enforcement of the existing antitrust laws will also cause severe headaches for many high market-share companies.

There are, however, two qualifications to these risks:

1. *The degree of risk depends on how the company has obtained its high market share.* To the extent that its success is based on continuous innovation and/or lowering of costs and prices to buyers, consumers and the government may feel less hostile to the company, and competitors may feel less able to attack it. To the extent that its success is based on using an expiring patent, on bundling services, or on tying up a particular channel of distribution, these parties may be more inclined to attack it.

2. *The degree of risk depends on the resources of the other parties.* For example, risk from competitors is not very great if they cannot afford to mount counteradvertising campaigns or private antitrust suits. The risk of consumer and government intervention is not very great if the social milieu has changed from one of widespread business criticism to one of more traditional acceptance of business practices.

Unfortunately, there has been little discussion of either the problems of market-share management facing the high market-share company or of the actions it should consider. Much has been written about how a company should go about attaining increases in its market share, but little about what it should do once it has attained a large share. That is the question we shall consider here, but first we shall discuss the way in which a business decides on its optimal market share.

Determining an Optimal Market Share

Most companies think and plan not only in terms of profit and sales volume but also in terms of market share. They see market-share gains as the key to long-run profitability. The Boston Consulting Group, for example, has proposed that, in product areas characterized by a strong learning curve, companies pursue *market share maximization* instead of *current profit maximization.*[3]

Despite this recommendation, we feel that an organization's goal should not be to maximize market share, but rather to attain the optimal market share. *A company has attained its optimal market share in a given product/market when a departure in either direction from the share would alter the company's long-run profitability or risk (or both) in an unsatisfactory way.* A company finding its current share below the optimal level should plan for market-share gains; a company that is at its optimal market share should fight to maintain it; and a company that has exceeded it should seek to reduce its current share.

How can a company determine where its optimal market share lies? It must go through the following three-step procedure:

1 Estimate the relationship between market share and profitability.
2 Estimate the amount of risk associated with each share level.
3 Determine the point at which an increase in market share can no longer be expected to bring enough profit to compensate for the added risks to which the company would expose itself.

Estimating Profitability as a Function of Market Share

Both economic theory and empirical evidence suggest that profitability increases with market share. Consider the case of a company with a fixed plant size. In this case, its sales volume breakeven point is determined by the slopes of the cost and revenue curves. Beyond the breakeven point, the company's profits increase with its sales volume. This may continue until output levels reach a high percentage of capacity and thereby cause direct costs to increase dramatically.

Now consider the company that can expand its plant and market size. Usually this permits economies of scale in production, distribution, and marketing. A larger company can afford better equipment or more automation that lowers unit costs. It can obtain volume discounts in media advertising, purchasing, warehousing, and freight. It can attract the more lucrative customer accounts that want fuller services. And it can gain distributor acceptance and cooperation at a lower cost. Empirical studies bear this out. One of the best and most recent is the Marketing Science Institute's "Profit Impact of Market Strategies" (PIMS) project. This study found that:

> The average ROI for businesses with under 10% market share was about 9%. . . . On the average, a difference of 10 percentage points in market share is accompanied by a difference of about 5 points in pretax ROI.[4]

The PIMS study shows that businesses with market shares above 40% earn an average ROI of 30%, or three times that of those with shares under 10%.

However, the PIMS study does not reveal whether profitability eventually turns down at very high market-share levels. The study lumps together all market shares above 40%; therefore, the behavior of ROI in response to still higher market shares is undisclosed. Consequently, a high market-share company must itself analyze whether profitability will fall with further gains in market share. For the following reasons, it could drop dramatically:

☐ Holdout customers may be loyal to competitors, so the cost of attracting them might exceed their value as new customers.

☐ The needs of these customers may be unique and not worth the cost of catering to.

☐ Companies seeking to enlarge their share of market may have to carry extra costs of legal work, public relations, and lobbying to defend their larger market share against criticism and regulation.

When these factors begin to offset further gains in production and distribution efficiency, the optimal market share has been reached.

Estimating Risk

At different levels of market share, a company's risk also changes. Risk is high for low market-share companies, declines as market share increases, and then increases again at very high share levels. Risk is high at low market-share levels because a business is subject to competitive forays by stronger competitors, cannot afford adequate marketing research and promotional spending, and is vulnerable to sudden changes in consumer tastes or spending. Risk starts to fall with increased market share because an organization can engage in more market research, operate better information systems, recruit more experienced marketing personnel, and spend more on marketing. Risk reaches a low point at a high share level and then may begin to increase at higher levels because of the growing probability that the government, consumers, and competitors will single the business out for specific attack.

Finding the Optimal Level

This third step calls for top management to compare the changes in profitability and risk that it expects in seeking other levels of market share. Starting with its current share, management can analyze:

1 The expected cost of achieving a specified higher level of market share.

2 The expected profitability associated with that market share.

3 The expected increase in risk.

The increase in long-run profitability must compensate for the cost of achieving the higher share and the higher attendant risk. If not, the specified higher market share is not optimal.

Management should also examine a specified lower share level, taking into consideration the cost, profitability, and decrease in risk at each level. If a lower level of risk does not compensate for the reduced profitability (which may or may not exist, since prices may be higher or marketing costs lower and profitability unchanged) and for transitional costs, then the specified lower market share is not optimal. If the company uses this technique for a number of alternative market-share levels and cannot find one that offers a more satisfying balance of profitability and risk, then it is at its optimal level.

Market-Share Management Strategies

Thus far, we have shown how a high market-share company can locate its optimal market share. We shall now discuss the various strategies a company can use either to attain or maintain this optimal share or to shift it to a higher level.

Market-share management strategies fall into four broad categories: (1) share building, (2) share maintenance, (3) share reduction, and (4) risk reduction.

Share Building

The majority of companies that analyze their market position conclude that they are operating *below* their optimal market share. They are not exploiting their plant fully or have not been able to build a plant at the most economical size; they are not quite large enough to achieve promotional and/or distributional economies; and they cannot attract the strongest talent. In sum, they see a higher market share as promising greater profitability without commensurately greater risk—indeed, often as reducing that risk.

Share-building strategies must be designed to meet several considerations—whether (1) the primary market is growing, stable, or declining, (2) the product is homogeneous or highly differentiable, (3) the company's resources are high or low in relation to its competitors' resources, and (4) there are one or several competitors and how effective they are.

The most effective strategy for market-share gain is *product innovation*. Its weak sister, product imitation, may be appropriate for growth in a growing market, but it will probably not alter existing market shares. Such companies as Xerox, Zenith, Control Data, and Polaroid made their mark because they found a better product. At the same time, innovation is an expensive and risk-laden strategy requiring a careful analysis of market needs and preferences, a large investment, and astute timing.

Market segmentation may also be used to build share. Many dominant companies concentrate on the mass market and neglect or undersatisfy various fringe markets. This mistake is illustrated by the big three American auto makers, who for years sought the majority market, concluding that the small-car market segment was too small to be profitable. The vacuum they created was first filled by Volkswagen and then later by other European and Japanese auto companies at a high profit.

A third strategy for building market share is *distribution innovation*. In this instance, the company finds a way to cover a market more effectively. Timex achieved its growth as a watch manufacturer by entering unconventional outlets like drugstores and discount stores. These outlets then refused to carry additional brands of low-priced watches, leaving Timex king of the mountain. Avon achieved its spectacular growth as a leader in cosmetics by resurrecting the old and neglected channel of door-to-door selling rather than by fighting bloody battles for space in conventional retail outlets.

A final strategy for share building is *promotional innovation*. Consider Philip Morris's "Marlboro man" or Avis's "We're No. 2, We Try Harder." A clever and distinctive campaign or promotion, once established, is hard to duplicate or offset. At the same time, however, too many organizations emphasize promotional innovation when they should be searching for real product, segment, or distributional innovations. Flashy promotion has a hollow ring when unsupported by improvements in consumer value.

Share Maintenance

In evaluating their market positions, some companies will find that they are in fact operating at an optimal share level. The cost or risk of increasing their share would cancel out any gains. On the other hand, a decline in their current share would reduce their profitability. These companies are intent on maintaining market share.

Such organizations find, however, that stabilizing their share is almost as challenging as expanding it.

Underdog competitors are constantly chipping away at the stable company's share. They introduce new products, sniff out new segments, try out new forms of distribution, and launch new promotions. One of the most annoying and common forms of attack is price cutting. The high-share company is always wrestling with the question of whether to meet price cuts and maintain its share or give up a little share and maintain its margins. If the high-share company maintains its prices, it loses share. If it loses more than it expects, it may discover that rebuilding costs more than the gains from holding prices.

In general, the best defense for maintaining market share is a good offense—product innovation, the same strategy that works so well for the underdog. A dominant company must refuse to be content with the way things are. It has to anticipate its own obsolescence by developing new products, customer services, channels of distribution, and cost-cutting processes.

A second line of defense is *market fortification*. The dominant company plugs market holes to prevent competitors from moving in. This is the essence of the *multibrand strategy* perfected by P&G. P&G will introduce a number of brands competing with each other; the effect is to tie up scarce distribution space and lock out some of the competition.

A third and less attractive defense for share maintenance is a *confrontation strategy*. Here the dominant company defends its empire by initiating expensive promotional or price-cutting wars to discipline upstart competitors. It may even resort to harassment—pressuring dealers and suppliers into ignoring upstarts to avoid losing the dominant company's goodwill. Confrontation may work, but it is undertaken at some risk and contributes less to social welfare than would more innovative responses. Furthermore, such tactics suggest a senescence in the dominant organization.

Share Reduction

Some companies analyzing the profitability and risk associated with their current market share may come to the conclusion that they have overextended themselves in the overall market or in certain sub-markets. Their large share puts them on the "hot seat" too often or includes too many marginal customers. These factors can lead the company to think about how to reduce its presence in the market.

Share reduction calls for the application of general or selective demarketing principles.[5] *Demarketing is the attempt to reduce, temporarily or permanently, the level of customer demand.* It may be directed at the market or selected market segments. It calls for reversing the normal direction of marketing moves: raising price, cutting back advertising and promotion, reducing service. It may involve more extreme measures such as reducing product quality or convenience features. In a period of prolonged shortages, these steps may be especially necessary.

Several high market-share companies have apparently used demarketing to reduce their shares to less risky levels. Procter & Gamble, for example, has allowed its share of the shampoo market to slip from around 50% to just above 20% of its competitors. In this period, the company has delayed reformulating its old brands (Prell and Head & Shoulders), has tried to introduce only one new brand (which was withdrawn twice from test markets), and has not attempted to "buy" back its share with heavy spending on advertising and promotion.[6] It seems fair to speculate that Procter & Gamble's passive response to its decline in market share is deliberate; it may be motivated by a desire to avoid antitrust difficulties like those it has encountered with Clorox and, recently, with its detergent products.[7]

An example of a company that has used demarketing more selectively is Kellogg in its delay in entering the natural cereal market. The company may have decided to allow others to dominate this segment of the market to improve its chances of emerging from current antitrust difficulties without too many scars.[8]

In the auto industry, observers have long noted how General Motors,

Ford, and Chrysler treat American Motors as a shield against antitrust attack. The big companies have apparently given AMC very little competition over lucrative contracts for government vehicles (postal and military jeeps, military trucks, and so on).[9]

Finally, the demarketing experience of ReaLemon Foods, a subsidiary of Borden, deserves comment. ReaLemon implemented a selective demarketing strategy to avoid antitrust problems, but it reversed its strategy too soon and paid a price. Until 1970, ReaLemon held about 90% of the reconstituted lemon juice market. According to industry sources, ReaLemon at that time began to allow companies on the West Coast and in the Chicago area to make inroads into its share through fear of antitrust attack. By 1972, however, a Chicago competitor, Golden Crown Citrus Corporation, had captured a share that ReaLemon considered too large. ReaLemon retaliated. As a result, the Federal Trade Commission filed a complaint in 1974 charging ReaLemon with predatory pricing and sales tactics.[10] The lesson to be learned from ReaLemon's experience is that once a high market-share company allows its share to fall, it must be careful if it decides to reverse itself.

It should be said parenthetically that demarketing can be both desirable and undesirable from a social point of view. To the extent that businesses selectively concentrate on those customer segments and product lines where they can market most efficiently and profitably, demarketing can lead to greater effectiveness, variety, and competition. However, where they demarket in ways that discriminate against the weaker or disadvantaged segments—such as when a big supermarket chain closes down its inner-city stores—the results can be unfortunate.

Risk Reduction

Companies concluding that their high share is dangerous may want to adopt strategies reducing the risk rather than strategies reducing the share. We have stated that the optimal market share is a function of both profitability and risk, and that any success in reducing the risk surrounding a high share is tantamount to optimizing that share.

Companies can consider a number of measures to reduce the insecurity surrounding their high market share, including (1) public relations, (2) competitive pacification, (3) dependence, (4) legislation, (5) diversification, and (6) social responsiveness.

Public Relations. It is becoming common for companies in dominant positions to spend large sums of money on advertising and other public relations efforts to improve their images. In many cases, such companies hope their efforts will undercut public support for legislative, government agency, or consumer group actions that would hurt their interests.

Public relations strategies are used with good cause to publicize genuine efforts that serve the public interest. But they are also used to cover up weak or nonexistent attempts—the case of a public utility that spent $50,000 to clean up the environment and $400,000 to publicize the action comes to mind. When a company spends more on good words than good deeds, it is giving its critics ammunition.

Organizations have also used public relations and advertising to publicize their position on a controversial issue. Major oil companies took out expensive newspaper ads during the oil and gas shortages to defend their high profits—arguing that they were needed either to finance future energy growth or to make up for depressed profits in the past. These ads probably did not convince a single skeptic and, if anything, made the public angrier at the thriftlessness of full-page spreads defending oil profits. Some critics have called this "ecopornography" and have complained that these ads reduce government tax revenues, since corporations, unlike private citizens, can treat the cost of political messages as a legitimate business expense.

Competitive Pacification. The high share company may attempt to reduce the risks associated with its position by cultivating better relations with its competitors. There are numerous ways in which this can be done. Organizations may help find supplies of raw materials, or even sell the material outright. They may conduct advertising campaigns that promote the product category rather than their specific brands. They may refrain from reacting strongly to the strategy changes of their rivals. They may supply valuable research data and other assistance to smaller competitors through trade association activities. They may provide price umbrellas. And they may hold back the rate of new product introduction. (Of course, the company that chooses to use competitive pacification strategies must be careful to avoid behaving in what could be considered a collusive manner.)

Pacified smaller competitors exist in many industries. General Motors and Ford have apparently recognized that it is in their best interests to keep Chrysler and American Motors friendly. Similarly, the smaller cereal companies are on good terms with giant Kellogg.

Because competitive pacification strategies permit weak competitors to survive and even to prosper, they provide a public service by giving consumers a wide variety of products to choose from. However, to the extent that these strategies lead to a misallocation of resources and higher prices, they may do a disservice to the American public. It should be remembered that consumers can also benefit from counteradvertising, antitrust suits, and other aggressive actions initiated by these same unpacified smaller competitors.

Dependence and Legislation. Dependency strategies forge a link between the high market-share company and the government. By making government institutions and officials dependent on it for various products (particularly defense-related commodities), for help in keeping unemployment down, or for political campaign funds, a company can acquire considerable power over policy makers and lessen its chances of being the target of government legislation and lawsuits.

Both the Justice Department and the Federal Trade Commission have been the butt of dependency strategies. In a chapter entitled "The Politics of Antitrust," the authors of *The Closed Enterprise System* (a Ralph Nader venture) cite numerous cases in which the Justice Department has been subjected to and has sometimes succumbed to pressures by elected officials to curtail antitrust actions.[11] The most noteworthy example, of course, is the ITT case. Similarly, the supposedly independent FTC has not found itself totally immune from pressures by elected officials, since Congress appropriates its budgets and the President appoints its commissioners. Many elected officials are willing to exert pressure on these and other enforcement agencies because they fear that they will lose campaign funds and other forms of political support, defense supplies, and employment opportunities for their constituencies if large, powerful companies are successfully prosecuted under antitrust or other laws.

It is unfortunate that our antitrust laws have encouraged the use of dependency strategies. The laws were originally designed to prevent this type of behavior. However, it is just as true that the procedures developed over the years for enforcing these laws have allowed dependency strategies some success. This success has resulted in a reduction of the political influence of individual citizens and a lessening of competition in many economic sectors.

Closely related to dependency strategies are legislative ones. A high market-share company can attempt to convince Congress to pass legislation giving it special treatment under the law. For example, labor unions, professional athletic leagues, banks, and newspapers have all received special treatment under the antitrust laws. Special legal treatment has also been offered to many companies in the form of subsidies, tax loopholes, and tariff reductions. Thus successful use of legislative strategies can practically eliminate a company's risk of being the target of an antitrust attack and/or help stabilize earnings at high levels.

It is difficult to say a priori whether a company's use of legislative strategies will or will not benefit society. The organization that lobbies for an antitrust exemption, special tariff treatment, or tax loopholes is acting in its own interest. Yet this does not mean that its interest will not ultimately coincide with that of the public. The biggest objection to the use of legislative strategies by high market-share companies is that it involves asking for special treatment rather than equality under the law, and it shelters the company or industry from the fresh winds of competition.

Diversification. By diversifying successfully into markets that are different from the one it dominates, a company can ensure that a steady stream of profits will continue even after something as drastic as an antitrust divestiture has occurred.

Many high market-share companies have done just this. For example, the Brookings Institution's classic examination of the pricing practices of

20 major corporations (including General Motors, General Electric, General Foods, and U.S. Steel) revealed that antitrust concerns seemed to motivate several high-share companies to diversify. The report states:

> A broader impact of the antitrust laws may be their effect on market-share policy. Many of the companies interviewed expressed a preference for making their way into new markets, wherein their share would be a minor fraction, to dominating the market in the established product.[12]

In addition, fear of competition in established markets can lead companies to diversify. A more recent example of a high-share company that has diversified extensively is Gillette. It has expanded from shaving-related products to deodorants, pens, shampoos, hairdryers, and other product categories.

The adoption of diversification strategies by dominant organizations normally has positive social benefits. Their movement into new industries tends to create healthy competition throughout the entire economy.[13]

Social Responsiveness.   The most constructive way for a high market-share company to reduce its risk is to demonstrate a responsiveness to emerging consumer and social needs. Certain companies have gained the trust of the buying public because of their continuous efforts to respond to such social needs—one thinks immediately of Sears, Zenith, and Whirlpool. Trust is not the result of a sustained and clever public relations campaign, but rather of the satisfaction that customers and the public receive in dealing with a company.

A high market-share company that has successfully won the public trust is Giant Foods, a major food chain in the Washington, D.C., area.[14] Giant Foods interpreted the various consumer criticisms of the late 1960s not as presenting unwelcome problems but as offering useful new opportunities. So it took the initiative and introduced such consumer-oriented programs as unit pricing, open dating, and some nutritional labeling. It also carried an extensive supply of less expensive private labels to enable consumers to hold down their costs. It publicized money-saving food buys and supported the meat boycott to bring down consumer costs. And it appointed Esther Peterson, former White House special assistant for consumer affairs, as a consumer affairs advisor. All of these steps made it a consumer champion and won it many friends and patrons.

Nonetheless, evidence is still needed to prove that a company assuming the role of consumer champion, with all the expense this entails, is compensated in terms of either market share or lower risk. It seems to be a part that only one company in each industry can play meaningfully, since others are typed as weak imitators. However, in an age of such formidable social problems as high prices, environmentalism, shortages, antibusiness sentiment, and changing life-styles, these problems should be regarded as disguised opportunities for the companies that have the courage and imagination to perceive them.

Filling Societal Needs

Because it is exposed to a large and unique set of risks, the high market-share company is confronted with difficult problems. It cannot seek an ever larger market share as freely as its smaller competitors. Instead, it must carefully analyze the relationship of its current share to its optimal market share, and it must plan how to make these two shares coincide.

More often than not, the high market-share organization will find that it must use share-reduction or risk-reduction strategies to align these two shares. Unfortunately, the use of many share- and risk-reduction strategies can have undesirable social consequences. Demarketing strategies of a highly discriminatory nature, certain public relations strategies, competitive pacification strategies, dependency strategies, and legislative strategies can all produce outcomes that are not in the best long-term interests of major portions of society. Therefore, the high market-share company should give serious consideration to those strategies that not only fill its coffers but also respond to consumer and social needs.

Notes

1. For a detailed discussion of the relationship between market share and profitability, see Robert D. Buzzell, Bradley T. Gale, and Ralph G.M. Sultan, "Market Share—A Key to Profitability," *HBR*, January-February 1975, p. 97.

2. Ernest Holsendolph, "New Challenges in Antitrust," *New York Times*, January 21, 1973.

3. See *Perspectives on Experience* (Boston: The Boston Consulting Group, Inc., 1968).

4. Buzzell, Gale, and Sultan, "Market Share," pp. 100 and 97; for further evidence, see Bradley T. Gale, "Market Share and Rate of Return," *Review of Economics & Statistics*, November 1972, p. 412.

5. See Philip Kotler and Sidney J. Levy, "Demarketing, Yes, Demarketing," *HBR*, November-December 1971, p. 74.

6. Nancy Giges, "Shampoo Rivals Wonder When P&G Will Seek Old Dominance," *Advertising Age*, September 23, 1974. p. 3.

7. "Investigation of Heavy-Duty Detergent Industry Announced," *Federal Trade Commission News Summary*, June 20, 1975, p. 4.

8. For information on Kellogg's antitrust difficulties, see "The Cereal Case," *Antitrust Law and Economics Review*, Fall 1971, p. 71.

9. "The Mouse That Varoomed," *Time*, November 20, 1972, p. 82.

10. Dennis D. Fisher, "ReaLemon Sales Tactics Hit," *Chicago Sun-Times*, July 4, 1974.

11.   See Mark J. Green, Beverly C. Moore, Jr., and Bruce Wasserstein, *The Closed Enterprise System* (New York: Grossman Publishers, 1972), pp. 30–62.

12.   Abraham D.H. Kaplan, Joel B. Dirlam, and Robert F. Lanzillotti, *Pricing in Big Business* (Washington, D.C.: The Brookings Institution, 1958), p. 268.

13.   See Bruce R. Scott, "The Industrial State: Old Myths and New Realities," *HBR*, March-April, 1973, p. 133.

14.   See Esther Peterson, "Consumerism As a Retailer's Asset," *HBR*, May-June 1974, p. 91.

32
Pyrrhic Victories in Fights for Market Share

WILLIAM E. FRUHAN, JR.

Business in the United States has a way of growing compulsively; companies tend to want "in" where a lively market is concerned, and once they are in, they want first place. There are times, as the author shows, when a little self-restraint is an admirable thing. When a company can be sure that moving into a new area or moving up the ladder is going to cost it its lifeblood; when a company can see the hand of government writing restrictive legislation on the wall; when a company must race an established competitor to exhaustion just to get a foothold in a new market—these are times when management should put the ceiling of realism on its ambitions. The author cites examples of disasters stemming from overambition of this kind, from the computer industry, the food business, and the airline companies.

In many U.S. industries, profitability is closely linked to market share. ROI statistics demonstrate this characteristic quite clearly for automobile manufacturing, for example, as Exhibit 1 illustrates.

Since profits can jump impressively in many industries as a company's position in the market-share pecking order advances, market-share battles are often waged with energy; but unfortunately, in spite of the tremendous stakes involved, companies tend to launch their campaigns for building market share without much foresight.

Specifically, they tend to ignore three basic questions:

☐ *Question 1.* Does the company have the financial resources necessary to win—and then support—the level of sales implied by its market-share target; or, if it does not have these resources, can it acquire them at acceptable cost?

Published 1972.

☐ *Question 2.* Will the company find itself in a viable position if its drive for an expanded market share should be thwarted—by antitrust action, say–before it has reached its market-share target?

☐ *Question 3.* Will regulatory authorities permit the company to achieve its objective with *the strategy it has chosen to follow?*

To demonstrate the importance of these questions to expansion strategies, let me review the experiences of a number of companies, operating in quite separate industries, that fought, by-and-large disastrously, to increase their market shares.

Main-Frame Computers

Recently, two companies opted out of the main-frame computer manufacturing industry. Prior to their exit from the business, both of these companies had committed themselves to increasing their market shares:

☐ According to press reports during September 1970, General Electric's studies indicated that it had to have a 15% market share if the company were to become competitive in the industry.[1]

☐ About the same time, RCA concluded that it needed a 10% share to become competitive; and the company committed itself, publicly, to meeting that goal by the mid-1970s.[2]

Modest as they might first appear, these market-share objectives represented a more than threefold advance from these companies' 1969 industry standings, which are given in Exhibit 2. Further, both companies planned to meet these objectives solely through internal growth. Both probably felt that antitrust regulations ruled out a strategy for expansion through acquisition of other domestic computer manufacturers, and hence decided to seek their expanded shares through internal means.[3]

A strategy of internal growth in the computer industry, however, demands a major financial commitment. Since a large fraction of manufacturers' output is marketed via leases, operations are capital-intensive. For example, in 1969 IBM required a capital base of about $5.9 billion to support shipment

Exhibit 1. Return on Equity for Automobile Manufacturers, Ranked by Market Share

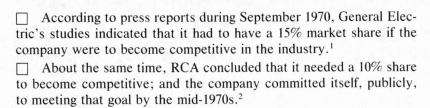

Company	Market-share rank	1960	1962	1964	1966	1968	1970
General Motors	1	16.9%	21.3%	23.5%	21.2%	18.2%	6.1%
Ford	2	15.6	14.6	12.9	13.3	13.0	9.4
Chrysler	3	4.6	8.8	20.4	11.4	14.1	−0.3

Exhibit 2.   Competitors' Standings in the 1969 Main-Frame Computer Market (dollar figures in millions)

Company	Sales Value of Computers Shipped	Market Share	Total Corporate Capital[a] 1969	Total Corporate Revenue 1969	Percent of Total Revenues from Computers
IBM	$4,950	69.0%	$5,906	$7,197	83%
Sperry Rand	400	5.6	977	1,710	36
Honeywell	340	4.7	956	1,281	27
Burroughs	305	4.3	907	759	36
GE	290	4.0	3,554	8,448	3
Control Data	255	3.6	984	1,084	53
RCA	230	3.2	1,875	3,222	7
NCR	195	2.7	1,104	1,255	16
Xerox	75	1.1	1,099	1,483	8
Others	130	1.8	—	—	—
Industry total for year	1969 $ 7,170	100.0%			
Projections of industry shipments	1970 $ 7,720				
	1971 8,940				
	1972 10,300				
	1973 11,800				
	1974 13,400				

Source: International Data Publishing Co., annual reports, and author's estimates.
[a]Includes short-term loans, long-term debt, and shareholders' equity.

estimated at $4.95 billion, as indicated in Exhibit 2. These figures suggest that, given a stable market share, $1 in annual shipments requires the support of about $1.20 of firm capital in this industry.

This degree of capital intensity, coupled with the absolute size of the computer industry and the speed with which RCA (and presumably GE, too) wished to reach its market-share objectives, leads to one inescapable conclusion: the market-share aspirations of GE and RCA required a capital commitment quite out of proportion to their capital-generating ability.

Exhibit 3 shows this clearly. The combined retained earnings and the additions to debt capital which the earnings retentions of GE and RCA might have supported at their debt/equity ratios in the late 1960s were insufficient to meet the future capital needs arising solely from the *computer divisions* of these diversified companies. Yet, in 1969, the computer divisions' revenues accounted for less than 10% of total corporate revenues in the two companies.

The implications are clear. The debt/equity ratios of GE and RCA

Exhibit 3.   Severe Capital Intensity In The Main-Frame Computer Industry
(dollar figures in millions)

A. All-Industry Figures

Year	Projected Industry Computer Shipments	Industry Capital/ Shipments Ratio	Total Capital Required by Industry
1969	$ 7,170	1.2	$ 8,600
1970	7,720	1.2	9,270
1971	8,940	1.2	10,710
1972	10,300	1.2	12,350
1973	11,800	1.2	14,200
1974	13,400	1.2	16,100

B. RCA Projected Goals

Year	Share of Market Projection	Total Capital Required	New Capital Required
1969	3.2%	$ 276	—
1970	4.0	371	$ 95
1971	5.0	536	165
1972	6.3	778	242
1973	8.0	1,135	357
1974	10.0	1,610	475

C. GE Projected Goals

Year	Share of Market Projection	Total Capital Required	New Capital Required
1969	4.0%	$ 344	—
1970	5.2	482	$138
1971	6.8	730	248
1972	8.9	1,100	370
1973	11.5	1,635	535
1974	15.0	2,420	785

D. Capital Generation

	RCA—1969	GE—1968
Profit after taxes	$151	$357
Dividends	68	235
Earnings retentions	$ 83	$122

Exhibit 3. (*Continued*)
D. Capital Generation

	RCA—1969	GE—1968
Debt/equity ratio[a]	× .45	× .27
Debt potential at D/E ratio	37	33
Total capital generation potential	$120	$155

[a]Includes long-term debt only; in the case of RCA, does not include debt of the Hertz Corporation.

(already high by IBM standards) would have had to be raised sharply, or equity securities would have had to be sold (at low P/E ratios by IBM standards) before these companies could have come close to achieving their market-share objectives. Exhibit 4 gives the statistics for the competing companies.

As *this* exhibit implies, the prospects for GE and RCA were not always quite this dim. Back in 1955, both companies had sufficient corporate resources (in terms of total profit or cash flow) to challenge IBM. By 1961, however, this ability, even for GE, was somewhat questionable. By the mid-1960s, and certainly after the IBM System 360 became a demonstrated success, the contest was over. IBM had so far outdistanced its nearest competitors, and its markets had grown to enormous size so rapidly, that the simple passage of time was raising market-entry barriers to insurmountable heights.

All that remained were the acknowledgments—which finally came in 1970 and 1971—that neither GE nor RCA could marshal the resources necessary to achieve, without domestic acquisitions, even a marginal market share in the computer industry at acceptable cost. Had they asked my Question 1 somewhat earlier than 1970, both GE and RCA might have greatly reduced their losses in the computer business.

Retail Groceries

The retail grocery trade is a second industry in which the fight for market share is well worth examining.

In food retailing, the Federal Trade Commission has found a high correlation between the *profit contribution* of chain stores in a given geographic market area—usually a city or metropolitan area—and the *market share* achieved by those chain stores in the same market area. (Exhibit 5 demonstrates the strength of this correlation.) Indeed, in reference to one company operating in this industry, the FTC's chief economist has stated, "I have never seen a closer relationship between the market dominance of a firm in an individual market, or group of markets, and its profitability. . . ."[4]

Exhibit 4. Financial Statistics for Major Computer Manufacturers, 1955–1969

Company	1955	1957	1959	1961	1963	1965	1967	1969
A. Debt/Equity Ratio								
Burroughs	33%	70%	62%	61%	65%	56%	48%	58%
Control Data	—	—	0	0	103	78	163	39
GE	0	25	19	14	11	17	31	27
Honeywell	18	28	24	28	35	42	65	77
IBM	102	60	50	36	27	15	13	10
NCR	50	59	24	41	51	38	69	61
RCA	97	85	76	52	48	43	50	45
Sperry Rand	—	65	60	62	70	58	31	36
Xerox	38	23	28	59	64	72	52	35
B. Average P/E Ratio								
Burroughs	13.1%	24.0%	22.4%	21.3%	24.5%	15.7%	32.4%	43.1%
Control Data	—	—	32.6	95.3	49.9	55.1	53.3	43.2
GE	22.3	21.9	25.8	25.5	26.7	27.1	24.5	28.4
Honeywell	19.2	29.8	30.6	42.2	23.3	26.3	29.6	32.7
IBM	22.7	31.0	42.0	54.9	34.6	35.8	43.5	40.4
NCR	14.3	17.7	23.0	27.0	27.6	22.8	26.3	32.1
RCA	14.3	13.3	23.6	29.8	20.5	22.2	23.5	17.8
Sperry Rand	13.7	22.0	18.7	32.6	18.3	14.4	23.7	18.6
Xerox	30.6	27.4	45.8	78.5	43.8	54.7	62.3	45.7
C. Profit After Taxes (in millions of dollars)								
Burroughs	$ 12	$ 10	$ 11	$ 11	$ 9	$ 18	$ 35	$ 55
Control Data	—	—	—	1	3	8	8	52
GE	201	248	280	242	271	355	361	278
Honeywell	19	21	29	25	35	38	42	63
IBM	73	111	176	253	363	477	652	934
NCR	18	23	22	30	22	29	35	44
RCA	48	39	40	36	66	101	148	151
Sperry Rand	46	28	37	24	27	32	64	81
Xerox	1	1	2	5	23	62	100	161

Source: Annual reports; *Moody's Industrial Manual*, 1970; *Value Line Investment Survey*.

Stated another way, the profitability of an individual company in gro-cery retailing depends not so much on its total industry market share but, rather, on its weighted-average market share in the various city-market areas in which it participates. This relationship between profitability and city-market share suggests that a growth-minded retail company planning to expand its market position rapidly faces a strategic dilemma: Should it gain

Exhibit 5.   Market Shares Charted against Store Contribution to Corporate Profit, by Groups of Cities (1958)

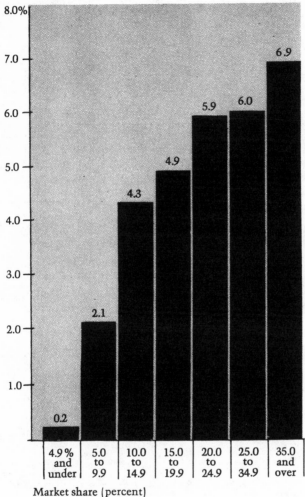

Average contribution
to corporate profit
(percent of sales)

Market share (percent)	Average contribution to corporate profit
4.9% and under	0.2
5.0 to 9.9	2.1
10.0 to 14.9	4.3
15.0 to 19.9	4.9
20.0 to 24.9	5.9
25.0 to 34.9	6.0
35.0 and over	6.9

Market share (percent)

toehold positions in a large number of city-market areas (via acquisitions, for example), and then build its share in each city from this limited base later? Or should it devote its resources to building a dominant position in one-city market area at a time?

Many large chains operating in the industry faced precisely this dilemma between 1948 and 1958, a period when the retail food industry was consolidating itself rapidly through mergers. (Exhibit 6 shows the trend

Exhibit 6.   Percentage Distribution of Food Store Sales, by Type of Retailer, for 1948, 1954, and 1958

Type of Retailer	Percent of Food Store Sales		
	1948	1954	1958
Top 20 chains	24.0%	30.1%	34.0%
Other chains	5.2	6.7	9.8
Cooperative members[a]	7.7	12.7	18.8
Voluntary members[a]	4.6	10.0	12.0
Unaffiliated independents	58.5	40.5	25.4
Total	100.0%	100.0%	100.0%

[a]Arrangements between wholesalers and independents have assumed two basic forms: the retailer-owned cooperative food wholesaler and the wholesaler-sponsored voluntary retail group. Groups of independents so affiliated with a particular wholesaler commonly are referred to as voluntary or cooperative groups or chains.

toward consolidation in those years.) In that decade, the most active acquirer in the field, National Tea, opted for the "toehold" strategy on a nationwide basis, as did many of its competitors. These companies found themselves spread quite thin in numerous markets just at the critical moment in 1958, when (a) the last of the large-store independents were disappearing via merger into competitive chain operations, and (b) the FTC was taking decisive action to halt the consolidation movement by blocking future mergers in this industry.

In short, these companies found themselves in disadvantaged competitive positions and without usable strategies. The detrimental effect on ROI, in the case of National Tea, is clear from the figures in Exhibit 7. What National Tea and many of the others in the group had failed to do was adequately test their strategies against my Questions 2 and 3: they had failed to consider their positions, should they have to shelve their strategies midway

Exhibit 7.   ROI and Acquisition Activity of Three Retail Grocery Companies

Company	Share of U.S. Food Store Sales in Countries Where Company Operates, 1958	ROI				Number of Stores Acquired, 1949–1958	Share of U.S. Food Store Sales, 1958
		1955	1960	1965	1970		
Winn-Dixie	17.2%	17.7%	19.8%	20.6%	18.3%	306	1.3%
A&P	12.6	10.5	12.1	8.8	7.4	0	9.7
National Tea	8.6	9.5	9.1	8.4	5.5	485	1.6

to their goals, and they had failed to prepare themselves for restrictive government regulation.

In contrast, Winn-Dixie—the second most active acquirer in the retail grocery field—appears to have tested its strategies well, judging by the figures given in Exhibit 7. And, in fact, in planning its acquisitions in the 1948–1958 period, Winn-Dixie drove for market depth in a limited geographic area, namely, the Southeast. The company continues to reap the benefits of this bit of foresight in strategy formulation even today. Clearly, there can be an enormous profit payoff in keeping a relatively modest exposure to adverse regulatory responses which might be expected to occur in the middle of a share expansion drive.

Air Transport

My third and final example of a heroic but less-than-successful fight for market share is taken from the air transportation industry.

In this field, consumer buying habits and basic industry economics seem to have entered into a conspiracy to make market-share duels look like very attractive investment opportunities. In making plans, first of all, many air travelers initially contact the air carrier that they believe has the most daily flights to their destination city, which is a natural thing to do. But because of this customer trait, the frequency of a carrier's flight departures in relation to those of its competitors often becomes the crucial factor determining the carrier's share of the passenger traffic in a particular city-pair market. Just as a relatively larger allocation of shelf space in a supermarket might help a cereal manufacturer gain an edge over his competitors, so an added round-trip flight each day between Boston and Chicago might help an airline boost its share of the passenger traffic moving between these cities.

In air travel, the relationship between product availability and market share is especially dramatic. In a city-pair market served by only two air carriers, for example, a carrier with 70% of the "daily flight frequencies" might attract 80% of the passenger traffic (see Exhibit 8).

Equally, the carrier with only 30% of the flights in this situation might get only 20% of the traffic. This relationship between frequency share and market share is, of course, moderated by differences in carrier promotion and quality of service; but it seems to hold true where competitors can be distinguished only by service frequency.

Now, what are the economics in this situation? Since most flights operate at a loss unless passengers occupy at least 40% of the seats available, the minority carriers on many routes operate at a significant loss. In the example I just mentioned, where one carrier has 70% of the capacity and 80% of the business, and his competitor has only 30% of the capacity and 20% of the business, the competitor is almost certain to lose money on his operation. The dominant carrier, on the other hand, often achieves the very

Exhibit 8. Market Share and Capacity Share on a Two-Carrier Route

Market: passengers flown

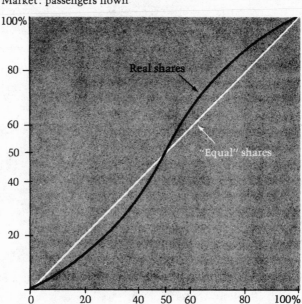

Capacity: seats flown

substantial profits implied by relatively high load factors. (Exhibit 9 presents the details of this situation.)

Thus, in the long run, the air carrier with sufficient financial resources to purchase the extra aircraft and fly the extra flight frequencies necessary to achieve a dominant capacity share in particular city-pair markets is almost bound to come out ahead.

If my analysis is correct, one might expect the history of the airline industry to reflect (a) chronic capacity competition, (b) poor profitability, and (c) frequent failures among the smaller carriers, as the larger carriers

Exhibit 9. Hypothetical Market Shares of Two Carriers Competing in a City-Pair Market

Carrier	Seats Flown per Year	Share of Seats on Route	Share of Market	Total Passengers Flown	Passenger Load Factor
Dominant	70,000	70%	80%	44,000	62.8%[a]
Minority	30,000	30	20	11,000	36.7%[a]
Total	100,000			55,000	

[a]Overall passenger load factor on route—55%.

build their market shares by overwhelming smaller rivals via capacity competition.

While one does indeed find the first two characteristics, a closer look at the record (see Exhibits 10 and 11) illustrates the market shares of the largest carriers shrinking over the past 15 years and the highest level of profitability among the smallest carriers. Frequent failures among the smaller carriers have just not taken place—quite the reverse. Hence, on this point, either my analysis has led us down a blind alley, or something must have intervened in the competitive environment to neatly reverse the anticipated and the actual outcomes. The "something" is, of course, the Civil Aeronautics Board (CAB). This government regulatory body has become, in practice, an allocator of market shares and relative profitability for the domestic trunk air carriers.

Regulatory Inversion

The CAB has been able to accomplish this rather remarkable inversion of free market results for two principal reasons. First, it has the power to grant or withhold licenses permitting air carriers to fly in various markets. Second,

Exhibit 10. Average Market Shares for the 11 Domestic Trunk Air Carriers (Domestic Operations), 1954–1970

Airlines	1954	1958	1962	1966	1970
Big 4					
American	23.7%	22.3%	20.5%	19.0%	17.4%
Eastern	16.9	17.1	12.3	12.6	13.0[a]
Trans World	16.0	14.8	13.7	14.1	12.8
United	20.2	20.9	24.5[b]	21.9	23.7[a]
Little 7					
Braniff	3.7%	4.2%	3.8%	3.8%	3.8%
Continental	1.3	1.9	3.1	4.0	4.6
Delta	5.1	6.1	8.3	9.3	10.1
National	4.1	4.0	4.2	4.8	3.9
Northeast	1.0	1.6	2.4	1.6	2.1
Northwest	5.0	4.5	4.1	5.1	4.7
Western	2.7	2.7	3.3	3.7	3.9
Total for Big 4	76.8%	75.0%	70.9%	67.7%	66.9%
Total for Little 7	23.2	25.0	29.1	32.3	33.1

[a]Data for 1970 show a rising market share for two of the Big 4 carriers. This was due to strikes at National and Northwest which temporarily but significantly reduced their market shares during the year.

[b]Includes Capital Airlines, which merged into United in 1961 and which accounted for 5.6% of domestic trunk revenues in 1960.

Exhibit 11.   ROI for the 11 Domestic Trunk Air Carriers, 1954–1970

Airlines	1954	1958	1962	1966	1970
Big 4					
American	15.6%	12.4%	5.7%	20.2%	− 7.8%
Eastern	13.1	6.3	−16.7	7.4	− 1.1
Trans World	18.7	2.7	−20.2	7.4	−33.9
United	10.8	11.2	1.9	8.8	− 7.2
Little 7					
Braniff	28.4%	10.5%	11.4%	33.0%	− 10.1%
Continental	11.3	− 1.7	6.9	31.7	3.9
Delta	15.7	9.9	26.5	37.2	16.1
National	10.7	4.5	24.5	22.6	− 4.9
Northeast	3.0	—	—	0	—
Northwest	9.7	8.4	6.4	20.2	8.7
Western	13.1	7.3	11.7	23.3	− 3.4
Big 4	14.0%	8.9%	− 3.2%	11.5%	−11.0%
Little 7	13.4	4.5	12.6	27.3	5.2
Industry	13.9	7.7	1.3	17.2	− 4.5

it can control the number of participants in any given city-pair market. This power is significant because the number of carriers competing in a city-pair market has a very heavy impact on that market's profit potential. So pronounced is the impact of competition, in fact, that one carrier's monopoly routes, although they generated less than 10% of its revenue, supported the fraction of its traffic—more than 50%—which was carried at a loss.

Thus the CAB exercises tremendous profit control over the individual carrier. By making the largest new-route awards to smaller carriers, it can, over a long period of time, regulate a carrier's market share of the total industry traffic.

How has the CAB used this great regulatory power? Exhibits 10 and 11 show that since the carriers were removed from government subsidy in the mid-1950s, the air-carrier market shares have slowly been leveling out. Even at that early date, the CAB may well have looked at the air transportation industry in the context of my Question 1 and come to the conclusion that, without its intervention, small carriers would simply be unable to withstand market-share battles waged by bigger rivals with greater financial resources.

Hence, to avoid capacity duels that might end in small-carrier bankruptcy, and to offset the advantages large carriers have in raising expansion capital, the CAB has tended to give the small carriers a dramatic edge in relative profitability.

Exhibits 10 and 11 point out a meaningful contrast between the growth and profit opportunities of the smallest large carrier (Eastern) and the largest small carrier (Delta). The essence of this contrast was exquisitely penned by Paul H. Frankel 24 years ago, in his study of the petroleum industry:

> There is no more enthusiastic satellite than the biggest operator outside the ring—But the more successful he becomes the greater his danger of cutting off the branch upon which he is sitting. For, beyond a certain point . . . he is faced with . . . joining the inner circle himself. Thus, while the position of the biggest "outsider" is the most desirable, the lot of the smallest "insider" is the most uncomfortable.[5]

The game rules for profitability apply very differently to companies on the two sides of the regulatory fence; and companies which plan to climb that fence had better recognize the fact explicitly.

Further, the intent of the CAB's regulations is to maintain the number of competitors for market share, both large and small; and its resulting regulations may have created, in effect, a no-win market environment for the Big Four carriers.

Unfortunately, this no-win environment does not seem to have muted the willingness of the Big Four carriers to wage wasteful and expensive capacity wars. Indeed, these firms seem quite unwilling to address the implications of Question 3—their need to devise more creative and effective strategies for gaining larger shares.

Word of Warning

Most companies have committed themselves to fight for larger market shares. I contend that companies often make this commitment before they have adequately considered my three basic questions:

1 Are company financial resources adequate?
2 If the fight is stopped short for any reason, will the company's position be competitively viable?
3 Will government regulators permit the company to follow the strategy it has chosen?

In computer manufacturing, GE and RCA both pursued dramatic increases in their market shares long after the evidence indicated that their goals were financially impossible. In choosing an internal-growth rather than an acquisitions strategy, these companies showed they had considered the antitrust aspects of Question 3, but they were quite late in acknowledging the relevance of Question 1.

In grocery retailing, National Tea and many of its competitors evidently neglected Questions 2 and 3. As a result, halfway to their market-share goals, they were trapped in competitively disadvantaged positions. Winn-Dixie's strategy dealt more successfully with Questions 2 and 3, and this company remains a consistent leader in terms of industry profitability.

Finally, in the air transport industry, the CAB has structured a no-win environment for the larger carriers. These companies are simply not permitted to build their market shares through the traditional avenue of internal expansion. For their part, the larger carriers have yet to identify a market-share expansion strategy that recognizes my Question 3—the *feasibility* question—as the capacity wars and eroded profits of recent years demonstrate; yet their taste for doing battle with losing strategies seems undeterred.

Here, as in all the examples I have cited earlier, the cost of ignoring or failing to gather evidence relating to the three questions I posed initially has been frightfully high.

I could continue to add examples, but let me recommend some points for thought instead:

☐ Are you operating in an industry where extremely heavy financial resources are required?

☐ Are you in an industry where an expansion strategy might be cut off abruptly by a regulatory agency?

☐ Are you in an industry where some agency is even now planning some new regulatory hurdles?

If the answer to any of those questions is *yes*, and if yours is the kind of company that fights for market share, reassess your battle plan.

Notes

1. "Honeywell Tries to Make Its Merger Work," *Business Week*, September 26, 1970, p. 93.

2. Gene Smith, "RCA Profits Topple, Kodak Sets Mark," *The New York Times*, October 15, 1970.

3. Allan T. Demaree, "G.E.'s Costly Ventures Into Futures," *Fortune*, October 1970, p. 158.

4. U.S. Federal Trade Commission, *In the Matter of National Tea Co., Findings as to the Facts, Conclusions, and Order*, Docket #7453, March 4, 1966, p. 57.

5. *Essentials of Petroleum* (London, Chapman & Hall, Ltd., 1946), p. 86.

About the Authors

William J. Abernathy, *now deceased, was professor of business administration at the Harvard Business School. He was a leading authority on the automobile industry. Mr. Abernathy was the author of* The Productivity Dilemma: Roadblock to Innovation in the Automobile Industry *and co-author of* Industrial Renaissance.

John E. Bishop *is professor of business administration at the Harvard Business School, where he is a member of the production and operating management area. A specialist in decision theory and operations research, he has been involved in the Harvard Business School development of quantitative techniques in the analysis of business decisions. Currently he is doing research in manufacturing planning and control.*

Paul N. Bloom *is visiting associate professor of business administration at the University of North Carolina at Chapel Hill. He is on leave for the 1984–1985 year from the University of Maryland, where he has taught since receiving his Ph.D. in marketing from Northwestern University in 1974. He also spent the 1980–1981 year as visiting research professor at the Marketing Science Institute. His research has been primarily in public policy toward marketing, marketing for nonprofit organizations, and marketing of professional services. He is the author or co-author of over forty articles and papers and three books, the latest of which is* Marketing Professional Services *(written with Philip Kotler).*

Ben Branch *is a professor of finance at the University of Massachsetts, School of Management. Since receiving his Ph.D. in economics from the University of Michigan in 1970, he has published extensively in finance and economics journals (including* Journal of Political Economy, Journal of Finance, Journal of Financial and Quantitative Analysis, Antitrust Bulletin,

Publisher's Note. Biographical information was not available on all authors at the time of publication.

529

Journal of Business Strategy) *as well as having written several books on investing. He served as president of the Eastern Finance Association in 1983–1984. His research interests include capital market efficiency, strategic planning, industrial organization, and environmental economics.*

Robert D. Buzzell *is the Sebastian S. Kresge Professor of Marketing at Harvard Business School. Before joining the HBS faculty in 1961, he taught at the Ohio State University, where he earned a Ph.D. degree. Mr. Buzzell was instrumental in the development of the PIMS research program, initially at the Marketing Science Institute (where he served as executive director, 1968–1972) and later at the Strategic Planning Institute. He is the author or co-author of several texbooks and numerous articles and case studies and serves on the boards of directors of four New York Stock Exchange-listed companies.*

Kim B. Clark *is an associate professor at the Harvard Business School, where he currently teaches manufacturing policy and productivity, technology and operations management. Mr. Clark received the B.A., M.A., and Ph.D. degrees in economics from Harvard University and has been on the Harvard faculty since 1978. Mr. Clark has participated in consulting, executive seminars, and field research with leading firms in North America, Europe, and Japan. He has served at the U.S. Department of Labor and is a member of the National Materials Advisory Board. Professor Clark is co-chairman of the 75th Anniversary Colloquium on Productivity and Technology at HBS, and a Research Associate of the National Bureau of Economic Research. Professor Clark's research interests are in the areas of technology and productivity and operations strategy. He has studied technological steel, semiconductors, computers, and advanced ceramics. His current research focuses on management and productivity at the plant level and on the product/process development cycle. Mr. Clark's recent publications include* The Competitive Status of the U.S. Auto Industry *(1981);* Industrial Renaissance *(with William J. Abernathy and Alan M. Kantrow; 1983); "The New Industrial Competition" with W.J. Abernathy and A.M. Kantrow—winner of the McKinsey Prize for 1981); and "Innovation: Mapping the Winds of Creative Destruction" (with W.J. Abernathy, 1984).*

Arnold C. Cooper *is Louis A. Weil, Jr. Professor of Management at the Krannert Graduate School of Management, Purdue University. He received a B.S. (Chemical Engineering) and M.S. (Management) from Purdue University and a D.B.A. from Harvard. He has also served on the faculties of the Harvard Business School, Stanford University, Manchester Business School (England), and IMEDE Management Development Institute (Switzerland). His primary teaching and research interests are in entrepreneurship and strategic management. He is author, co-author, or co-editor of five books and a number of articles on entrepreneurship, strategic planning, and the management of technology.*

William E. Fruhan, Jr. *is a professor of business administration at the Harvard Business School. He received his S.B. degree from Yale University and his M.B.A. and D.B.A. from Harvard University. Mr. Fruhan is the author of* Financial Strategy *and* The Fight for Competitive Advantage. *He is co-editor of* Case Problems in Finance. *In 1980 Mr. Fruhan won the Financial Analysts Federation's Graham and Dodd Award for his feature article entitled "Levitz Furniture: A Case History in the Creation and Destruction of Shareholder Value." Mr. Fruhan has served as course head for finance in the first year of Harvard's M.B.A. program and as faculty chairman for the Corporate Financial Management executive education program.*

Richard G. Hamermesh *received the A.B. degree from the University of California (1969) and the M.B.A. (1971) and D.B.A. (1976) degrees from Harvard University. He has been member of the Harvard Business School faculty since 1976, teaching business policy in the M.B.A. program. Professor Hamermesh's research has been on the implementation of strategic planning systems. He has written over twenty case studies, four articles that have appeared in the* Harvard Business Review, *one article for the* Academy of Management Review, *is a co-author of* Business Policy: Text and Cases, *the editor of* Strategic Management, *and the author of* Making Strategy Work. *Professor Hamermesh has been a consultant to companies in the fields of strategic planning, organization design, and antitrust. He has also been a consultant to the executive development programs of General Electric and Honeywell. Professor Hamermesh is a member of the board of directors of Bishopric, Inc. and of the editorial board of the* Harvard Business Review.

Mack Hanan *is president of The Wellspring Group, management consultants in growth and diversification. He consults and lectures internationally, and has written* Fast-Growth Management, Accelerated Growth Planning, Venture Management, Leading-Edge Growth Strategies, *and* High Tech Growth Strategies. *Mr. Hanan is an authority on emerging growth technologies.*

Kathryn Rudie Harrigan *is associate professor at the Columbia University Graduate School of Business. She received her D.B.A. from the Harvard Business School and her M.B.A. from the University of Texas at Austin. Dr. Harrigan's publications include three books—*Strategies for Declining Businesses, Strategies for Vertical Integration, *and* Strategies for Joint Ventures—*and many articles in such journals as* Academy of Management Review, Strategic Management Journal, *and* Journal of Business Strategy.

Robert H. Hayes' *current research is concerned with the facilities investment and productivity improvement activities of manufacturing companies both here and abroad. He has published over two dozen articles, including "Managing Our Way to Economic Decline" (1980) and "Managing as if Tomorrow Mattered" (1982), both of which won McKinsey Awards for the best article published in the* Harvard Business Review *during their respective years. His* *article "Why Japanese Factories Work" was runner-up for the McKinsey Award in 1981. He recently wrote a book with Professor Steven C. Wheelwright of Stanford University entitled* Restoring Our Competitive Edge: Competing Through Manufacturing, *which won the PSP Award of the American Association of Publishers for the best business book of 1984.*

Philip Kotler *is one of the leading scholars in marketing today. He is the Harold T. Martin of marketing at the J. L. Kellogg Graduate School of Management, Northwestern University. A graduate of the University of Chicago and M.I.T., Dr. Kotler is the author of the world's leading graduate textbook in marketing,* Marketing Management *(now in its fifth edition). He is also the author of* Marketing for Nonprofit Organizations *(second edition) and* Marketing Professional Services. *Dr. Kotler has won several prizes for his original contributions to marketing, including the Leader in Marketing Thought Award (1975), the Paul D. Converse Award (1978), and the Stuart Henderson Britt Award (1983). Besides teaching and writing, he is an active management consultant and has worked with General Electric, AT&T, Apple Computer, Bank of America, Arthur Andersen & Co., and several other companies on marketing strategy.*

Robert A. Leone *is a lecturer in public policy at the Kennedy School of Government, Harvard University. He has published extensively in the area of competitive strategy and public policy. Professor Leone served for nine years on the faculty of the Harvard Business School and recently served as senior staff economist at the President's Council of Economic Advisers, where he addressed a wide range of regulatory and industrial policy issues. Dr. Leone also maintains a consulting practice, advising clients both in the private and public sectors on issues involving the competitive consequences of governmental action.*

Theodore Levitt *is the Edward Carter Professor of Business Administration, Harvard University Graduate School of Business Administration. He is the author of numerous articles on economic, political, management, and marketing subjects, including the prize-winning article, "Marketing Myopia,"* in the Harvard Business Review; *a four-time winner of McKinsey Awards for articles in the* Harvard Business Review; *winner of Academy of Management Award for one of the outstanding business books of the year 1962, for* Innovation in Marketing; *winner of John Hancock Award for Excellence in Business Journalism in 1969; recipient of Charles Coolidge Parlin Award as Marketing Man of the Year, 1970; recipient of the George Gallup Award for Marketing Excellence, 1976; recipient of the 1978 Paul D. Converse Award of the American Marketing Association for Major Contributions to Marketing. Mr. Levitt is the author of* Industrial Purchasing Behavior: A Study in Communcations Effects *(1965);* The Marketing Mode: Pathways to Corporate Growth *(1969);* The Third Sector: New Tactics for a Responsive Society *(1973);* Marketing for Business Growth *(1976);* The Marekting Imag-

ination *(1983); and co-author of* Marketing: A Contemporary Analysis *(1972).*
He is on the board of directors of Consolidated Natural Gas Company, GCA
Corporation, AM International, the Gintel Fund, Inc., Gintel ERISA Fund,
Inc.; Trustee, Marketing Science Institute; and consultant to a large number
of major international corporations in manufacturing, finance, natural re-
sources, and trade.

John R. Meyer *is the James W. Harpel Professor of Capital Formation and*
Economic Growth at Harvard's Center for Business and Government. He
has been a member of the Harvard faculty since 1953, with a five-year period
of service at Yale from 1968 to 1973. He also served as president of the
National Bureau of Economic Research from 1967 to 1977 and has written
many social and economic studies, ranging from the Economics of Slavery
in the Ante-Bellum South *to various studies of the economic effects of*
government regulation on such industries as transportation and tele-
communications.

Michael E. Porter *is a professor at the Harvard Business School and a leading*
authority in the field of competitive strategy. He received a B.S.E. from
Princeton University, an M.B.A. from Harvard, where he was a George F.
Baker Scholar, and a Ph.D. in Business Economics from Harvard. Professor
Porter is the author of six books and numerous articles. His award-winning
bestseller, Competitive Strategy: Techniques for Analyzing Industries and
Competitors, *is widely recognized as an important work in its field. Professor*
Porter serves as a director or strategic consultant to many U.S. and inter-
national companies.

Lawrence Revsine, *Ph.D., CPA, is the Eric L. Kohler Professor of Accounting*
and Information Systems at the Kellogg Graduate School of Management,
Northwestern University. He is the author of Replacement Cost Accounting
and several other books; in addition, Professor Revsine has published nu-
merous articles in such journals as Accounting Review, Journal of Accounting Research, Journal of Accountancy, Wall Street Journal, *and* Financial
Analysts Journal. *He has served as a consultant to the SEC, FASB, and*
AICPA as well as to numerous corporations. Professor Revsine has extensive
experience as an instructor in management development programs and was
voted Teacher of the Year, 1983, by students of the Kellogg Graduate School
of Management.

Thomas S. Robertson *is an associate dean and professor of marketing at the*
Wharton School, University of Pennsylvania. One of the ten most frequently
cited authors in marketing, his publications have appeared in most of the
leading business journals. His current research interests are in marketing
strategy, deregulation strategy, and consumer behavior. His business re-
lationships include the board of directors of Time Energy Systems, Inc. Dr.
Robertson holds his Ph.D. in marketing as well as an M.A. in sociology

from Northwestern University. He taught previously at Harvard Business School and UCLA.

Malcolm S. Salter *has been a member of the Harvard Business School faculty since 1967, teaching courses in business policy and managing Diversification. He served as head of the Business Policy Teaching Group from 1979 to 1983 and is currently faculty chairman of the International Senior Managers Program. Professor Salter is also a member of the faculty of the John F. Kennedy School of Government. Professor Salter is co-author of* New Alliances: The Politics of an American Industry, Policy Formulation and Administration *(1980),* Merger Trends and Prospects for the 1980s *(1980),* Diversification Through Acquisition *(1979), and many articles addressing general management issues. He is also a consultant in the fields of corporate strategy and organization and has led consulting projects and executive development seminars in the U.S., Europe, and Japan. He is a director of Schlegel Corporation, an overseer of the Boston Museum of Fine Arts, and a trustee and former treasurer of the Shady Hill School of Cambridge. Professor Salter received his A.B., M.B.A., and D.B.A. degrees from Harvard University.*

Raymond Vernon *is Clarence Dillon Professor of International Affairs Emeritus, Harvard University. He is the author of numerous books, including* Manager in the International Economy *(with L. T. Wells, Jr.),* Two Hungry Giants, Storm over the Multinationals, *and* Sovereignty at Bay. *For many years he occupied the Herbert F. Johnson Chair in Internaitonal Business Management at the Harvard Business School. He is a fellow of the Academy of International Business.*

Scott Ward *is professor of marketing at the Wharton School of the University of Pennsylvania. He has published over fifty articles in journals such as* Harvard Business Review, Journal of Marketing Research, The Corporate Board, *and the* Journal of Consumer Research. *His most recent books are* Problems in Marketing *(with E. Corey and C. Lovelock) and* Consumer Behavior *(with T.S. Robertson and J. Zielinski). His teaching interests are in the area of marketing strategy and implementation. Professor Ward serves on the boards of several companies and organizations and is a consultant to many Fortune 500 companies.*

Wolf A. Weinhold *and his associates of Wolf Weinhold and Co. offer general management consulting and executive education seminars. The company is a merchant banking operation, providing financial advice, capital, and investment services to selected clients. It holds a diversified portfolio of real property assets, equity participations, and marketable securities. A graduate of M.I.T.'s Sloan School of Management with simultaneous bachelor's and master's degrees, Mr. Weinhold has been associated with the Harvard Business School since 1975. He is co-author of* Diversification through Acquisition: Strategies for Creating Economic Value *(1979) and has written for such publications as* The Wall Street Journal, The New York Times, *and* Harvard Business Review.

Carolyn Y. Woo *is an assistant professor at Purdue University. Her current research involves a critical assessment of market share building as a means to effective performance, and identification of strategic alternatives for long-term corporate value creation. Her publications have appeared in the* Harvard Business Review, Management Science, *and* Strategic Management Journal. *Her thesis,* Strategies of Effective Low Share Businesses, *placed second in the A.T. Kearney Award for Outstanding Research in General Management, 1981. Professor Woo has been a consultant at Strategic Planning Associates and was elected to the Executive Board of the Business Policy and Planning Division of the Academy of Management.*

Author Index

537

Subject Index